Adobe InDesign CS

one-on-one™

Adobe InDesign CS

one-on-one™

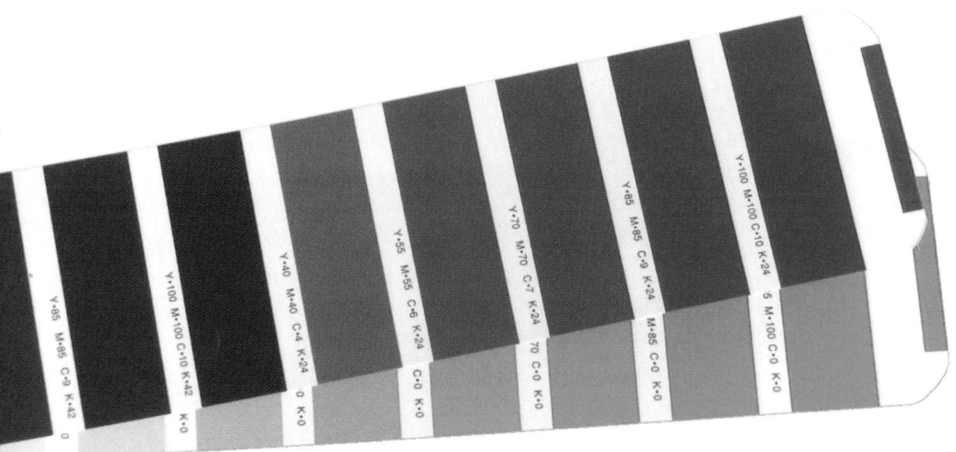

DEKE McCLELLAND

BEIJING • CAMBRIDGE • FARNHAM • KÖLN deke™ PRESS O'REILLY® PARIS • SEBASTOPOL • TAIPEI • TOKYO

Adobe InDesign CS One-on-One

by Deke McClelland

Printed in the United States of America.

This title is published by Deke Press in association with O'Reilly Media, Inc., 1005 Gravenstein Highway North, Sebastopol, CA 95472.

O'Reilly Media books may be purchased for educational, business, or sales promotional use. Online editions are also available for most titles (*safari.oreilly.com*). For more information, contact O'Reilly's corporate/institutional sales department: 800-998-9938 or *corporate@oreilly.com*.

Managing Editor:	Amy Thomas Buscaglia
Additional Content & Puppetry:	Galen Fott
Project Editor:	Robert Luhn
Copyeditor:	Susan Pink
Indexer:	Julie Hawks
Technical Editors:	Tim Cole and Kacey Crouch
Production Manager:	Claire Cloutier
Cover Designer:	Emma Colby
Interior Designer:	David Futato
Video Directors:	Brian Maffitt and Jason Woliner
Video Editor:	Denise Maffitt
CD Producer:	Barbara Ross
CD Graphic Designer:	Barbara Driscoll
Video Compression:	Carey Matthew Brady
Video Interface Programmer:	Marc Johnson
Fog Machine:	James Thomas

Print History:

September 2004: First edition.

Special thanks to John Bell, Dave Murcott, J. Scott Klossner, Jodi Richter, Richard Lainhart, Barbara Stilwell, Melissa Symolon, Laura Fott, Jerry Hunt, Andrew Faulkner, Michael Mabry, Kevin O'Connor, Marjorie Baer, Rebecca Ross, Timothy Nicholls, Barbara Rice, David Rogelberg, Sherry Rogelberg, Stacey Barone, Sue Willing, Glenn Bisignani, Laurie Petrycki, Mark Brokering, and Tim O'Reilly, as well as Patrick Lor and the gang at iStockPhoto.com.

This book was typeset using Adobe InDesign CS and the Adobe Futura, Adobe Rotis, and Linotype Birka typefaces.

0-596-00736-1
[C]

RepKover. This book uses RepKover™, a durable and flexible lay-flat binding.

To my two
favorite teachers,
Mom and Elle.

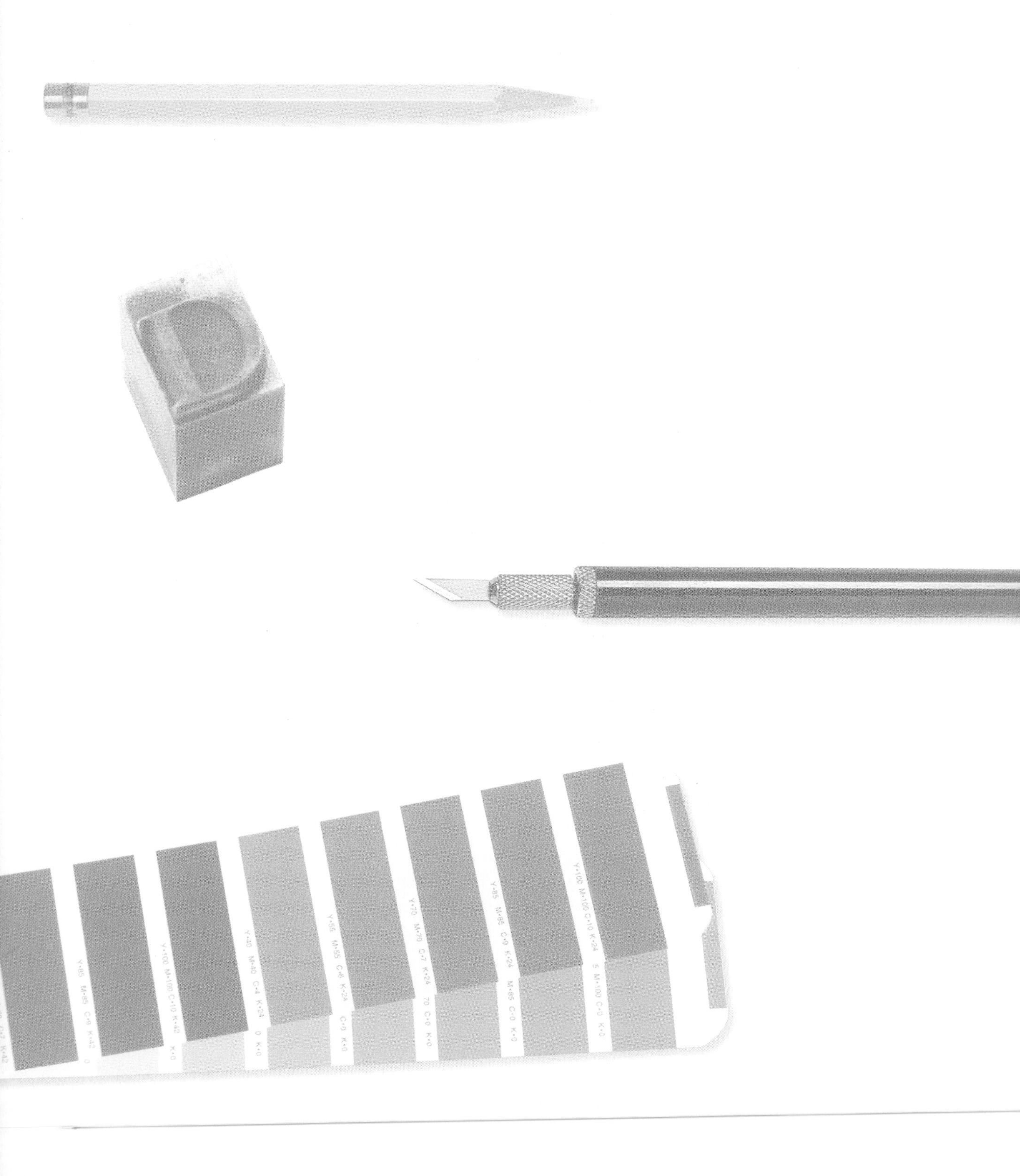

CONTENTS

PREFACE

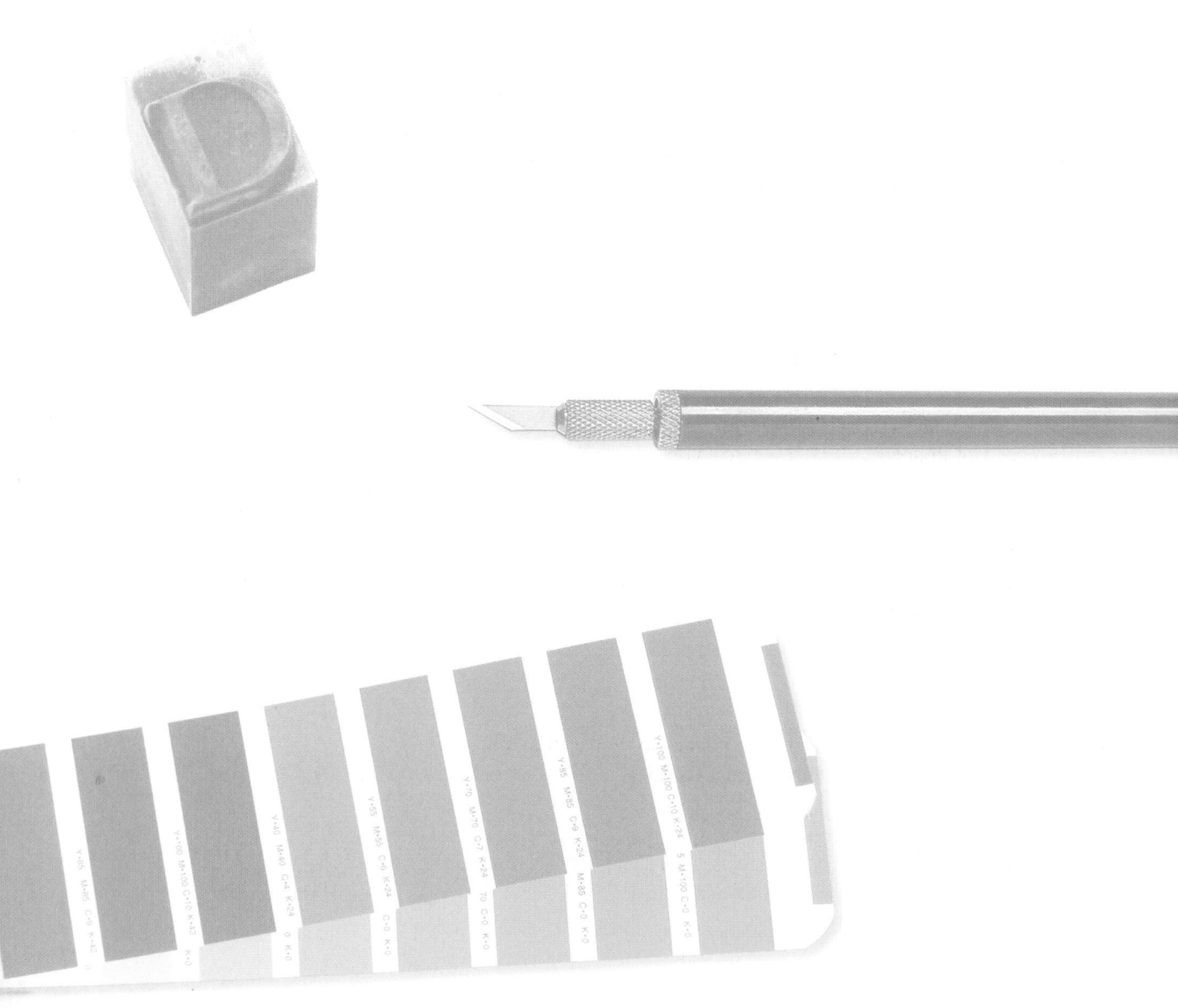

HOW ONE-ON-ONE WORKS

Welcome to *Adobe InDesign CS One-on-One*, the second in a series of highly visual, full-color titles that combine step-by-step lessons with two hours of video instruction. As the name *One-on-One* implies, I walk you through InDesign just as if I were teaching you in a classroom or corporate consulting environment. Except that instead of getting lost in a crowd of students, you receive my individualized attention. It's just you and me.

I created *One-on-One* with three audiences in mind. If you're an independent designer or graphic artist—professional or amateur—you'll appreciate the hands-on approach and the ability to set your own pace. If you're a student working in a classroom or vocational setting, you'll enjoy the personalized attention, structured exercises, and end-of-lesson quizzes. If you're an instructor in a college or vocational setting, you'll find the topic-driven lessons helpful in building curricula and creating homework assignments. *Adobe InDesign CS One-on-One* is designed to suit the needs of beginners and intermediate users. But I've seen to it that each lesson contains a few techniques that even experienced users don't know.

Read, Watch, Do

Adobe InDesign CS One-on-One is your chance to master Adobe's revolutionary layout application under the direction of a professional trainer with nearly 20 years of computer design and imaging experience. Read the book, watch the videos, do the exercises. Proceed at your own pace and experiment as you see fit. It's the best way to learn.

Figure 1.

Adobe InDesign CS One-on-One contains twelve lessons, each made up of three to six step-by-step exercises. Every book-based lesson includes a corresponding video lesson (see Figure 1), in which I introduce the key concepts you'll need to know to complete the exercises. Best of all, every exercise is project-based, culminating in an actual finished document worthy of your labors (see Figure 2). The exercises include insights and context throughout, so you'll know not only what to do but, just as important, why you're doing it. My sincere hope is that you'll find the experience entertaining, informative, and empowering.

All the sample files required to perform the exercises are included on the CD-ROM at the back of this book. The CD also contains the video lessons. (This is a data CD, not a music CD or DVD. It won't work in a set-top device; it works only with a computer.) Don't lose or destroy this CD. It is as integral a part of your learning experience as the pages in this book. Together, the book, sample files, and videos form a single comprehensive training experience.

The goal: Start here...

and end here. No head scratching allowed!

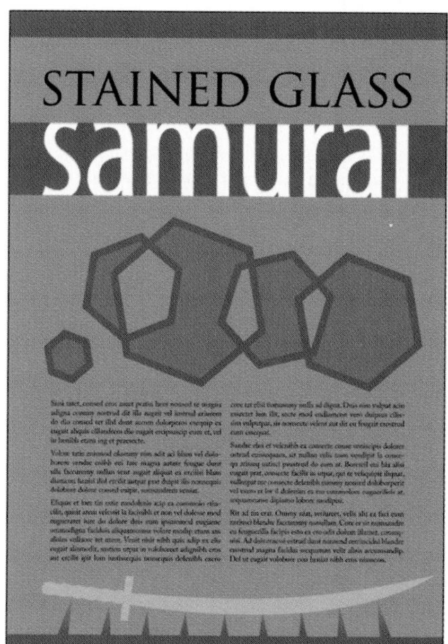

Figure 2.

One-on-One Requirements

The main prerequisite to using *Adobe InDesign CS One-on-One* is having Adobe InDesign CS (also known as InDesign 3) installed on your system. You may have purchased InDesign CS as a stand-alone package or as part of Adobe's full Creative Suite, both pictured in Figure 3. (InDesign CS is included in both the Standard and Premium editions of the Creative Suite.) You can work through many of the exercises using InDesign 2 and earlier versions, but some steps and some entire exercises will not work. All exercises have been fully tested with Adobe InDesign CS but not with older versions.

Adobe InDesign CS One-on-One is cross-platform, meaning that it works equally well whether you're using InDesign installed on a Microsoft-Windows-based PC or an Apple Macintosh. Any computer that meets the minimum requirements for InDesign CS also meets the requirements for using *Adobe InDesign CS One-on-One*. Specifically, if you own a PC, you will need an Intel Pentium II, III, or 4 processor running Windows XP or Windows 2000 with Service Pack 2. If you own a Mac, you need a PowerPC G3 processor or faster running Mac OS X version 10.2 or higher.

Figure 3.

Regardless of platform, your computer must meet the following minimum requirements:

- 128MB of RAM
- 600MB of free hard disk space (350MB for InDesign and 250MB for the One-on-One project and video application files)
- Color monitor with 16-bit color video card
- 1,024-by-768-pixel monitor resolution
- CD-ROM drive

If your computer is better equipped—say, with 256MB of RAM and a DVD drive—all the better.

To play the videos, you will need Apple's QuickTime Player software version 5.0.2 or later. Many PCs and all Macintosh computers come equipped with QuickTime; if yours does not, you will need to install QuickTime using the link provided on the CD included with this book.

Caflisch Script Pro
Regular only

Adobe Caslon Pro
Regular, *Italic*, **Semibold**, ***Semibold Italic***, **Bold**, ***Bold Italic***

Adobe Garamond Pro
Regular, *Italic*, **Semibold**, ***Semibold Italic***

Adobe Jenson Pro
Light, *Light Italic*, Regular, *Italic*, **Semibold**, ***Semibold Italic***, **Bold**, ***Bold Italic***

Letter Gothic Standard
Medium, *Slanted*, **Bold**, ***Bold Slanted***

LITHOS PRO
EXTRA LIGHT, LIGHT, REGULAR, **BOLD**, **BLACK**

Myriad Pro Condensed (and *only* condensed)
Light, *Light Italic*, Condensed, *Italic*, **Semibold**, ***Semibold Italic***, **Bold**, ***Bold Italic***, **Black**, ***Black Italic***

Poplar Standard Black

TRAJAN PRO
REGULAR, **BOLD**

Figure 4.

Finally, you'll need to install the *One-on-One* project files from the CD that accompanies this book, as explained in the next section. All sample files use the fonts pictured in Figure 4. These fonts install automatically with all versions of InDesign CS. If you discover that any of them are missing, you will need to reinstall InDesign.

One-on-One Installation and Setup

Adobe InDesign CS One-on-One is designed to function as an integrated training environment. Therefore, before embarking on the lessons and exercises, you must first install a handful of files onto your computer's hard drive. These are:

- QuickTime Player software (if it is not already installed)
- All sample files used in the exercises (170MB in all)
- Total Training video training software
- *One-on-One* InDesign preference settings, color settings, and keyboard shortcuts (optional, but very much recommended)

All of these files are provided on the CD that accompanies this book. To install the files, follow these steps:

1. ***Quit InDesign.*** If InDesign is running on your computer, you must exit the program before you install the *One-on-One* files. On the PC, choose the **Exit** command from the **File** menu or press Ctrl+Q or Alt+F4. On the Mac, choose **Quit InDesign** from the **InDesign** menu or press ⌘-Q.

2. ***Insert the One-on-One CD.*** Remove the CD from the book and place it in your computer's CD or DVD drive.

3. ***Open the Adobe InDesign CS One-on-One Launchpad.*** On the PC, the Launchpad window (see Figure 5) should open automatically. If it doesn't, choose **My Computer** from the **Start** menu and double-click the *ID1ON1* CD icon.

   On the Mac, double-click the *ID1ON1* CD icon on your computer's desktop. (The CD icon sports the blue-and-white Total Training logo, shown in Figure 6 on the facing page.) Then double-click the *ID1ON1 Installer* file icon to display the Launchpad window.

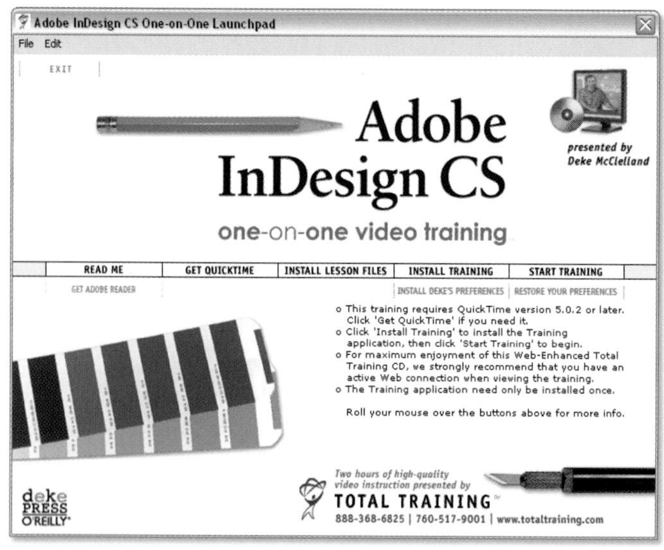

Figure 5.

The Launchpad includes everything you need to install files and play the videos. You perform these operations by clicking the buttons in the horizontal strip, just below the words *one-on-one video training.*

4. ***If necessary, get QuickTime.*** If your computer does not include the QuickTime Player software, make sure you're connected to the Internet, and then click the **Get QuickTime** button in the **Launchpad**. This takes you to Apple's QuickTime download page, *www.apple.com/quicktime/download*. Under **Download the free player**, select your operating system. Then scroll down to the bottom of the page, click the **Download QuickTime** (or **Download QuickTime + iTunes**) button, and follow the installation instructions. (This site is subject to change, so the specific installation process may change by the time you read this.)

5. ***Install the Lesson files.*** Back inside the **Launchpad** window, click the **Install Lesson Files** button to copy to your hard drive the sample files required to complete the exercises. Then click the **Desktop** button to install the files inside a folder on your computer's desktop, which is generally the easiest place to find them. (If you prefer to put the files elsewhere, click **Other Location** and specify where.) The copy operation may take a minute or two. When it completes, you'll find a new folder called *Lesson Files-IDcs 1on1* on your desktop.

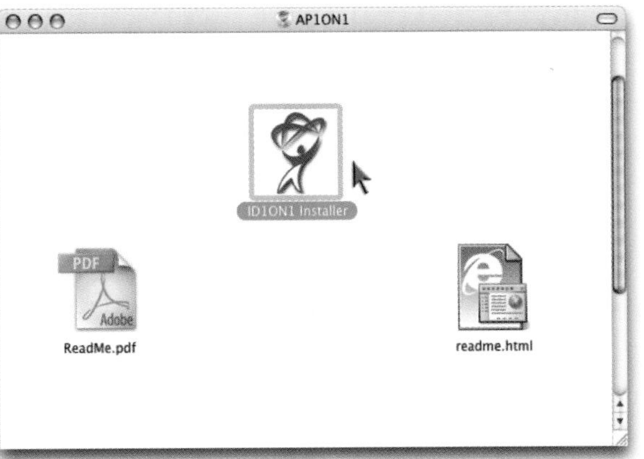

Figure 6.

6. ***Install the video training software.*** To watch the video lessons, you must install a small piece of software from the good folks who produced the videos, Total Training. To do so, click the **Install Training** button. A *Total Training* folder is added to the *Program Files* folder on the PC or the *Applications* folder on the Mac.

7. ***Install the preference, color, and shortcuts settings.*** *Preference settings* govern the way InDesign behaves under certain circumstances. To ensure that you and I are on the same page during the exercises, it's necessary for our settings to match. Therefore, click the gray **Install Deke's Preferences** button located directly below the Install Training button. These files are very small, so the operation completes almost immediately.

If you're an experienced InDesign user or an instructor using this book as a teaching resource, you may be perfectly happy with the InDesign preferences you've already established. With this in mind, the Install Deke's Preferences button automatically backs up your preferences before it installs new ones. If, after completing the exercises in this book, you want to restore your original preferences, just click the **Restore Your Preferences** button.

8. ***Close the Launchpad (or don't).*** We're done with the Launchpad for the moment. If you like to keep your on-screen world tidy, close the Launchpad by clicking the **Exit** button in the top-left corner of the screen. But bear in mind, the Launchpad is your gateway to the videos. If you plan on watching them in the near future (and there is one I'd like you to watch right away, as I discuss in "Playing the Videos" on page xviii), then leave the Lanchpad open.

9. ***Start InDesign.*** On the PC, go to the **Start** menu and choose **Adobe InDesign CS**. (The program may be located in the **Programs** or **All Programs** submenu, possibly inside an **Adobe** submenu.) On the Mac, go to the desktop level and choose **Go→Applications**. Double-click the *Adobe InDesign CS* folder and then double-click the *Adobe InDesign CS* application icon.

10. ***Close the Welcome Screen.*** After InDesign launches, click the **Close** button in the **Welcome Screen** window to make it go away.

To make the Welcome Screen go away for good, turn off the **Show this dialog at startup** check box before clicking **Close**.

11. ***Change the color settings to Best Workflow.*** The color settings and keyboard shortcuts files will be installed, but you have to activate them manually to use them. Choose **Edit→Color Settings**. Inside the **Color Settings** dialog box, turn on the **Enable Color Management** check box. Then click the **Settings** option to display a pop-up menu and choose **Best workflow** (see Figure 7). To accept your changes, click the **OK** button. Now the colors of your images will match (or very nearly match) those shown in the pages of this book.

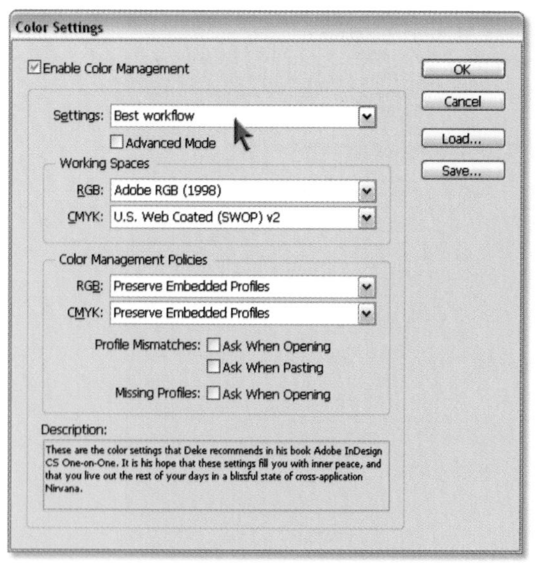

Figure 7.

12. ***Load the Deke Keys shortcuts.*** Choose **Edit→Keyboard Shortcuts**. Inside the **Keyboard Shortcuts** dialog box, click the **Set** pop-up menu and choose **Deke Keys** (see Figure 8). Then click **OK**. This loads a few keyboard shortcuts for some of InDesign's most essential functions, and ensures that you and I will be on the same page throughout the exercises. (Don't worry, the Deke Keys settings don't harm any of InDesign's default shortcuts.)

13. ***Quit InDesign.*** You've come full circle. On the PC, choose **File→Exit**; on the Mac, choose **InDesign→Quit InDesign**. Quitting InDesign not only closes the program but also saves the changes you made to the color settings and keyboard shortcuts.

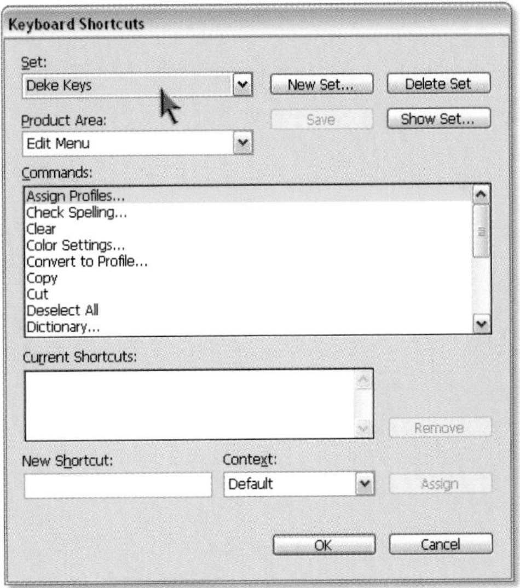

Figure 8.

Congratulations, you and I are now in sync. Just one more thing: If you use a Macintosh computer equipped with Mac OS X 10.3 (AKA, Panther), you may find that a few of InDesign's palette shortcuts get interrupted by the default shortcuts for Exposé, Apple's excellent window-management software. To fix this problem, read the following important message. If you use a PC or another version of the Mac OS, feel free to skip this message and move along to the next section.

Normally when using InDesign for the Mac, pressing F9, F10, or F11 displays or hides one of three of the program's most essential palettes. But in OS X 10.3 (Panther), these keys tile or hide windows according to the dictates of Apple's Exposé. To rectify this conflict, choose **System Preferences** from the menu. Click **Show All**, and then click the **Exposé** icon. Notice the three pop-up menus in the **Keyboard** area, circled in **Figure 9**? To change these so as to avoid conflict with InDesign, press and hold the ⌘ key (which also bears the logo). Keep the key pressed and choose F9 from the **All windows** menu, F10 from the **Application windows** menu, and F11 from the **Desktop** menu. Now release the ⌘ key. Each option should now bear the ⌘ insignia, as in the figure. From now on, you'll press ⌘ with a function key to invoke Exposé, or the function key by itself to access the corresponding InDesign palette.

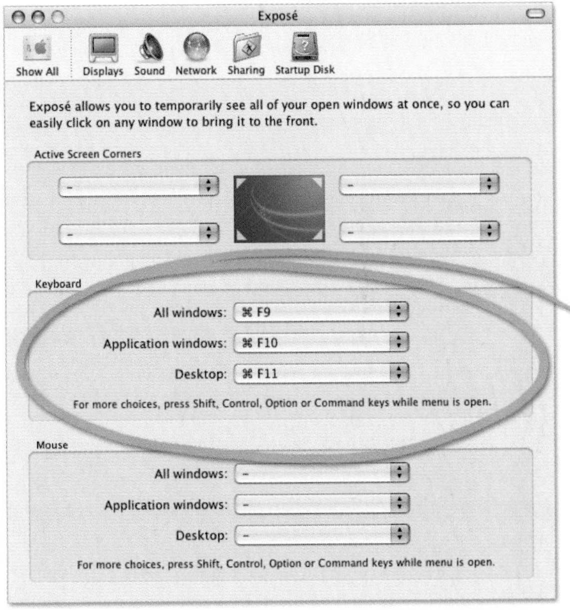

Figure 9.

Playing the Videos

At the outset of each book-based lesson, I ask you to play the companion video lesson from the CD. Ranging from 8 to 13 minutes apiece, these video lessons introduce key concepts that make more sense when first seen in action.

The fact that I provide these videos on CD may lead you to question their playback quality. If so, you're in for a surprise. Produced by the computer training pioneers at Total Training, each video is rendered at a resolution of 640 by 480 pixels, roughly the equivalent of broadcast television. (If the video looks smaller on your computer monitor, bear in mind that your monitor packs in way more pixels than a TV.) Total Training employs state-of-the-art capture technology and gold-standard Sorenson compression to pack these vivid, legible videos onto the relatively small space available to a CD. This is video training at its finest.

Figure 10.

To watch a video, do the following:

1. ***Insert the One-on-One CD.*** You must have the CD in your computer's CD drive to watch a video.

2. ***Open the Adobe InDesign CS One-on-One Launchpad.*** Again, the Launchpad window opens automatically on the PC. On the Mac, double-click the *ID1ON1* icon and then double-click the *ID1ON1 Installer* file.

3. ***Click the Start Training button.*** Click the button on the far right side of the Launchpad, which is highlighted in Figure 10. Assuming that you've installed the Total Training video training software (see Step 6, page xv), you'll be treated to a startup screen (see Figure 11) followed by a welcoming message from your genial host, me.

Figure 11.

4. ***Switch to the video lesson you want to watch.*** The thirteen videos are divided into four sets of three to four lessons each. To switch between sets and lessons, click the buttons in the upper-right corner of the player window (see Figure 12 on the facing page). Set 1 contains the Preface lesson as well as Lessons 1 through 3; Set 2 contains Lessons 4 through 6; and so on. You can watch any video lesson in any order you like.

However, the video lessons make the most sense and provide the most benefit when watched at the outset of the corresponding book-based lesson.

The video is surrounded by an interface of navigational buttons and play controls. To hide the interface and view only the video, move your cursor inside the video image; when the cursor changes into a magnifying glass, click. If you prefer to magnify the video so it fills your entire screen, press the Alt key (or Option on the Mac) and click. To restore the video to its normal state, with interface and all, click anywhere inside the video.

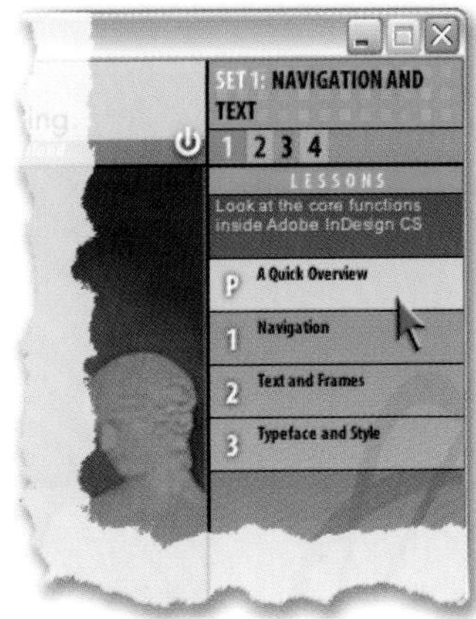

Figure 12.

Use the play controls in the lower-left corner of the screen (see Figure 13) to play, pause, and fast-forward the video. You can also take advantage of the following keyboard shortcuts:

Figure 13.

- To pause the video, press the spacebar. Press the spacebar again to resume playing.
- To skip to the next lesson, press the → key. This is also a great way to play the next lesson after the current one ends. For example, after viewing the initial personal introduction, press the → key to play Video Lesson 1.
- To return to the previous lesson, press ←. For example, you might revisit one of my personal introductions after watching a lesson.
- Adjust the volume by pressing the + and − (plus and minus) keys.

Finally, for help on any element of the interface, click the yellow-on-blue ? icon in the lower-right portion of the screen.

5. ***Play the first video.*** Before going any further, I urge you to watch the 10-minute 49-second video that I've provided specifically to accompany the Preface. To do just so, click the **P** item in the upper-right list, as I'm doing in Figure 14. Titled **A Quick Overview**, this video lesson provides you with a brief and insightful overview of how InDesign works and what it can do. It's the perfect way to kick off your learning experience.

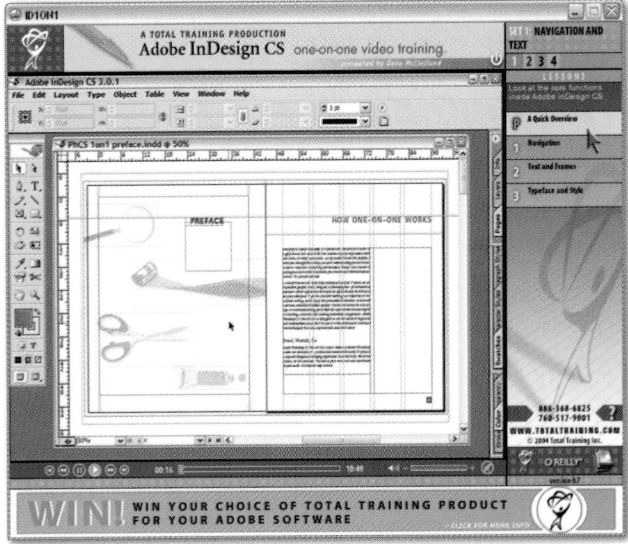

Figure 14.

Structure and Organization

Each of the dozen lessons conforms to a consistent structure designed to impart skills and understanding through a regimen of practice and dialog. As you build your projects, I explain why you're performing the steps and why InDesign works the way it does.

Each lesson begins with a broad topic overview. Turn the page, and you'll find a section called "About This Lesson," which lists the skills you'll learn and directs you to the video-based introduction.

Next come the step-by-step exercises, in which I walk you through some of InDesign's most powerful and essential page-layout functions. A CD icon, like the one on the right, appears whenever I ask you to open a file from the *Lesson Files-IDcs 1on1* folder that you installed on your computer's hard drive. To make my directions crystal clear, command and option names appear in bold type (as in, "choose the **Open** command"). Figure references appear in colored type. More than 600 full-color, generously sized figures diagram key steps in your journey so you're never left scratching your head, puzzling over what to do next. And when I refer you to another step or section, I tell you the exact page number to go to. (Shouldn't every book?)

PEARL OF WISDOM

Along the way, you'll encounter the occasional "Pearl of Wisdom," which provides insights into how InDesign and the larger world of digital imaging work. While this information is not essential to performing a given step or completing an exercise, it may help you understand how a function works or provide you with valuable context.

More detailed background discussions appear in independent sidebars. These sidebars shed light on the mysteries of OpenType technology, the Flattener Preview palette, web-offset lithography, and other high-level topics that are key to understanding InDesign.

A colored paragraph of text with a rule above and below it calls attention to a special tip or technique that will help you make InDesign work faster and more smoothly.

EXTRA CREDIT

Some projects are quite ambitious. My enthusiasm for a topic may even take us a bit beyond the stated goal. In such cases, I cordon off the final portion of the exercise and label it "Extra Credit." If you're feeling oversaturated with information, go ahead and skip to the next exercise. If you're just warming up, then by all means carry on and you will be rewarded with a completed project and a wealth of additional tips and insights.

Each lesson ends with a section titled "What Did You Learn?" which features a multiple-choice quiz. Your job is to choose the best description for each of 12 key concepts outlined in the lesson. Answers are printed upside-down at the bottom of the page.

The Scope of This Book

No one book can teach you everything there is to know about InDesign, and this one is no exception. If you're looking for information on a specific aspect of InDesign, here's a quick list of the topics and features discussed in this book:

- Lesson 1: Ways to start a document, including opening a file created in InDesign or QuarkXPress, creating a new document, setting up guides, and saving a document
- Lesson 2: Adding text to a document, including flowing text between multiple frames, editing and selecting text, the Check Spelling command, and the path type tool
- Lesson 3: Formatting attributes, including font, type size, leading, color, paragraph spacing, alignment, justification, hyphenation, and paragraph composition, as well as glyphs and OpenType
- Lesson 4: Assembling lists and tables, including drop caps, tabbed lists, hanging indents, line breaks and spacing characters, the Tabs palette, and the Table function
- Lesson 5: Style sheets, including the eyedropper, paragraph styles, character styles, and nested style sheets
- Lesson 6: Drawing tools and path attributes, including the line, pencil, pen, and shape tools; the Color, Gradient, Align, and Pathfinder palettes; and the Compound Paths command

- Lesson 7: Working with imported artwork, including cropping, the scale and free transform tools, the Transform and Text Wrap palettes, and inline graphics
- Lesson 8: Applying transparency, including the Transparency palette, blend modes, the Drop Shadow and Feather commands, clipping paths, alpha channels, layered PSD images, and the Flattener Preview palette
- Lesson 9: Document structure, including page numbering, sections, master pages, layers, the Structure bay, the Tags palette, and XML automation
- Lesson 10: Long-document functions, including making books, file synchronization, the Table of Contents command, and the Index palette
- Lesson 11: Creating an interactive PDF document, including the Bookmarks, Hyperlinks, and State palettes, embedding sounds and movies, and the Export command
- Lesson 12: Print functions, including the Print command, overprinting, and the Trap Presets palette, as well as the Preflight and Package commands

To find out where I discuss a specific feature, please consult the Index, which begins on page 461.

While I cover almost every single aspect of InDesign—more than any other tutorial guide on the market—there are a few specialized topics that fall outside the scope of this book. These include scripting, the Library palette, Version Cue (which is included only with the Creative Suite), Package for GoLive, and all functions that are unique to InDesign CS PageMaker Edition. If these topics are important to you, please consult *Total Training for Adobe InDesign CS* or one of the other fine training products available from Total Training at *www.totaltraining.com.*

I now invite you to turn your attention to Lesson 1, "Starting a Document." I hope you'll agree with me that *Adobe InDesign CS One-on-One*'s combination of step-by-step lessons and video introductions provides the best learning experience of any InDesign training resource on the market.

LESSON 1

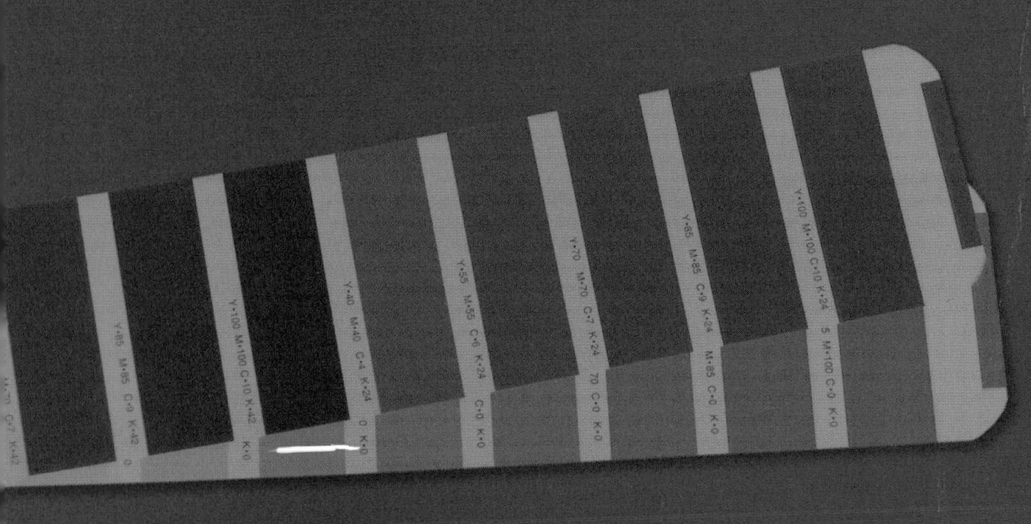

Y•100 M•100 C•10 K•24
Y•85 M•85 C•9 K•24
Y•70 M•70 C•7 K•24
Y•55 M•55 C•6 K•24
Y•40 M•40 C•4 K•24
Y•100 M•100 C•10 K•42
Y•85 M•85 C•9 K•42

STARTING A DOCUMENT

EVEN BY computer industry standards, digital publishing is a volatile business. Adobe's PostScript printing language gave us the ability to combine text and graphics without traditional paste-up, but has since conceded cutting-edge functions like transparency to the more flexible Portable Document Format (PDF). PageMaker single-handedly created a multimillion-dollar desktop publishing industry and then watched with bewilderment as QuarkXPress charmed away its professional design audience just a few years later. Apple, the sole supplier of early publishing machines, now garners most of its revenues from its mobile, consumer, and music products. Even the industry's original moniker, *desktop publishing*, is shunned as hopelessly outdated. Today's cyber elite bandy words like *digital*, *production*, and *design*, but never *desktop*.

So I guess it figures that nearly 20 years after the publishing revolution began, it appears primed for yet another coup in the form of InDesign. Half a decade since Adobe released what many gleefully termed its "Quark killer," XPress remains in heavy use, especially for laying out books, newspapers, and magazines. But unfortunately for Quark, most of its users aren't upgrading; they're making do with what they have. To a person, the hundreds of XPress and PageMaker users I've talked to agree that, whatever their personal preferences, the writing is on the wall. InDesign may not be the most popular page layout and design tool at this moment, but give it time. PageMaker is dead and XPress is withering. InDesign is the tool with a future.

Fortunately for us users, the tool with a future just so happens to be really great. No, I take that back. Not really great—outrageously, unbelievably, profanity-inspiringly great. That's why I want you to put this book down for a moment—if not now, well then, when you get a moment—and pat yourself on the back. You made a very wise decision the day you decided to take on InDesign.

ABOUT THIS LESSON

Project Files

Before beginning the exercises, make sure that you've installed the lesson files from the CD, as explained in Step 5 on page xv of the Preface. This should result in a folder called *Lesson Files-IDcs 1on1* on your desktop. We'll be working with the files inside the *Lesson 01* subfolder.

Before you can take advantage of InDesign's state-of-the-art page-composition functions, you must know how to open a file, set up a new document, adjust columns and guides, and save your work to disk. In this lesson, you'll learn how to:

Video Lesson 1: Navigation

Another topic I urge you to master as soon as possible is navigation. Not *doing* anything to a document, mind you, just moving around inside it: magnifying an area in a document, panning to a different part of a page, or advancing from one page to the next.

Navigation is the subject of the first video lesson included on the CD. To view this video, insert the CD, click **Start Training**, and then select **1, Navigation** on the right side of the screen. The movie lasts 12 minutes and 32 seconds, during which time you'll learn these shortcuts:

Operation	Windows shortcut	Macintosh shortcut
Highlight zoom value	Ctrl+Alt+5	⌘-Option-5
Alphabetize menu	Ctrl+Shift+Alt-click menu name	⌘-Shift-Option-click menu name
Zoom to 100 percent view size	Ctrl+1	⌘-1
Fit page or spread in window	Ctrl+0 (zero), Ctrl+Alt+0	⌘-0, ⌘-Option-0
Zoom in or out	Ctrl+[+] (plus), Ctrl+[–] (minus)	⌘-[+], ⌘-[–]
Zoom in with magnifying glass	Ctrl+spacebar-click in document	⌘-spacebar-click in document
Zoom out with magnifying glass	Ctrl+Alt+spacebar-click	⌘-Option-spacebar-click
Scroll with the hand tool	Alt+spacebar-drag in document	Option-spacebar-drag in document
Switch to the next or last page	Shift+Page Down, Shift+Page Up	Shift-Page Down, Shift-Page Up
Expand or collapse docked palettes	Ctrl+Alt+Tab	⌘-Option-Tab
Hide or show toolbox and/or palettes	Tab, Shift+Tab	Tab, Shift-Tab
Switch in and out of preview mode	W	W

What Is InDesign?

Like any great page-composition program, InDesign lets you combine elements from a variety of sources to make multipage documents. You can import text from a word processor or enter text directly in InDesign. You can import photographs and high-resolution line art, as well as create artwork with InDesign's drawing tools. In this regard, InDesign is a kind of page-making mill. You pour text and graphics into its hopper, mix them together using your carefully practiced design skills, and eventually produce fully-rendered pages, like the one pictured at the end of Figure 1-1.

Once the raw materials are in the hopper, InDesign invites you to place them on the page. You can establish regular columns of type, as in a newspaper, or adjust each column independently. You can align text and graphics using a variety of grids and guidelines. You can wrap text around graphics, place text along curved lines, and even insert graphics into text blocks as if they were characters of type. And all the while, text and graphic objects are independently editable. You have only to drag an object to move it to a new location, scale it, or even slant it to a more interesting angle.

Although InDesign is more than adequate for designing single pages, it really comes to life when laying out multipage documents. You can add and reorder pages with ease, automatically number pages, and repeat regular design elements from one page to the next. When constructing long documents like books, InDesign helps you generate a table of contents and an index. And you can even create automated templates to expedite the layout of newsletters and other periodicals.

Most InDesign documents are bound for print, so it makes sense that the program is well versed in outputting full-color pages and separating inks for commercial reproduction. But print isn't your only option. InDesign exports directly to PDF, ideal for designing interactive documents with bookmarks, hyperlinks, and other navigation functions.

Plainly put, there's no better program for designing documents, especially those that are two pages or longer. InDesign lets you control every phase of the page-layout process with glorious precision and unparalleled control. As proof of my commitment, I submit to you this very document. I used InDesign to create every page of this book—not to mention a few thousand pages before them.

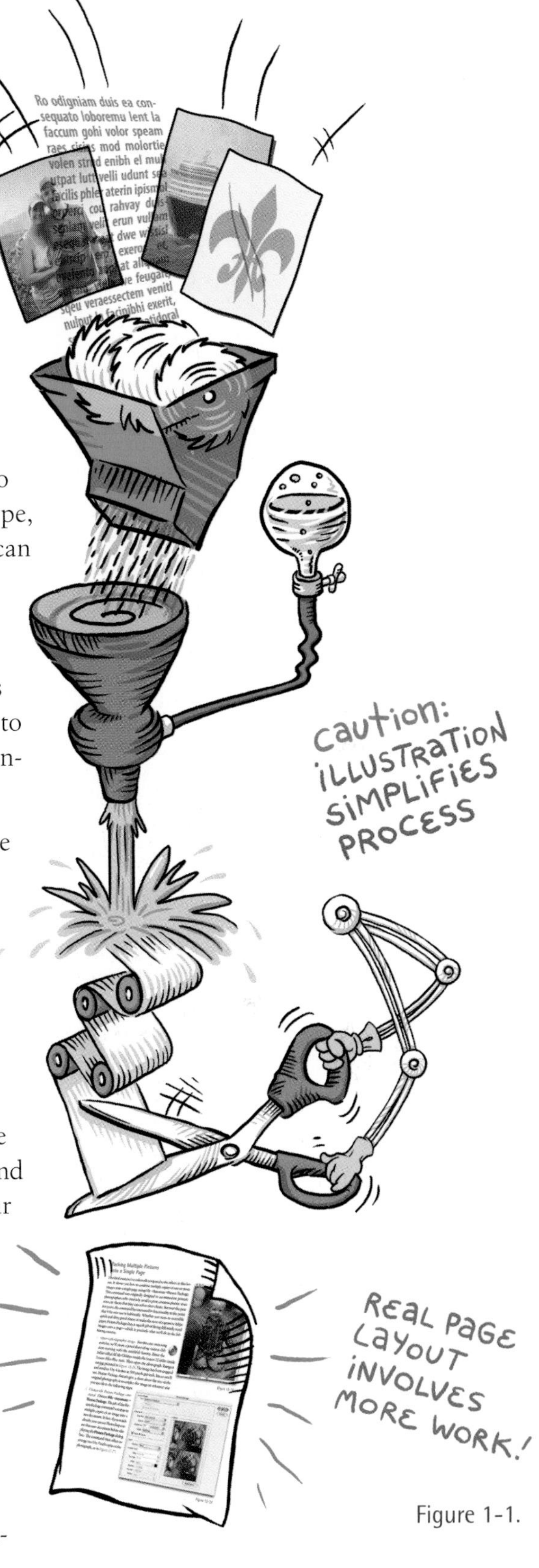
caution: illustration simplifies process
Real page layout involves more work!

Figure 1-1.

Opening an InDesign Document

Opening an InDesign document is pretty much like opening a document in any application, Adobe or otherwise. It all begins with the Open command. That said, there are a few possible stumbling points, which this exercise shows you how to circumnavigate.

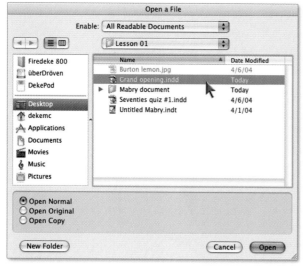

Figure 1-2.

1. ***Choose File→Open.*** Alternatively, you can press Ctrl+O (⌘-O on the Mac). Either way, you get the **Open a File** dialog box. Figure 1-2 shows the dialog box as it appears on the Mac under OS X 10.3.

2. ***Navigate to the Lesson 01 folder.*** Assuming you followed my advice in the Preface and installed the lesson files on your desktop, here's how to get to the *Lesson 01* folder:

   - Click the **Desktop** icon located along the left side of the dialog box to display the files and folders on your computer's desktop. (If you don't see a Desktop button on the Mac, press ⌘-D instead.)
   - Locate and double-click the *Lesson Files-IDcs 1on1* folder.
   - Finally, double-click the *Lesson 01* folder. You're in like Flynn.

3. ***Select a file.*** Click the file called *Grand opening.indd* to select it. In this opening exercise about opening files, it seems appropriate to open a document about an opening. Assuming you're open to that, of course.

Figure 1-3.

PEARL OF WISDOM

If you're using a Windows-based PC and you don't see the document you're looking for, you probably need to change the setting in the Files of Type pop-up menu at the bottom of the Open a File dialog box, shown in Figure 1-3. While this menu is useful for narrowing down the choices in a folder full of files—you might want to view only PageMaker files, for example—it can prevent you from seeing the InDesign document you're looking for. For day-to-day work, the default setting of All Readable Files is usually your best bet.

4. ***Select an Open As option.*** The bottom-left corner of the Open a File dialog box has three options that let you specify how you would like to open a document. These options generally come into play when you are working with templates. A *template* is a special type

of InDesign file that you can create to serve as the starting point for a series of similar documents. For instance, if you publish a weekly newsletter, you can create a template that contains the basic layout and formatting for the newsletter.

Here's a rundown of how the Open As options work:

- Most of the time, you'll want to leave the Normal radio button (called Open Normal on the Mac) selected. Doing so opens the original of a regular InDesign file, but opens an untitled copy of a template file so that the original template is preserved.
- If you do want to make changes to an actual template file, select the Original (or Open Original) radio button.
- If you want to work with a copy of a regular InDesign file and preserve the original, select the Copy radio button (named Open Copy on the Mac).

For our purposes, please select **Normal** (**Open Normal** on the Mac). But for the record, in this instance choosing Original (Open Original on the Mac) would produce the same result because *Grand opening.indd* is not a template file.

5. ***Click the Open button.*** Click the **Open** button or press the Enter or Return key to open the document inside InDesign. If the document appears on screen, then all is well. But be aware that InDesign may ask you to respond to an alert message or two before opening a file. For example, it's possible (though unlikely) that InDesign will complain that one or more fonts used in the document are missing from your system. If so, stay tuned for the next exercise, "Opening a QuarkXPress Document," in which you'll learn how to address this problem. More likely, InDesign will greet you with the **Embedded Profile Mismatch** message (see Figure 1-4), which warns you about a discrepancy in the color settings. To address this message, read the next step.

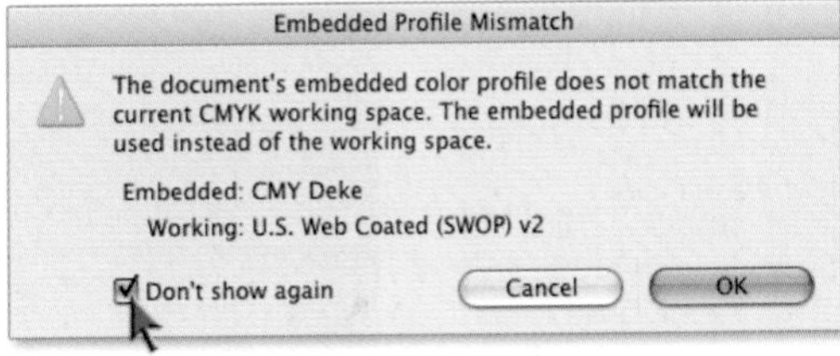

Figure 1-4.

6. ***Disable the color warning.*** I trust that you followed my advice in the Preface and set your Color Settings to Best Workflow (see Step 11, page xvi). Part of what the Best Workflow setting does is to tell InDesign to keep mum when a document's color profile doesn't match your current color space. And yet, in direct violation of this request, InDesign sees fit to bug you anyway, just to let you know what it's doing. It's kind of like asking a three-year-old child not to bang her spoon on her plate, and she responds by banging it on the table instead.

Interface and Document Window

The first time you run InDesign CS, the interface is so streamlined you hardly notice it's there. But a few minutes of opening files and poking around unleash a Pandora's Box, one bursting with all varieties of commands, buttons, and gizmos, as in the figure below. If you've been using a computer for any amount of time, much of it will appear familiar. But to make sure you and I are on the same page—and to square away some important vocabulary—the following list explains some of the more pivotal interface elements in alphabetical order.

- **Cursor:** The cursor is your mouse's on-screen representative. It tracks mouse movements and changes to reflect the active tool or operation. Keep an eye on it and you'll have a better sense of what you're doing.
- **Control palette:** Located at the top of the screen by default, this horizontal strip provides access to the most commonly used options in InDesign. Better yet, the palette is context-sensitive, changing to accommodate the selected object or active tool.

Press Ctrl+Alt+6 (⌘-Option-6 on the Mac) to hide or show the palette. Press Ctrl+6 (⌘-6) to highlight the first value. Then press Tab to advance or Shift+Tab to back up.

- **Document window:** Each open document appears in a separate window, thus permitting you to open multiple documents at once. This is where you edit text, position graphics, and assemble your pages. Drag the *size box* in the lower-right corner to resize the window.
- **Guides:** The colored lines in the document window are nonprinting, "magnetic" guides, meaning that objects snap into place when dragged close to them. See "Adjusting Margins and Guides" on page 26 for more info.

To hide all nonprinting elements, press the W key or click the bottom-right icon in the toolbox. Press W again or click the bottom-left icon to bring the guides back.

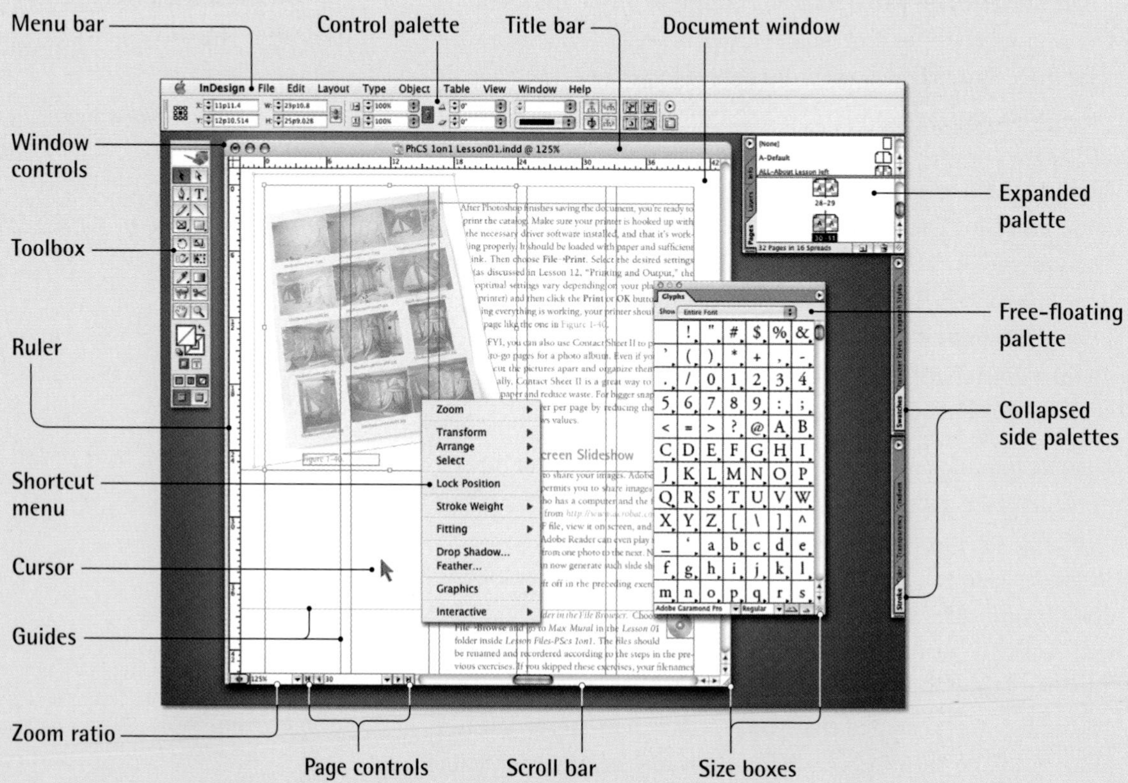

- **Menu bar:** Click a name in the menu bar to display a list of commands. Choose a command by clicking on it. A command followed by three dots (such as Export...) displays a window of options called a *dialog box*. Otherwise, the command works right away.

- **Page controls:** The controls in the bottom-left corner of the document window let you switch pages, either sequentially or by entering a specific page number.

Press Shift+Page Down to go to the next page or Shift+Page Up to go to the previous one. To go to a specific page, press Ctrl+J (⌘-J on the Mac), type a page number, and press the Enter or Return key.

- **Palettes:** A *palette* is a window of options that remains on-screen regardless of what you're doing. In InDesign CS, a palette may attach sideways to the side of the screen. Click a wedge-shaped tab to expand or collapse the corresponding palette. You can also click tabs to switch between grouped palettes.

You can customize the arrangement of palettes by dragging a tab from one group to another. Drag a tab away from the right side of the screen to create a free-floating palette. Press Alt (or Option) and drag a tab to move all grouped palettes at once. Drag a tab to the left or right side of your screen to tuck the palette away.

- **Ruler:** Press Ctrl+R (or ⌘-R) to frame the document window with two rulers, one above and one to the left. Tick marks track your movements. By default, the unit of measure for the rulers is *picas*, where a pica is ⅙ inch. To change the unit of measure, right-click (or Control-click) a ruler and choose a setting from the shortcut menu.

Right-clicking changes one ruler independently of the other. Press Ctrl+Shift+Alt+U (⌘-Shift-Option-U on the Mac) to cycle both rulers from one unit to the next.

- **Scroll bars:** Located opposite the rulers, the scroll bars let you pan the document horizontally or vertically to display hidden areas. For more information, watch Video Lesson 1, "Navigation," on the CD (see page 4).

- **Shortcut menu:** Click the right mouse button to display a shortcut menu of options. Like the Control palette, these options are context-sensitive, changing to suit a selected object or the active tool. When in doubt, right-click. If your Macintosh mouse doesn't have a right mouse button (Apple's mice don't), press the Control key and click.

- **Title bar:** The title of the last-saved version of a file appears at the top of the document. Click this title bar to make a document active so you can edit its contents; drag the title bar to move a document window.

To switch between open windows from the keyboard, press Ctrl+[~] (⌘-[~] on the Mac). Typically, the [~] key is located in the upper-left corner of the keyboard, next to the [1].

- **Toolbox:** Click an icon in the toolbox to select a tool; then use the tool in the document window. A small black triangle to the bottom-right of an icon shows that multiple tools share a single *slot*. Click and hold the icon to display a flyout menu of alternate tools. Or press Alt (or Option) and click a slot to cycle between tools.

Press the Tab key to hide the toolbox and all palettes. Press Tab again to bring them back. To hide or show all palettes except the toolbox and Control palette, press Shift+Tab. To expand or collapse palettes attached to the sides of the screen, press Ctrl+Alt+Tab (⌘-Option-Tab on the Mac).

- **Window controls:** The title bar contains three controls that let you hide, size, and close a document window. The Mac controls are on the left; the Windows controls are on the right.

- **Zoom ratio:** The percentage value in the lower-left corner of the document window lists the magnification of the document on screen. Raise the value to zoom in on a page; lower the value to zoom out. For more information, watch Video Lesson 1, "Navigation," on the CD.

To highlight the zoom ratio value, press Ctrl+Alt+5 (or ⌘-Option-5). Then type a value between 5 and 4,000 percent and press Enter or Return. When the value is highlighted, press the ↑ or ↓ key to zoom in 25-percent increments.

No matter; InDesign can be silenced far more easily than any toddler. Just turn on the **Don't show again** check box and click **OK**. Now InDesign really won't bug you again—not about embedded profiles, anyway.

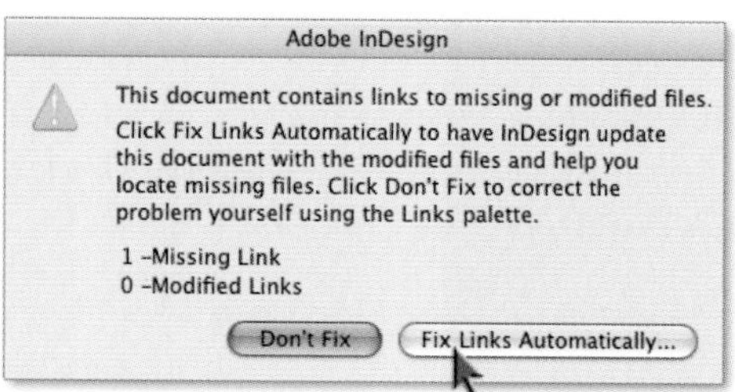

Figure 1-5.

7. ***Fix any missing or modified links.*** There's also a good chance you'll encounter the alert message shown in Figure 1-5. When you import a graphic into a document, InDesign avoids any unnecessary duplication of information by creating a link to the graphic file on disk. But if the graphic file has been moved since the last time the InDesign document was saved—as invariably occurs when copying files from a CD to your hard drive, for example—InDesign may get confused and be unable to find the graphic. If it does, do the following:

Figure 1-6.

- Click the **Fix Links Automatically** button to tell InDesign to hunt down the graphic file and reestablish the links on its own.
- If clicking the button takes you to a **Find** dialog box, look for *Burton lemon.jpg* in the *Lesson 01* folder. When you find it, select the file and click **Open**. A few moments later, InDesign displays the document in a new document window, as in Figure 1-6.

Incidentally, I'll be asking you to open and modify lots of documents throughout this book. When you arrive at the successful conclusion of an exercise, as you have now, you may do with the document as you will. You can inspect it, modify it, or ignore it altogether. To tidy up your screen and move on, click the ☒ icon in the title bar (⊗ on the Mac). Alternatively, you can choose **File→Close** or press Ctrl+W (⌘-W on the Mac).

Opening a QuarkXPress Document

If QuarkXPress was previously your page-layout application of choice, then you've undoubtedly heard how InDesign can open Quark files. But while InDesign gets an A for effort, I'd give it a C for its average rate of success. That's not to say InDesign won't open your Quark documents; it usually will. But expect to lose something in the translation.

The fact is, it's always difficult for one application to open another's native file format. After all, the native format—in Quark's case, QXD—is designed to work with one program and one program only. A QXD file takes advantage of features and settings that have long existed in QuarkXPress but may be significantly different or altogether missing in InDesign. The problem is compounded by the fact that Quark has never published its format so that other software developers can use it. Quark considers QXD proprietary, so as you might imagine, it isn't the least bit interested in helping Adobe crack the code.

PEARL OF WISDOM

I should mention that InDesign can read files saved in QuarkXPress 3.3 through 4.1 only. Why not Quark 5 and 6 files? Encryption. Quark is so anxious about other programs siphoning away its documents that it equipped XPress 5 and later with the ability to save a QXD file in a manner that's incomprehensible to any outside application, including InDesign. While Quark argues it has the right to protect its intellectual property, encryption turns recent versions of XPress into the software equivalents of the *Hotel California:* you can check out, but you can never leave—not with your files, anyway. If you ask me, it's yet another reason to get out of Quark while the getting is good.

My advice: Think of InDesign not as capable of opening QXD files, but rather as pretty darn good at interpreting them. In the following steps, we'll see how to interpret one such QXD file, respond to the error messages that may occur, and resolve the worst of the misinterpretations. And lest you think the lessons learned in this exercise apply to Quark files only, these steps also work when opening a PageMaker document. InDesign is a little better at interpreting PageMaker files, but chooses to limit its support to documents created in PageMaker 6.5 and 7.

1. ***Open a QuarkXPress document.*** Choose **File→Open**. Go to the *Lesson 01* folder inside *Lesson Files-IDcs 1on1*. Therein, you'll find a subfolder called *Mabry document*. Open it and then double-click the file called *AMC-DI Mabry.qxd*. This file contains six pages from a book I wrote called *Adobe Master Class: Design Invitational* (Peachpit Press, 2002), pictured in Figure 1-7 on the next page. Although the book centers on Adobe and its products, the designer, Andrew Faulkner, decided to lay out the pages in Quark. As you can imagine, some inside Adobe took offense. But I say, why worry? Andrew did a terrific job, the book looked great, and lo these many years later, we still have the option to convert the document over to InDesign.

Figure 1-7.

Converting QuarkXPress document

Converting regular spreads...

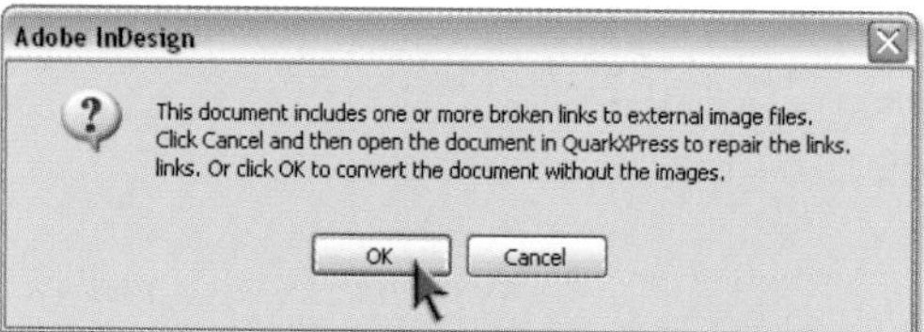

Figure 1-8.

2. ***Respond to the alert message.*** After a moment or two, InDesign warns you that your document includes "broken links," which is to say, InDesign can't locate the graphics that are associated with this file. Pictured in Figure 1-8, the message recommends that you return to Quark and fix the links there. But that's nuts. Truth is, you can just as easily restore the links in InDesign. So click the **OK** button to acknowledge the message and move on.

3. ***Read the warnings.*** A moment later, InDesign graces you with another alert message, this time listing everything about the Quark document that won't work properly in InDesign. Although the list seems interminable (Figure 1-9), it documents just three kinds of problems:

   - **Shortcuts.** InDesign can't honor some of the keyboard shortcuts Andrew assigned to his custom styles because they conflict with other shortcuts. I tell you more about style shortcuts in Lesson 5, "Using Style Sheets." But between you and me, it's a nonissue. Ignore.

   - **Objects.** Some of the text and graphic objects in Andrew's document are locked in ways that InDesign can't interpret. So it might have to lock one or two objects that weren't locked, or vice versa, all of which you can override at your leisure. In other words, ignore.

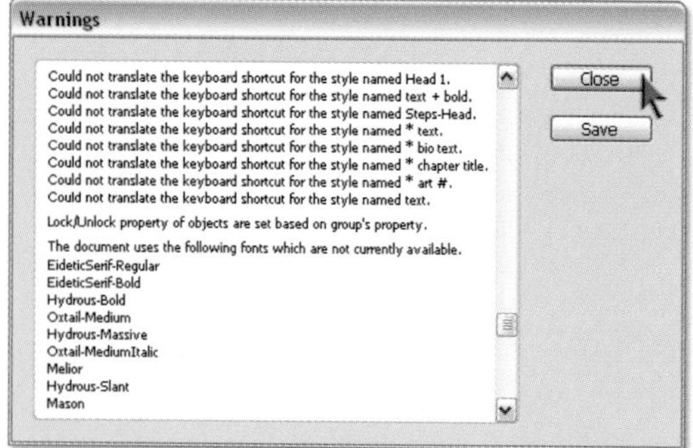

Figure 1-9.

- **Fonts.** Andrew used a bunch of fonts from Psy/Ops, a San Francisco-based type house. Wonderful typefaces, but I don't happen to have any on my system—and most likely you don't either. As a result, InDesign complains. This is a legitimate issue, one that we'll address shortly.

If you care to examine the list in detail, you can save it to a text file by clicking the **Save** button. Otherwise, click **Close** to move on.

4. ***Review your document for problems.*** By now, InDesign has opened the QXD file inside a new, untitled document window, as in Figure 1-10. This tells you that the document has been converted from a non-native file format and that the converted document has not been saved. (This happens when opening documents saved in InDesign 2.0 and earlier as well.)

Figure 1-10.

By default, InDesign reduces the first couple of pages so they fit within the dimensions of your screen. Even this far zoomed out, you can see that the text is covered in a Pepto-Bismol pink, which is InDesign's way of telling you the typefaces are all wrong. To check out other problems, zoom in. I suggest pressing Ctrl+spacebar (⌘-spacebar on the Mac) and clicking three or four times close to the cartoon face, as indicated by the zoom tool cursor in Figure 1-11 on the next page. At a magnified zoom level, you can clearly see that the graphics are jagged, a function of the fact that InDesign can't locate the

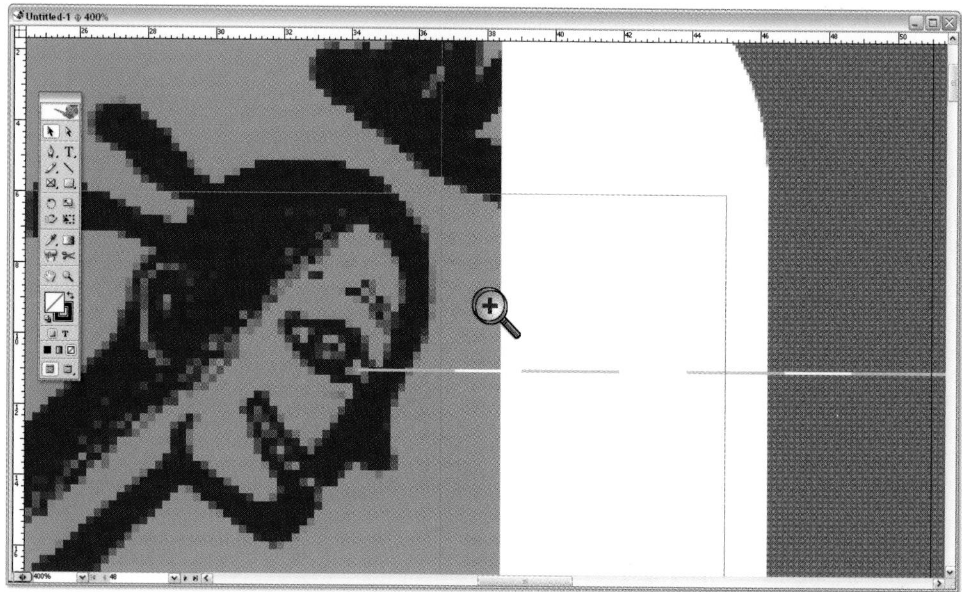

Figure 1-11.

high-resolution graphics on disk. Also, there's a big white gap between the cartoon and the vertical bar to the right of it. These are all problems you'll fix in the next steps.

5. ***Choose the Find Font command.*** First press Ctrl+Alt+0 (or ⌘-Option-0) to zoom out so you can take in the entire document. Then choose **Type→Find Font** to display the **Find Font** dialog box. Pictured in Figure 1-12, this dialog box lets you replace all instances of any typeface used in your document with a different typeface.

6. ***Replace Eidetic Serif Regular with Jenson Pro Light.*** We'll start by replacing the most popular font in the document, which happens to go by the name Eidetic Serif. Here's what I want you to do:

   - Click the font **EideticSerif-Regular** in the scrolling list on the left side of the dialog box. This is the second font down, between EideticSerif-Bold and Hydrous-Bold.

   - Click the **More Info** button. InDesign expands the dialog box to show you more information about the font, such as how many characters of type are set in the font, which happens to be 33,023.

   - If you're feeling adventurous, you can look for occurrences of the selected font in the document window by clicking the **Find First** button. In this particular case, InDesign locates

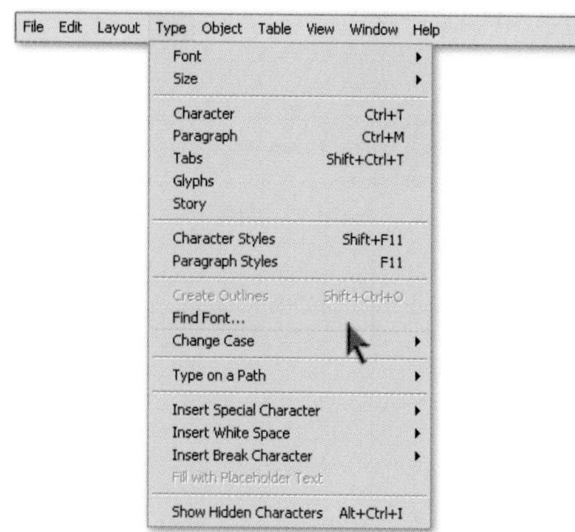

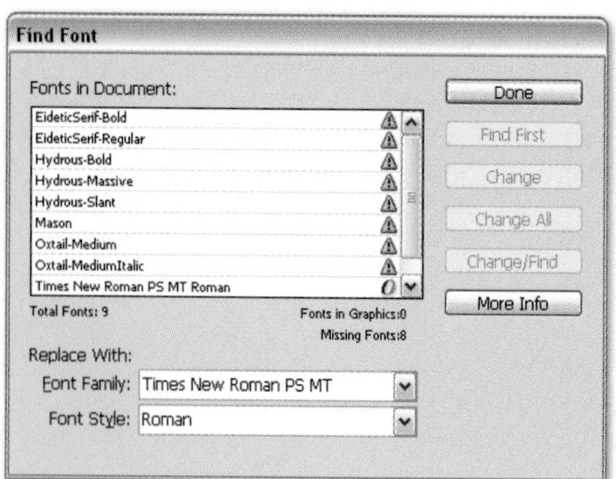

Figure 1-12.

an invisible character (specifically a paragraph return) at the outset of the main text. If that's not terribly satisfying, click **Find Next** to find the next occurrence of the font. This will take you to the next page, where the long string of found text ends.

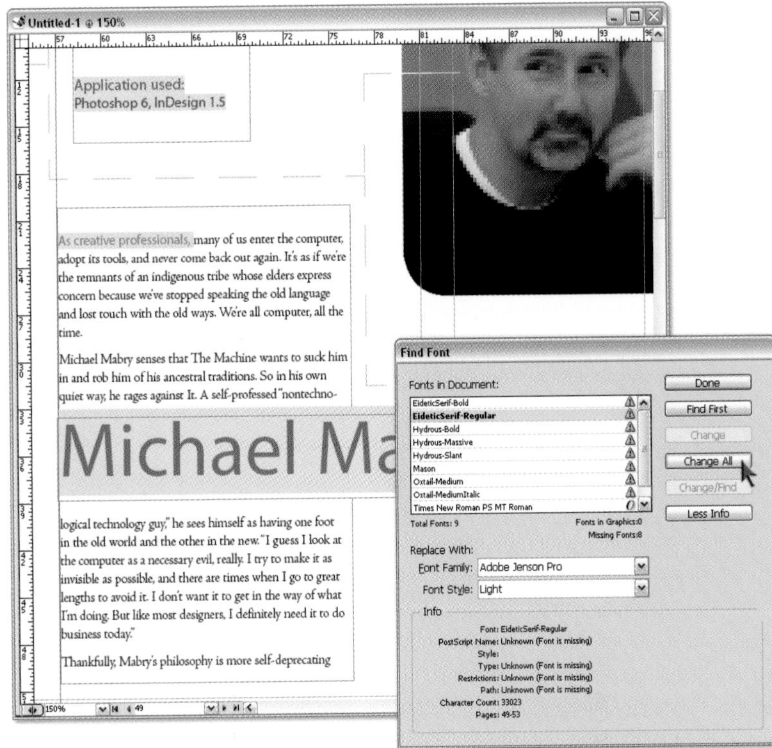

Figure 1-13.

- If you performed the previous Find operations and you'd like to return to the beginning of the document, select the top font, **EideticSerif-Bold** and click **Find First**. Then (very important!) select **EideticSerif-Regular** to make it active again.
- Choose a replacement typeface and style from the **Replace With** pop-up menus in the middle of the dialog box. I recommend setting **Font Family** to **Adobe Jenson Pro**—alphabetized among the J's—and **Font Style** to **Light**. (As I explained in the Preface, Jenson Pro is installed automatically with InDesign CS, so it should be available to your system just as it is to mine.)
- Click the **Change All** button to replace all occurrences of EideticSerif-Regular with Jenson Pro Light.

The result is a welcome lifting of much of the Pepto-Bismol pink, not to mention a marked improvement in the appearance of the *body text* (the main text in the article), as in Figure 1-13.

7. ***Replace the other fonts.*** In all, this document contains a total of eight missing fonts, seven of which we have yet to address. So let's address them. Here are my suggestions (though by all means, feel free to try out different typefaces):

   - Replace EideticSerif-Bold with Adobe Jenson Pro Semibold. (The fact that Jenson Pro remains in effect from the last font change should save you some time.) Don't forget to click **Change All**. When you do, InDesign updates the words at the outset of the first paragraph.

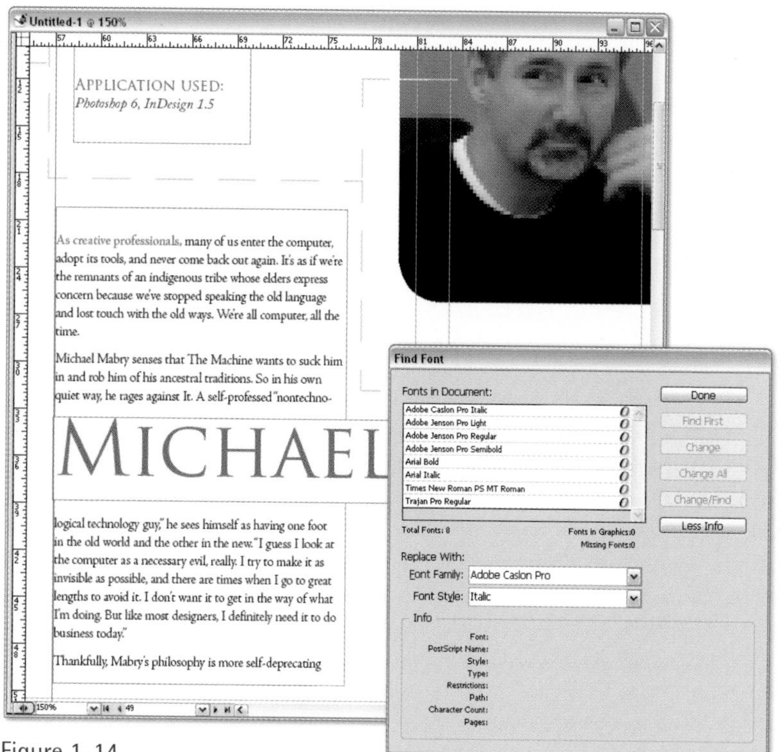

Figure 1-14.

- Replace Mason with Adobe Jenson Pro Regular. This will fix the big ornamental braces, like the ones that appear on page 50 above the pull quote.
- The various Hydrous styles are used for the page number entries at the bottom of each page. Change both Hydrous-Bold and Hydrous-Massive to the family Arial and the style Bold. Change Hydrous-Slant to Arial Italic.
- The remaining Oxtail fonts are used for chapter names, subheads, and other display text. Select Oxtail-Medium and change it to Trajan Pro Regular (another font that ships with InDesign CS).
- Trajan doesn't have an italic style, so you'll have to find another font. I suggest changing Oxtail-MediumItalic to Adobe Caslon Pro Italic (alphabetized with the C's).

When changing typefaces, you may find it easier to double-click in the Font Family option and enter the first few letters of the font name from the keyboard. For example, typing A-D-O selects the first font with the word *Adobe* in its name, most likely Adobe Caslon Pro. You can also use the ↑ and ↓ keys to move from one font or style to the next.

When you finish, the Find Font dialog box should look like the one shown in Figure 1-14. (On the Mac, Times goes by a different name, and the icons to the right of the fonts Times and Arial will look different, but it's all good.)

8. ***Click the Done button.*** Your work here is done. So click **Done** to leave the dialog box and return to the document window.
9. ***Display the Links palette.*** Next I ask you to turn your attention from text to graphics. To wit, you need to relink all the graphic files so that they look good on screen and print super smooth and color-accurate. Choose **Window→Links** or press Ctrl+Shift+D (⌘-Shift-D on the Mac) to display the **Links** palette, as shown in Figure 1-15 on the facing page. The palette lists nine graphic files, all followed by ❷ icons and the page on which they appear in the document. This tells you InDesign

knows that the graphics were used in the document, but it has no idea where the original graphics are on disk.

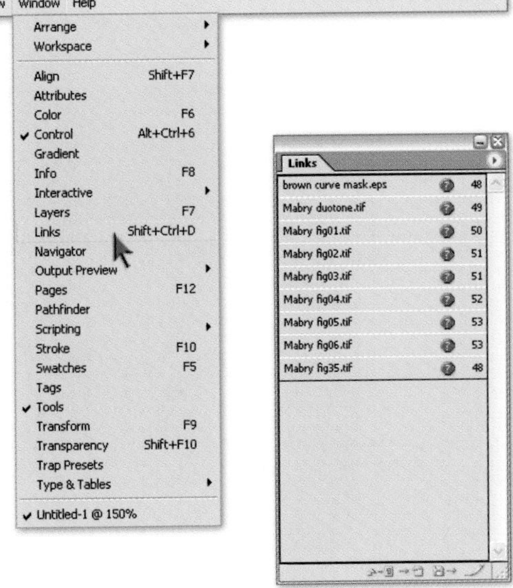

Figure 1-15.

10. ***Select one of the graphics.*** Click the first item in the list, **brown curve mask.eps**, which corresponds to the vertical bar that appears selected in Figure 1-16. To display this graphic in the document window, click the small →⎕ icon at the bottom of the Links palette, as demonstrated to the right of the figure.

11. ***Relink the graphic.*** The bar is colored wrong, and it includes a white background that covers up the cartoon man. That's because this isn't the real graphic at all; it's just an imprecise stand-in. To see the real thing, you must relink the graphic. Click the first icon along the bottom of the Links palette (the one that looks like ⇨⎕) to display the **Find** dialog box. Then burrow your way into the following folders: *Lesson Files-IDcs 1on1*, *Lesson 01*, *Mabry document*, and *Artwork*, until you come to a file called *brown curve mask.eps*. Select that file and click **Open**. InDesign loads the graphic and displays it the way it's supposed to look: as the solid brown bar butting right up against the cartoon that you see in Figure 1-17 on the next page.

Figure 1-16.

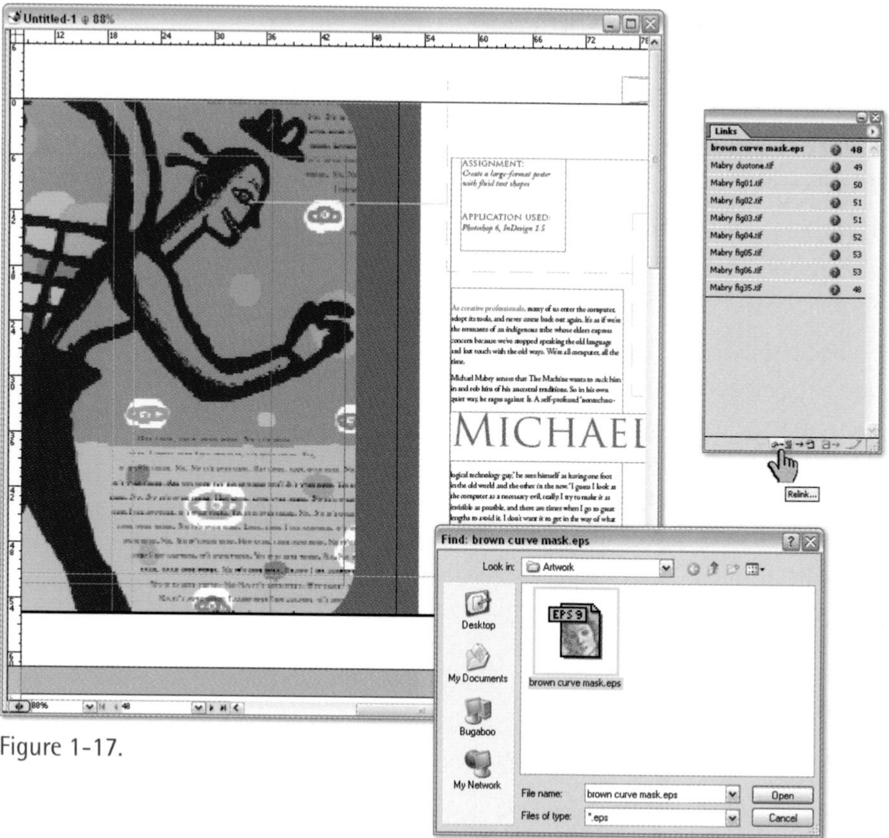

Figure 1-17.

If your bar doesn't look any different after relinking it, it's probably because InDesign's display performance is set wrong. Choose **View→Display Performance→High Quality Display**. Or, assuming you loaded the Deke Keys shortcuts as suggested on page xvii of the Preface, just press F3 at the top of your keyboard.

Figure 1-18.

12. ***Update the other links.*** Now that you've told InDesign where the graphics are, you should be able to update the other links more easily. Click the **Mabry duotone.tif** item at the top of the Links palette. Then press the Shift key and click the Mabry image at the bottom of the list, **Mabry fig35.tif**, to select the range of items in between, as shown in Figure 1-18. Click the ⇨▯ icon at the bottom of the Links palette to fix all selected graphics at once. At this point, one of two things will happen:

    - If a series of yellow ⚠ icons replace the ❓ symbols along the right side of the palette, you're in luck. This means InDesign was smart enough to figure out where the other graphic files were and link to them. Click the ▤→ icon at the bottom of the Links palette—pictured in Figure 1-18—to update the images inside the document window.

- If InDesign instead presents you with a **Relink** dialog box, as in Figure 1-19, you have to link each file manually. Click the **Browse** button, find the image in the *Artwork* folder, click the **Open** button, and repeat for each of the other graphics.

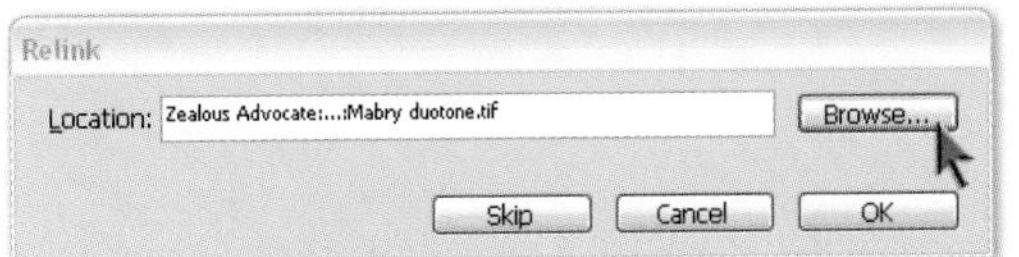

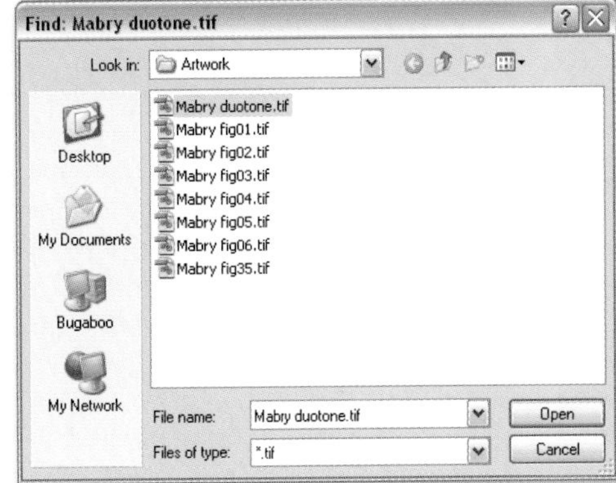

Figure 1-19.

Whether InDesign lets you reestablish links the easy way or makes you do it the hard way, you'll end up with a palette full of happily linked graphics. When you finish, feel free to close the Links palette.

13. ***Review your document again.*** Now that you've had a chance to swap out the fonts and relink the graphics, take a step back and evaluate your document. In all likelihood, you'll have to manually tweak a few elements to put them right. For example, Figure 1-20 shows our document thus far. The text and graphics are dramatically improved over their appearance back in Figure 1-10. But they're hardly perfect. A few problems:

    - The name of the artist, Michael Mabry, no longer fits on one line. I'll need to reduce the type size.
    - The last line of body text on page 49 of the sample document—the one that starts with *Thankfully, Mabry's philosophy*—should begin on the next page. Many of the line breaks aren't right either. A large type size and some adjustments to the text box are in order.

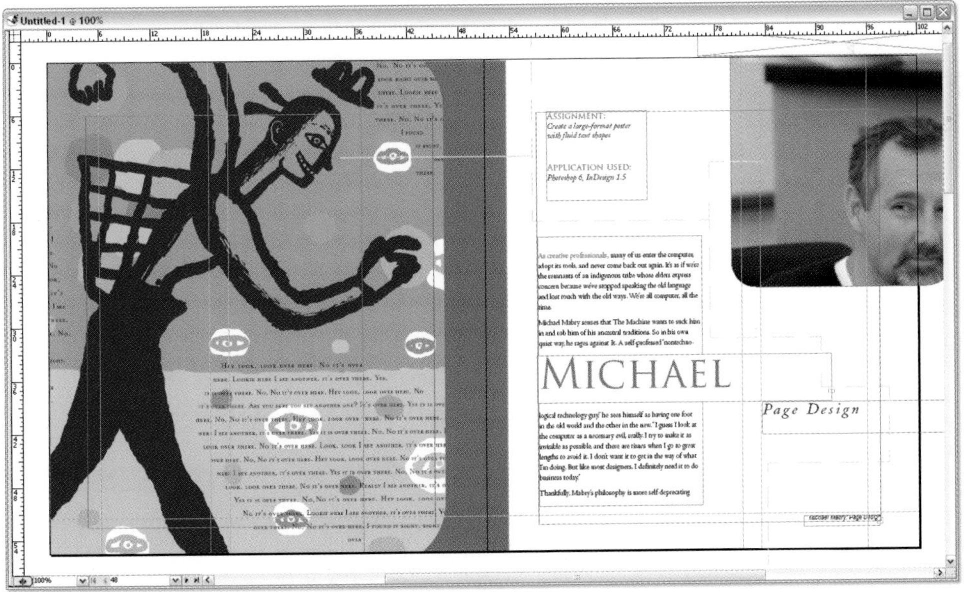

Figure 1-20.

- In the bottom-right corner of the right-hand page, the page number is cut off. It looks like I need to enlarge the text box a bit.
- Michael's head shot no longer fits properly in its frame. Updating the link also restored the image to full size. I'll need to resize it and adjust the positioning.

Figure 1-21 shows the page spread after 15 or so minutes of manual adjustments and fine tuning. The text is sized to fit, the page number is visible, and Michael's head is back in the frame. I also changed the color of the title text to match the finished book. (The figure shows the document in the preview mode, which hides guides and frame outlines. To enter the preview mode, click the icon in the toolbox or press the W key.)

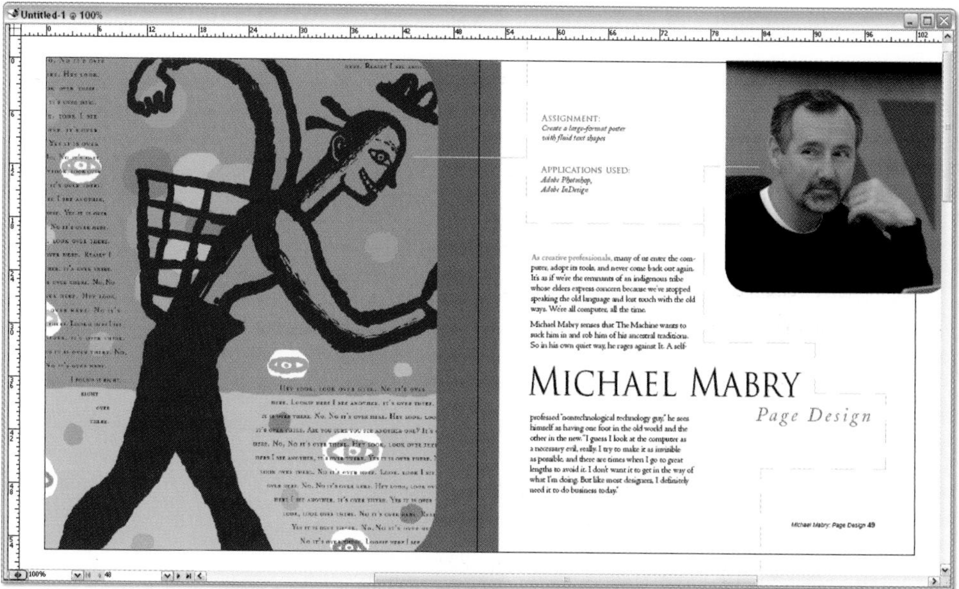

Figure 1-21.

The adjustments applied in Figure 1-21 fall under the category of general edits, the kind of day-to-day operations that you apply to any InDesign document, whether it started in QuarkXPress or elsewhere. Therefore, we'll explore them in detail in later lessons. Specifically, I'll show you how to modify text blocks in Lesson 2, adjust type sizes in Lesson 3, and scale and crop graphics in Lesson 7.

After all this work, you'll probably want to save your document so you don't lose the conversion and other changes. To do so, choose **File→Save**, give the document a name, specify a location, and click the **Save** button. To learn more about this process, skip ahead to the "Saving Your Document" exercise which begins on page 39.

Setting Up a New Document

All layout programs let you create new documents, but few let you do so as meticulously as InDesign. And with good reason. Meticulous controls permit you to establish solid foundations, which in turn serve as backbones for successful designs. Armed with an established regimen of margins, columns, and bleeds, you have everything you need to structure your content, solve problems, and concentrate your creative energies. Without that foundation, all you have is an empty page.

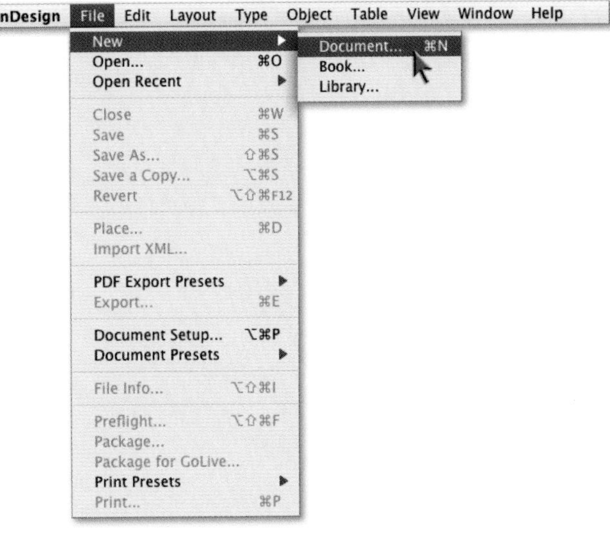

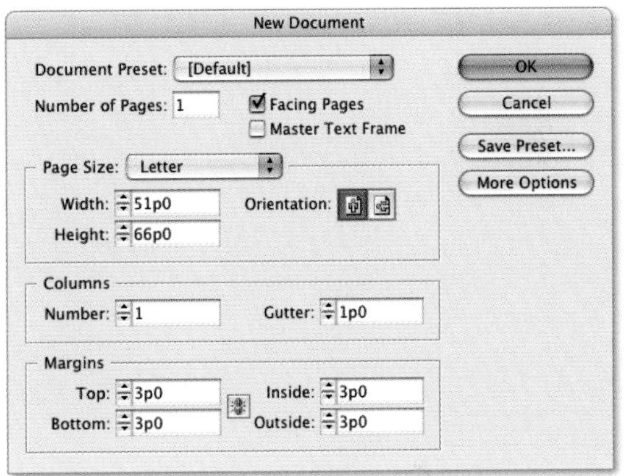

Figure 1-22.

The goal of the next exercise is to create a new multipage document. For the sake of example, we'll create a document that subscribes to the page dimensions and margins at work in this very book.

1. ***Choose the New command.*** Choose **File→New→Document** or press Ctrl+N (⌘-N on the Mac). InDesign displays the **New Document** dialog box, as in Figure 1-22.

2. ***Enter the number of pages.*** Ever helpful, InDesign highlights the very first option, **Number of Pages**, so you can dig right in. Change the value to 12.

   Why 12? First, it's an even number, so the document will start on a right-hand page and end on a left one. Second, if you don't know exactly how long a final document will run, 12 pages give you room to experiment without running so long that you have to delete pages later. In other words, it's an educated shot in the dark.

PEARL OF WISDOM

Bear in mind, every value that you enter into the New Document dialog box can be modified at a later date. You can add and delete pages, change margins and columns, even set up new pages with independent margins and columns. So if you have only a very vague idea of how you want to set up your new document, don't fret. Just rough in some numbers and consider the resulting document a work in progress.

3. ***Turn on Facing Pages.*** As illustrated in Figure 1-23 on the next page, your everyday average multipage publication comprises many pairs of facing pages.

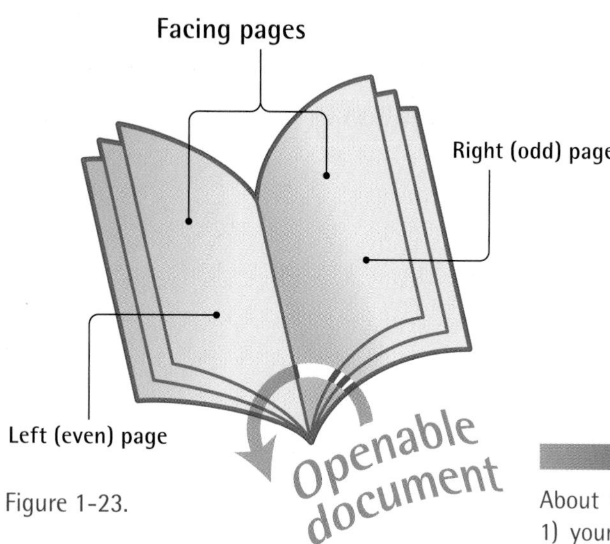

Figure 1-23.

Examples include newsletters, magazines, books—anything printed on both sides of a page and bound along a spine. The left-hand page bears an even page number, and hence is called the *even page*; the one on the right sports an odd number, making it the *odd page*. If you intend to create such a document, then select the **Facing Pages** check box, as by default. When this option is on, InDesign makes each pair of pages symmetrical. This means the two inner margins (the right margin on the even page and the left on the odd) are the same, as are the outer margins (left on even, right on odd).

PEARL OF WISDOM

About the only times you want to turn Facing Pages off are when: 1) your final document includes strictly single-sided pages, as in the case of a legal contract, or 2) you plan on outputting the file to PDF and distributing it electronically, in which case the traditional spine-bound document metaphor (Figure 1-23) doesn't apply. When Facing Pages is off, InDesign treats each page the same, with consistent left and right margins unless you specify otherwise.

4. ***Leave Master Text Frame turned off.*** If you're used to working with QuarkXPress, then you're used to creating boxes to house your text. XPress even lets you create automatic text boxes when making a new document. The same is true for InDesign, with two exceptions. First, InDesign calls its boxes *frames*. Second, you can create frames on the fly—as you type in or import text—so there's little advantage in having InDesign create automatic frames in advance. To see the Master Text Frame check box in action, watch Video Lesson 2, "Text and Frames," on the CD (see page 48). But for the present, leave the option off.

5. ***Adjust the page dimensions.*** If you want your pages to conform to a common paper format, such as letter or tabloid, choose the size from the **Page Size** pop-up menu. But don't think those two choices are the only ones available. Although your inkjet or laser printer may limit you to certain paper formats, commercial printers can trim paper to any size you like (provided, of course, that the page fits on the press). And if you intend to publish your document to PDF, why then no paper, no problems.

   The pages in this book happen to measure 8 inches wide by 9¾ inches tall, shorter and slightly narrower than a letter-sized page but quite large by book standards. To create such a page, enter the desired dimensions into the **Width** and **Height** option boxes. Only problem is, InDesign's default units of measure are *picas* and *points*. A pica is 1/6 of an inch; a point is 1/12 of a pica, or 1/72 inch. The default Width value of 51p0 means 51 picas and 0 points, which translates to 8 1/2 inches. If you don't like picas, you can choose Edit→Preferences (InDesign→Preferences on the Mac) and click Units & Increments to switch to inches or some other unit. But I urge you not to, if only to strike accord with the rest of the design community. Picas and points are the standard for page layout in the U.S. and England, and they enjoy wide support across all varieties of design applications and hardware.

9.75 inches	702 points	247.65 millimeters
9.75inches	702 point	247.65mm
9.75 inch	702pt	24.765 centimeters
9.75inch	picas 702	24.765cm
9.75 in	pica 702	24cm+7.65mm
9.75in	pica702	24765/100mm
9.75i	p702	54.9 ciceros
9.75"	9i+4.5p	54.9 cicero
9"+.75"	9i+4p6	54.9c
10"-0.25"	9i+54pt	54 cicero 10.8
39/4"	9i+p54	54cicero10.8
39*0.25"	10i-1.5p	54c10.8
58.5 picas	10i-1p6	ciceros 658.8
58.5 pica	10i-18pt	cicero658.8
58.5pica	10i-p18	c658.8
58.5p		
58 pica 6		
58pica6		
58p 6		
58p6		

50 different ways to say "9 3/4 inches" in InDesign

Figure 1-24.

And besides, why switch when you can convert from inches on the fly? Here's how. Press the Tab key one or more times to advance to the Width value. Then type "8 inches" ("8in" or "8i" for short). Press Tab to advance to the Height value. The moment you do, InDesign converts your inches to picas, making the Width value 48p0, or 48 picas. Next, enter "9.75 inches" (or "9.75in") and press Tab again. The Height value becomes 58p6, which is 58 picas 6 points, or 58.5 picas.

Just for fun, Figure 1-24 shows the many other ways to enter alternative measurements, including millimeters and ciceros. (Like a pica, the European *cicero* comprises 12 points, but each point—sometimes called a *didot*—is about 1/68 inch.) Note that you can spell out units or use a number of abbreviations. You can also perform small bits of math.

6. ***Specify two columns.*** The **Columns** values determine how many columns of type you intend to place on a page. InDesign will automatically flow text into these columns, but you can modify the dimensions of a text frame and adjust the column guides at any time you like.

   This book employs a loose two-column design with text on the inside of the page and graphics on the outside. So enter 2 for the **Number** value. The **Gutter** value defines the distance between columns; leave this set to 1p0, or 1 pica. Note that InDesign delivers columns of equal width. If you want to create columns of different widths, like the ones in this book, you'll have to adjust the columns manually, as I explain in the next exercise ("Adjusting Margins and Guides," page 26).

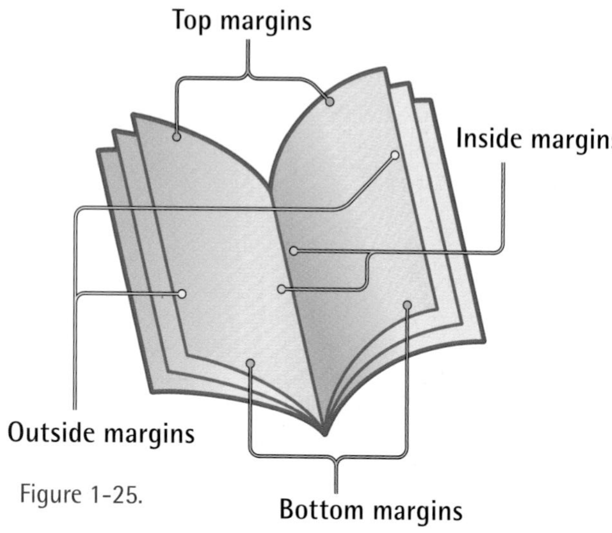

Figure 1-25.

7. ***Increase the margins.*** The **Margins** values define the amount of room between the far edge of your content and the perimeter of the page. When Facing Pages is active (Step 3, page 21), InDesign calculates inside and outside margins, as well as top and bottom margins (see Figure 1-25). If Facing Pages is off, you must set the left and right margins.

   The default Margins values of 3 picas (½ inch) apiece give a design room to breathe and guarantee that nothing will get clipped when the final pages are trimmed. This book includes a roomier bottom margin to accommodate the page number, as well as some extra space along the inside margin to account for the area lost in the deep furrow where the pages meet the spine. Change both the **Bottom** and **Inside** values to 4p6 (¾ inch). Leave the **Top** and **Outside** values at 3p0.

8. ***Expand the dialog box.*** Click the **More Options** button in the upper-right area of the dialog box to reveal the Bleed and Slug options (see Figure 1-26), which permit you to increase the size of the printable area of a page beyond its strict Page Size boundaries.

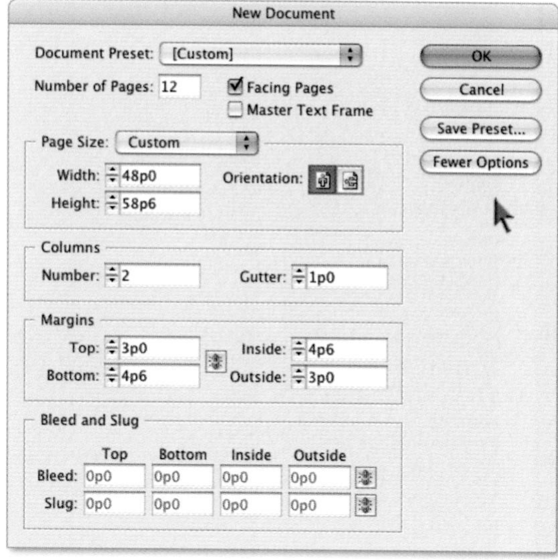

Figure 1-26.

PEARL OF WISDOM

If you want a text or graphic object to extend all the way to the edge of a page—like the big, colorful artwork at the outset of each lesson in this book—then you have to add an extra margin outside the page boundary called a *bleed*. This gives your commercial printer some wiggle room when trimming the page, so that the finished product doesn't end up with a tiny sliver of exposed, uninked paper. The *slug* is an additional area beyond the bleed that contains project titles, handling instructions, and whatever other stuff you want to communicate to your commercial printer. In Figure 1-27, the slug boundary appears as a thin blue line, the bleed boundary is red, and the trim size is yellow. Nothing beyond the trim size (as indicated by the crop marks) will appear in the final product you receive back from the printer.

9. ***Set all Bleed values to 1 pica.*** Typical bleeds range anywhere from half a pica to 1.5 picas. We'll split the difference. To change all **Bleed** values at once, click the broken chain icon () to the right of the final option (**Outside**) to link the values. Change any of the values to 1p0, and then press Tab to update the others.

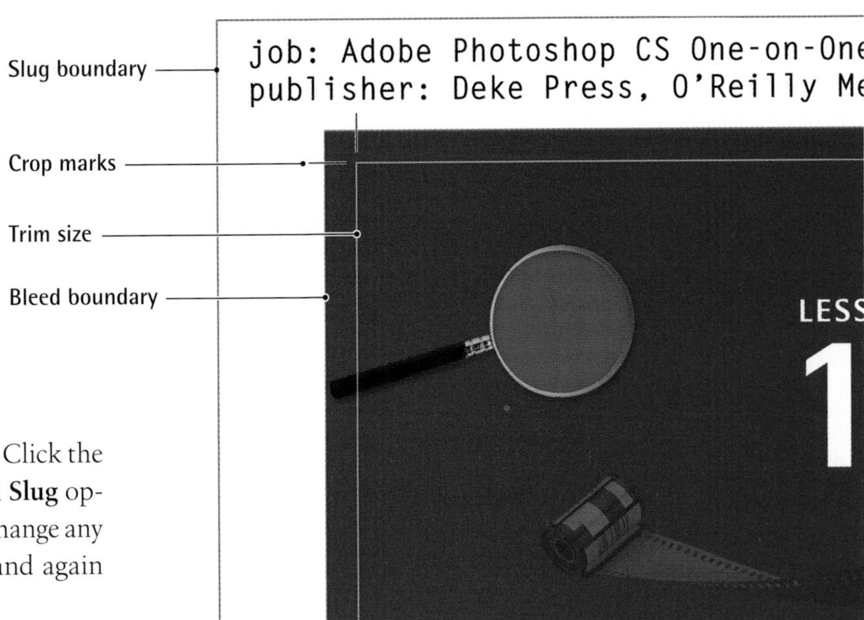

Figure 1-27.

10. ***Set all Slug values to 3 picas.*** Click the icon to the right of the final **Slug** option to turn the link on. Then change any Slug value to 3p0 (or 0.5in) and again press the Tab key.

11. ***Save your settings as a new document preset.*** After putting this much work into the New Document dialog box, you don't want to lose it. To save your settings—even if you think there's just a hint of a chance that you might want to use them again—click the **Save Preset** button. Then name the new preset "One-on-One," as in Figure 1-28, and click **OK**. A new option called **One-on-One** appears in the **Document Preset** pop-up menu at the top of the dialog box. In the future, choosing that option loads all the settings you applied in this exercise.

12. ***Click the OK button.*** Or press Enter or Return to accept your settings and create a blank document inside a new document window. Your document should look like the one in Figure 1-29 on the next page, with purple page margins, a red bleed boundary, and a blue slug.

Now that you've created a pristine new document, you'll learn a few ways to change it in the next exercise.

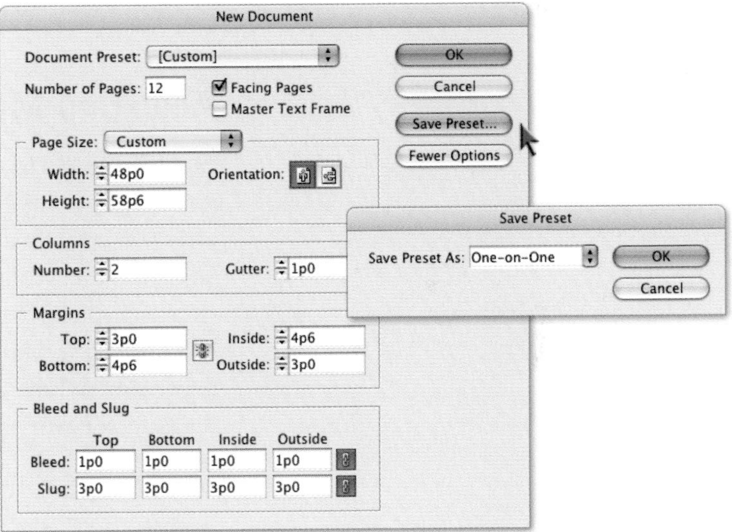

Figure 1-28.

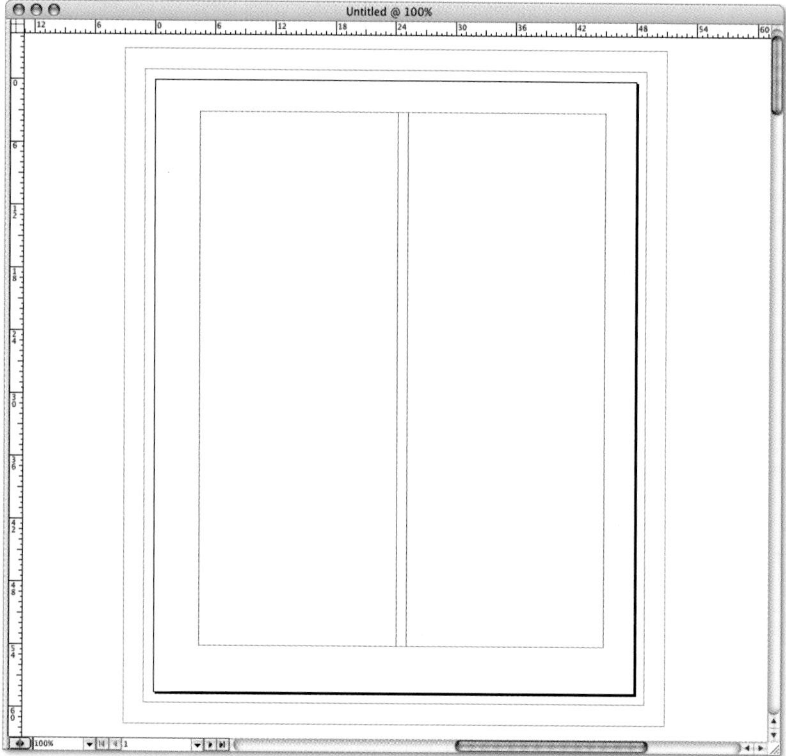

Figure 1-29.

Adjusting Margins and Guides

As I mentioned in the previous exercise, every page attribute that you specify in the New Document dialog box can be changed long after you create a document. The only difference is that instead of adjusting everything from a single dialog box, as in the previous exercise, you have to flit back and forth between many. One dialog box affects the whole document, another changes one or two active pages, and a third offers access to options that the New Document dialog box never heard of.

This exercise explores how to change margins, columns, page numbers, and custom guidelines in the new document you just created to make it better match the layout used to create the lessons in this book.

1. ***Make your new document.*** If the new document from the previous exercise remains open, then skip to Step 2. Otherwise, choose **File→New→Document** to display the New Document dialog box. Then choose **One-on-One** from the **Document Preset** pop-up menu to load the settings that you saved in Step 11 on the preceding page (see Figure 1-30). To make the document, click **OK**.

By saving the preset back in Step 11 of the preceding exercise, you established new default settings. To bypass the New Document dialog box and put these settings into play, eschew File→New and press Ctrl+Alt+N (⌘-Option-M on the Mac) instead.

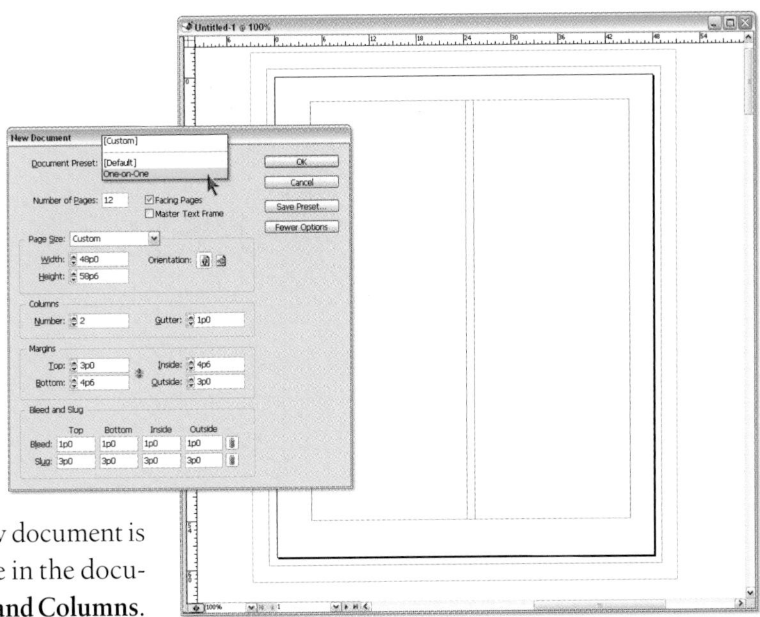

Figure 1-30.

2. ***Choose the Margins and Columns command.*** The first page of a document is generally where you put the title of the publication or chapter, so it's the one that's most likely to vary from the others in its placement of margins and guides. Naturally, your new document is no exception. With the first page visible in the document window, choose **Layout→Margins and Columns**. Alternatively, if you loaded my shortcuts as suggested on page xvii of the Preface, you can access the command from the keyboard by pressing Ctrl+/ (⌘-/ on the Mac). As shown in Figure 1-31, the **Margins and Columns** dialog box contains only those options from the New Document dialog box that are applicable to a single page at a time.

3. ***Increase the Top margin value.*** Lower the top margin by changing the **Top** value to 2.75in. When you press Tab, InDesign converts the value to its equivalent in picas, 16p6. Then click the **OK** button to accept the change. The resulting margin boundaries will house the body text. The chapter title will sit in the empty area above.

Before clicking the OK button, you can preview the effect of your change by turning on the **Preview** check box. As witnessed in Figure 1-32 on the next page, this is a fantastic way to gauge the results of your changes before making a commitment.

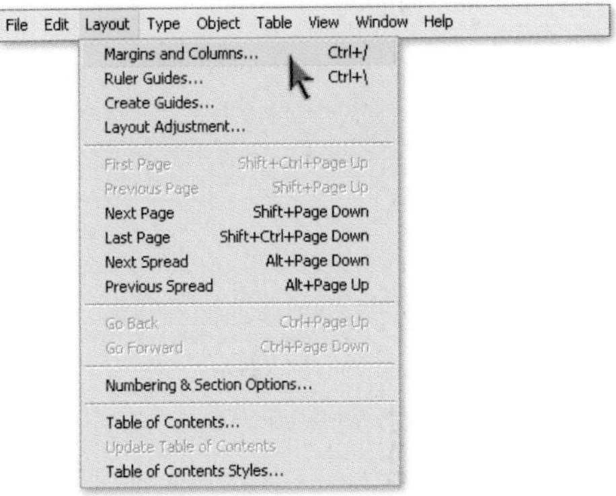

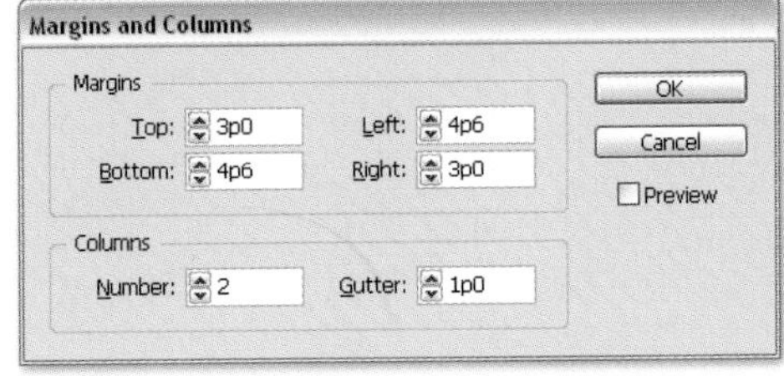

Figure 1-31.

4. ***Add two vertical ruler guides.*** In clearing a space for the chapter title, you've also managed to remove all constraints from the top portion of the page. Fortunately, you can establish custom constraints by adding *ruler guides*, or just plain *guides* for short. As in QuarkXPress, Photoshop, and other programs, you create a ruler guide by dragging from one of the two rulers, hence the name. But that's where the similarities end. As you'll see over the next few steps, InDesign implements the humble ruler guide better than any other program on the market.

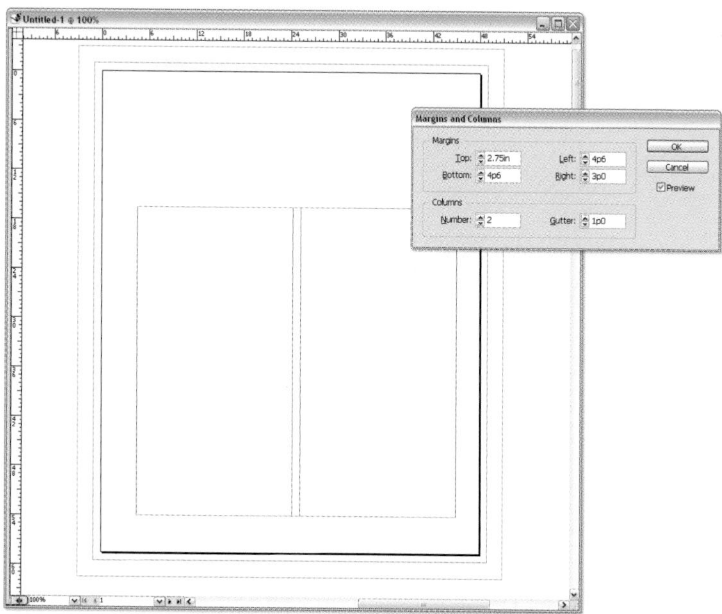

Figure 1-32.

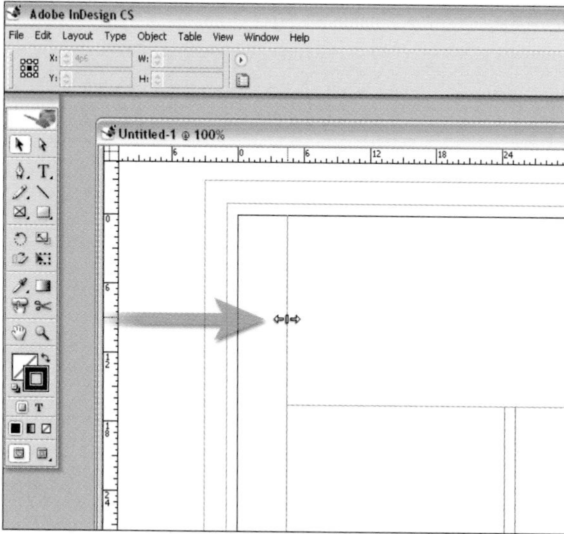

Figure 1-33.

We'll start by adding two vertical guides, one in line with the left margin and the other in line with the right.

- Drag from the middle of the vertical ruler on the left side of the document window until your cursor snaps into alignment with the left margin. At the moment of the snap, your cursor changes from black to white, as in Figure 1-33. Just to be sure, you can also monitor the faint **X** value in the Control palette at the top of your screen. When the guide is properly aligned, the value will read 4p6, the location of the inside margin.
- Drag another guide from the vertical ruler so that it snaps into alignment with the right margin. The newly black **X** value in the Control palette will read 45p0.

PEARL OF WISDOM

If the guide does not snap and your cursor does not turn white, then click the **View** menu, check to see if the **Snap to Guides** command has a check mark in front of it, and assuming it doesn't, choose the command. The Snap to Guides command controls not only whether objects snap into alignment with the guides, but also whether the guides snap into alignment with selected objects and other guides as you drag them.

5. ***Make a horizontal guide at 8p6.*** Now to constrain the top and bottom of the title text. Drag a guide from the horizontal ruler at the top of the screen and drop it at the point where the **Y** value in the Control palette reads 8p6.

To snap the guide into alignment with the regular tick-mark increments in the ruler, press the Shift key as you drag the guide. The Shift key does not have to be down when you start dragging (in other words, you can press it mid-drag), but it does have to be down when you release the mouse button. Because the guide is snapping, your cursor will again appear white, as in Figure 1-34 on the facing page. Bear in mind that the number of tick marks increases as you magnify a document, and more tick marks means more snap points when Shift is down.

If you're still having problems getting the guide into position, here are a few other tricks to try:

- After releasing the guide, press the ↑ or ↓ key to nudge the guide up or down in 1-point increments. Press Shift+↑ or ↓ to move the selected guide in 10-point increments.
- Highlight the **Y** value in the Control palette and change it to 8p6. Then press Enter or Return to move the guide.

Note that the guide has to be selected for these techniques to work. A selected guide is colored a medium blue (as opposed to the deselected guides, which are cyan). If the guide is not selected, click on it with the black arrow tool.

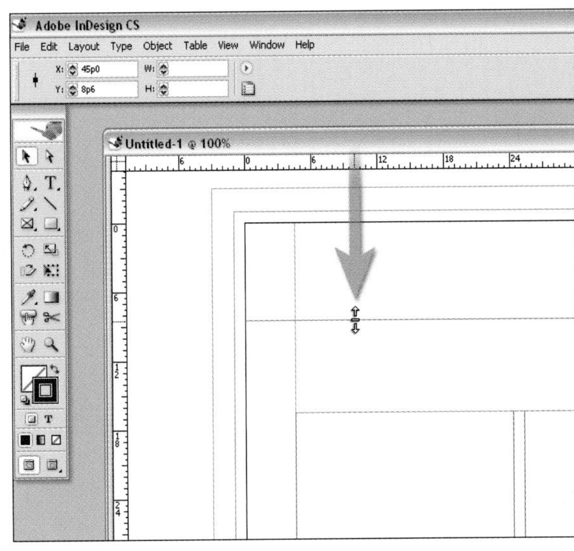

Figure 1-34.

6. ***Create another horizontal guide at 13p0.*** Let's now create a bottom guide for the chapter title. There are two ways to do this. One is the ho-hum way we've been doing things. Drag the guide from the horizontal ruler, press Shift if necessary, and drop the guide when the Y value reaches 13p0. But if you're looking for something new, try this technique instead:
   - First, make sure the horizontal guide you created in Step 5 is selected. (Click it if necessary.)
   - Highlight the **Y** value in the Control palette.
   - Change the value to 13p0.
   - Press Alt+Enter (or Option-Return on the Mac). InDesign clones the guide to the new position.

PEARL OF WISDOM

Our next chore is to adjust the width of the columns. As you may have noticed, while the page you're currently reading is divided into two columns—one for text and the other for graphics—the text column is several picas wider. Although the Margins and Columns command is limited to regular columns, you can create uneven columns as easily as dragging the column guide directly in the document window. But there are two problems with this approach: First, unlike ruler guides, column guides don't remain selected when you click on them, so you can't nudge them from the keyboard or specify a precise numerical position in the Control palette. Second, changing the location of a column guide on one page affects that page only, hamstringing your ability to make global edits. Like the problems, the solutions are twofold: Recruit ruler guides for their precision and master pages for their global influence, as the following steps explain.

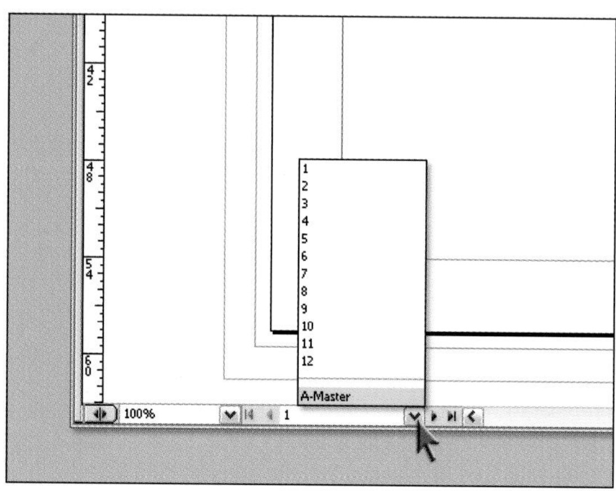

Figure 1-35.

7. ***Go to the master page.*** Behind every page is a *master page*. The purpose of the master page is to carry recurring objects such as page numbers and, happily for us, guides. To visit the master page, click the ▼ icon to the right of the page number in the bottom-left corner of the document window. As shown in Figure 1-35, this displays a pop-up menu of pages. Choose the last option, **A-Master**.

To go to the master page even faster, press Ctrl+J to highlight the page value, type the letter A, and press the Enter key. (On the Mac, press ⌘-J, A, Return.)

Whatever your method, you should now find yourself looking at a pair of humble-looking but terribly powerful master pages. For a detailed examination of master pages, read the exercise "Setting Up Master Pages" that begins on page 334 of Lesson 9. But in the meantime, know this: Any change made to these masters will affect every other page in this document.

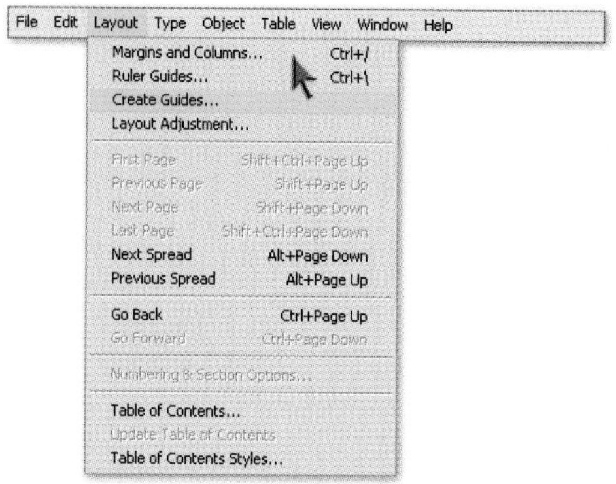

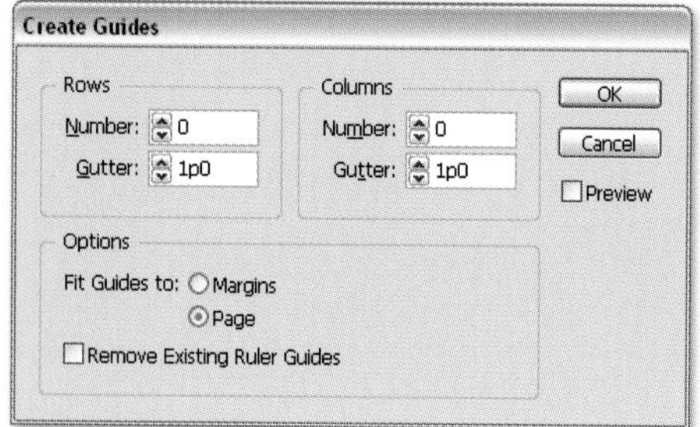

Figure 1-36.

8. ***Choose the Create Guides command.*** If you were to scrutinize the printed page that you're currently reading, you might notice that the outside graphics column is $2/3$ as wide as the inside text column. Two parts graphics to three parts text adds up to five parts altogether. So to exactly align our uneven columns, we need to divide the page into fifths. As luck would have it, InDesign can do this for us by automatically laying down guides. To take advantage of this wonderful function, choose **Layout→Create Guides** to display the **Create Guides** dialog box, as in Figure 1-36.

9. ***Create five columns of guides.*** The Create Guides dialog box lets you create a series of ruler guides—horizontal or vertical or both—at regular increments. The guides may even include gutters, like column guides. Here's how I want you to fill out the options:

   - First, turn on the **Preview** check box. You'll want to see what you're doing.
   - This design demands regular columns, so Tab your way to the **Columns** options and change the **Number** value to 5. The **Gutter** value is fine as is, at 1p0.
   - The guides need to fit inside the margins. So set the **Fit Guides to** option to **Margins**.

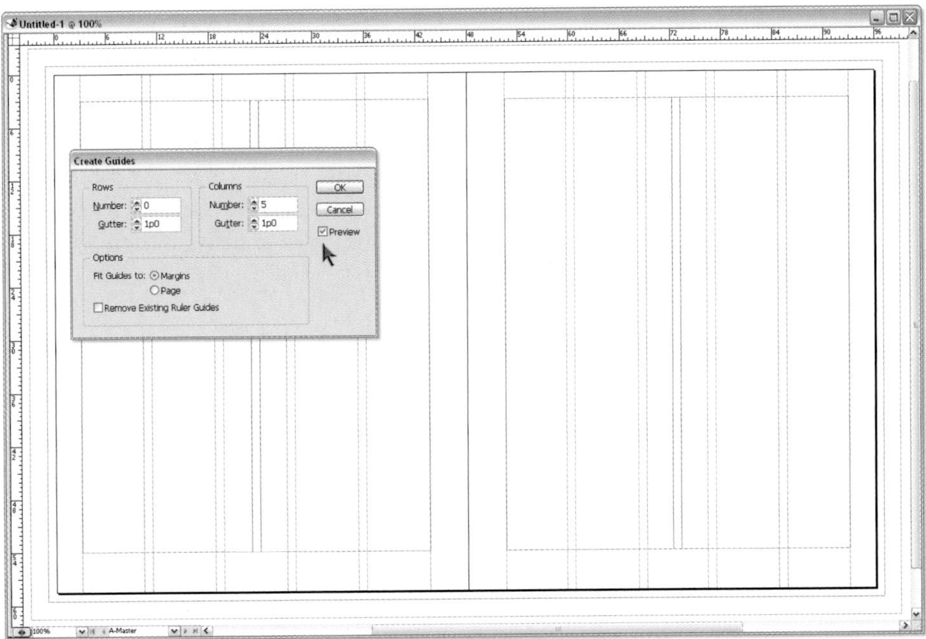

Figure 1-37.

You should get the results shown in Figure 1-37. When you do, click **OK** to make those guides.

10. ***Move the column guides into alignment.*** Drag either side of the purple column guide in the middle of the left master page so it snaps into alignment with the dual ruler guides just to the left of it, as in Figure 1-38. Then scroll to the right master page and drag its column guide to the right. You should end up with two outer columns that are ⅔ as wide as the inner columns.

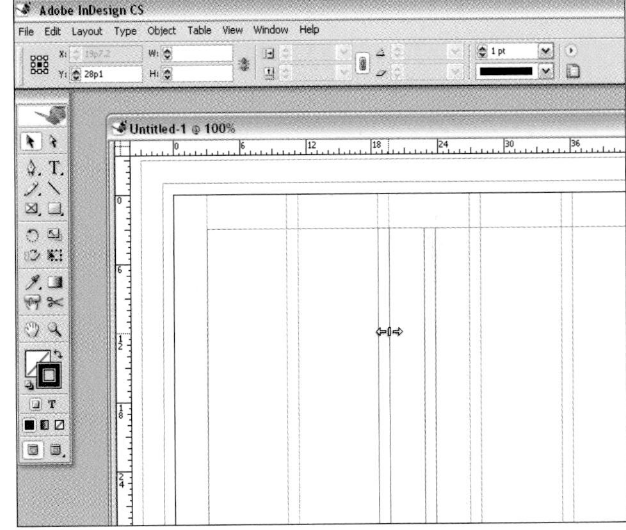

Figure 1-38.

PEARL OF WISDOM

Now that the column guides are positioned properly, we don't really need the cyan-colored ruler guides anymore. And leaving them in place might prove a little confusing, since they sort of clutter up the page. One solution is to delete them. But I hate to delete anything I've created. As I've learned from hard experience, something you need once is something you may very well need again. Fortunately, there's a way to hide the guides and still keep them around. Permit me to explain.

11. ***Select all the ruler guides.*** As you may have gathered by now, InDesign treats guides as selectable objects that you can move, modify, and delete independently of each other. For example, you can select any one of the cyan guides by clicking on it. Press Shift and click to select multiple guides.

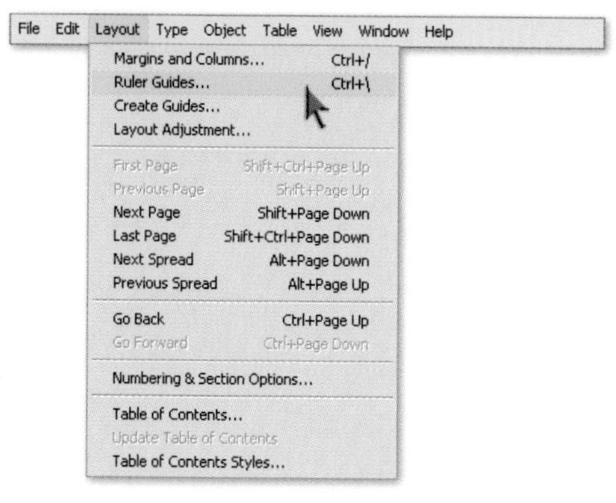

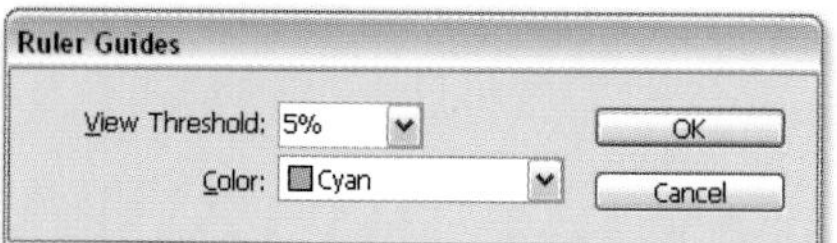

Figure 1-39.

For our part, we'll change all guides across both master pages. But clicking and Shift-clicking on 20 separate guidelines is just too much work. Fortunately, InDesign provides a most excellent shortcut.

To select all ruler guides on the active page or *page spread* (a pair of facing pages), press Ctrl+Alt+G (⌘-Option-G on the Mac). Even if the pages contain text and graphics, InDesign selects only the ruler guides.

Note that there's no menu command for this operation. Like so many things in InDesign, the shortcut *is* the feature.

12. ***Choose the Ruler Guides command.*** This is the point at which you could delete the guides just by pressing the Backspace or Delete key. But let's not; let's modify them instead. To do so, choose **Layout→Ruler Guides**. Or, if you loaded the Deke Keys shortcuts as suggested on page xvii of the Preface, you can take advantage of the shortcut Ctrl+\ (⌘-\ on the Mac). InDesign displays the small **Ruler Guides** dialog box shown in Figure 1-39, which lets you modify the color of the guides and their visibility.

13. ***Change the color and visibility of the guides.*** Make two adjustments to this dialog box:

    - Change the **View Threshold** value to 125 percent. This tells InDesign to display the guides when you magnify the document to 125 percent or greater. When zoomed farther out—say, to 100 percent—the guides are invisible. Bear in mind, however, that just because they're out of sight doesn't mean they're gone. Objects will continue to snap to the guides at all zoom ratios.
    - Click the **Color** pop-up menu and choose the most unobtrusive color possible, **Light Gray** (see Figure 1-40). Even when you do see the guides, they won't attract attention.

    When you finish, click **OK** to accept your changes. If you're zoomed out, the guides will disappear. If you're zoomed in to 125 percent or closer, the guides remain medium blue because they're selected. Choose **Edit→Deselect All** or press Ctrl+Shift+A (⌘-Shift-A) to see their true coloring.

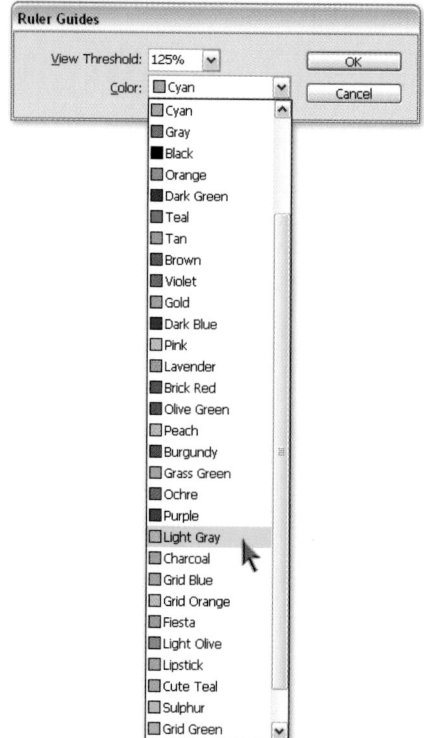

Figure 1-40.

14. ***Add two full-spread ruler guides for the page numbers.*** Note that your changes affect the selected guides only. All other ruler guides, past and future, remain cyan. To see what I mean—and learn another cool trick—let's add a couple more guides.

Drag a horizontal guide from the top ruler to the bottom of the page, where the **Y** value in the Control palette reads 55p0. (Because no guide was previously selected, the Y value again appears faint.) But rather than merely dropping the guide into place, press and hold the Ctrl key (⌘ on the Mac) midway into the drag. This extends the ruler guide across both pages in the spread. Be sure to hold Ctrl (or ⌘) until after you release the mouse button.

Then, with the newest guide selected, highlight the **Y** value (55p0) in the Control palette, change it to 56p0, and press Alt+Enter (or Option-Return). Pictured in Figure 1-41, the result is two guides that span the entire master page spread and define the upper and lower boundaries of the page numbers.

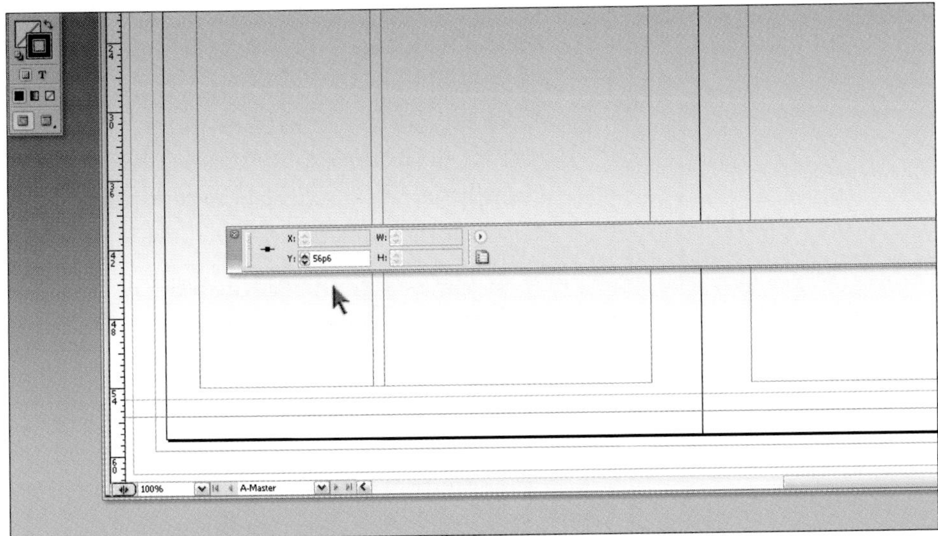

Figure 1-41.

15. ***Return to the main document.*** Switch to page 2 of the document (see Figure 1-42 on the next page). On the PC, you can also press Ctrl+J, 2, Enter. On the Mac, try ⌘-J, 2, Return. Then choose **View→Fit Spread in Window** to take in the entirety of pages 2 and 3. The columns are wide on the inside and a bit narrower on the outside, the 20 gray ruler guides are hidden, and two page number guides grace the bottom of the document. Zoom in and you'll see the gray guides suddenly pop into view at 125 percent. True to our expectations, changing the guides on the master page has affected all other pages as well.

16. ***Fix the first page.*** Well actually, there is *one* page that hasn't been affected, and like this book, it goes by the name *One*. Choose **Layout→First Page** or press Ctrl+Shift+Page Up (⌘-Shift-Page Up on the Mac) to go to page 1. There you'll notice that, despite

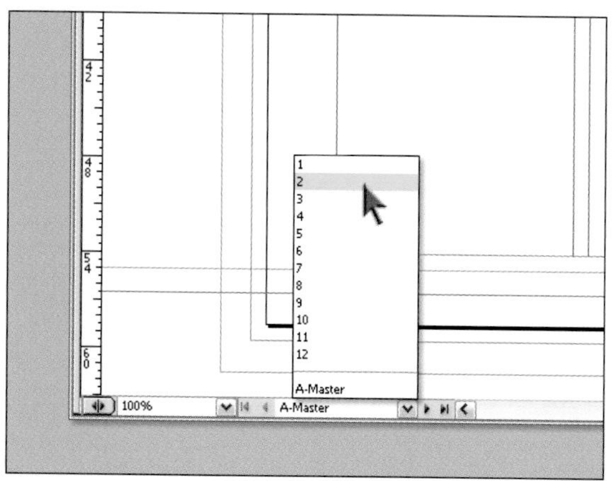

Figure 1-42.

Figure 1-43.

all your efforts, the columns remain resolutely equal in width. By manually changing the margins of this page back in Step 3 (page 27), we broke the link between the page 1 guides and those on the master pages. Alas, such is life—and so we must repeat a bit of work.

First, zoom in close enough to the page so you can see the gray ruler guides. Then drag the purple column guide so it snaps into alignment with the gray ruler guides immediately to the right of it, as in Figure 1-43. Just like that, problem solved.

17. ***Recolor the title guides.*** To better set off the chapter title boundaries, I suggest we change the color of the two horizontal guides at the top of page 1.

    - First, drag around the guides with the black arrow tool to select them, as demonstrated in Figure 1-44. Clicking and dragging from an empty portion of a document creates a dotted rectangular *marquee*; anything inside the marquee becomes selected, making it yet another nifty way to select multiple objects.
    - Next, choose **Layout→Ruler Guides** or press Ctrl+\ (⌘-\ on the Mac). Change the **Color** to **Gold** and click **OK**. Click off the guides to deselect them and see their new color.

    This seemingly simple action does something you can't do in any other layout program—create color coded guides. Now if you tell your fellow layout artists, "Use the cyan guides to position the page number and the orange guides for the title," they'll know exactly what you mean.

You've put in a lot of work, so may want to save your document. To do so, choose File→Save As, enter a name, and click the Save button. For more information, read the "Saving Your Document" exercise on page 39 of this lesson.

Creating Custom Workspaces

Like most Adobe software, InDesign's interface can be described as palette-intensive. Lurking under the Window menu are 35 different palettes, though mercifully only 12 of them appear on screen by default. A palette can either stand on its own or nest together with other palettes in a common palette window. InDesign's default workspace places three

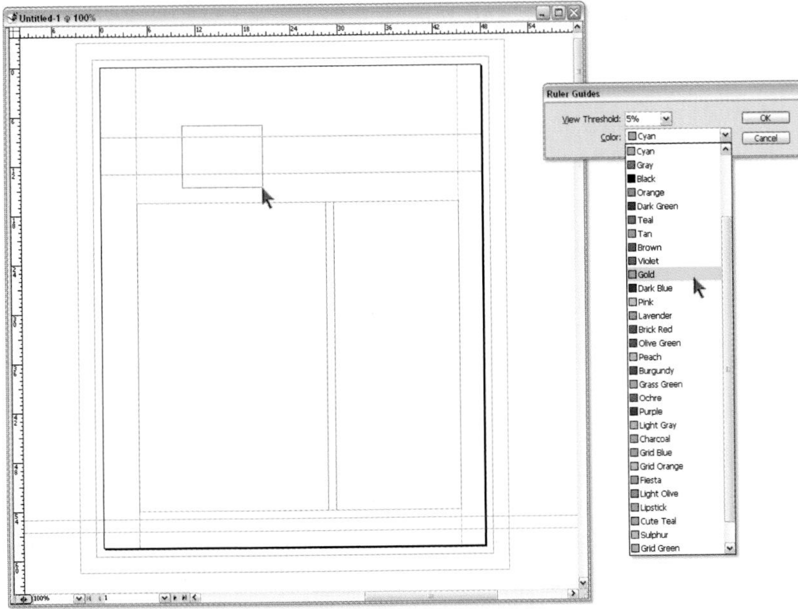

Figure 1-44.

groups of nested palettes on the right side of the screen, as you can see in Figure 1-45. (The blue pattern in the center is my computer's desktop image.) If this default palette setup doesn't suit you, not to worry. InDesign lets you create and save your own custom workspaces so that you can call up different arrangements of palettes for different tasks.

By way of example, this exercise shows you how to set up and save a custom workspace well suited for using InDesign's drawing tools. You'll also learn how to switch back and forth between the custom workspace and the default.

Figure 1-45.

My screen resolution for this exercise is set to 1024 by 768 pixels, which is definitely on the skimpy side when using a program like InDesign. I hope you're using a monitor with a higher resolution, possibly even a couple of monitors, one for the document window and another for palettes. In other words, the figures in this exercise demonstrate a sort of worst-case scenario, so if things on your screen don't look exactly like they do here in the book, just relax and breathe a hearty sigh of relief. But try not to gloat; it's unbecoming.

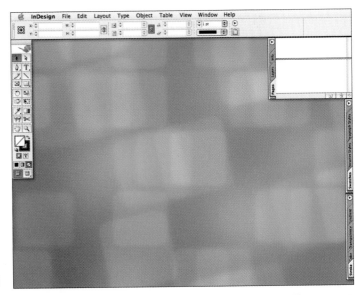

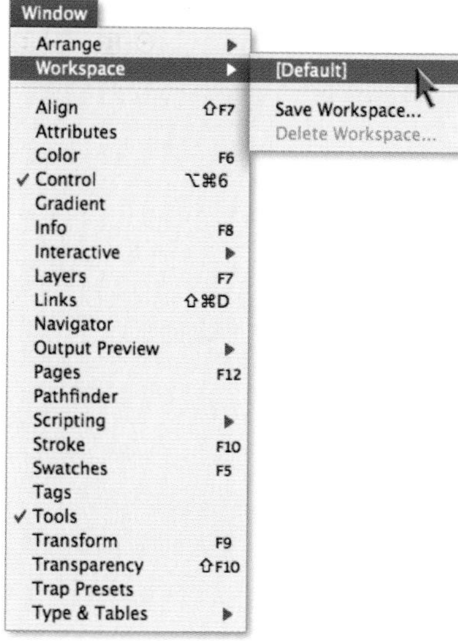

Figure 1-46.

1. ***Restore the default palette locations.*** Assuming that you haven't done any palette redecorating that you care to keep, let's get on the same page by choosing **Window→Workspace→[Default]**. Shown in Figure 1-46, this unassuming command resets all palettes to their default locations, just as if you were starting InDesign CS for the very first time.

2. ***Open a sample document.*** This makes sure we're all *literally* on the same page. Open the file named *Seventies quiz.indd* located in the *Lesson 01* folder inside the *Lesson Files-IDcs 1on1* folder. The document appears on screen, as shown in Figure 1-47.

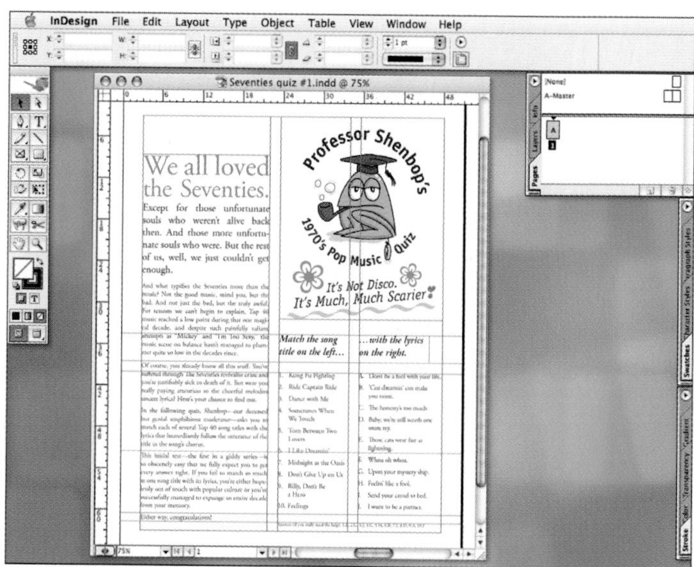

Figure 1-47.

3. ***Zoom in on the area above the text.*** Let's assume we want to draw near the top of the document, and we want to be zoomed in close to do fine detail work. Press Z to get the zoom tool, and then click in the upper-left corner of the document directly below the first *e* in *We all loved*. (The exact position isn't all that important; the *e* is just a landmark so that you and I are seeing more or less the same thing.) Keep clicking until you're zoomed in to 400 percent, as shown in Figure 1-48. In my case, it took six clicks, but it may be different for you.

4. ***Resize the document window.*** Click the size box in the lower-right corner of the document window and drag upward, as shown in Figure 1-49, so that only a small amount of the introductory text is visible.

Figure 1-48.

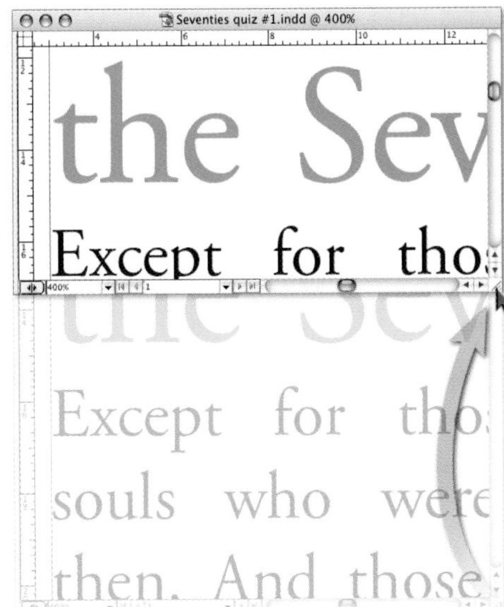

Figure 1-49.

5. *Close the Pages and Layers palettes.* Drag the **Pages** palette tab to the center of the screen. Then click the wee little ☒ or ⊗ button in the palette's title bar, as in Figure 1-50. Repeat this process for the **Layers** palette. This leaves the Info palette—handy for tracking the position, size, and color of objects—in the upper-right corner of the screen.

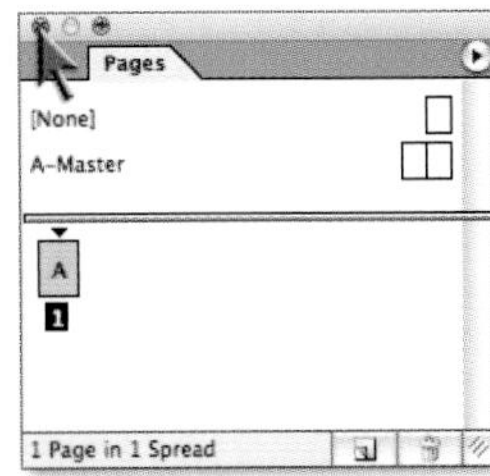

Figure 1-50.

6. *Close the Swatches, Character Styles, and Paragraph Styles palettes.* You could drag each palette to the middle of the screen and close it independently, as in the previous step. But there's an easier way: Press the Alt key (Option on the Mac) and drag the **Swatches** palette tab to the center of the screen. This moves all grouped palettes together. Now click ☒ or ⊗ to kill three birds with one stone. Poor birds.

7. *Reshape the toolbox.* Double-click the toolbox title bar and it stretches vertically. Another double-click stretches the toolbox horizontally across the top of the screen, as in Figure 1-51.

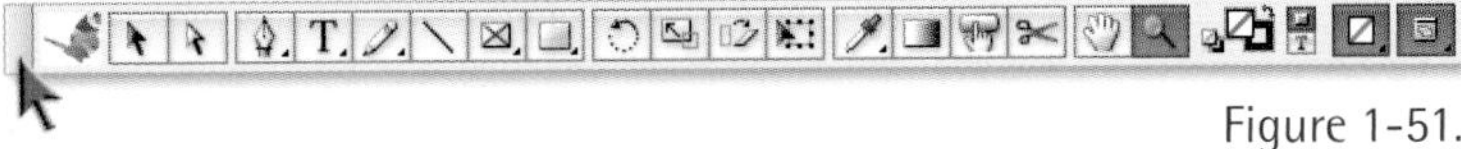

Figure 1-51.

8. *Open the Pathfinder and Align palettes.* Choose **Window→Pathfinder** to display the **Pathfinder** and **Align** palettes, both of which are exceedingly useful to have around when drawing line art inside InDesign. As shown in Figure 1-52 on the next page, these tiny palettes float free in the middle of the screen.

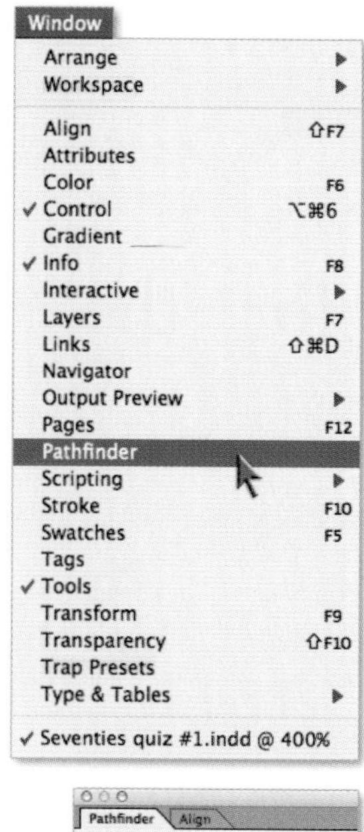

Figure 1-52.

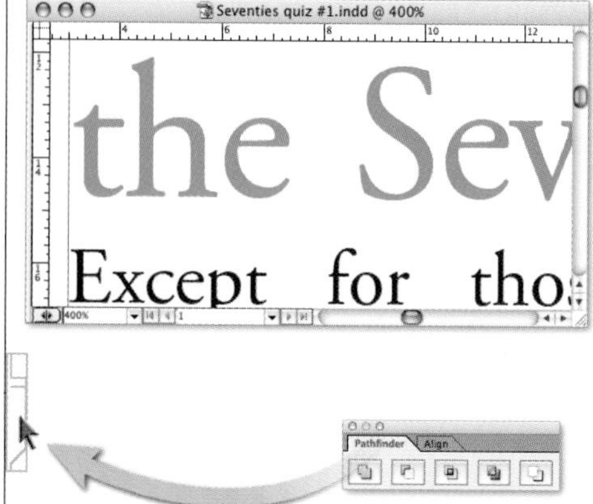

Figure 1-53.

9. ***Collapse the new palettes to the left side of the screen.*** Hold down Alt (or Option) and drag the Pathfinder palette tab to the left side of the screen. When the docking outlines appear, as in Figure 1-53, release the mouse button and key. The Pathfinder and Align palettes will collapse to the left side of the screen.

10. ***Rearrange the other palettes as you see fit.*** All the palettes you're likely to need for drawing are now open. But you may want to separate the Stroke/Color/Transparency/Gradient cluster to make each palette more convenient to access. How you do so is up to you. Some tricks to try:

    - Drag a nested palette away from its mates.
    - Move a palette from one side of the screen to the other.
    - Create your own nested groups of palettes.
    - When working with a free-floating palette, click the ♦ icon in the tab to cycle between different expansion settings. Or double-click the palette's title bar.

    In short, go nuts. My nutty workspace appears in Figure 1-54.

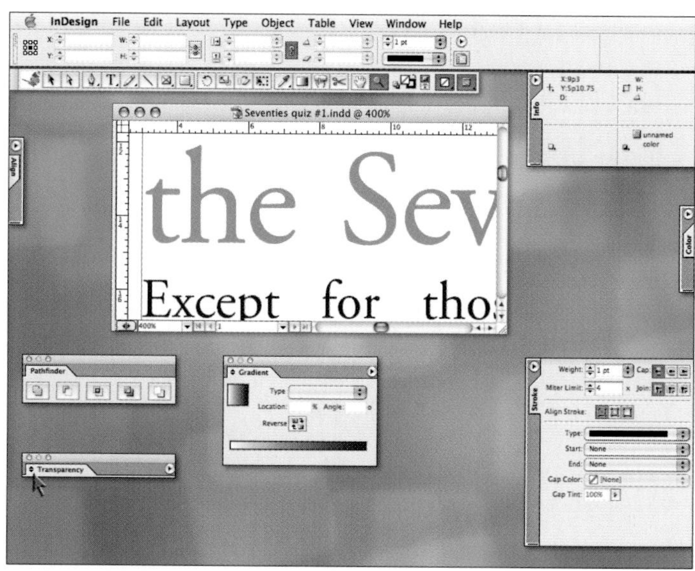

Figure 1-54.

11. ***Save your altered workspace.*** Now that you have your workspace just the way you want, make InDesign remember it by choosing **Window→Workspace→Save Workspace**. Then name the workspace "Drawing Workspace," as in Figure 1-55 on the facing page. And click the **OK** button.

12. ***Again restore the default workspace.*** Having saved your drawing workspace, you can now switch between it and any other workspace, including InDesign's default. Choose **Window→Workspace→[Default]**. Your drawing workspace vanishes, replaced by the original palette orientation.

13. ***Bring back the drawing workspace.*** Now comes the real test. Display your workspace by choosing **Window→Workspace→Drawing Workspace**. Presto, your saved workspace reappears, ready for you to start drawing.

To delete a saved workspace, choose Window→Workspace→Delete Workspace. Then choose the name of the workspace you want to delete from the Name pop-up menu and click Delete.

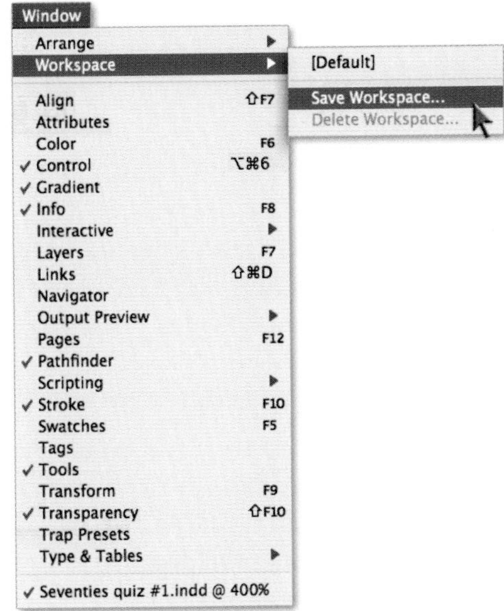

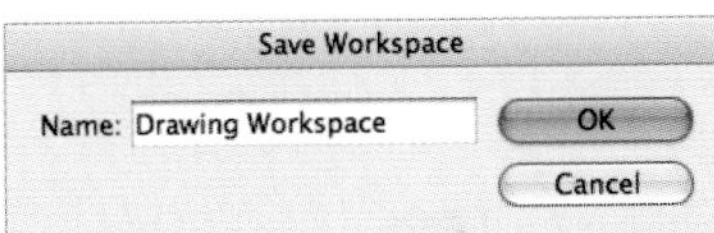

Figure 1-55.

PEARL OF WISDOM

While the Save Workspace command may seem to give you complete control over your interface, it actually has no bearing on the document window itself. Settings applied to the document window, such as zoom level and position, are stored with the document itself, not with custom workspaces.

Saving Your Document

InDesign has gobs of sexy features. It's packed to the gills with state-of-the-art functions that make QuarkXPress look as backward and archaic as an AMC Gremlin. But if I had to choose the best command in the whole program, it would be that oldie but goodie, the Save command. Without File→Save, you couldn't preserve your work. Goodbye efficiency, adieu automation. Your only choice would be to do the same old thing over and over again, just like we did in the days before digital.

So it is with a mixture of delight and relief that I confirm that, yes, InDesign offers a Save command and, yes, you'll learn how to use it in this exercise. Not only that, InDesign has the quite fortunate habit of automatically saving your work to a separate backup file behind your back (see the sidebar "InDesign Saves Your Sanity," page 40). Here's how saving works:

1. ***Open a document.*** Choose **File→Open** or press Ctrl+O (⌘-O on the Mac). Then open the document named *Untitled Mabry.indt* in the *Lesson 01* folder inside *Lesson Files-IDcs 1on1*. (If you get the modified links message, click the Fix Links Automatically button to refresh the graphics.) This is that same *Adobe Master Class: Design Invitational* document

InDesign Saves Your Sanity

These days, operating systems seldom crash. It's a rare day when you see the "blue screen of death" on the PC or a restart message on the Mac. But while the operating system does a splendid job of protecting itself (and you in the process), applications still go down. Even an application as virtuous as InDesign encounters the occasional fatal error. And when the program goes down, your data goes with it.

At least, that's how it works in a normal program. Fortunately for us, however, InDesign is anything but normal. The entire time you work, InDesign is thinking, "I could mess up—never know, I could mess up!" while furiously anticipating just such a mishap. Every time you perform what InDesign regards to be a critical event—often something as simple as drawing a rectangle or adding a page—the program saves a backup of the file to its top-secret *InDesign Recovery* folder. That way, when the worst does happen (as it inevitably does), you have something to work from. The recovered file may not reflect every last edit you performed, but it's typically no more than a few operations behind. So instead of losing a half hour of work, you lose two or three minutes.

To see it for yourself, try this:

- Close all open documents. (Otherwise, InDesign is faced with the proposition of recovering multiple documents, which works but takes extra time.)
- Start by creating a new document. Just to keep things simple, make it one page long.
- Click the pencil tool icon, the third tool down on the left side of the toolbox. It's not a particularly useful tool—if you like, you can watch me malign it in Video Lesson 6, "Pencil versus Pen"—but it is easy to use, which suits our purposes for now.
- Scribble in the document window. The figure below gives you an idea of what I have in mind. But it really doesn't matter—just have fun.
- See those two pop-up menus on the right side of the Control palette? One reads 1 pt and the one directly below looks like a black bar. Use these options to select different line thicknesses and styles for your doodling.

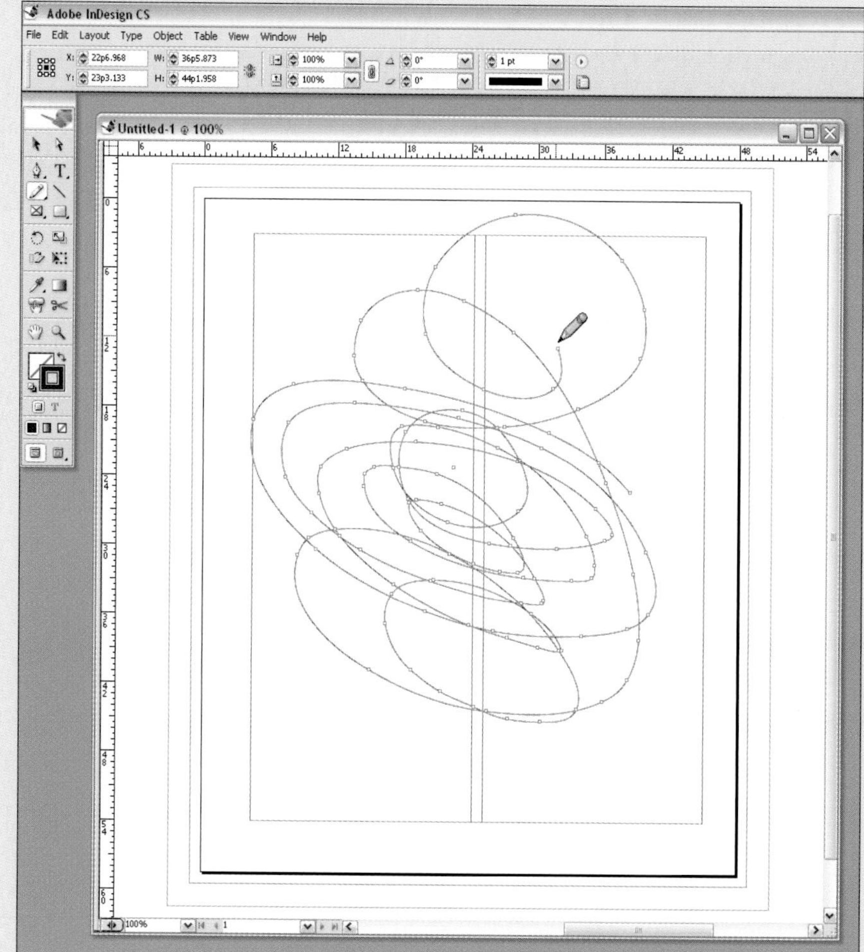

- Press Ctrl+Shift+P (⌘-Shift-P on the Mac). This adds a new blank page to the document. (I'll introduce the equivalent command in Lesson 9, "Pages, Layers, and XML," but for now just press the keys.)
- Repeat the last three steps—draw a squiggle with the pencil, modify the outline from the Control palette, and add another page by pressing Ctrl+Shift+P—a few times.
- Now to simulate a crash by force quitting the application. On the PC, press Ctrl+Alt+Delete to make Windows bring up the Task Manager window. Select Adobe InDesign CS and click End Task. An alert message will appear, asking whether you want to save the file. Ignore it! Shortly thereafter, Windows complains that "The system cannot end this program because it is waiting for a response from you." Click the End Now button to abruptly terminate InDesign, as shown on the right. Then close the Task Manager by clicking the ☒ button in the title bar.

  On the Macintosh, things work a bit differently. First, to force quit InDesign, press ⌘-Option-Escape. Then select InDesign from the list and click the Force Quit button, as in the figure on the right. When the alert message appears, click Force Quit again. Then close the Force Quit window by clicking the ⊗ on the left side of the title bar.
- Wait about a minute or so for the application to completely empty out of memory. Then restart InDesign. During the startup process, the program may display a message like the one on the right, asking if you want it to begin automatically recovering files. In this case, click Yes. Otherwise, InDesign will set about recovering unsaved files without your consent.

In a few moments, you will see a recent version of your document. It may contain one page, it may contain many pages. It may include all your pencil squiggles, or it may just include the very first squiggle. Whatever the case, it's welcome news: InDesign managed to save something, which is more than you saved. It's still no substitute for not saving your documents as frequently as humanly possible, but it's a heck of an insurance policy.

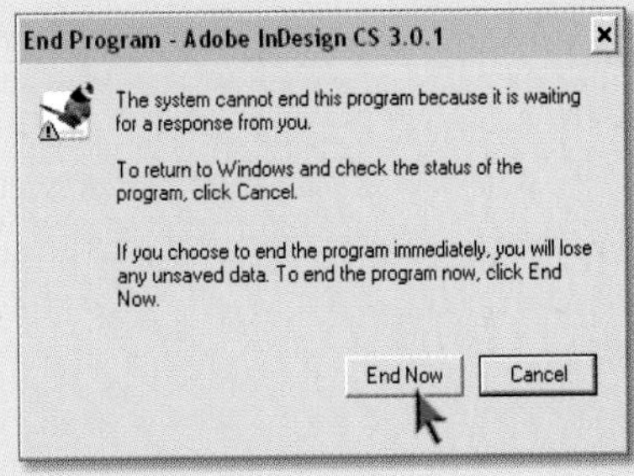

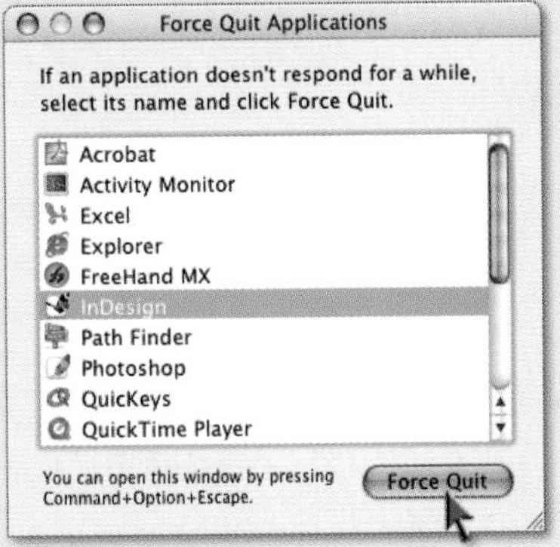

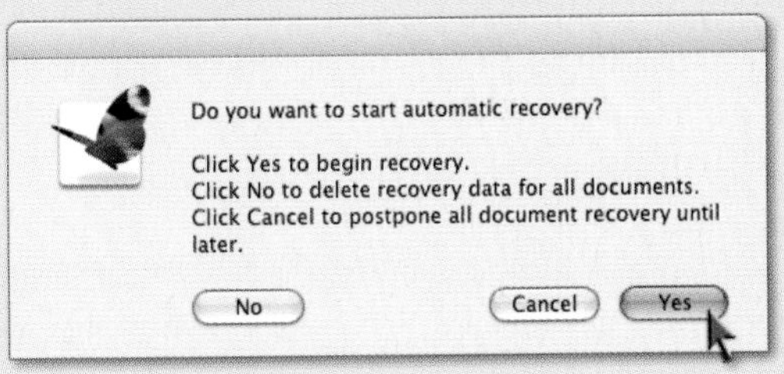

featured in "Opening a QuarkXPress Document" (page 10). The only difference is that I've taken the liberty of advancing a few pages for variety's sake (see Figure 1-56). Imagine that you've just converted this document from Quark, replaced the fonts, fixed the links, and made a few manual adjustments to the text and graphics. You are now ready to save the document for posterity.

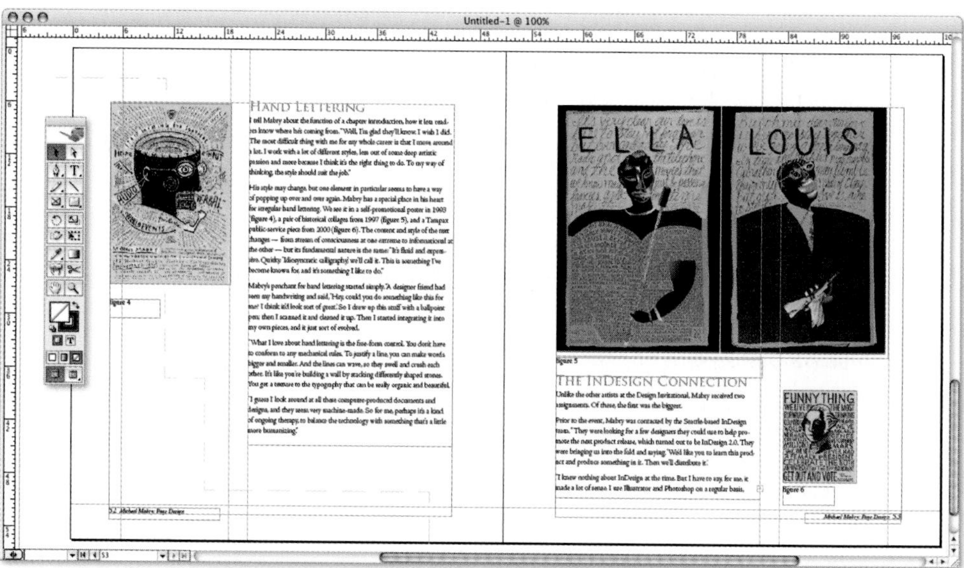

Figure 1-56.

Because this file was last saved as a template (hence the *.indt* extension), InDesign opens an untitled copy of the file. This prevents you from accidentally saving over the original. More importantly where this exercise is concerned, it exactly simulates the experience you would have if you were to open a Quark file or create a new document—so far as InDesign is concerned, the document has never been saved.

2. ***Consult the File Handling preferences.*** This step is not essential to saving a file; it merely establishes a few preferences and provides you with some information about how your system is configured. Choose **Edit→Preferences→File Handling** (under the **InDesign** menu on the Mac). Pictured in Figure 1-57, these options control how InDesign saves its files. Here's how the options work:

   • The first option, **Document Recovery Data**, determines where InDesign stores its auto-saved documents. To learn more, read the sidebar "InDesign Saves Your Sanity" on page 40.

- As long as we're here, you might as well turn on the **Save Document Preview Image** check box. This embeds a thumbnail preview so you can identify a file at a glance from within the Open a File dialog box.
- Now we come to the reason I had you choose Preferences→File Handling in the first place. Take a look at the setting of **Enable Version Cue**. If the check box is off (as I recommend unless you're working with a company that has bought into Version Cue), then great. If the box is checked, no problem, just make a mental note. It'll make a difference in Step 4.

Click the **OK** button to exit the dialog box and accept your changes (assuming you made any).

3. *Choose the Save command.* Press Ctrl+S (⌘-S) or choose **File→Save**. If the document had been saved before, InDesign would update the file on disk. But because it hasn't, the **Save As** dialog box appears, as in Figure 1-58.

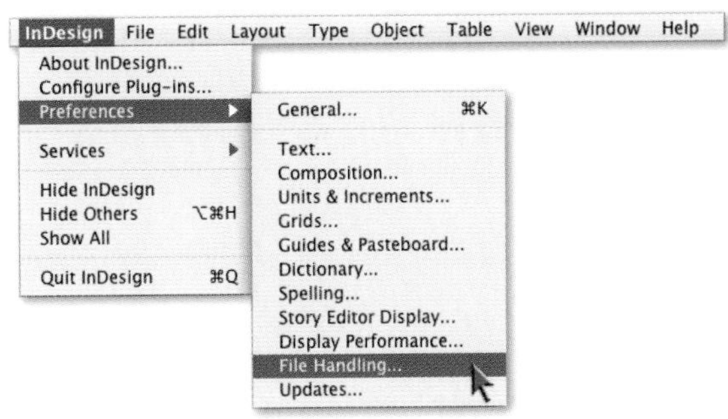

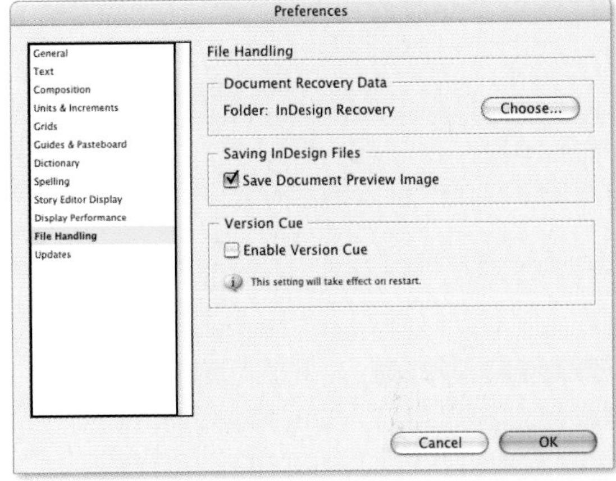

Figure 1-57.

PEARL OF WISDOM

Typically, you can also save a document by closing it. Just click ☒ or ⊗ in the title bar or choose File→Close. When asked to save the document, click Yes or Save and away you go. But if you ask me, relying on a force-save is a trifle cavalier. If you accidentally click No or Don't Save—or press the N or D key—*you lose your changes with no way to get them back!* My suggestion: When you want to close a document, first choose File→Save and then close it.

4. *Click the Local Files icon.* Remember the Enable Version Cue check box in Step 2? If it was off, skip to the next step. If it was on, check to make sure that you see an icon labeled **Version Cue** in the lower-left corner of the dialog box, as in Figure 1-58. If so, it means you are saving normally (that is, *without* Version Cue), and all is well. If, on the other hand, you see an icon labeled **Local Files**, as in Figure 1-59 on the next page, click this icon to turn Version Cue off and save the file normally.

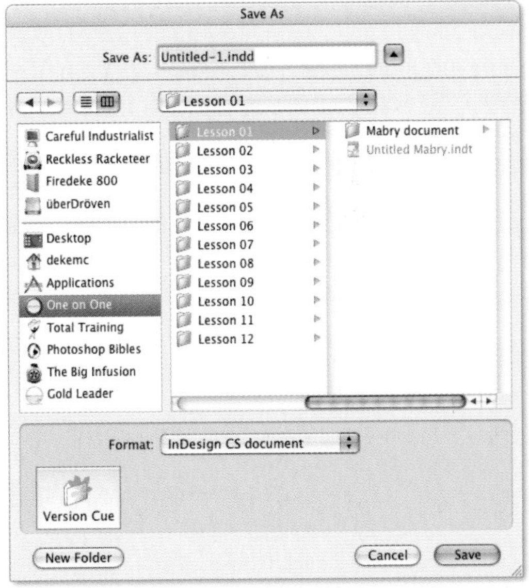

Figure 1-58.

PEARL OF WISDOM

Included with the full Creative Suite, Version Cue is Adobe's automated file-management environment, which lets you organize project files and share them with other users. While interesting in theory, I've found the current implementation to be shockingly flaky. (As if in acknowledgment, Adobe titles the *first* section of its Version Cue documentation "Adobe Version Cue uninstallation.") Besides, InDesign CS works just fine without it—and so, dear reader, shall we.

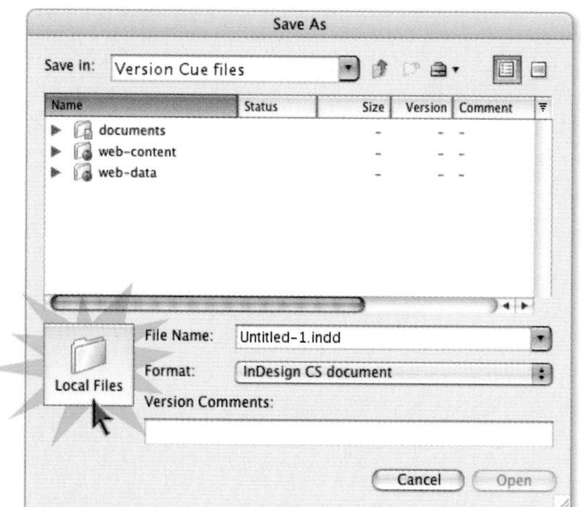

Figure 1-59.

5. ***Choose the desired format.*** By default, the **Save as Type** option (called **Format** on the Mac) is set to **InDesign CS document**. This saves the file as an everyday average native file that opens as a titled document. If you prefer to save the file as a template that opens untitled, as this one did, then choose **InDesign CS template**. This ensures that InDesign opens a copy of the document, making it harder to overwrite.

6. ***Specify a name and location.*** I recommend you save the file inside the same *Lesson 01* folder that contains the *Untitled Mabry.indt* document. This keeps the file in close proximity to the linked images in the *Mabry document* folder. That way, even if you were to copy the *Lesson 01* folder to a different location, all links would remain intact.

You can name the file as you like, with one proviso: Leave the extension set to *.indd* for an InDesign document or *.indt* for an InDesign template. It's very difficult to override this on the PC, but it's very easy on the Mac. *Don't do it!* Files without extensions won't successfully transport across platforms (via email or servers), they go unrecognized by Windows, and they may not work properly under future versions of the Mac OS.

---

7. ***Click the Save button.*** Or press Enter or Return to save the file to disk. From this point on, you can update the file to reflect any changes you make by choosing File→Save. To again invoke the Save As dialog box—whether to save a different version of the document or store it in a different location—choose **File→Save As** or press Ctrl+Shift+S (⌘-Shift-S on the Mac).

The Save As command has one other bonus: It rebuilds the file and makes it more efficient. Normally, when you choose File→Save, InDesign appends the new information onto the old. This saves time and makes for a more efficient working experience, but it also balloons the file over time, causing it to grow incrementally larger with every press of Ctrl+S. To streamline the file, periodically choose File→Save As. (I generally add a version number to the end of the filename, such as "-1" or "-2.") If it's been a long time since your last Save As, it's not unusual to see the file size drop by half or more.

Regrettably, there's no way to save a document that's compatible with older versions of InDesign. According to InDesign's documentation, you can save a document for use in InDesign 2.0 by choosing File→Export and then setting the Save as Type option to InDesign Interchange. But this turns out to be false. Adobe never fully implemented the InDesign Interchange (INX) format, and no program beyond InDesign CS supports it. InDesign is similarly incapable of saving files for use in InDesign 1.5 or older and incapable of exporting to another program's native file format, such as Quark's QXD.

WHAT DID YOU LEARN?

Match the key concept in the numbered list below with the letter of the phrase that best describes it. Answers appear upside-down at the bottom of the page.

Key Concepts

1. Template
2. Embedded Profile Mismatch
3. Control palette
4. Fix Links Automatically
5. Find Font
6. Pica
7. Point
8. Gutter
9. Bleed
10. Slug
11. Ruler guide
12. Custom workspace

Descriptions

A. The space between columns, as distinguished from the margins, which are the area outside the columns.

B. A nonprinting horizontal or vertical line that serves both as a visual marker and a magnetic alignment tool.

C. A button that seeks to reestablish connections to all graphic files that have been moved or modified since the last time an InDesign document was saved.

D. A unit of measurement equal to $^{1}/_{72}$ of an inch, useful for measuring type and other small page elements.

E. This special kind of InDesign file contains page specifications and placeholder frames that will serve as the starting point for a series of similar documents.

F. A preset that saves the position, docking, and visibility of palettes, but has no bearing on the document window.

G. An area outside the page boundary that holds the excess from artwork and other objects that are intended to extend to the very edge of the page and will be cut away when the pages are trimmed.

H. A context-sensitive palette located by default at the top of the screen that changes to accommodate the selected object or active tool.

I. A portion of the pasteboard outside the bleed that holds printing information such as project titles and handling instructions.

J. A unit of measurement equal to 12 points, or $^{1}/_{6}$ inch, which you can annotate inside an InDesign option box by entering the letter *p*.

K. This alert message warns you that you're about to open a document that uses a different color space than you specified in the Color Settings dialog box.

L. This command lets you replace all instances of any typeface used in your document with a different typeface.

Answers

1E, 2K, 3H, 4C, 5L, 6J, 7D, 8A, 9G, 10I, 11B, 12F

LESSON 2

Y•85 M•85 C•9 K•42
Y•100 M•100 C•10 K•42
Y•40 M•40 C•4 K•24
Y•55 M•55 C•6 K•24
Y•70 M•70 C•7 K•24
Y•85 M•85 C•9 K•24
Y•100 M•100 C•10 K•24
M•85 C•0 K•0
M•100 C•0 K•0

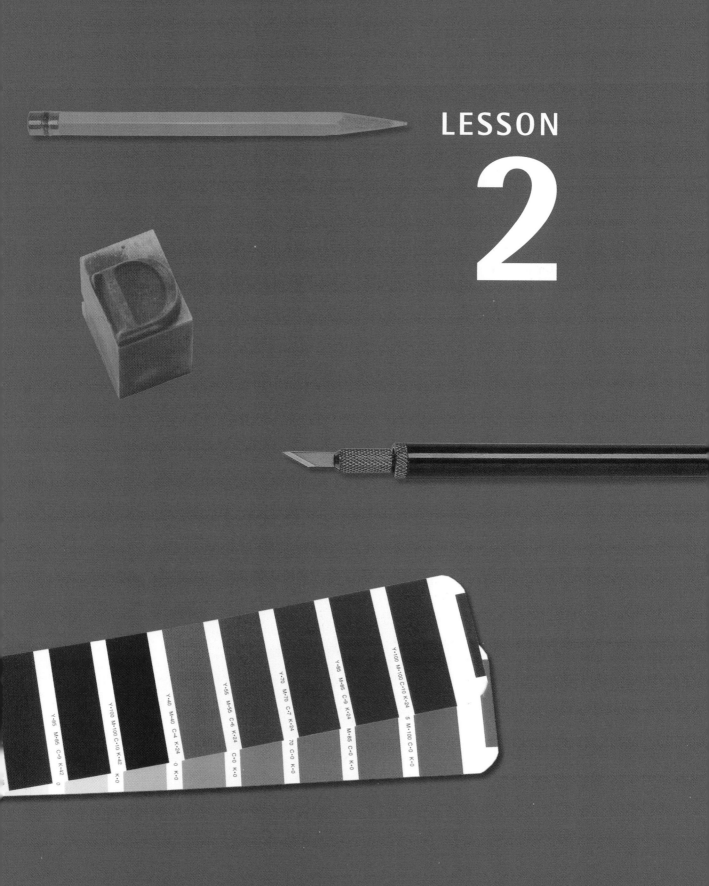

CREATING AND FLOWING TEXT

WHEN IT COMES to working on computers, most serious writing—including the writing I'm writing right now—takes place in Microsoft Word. I'm going to climb out on a limb and guess that you use Word, too. InDesign and Quark may be butting heads for a while yet, but Word managed to shake off serious competition years ago. And while Microsoft's reputation for consistently creating quality software isn't exactly stellar, they got a lot of things right in the case of Word.

Heck, Microsoft has even crammed a fair amount of actual page-layout features into the program. But I'm going to climb out even further on this limb here and guess that you don't use them. Maybe, just *maybe* you've created a two-column spread in Word, but that's probably it. And frankly, I commend you for getting that far. Word's page-layout capability reminds me of Samuel Johnson's comment about a dog walking on its hind legs: "It is not done well; but you are surprised to find it done at all."

I bring this up because Word has shaped many people's notions of how computer applications should handle text. Word processors make it easy for you to quickly enter and edit text. They'd better; that's their main reason for existing. But when it comes to controlling how that text appears on the printed page, a word processor pretty much expects you to create single columns of text that flow in regular procession from one page to the next.

Not so with InDesign. To say that InDesign makes easy work of composing multicolumn documents is true, but it doesn't begin to tell the story. As we saw in the previous lesson, you can specify different column settings on different pages and even make neighboring columns different widths. But the real genius of InDesign and other layout programs is that you don't have to adhere to your column settings at all. Every character of type exists inside an independent, free-floating container called a *frame*. That frame can be rectangular,

ABOUT THIS LESSON

Project Files

Before beginning the exercises, make sure that you've installed the lesson files from the CD, as explained in Step 5 on page xv of the Preface. This should result in a folder called *Lesson Files-IDcs 1on1* on your desktop. We'll be working with the files inside the *Lesson 02* subfolder.

In this lesson, we'll look at the many ways to create, import, edit, and correct text in InDesign. You'll learn how to:

Video Lesson 2: Text and Frames

Adding text to a document is a matter of drawing frames, placing a story saved in a word processor, and entering or modifying words with InDesign's text tool. If you're familiar with PageMaker or QuarkXPress, this may sound like child's play. But like any program, InDesign throws a few curve balls, enough to occasionally frustrate even seasoned users.

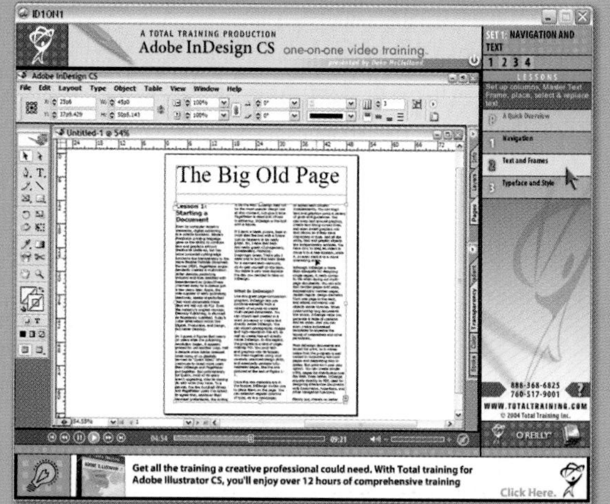

To get a feel for how you import and adjust text in InDesign, watch the second video lesson included on the CD. To view this video, insert the CD, click the **Start Training** button, and then select **2, Text and Frames** from the Lessons list on the right side of the screen. During this 9-minute 23-second movie, you'll learn about the following commands and shortcuts in the order listed below:

Operation	Windows shortcut	Macintosh shortcut
Create a new document	Ctrl+N	⌘-N
Place text into a document	Ctrl+D	⌘-D
Undo placement and reload text cursor	Ctrl+Z	⌘-Z
Change the text frame options	Ctrl+B	⌘-B
Switch to the type tool	T, or double-click in text frame	T, or double-click in text frame
Select word or line of type	Double-click word, triple-click line	Double-click word, triple-click line
Select entire story	Ctrl+A	⌘-A

geometric, elliptical, or any shape you like, as Figure 2-1 illustrates. You can move and scale the frame just by dragging it. And you can drop the frame literally anywhere on the page. I commend Word and other word processors for their text-editing prowess. But when it comes time to put the text on the page, I simply couldn't manage without a program like InDesign.

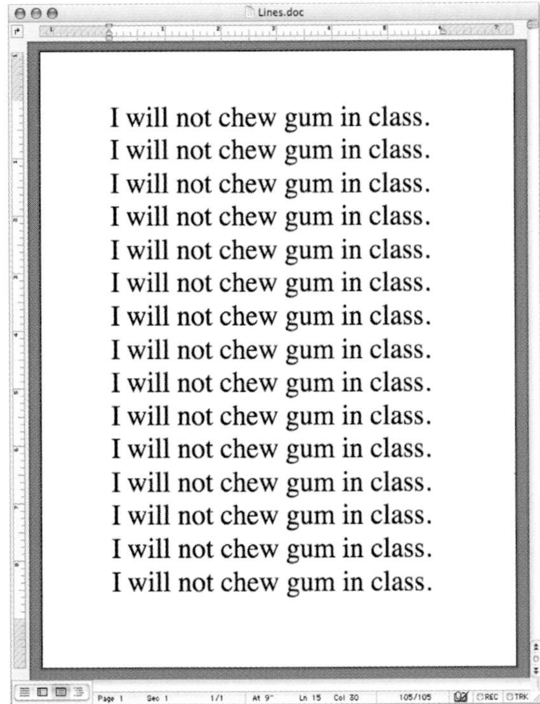

A single column of type in Word

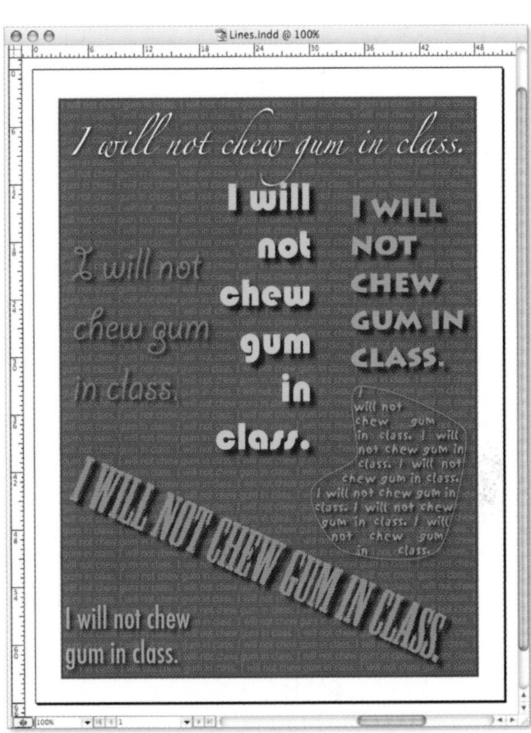

Text arranged in free-form frames in InDesign

Figure 2-1.

The Mechanics of Frames

If you come from QuarkXPress or PageMaker, you know that text frames are nothing new. These programs use different terminology—Quark calls them *text boxes* and PageMaker calls them *text blocks*—but they're one and the same. (I still use the term text block to mean a frame that's filled with text.) For those to whom page-layout is a new experience, a few words about how frames work: InDesign regards the text frame as an independent object, just like a line or shape. The main difference is that instead of being filled with color, it's filled with type. Double-click inside the frame and start typing away. Or, if you've already done your typing in a word processor, import the text from a file on disk, or copy it from the word processor and paste it into InDesign. The text automatically wraps from one line to the next inside the confines of the frame.

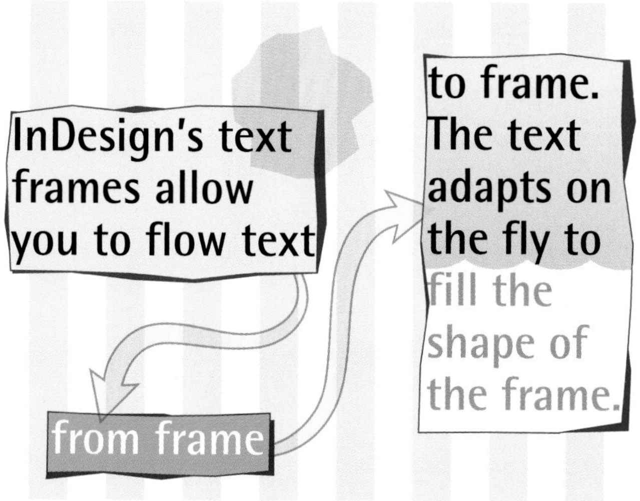

Figure 2-2.

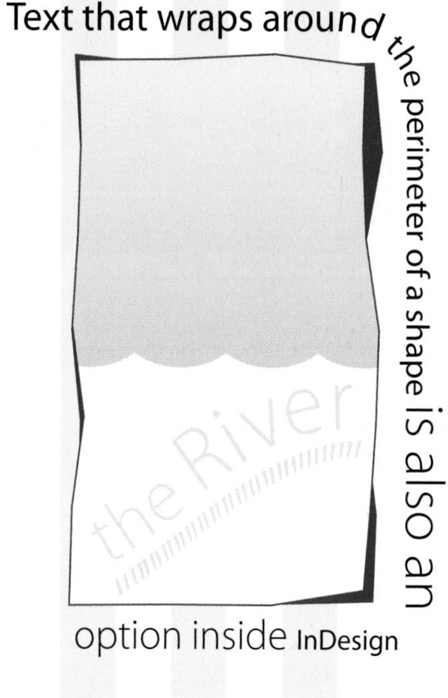

Figure 2-3.

It's rare that a single text frame can contain all the text in a document, so you can draw many text frames and link them together. This way, a long text document can flow from one frame to another to create multiple columns and pages of type. You can draw and link frames manually, as in Figure 2-2. Or you can watch your text roar through scores of columns and pages with a single click.

Whether empty or full, the outline of a text frame can be edited to suit your shifting layout needs. The black arrow in the toolbox lets you scale the frame; the white arrow lets you change the frame's shape. Either way, InDesign rewraps and reflows the text immediately and automatically, permitting you to concentrate on the page design without having to fuss over each and every character of content. And while text usually flows inside the frame, it doesn't have to. You can also wrap text around the perimeter of a frame, as illustrated in Figure 2-3.

When it comes time to fuss over the content—sadly, misspellings and typos are a fact of life—InDesign is good at that, too. You can edit the text directly inside a frame, great for staying abreast of how your changes affect flow and hyphenation. Or you can switch to the new Story Editor, a no-frills text editing environment that InDesign inherited from its progenitor, PageMaker. The Story Editor not only allows you to focus on your text, free from the distractions of layout. It also works faster, saving up InDesign's more time-consuming rewrap and reflow calculations until the editing is complete. And like any self-respecting layout program, InDesign lets you spell check your text, both in the standard layout and Story Editor modes.

InDesign's combination of flexible, frame-based layout and eternally editable text makes it a cinch for you to "suit the action to the word, the word to the action," as the melancholy Hamlet put it. (Oh, had he only lived to be a electronic designer; how much happier he might have been.) Assimilate the information presented in this lesson, and you'll be one major step forward on the road to mastery of InDesign. But enough words already; let's get down to action.

Flowing Text into Frames

It's easy enough to enter text into a lone frame, as I demonstrate in Video Lesson 2, "Text and Frames." (If you haven't watched the video, this is a good time to do so.) The trick is making text flow from column to column in multiple frames. *Flow* is the perfect word, too. Text in InDesign courses like a tenacious little river, filling every vessel it comes into contact with. It swells to fill wide frames and dribbles through narrow ones. The similarities between text and liquid are so downright palpable that many designers refer to the act of importing text into linked frames as "pouring a document." In other words, text is fluid, baby.

This exercise shows you how to import text from a Word file and set it gushing through a multicolumn InDesign document. The goal is to lay out a cookie recipe for publication in a food magazine. In the process, you'll learn how to draw text frames, link them together, and auto-pour long documents.

1. ***Open a document.*** Open the file named *Cookie recipe 1.indd* located in the *Lesson 02* folder inside *Lesson Files-IDcs 1on1*. Figure 2-4 shows the first page of this two-page document. The page contains a single photo; the text eagerly awaits.

Figure 2-4.

2. ***Select the type tool and draw a text frame.*** We need to draw a text frame to hold the title of the recipe and the byline at the top of the first page. Press T to get the type tool and drag to draw a rectangle from the upper-left corner of the first column to the intersection of the cyan guide and the right margin, as shown in Figure 2-5 on the next page. The frame should snap to the guides. (If not choose View→Snap to Guides to turn snapping on.) You should see a blinking insertion marker in the upper-left corner of the resulting text frame. Since you drew the text frame with all its edges aligned to columns and guides, you can't see the frame itself. If you like, choose **View→Hide Guides** or press Ctrl+; (⌘-; on the Mac) to hide the guides so you can see the frame. Just make sure you press the shortcut again (or choose **View→Show Guides**) to turn the guides back on before continuing.

3. ***Place a document from a word processor.*** Choose **File→Place** or press the shortcut Ctrl+D (⌘-D) to display the **Place** dialog box.

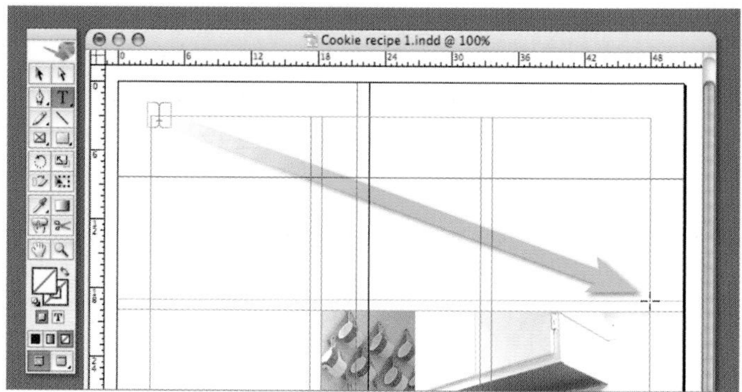

Figure 2-5.

Go to the *Lesson 02* folder and select the *Puppet text.doc* file. Turn on the **Show Import Options** check box, and click the **Open** button. (Or leave the check box off and Shift-click the Open button.) InDesign displays the **Microsoft Word Import Options** dialog box (see Figure 2-6), which presents you with the following options:

- If your document contains a table of contents, footnotes, or an index, use the three Include check boxes to specify whether or not you want to import these elements. Our document doesn't contain any of this stuff, so it doesn't matter if the options are on or off.

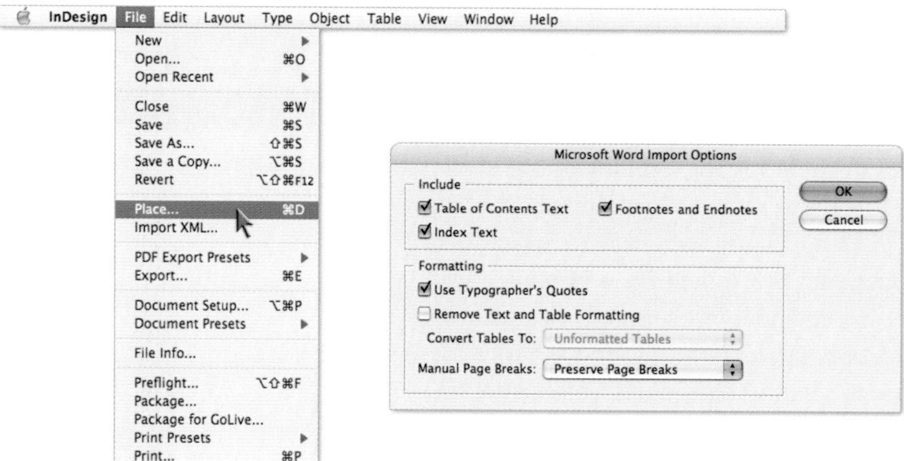

Figure 2-6.

- The Use Typographer's Quotes check box lets you choose to convert any straight quotes in your Word file into typographer's quotes (also known as "curly" quotes, because they typically curl around the text inside the quotes). This check box also substitutes straight apostrophes with curled ones. Leave it turned on.

- The Remove Text and Table Formatting option controls whether InDesign respects or ignores the font, type size, and other attributes applied inside the word processor. We want to retain the formatting used in this document, so leave this option off.
- Word and other word processors let you insert page breaks to define where one page ends and another begins. But Word pages almost never correspond to InDesign pages. To let your documents flow freely, set the **Manual Page Breaks** option to **No Breaks**.

To recap, set Manual Page Breaks to No Breaks and leave the other options as is. Then click **OK**. The first part of the text appears within the frame you drew in the last step, which results in a filled text block. Of course, this cookie recipe consists of more than a title and a byline. InDesign tells you that there's more to come by setting the *out port*—the box in the lower-right corner of the text block, labeled in Figure 2-7—to a red ⊞. This indicates that the entire amount of text—known in InDesign parlance as the *story*—doesn't fit inside the text frame. Think of the out port as a faucet that has been turned off so that the story can't flow any further. Your job is to open the faucet and give the story another container to flow into.

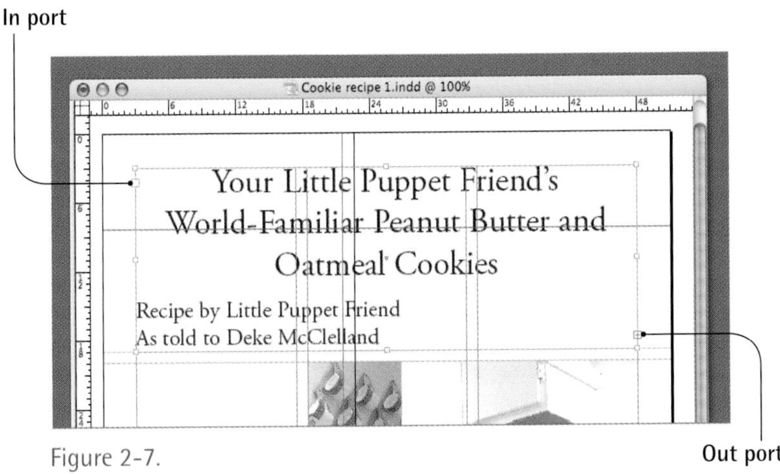

Figure 2-7.

4. *Select the black arrow tool.* Click the black arrow in the upper-left corner of the toolbox. Adobe calls this the selection tool, but I prefer to call it what it is, the black arrow tool.

If you loaded my Deke Keys keyboard shortcuts as directed on page xvii of the Preface, you can get to the black arrow at any time by pressing the Enter key on the numerical keypad. If you remember none of my other keyboard shortcuts, remember this one: it really will save you scads of time (though I must admit, scads are difficult to measure).

5. ***Click in the text frame's out port.*** Click the red ⊞ in the text frame's out port. The cursor changes to ▤, which tells you that the cursor is loaded with text that's ready to be placed.

6. ***Draw a second text frame.*** Position the cursor at the intersection of the left edge of the left column and the magenta ruler guide (directly below the cyan one). The black arrow in the loaded text cursor turns white when the cursor is next to a guide, as in ▤. This color change means that you are about to create a text frame that snaps in alignment with the guide. With the cursor positioned as I've described, drag to draw a second text frame within the first column. As Figure 2-8 shows, the text automatically flows from the first text frame into the second. The upper-left corner of this second frame sports a blue *in port*. The in port happens to contain an arrowhead (▶), which shows that text flows from another text frame into this one. You'll also see that this frame ends with a red ⊞ out port, signifying that still more text waits to flow.

   Before we let this dammed text flow—note the spelling on that one—take a moment to click inside the first text block. The first frame's out port is now a blue ▶, which indicates that text flows out of it into another text frame. This frame also has an in port, but because the frame is the first text block in the string of blocks that will contain this story, the in port is empty.

Figure 2-8.

7. ***Load the text cursor and go to page 2.*** Let's continue the text flow on the second page of the document. Click in the second text frame's out port to load the text cursor, press Ctrl+J (⌘-J on the Mac) to highlight the page number in the lower-left corner of the document window, type the number 2, and press Enter or Return to go to page 2.

8. ***Create a new text frame.*** This time, instead of dragging to draw a text frame, simply click on the cyan guide somewhere in the first column. As Figure 2-9 shows, InDesign creates the text frame automatically, positioning the top of the frame at the point where you clicked and pouring text into the remaining length of the column.

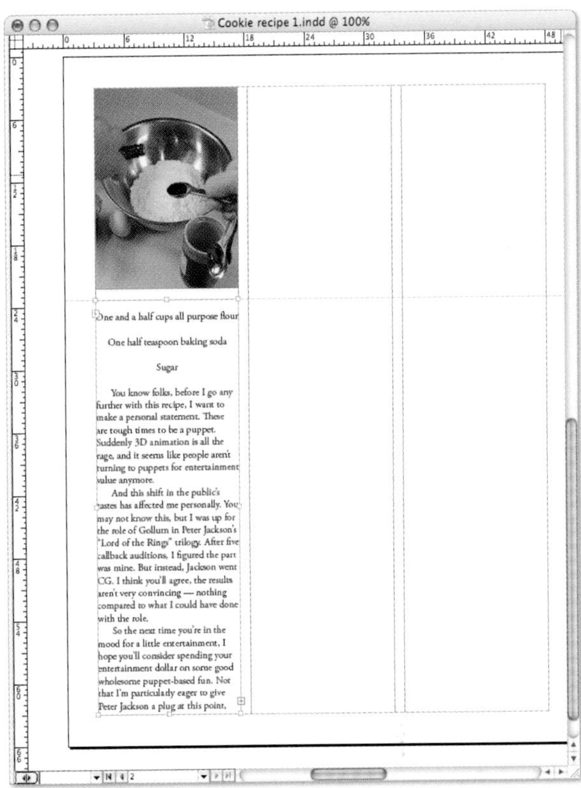

Figure 2-9.

PEARL OF WISDOM

Modeled after a function introduced by the first incarnation of PageMaker but inexplicably never added to QuarkXPress, automatic frame making is InDesign's alternative to drawing frames by hand. You can use this trick anytime you want a text block to be the same width as a column—as in Step 6, for example. But if you intend to violate columns, as you did in Step 2, drawing the frame by hand is your only option. My recommendation: Let InDesign be in charge of frames when you can, draw frames when you must.

9. ***Display the text threads.*** As you might imagine, with text flowing from one page to the next, potentially skipping pages and intertwining with other stories, it may become difficult to follow exactly how a single article flows from one frame to the next. Choose **View→Show Text Threads** or press Ctrl+Alt+Y (⌘-Option-Y on the Mac) to display blue lines between the out ports and in ports of linked, or *threaded*, text blocks. The result is that you can more easily follow the flow of a story, as in Figure 2-10 on the next page.

If it took you a while to find the Show Text Threads command in the View menu, remember the nifty trick from Video Lesson 1: Press Ctrl+Shift+Alt (that's ⌘-Shift-Option on the Mac) and click View to alphabetize the commands in the menu. This technique works with all menus, but Adobe added it with the convoluted View menu in mind.

As you can imagine, it would take quite a while to lay out a large amount of text by clicking or dragging to create a text frame, clicking the frame's out port to load the cursor, clicking or dragging to create another text frame, clicking that frame's out port, and so on. Luckily, InDesign gives you several ways to speed the process along.

10. ***Load the text cursor.*** Click the last frame's out port to load the cursor.

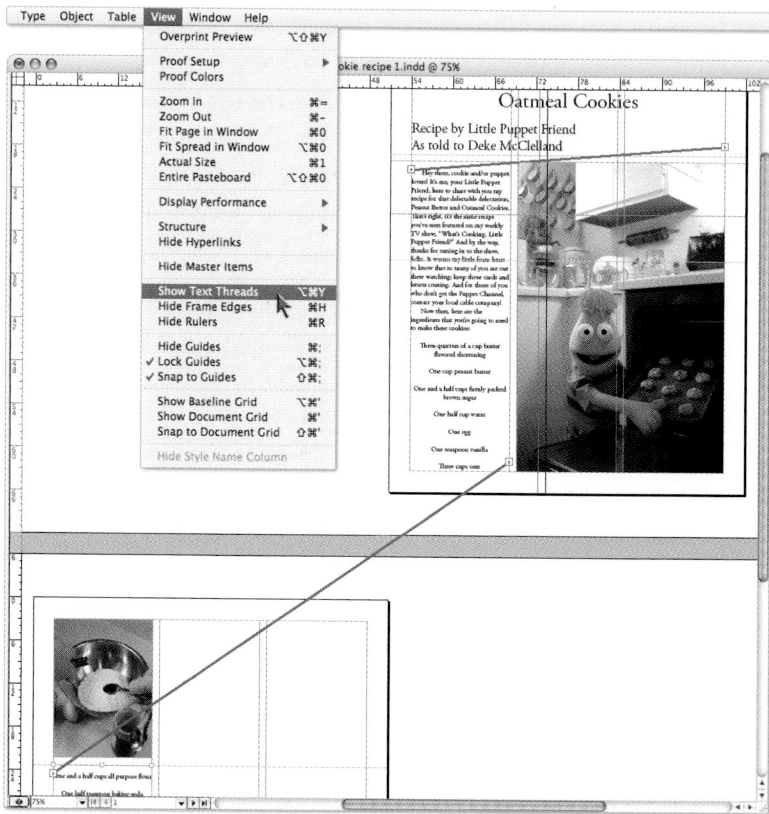

Figure 2-10.

11. *Alt-click at the top of the second column on the second page.* Press the Alt key (Option on the Mac) to change the cursor to the *semi-autoflow* cursor (). To see exactly what it does, go ahead and click while keeping Alt (or Option) down. The second column fills with text, as shown in Figure 2-11, but nothing more. So what's so automatic about that? How did that save any time? Release the key and take a look at your cursor. It's already loaded and ready for you to continue pouring text. No need to click the out port first. You saved yourself one whole click!

12. *Choose the Undo command.* All right, so maybe saving yourself a single click doesn't measure up to your idea of slick, state-of-the-art automation. Fortunately, InDesign has a couple more tricks up its sleeve. To test them out, first choose **Edit→Undo Place** or press Ctrl+Z (⌘-Z) to undo the last operation. And *voila*, you still have a loaded text cursor. I don't know about you, but I'm impressed.

What if you *don't* want InDesign to reload your cursor? To regain the black arrow tool, press the Enter key on the keypad (courtesy of Deke Keys), or just press Ctrl+Z (⌘-Z) again.

---

13. ***Shift+Alt-click at the top of the second column.*** Press and hold the Shift and Alt keys (Shift and Option on the Mac). This time, you get the *autoflow document* cursor, which looks like . With the keys still down, click at the top of the second column. As illustrated in Figure 2-12, the flowing text fills all the remaining columns in the document. You have to admit, *this* is automation.

14. ***Choose Undo again.*** Oh, but take a look at the bottom of the last column: we still have a red ⊞ out port. Obviously, my verbose Little Puppet Friend (I call him LPF) has provided us with a very lengthy cookie recipe, longer than these two pages can accommodate. This brings us to InDesign's third text-flowing shortcut. To see it in action, I ask you to once again press Ctrl+Z (or ⌘-Z) to undo the last action and reload that cursor.

15. ***Shift-click at the top of the second column.*** Press and hold the Shift key on its own to get yet another variety of the loaded text cursor, this time with a solid loopy arrow as in . This is the Superman of text flow functions, the *autoflow* cursor. Still pressing Shift, click at the top of the second column and as quick as you can say "Houdini never did this," InDesign not only fills all columns to the end of the document but actually creates a brand new page to accommodate the overflow text, as shown in the large Figure 2-13 on the next page. If LPF had written a novel instead of a cookie recipe, InDesign would have added as many pages as needed to contain the text, automatically generated the necessary frames, and threaded the text through them. Conclusion: Shift-clicking is the finest method for roughing out text into pages yet divined by man, woman, or puppet.

16. ***Save your document.*** If you want to make sure you're at the end of the article, click the final column on the new third page, and notice the empty out port at the bottom of the column. This signifies that, indeed, that's all he wrote. Then choose **File→Save As**. Name your modified document "My cookies 1.indd" and save it in the same *Lesson 02* folder inside *Lesson Files-IDcs 1on1*.

Incidentally, if you're planning to speed directly into the next exercise, keep this document open. We're not done with it yet.

Figure 2-11.

Figure 2-12.

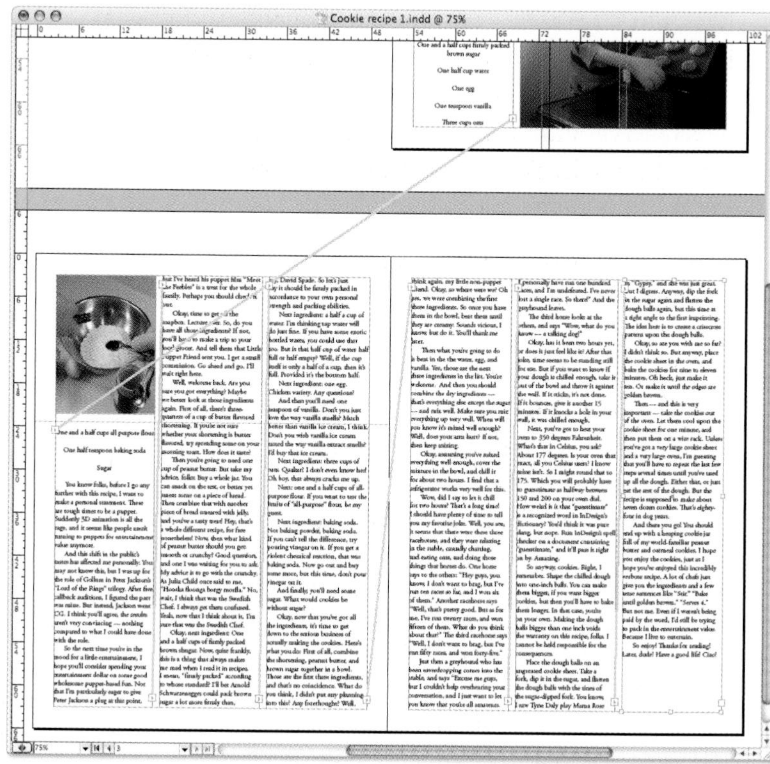

Figure 2-13.

Adjusting Text Blocks

InDesign's text frames are infinitely adjustable, so if you don't get everything perfect when you first lay out your frames, you can go back and tinker with them until they're exactly right. In the following steps, we'll adjust the text blocks we created in the previous exercise. And with a song in our hearts, we'll see how that Ol' Text River, he just keeps flowing along, even into non-rectangular text frames.

1. *Open a document.* This exercise picks up where the last one left off. So if you still have open the *My cookies 1.indd* document that you saved in the preceding exercise, you can skip to Step 2. If you didn't work through the last exercise, I have you covered. Open the file *Cookie recipe 2.indd* located in the *Lesson 02* folder inside *Lesson Files-IDcs 1on1*.

2. *Crop the graphic on the first page.* We have to make some serious adjustments to the text on the first page, but first you need to resize the frame for the graphic. That's right, just like text, graphics reside inside frames. And by resizing the frame, you crop the photograph. (For complete details on cropping graphics, see "Cropping and Scaling Artwork" on page 249 in Lesson 7.)

If the black arrow tool is active, great; if not, click its icon in the toolbox or press Enter on the keypad. Then click the graphic to activate its frame. Small white boxes called *handles* appear in the corners of the frame and in the middle of each side. You can click and drag these handles to change the size of the frame.

Move your cursor over the handle at the top center of the frame. When the cursor turns into a two-headed arrow, drag downward until the top edge of the frame snaps to the yellow guide. Then click the middle handle on the left side of the frame and drag it to the right until it snaps to the vertical black guide. Figure 2-14 demonstrates both operations.

Figure 2-14.

3. ***Scale the text block in the first column.*** Click the bottom-left text block—the one that begins *Hey there, cookie and/or puppet lovers*—to activate it. Then drag the handle on the right side of the frame to the right until it snaps to the red guide. Notice how the text reflows to accommodate the larger frame. Then drag the top handle down until it snaps to the yellow guide. Figure 2-15 shows how your document should look after these changes.

4. ***Make the top text block bigger.*** Turns out, I want the first couple of paragraphs to appear in the top text block. To accomplish this, we'll enlarge the top frame. Click on the frame to select it. Then drag the handle on the bottom edge downward until it snaps to the green guide. The last line in the top text block should begin *Now then, here are the ingredients*, with *Three-quarters of a cup butter flavored shortening* leading off the bottom block. Figure 2-16 on the next page shows what I'm talking about.

5. ***Move the top text block down.*** There's too much space between the top text block and the other elements on the first page, so let's move the entire text block down. With the top text block selected, click inside it and drag down until the top edge snaps to the dark blue guide, as in Figure 2-17. You can press the Shift key while you drag to help constrain the movement of the frame straight downward. (The Shift key constrains the angle of a drag to a

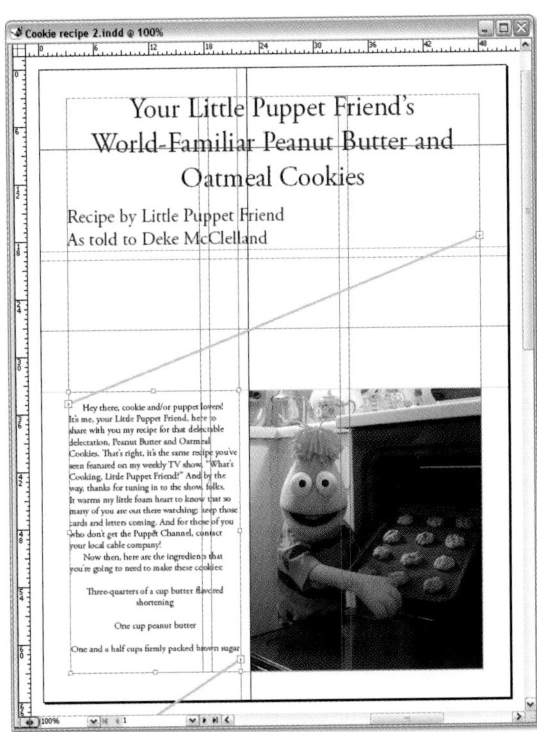

Figure 2-15.

Figure 2-16.

Figure 2-17.

multiple of 45 degrees, so you still have to make some effort to drag in a vertical direction.) But because View→Snap to Guides is turned on, it's just as easy to drag the frame straight down without using Shift.

If you need to move more than one text block at a time, select the additional text blocks by Shift-clicking with the black arrow tool. Meanwhile, Shift-clicking a selected text block deselects it. You can also drag from an empty portion of the document window to draw a rectangular *marquee*. When you release the mouse button, any objects even partially inside the marquee become selected.

---

6. ***Delete the bottom-left block on the first page.*** I have something else in mind for the bottom-left text block: I want to replace its rectangular frame with an oval one. As opposed to trying to convert the rectangle to an ellipse—an arduous, inexact process at best—we're better off deleting the rectangle and drawing the ellipse in its place. Select the bottom-left text block and press the Backspace or Delete key. The frame disappears, but as Figure 2-18 illustrates, the text remains intact, flowing from the top block into the first frame on the next page. (You may want to scroll down in the document window to observe this. Clicking a text frame makes the text threads visible.)

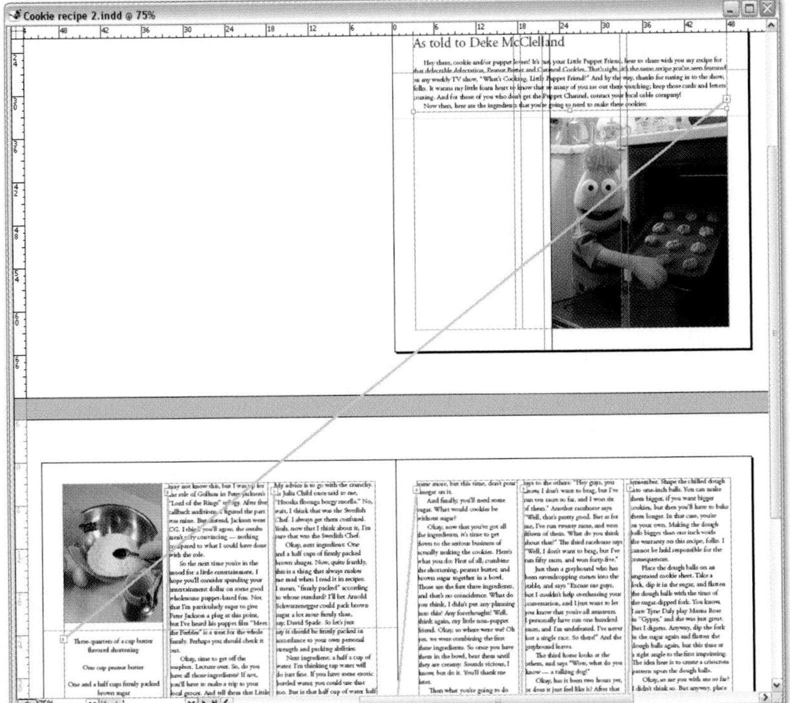

Figure 2-18.

7. *Select the ellipse tool.* InDesign provides two tools that let you draw oval text frames: the ellipse frame tool and the standard ellipse tool. As shown in Figure 2-19, the ellipse frame tool is located in the frame tool flyout menu on the left side of the toolbox; the ellipse tool shares a flyout menu with the shape tools on the right side of the toolbox. You can select the latter from the keyboard by pressing the L key.

   As I mentioned, either tool is perfectly capable of creating a frame for holding text. The only difference is that, by default, the ellipse tool draws a frame with a visible border, called a *stroke*. The ellipse frame tool includes no border. I have in mind a frame with a border, so press the L key to select the standard ellipse tool.

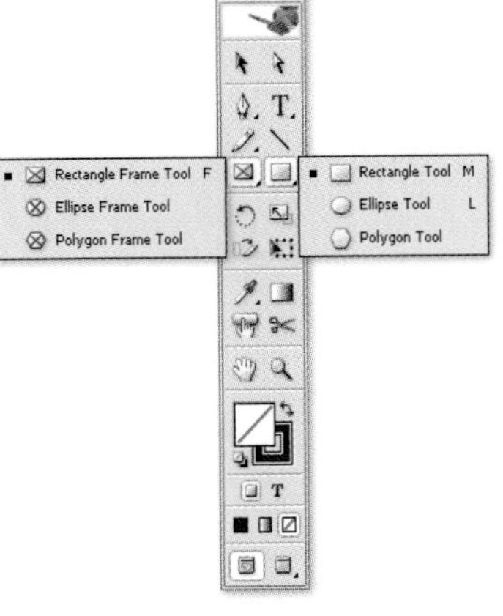

Figure 2-19.

8. *Draw an oval frame in place of the deleted frame.* To draw the oval frame, begin dragging at the intersection of the yellow and red guides, as in Figure 2-20. Then drag down and to the left until the cursor is even with the lower-left corner of the first column. When you release the mouse, the oval appears.

9. *Click the text frame's out port.* Now that we have an elliptical frame in place, let's reflow the text into the frame. To do so, first press the V key (or Enter on the keypad if you loaded

Figure 2-20.

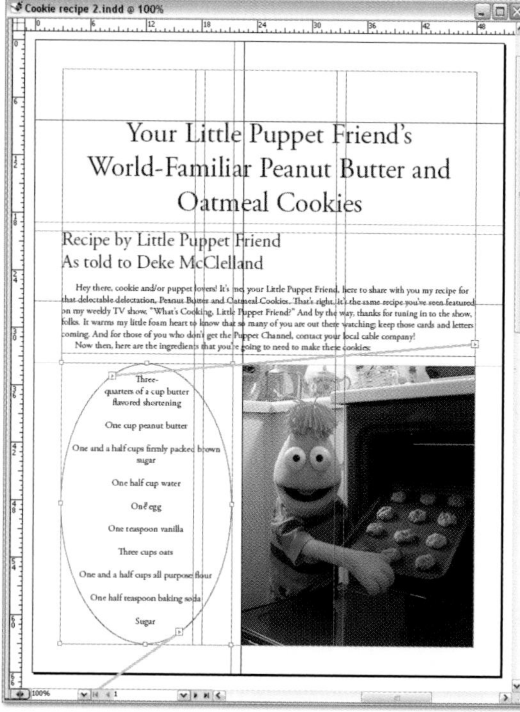

Figure 2-21.

my shortcuts) to return to the black arrow tool. Click the top text block, and then click its out port. Once again, you have loaded your cursor.

Pressing the V key is the standard shortcut for the black arrow tool. This may cause you to scratch your head a bit. If V already exists, why did I go to the trouble of creating my own shortcut, Enter? Consider for a moment what happens if text is highlighted. Pressing V replaces the type with a lowercase *v*. The Enter key works whether text is active or not, making it my shortcut of choice for the black arrow tool.

---

10. *Flow the text into the oval frame.* If you hover your cursor over the text block on which you just clicked, you'll notice that the cursor changes from into , a broken chain. This tells you that another click of the mouse will break the link to all subsequent frames. After that, you can flow the text in a different direction.

    That might be one way to steer the text into the ellipse, but it would involve reflowing the article onto the second page. Here's a better technique: Move the cursor into the ellipse. You should see yet another variation of the loaded cursor that looks like . This *area text* cursor indicates that you are about to flow text into an existing shape. Click in the ellipse to fill it with text, as in Figure 2-21. The ingredient list flows up from the second page and perfectly fills the oval frame.

11. *Save your document.* Choose **File→Save As** and name your document "My cookies 2.indd." As before, save it in the *Lesson 02* folder inside *Lesson Files-IDcs 1on1*.

Editing Your Text

Now that you've placed some text and had a crack at creating and modifying frames, it's high time we took a look at ways to edit the text inside those frames—replace letters, add words, fix typos, that kind of thing. InDesign provides two basic methods of doing this: you can edit text directly inside the document window, or you can switch to the pared-down Story Editor. Either way, InDesign makes the process as straightforward and obvious as reasonably possible. What isn't obvious is the plethora of handy shortcuts that permit you to edit with greater speed and less cursing. This exercise shows off some of InDesign's best text editing techniques.

1. ***Open a document.*** As before, this exercise is a continuation of its predecessor. If you still have *My cookies 2.indd* up on screen, wonderful. You might want to press Ctrl+; (or ⌘-;) to hide the guides, because we don't need them anymore. Then move on to Step 2. Otherwise, open the file named *Cookie recipe 3.indd* located in the *Lesson 02* folder inside *Lesson Files-IDcs 1on1*, which has the guides turned off by default. (Do you see how I help you?)

2. ***Identify the text to be deleted.*** As I read through LPF's recipe, I see that he didn't exactly stick to the topic of making cookies. We'll edit out one of his more egregious tangents, which starts with the first paragraph on the second page and ends two sentences into the fourth paragraph. In fact, let's work from the bottom up, deleting those two offending sentences first.

3. ***Delete the first two sentences of the fourth paragraph on the second page.*** Scroll to the bottom-left corner of the second page of the document until you see the paragraph that begins *Okay, time to get off the soapbox*. Double-click inside the text to switch to the type tool and position the blinking insertion marker. Then select the first two sentences of this paragraph using one of the following techniques:

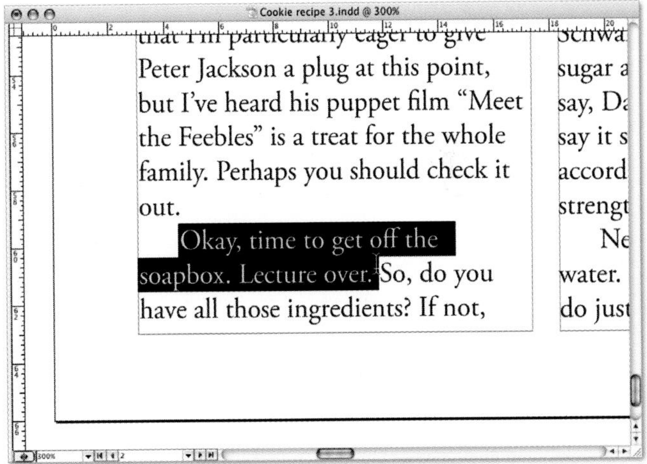

Figure 2-22.

   - Drag from the left edge of the *O* in *Okay* to the left edge of the *S* in *So*. Be sure to select the period and space between *over* and *So*. The first two sentences should now appear highlighted, as in Figure 2-22.

   - Click in front of the *O* in *Okay*. Then press the Shift key and click in front of the *S* in *So*. This selects the entire range of characters between the click and Shift-click points.

   - Double-click the word *Okay*, keeping the mouse button down on the second click. (So it's a click-press, as opposed to a standard double-click.) Now drag to select the text in whole word increments. Drag down one line and to the right until you've selected the first two sentences, including the space before *So*.

   After you have the sentences selected, press the Backspace or Delete key to remove them.

4. ***Delete the third paragraph on the second page.*** To make things more interesting—and to demonstrate some useful techniques—I'd like you to select and delete the first three paragraphs on this page using only the keyboard. Start with the third paragraph:

   - At this point, the insertion marker should be blinking immediately in front of the word *So*. Press the ↑ key once to move the insertion marker to the end of the third paragraph, after the word *out*.
   - Now, hold the Shift key and press →. This highlights the period at the end of the paragraph. Press Shift+→ again to select the letter *t*. Keep pressing Shift+→ to expand the selection one character at a time.
   - Finding this agonizingly slow? Try adding the Ctrl key (⌘ on the Mac) to the mix. Press Ctrl+Shift+→ (or ⌘-Shift-→) to select an entire word at a time.
   - If you select too many words, you can deselect a few by pressing Ctrl+Shift+← (⌘-Shift-←). Watch out though: if you go too far, you'll start selecting words in the direction of the fourth paragraph.
   - Another trick to try: Press Shift-↑ to expand the selection by a line at a time.
   - Press Shift-↑ until you've selected part of the first line in the paragraph, *So the next time you're in the*. Then press Ctrl+Shift+← several times more to expand the selection past the word *So*, past the indent, to the sliver of space after the period at the end of the second paragraph.

   Your selection should look like the one in Figure 2-23, with a little bit of highlight poking above the first line in the selection. Press Backspace or Delete to delete the text.

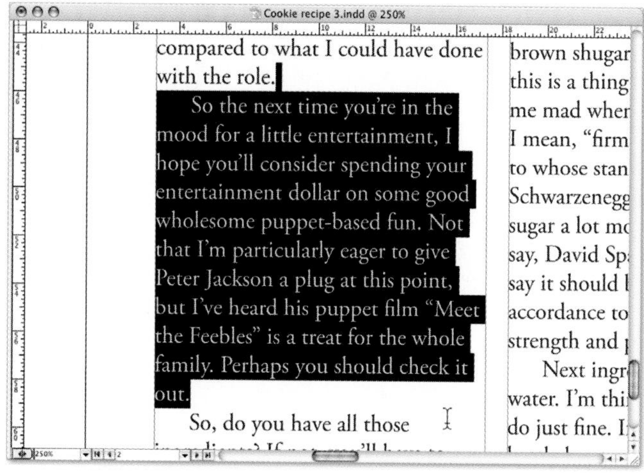

Figure 2-23.

5. ***Delete the first two paragraphs.*** You should see the insertion marker pulsing away after the period at the end of the second paragraph. Now let's select and delete the first two paragraphs on the page even more quickly than we removed the first:

   - Press Ctrl+Shift+↑ (⌘-Shift-↑ on the Mac) to select the entire second paragraph.

- Press Ctrl+Shift+↑ (⌘-Shift-↑) again to select the first paragraph as well, as shown in Figure 2-24.
- With the first two paragraphs selected, press Backspace or Delete.
- Finally, press the ← key and then press Backspace or Delete to eliminate the blank line at the top of the text frame. Or press the forward delete key, called Delete on the PC (marked by a ⌦ on the Mac).

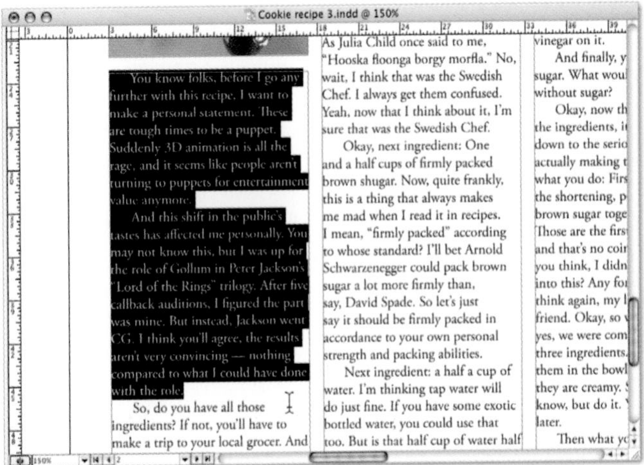

Figure 2-24.

PEARL OF WISDOM

As you're editing, InDesign may seem a little sluggish, especially when compared to a word processor. If you think about it, this is perfectly understandable; an edit you make early in a lengthy story can cause changes that ripple throughout many text frames and pages. InDesign has a lot to keep track of, so it can be excused for being a little slow to respond. For heavy editing tasks, the more practical route is to switch to the Story Editor, a sort of miniature word processor built into InDesign.

6. *Switch to the Story Editor.* Flipping over to the Story Editor is a snap. Just choose **Edit→Edit in Story Editor** or press Ctrl+Y (⌘-Y on the Mac). InDesign displays the **Story Editor** window featured in Figure 2-25. Bear in mind, the Edit in Story Editor command is available only when a text frame is selected or there's an active insertion marker in the text. This is necessary to tell the Story Editor what story you want to edit. If the command appears dimmed, click inside the story and try again.

   The Story Editor is a no-frills environment—no fonts, no styles, no hyphenation, just plain old text—where you can edit a story without having to wait while InDesign adjusts the layout to accommodate your changes. InDesign divides the window into two panes: one on the right that displays the text, and one on the left that lists the style sheets. For the

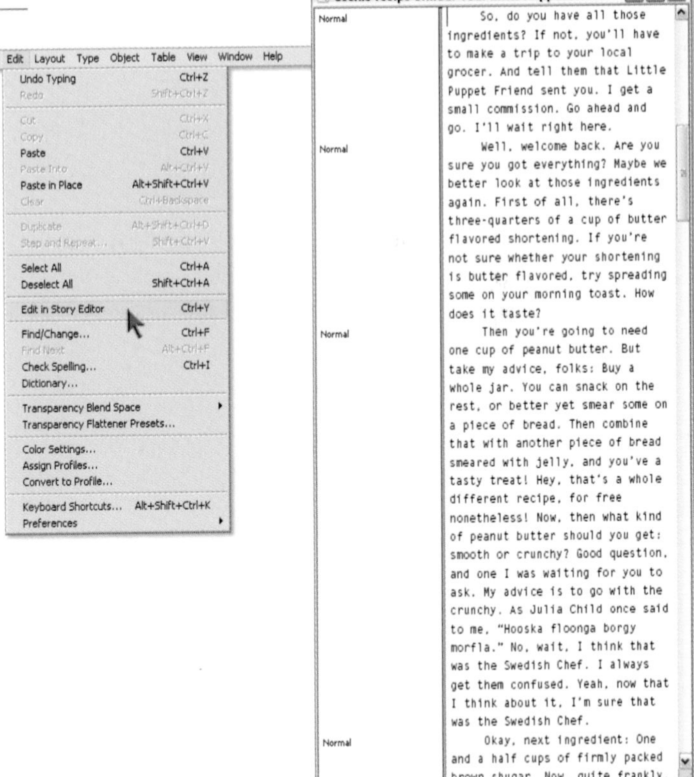

Figure 2-25.

present, we're going to ignore the style sheets—in our case, they're all set to Microsoft Word's default, Normal—but rest assured, you'll be well versed with them by time you complete this book. In fact, I devote an entire lesson to the topic of style sheets, namely Lesson 5, "Using Style Sheets."

To give yourself more room to work, you may want to drag the vertical divider line to the left. After all, we're not concerned with the style sheets, so might as well squish them out of view. If you want to see how your edits affect the document—which periodically updates to reflect your changes—choose Window→Arrange→Tile to see both document window and Story Editor at the same time. You might well wonder, doesn't viewing the frills from inside the no-frills environment sort of defeat the purpose? Not really. Because you're in the Story Editor, it has precedence, so InDesign resists updating the document window until it senses a lull in your activity. In other words, your edits occur lightning fast no matter what may be happening in the background document.

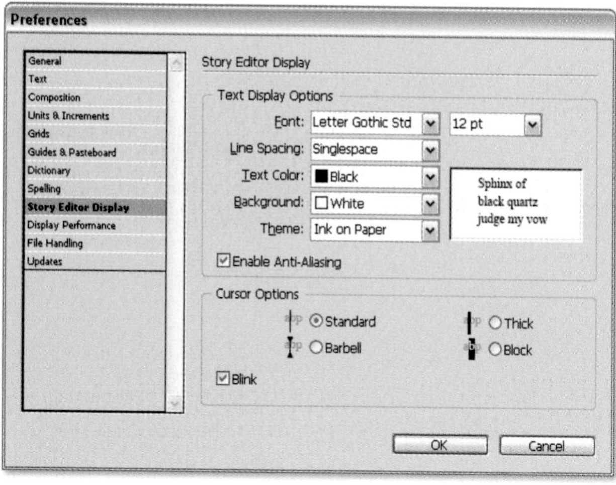

Figure 2-26.

7. *Display the Preferences dialog box.* If nothing else, text in the Story Editor should be easy to read. If you're experiencing eye fatigue or simply don't like the way the type looks, you can customize the size and appearance of type by visiting the Preferences dialog box. Choose **Edit→Preferences→Story Editor Display** (that's **InDesign→Preferences→Story Editor Display** on the Mac), or press Ctrl+K and then Ctrl+9 (⌘-K, ⌘-9). InDesign responds with the Story Editor Display panel of the Preferences dialog box (see Figure 2-26), which is worth visiting if only so you can see the deathless line of prose *Sphinx of black quartz, judge my vow!* Not only does this deranged passage contain all 26 letters in the alphabet, it updates to show you how the Story Editor text will appear when you change the Text Color, Background, or Anti-Aliasing settings. Oddly, it doesn't show font and spacing changes, but I suppose odd behavior is to be expected from such an odd sentence.

8. *Set the Theme to Classic System.* The **Theme** pop-up menu lets you choose between four preset Text Color and Background combinations. Choose **Classic System**, which emulates the ancient terminal systems used by newspaper editors and the like. (Personally, I like it because it reminds me how happy I am that I don't have to

use DOS ever again.) Then click **OK** to exit the Preferences dialog box. The Story Editor updates to reflect your changes, as in Figure 2-27.

9. ***Position the cursor at the beginning of the story.*** Let us now make an editorial change in the Story Editor and learn another keyboard shortcut in the process. If you left a blinking insertion marker in the text in the layout view, that insertion marker is automatically carried over into the Story Editor, with the window scrolled so that the insertion marker appears at the top. I'd like you to make a change to the very beginning of the story. The easiest way to get there is to press Ctrl+Home (⌘-Home on the Mac).

Note that this and other editing shortcuts work equally well in either the document window or the Story Editor. Pressing the Home key without the Ctrl (or ⌘) key moves the insertion marker to the beginning of the current line.

---

10. ***Delete the first word in the title.*** Press Ctrl+Shift+→ (or ⌘-Shift-→) to select the word, as in Figure 2-28. And then press Backspace or Delete to delete it.

11. ***Advance the cursor to the end of the story.*** Ctrl+Home takes you to the beginning of a story, so it only stands to reason that you can press Ctrl+End (⌘-End) to go to the end.

12. ***Replace the last two words.*** Press Ctrl+Shift+→ (⌘-Shift-→ on the Mac) four times to make the selection—one each for the exclamation points and once each for the words *life* and *Ciao*. Then type the phrase, "wholesome glass of milk with the cookies!" The new entry replaces the selected type.

13. ***Scroll to the same point in the document window.*** Choose **Edit→Edit in Layout** or press Ctrl+Y (⌘-Y on the Mac) to send the Story Editor to the back and display the newly edited text in the document window. InDesign even auto-scrolls you to the most recently modified text, which happens to be in the third column of page 3, as in Figure 2-29 on the next page.

14. ***Save your document.*** I expect you know the drill by now, but I'm going to tell you anyway. Choose **File→Save As**, name the document "My cookies 3.indd," and save it in the *Lesson 02* folder. We're done with the Story Editor, so if you like, you can close it by clicking inside it and pressing Ctrl+W (⌘-W). Or leave it running in the background—it won't hurt a thing.

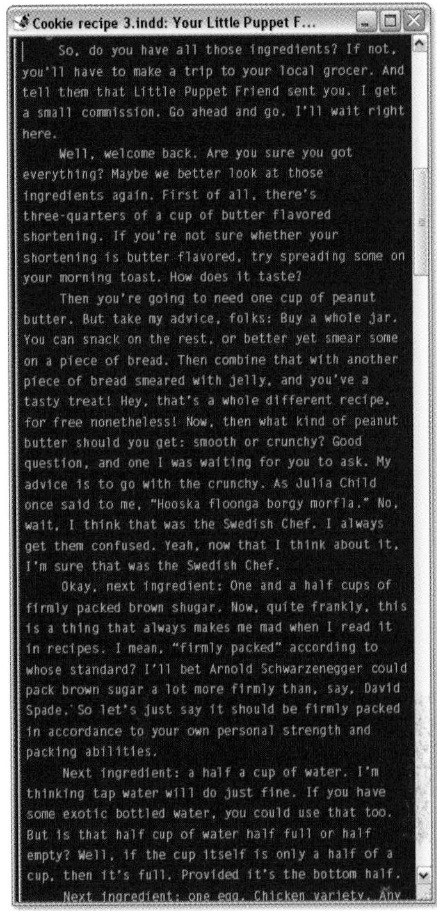

Figure 2-27.

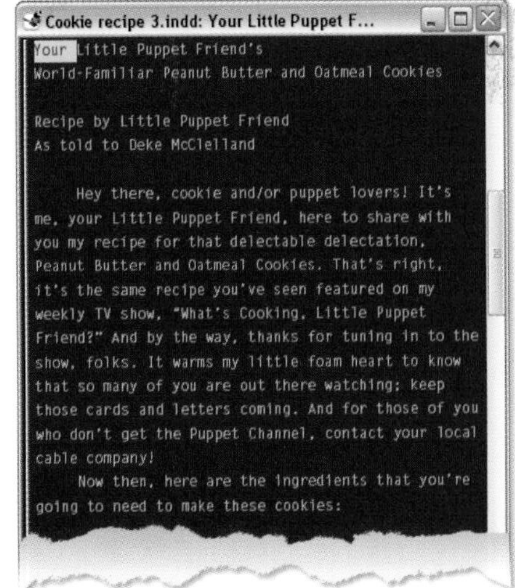

Figure 2-28.

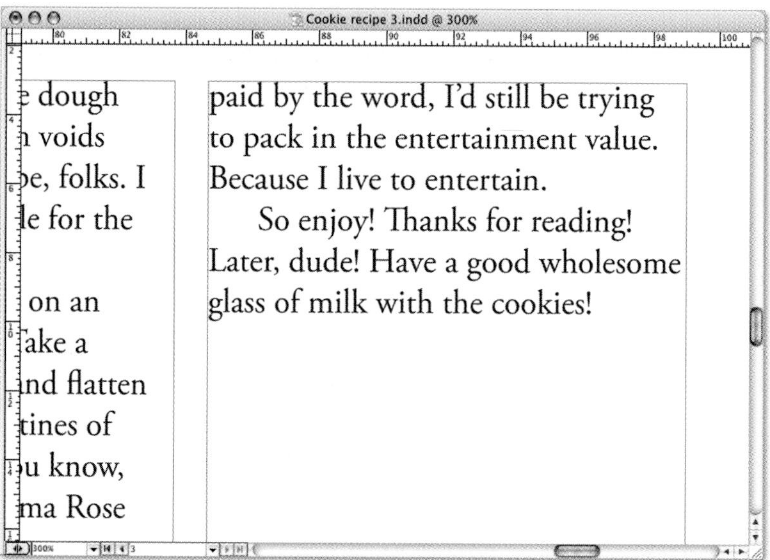

Figure 2-29.

Checking Your Spelling

InDesign lets you check the spelling of your text. If your text was written in a word processor, I would hope that you already checked the spelling there. But the Story Editor provides an open invitation for last-minute tinkering and rewriting. And when rewriting occurs, spelling mistakes can sneak in. So it's a good idea to submit your text to a final spell check.

PEARL OF WISDOM

I should say, I don't regard InDesign's spell checker as one of its best features. You can't instruct it to ignore words in all caps, hyphenated words, or filenames and Web addresses containing numbers and periods. Plus, the dictionary lacks a troubling number of routine words. Missing are *resize*, *hyperlinks*, *multipage*, *workspaces*, *inkjet* (!), *email* (!!), *QuarkXPress* (no surprise there), *Deke* (et tu, InDesign?), and my absolute favorite, *CS*. As a result, it flags way more spelling errors than it ought to. I am at least thankful it recognizes *InDesign*. More importantly, you can add words to a custom dictionary that is shared by fellow Adobe products Photoshop and Illustrator.

Anyhoo, better a ponderous spell checker than none at all. Let's see how to use it.

1. *Open a document.* This is the last exercise in this lesson that picks up where the previous one left off. If you have ready access to the file you saved in Step 14, *My cookies 3.indd*, open it up. Otherwise, you can use *Cookie recipe 4.indd* located in the *Lesson 02* folder inside *Lesson Files-IDcs 1on1*.

2. *Activate the story.* Scroll to the first page in the document. Armed with the type tool, click anywhere in the story. Then press Ctrl+Home (⌘-Home) to begin spell checking from the very beginning.

3. *Choose the Check Spelling command.* Choose **Edit→Check Spelling** or press Ctrl+I (or ⌘-I) to display the **Check Spelling** dialog box, pictured in Figure 2-30.

4. *Set search parameters.* Your first order of business is to tell InDesign exactly what you want to spell check by choosing an option from the Search pop-up menu. You can choose to search the Story (that is, all text in a series of threaded text blocks), the entire Document (which might contain several stories), All Documents that you have open, or from the insertion marker To End of Story. If you have text selected when you choose the Check Spelling command, a fifth option, Selection, appears. Our document contains just one story, so set the **Search** option to either **Story** or **Document**, your choice.

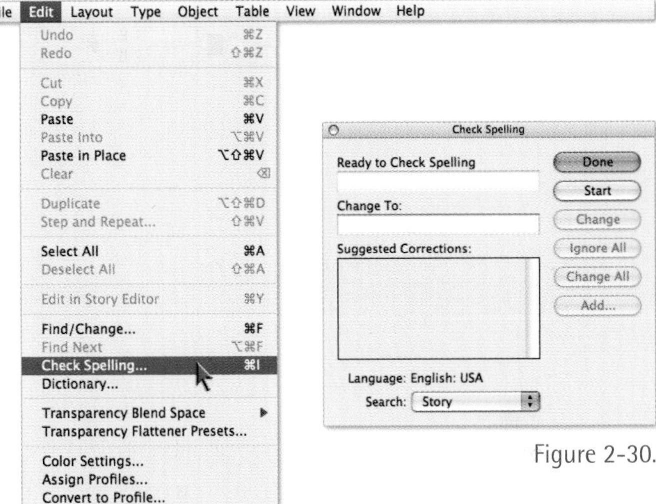

Figure 2-30.

5. *Click the Start button.* Almost immediately, InDesign locates and selects the first questionable word in the story—my name, naturally—and offers a number of possible corrections, virtually all of which I was called at some point in time in junior high.

6. *Select the first suggested correction and click Ignore.* Click **Duke** in the **Suggested Corrections** list, as in Figure 2-31. The four Change and Ignore buttons become active:

   - Change swaps the currently selected occurrence of *Deke* with *Duke.*

   - Change All changes this and all future occurrences of *Deke* to *Duke.*

   - Ignore skips this word and moves on to the next suspect word.

   - Ignore All skips *Deke* in this and every other document until the next time you quit and restart InDesign.

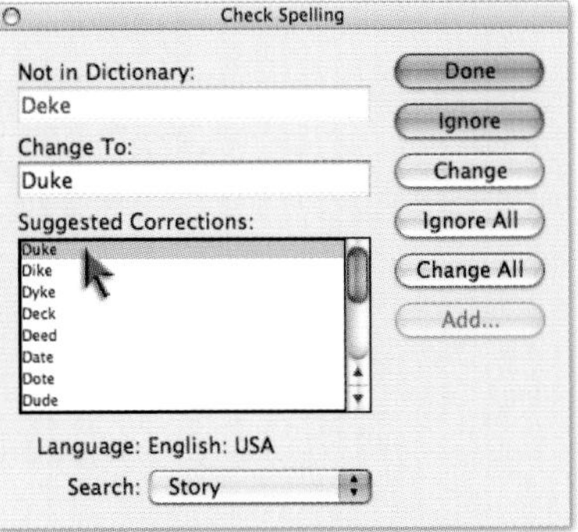

Figure 2-31.

The thing is, while I do rather remind myself of John Wayne—check out the videos, I'm the spitting image—I have no desire to change my name to *Duke*. And if you scroll down the list, it only gets worse. So do me a big favor, and click the **Ignore** button to move on. You could also click Ignore All, but as it just so happens, there are no more occurrences of *Deke* in this story.

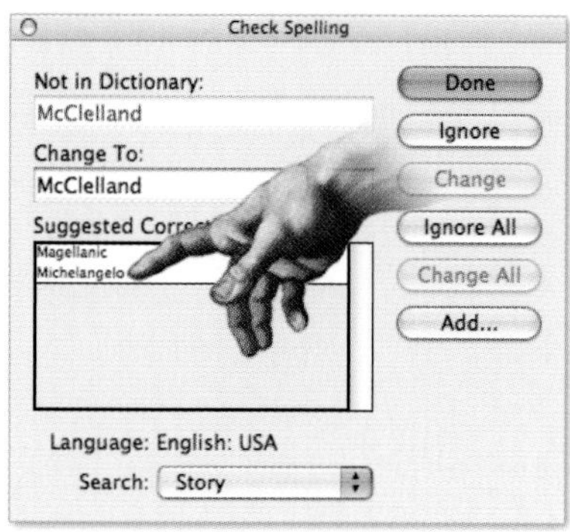

Figure 2-32.

7. *Click Ignore again.* InDesign moves on to the next unfamiliar word, which happens to be my last name, *McClelland*. Although I rather like that second suggestion (see Figure 2-32), it ain't me. Click **Ignore** to move on.

9. *Click Ignore four more times.* This bypasses LPF's Swedish-gibberish quote and brings up the next unfamiliar word, *shugar*.

10. *Correct the misspelling.* It's unusual to see a renowned cookie expert misspell such a sweet word, but puppets are notoriously bad typists. To set the record straight, click the first choice, **sugar**, in the Suggested Corrections list. Just in case *shugar* pops up again, click **Change All** to correct all occurrences of the word. A message appears, telling you that there was only one instance of *shugar* in the document. Click the **OK** button to confirm and move on.

11. *Add* Schwarzenegger *to the dictionary.* The spell checker next questions the word *Schwarzenegger*. As a California corporation, I know Adobe has heard of this guy, but proper nouns are not InDesign's strong suit. Still, the name has rather pervaded the public consciousness, so I reckon it ought to be part of the dictionary. Click **Add** to bring up the **Dictionary** dialog box. It contains a lot of options and we need them all to properly add the famous muscleman's name. So here's a quick rundown:

    - The Target pop-up menu lets you specify whether you want InDesign to store your changes in the User Dictionary—specifically, in a file called *ENG.UDC* buried several folders deep along with the system files on your hard drive—or directly inside any open document so that others who open that file will also have access to your saved words.

    - The Language pop-up menu lets you select the language that you're working in. If you spend a lot of time editing text in a foreign or specialized language—such as, say, English: USA Medical—then you can specify a different default setting in the Dictionary panel of the Preferences dialog box.

- The Dictionary List pop-up menu contains two settings. Select the first, Added Words, to add a word that is unfamiliar to InDesign (such as *Schwarzenegger*) to the custom dictionary. Select the second option, Removed Words, to force InDesign to question a word that is in its main dictionary but you consider to be wrong. For example, InDesign likes to spell the word email as *e-mail*, which is out of step with many publications. To set InDesign right, you'd add *email* to the Added Words list and *e-mail* to the Removed Words list.
- The Word option shows the word in question, the one you are poised to add to the dictionary. You can use that word or enter another.
- Click the Hyphenate button to ask InDesign to automatically hyphenate your word. Our man's name just cries out to be hyphenated, so give **Hyphenate** a click. The result, *Schwar~~zeneg~~~ger*, includes two hyphenation points, with fewer tilde (~) characters getting the higher priority. So this word is more likely to hyphenate as *Schwar-zenegger* than *Schwarzeneg-ger*. You can edit the tildes if you like.

To request that a word *never* be hyphenated, enter a tilde in front of the word, as in *~Schwarzenegger*. I don't recommend that with a word this long, but it might make sense with *~Deke*.

Here's what I want you to do:

- Set **Target** to **User Dictionary**. Leave **Language** set to its default (which varies depending on where you are on the face of our fair planet).
- Make sure **Dictionary List** is set to **Added Words**.
- Change the spelling of the contents of the **Word** option box to *Schwar~ze~~neg~~~ger*. Again, the word is more likely to be hyphenated where there are fewer tildes.
- Click the **Add** button to add our new vocabulary word to the list under the Word option, as in Figure 2-33.
- Click **Done** to return to the Check Spelling dialog box.

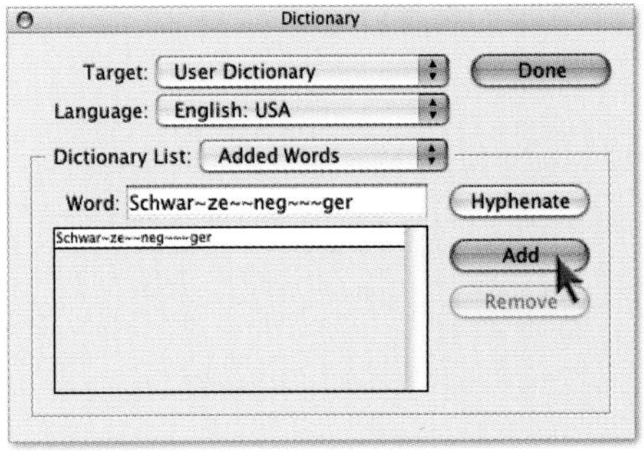

Figure 2-33.

12. ***Prod InDesign to move along.*** Seems like InDesign should go ahead and continue to check the document after you leave the Dictionary dialog box, but you have to give it a little nudge. Click **Ignore** and the Check Spelling dialog box goes on about its business.

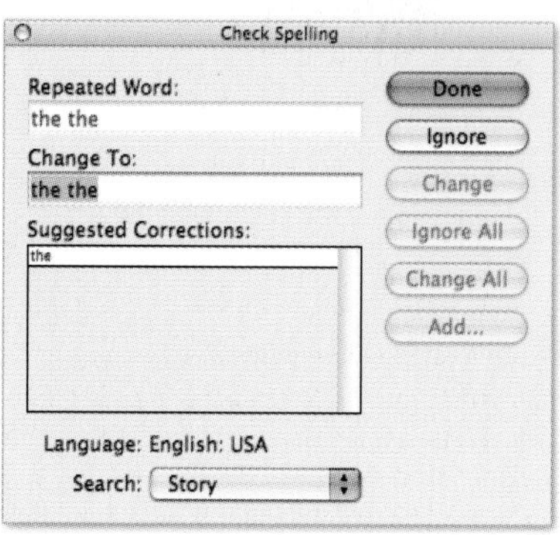

Figure 2-34.

13. *Fix the repeated words.* The next point of business happens to be *the the*—not the undeservedly obscure pop music act of the 1980s (*www.thethe.com*), but rather an all-too-common instance of a repeated word. As shown in Figure 2-34, the option at the top of the dialog box changes from Not in Dictionary to Repeated Word, and the Add button becomes dimmed. (You can't add a repeated word to the dictionary.) Select **the** in the Suggested Corrections list and click **Change**. The double world becomes one.

14. *Add* **ungreased** *to the dictionary.* After making the correction, the spell checker moves to the word *ungreased*. According to *Webster's* and other sources, this is not a word. Strunk and White urged us to avoid made-up words when plain words will do. But no other word will do. The cookie demands a baking sheet free of grease, thus ungreased it must be. So click the **Add** button to bring up the Dictionary dialog box. I'm not sure I'm ready to add this word to the user dictionary—this is one of those words that raises eyebrows outside the culinary world—so it's best to keep it inside this document. Choose your document's name from the **Target** pop-up menu. Click **Add** to sanctify the word inside this file, and click **Done** to return to the Check Spelling dialog box.

15. *Click Ignore three times.* The first click of the **Ignore** button prods the spell checker to keep searching the document. The next two clicks skip past more proper nouns that you're unlikely to use again—unless you're a big "Cagney and Lacey" fan, that is.

16. *Wrap it up.* A moment later, InDesign tells you that the spell check is complete. Click **OK** to dismiss the message, and then click **Done** to close the Check Spelling dialog box. My friend, you are done.

That's it for this file. Feel free to save your changes—after all, you fixed the spelling of a word, deleted a repeated word, and added a word to the document's internal dictionary. After you've saved the file, close the cookie recipe in anticipation of the next exercise.

Joining Type to a Curve

In addition to placing text inside a rectangular frame or other shape, you can flow text around the outside of a shape. Figure 2-35 offers a few examples. For the sake of comparison, the central text is set inside an oval. The rest flows around curves. In Adobe parlance, these curves are *paths*, and so each line of type is called *type on a path*, or just plain *path type*. In all, Figure 2-35 contains 10 independent lines of path text—two in white, two dark red, and six in black.

In this exercise, you'll create two lines of type, one along the top of a circle and the other along the bottom. In addition to binding text to the shape, you'll learn how to move the text along the path outline, flip it to one side or the other, and space the letters to keep them legible.

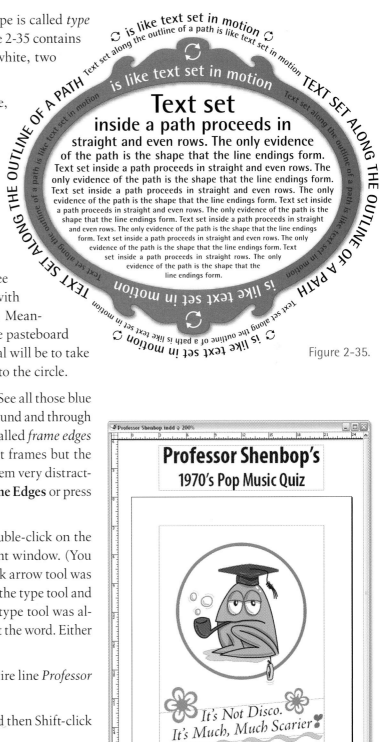

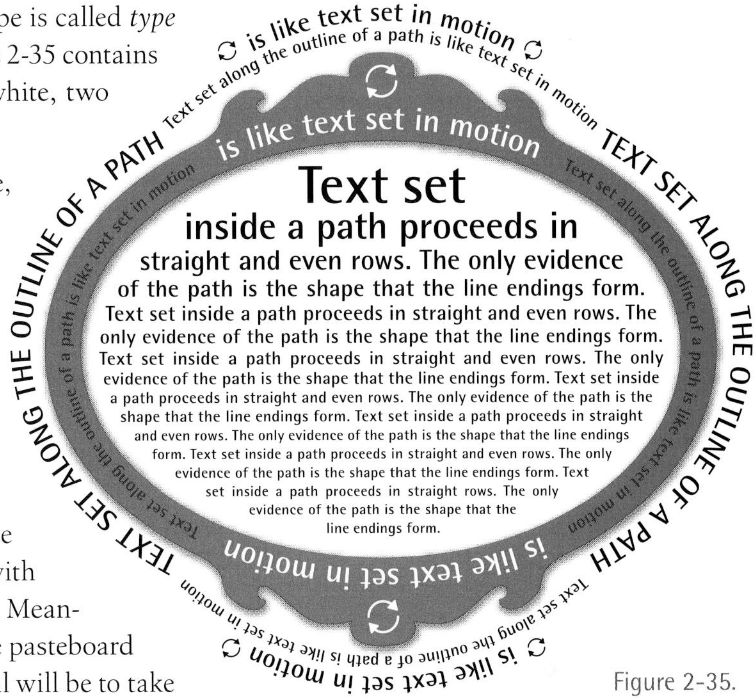

Figure 2-35.

1. ***Open a document.*** Open the *Professor Shenbop.indd* file in the *Lesson 02* folder inside *Lesson Files-IDcs 1on1*. Here we see a small page bearing a cartoon of a frog with a pull-string surrounded by a red circle. Meanwhile, two lines of type lay waiting in the pasteboard above the page (see Figure 2-36). Our goal will be to take this text from the pasteboard and join it to the circle.

2. ***Hide the frame edges and path outlines.*** See all those blue lines running around the text as well as around and through the objects in the illustration? These so-called *frame edges* mark not only the boundaries of the text frames but the path outlines as well. Personally, I find them very distracting. If you agree, choose **View→Hide Frame Edges** or press Ctrl+H (⌘-H on the Mac) to hide them.

3. ***Activate the text in the pasteboard.*** Double-click on the word *Professor* at the top of the document window. (You may have to scroll up to see it.) If the black arrow tool was active, double-clicking will switch you to the type tool and enter a blinking insertion marker. If the type tool was already active, double-clicking will highlight the word. Either way, you're set.

4. ***Select the first line of type.*** Select the entire line *Professor Shenbop's*. A few ways to do this:

   - Click in front of the *P* in *Professor* and then Shift-click after the final *s* in *Shenbop's*.

   - Double-click a word; on the second click, hold the mouse button and drag to highlight the other word.

   - Triple-click inside a word to select the entire line.

Figure 2-36.

Or don't click at all. Just press Ctrl+Shift+[icon] (or ⌘-Shift-[icon]) to extend an existing selection to include an entire line of type. It's a weird keyboard shortcut, but extremely useful if you can remember it.

5. ***Copy the selected text.*** In some programs, you join text to a path by creating the text and the path independently and then combining the two. In Adobe apps, you enter the text directly onto the path. To use existing text, like the stuff we have here, you have to copy the text and then paste it onto the path. To start the process, choose **Edit→Copy** or press Ctrl+C (⌘-C) to copy the text to InDesign's clipboard.

PEARL OF WISDOM

Our next task is to prepare the circle to receive the text. Because we have two lines of type—one for the top of the circle and the other for the bottom—we need two separate paths. (Sadly, InDesign won't let you join two lines of type to one circle.) The trick: cut the circle into two halves, one upper and one lower. That's a job for the scissors tool.

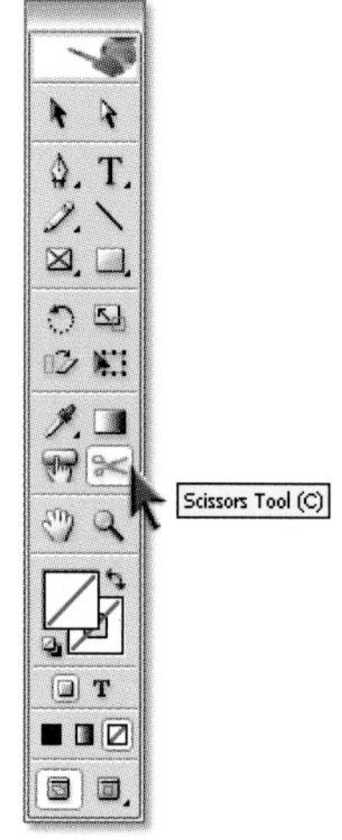

Figure 2-37.

6. ***Select the scissors tool in the toolbox.*** Press Ctrl+Shift+A (⌘-Shift-A on the Mac) to deselect the text. Then click the scissors tool in the toolbox, as in Figure 2-37, or press the C key. The purpose of the scissors tool is to snip apart path outlines.

7. ***Snip the circle.*** Now to click both the left and right sides of the circle, thus separating the top and bottom halves. Sounds simple enough, but you have to do it just right:

   - First, move the scissors tool cursor over the inside edge—I repeat, the *inside* edge—of the leftmost point in the circle. (If you're keeping an eye on the Control palette, move the cursor until the dimmed coordinate values read X: 5p2, Y: 12p0.) When the cursor changes from a cross to a tiny bullseye (as in ⌖), click. The red outline shifts inward, from outside the thin blue line—which is the path of the circle—to inside. Blue lines also appear. These are the control handles. I discuss control handles in Lesson 6, "Drawing inside InDesign." For now, don't worry about them.

   - Now click the rightmost point in the circle, which has shifted to the outside edge. Again, watch for the cursor to change before you click.

   The orange arrows in Figure 2-38 on the facing page show the proper click points. This screen shot was taken after creating the points, so the red outline has already shifted to the inside of the blue path.

8. ***Select the type-on-a-path tool.*** Click and hold the type tool icon in the toolbox to display a flyout menu, and then choose the type-on-a-path tool, as in Figure 2-39. Or Alt-click (Option-click) the type tool icon. Or just press the keyboard shortcut Shift+T. However you do it, you'll arm yourself with the tool used to put type along a curve in InDesign.

9. ***Click anywhere along the top half of the circle.*** Move your cursor to the outside edge of the top of the circle. When a plus sign appears next to the cursor (I+), click. The path is now ready to accept text.

10. ***Paste the copied text.*** It's been five steps since you copied the text, but that doesn't matter. The clipboard retains its information until the next time you choose Edit→Copy or Cut. So choose **Edit→Paste** or press Ctrl+V (⌘-V) to paste the text along the top half of the circle.

PEARL OF WISDOM

Unexpectedly, InDesign pastes the text upside-down and along the inside of the circle, as in Figure 2-40. The reason: Every path has a direction, and InDesign thinks this particular path goes counterclockwise. So the text goes under the hump instead of over it. Fortunately, this minor irritation is easily fixed.

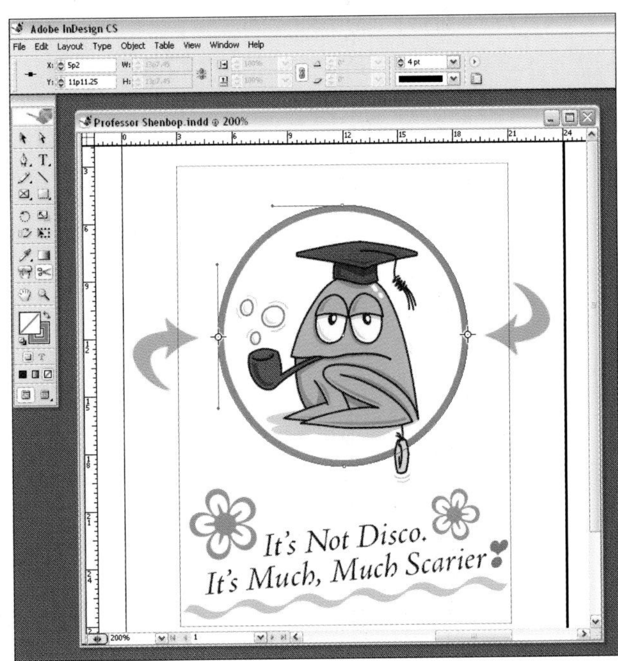

Figure 2-38.

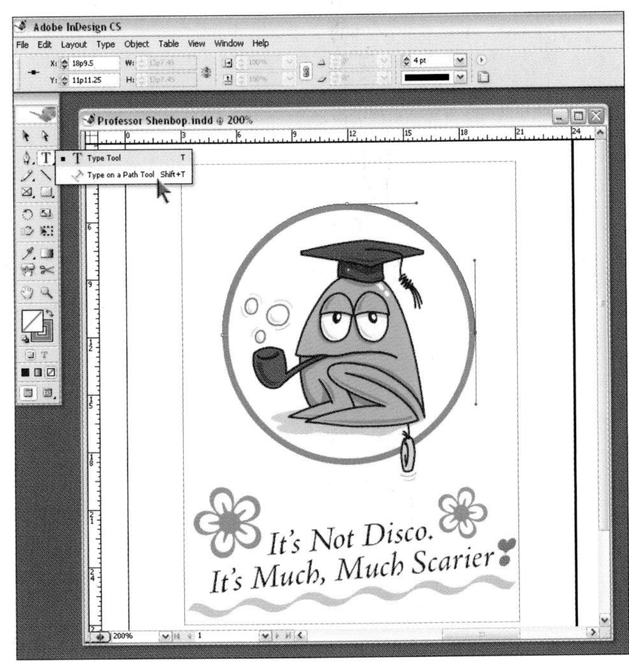

Figure 2-39.

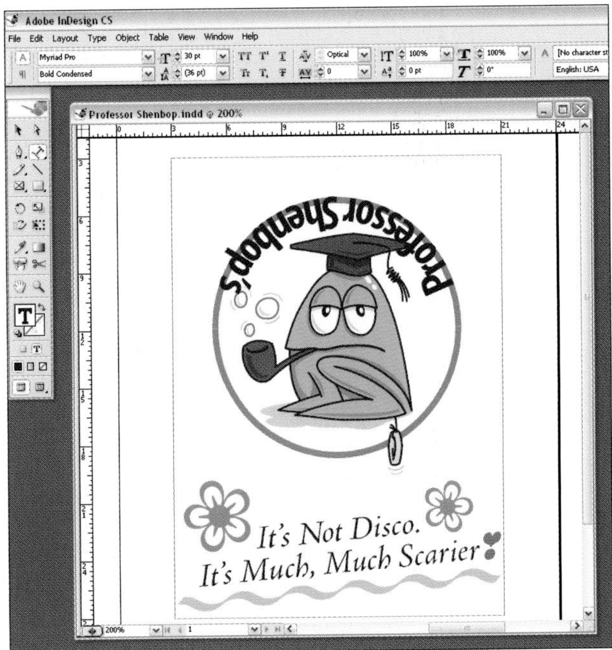

Figure 2-40.

11. ***Switch to the black arrow tool.*** If you loaded my keyboard shortcuts as directed on page xvii of the Preface, then press the Enter key on the numeric keypad. Otherwise, click the black arrow in the upper-left corner of the toolbox.

12. ***Flip the text to the other side of the path.*** If you look very closely at the handle (the blue square) centered atop the rectangular bounding box around the text, you should see a tiny blue crossbar that intersects the end of the *S* in *Shenbop's*. (It's actually a little ⊤, but it's hard to make out because of the bounding box.) This all-too-subtle indicator lets you control which side of an object the text is on. To flip the text, drag the tiny crossbar upward. As illustrated in Figure 2-41, this sends the text to the other side of the hump.

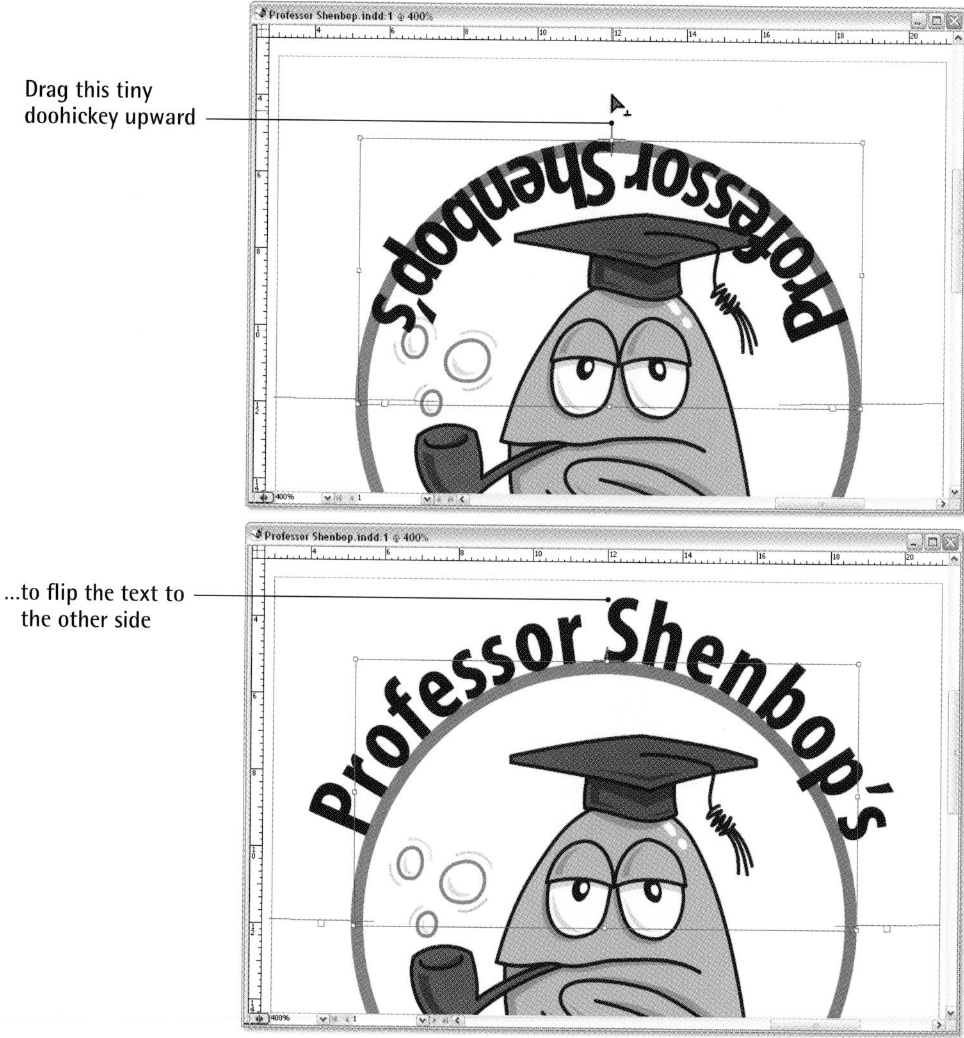

Figure 2-41.

Can't locate the crossbar? Just don't feel like monkeying with it? Have I got the solution for you: Choose **Type→Type on a Path→Options**. When the dialog box appears, select the **Flip** check box (if necessary, turn on **Preview** to make sure it works) and click **OK**.

13. ***Make the outline transparent.*** Now that you've flipped the text, the next problem is that thick red outline. It should not be there. To get rid of it, click the red ◱ control near the bottom of the toolbox, as indicated by the purple arrow cursor in Figure 2-42. This shifts the focus to the border, or *stroke*, of the path. Then click the ☒ icon below the stroke control, as indicated by the green cursor in the figure, to change the outline to transparent.

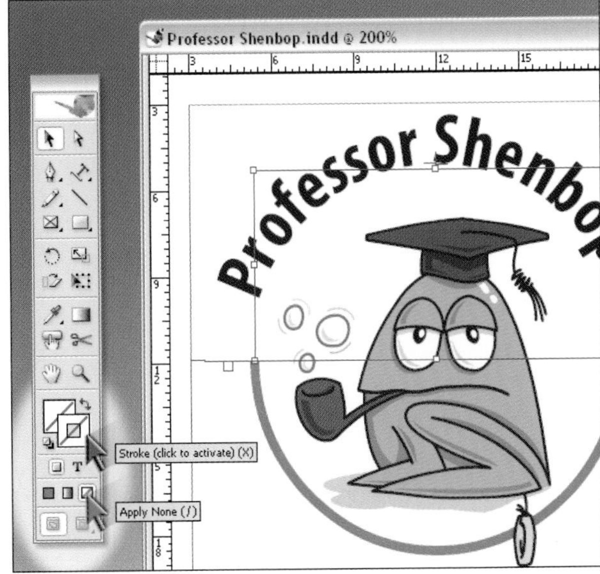

Figure 2-42.

To do the same from the keyboard, press the X key to switch to the stroke and then press the / key to make the stroke transparent. For more information on how to change the stroke of an object, see the "Fill, Stroke, and Color" exercise on page 211 of Lesson 6.

EXTRA CREDIT

One line of path type down, one more to go. So far, you've seen how to attach type to a path and how to account for one potential problem that may occur when adding type to a convex curve, where the text is on the outer surface of the arc. Now we'll take a look at the special issues that may arise when adding text to a concave curve, where the text needs to go on the inner surface of a curve. Naturally, you don't have to participate. If you've had enough path type for now, skip ahead to "What Did You Learn?" (page 83). But if you're still itching to learn more—and I hope that you are because there's some good stuff coming up—keep reading.

14. ***Repeat the previous steps on the bottom half of the circle.*** Specifically, repeat Steps 4, 5, 9, and 10. Needless to say, I wouldn't think of asking you to go back and reread those paragraphs. So here's the skinny:

    - Select the type-on-a-path tool in the toolbox. If you like keyboard shortcuts, press Shift+T.
    - Select the second line of type in the pasteboard, the one that reads *1970's Pop Music Quiz*. Notice that the type-on-a-path tool is equally adept at selecting normal text as it is at creating and editing path type.

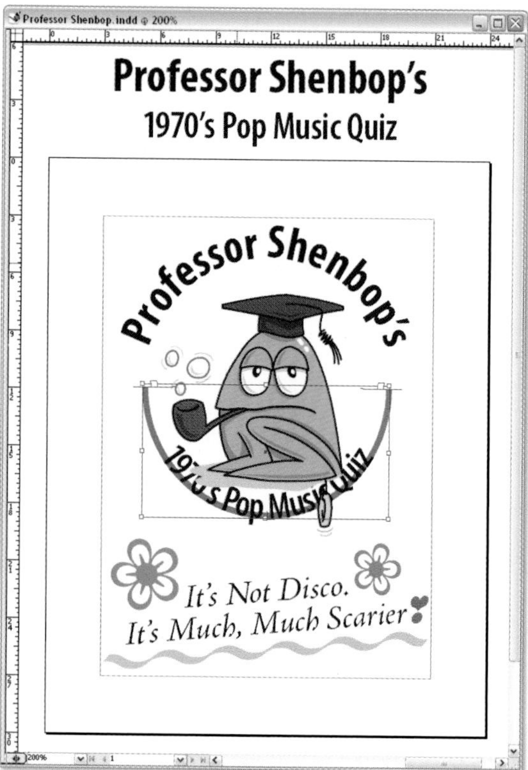

Figure 2-43.

- Press Ctrl+C (or ⌘-C) to copy the text.
- Using the same type-on-a-path tool, click anywhere along the bottom half of the circle. (Make sure the cursor shows a plus sign before you click.)
- Press Ctrl+V (or ⌘-V) to paste the text.

At this point, your document should look like the one pictured in Figure 2-43. For now, we'll leave the red stroke intact; it serves as a helpful point of reference. Although the bottom line of type flows in the proper direction, left-to-right, InDesign has aligned it to the inside of the half circle rather than the outside. As a result, the letters appear squished, not to mention directly under Shenbop's nether regions. This is entirely unacceptable—we shall fix it.

15. *Open the Type on a Path Options dialog box.* Choose **Type→Type on a Path→Options** to display the **Type on a Path Options** dialog box shown in Figure 2-44. These options permit you to change how InDesign aligns text to a curve.

Strictly speaking, there is no shortcut for this command. But if you're using the Windows version of InDesign, you can take advantage of an Alt-key equivalent. Press Alt+T to open the Type menu, and then press T for Type on a Path and O for Options. Again, that's Alt+T, T, O.

---

16. *Align the letters by their ascenders.* First, make sure the **Preview** check box is on. Then select **Ascender** from the **Align** pop-up menu. This aligns the topmost portions of the letters with the path, shifting the characters below the circle, as in Figure 2-45 on the opposite page. Granted, this setting drops the letters too far, but it's the only Align option that comes close to satisfying our needs. Fortunately, you can fine-tune the vertical alignment once you leave the dialog box.

17. *Bring the letters together.* In shifting the characters down, InDesign has also spread them farther apart. As a result, we have too much space between the characters. To squish them together a bit, change the **Spacing** value to –5.

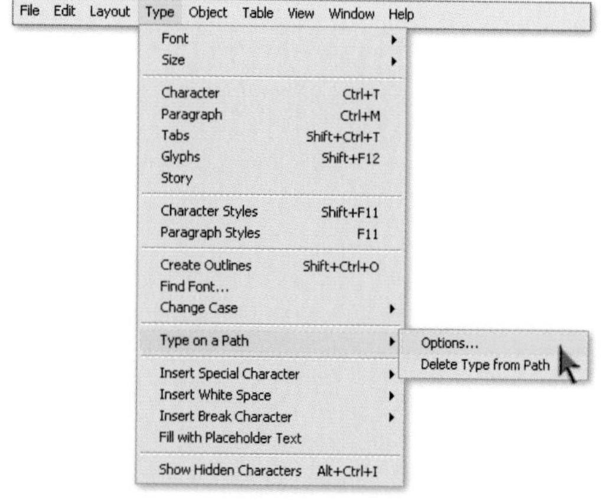

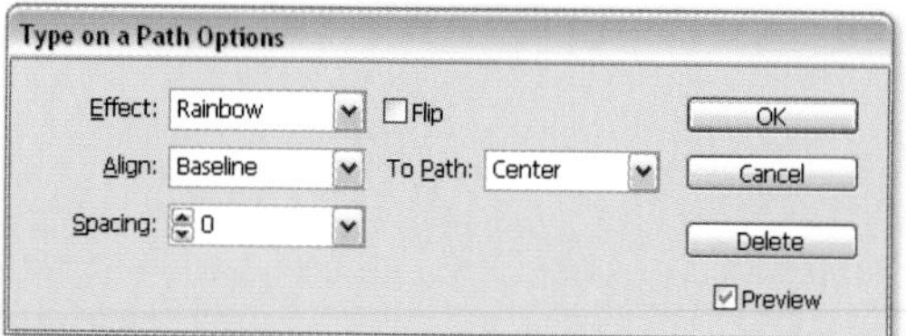

Figure 2-44.

18. *Leave the Effect option set to Rainbow.* While **Rainbow** might sound like an ethereal, impractical setting, it's actually the most buttoned-down path type effect you can apply. Figure 2-46 illustrates all five options you can choose from the **Effect** pop-up menu. Skew is sometimes useful for simulating text wrapping around an object. But otherwise, Rainbow is the way to go.

19. *Click the OK button.* Or press Enter or Return to accept your changes. Things are certainly looking better, but some issues remain. The text needs to be closer to the line, and the words need to be spaced around the yellow ring attached to the pull string coming out of Shenbop's . . . foot. Let's start things off by adding some space.

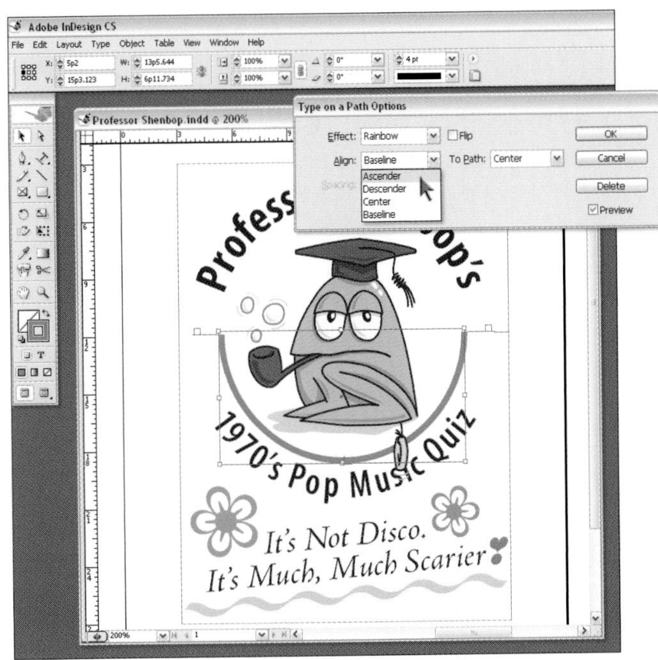

Figure 2-45.

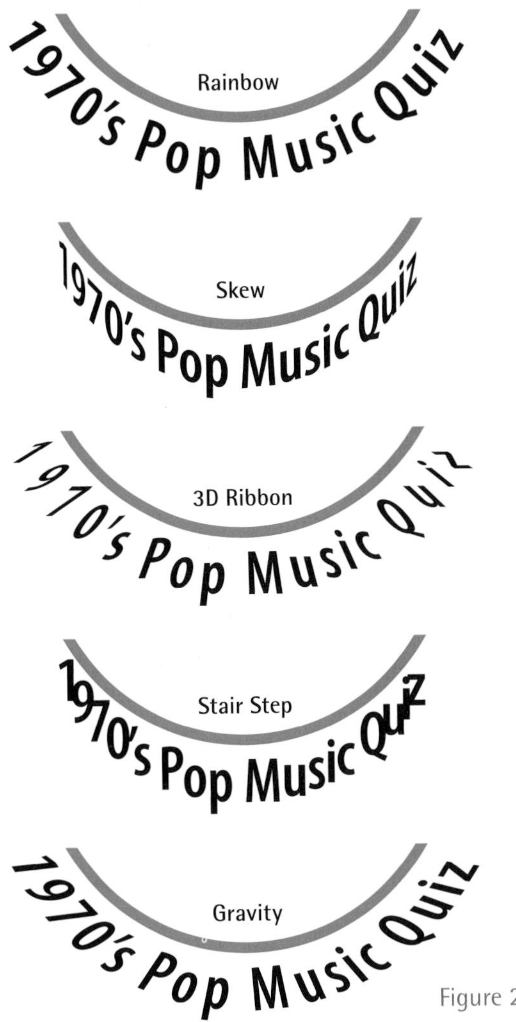

Figure 2-46.

20. ***Increase the space before*** Quiz. Press the T key to get the type tool (or Shift+T for the type-on-a-path tool—either way works). Then highlight the space character between *Music* and *Quiz*. Currently, this is a standard, everyday space created with the spacebar. But InDesign gives you several other spaces to choose from. For the thickest space possible, right-click on the selected space (or Control-click if your Macintosh mouse has just one mouse button). Then choose **Insert White Space→Em Space**, which inserts a space as wide as the type size, as in Figure 2-47. This is 24-point type, so the space is 24 points wide. (To learn more about spaces and other special characters, see "Dashes, Spaces, and Breaks" on page 143 of Lesson 4.)

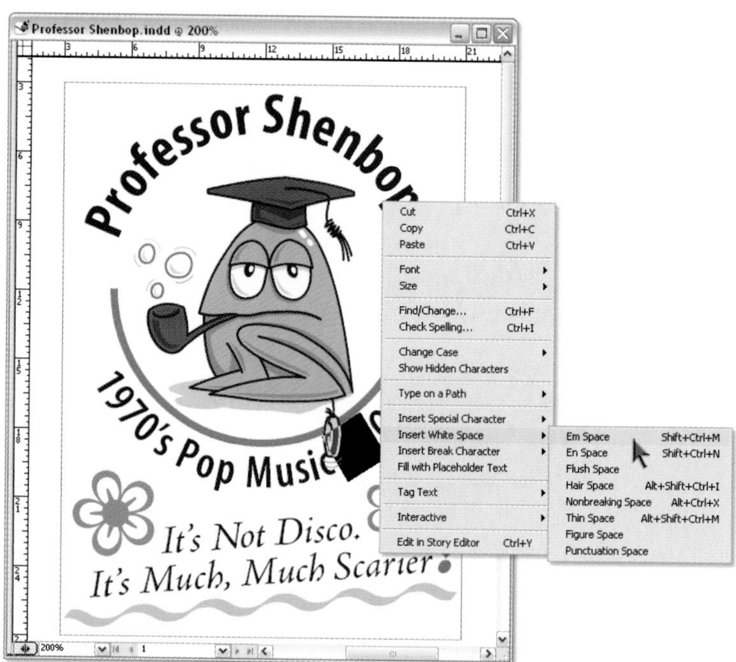

Figure 2-47.

21. ***Adjust the baseline shift.*** Now it's time to move the text closer to the line. Press Ctrl+Shift+\ (or ⌘-Shift-\) to select the entire line. Then go to the Control palette at the top of the screen and click the icon that looks like a capital letter paired with a superscript one ($\underline{A}^{a}$). This selects the baseline shift value, which lets you nudge characters up or down. Change the value to 5 and press Enter or Return. The letters move up 5 points until they just barely touch the red path, as in Figure 2-48. Notice that the letters also scoot closer together, which happens to work out perfectly.

Figure 2-48.

22. ***Switch back to the black arrow tool.*** The text is joined nicely to its path, and the em space permits plenty of room for the ring. Only problem is, the space isn't aligned with the ring. You need to move the type slightly to the left, which you can do with the black arrow tool. Either click the black arrow icon in the toolbox or (assuming you loaded Deke Keys as advised back on page xvii of the Preface) press Enter on the keypad.

23. ***Drag the end bar.*** See the blue bars at both ends of the red half circle? These are the equivalent of column markers, the points at which the text begins and ends on the path. But they also permit you to move text along the path. For example, to move the text to the left, drag the right bar down and to the left, as demonstrated in Figure 2-49. A simple adjustment or two moves the space directly over the ring.

Figure 2-49.

You can also move text using the tiny crossbar ⊤, first introduced in Step 12 (see page 76). After (and only after) you move in one of the end bars, you can drag the crossbar (presently located above the M) to move the text back and forth. Just be careful not to drag the bar to the other side of the path or you'll flip the text.

24. ***Make the outline transparent.*** The final step is to get rid of the thick red outline. Thanks to Step 13, the stroke should still be active. So just press [/] to make it invisible.

Figure 2-50 shows the final piece of artwork. Notice that I adjusted the top line of type, *Professor Shenbop's*, by dragging its left end bar up and to the right. This made the text more symmetrical with the lower curved line of type, so that the amount of empty space on either side of the charismatic Shenbop is equal. The text is a bit off-kilter, which I regard as perfect for my kooky cartoon.

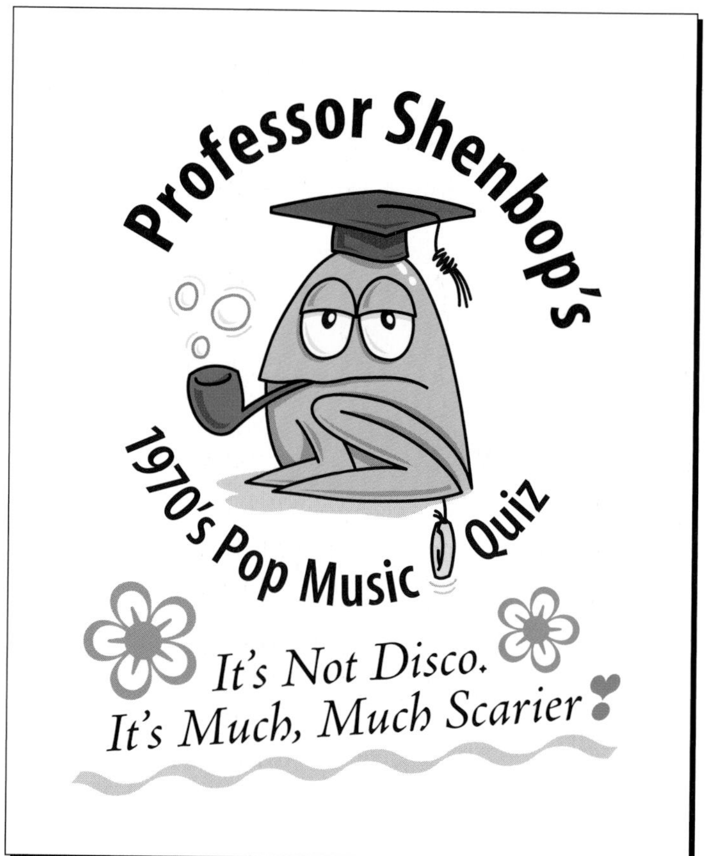

Figure 2-50.

WHAT DID YOU LEARN?

Match the key concept in the numbered list below with the letter of the phrase that best describes it. Answers appear upside-down at the bottom of the page.

Key Concepts

1. Frame
2. Place
3. Typographer's quotes
4. Out port
5. Story
6. Text threads
7. Autoflow
8. Area text
9. Story Editor
10. Check Spelling
11. Path type
12. Frame edges

Descriptions

A. InDesign's ability to flow all text from a story in a single click—whether into frames or empty columns—and even generate pages.

B. Located in the lower-right corner of a text block, this box shows whether the frame hides overflow text ⊞ or passes it to another frame ▶.

C. Among other things, this command allows you to add words to a custom dictionary and even specify hyphenation preferences.

D. A continuous body of text that may exceed the confines of a frame or page and flow from one text frame to another.

E. The boundaries of a selected text or graphic container, which can be hidden with a command from the View menu or by pressing Ctrl+H (⌘-H on the Mac).

F. Punctuation marks that curl or bend toward the text they bracket, as opposed to remaining invariably straight.

G. Nonprinting lines that show how text flows from one frame to another.

H. This command permits you to import all varieties of content into InDesign, including both text from a word processor and graphics.

I. Type set inside an existing shape, regardless of what tool you used to draw the shape in the first place.

J. An independent, free-floating container that may contain text or an imported graphic.

K. InDesign's built-in text processor, which omits formatting in an attempt to streamline the correction process and permit you to focus on content exclusive of design.

L. Text that follows the contours of a curve.

Answers

1J, 2H, 3F, 4B, 5D, 6G, 7A, 8I, 9K, 10C, 11L, 12E

LESSON 3

Y•85 M•85 C•9 K•42
Y•100 M•100 C•10 K•42
Y•40 M•40 C•4 K•24
Y•55 M•55 C•6 K•24
Y•70 M•70 C•7 K•24
Y•85 M•85 C•9 K•24
Y•100 M•100 C•10 K•24

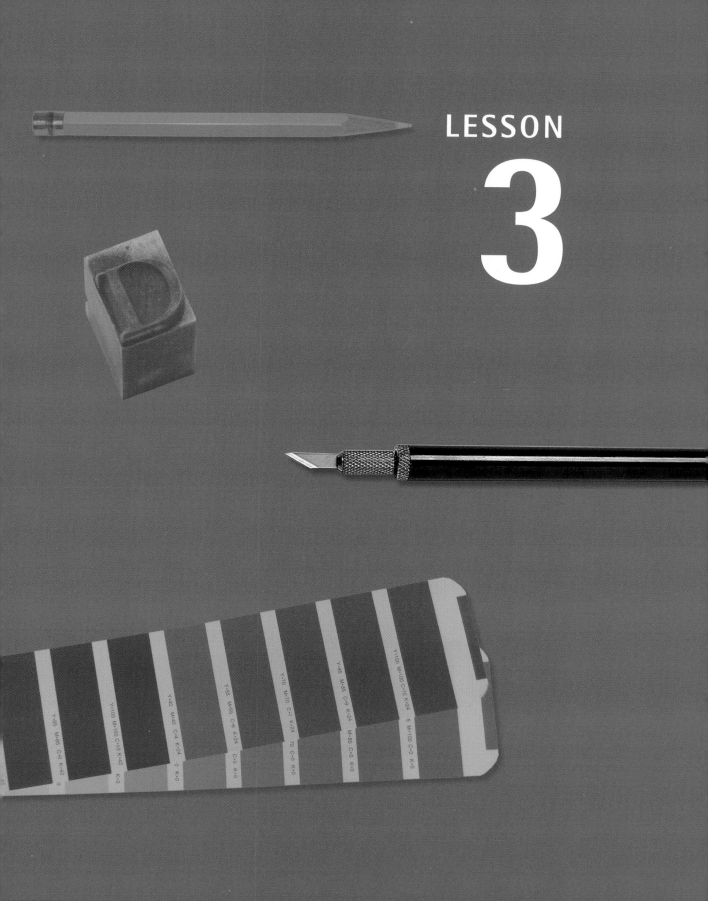

BASIC TEXT FORMATTING

IF YOU'RE NEW to page design, or merely a pragmatist at heart, you might have difficulty understanding why so many people devote so much time and effort to changing the appearance of a handful of letters. If you've seen one typeface, you've seen them all. Why not just enter the text, print it, and be done with it?

Even in my capacity as a gung-ho type enthusiast (read: type nerd), I have to admit, the differences between one typeface and another are at times incredibly subtle. Consider Figure 3-1. Here we have uppercase O's from seven different sans serif fonts. (To learn more about serif and sans serif typefaces, see the sidebar "The Look of Type" on page 94.) A type nerd like me could draw you a diagram to explain how remarkably diverse these letters are, hailing from as many as three distinct sans serif traditions: Grotesque, Geometric, and Humanist (see Figure 3-2 on page 87). But to the untrained eye, the letters are just a bunch of ovals. Some look like hula hoops, others more like donuts. But they're all ovals. The overwhelming majority of your readers can't tell a Grotesque O from a Humanist O, and furthermore they probably don't care. It makes you wonder why Max Miedinger put so much care into creating his ubiquitous Haas-Grotesk (renamed Helvetica in 1960)—not to mention, why in the world I know that he did.

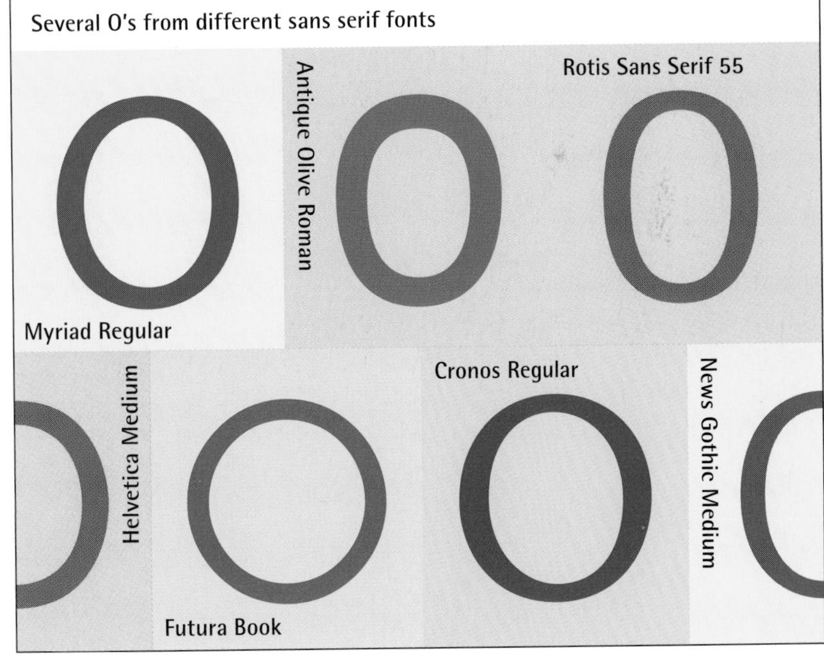

Figure 3-1.

ABOUT THIS LESSON

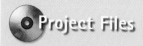

Project Files

Before beginning the exercises, make sure that you've installed the lesson files from the CD, as explained in Step 5 on page xv of the Preface. This should result in a folder called *Lesson Files-IDcs 1on1* on your desktop. We'll be working with the files inside the *Lesson 03* subfolder.

This lesson introduces you to InDesign's state-of-the-art character and paragraph formatting controls. We'll also take a look at Adobe's OpenType font technology. You'll learn how to:

- Change the typeface, type size, line spacing, and color of selected characters of type . . . . page 89
- Adjust the horizontal space between letters using kerning and tracking . . . . page 96
- Add vertical space between paragraphs, as well as justify and center lines of text . . . . page 103
- Fix stacks, widows, and spacing irregularities by adjusting hyphenation and justification . . . . . page 109
- Access ligatures, small caps, fractions, and other special characters from the Glyphs palette. . . . . . page 116

Video Lesson 3: Typeface and Style

Like any publishing program, InDesign divides its formatting capabilities into two groups: those that affect individual characters of type and those that affect entire paragraphs at a time. Character attributes appear in the Character palette; paragraph attributes appear in the Paragraph palette. And when editing text with the type tool, you can get to both kinds of attributes from the Control palette.

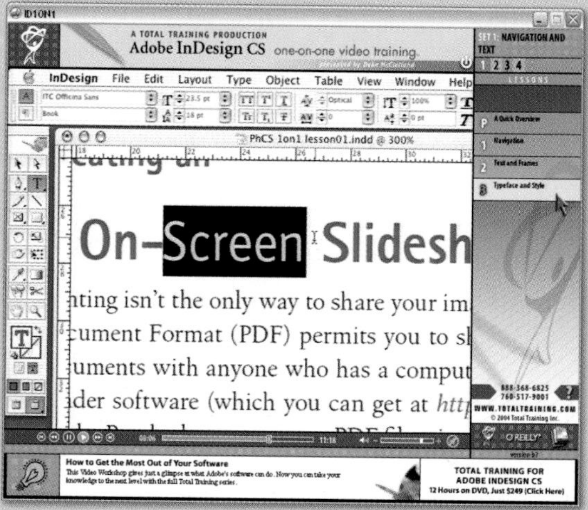

To see how these palettes work, watch the third video lesson on the CD. Insert the CD, click **Start Training**, and then select **3, Typeface and Style** from the Lessons list on the right side of the screen. This 11-minute 20-second movie shows you how to apply some basic formatting options and acquaints you with the following shortcuts:

Operation	Windows shortcut	Macintosh shortcut
Display the Character palette	Ctrl+T	⌘-T
Display the Paragraph palette	Ctrl+Alt+T	⌘-Option-T
Switch options in Control palette	Ctr+Alt+7, or F4*	⌘-Option-7, or F4*
Apply underline or all caps style	Ctrl+Shift+U, Ctrl+Shift+K	⌘-Shift-U, ⌘-Shift-K
Apply bold or italic style (if available)	Ctrl+Shift+B, Ctrl+Shift+I	⌘-Shift-B, ⌘-Shift-I

* Works only if you loaded the Deke Keys keyboard shortcuts (as directed on page xvii of the Preface).

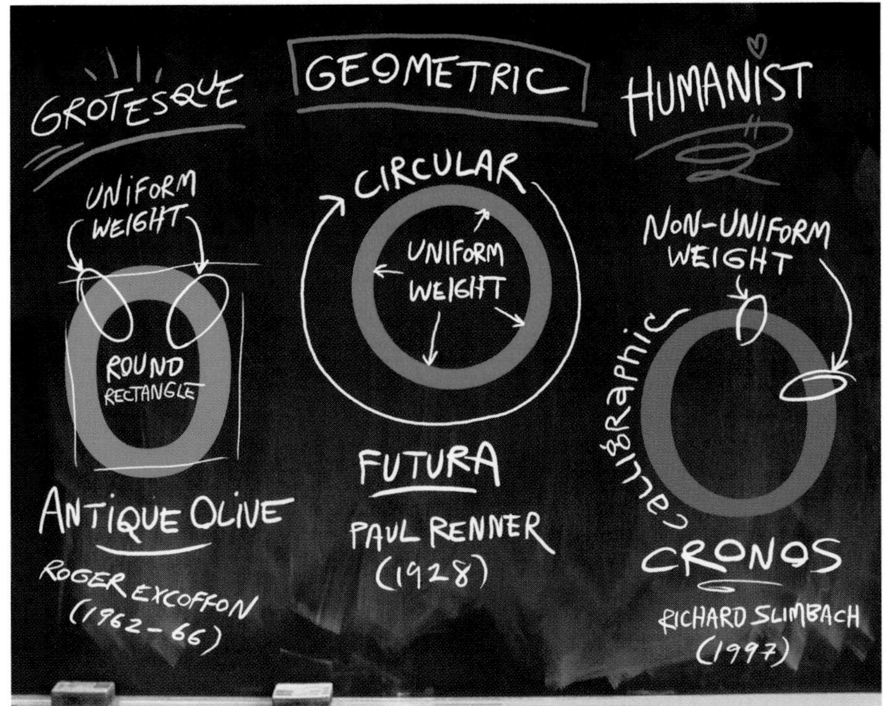

Figure 3-2.

Well, I'm here to tell you, Miedinger and the others did what they did because the appearance of type can determine whether or not it gets read. While single letters are endlessly entertaining to us type nerds, fonts and other type characteristics take on real meaning when applied to larger passages of text. By way of example, Figure 3-3 on the following page shows each of the typefaces from Figure 3-1 applied to a full sentence. (Believe it or not, the size specifications are consistent throughout.) Suddenly it becomes evident just how much a typeface—in addition to color and other factors—can affect our perception of what we read. Each face imbues a page with its own particular weight, texture, and style, which in turn affect the appeal and legibility of your text. Much as I love graphics, text is the reason most printed documents (including this one) exist. And that makes the humble font the single greatest contributor to the look and feel of a page.

Applying Formatting Attributes

To *format* type is to define its appearance. Therefore, the specific physical traits of type are called *formatting attributes*. InDesign's extensive and far-flung formatting options control everything from the way a single letter looks to the relationship between neighboring letters. In addition to typeface, examples include the slant or thickness of a letter

Helvetica Medium

Meanwhile, each of those same fonts appl
phrase or sentence imparts a unique look a

Myriad Regular

Meanwhile, each of those same fonts applied t
phrase or sentence imparts a unique look and fe

Futura Book

Meanwhile, each of those same fonts applied to a
phrase or sentence imparts a unique look and feel.

Antique Olive Roman

Meanwhile, each of those same fonts a
phrase or sentence imparts a unique lo

Cronos Regular

Meanwhile, each of those same fonts applied to a
phrase or sentence imparts a unique look and feel.

Rotis Sans Serif 55

Meanwhile, each of those same fonts applied to a
phrase or sentence imparts a unique look and feel.

News Gothic Medium

Meanwhile, each of those same fonts applied
phrase or sentence imparts a unique look and

Figure 3-3.

(style), its height (type size), the distance from one row of type to the next (leading), how the rows line up with each other (alignment), and the placement of tabs and indents, to name a few.

To format text, you must first select it, either with the black arrow tool or the type tool:

- If you use the black arrow tool, InDesign changes all type inside the selected frame. Before changing the color of type selected with the arrow tool, be sure to click the T icon at the bottom of the toolbox, as in Figure 3-4. Otherwise, you'll change the color of the frame instead (which also has its uses, as you'll see in the first exercise). Note that you can use the arrow tool to modify a stand-alone text block only; if the block is linked to other frames, you have to use the type tool instead.
- If you select one or more letters with the type tool, the results of your formatting depend on the kind of formatting you apply. Choosing a font, type size, or other *character-level attribute* affects the selected text only. Changing the alignment, indent, or other *paragraph-level attribute* affects the entire paragraph. For more information on character versus paragraph formatting, watch Video Lesson 3, "Typeface and Style," on the CD (see page 86).

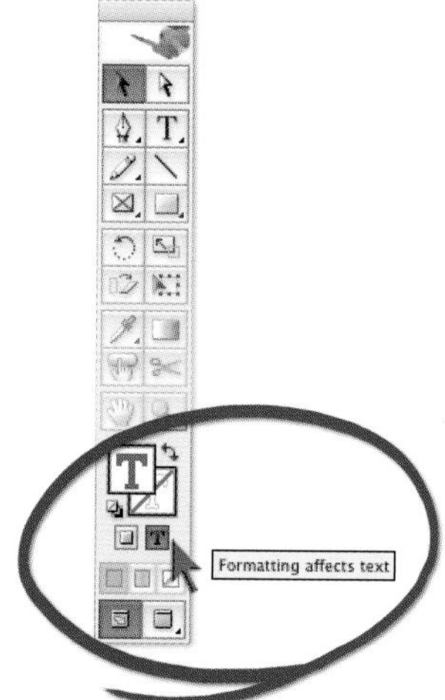
Formatting affects text

Figure 3-4.

After selecting your text, you can apply formatting attributes from the Control palette, the Type menu, or one of eight—count them, *eight*—other palettes. And even then, you have to look to other palettes to color your text. If this sounds extreme, bear in mind two things. First, there's a lot of duplication. You can change the type size from four different locations and the font from five. Fortunately, this book focuses on *best* methods (not all methods), so that's not a problem. Second, InDesign's range of formatting attributes goes well beyond those included in QuarkXPress and PageMaker. They are so vast, in fact, that we'll spend this and the next two lessons exploring them.

Don't consider yourself a type nerd? Reckon you have better things to do than obsess over type? No problem. You'll be one of us by the end of Lesson 5.

Font, Size, and Color

While a skilled writer can pack a string of words with nuance, emotion, and meaning, a skilled designer can take those words and amplify their effect through careful use of font, size, and color. These three components are vital tools for enhancing legibility and drawing attention to important words and phrases in your document. Luckily, InDesign gives you plenty of ways to apply these crucial formatting attributes, as we'll see in this next exercise.

1. ***Open a document.*** Open the file *Seventies quiz #1.indd*, which you'll find in the *Lesson 03* folder inside *Lesson Files-IDcs 1on1*. As pictured in Figure 3-5, the first column of type features an odd color scheme, sure to discourage even the most eager reader. Although you may never encounter a formatting blunder of this magnitude in your workaday routine, learning how to fix it provides us with a swell introduction to InDesign's text-coloring capabilities.

2. ***Select the ugly text frame on the left.*** Get the black arrow tool and click the text frame to select it.

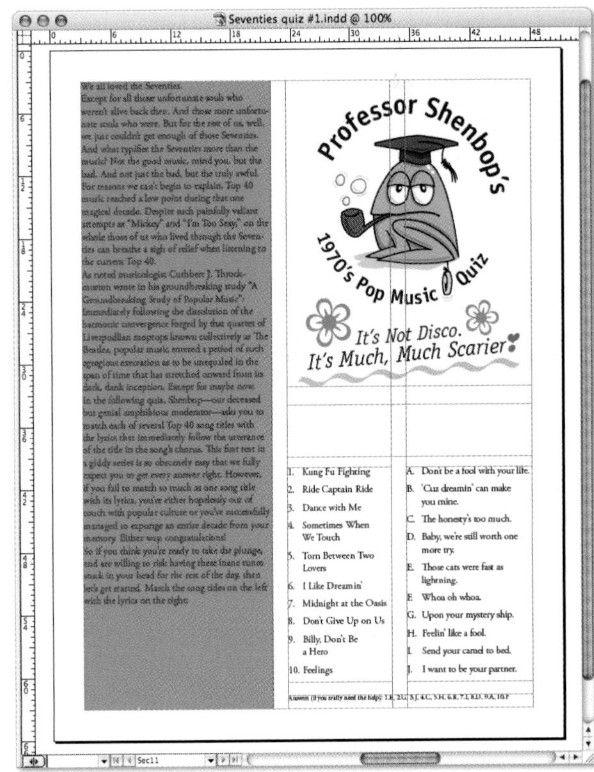

Figure 3-5.

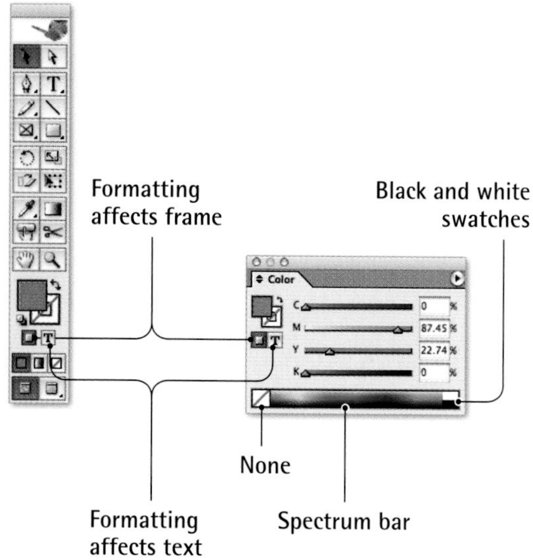

Figure 3-6.

3. ***Change the background color of the text frame.*** Our first point of business is to get rid of that ghastly pink background. Choose **Window→Color** or press F6 to access the **Color** palette. Figure 3-6 shows a labeled version of the palette, along with the corresponding options in the toolbox. You can use either palette or toolbox to perform the following:

   - Click the pink fill icon ( ). This makes the interior of the text frame active.
   - Below the pink fill icon are two small icons. The [□] icon affects the interior of the frame; the [T] icon affects the text. The [□] icon should be selected; if it isn't, click it.
   - Click the [/] icon in the bottom-left corner of the Color palette, or press the [/] key. The pink in the text frame goes away.

4. ***Change the color of the text to black.*** Click the [T] icon below the [ ] icon in the Color palette or toolbox to modify the text inside the frame. Then click the black swatch in the lower-right corner of the Color palette. The text turns black, as in Figure 3-7.

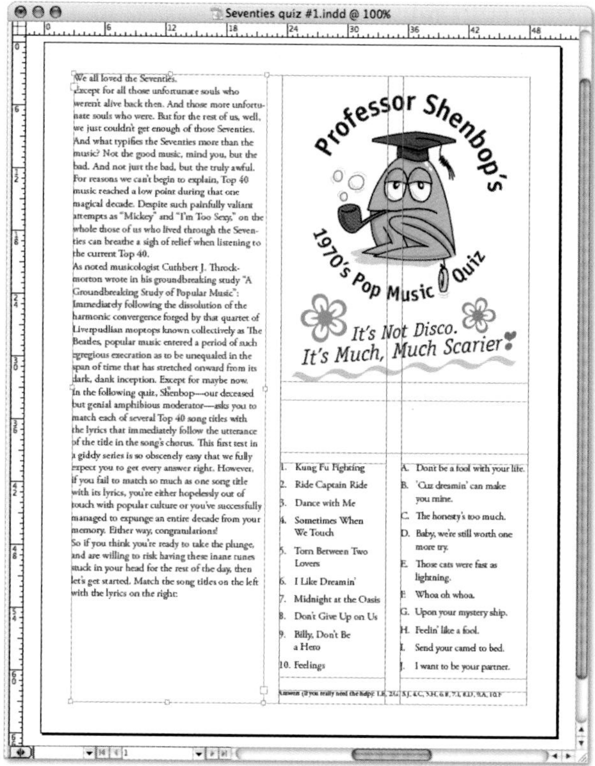

Figure 3-7.

5. *Select the first line of text.* Having changed the entire text block, let's look at a few ways to format individual words and lines of type. To accomplish this, you'll need the type tool. Double-click the text frame to automatically switch to the type tool and position the blinking insertion marker. Now triple-click any word in the first line of text to select the entire line, as in Figure 3-8.

6. *Bring up the Character palette.* One way to apply formatting attributes is to use the character-level options in the Control palette, labeled in Figure 3-9. If you don't see the options, click the A icon in the upper-left corner of the palette. But for the time being, we'll focus on the **Character** palette, which is a little easier to navigate. Choose **Type→Character** or press Ctrl+T (⌘-T on the Mac) to display the Character palette, also labeled in Figure 3-9. Happily, the first option in the palette—the font name—is already highlighted.

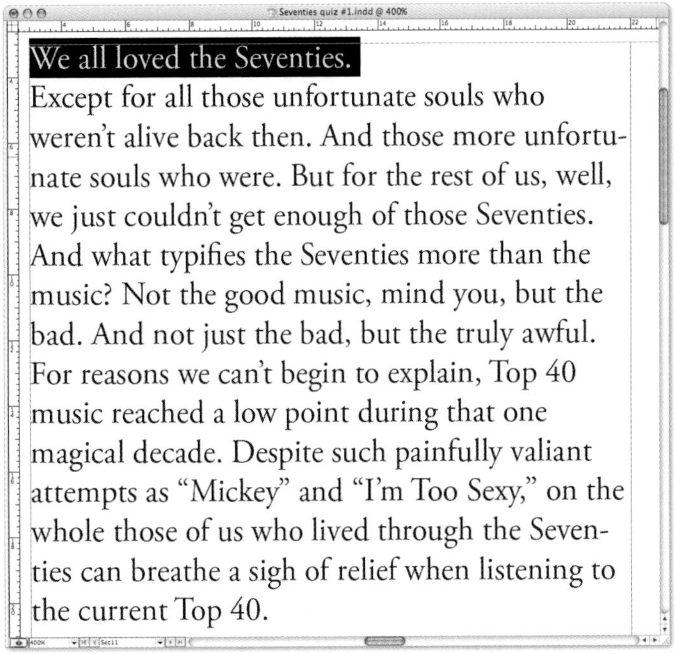

Seventies quiz #1.indd @ 400%

We all loved the Seventies.
Except for all those unfortunate souls who weren't alive back then. And those more unfortunate souls who were. But for the rest of us, well, we just couldn't get enough of those Seventies. And what typifies the Seventies more than the music? Not the good music, mind you, but the bad. And not just the bad, but the truly awful. For reasons we can't begin to explain, Top 40 music reached a low point during that one magical decade. Despite such painfully valiant attempts as "Mickey" and "I'm Too Sexy," on the whole those of us who lived through the Seventies can breathe a sigh of relief when listening to the current Top 40.

Figure 3-8.

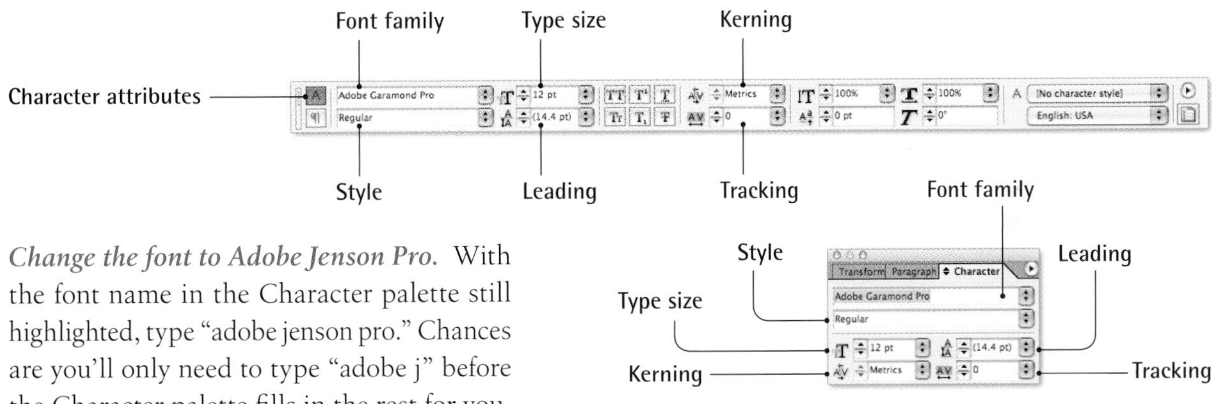

Figure 3-9.

7. *Change the font to Adobe Jenson Pro.* With the font name in the Character palette still highlighted, type "adobe jenson pro." Chances are you'll only need to type "adobe j" before the Character palette fills in the rest for you. Press Tab to apply the font, as in Figure 3-10 on the next page. Swapping one serif typeface for another is a subtle change; but given our limited collection of shared fonts, it'll do.

8. *Change the type style to Bold.* Choose **Bold** from the second pop-up menu in the Character palette (labeled *Style* in Figure 3-9) or press Ctrl+Shift+B (⌘-Shift-B on the Mac). Either way, the selected text becomes bold, as in Figure 3-11.

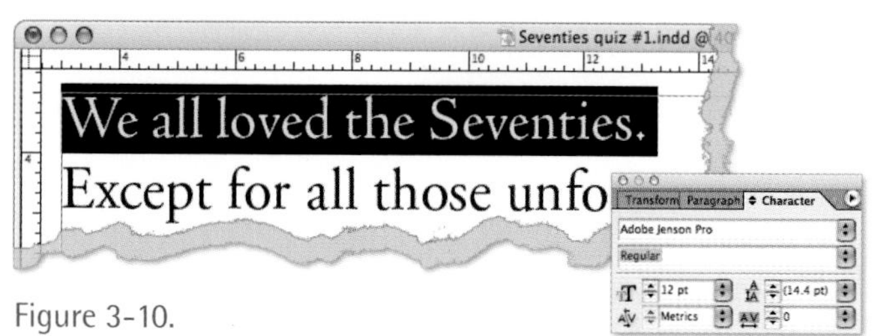

Figure 3-10.

9. ***Increase the type size to 30 points.*** Choose **30 pt** from the type size pop-up menu. Or type 30 in the option box and press Enter or Return.

You can also change the type size from the keyboard. Press Ctrl+Shift+> or Ctrl+Shift+< (that's ⌘-Shift-> or ⌘-Shift-< on the Mac) to enlarge or reduce text, respectively, in 2-point increments. Add in the Alt (or Option) key to increase or decrease the type size by five times that amount, or 10 points by default.

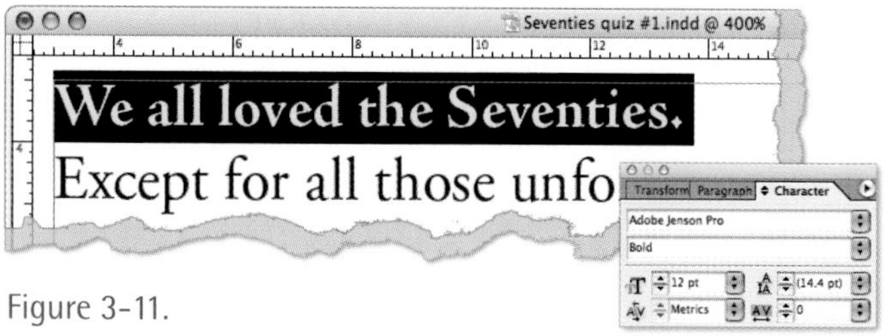

Figure 3-11.

10. ***Decrease the leading to 30 points.*** Increasing the type size bumped the text to two lines. Next we're going to decrease the vertical distance between those two lines, which is known as *leading*. (See the upcoming sidebar "The Look of Type" on page 94 for a thorough discussion of leading, baseline, and other key formatting terminology.) By default, InDesign applies Auto leading, which is equal to 120 percent of the type size. For instance, the Auto leading for our 30-point text is 120 percent of 30, or 36 points, as the value in the Character palette shows.

A glance at the Character palette confirms whether or not Auto leading is in effect. If the value appears in parentheses, then Auto leading is on; otherwise a manual leading value prevails. Auto leading changes automatically with the type size; manual leading does not.

Figure 3-12.

Large text such as headlines often look best when the leading matches the type size, a treatment known as *solid* leading. You can achieve this by performing either of the following:

- Select the value and change it to 30. Press Enter or Return to apply the value.
- Pressing Alt+↓ or Alt+↑ (on the Mac, Option-↓ or Option-↑) expands or reduces the leading in 2-point increments. So to reduce the leading from 36 to 30 points, press Alt+↑ three times in a row. Your headline should now look like the one in Figure 3-12.

When adjusting leading from the keyboard, add the Ctrl (or ⌘) key to increase the increment by a factor of five. For example, pressing Ctrl+Alt+↓ reduces the leading by 10 points. To restore Auto leading, press Ctrl+Shift+Alt+A (⌘-Shift-Option-A on the Mac). Consult the "Formatting Shortcuts" sidebar on page 100 for these and many other handy keyboard shortcuts.

PEARL OF WISDOM

If you come from QuarkXPress, you may find it disconcerting that the leading option is located in the Character palette rather than the Paragraph palette. The reason is that InDesign lets you apply leading on a line-by-line basis. Personally, I prefer this approach because it makes it easier to squeeze or expand lines to better fit the length of a column. But I know Quark devotees who absolutely have a conniption over this. If you feel a conniption coming on, here's what to do: Press Ctrl+K followed by Ctrl+2 (⌘-K, ⌘-2 on the Mac) to display the Text panel of the Preferences dialog box. Then turn on the Apply Leading to Entire Paragraphs check box. Now InDesign will apply leading to entire paragraphs, just like Quark.

11. ***Bring up the Units & Increments panel of the Preferences dialog box.*** By default, InDesign's formatting shortcuts change the type and leading values in 2-point increments. While this is appropriate for grand, sweeping changes, my experience suggests that 2 points is too much for everyday work. So let's change it. Press Ctrl+K and then Ctrl+4 (⌘-K, ⌘-4) to display the **Units & Increments** panel in the **Preferences** dialog box, as in Figure 3-13.

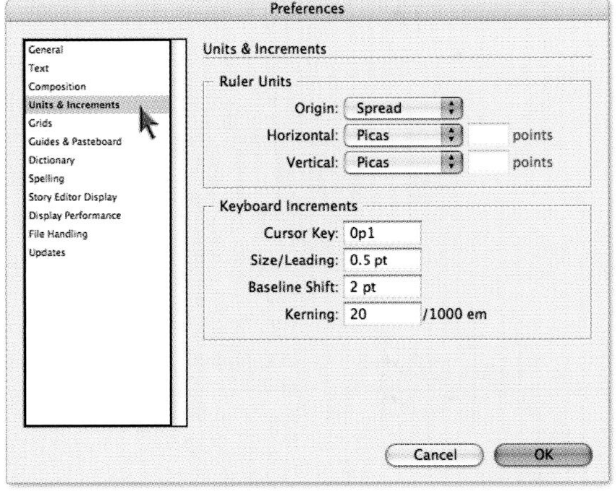

Figure 3-13.

12. ***Change the Size/Leading value to 0.5 pt.*** Tab your way down to the **Size/Leading** value and change it to 0.5 point, which gives you finer control when making keyboard modifications. After you make the change, click the **OK** button to exit the Preferences dialog box.

13. ***Select the paragraph below the headline.*** Quadruple-click with the type tool somewhere in the first paragraph below the headline. This selects the entire paragraph.

14. ***Increase the type size to 15.5 points.*** Now that you've set the Size/Leading value in the Preferences dialog box to 0.5 point, the fastest way to increase the type size from 12 to 15.5 points is as follows:

    - Press Ctrl+Shift+Alt+> (⌘-Shift-Option->). This raises the type size by 2.5 points, or to 14.5 points.

The Look of Type

Subtle crafts demand meticulous tools, and typography has more meticulous tools than you can shake a finely carved stick at. Let's begin at the beginning, with fonts—specifically, the two fonts that ushered in desktop publishing, Times and Helvetica, both pictured below. In Times, the lines of each character change gradually in thickness and terminate in tapering—or *bracketed*—wedges called *serifs*. Created in 1931 by Stanley Morison for *The Times* of London, the font was designed as a revival of the 18th-century Transitional serif faces. Meanwhile, the "naked" sans serif Helvetica drew its inspiration from the turn of the previous century. With its uniform strokes and disdain for ornamentation, Helvetica came to dominate typesetting and remains one of the top 10-selling fonts to this day. It even inspired its own revival, Robin Nicholas's 1982 Arial, now an online standard.

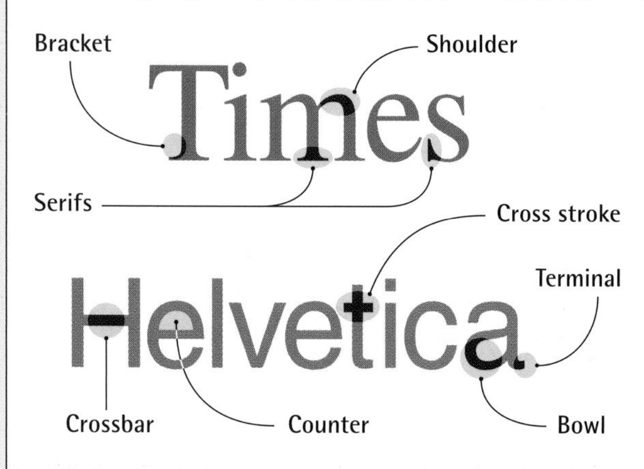

Naturally, the number of fonts available to digital publishers has grown exponentially over the last 20 years. In addition to a few thousand serif and sans serif faces, you can choose from slab serif, monospaced, blackletter, script, display, symbol—the list goes on and on. Fortunately, even the wackiest of these fonts subscribes to a few basic formatting conventions.

For example, regardless of font, type is measured in points, from roughly the top of the highest letter to the bottom of the lowest. But that doesn't mean that 12-point text set using one typeface matches the size of another—in fact, far from it. To show why, the illustration at the top of the opposite page shows three lines of 52-point type. Only the font changes, from Century Old Style on top to Künstler Script and finally the display face Tekton. The first line appears the largest thanks to its relatively tall lowercase letters. Like most script faces, Künstler offers short lowercase letters and thus appears the smallest.

When gauging type size, bear in mind the following:

- Each row of characters rests on a common *baseline*. The parts of characters that drop below the baseline—as in *g*, *j*, *p*, *q*, and *y*—are called *descenders*.
- The line formed by the tops of most lowercase letters—*a*, *c*, *e*, and others—is the *x-height*. Those characters that fit entirely between the baseline and x-height are called *medials*. Large medials usually translate to a larger looking font and remain legible at very small sizes.
- The parts of lowercase letters that rise above the x-height—*b*, *d*, and the rest—are called *ascenders*. Two letters, *i* and *t*, do not rise to full height and are considered medials.
- The unlabeled white lines in the upper-right illustration indicate the *cap heights*, which mark the top boundary of the capital letters. When working with a standard text face like Century Old Style (as well as Times, Helvetica, and the others), the cap height falls slightly below the ascenders. Künstler Script raises the cap height well above the ascenders; the display face Tekton makes caps and ascenders the same height.

In the old days of metal typesetting, *point size* was calculated by measuring the piece of lead that held the letter. This meant the size was slightly larger than the largest character of type. Typesetters added room between lines of type by inserting additional blank strips of lead. Now that everything's digital, the lead is gone but not forgotten. Designers still call line spacing *leading* (pronounced *ledding*). And while modern type houses can size their characters any way they want, the actual height of the characters is typically smaller than the prescribed size. For example, in the upper-right illustration, each colored bar is exactly 52 points tall; the characters fit inside the bars with a few points to spare.

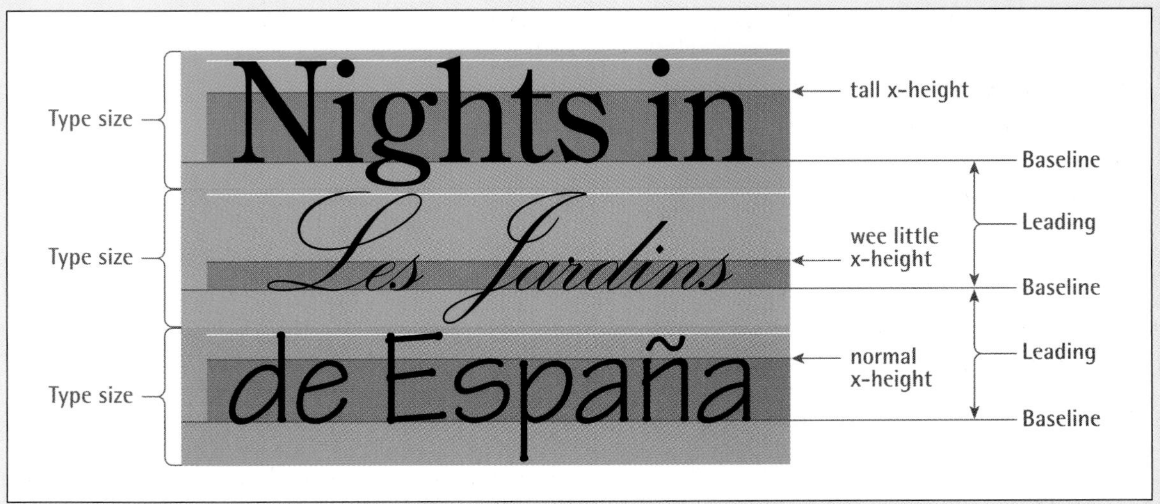

In addition to height, you can measure type by its width and weight. The difference is that you don't typically scale these attributes numerically. Rather, you select from predefined styles, like those pictured for the fonts Myriad and Moonglow to the right. Because few fonts include width variations, InDesign lets you stretch or squish the letters manually. But doing so can make the text look ridiculous. As indicated by the brown text in the right-hand figure, scaling the width of a letter changes the proportions of its strokes as well as its proximity to other letters. If you choose to stretch, I recommend going no narrower than 80 percent and no wider than 125 percent.

Most font families include at least one italic or oblique style. These slanted variations are used to stress foreign or unfamiliar phrases, as well as titles of books and other publications. Although InDesign also offers underlines, they aren't commonly used. (You may notice that underlines never appear in this book, for example.) These days, the underline is relegated to marking hyperlinks, such as those on the Web, and that's about it. So in virtually all cases, if you're tempted to underline, use italics instead. If an italic style is not available, InDesign lets you slant text manually by entering a skew value in the Control palette (as I show in Video Lesson 3, "Typeface and Style," on the CD). A value of 12 degrees or lower is generally sufficient.

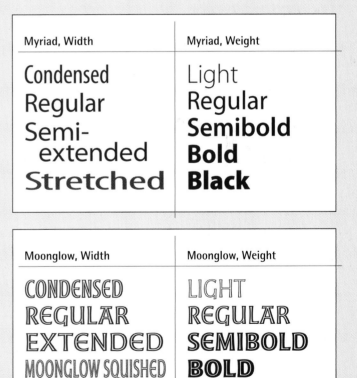

Myriad, Width	Myriad, Weight
Condensed	Light
Regular	Regular
Semi-extended	Semibold
Stretched	Bold
	Black

Moonglow, Width	Moonglow, Weight
CONDENSED	LIGHT
REGULAR	REGULAR
EXTENDED	SEMIBOLD
MOONGLOW SQUISHED	BOLD

We all loved the Seventies.

Except for all those unfortunate souls who weren't alive back then. And those more unfortunate souls who were. But for the rest of us, well, we just couldn't get enough of those Seventies.

Figure 3-14.

We all loved the Seventies.

Except for all those unfortunate souls who weren't alive back then. And those more unfortunate souls who were. But for the rest of us, well, we just couldn't get enough of those Seventies.

Figure 3-15.

- Then press Ctrl+Shift+⍐ (⌘-Shift-⍐) twice to nudge the type the last extra point. The result appears in Figure 3-14.

15. ***Change the headline to red.*** As a final touch, let's assign the headline a bold, vibrant, 1970s color. Quadruple-click anywhere in *We all loved the Seventies* to select the entire headline. In the Color palette, make sure you see four slider bars, one each for C, M, Y, and K. (If you see just one slider, labeled *[Black]*, click the ⦿ arrow in the upper-right corner of the palette and choose **CMYK**.) Change the Magenta and Yellow (**M** and **Y**) values to 100 percent; then change the Black (**K**) value to 0. Press Enter or Return to apply the color.

16. ***Deselect the text.*** Press Ctrl+Shift+A (⌘-Shift-A on the Mac) to deselect the text and see the results of your changes. As Figure 3-15 shows, the revised headline is a lovely ruby red, just the sort of color you'd expect from Lipps, Inc. or some similar ultrafunky, chart-topping, dead-the-second-the-decade-ended act of the Seventies.

That's not to say the text looks *good*, necessarily. It has spacing problems, the lines break badly—in short, it's a mess. Which is why we'll continue to work on this very document in the next exercise.

Kerning and Tracking

In the preceding exercise you learned, among other things, how to adjust the vertical space between lines of text. In this exercise you'll work on controlling the horizontal space within lines of text using two strangely named properties, kerning and tracking. In publishing, *kerning* changes the space between two adjacent characters of type; *tracking* affects a range of selected characters at a time. It works like this:

- Every character of type includes a fixed amount of left and right space, called *side bearing*. The side bearing is defined by the font; you can't change it. Together, the right bearing of one character and the left bearing of the one that follows it determine the base spacing between two characters of type.

- The base spacing satisfies most pairs of characters, but when it doesn't, kerning is there to compensate. For example, consider the classic *WA* combo illustrated in Figure 3-16. The letters slant parallel to each other, resulting in a big gap between them. *WA* is such a well-known combo that the font contains instructions to kern it automatically. Hence, *WA* is termed a *kerning pair.*
- If you don't like InDesign's automatic kerning—or none was applied—you can enter a custom kerning value to override the space between a pair of characters. Measured as a fraction of an em space (that is, a fraction of the width of the active type size), the kerning value is added to or subtracted from the bearing space.
- Finally, you heap tracking on top of the side bearing and kerning settings to adjust the spacing of many characters at a time. Like kerning, tracking is measured in fractions of an em space, so it automatically adjusts to suit changes in type size.

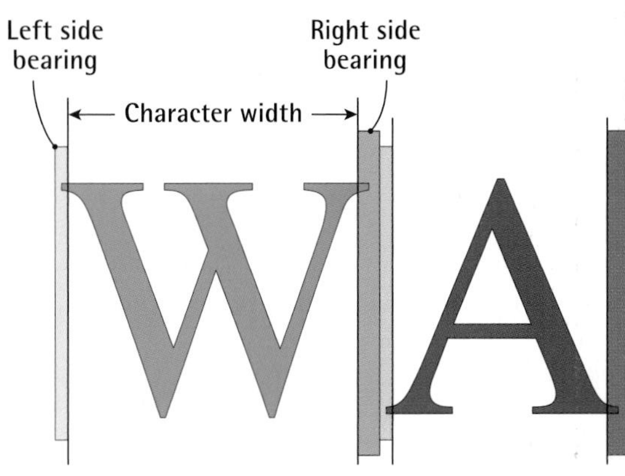

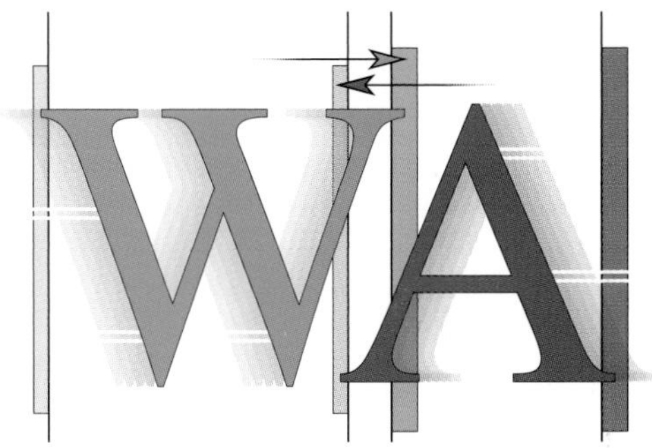

Figure 3-16.

Together, kerning and tracking let you fine-tune a font's already good default character spacing to create more attractive, easier-to-read text, as I shall demonstrate in the following exercise.

1. *Open a document.* Open the next file I've prepared for you, *Seventies quiz #1a.indd* in the *Lesson 03* folder inside *Lesson Files-IDcs 1on1*. Or if you just completed the preceding exercise, you can simply forge ahead with the file you already have open. Either way, your document should look like the one shown in Figure 3-17.
2. *Select the first column of text.* We'll start by modifying the spacing of all the text in the left column. So get the black arrow tool and click the left frame.
3. *Magnify the red headline at the top of the column.* Although we're going to adjust the kerning for *all* the text in the frame, spacing changes can be subtle, so I recommend that you zoom in on a representative portion of the text to better see what's going on. Press Ctrl+spacebar (⌘-spacebar on the Mac) and drag to draw a marquee around the headline and the following paragraph. You should be able to achieve a zoom similar to the one pictured in Figure 3-18 on the next page.
4. *Apply optical kerning.* Virtually all type designers embed kerning specifications (or *metrics*) directly into their fonts. This so-called *metrics kerning* ensures that well-known kerning pairs—such as *Av*, *Ye*, and even *r.* (that is, an *r* followed by

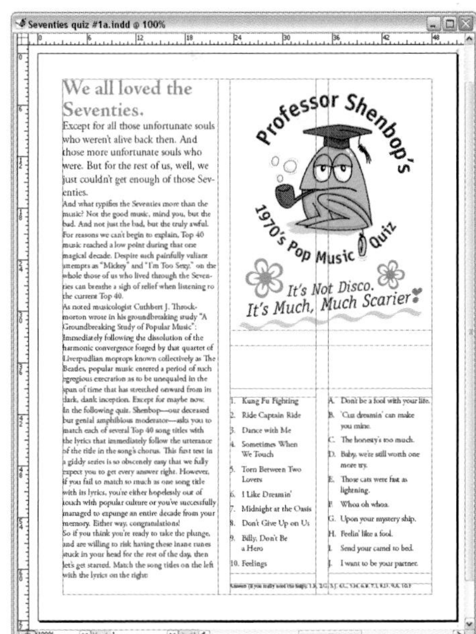

Figure 3-17.

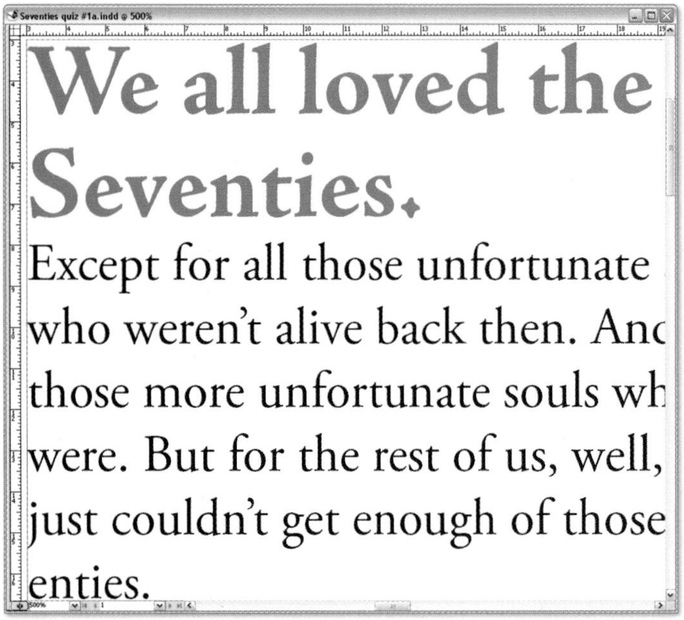

Figure 3-18.

Figure 3-19.

a period)—are not interrupted by unintended gaps. Like other publishing programs, InDesign abides by a font's metric kerning specifications by default. But while metric kerning is the industry standard, it relies heavily on the skills and thoroughness of the font designer. Some fonts (such as Adobe's OpenType collection) contain hundreds or thousands of carefully defined kerning pairs. Others describe only the most obvious pairs and give those minimal attention.

If you find yourself working with a badly kerned typeface—even beautiful type designs may include flawed kerning info—InDesign provides an alternative. Inside the Character or Control palette, choose **Optical** from the kerning (A͟V) pop-up menu. This applies Adobe's exclusive *optical kerning* function, which automatically evaluates character outlines to produce what InDesign considers to be the most attractive results possible. This isn't always the case—hey, what does a cold, heartless piece of software know about aesthetics?—but it's better than bad metrics kerning. Case in point: The text you're reading now is set in Linotype's Birka, which is a prime example of a delicate, legible typeface with rotten kerning. No problem with optical kerning. While I hand-tweaked a few characters here and there, most of what you see is kerned automatically by InDesign.

When you choose the Optical option, you'll see a slight shift in the letters. Using the headline as an example, Figure 3-19 illustrates exactly how the letters shift: the blue letters show metrics positioning, the red letters show optical, and the black areas indicate overlap. Frankly, this is a modest adjustment, and some might argue against it. Adobe's product manager of Western Type Department argues against applying optical kerning to any of Adobe's OpenType fonts. After all, optical kerning is a demanding operation that can slow InDesign's performance slightly, and OpenType fonts already include lots and lots of kerning pairs. But OpenType fonts are all we have, and I want you to see the feature in action.

PEARL OF WISDOM

If you are using a script font such as Caflisch Script Pro, do *not* use optical kerning! The characters in a script font are drawn and kerned specifically to emulate cursive writing so that the characters touch when metrics kerning is applied; optical kerning can destroy this handwritten effect.

5. ***Decrease the kerning keystroke increment.*** All right, so much for automatic kerning; let's get down to the manual stuff. But before we do, I want you to reduce InDesign's clunky kerning increments. Press Ctrl+K and then Ctrl+4 (⌘-K, ⌘-4 on the Mac) to again access the Units & Increments panel of the Preferences dialog box. Tab down to the **Kerning** value and lower it from 20/1000's of an em space—equal to a relatively whopping 0.6 point in the case of our 30-point headline—to 5/1000's of an em. (You just have to enter 5.) Then click **OK**. This will result in more precise keyboard kerning adjustments, as you'll experience in the next step.

6. ***Adjust the kerning of the word*** We. Kerning problems most frequently appear when using letters with negative space, especially prevalent among capital letters such as *L*, *T*, and *V*. In our case, the negative space in a *W* creates a bit of an empty pocket inside the word *We*. Click with the type tool between the letters *W* and *e*, as in Figure 3-20. Notice that the kerning value in the Character palette appears as (–89). The parentheses tell you that InDesign automatically applied this value, either using metrics or optical kerning.

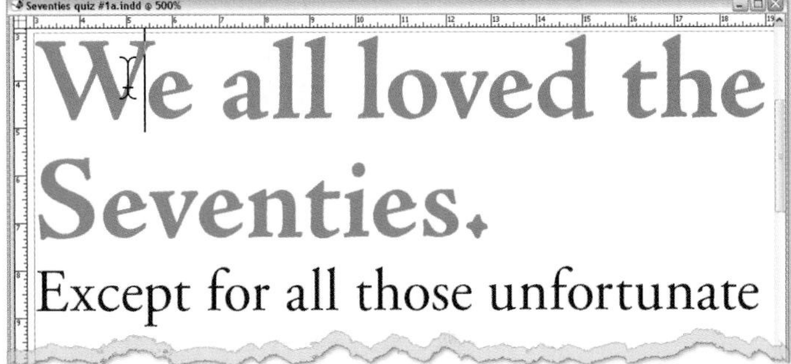

Figure 3-20.

To nudge these letters closer together, do the following:

- Press Alt+← (Option-← on the Mac) to move the *e* exactly 5/1000 em space toward the *W*. When the type size is set to 30 points, 5/1000 em is 0.15 point, or 1/480 inch. That's a small nudge, all right. Perhaps too small.
- Press Ctrl+Alt+← (or ⌘-Option-←) to nudge the letters 5 times the specified kerning increment, or 25/1000 em.

Most of the time, you'll want to kern characters closer together. But for those occasional times when you need to kern letters apart, pressing Alt+→ (Option-→ on the Mac) does the trick. Press Ctrl+Alt+→ (⌘-Option-→) to multiply the increment by a factor of five.

Formatting Shortcuts

When it comes to formatting, InDesign is shortcut crazy. And for good reason—shortcuts let you experiment with various text settings while keeping your eyes on the results. Quite simply, by assigning a few keyboard shortcuts to memory, you can dramatically increase the speed at which you work. Assuming you have a rough feel for the location of keys on the keyboard, you can adjust formatting settings almost as fast as you can think of them.

I should note that I'm not asking you to do anything I wouldn't ask of myself. This is not a comprehensive list that I've assembled by pouring through menus and help files. These are the shortcuts that I routinely use, all lodged in the nether regions of my brain. Sure I had to displace some information—my home phone number, my kids' birthdays, what my mom looks like—but it was worth it.

Before trying out these shortcuts for yourself, I recommend that you confirm the keyboard increments in the Preferences dialog box. Choose Edit→Preferences→Units & Increments (InDesign→Preferences→Units & Increments on the Mac) or press Ctrl+K, Ctrl+4 (⌘-K, ⌘-4). Then Tab your way down to the Keyboard Increments options. As I mentioned in the previous exercises, I recommend setting Size/Leading to 0.5 point and Kerning to 5/1000 of an em space. I also suggest you change Baseline Shift to 0.5 point, as shown below. Then click OK to confirm.

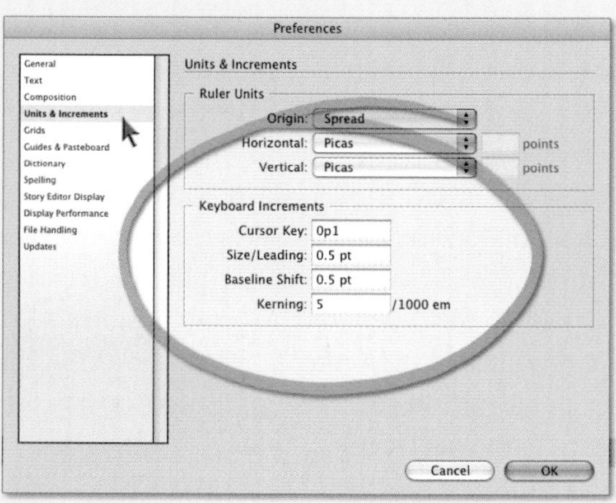

Whatever values you decide on, bear in mind that this is an editable function and you can change it anytime you like. Because these increments are variables, I refer to them in the following table by their initials—*SL* for the Size/Leading increment, *BI* for the Baseline Shift increment, and *KI* for the Kerning increment. In all cases, text has to be selected for the keyboard shortcut to work. (For paragraph alignment and kerning, you need an active insertion marker.)

Operation	Windows shortcut	Macintosh shortcut
Apply bold type style (when available)	Ctrl+Shift+B	⌘-Shift-B
Apply italic type style (when available)	Ctrl+Shift+I	⌘-Shift-I
Underline selected text	Ctrl+Shift+U	⌘-Shift-U
Strikethrough selected text	Ctrl+Shift+/ (slash)	⌘-Shift-/ (slash)
Change text to all caps	Ctrl+Shift+K	⌘-Shift-K
Change text to small caps	Ctrl+Shift+H	⌘-Shift-H
Superscript selected text	Ctrl+Shift++ (plus)	⌘-Shift-+ (plus)
Subscript selected text	Ctrl+Shift+Alt++	⌘-Shift-Option-+
Restore regular or plain style	Ctrl+Shift+Y	⌘-Shift-Y
Increase type size by SL	Ctrl+Shift+. (period)	⌘-Shift-. (period)
Increase type size by 5× SL	Ctrl+Shift+Alt+.	⌘-Shift-Option-.

Operation	Windows shortcut	Macintosh shortcut
Decrease type size by SL	Ctrl+Shift+, (comma)	⌘-Shift-, (comma)
Decrease type size by 5× SL	Ctrl+Shift+Alt+,	⌘-Shift-Option-,
Increase leading by SL	Alt+↓	Option-↓
Increase leading by 5× SL	Ctrl+Alt+↓	⌘-Option-↓
Decrease leading by SL	Alt+↑	Option-↑
Decrease leading by 5× SL	Ctrl+Alt+↑	⌘-Option-↑
Reinstate Auto (120%) leading	Ctrl+Shift+Alt+A	⌘-Shift-Option-A
Increase baseline shift by BI	Shift+Alt+↑	Shift-Option-↑
Increase baseline shift by 5× BI	Ctrl+Shift+Alt+↑	⌘-Shift-Option-↑
Decrease baseline shift by BI	Shift+Alt+↓	Shift-Option-↓
Decrease baseline shift by 5× BI	Ctrl+Shift+Alt+↓	⌘-Shift-Option-↓
Increase kerning/tracking by KI	Alt+→	Option-→
Increase kerning/tracking by 5× KI	Ctrl+Alt+→	⌘-Option-→
Decrease kerning/tracking by KI	Alt+←	Option-←
Decrease kerning/tracking by 5× KI	Ctrl+Alt+←	⌘-Option-←
Increase word kerning by KI*	Ctrl+Alt+\ (backslash)	⌘-Option-\ (backslash)
Increase word kerning by 5× KI*	Ctrl+Shift+Alt+\	⌘-Shift-Option-\
Decrease word kerning by KI*	Ctrl+Alt+Backspace	⌘-Option-Delete
Decrease word kerning by 5× KI*	Ctrl+Shift+Alt+Backspace	⌘-Shift-Option-Delete
Restore kerning to Metrics and tracking to 0*	Ctrl+Alt+Q	⌘-Alt-Q
Reset horizontal scale to 100%*	Ctrl+Shift+X	⌘-Shift-X
Reset vertical scale to 100%*	Ctrl+Shift+Alt+X	⌘-Shift-Option-X
Toggle automatic hyphenation	Ctrl+Shift+Alt+H	⌘-Shift-Option-H
Toggle curly typographer's quotes	Ctrl+Shift+Alt+' (quote)	⌘-Shift-Option-' (quote)
Left-align paragraph	Ctrl+Shift+L	⌘-Shift-L
Right-align paragraph	Ctrl+Shift+R	⌘-Shift-R
Center-align paragraph	Ctrl+Shift+C	⌘-Shift-C
Justify all lines except last one	Ctrl+Shift+J	⌘-Shift-J
Justify that last line, too	Ctrl+Shift+F	⌘-Shift-F

* Okay, I admit, even I have a hard time remembering these. So you have my permission not to worry about them, guilt free. As for the others, you have some memorizing to do!

The AV value changes to –119. The parentheses go away, telling you that manual kerning is in force.

7. ***Kern the rest of the headline to taste.*** Why did I have you reduce the Kerning value in Step 5 only to multiply it by 5 a moment later? Because other letter pairs require smaller adjustments:

   - Click between the *o* and *v* in *loved*. Then press Alt+← (Option-←) twice to reduce the spacing by a slim 10/1000 em.
   - Then press the → key to move the insertion marker between the *v* and *e*, and press Alt+← (Option-←) twice again.
   - Next, click between the *v* and the second *e* in *Seventies*. These letters are spaced wider, so press Ctrl+Alt+← (⌘-Option-←) to move them together. If that's too far, press Alt+→ (Option-→) to nudge them slightly apart.

   Figure 3-21.

   Figure 3-21 shows the results of these kerning changes.

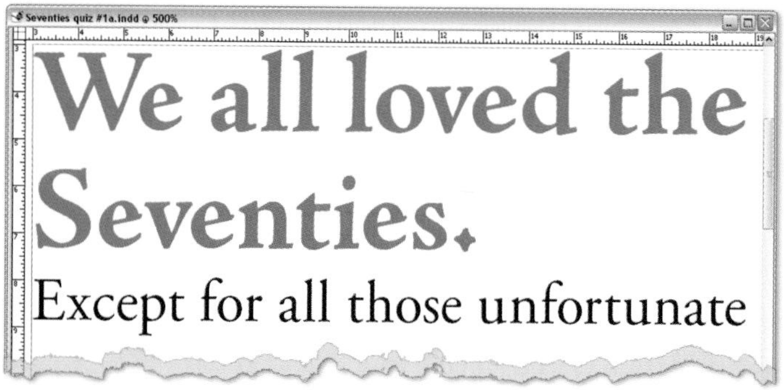

8. ***Adjust the tracking in the paragraph below the headline.*** Mind numbed by the sheer tedium of it? That's manual kerning for you—subtle, meticulous, but rarely the least bit exciting. Fortunately, you can affect multiple letters at a time using tracking. While it's not any more exciting, it tends to go faster. Professional designers typically use tracking for one of two purposes:

   - As characters grow, so does the space between them. As a result, headlines and other large text may appear more loosely set than, say, body copy. To offset this, track the letters in a headline closer together. (Quark and PageMaker go so far as to let you customize default tracking according to type size; InDesign does not.)
   - You can also use tracking to shift characters from one line of text to another, an operation known as *copyfitting*. Consider the partial word *enties* at the end of the first paragraph of body text. Tracking will unite it with the line above.

   Quadruple-click inside this paragraph to select the entire thing. The same keyboard tricks that kern letter pairs track text as well, and by the same increments. So press Alt+← (Option-← on the Mac) to track the letters 10/1000 closer than they were before. Note the AV values in the Character and Control palettes change to –10. Your text should end up looking like it does in Figure 3-22 on the facing page.

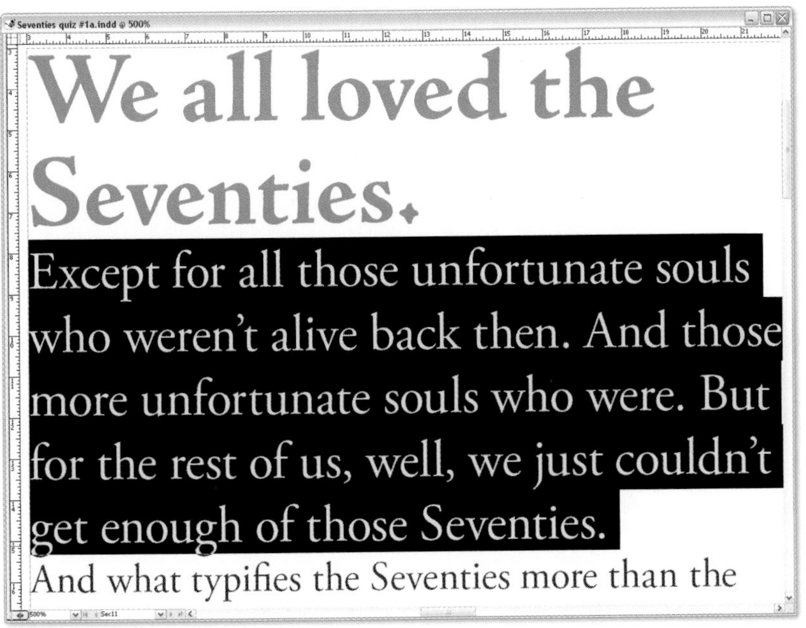

Figure 3-22.

Paragraph Spacing and Alignment

While the niceties of kerning and tracking are essential for regulating the relationship between letters and words, they rank among the subtlest adjustments you can apply in InDesign. In stark contrast, our next topics are as obvious as the entire paragraphs they influence. First, we'll look at *paragraph spacing*, which adds vertical space between one paragraph and its neighbor. Then, we'll modify the alignment of text to create centered and justified paragraphs. Finally, we'll use InDesign's Keep Options command to glue neighboring lines of type together, thus avoiding those lonely casualties of page layout, widows and orphans.

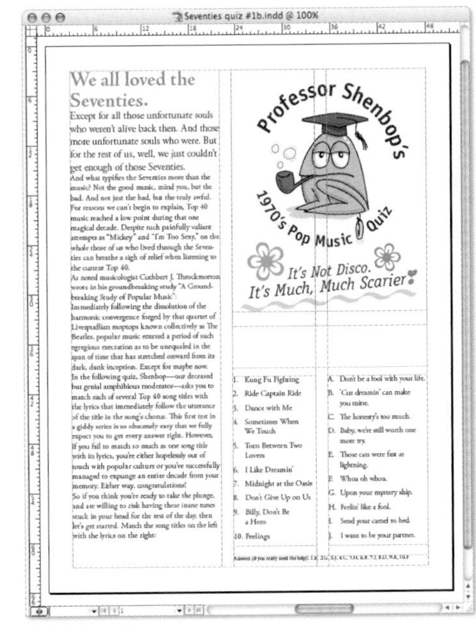

Figure 3-23.

1. *Open a document.* If you still have open the document from the preceding exercise, you're good to go. Otherwise, open the file titled *Seventies quiz #1b.indd* located in the *Lesson 03* folder inside *Lesson Files-IDcs 1on1*. As seen in Figure 3-23, the body copy in the left column suffers from what might be called "clumpiness," if only that were a word. The lines of text run together with nary an indent to indicate where one paragraph ends and the next begins. It's forbidding. It's unappealing. No one wants to read a clump. Fortunately, InDesign gives you all the tools you need to separate the paragraphs and make the clump go away.

2. ***Bring up the Paragraph palette.*** Most likely, the Paragraph palette appears grouped with its associate, the Character palette. If so, click the **Paragraph** tab to bring it to the fore. You can also press Ctrl+Alt+T (⌘-Option-T on the Mac) or choose **Type→Paragraph**. If you don't see all the options shown on the right side of Figure 3-24, click the ⊙ arrow and choose **Show Options** to view the palette in its expanded form. Or, if the palette is free-floating, click the ♦ next to the word Paragraph twice.

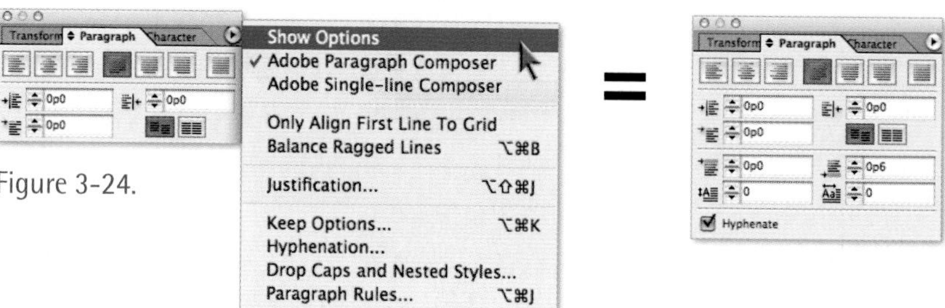

Figure 3-24.

Alternatively, you can use the paragraph options in the Control palette. To display these options, click the ¶ icon on the left side of the palette. Or press the keyboard shortcut Ctrl+Alt+7 (⌘-Option-7 on the Mac). That trick has never made much sense to me, which is why I've provided you with another one: If you loaded my Deke Keys shortcuts as described on page xvii of the Preface, press the F4 key to toggle between the character and paragraph formatting functions.

3. ***Apply paragraph spacing to the text in the left column.*** One way to rid your text of clumpiness is to add an indent to the first line of each paragraph. You can do that the old-fashioned way, by inserting a tab character like you would if using a typewriter. But that means pressing the Tab key at the outset of each and every paragraph. If first-line indents are your goal, you're better off entering a positive value into the first-line indent option (second option on the left, ⁺≣, in the Paragraph palette).

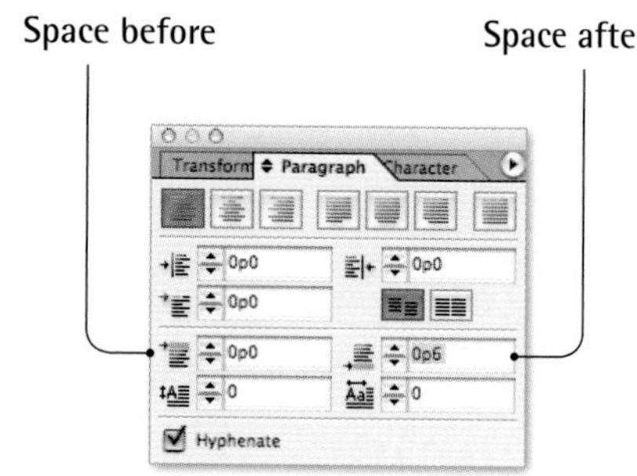

Figure 3-25.

PEARL OF WISDOM

The other way to offset paragraphs is to insert vertical space between them. The Paragraph palette offers two options for inserting paragraph space. As labeled in Figure 3-25, one adds space before a paragraph; the other adds space after. In a way, the two options are redundant. Whichever you choose, the spacing appears between paragraphs, and has no effect on the positioning of text with respect to the frame. So 1 pica of space after one paragraph looks the same as 1 pica of space before the next. So why does InDesign go to the trouble of supplying two options? To accommodate style sheets. Covered in Lesson 5, "Using Style Sheets," style sheets are customizable collections of formatting attributes. For example, you might create a Headline style that combines before and after spacing to add extra space above and below all headings in a document.

Just as I use paragraph spacing to offset the paragraphs in this book, you'll use it to separate the paragraphs in the first column of text. Click the first column in the document with the black arrow tool to select it. Then go to the Paragraph palette and enter 0p6 in the space after (‾≡) option box. Press the Enter or Return key to apply 6 points of space between each paragraph in the frame and the paragraph that follows it, as in Figure 3-25.

4. ***Add more space after the headline and first paragraph.*** While 6 points of space between paragraphs works nicely for the main body copy, the headline and first paragraph still look a little cramped. To fix this, double-click anywhere in the headline to switch to the type tool and position the insertion marker. Drag from anywhere in the headline to anywhere in the first paragraph to select portions of each. Then raise the ‾≡ value in the Paragraph palette to 1 pica.

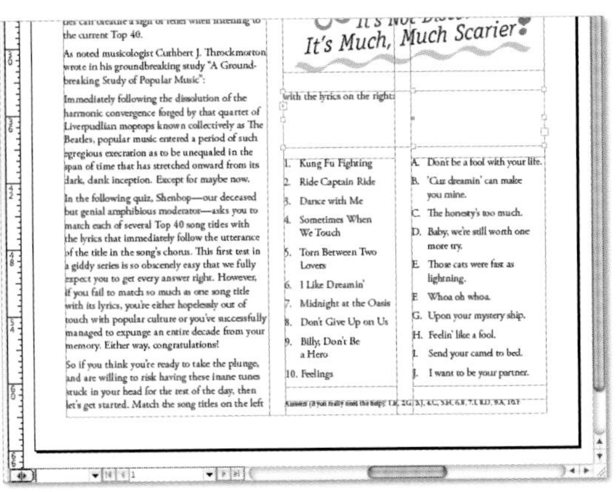

Figure 3-26.

5. ***Run overflow text into the empty frame.*** The added space forces the text to overflow the first column. Switch to the black arrow tool, click the left text frame's out port, and mouse over the empty text frame below the graphic on the right side of the document. When you see the link cursor (🔗), click. As Figure 3-26 shows, one line of text flows from the left-hand column into the newly created frame on the right. In the publishing world, it's considered bad form to leave the last line of a paragraph dangling all alone at the top of a column. They even have a word for it, *widow*. But other changes we make may fix the problem.

6. ***Indent the left side of the fourth paragraph.*** The fourth paragraph of body copy in the left column is actually a long quote. I want you to offset this block quote by indenting the left and right sides. Using the type tool, click anywhere in the fourth paragraph, the one that begins with the word *Immediately*. Enter 3 into the first option box (→≡) in the Paragraph palette and press the Tab key to indent the paragraph 3 picas to the left. This also advances you to the right indent option (≡←); enter 3 here and press the Enter or Return key. The result is the effect pictured in Figure 3-27.

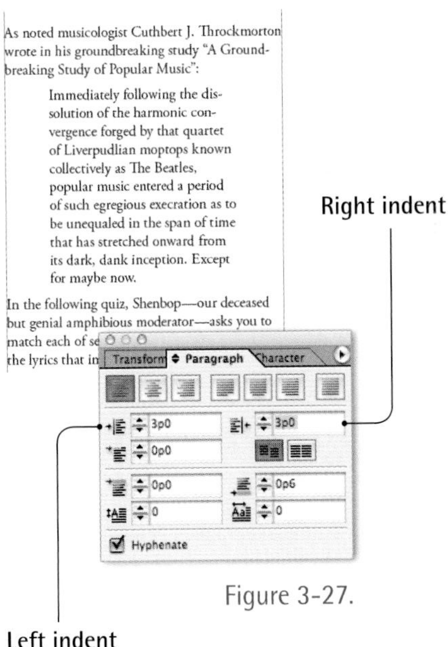

Figure 3-27.

7. ***Select all the body copy in the left column.*** The quote text continues to look unbalanced because of the ragged margin along the right side of the column. Therefore, we'll balance the body copy by justifying it. Using the type tool, select portions of all paragraphs in the left column *except* the red

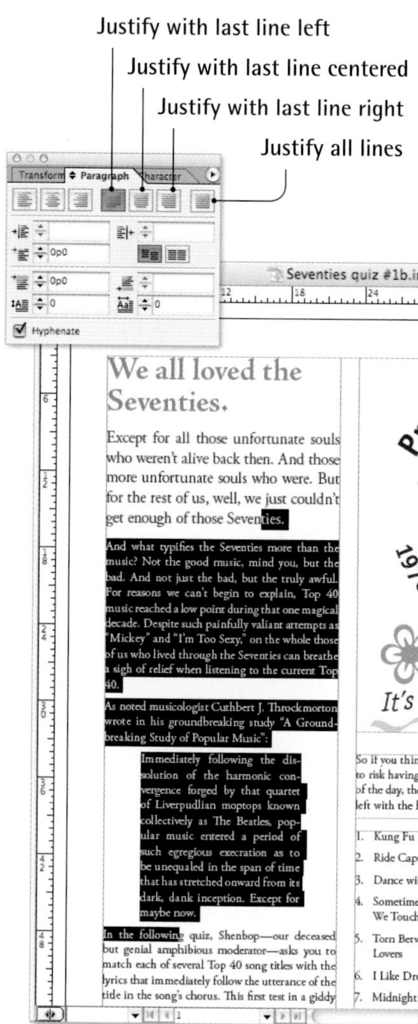

Figure 3-28.

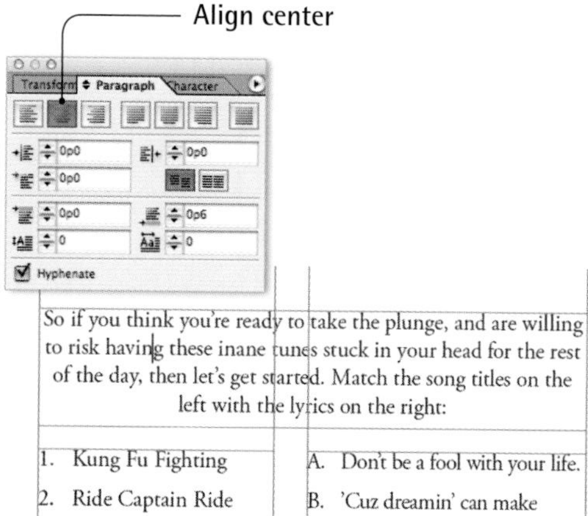

Figure 3-29.

headline. You don't have to be exact when making this selection. As long as so much as a single character in the first and last paragraphs is selected, all the body copy will receive the formatting you apply in the next step.

8. ***Justify the selected text, with the last line flush left.*** Notice that the first of the seven alignment icons at the top of the Paragraph palette (▤) is active. This tells you that the selected text is left aligned, or *flush left*, which means that each line in a paragraph begins at the same left edge. Let's change this so that the left and right edges are aligned, creating nice even edges on both sides of the text block. To do so, click the fourth icon (▤) at the top of the Paragraph palette, or press Ctrl+Shift+J (⌘-Shift-J on the Mac). Shown in Figure 3-28, the resulting text is said to be *fully justified*, or just plain *justified*. InDesign modifies the spacing between and within words to line up the left and right edges of the text.

PEARL OF WISDOM

Notice that the last line of each selected paragraph is still aligned left. But it doesn't have to be that way. The fifth, sixth, and seventh icons at the top of the Paragraph palette likewise justify text but offer different options for dealing with the last line of a paragraph. The last of these icons, ▤, spreads the words in the last line until they too appear justified. Such a paragraph is said to be *force justified*. You can force justify text from the keyboard by pressing Ctrl+Shift+F (or ⌘-Shift-F). But don't do that here; we'll stick with the last line flush left.

9. ***Center align the overflow text.*** You may not have noticed, but our modifications in the last three steps have moved an entire paragraph to the second column, thus reuniting the widow with the rest of her family. Inasmuch as this warms my heart, I have this nagging feeling that the family could use some help. Click anywhere inside the restored paragraph and click the second alignment icon (▤) in the Paragraph palette. Or press Ctrl+Shift+C (⌘-Shift-C on the Mac). Figure 3-29 shows how this centers the text.

As long as I'm handing out shortcuts, I might as well toss in a couple more: Press Ctrl+Shift (⌘-Shift on the Mac) plus a letter to align text. Thus, Ctrl+Shift+L (⌘-Shift-L) aligns text to the left; Ctrl+Shift+R (⌘-Shift-R) aligns it to the right.

10. ***Balance the red headline.*** The headline looks a bit uneven to me. Fortunately, a special InDesign command can fix it. Click anywhere in the headline with the type tool. Then click the ⊙

arrow in the Paragraph palette and choose **Balance Ragged Lines**. As pictured in Figure 3-30, InDesign bumps the word *the* down to the second line, thus evening out the first and second lines.

Transform
Paragraph
Character
0p0
0p0
0p0
0p0
0p0
1p0
0
0
Hyphenate
Hide Options
✓ Adobe Paragraph Composer
Adobe Single-line Composer
Only Align First Line To Grid
✓ Balance Ragged Lines ⌥⌘B
Justification... ⌥⇧⌘J
Keep Options... ⌥⌘K
Hyphenation...
Drop Caps and Nested Styles...
Paragraph Rules... ⌥⌘J
We all loved the Seventies.
Except for all those unfortunate souls who weren't alive back then. And those more unfortunate souls who were. But for the rest of us, well, we just couldn't get enough of those Seventies.

Figure 3-30.

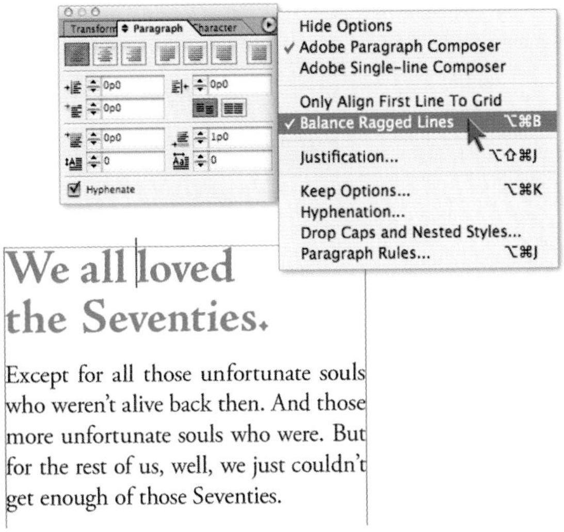

If you loaded my Deke Keys keyboard shortcuts (as directed on page xvii of the Preface), press Ctrl+Alt+B (⌘-Option-B on the Mac) to invoke the Balance Ragged Lines command.

---

11. ***Select the last three lines in the second paragraph.*** Generally speaking, justified type produces a crisp, tidy document. But for us, it creates a problem in the second paragraph. See that tiny *40* on its own line at the end of the paragraph? Let's fix this poor widow using a little-known function that Adobe calls *word kerning*, which lets you adjust the amount of space between words without affecting the space between the letters within the words. (Specifically, word kerning changes the space between the first letter in a word and the space before it.)

    Word kerning is a character-level attribute, so you start by selecting the letters you want to adjust. Select the last three lines of the second paragraph of body copy as follows:

    - Click anywhere in the third-to-last line in the second paragraph.
    - Press Ctrl+Shift+\ (⌘-Shift-\ on the Mac) to select the entire line.
    - Press Shift+↓ twice to select each of the remaining lines in the paragraph, as in Figure 3-31.

And what typifies the Seventies more than the music? Not the good music, mind you, but the bad. And not just the bad, but the truly awful. For reasons we can't begin to explain, Top 40 music reached a low point during that one magical decade. Despite such painfully valiant attempts as "Mickey" and "I'm Too Sexy," on the whole those of us who lived through the Seventies can breathe a sigh of relief when listening to the current Top 40.

Figure 3-31.

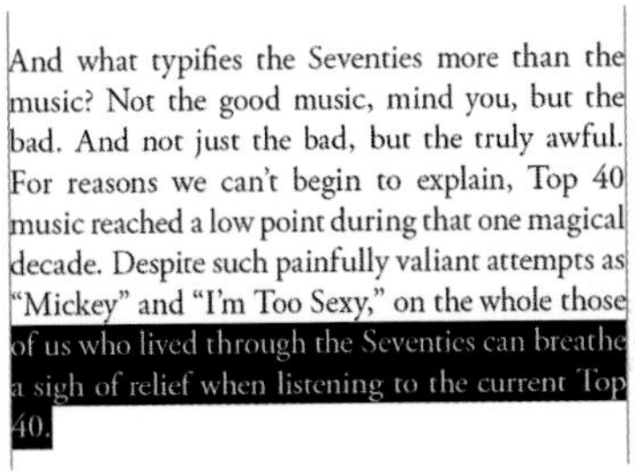

12. ***Tighten the word kerning.*** Word kerning is another of InDesign's secret features. You change it by keyboard shortcut only, using the same increment that you specified for the Kerning value in the Preferences dialog box (see Step 5 on page 99). Here's how:

    - To spread the selected words from their preceding spaces, press Ctrl+Alt+\ (⌘-Option-\).
    - To tighten the word kerning, press Ctrl+Alt+Backspace (or ⌘-Option-Delete). PC users, take note: that's Ctrl+Alt+Backspace, *not* Ctrl+Alt+Delete (which force-quits applications)!
    - To increase the kerning increment by a factor of five, add the Shift key.

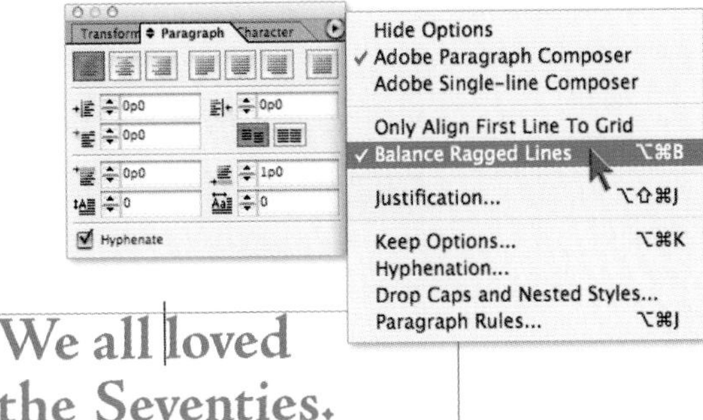

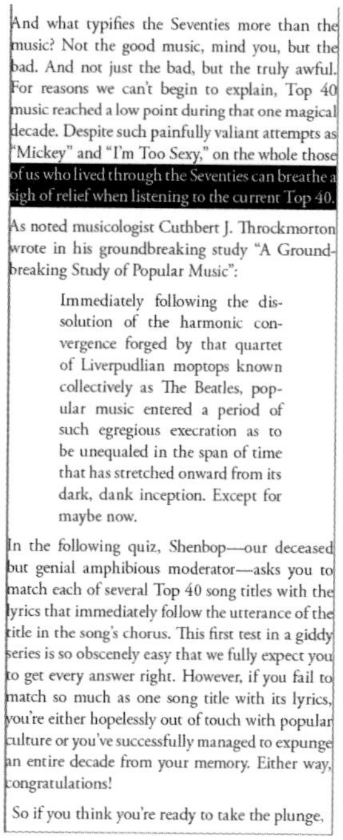

And what typifies the Seventies more than the music? Not the good music, mind you, but the bad. And not just the bad, but the truly awful. For reasons we can't begin to explain, Top 40 music reached a low point during that one magical decade. Despite such painfully valiant attempts as "Mickey" and "I'm Too Sexy," on the whole those of us who lived through the Seventies can breathe a sigh of relief when listening to the current Top 40.

As noted musicologist Cuthbert J. Throckmorton wrote in his groundbreaking study "A Groundbreaking Study of Popular Music":

> Immediately following the dissolution of the harmonic convergence forged by that quartet of Liverpudlian moptops known collectively as The Beatles, popular music entered a period of such egregious execration as to be unequaled in the span of time that has stretched onward from its dark, dank inception. Except for maybe now.

In the following quiz, Shenbop—our deceased but genial amphibious moderator—asks you to match each of several Top 40 song titles with the lyrics that immediately follow the utterance of the title in the song's chorus. This first test in a giddy series is so obscenely easy that we fully expect you to get every answer right. However, if you fail to match so much as one song title with its lyrics, you're either hopelessly out of touch with popular culture or you've successfully managed to expunge an entire decade from your memory. Either way, congratulations!

So if you think you're ready to take the plunge,

Figure 3-32.

It's a crazy keyboard shortcut, one I have problems remembering. But every so often, it comes in handy. And now's one of those times. With the last three lines highlighted, press Ctrl+Shift+Alt+Backspace (or ⌘-Shift-Option-Delete) twice in a row to reduce the word kerning to –50. (You can confirm this by clicking before the first letter of any of the kerned words and checking the AV value in the Character palette.) The reduced spacing causes the *40* to join the line above it.

13. ***Choose the Keep Options command.*** Alas, what's good for the widow doesn't always benefit the rest of the text family. As Figure 3-32 shows, our latest adjustment has created a new problem. The first line of the final paragraph has flowed out of the text frame on the right and into the bottom of the left column. This single stranded first line of a paragraph is known as an *orphan*, because it has been abandoned by its family—i.e., the other lines in the paragraph.

PEARL OF WISDOM

I should say, there is considerable disagreement over the exact definitions of widows and orphans. After consulting with a half-dozen type experts—all of whom voice slightly different opinions—I've decided to defer to Adobe's definition: Whatever the circumstances, an orphan is one or more abandoned lines at the beginning of a paragraph (and thus, the end of a column); a widow comes at the end of a paragraph (and thus, the beginning of a column). Whatever *you* decide to call them, one thing's for sure: InDesign, tenderhearted application that it is, gives you ways to help the poor widows and orphans of the text world.

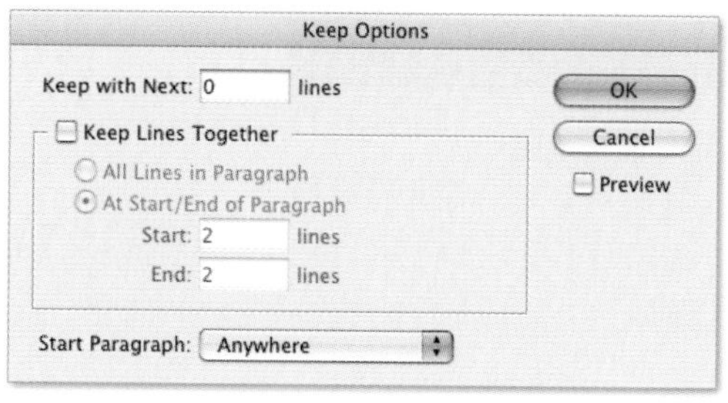

Figure 3-33.

Semantics aside, how do you fix the orphan? For starters, click either in the lone line at the bottom of the left column or in the overflow text block on the right. Then click the ⊙ in the corner of the Paragraph palette and choose the **Keep Options** command, or press Ctrl+Alt+K (⌘-Option-K on the Mac). Up comes the **Keep Options** dialog box, as in Figure 3-33.

14. ***Turn on Keep Lines Together.*** The simple act of turning on the **Keep Lines Together** check box is enough to reunite our orphan with its family. (To see it happen, also turn on the **Preview** check box.) But you probably want to know how all the options in this dialog box work, so here's a brief rundown:

   - The first option, Keep with Next, glues the last line of a paragraph to as many as five lines in the paragraph that follows it. Use this option to keep headlines with the text that follows them.

- After selecting Keep Lines Together, turn on All Lines in Paragraph to prevent the paragraph from breaking between frames and keep the paragraph forever whole.
- The next option, At Start/End of Paragraph, lets you specify how many lines will stick together at the beginning or end of the paragraph. In our case, the default Start setting of 2 lines means that as few as two lines in the selected paragraph can break away from the others. But since there isn't room for two lines at the end of the left column, the entire paragraph flows to the frame below the graphic.
- Finally, the Start Paragraph pop-up menu lets you decide where the reunited paragraph should appear. I rarely use this option, and any of the first three settings will give you the same happy result pictured in Figure 3-34.

Click the **OK** button to accept the changes to the selected paragraph. You are now done with this document. Feel free to close it. Save your changes or not; I leave that decision up to you.

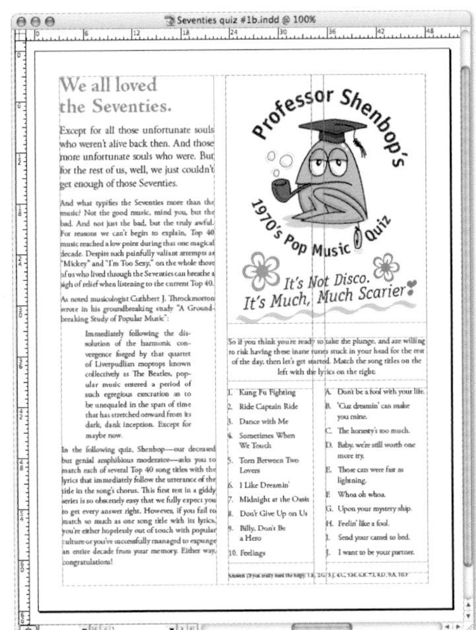

Figure 3-34.

Hyphenation and Composition

Like most other design programs, InDesign automatically hyphenates text to make lines wrap more neatly. The big difference is that it does so more intelligently than the rest, often evaluating multiple lines at a time before making its hyphenation decisions. Plus, InDesign gives you an enormous amount of control over the process, permitting you to not only increase or decrease the frequency of hyphenation, but even adjust spacing and change the general "color" of a paragraph. (Densely packed letters make for a dark paragraph; spread out letters make for a light one.)

To some, adjusting hyphenation may sound like a dreadfully dull way to while away a perfectly good half hour. And to be perfectly honest, even I, King of the Control Freaks, resort to hyphenation adjustment only when InDesign's default hyphenation doesn't look right. But I have to admit, there's something very satisfying about taking command of even a mundane process when that process is executed as expertly as InDesign's hyphenation engine.

In this exercise, we'll take a few paragraphs and change the amount of hyphenation and spacing that InDesign applies. At all times, it's InDesign's hyphenation and justification engine that's making the real decisions; we're just overseeing the process. The idea is, while you can wrest away control and hyphenate words manually, it's far more efficient to let InDesign do the heavy lifting subject to your occasional oversight. Also note that, although InDesign hyphenates flush-left type (as well as centered and flush-right), we'll be working with justified type. The reason: Justification includes some additional compositional controls that I want you to see.

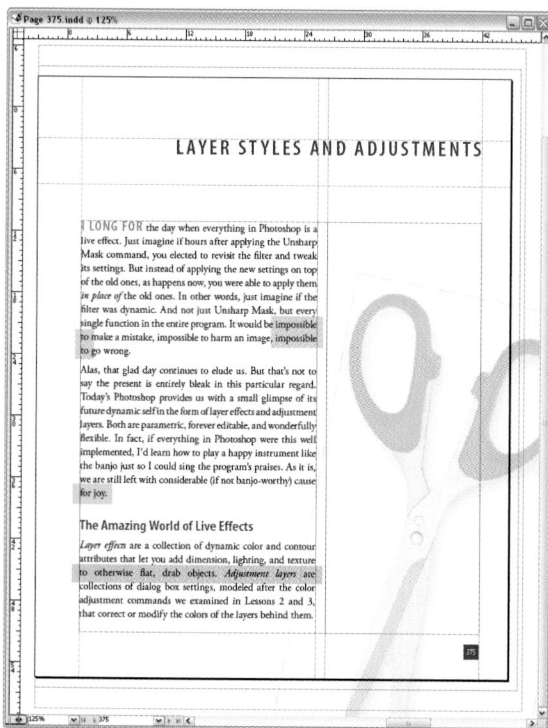

LAYER STYLES AND ADJUSTMENTS

I LONG FOR the day when everything in Photoshop is a live effect. Just imagine if hours after applying the Unsharp Mask command, you elected to revisit the filter and tweak its settings. But instead of applying the new settings on top of the old ones, as happens now, you were able to apply them *in place of* the old ones. In other words, just imagine if the filter was dynamic. And not just Unsharp Mask, but every single function in the entire program. It would be impossible to make a mistake, impossible to harm an image, impossible to go wrong.

Alas, that glad day continues to elude us. But that's not to say the present is entirely bleak in this particular regard. Today's Photoshop provides us with a small glimpse of its future dynamic self in the form of layer effects and adjustment layers. Both are parametric, forever editable, and wonderfully flexible. In fact, if everything in Photoshop were this well implemented, I'd learn how to play a happy instrument like the banjo just so I could sing the program's praises. As it is, we are still left with considerable (if not banjo-worthy) cause for joy.

The Amazing World of Live Effects

Layer effects are a collection of dynamic color and contour attributes that let you add dimension, lighting, and texture to otherwise flat, drab objects. *Adjustment layers* are collections of dialog box settings, modeled after the color adjustment commands we examined in Lessons 2 and 3, that correct or modify the colors of the layers behind them.

Figure 3-35.

1. ***Open a document.*** Open the file *Page 375.indd* in the *Lesson 03* folder inside *Lesson Files-IDcs 1on1*. Pictured in Figure 3-35, this single-page document is nothing less or more than page 375 from *Adobe Photoshop CS One-on-One*. It contains three paragraphs of body copy. The paragraphs look okay, but if you examine them closely, you'll see a few minor but vexing problems. Highlighted in Figure 3-35, these problems fall into three categories:

    - The pink boxes highlight *stacks*, in which identical words appear directly on top of each other. Stacks call attention to text wrap and can even cause a reader to skip a line of text.

    - The green box highlights a line of type that is much more loosely spaced than those immediately above and below it. Such inconsistencies in spacing look sloppy, to be sure. And when the space between words grows larger than the space between lines of type, it may hinder readability.

    - Finally, the yellow box highlights a couple of stray words at the end of a paragraph, similar to the lone *40* that we encountered in the preceding exercise. Because the stray words occur at the end of a paragraph, they are considered to be widows, albeit ones that the Keep Options don't address. In the last exercise, we fixed the placement of *40* using word kerning. But there's more than one way to fix a widow, as you will soon see.

As I said, these problems are minor, the design equivalent of forgetting to dot your *i*'s and cross your *t*'s. So no biggie, right? Except that you'd look like a twit if you didn't dot your *i*'s and cross your *t*'s, and the same is true in the design world if you left these problems in place. So let's fix them by adjusting the hyphenation and composition of the paragraphs.

2. ***Select the text.*** Hyphenation is a paragraph-level formatting attribute. If you want to adjust a single paragraph at a time, click inside the paragraph with the type tool. Or, since we want to fix all the text, select the text block with the black arrow tool.

3. ***Choose the Hyphenation command.*** If the type tool is active, click the ¶ icon in the Control palette to switch to the paragraph attributes. Then click the ⊙ arrow on the far right side of the palette to display the palette menu and choose the Hyphenation command. More likely, however, the black arrow is active, in which case the Control palette shows you transformation options. In this case, do the following:

   - Choose **Type→Paragraph**, or press Ctrl+Alt+T (⌘-Option-T on the Mac) to display the **Paragraph** palette.
   - Click the ⊙ arrow at the top of the palette and choose the **Hyphenation** command.

   Both alternatives are illustrated in Figure 3-36.

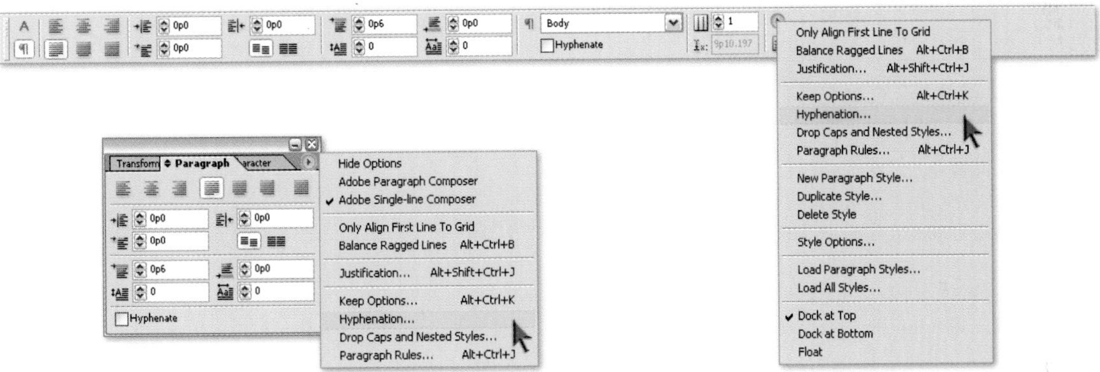

Figure 3-36.

4. ***Turn on the Hyphenate check box.*** Pictured in Figure 3-37, the **Hyphenation Settings** dialog box controls several aspects of hyphenation, including whether the feature is turned on. By default, hyphenation is active inside InDesign. But I've specifically turned it off so you can see how to turn it on manually, which you do by clicking the **Hyphenate** check box. To see the difference hyphenation makes, turn on the **Preview** check box as well (which like most Preview check boxes is off by default).

InDesign lets you activate and deactivate the automatic hyphenation function without setting foot in the Hyphenation Settings dialog box. Just press Ctrl+Shift+Alt+H (or ⌘-Shift-Option-H) to toggle the setting on or off.

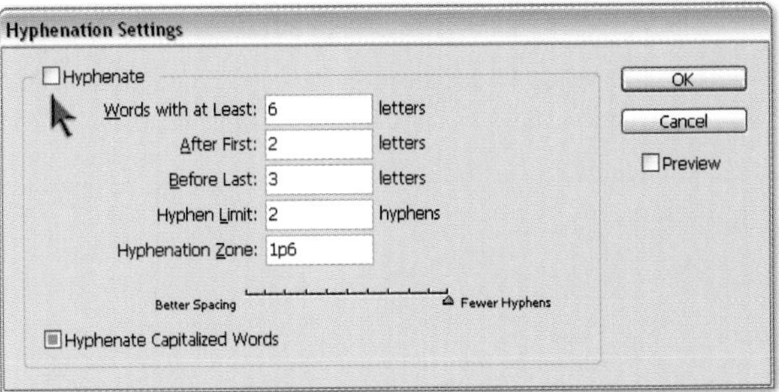

Figure 3-37.

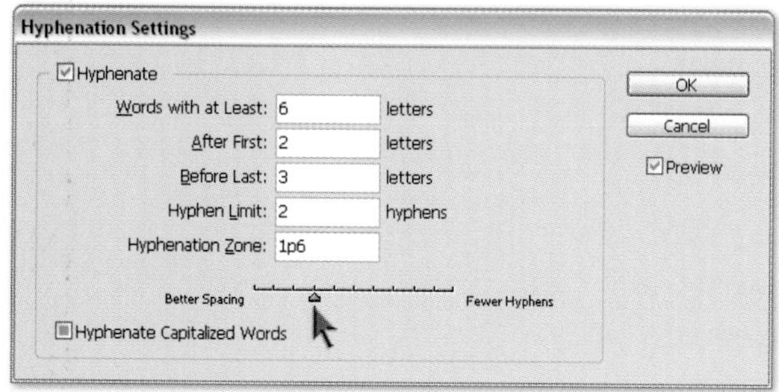

Figure 3-38.

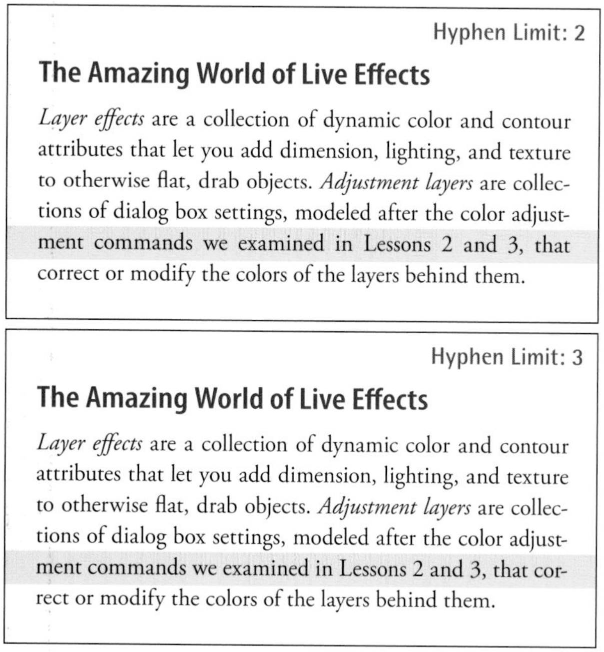

Hyphen Limit: 2

The Amazing World of Live Effects

Layer effects are a collection of dynamic color and contour attributes that let you add dimension, lighting, and texture to otherwise flat, drab objects. *Adjustment layers* are collections of dialog box settings, modeled after the color adjustment commands we examined in Lessons 2 and 3, that correct or modify the colors of the layers behind them.

Hyphen Limit: 3

The Amazing World of Live Effects

Layer effects are a collection of dynamic color and contour attributes that let you add dimension, lighting, and texture to otherwise flat, drab objects. *Adjustment layers* are collections of dialog box settings, modeled after the color adjustment commands we examined in Lessons 2 and 3, that correct or modify the colors of the layers behind them.

Figure 3-39.

5. ***Move the slider triangle closer to Better Spacing.*** The Hyphenation Settings dialog box is loaded with settings, but few of them are worth worrying about. The big exception is the slider bar between Hyphenation Zone and Hyphenate Capitalized Words, which lets you adjust the frequency of hyphenation. The rationale goes like this: Hyphenation interrupts the flow of a word, so you want as few hyphens as possible. But even word spacing looks better, and word spacing is improved by liberal hyphenation. So InDesign gives you the option of finding your own happy marriage.

   For this exercise, I recommend that you move the slider triangle about four ticks from the extreme **Better Spacing**, as I have in Figure 3-38. (If you're having problems getting it exactly right, don't fret. A tick mark one way or the other won't make any difference.) This favors consistent word spacing and permits InDesign as many hyphens as it needs, provided no more than two hyphenated lines appear in a row.

6. ***Raise the Hyphen Limit value.*** Now you might ask, "No more than two hyphenated lines in a row—where does that come from?" The answer is the one remaining useful option, **Hyphen Limit**, which is set to 2. Before you change it, take a look at the second-to-last line of type in the document window, the one near the bottom of the page that begins with the partial word *ment*. The line is a bit loose, but InDesign is prohibited from fixing it by the Hyphen Limit. The solution: Lift the prohibition. Change the value to 3 and press Tab to advance to the next option. Just like that, the line tightens and hyphenates. Figure 3-39 shows before and after views.

7. ***Click OK.*** That's all the good we can do in this dialog box. Click the **OK** button to close the dialog box and apply the hyphenation settings to the active text.

   Okay, if I were you, I'd be protesting, "Hey, how about those other options?" So here's the deal:

   - The first three are self-evident. By default, InDesign is limited to hyphenating words at least 6 letters long, with the hyphen occurring after the first 2 letters and before the last 3. I suggest you leave these as is.

- As for Hyphenation Zone, it determines the area in which a potential break must occur to receive a hyphen. The default value of 1p6 prevents the text from stretching or squishing any more than a quarter inch, which is a lot actually. Again, I recommend you leave this one alone.
- The final check box, Hyphenate Capitalized Words, helps prevent the splitting of product names, proper nouns, and other words that you may want to protect. That said, I usually leave it on for body copy and turn it off for headlines, which are capitalized and read better without hyphens.

EXTRA CREDIT

The text is considerably improved, and all of our problems—stacks, looseness, and the widow—are solved. In fact, under normal conditions, you might figure this is good enough and move on. But these aren't normal conditions. I'm still not quite satisfied with the text, and when teacher's not happy, no one's happy. Namely, even though I just sanctioned three hyphens in a row, I am secretly troubled by it. More to the point, I mark this as Extra Credit because from here on, we embark upon some very subtle adjustments. But one day, I assure you, you'll be glad you have these tools under your belt.

8. ***Choose the Justification command.*** With the text still selected with the black arrow, click the ⊙ arrow in the Paragraph palette and choose the **Justification** command. Or press Ctrl+Shift+Alt+J (⌘-Shift-Option-J on the Mac) to display the **Justification** dialog box, pictured in Figure 3-40. Most of these options control how InDesign automatically spaces and arranges characters inside justified paragraphs. And one option, Composer, goes so far as to control flush-left and otherwise-aligned text as well.

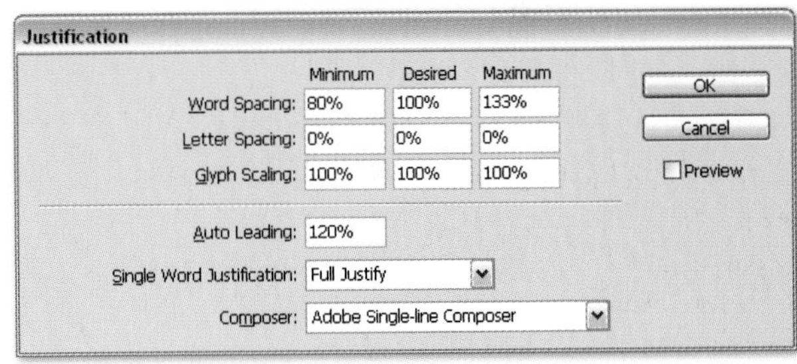

Figure 3-40.

9. ***Turn on Adobe Paragraph Composer.*** Click the **Composer** pop-up menu, which is currently set to Adobe Single-line Composer, and choose **Adobe Paragraph Composer**. Then turn the **Preview** check box on and off to see a few things happen in the document window. The stacked words *impossible* hyphenate differently, and the word *it* falls to the second-to-last line in the second paragraph. What's going on?
   - Prior to the step, InDesign distributed letters according to the *Single-line Composer*, which evaluates each line of text independently, as in PageMaker, QuarkXPress, and other layout

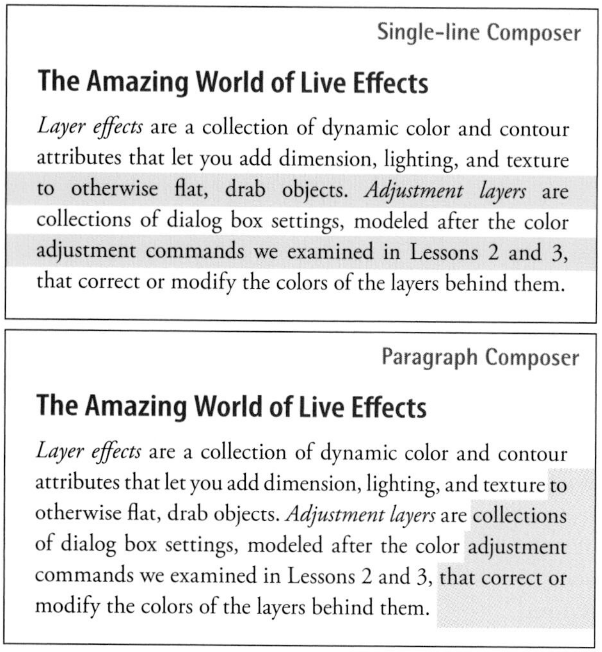

Single-line Composer

The Amazing World of Live Effects

Layer effects are a collection of dynamic color and contour attributes that let you add dimension, lighting, and texture to otherwise flat, drab objects. *Adjustment layers* are collections of dialog box settings, modeled after the color adjustment commands we examined in Lessons 2 and 3, that correct or modify the colors of the layers behind them.

Paragraph Composer

The Amazing World of Live Effects

Layer effects are a collection of dynamic color and contour attributes that let you add dimension, lighting, and texture to otherwise flat, drab objects. *Adjustment layers* are collections of dialog box settings, modeled after the color adjustment commands we examined in Lessons 2 and 3, that correct or modify the colors of the layers behind them.

Figure 3-41.

applications. The result can be wide variation in the spacing of justified lines or ragged endings of flush-left lines.

- InDesign's solution is the *Paragraph Composer*, which looks at all lines in a paragraph when distributing letters in any one of them. This creates more consistent spacing from one line to the next.

Sometimes, the Paragraph Composer makes an enormous difference, which is why it is active by default. (I turned it off for this specific document so you can see how it works.) And had you applied the Paragraph Composer before choosing Hyphenation in Step 3, you would have seen a big shift in the last paragraph. As illustrated in Figure 3-41, prior to Step 3, the third and fifth lines were extremely loose. Even without the aid of hyphenation, the Paragraph Composer managed to equalize the spacing, bringing the words highlighted in blue up a line.

In our post-Step 8 world, however, things are subtler. The Paragraph Composer affects at most four lines of type. The moral: When working with little or no hyphenation, turn it on; when permitting liberal hyphenation, as we are, experiment to see which setting works best.

Also bear in mind, the Paragraph Composer is a computationally intensive operation. So if you find InDesign behaving sluggishly, you might try switching to the relatively streamlined Single-line Composer. It usually quickens InDesign's performance—particularly when entering text from the keyboard—and you're no worse off in line spacing than you were with QuarkXPress.

For our purposes, however, leave the Paragraph Composer on. Every little spacing aid helps.

10. ***Adjust the Letter Spacing and Glyph Scaling values.*** The top of the Justification dialog box is occupied by a series of Minimum, Desired, and Maximum values that control the range of spacing InDesign can use to balance justified type. By default, InDesign permits fluctuations in word spacing only. But you can also allow it to vary letter spacing (the line-by-line tracking) and glyph scaling (the width of individual letters and other characters).

Here's what I want you to do:

- Click in the first **Letter Spacing** value. Then press the ↓ key to reduce the value to -1 percent. Right away, you'll see several lines shift. The result is better hyphenation and spacing in the second paragraph, but a return of the stacks in the first. We'll fix this in a moment.

- It's always nice to have symmetry. So Tab your way to the third Letter Spacing value and press ↑ to raise it to 1 percent. No change whatsoever—okay, it was worth a shot.

- Now Tab your way to the third and final **Glyph Scaling** value and press the ↑ key three times to raise the value to 103 percent. Huge difference! Much better hyphenation than anything we've seen so far plus a solution to the newest widow.

Isn't this exciting? I tell you, you're a born layout artist if you feel your heart flutter just a little bit when you see these kinds of changes. If not it just means you're normal, and people tell me that's okay, too.

11. ***Click OK.*** Figure 3-42 shows the changed settings. If yours match, you are welcome to click the **OK** button and be on your merry way.

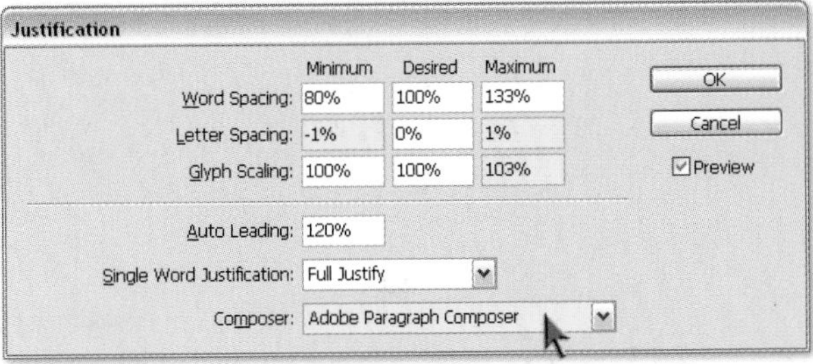

Figure 3-42.

12. ***Eliminate the stack manually.*** We've gone as far as we can with InDesign's automated controls. That means we'll have to fix those pesky stacks manually. And we'll do so using a line break. Double-click inside the text to switch to the type tool. Then select the space between the words *on* and *top* in the fourth line of the first paragraph. To swap the space for a line break, right-click in the text frame and choose **Insert Break Character→Forced Line Break**. InDesign knocks the word *top* to the next line without creating a new paragraph. Other lines adjust automatically, making the stack go away. Figure 3-43 on the next page shows a magnified version of the final page.

Note that I've highlighted the point at which you should have inserted the line break in the figure. I also turned on Type→Show Hidden Characters, which shows spaces and breaks as pale blue symbols. For more information on line breaks and hidden characters, see the exercise "Dashes, Spaces, and Breaks" on page 143 of Lesson 4.

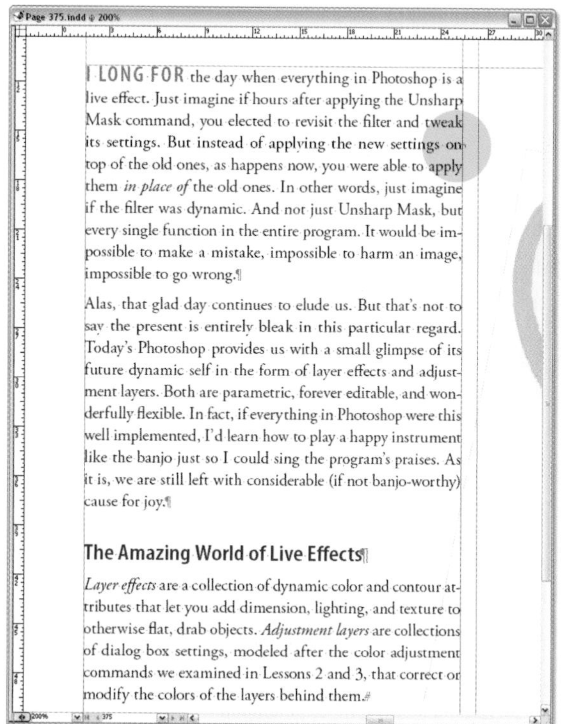

I LONG FOR the day when everything in Photoshop is a live effect. Just imagine if hours after applying the Unsharp Mask command, you elected to revisit the filter and tweak its settings. But instead of applying the new settings on top of the old ones, as happens now, you were able to apply them *in place of* the old ones. In other words, just imagine if the filter was dynamic. And not just Unsharp Mask, but every single function in the entire program. It would be impossible to make a mistake, impossible to harm an image, impossible to go wrong.

Alas, that glad day continues to elude us. But that's not to say the present is entirely bleak in this particular regard. Today's Photoshop provides us with a small glimpse of its future dynamic self in the form of layer effects and adjustment layers. Both are parametric, forever editable, and wonderfully flexible. In fact, if everything in Photoshop were this well implemented, I'd learn how to play a happy instrument like the banjo just so I could sing the program's praises. As it is, we are still left with considerable (if not banjo-worthy) cause for joy.

The Amazing World of Live Effects

Layer effects are a collection of dynamic color and contour attributes that let you add dimension, lighting, and texture to otherwise flat, drab objects. *Adjustment layers* are collections of dialog box settings, modeled after the color adjustment commands we examined in Lessons 2 and 3, that correct or modify the colors of the layers behind them.

Figure 3-43.

Accessing Special Characters

As I first mentioned on page xiv of the Preface, InDesign ships with several fonts from Adobe. They all happen to be OpenType fonts, which generally contain a wider selection of characters than their more common, non-OpenType counterparts. OpenType fonts also offer special intelligence that connects character variations (such as *a*, *á*, *â*, and so on), so that InDesign can find the exact letter or symbol to fit your needs. For a peek under the OpenType hood, read the sidebar "OpenType, Unicode, and Glyphs" on page 120. But frankly, it's not essential that you understand the technical stuff. All that really counts is that you know how to use an OpenType font, and you certainly will after this exercise.

In the next steps, we'll take a document with no special character treatments and go fairly nuts exploiting the letter-swapping capabilities of OpenType. Specifically, we'll add ligatures, small caps, fractions, ordinals, and more. If you don't know what some of those things are, don't worry. You will.

1. ***Open a document.*** Open the document *Max one-year.indd* contained in the *Lesson 03* folder inside *Lesson Files-IDcs 1on1*. Pictured in Figure 3-44, the document features an invitation to my eldest son's first birthday party. These days, he is much older. We actually wash him now.

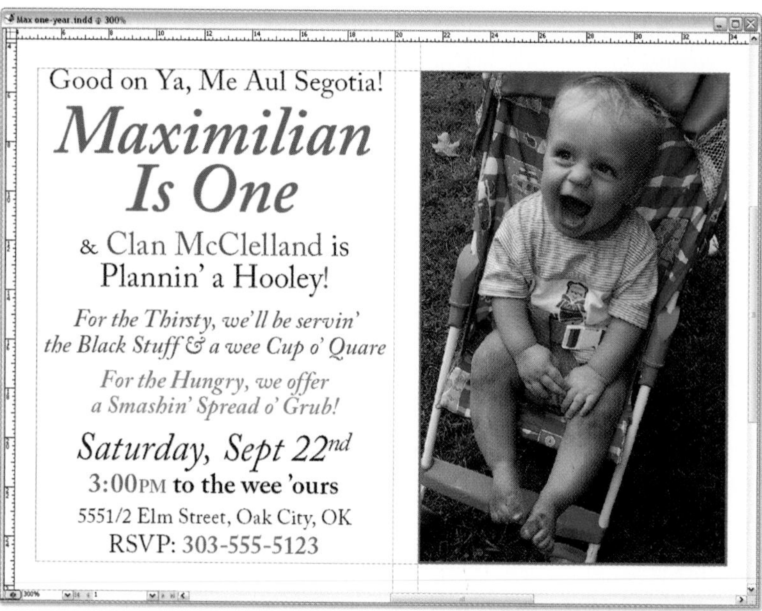

Figure 3-44.

2. ***Bring up the Character palette.*** Click the big text block with the black arrow tool to select it. Then choose **Type→Character** or press Ctrl+T (⌘-T on the Mac) to display the **Character** palette, which provides access to most of InDesign's automatic OpenType functions. The palette shows that the selected text is set entirely in the OpenType font Adobe Caslon Pro.

3. ***Turn on Ligatures.*** Although the invitation contains lots of weird text—it was a Celtic themed party so I threw in a lot of phrases that I no doubt used incorrectly—the document is pretty spare. It contains just 36 characters—24 letters (no *j* or *z*), 5 numbers, and 7 punctuation symbols. Counting capitals, lowercase, regular, and italic, I count a total of 80 character variations, or *glyphs*. Meanwhile, the regular and italic versions of the fonts contain close to 1,400 glyphs, or about 16 times what I managed to use here.

   What are those unused glyphs? Well, 20 or more of them are character combinations called *ligatures*. The idea is that some characters look wrong when combined with each other, usually because they overlap or almost touch in ways that type designers through the years have found unappealing. Figure 3-45 illustrates a handful of these character combos, both as separate letters (top) and as ligatures (bottom). The black characters are common ligatures; the blue ones are discretionary, old-fashioned ligatures.

   All letters expressed as independent characters

   With effort, the fly caught up with the wasp. "Make haste!" cried the junior insect. "The officers have finally amassed their armies between the orange juice and the waffles!"

   Certain combinations fused into ligatures

   With effort, the fly caught up with the wasp. "Make haste!" cried the junior insect. "The officers have finally amassed their armies between the orange juice and the waffles!"

   Figure 3-45.

   Most programs require you to enter ligatures manually (which means resorting to the Character Map utility on the PC) or employ a search-and-replace function. InDesign swaps ligatures out on the fly, and even spell checks them properly. All you have to do is turn on the Ligatures function.

   To do so, click the ⊙ arrow at the top of the Character palette and choose the **Ligatures** command from the palette menu, as in Figure 3-46. InDesign replaces three pairs of letters, the *ff*'s in *Stuff* and *offer*, and the *Th* in *Thirsty*.

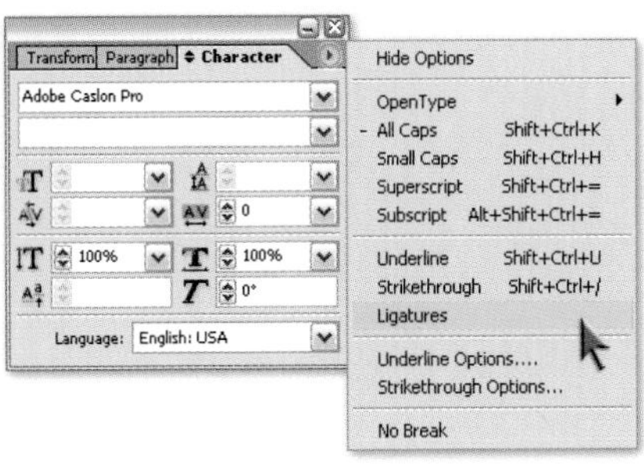

Figure 3-46.

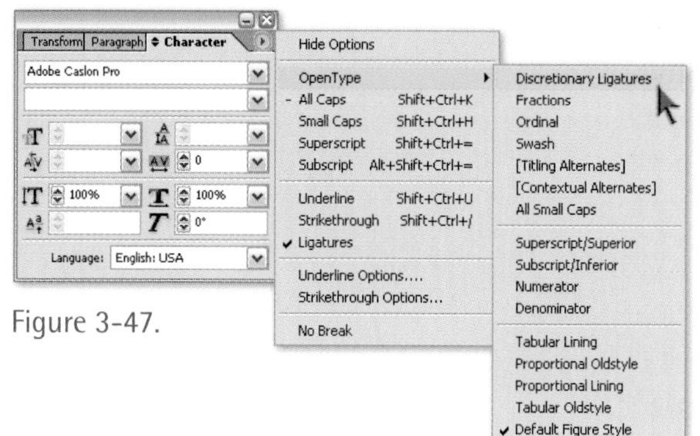

Figure 3-47.

4. ***Turn on Discretionary Ligatures.*** As you will have noted from Figure 3-45, standard ligatures are universally useful (which is why they're turned on by default in InDesign); discretionary ligatures aren't. But this is an old-timey sort of document, so discretionary ligs are apt. Again click the ⊙ arrow in the Character palette and choose **OpenType→Discretionary Ligatures**, as in Figure 3-47. InDesign makes just one change to the document, swapping out the *st* in *Thirsty*.

PEARL OF WISDOM

All commands in the OpenType submenu are exclusively applicable to selected text set in an OpenType font. Any command in brackets, such as [Titling Alternates] and [Contextual Alternates], does not apply to this specific typeface. So naturally, when using a non-OpenType font, *all* OpenType commands appear in brackets.

5. ***Switch out the* Th *lig.*** It just so happens that the type style in which *Thirsty* is set, Adobe Caslon Pro Semibold Italic, offers more than one *Th* ligature. To give priority to the second one, which looks better here, switch to the type tool and select the *Th*. Then choose **Ligatures** from the Character palette menu to turn it off. The primary ligature goes away and the secondary discretionary ligature takes over. Figure 3-48 shows this ligature along with the ones created in Steps 3 and 4.

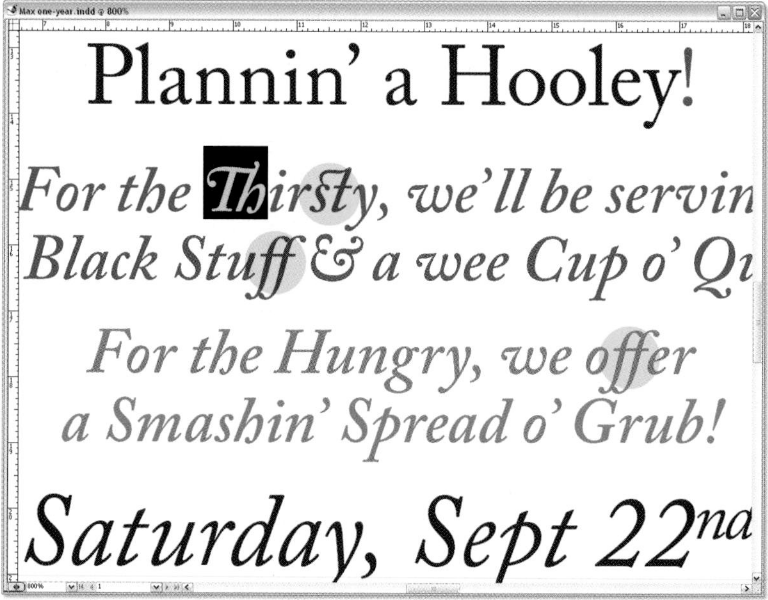

Figure 3-48.

6. ***Add some real small caps.*** Now we move on to another popular alternative letter, the x-height capital, or *small cap*. These are small capital letters that stand as tall as lowercase characters, most commonly used to call out common abbreviations such as 7AM, AD 456, and AKA Lloyd the Impaler.

   Still armed with the type tool, click between the green *3:00* and *PM* in the third-to-last line on the page. Notice that *PM* is already set in small caps, but these are fake small caps, set by reducing the type size of capital letters. Notice that the weight of the small caps is far lighter than that of the characters around them, even though the style is the same (Semibold). Simple reason: Reducing the size of letters reduces their weight.

   Solution? Do as follows:

   - Type *pm* in lowercase letters. Notice how much thicker these letters are?
   - Select the letters you just typed and choose **Small Caps** from the Character palette menu. Alternatively, you can click the Tt icon in the Control palette or press the shortcut Ctrl+Shift+H (⌘-Shift-H on the Mac). When using an OpenType font that offers small cap glyphs, as this one does, InDesign replaces the characters with those glyphs. The glyphs match the weight of surrounding characters, as Figure 3-49 illustrates.
   - Delete the old, puny small caps.

   Note that this technique works only when designer small caps are available, either from an OpenType font or a specialty font like the Expert Collection variety from Adobe. If such glyphs are not available, then InDesign merely capitalizes the letters and decreases their size.

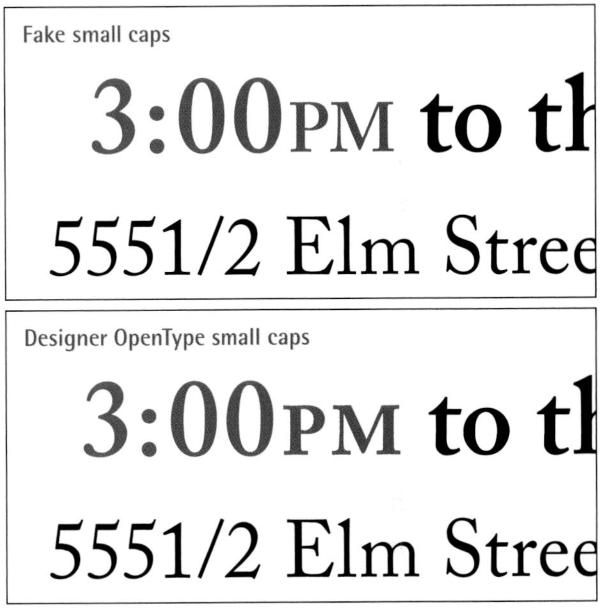

Fake small caps

3:00PM to th

5551/2 Elm Stree

Designer OpenType small caps

3:00PM to th

5551/2 Elm Stree

Figure 3-49.

7. ***Set the fraction.*** Directly below the green time is the address, which includes an improperly set fraction. Select the fraction *1/2* with the type tool, and then choose **OpenType→Fractions** from the Character palette menu. That's all it takes to replace a bad fraction with the proper prebuilt glyph. Figure 3-50 on page 122 shows the difference. I usually kern the fraction away from any normal numbers that precede it. In the figure, I used a kerning value of 75.

OpenType, Unicode, and Glyphs

Like any revolutionary technology, OpenType makes your life easier proportionally to the effort you put in. In other words, a little learning goes a long way. And by little, I mean very little. Read this page spread and you'll be up to speed.

OpenType serves three purposes: It expands the character set, it simplifies the installation process, and it permits applications to associate letter variations with their base characters. Before OpenType, most Western fonts were limited to 1 byte (8 bits) of data per character, which meant that a single font could offer no more than 256 *glyphs*, or character variations. By typewriter standards that's a lot, but by modern typesetting standards it's unacceptably low. By themselves, the letters (capital and lowercase), numbers, and punctuation shown on a U.S. typewriter or computer keyboard add up to 92 glyphs. Throw in some extra punctuation, a few fractions, the occasional symbol, and the bevy of accented letters used in the U.S. and elsewhere, and you hit the ceiling fast. The figure below shows samples from one of the italic styles from Adobe Jenson Pro. Although just four characters, they add as many as 81 glyphs. A 1-byte font simply can't handle this much variety.

The solution is the 2-byte (16-bit or double-byte) *Unicode* specification. By assigning 2 bytes per

Character: A, glyphs: 44

Character: G, glyphs: 15

Characters: T and/or H, glyphs: 22

All glyphs from Adobe Jenson Pro Light Italic

character, a Unicode-compatible font may comprise as many as 65,536 glyphs, enough to represent the most common characters in virtually every major language in use today, including Greek, Farsi, and Japanese. Font standards that support Unicode, such as OpenType, organize characters by address. For example, a lowercase, unaccented *a* is always character 0061. (If the font lacks an *a*, the address is blank.) This way, your character remains intact when you switch fonts. Even better, you can plug in a foreign keyboard—one with accented characters, for example—and the font will respect each key to the best of its ability.

But OpenType doesn't stop there. An OpenType font associates glyphs with their base characters. So an OpenType-aware program knows that an uppercase A, lowercase *a*, small cap A, swash *A*, and even the archaic ligature æ are all variations on one letter. The spell checker sees them as *A*'s, just as it rightly should. And if the program is as clever as InDesign, it can swap out glyphs and suggest alternatives automatically. To see this feature in action, work through the exercise "Accessing Special Characters," which begins on page 116.

Finally, OpenType fonts are more compact than their predecessors. A single OpenType file includes everything you need to use a typeface on your computer. So where an older font may require you to install separate screen, printer, and metrics files—not to mention extra files to hold overflow glyphs such as small caps and swashes—the OpenType font presents you with a single file (see below). This one file also happens to be cross-platform, so it serves PCs and Macs alike—and with identical kerning metrics, so there's no danger of having text reflow when you change platforms.

Incidentally, all the typefaces that ship with InDesign CS (as well as either version of the Creative Suite) are OpenType fonts. A font that contains the word *Pro* in its name contains a wider variety of glyphs, including accented letters used throughout Central Europe. A font that contains *Std* (for "standard") does not.

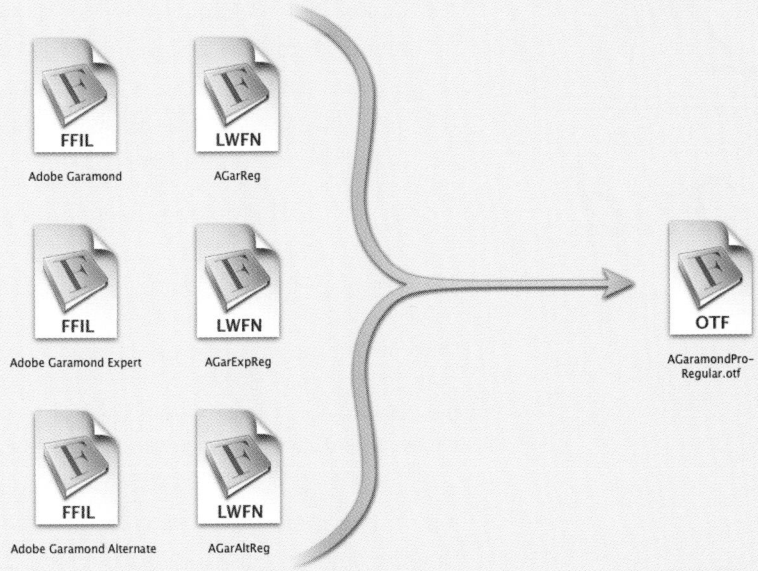

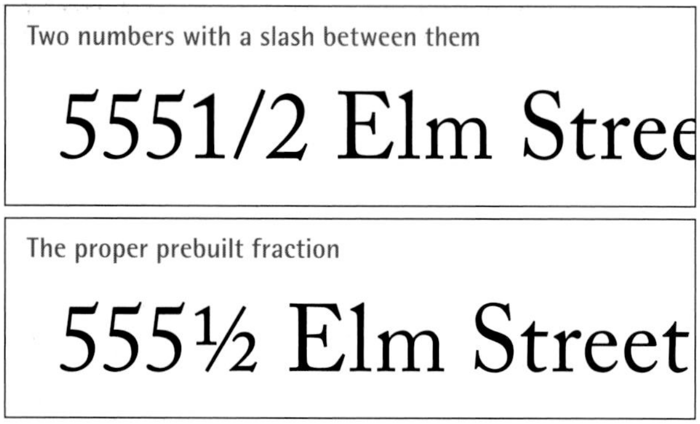

Two numbers with a slash between them

5551/2 Elm Stree

The proper prebuilt fraction

555½ Elm Street

Figure 3-50.

PEARL OF  WISDOM

OpenType fonts aren't the only ones that include fractions. In fact, most fonts include the fractions ½, ¼, and ¾. But unless you're using an OpenType font, you can't choose OpenType→Fractions to get to them. Instead, you select the fractions from the Glyphs palette, which I introduce in Step 12. On the PC, you can also access fractions by pressing Alt with numbers on the numeric keypad. Hold down the Alt key while typing 0-1-8-9 on the keypad (not along the top of the keyboard) to get ½. Alt+0-1-8-8 gets you ¼; Alt+0-1-9-0 gets you ¾.

Some OpenType fonts let you create much more complicated fractions than these. For example, just for fun, try selecting the entire address—*5551/2*—and selecting OpenType→Fractions. InDesign delivers the fraction 5551/2.

8. *Add some real ordinals.* Now for another strange-sounding type treatment, the ordinal. In typesetting, an *ordinal* is a superscripted sequence of letters following a number, like the *st* in 1st. Click between the *22* and *nd* at the end of the fourth-to-last line of text. Notice that the *nd* is a fake ordinal, created by superscripting standard text. As with fake small caps, the weight is all wrong. To fix the problem:

   - Type *nd* in lowercase letters.
   - Select the letters you just typed and then choose **OpenType→Ordinal** from the Character palette menu. Again, InDesign finds the designer-approved ordinal glyphs provided in Adobe Caslon Pro. The glyphs match the weight and letter spacing of the surrounding text, as in Figure 3-51.
   - Delete the bad old fraudulent ordinals.

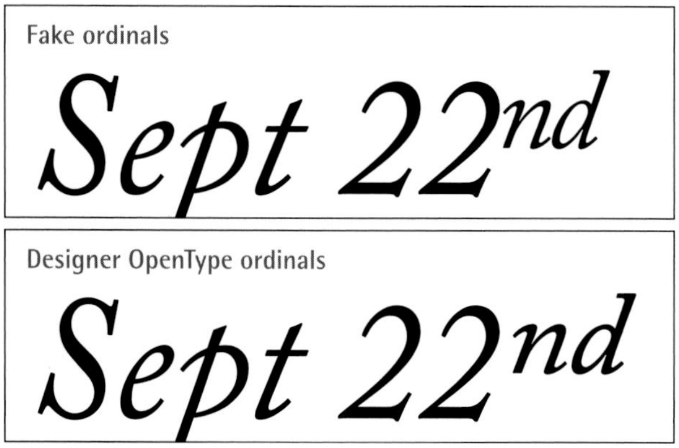

Fake ordinals

Sept 22nd

Designer OpenType ordinals

Sept 22nd

Figure 3-51.

The OpenType→Ordinal command is a little too smart for its own good. If you mistype the *nd*—even with something that could be an ordinal like *th*—InDesign refuses to participate unless it precisely goes with the preceding number. To override InDesign's faux intelligence, select the letters and choose **OpenType→Superscript/Superior** instead.

---

9. *Set the phone number in oldstyle numerals.* Directly down from the date you'll see a green phone number. Select the entire thing and choose **OpenType→**

Proportional Oldstyle from the Character palette menu. This replaces the standard numbers (sometimes called capital numbers because they are all the same height and sit on top of the baseline) with oldstyle numerals of differing heights with descenders. I've heard type experts argue that oldstyle numerals are more legible in text because of their height variation. But I imagine most readers view the numbers as antique, which suits this document but may not suit others.

PEARL OF WISDOM

To restore standard numbers, choose one of the two Lining commands in the OpenType submenu. Incidentally, the difference between Tabular and Proportional has to do with spacing. Choosing a Tabular command assigns every number the same width, so they line up in a table, as when adding sets of numbers. The Proportional command assigns less space to a skinny number like 1 than to a wide number like, well, everything else. This is typically the better choice when setting numbers inside lines of type.

---

10. *Set* RSVP *in small caps.* Given that they appear next to oldstyle numerals, the letters *RSVP* will probably look better in small caps. Double-click *RSVP* to select the abbreviation, and then press Ctrl+Shift+H (or ⌘-Shift-H) to set it in small caps. Nothing happens! The reason is that these letters are capitals, and InDesign only changes lowercase letters to small caps. So with the text still selected, choose **Type→Change Case→lowercase**. Now you have small caps. Figure 3-52 shows the last line as it looked before Step 9 and the way it looks now.

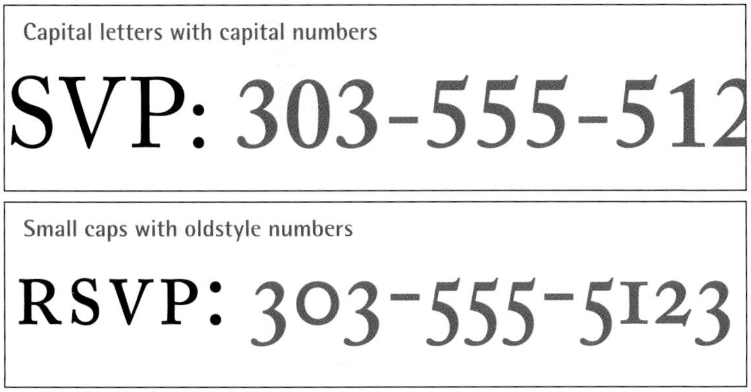

Capital letters with capital numbers

SVP: 303-555-512

Small caps with oldstyle numbers

RSVP: 303-555-5123

Figure 3-52.

11. *Replace the big green M with a swash.* Many italic OpenType fonts include cursive characters with additional flourish, known as *swash characters*. While it's easy to go a bit too nuts with swashes—I'll show you how in just a moment!—they can be very useful at the outset of a line or paragraph. To try one on

Figure 3-53.

for size, select the *M* at the beginning of *Maximilian* and then choose **OpenType→Swash** from the Character palette menu. Figure 3-53 features before and after views.

12. ***Bring up the Glyphs palette.*** One of the problems with selecting swash characters is that you never know if a specific character has a swash form (most don't) or what that swash looks like until you choose OpenType→Swash. Fortunately, InDesign provides you with a previewing tool that shows you every single character the font offers. Choose **Type→Glyphs**—or assuming you loaded the Deke Keys shortcuts (page xvii) press Shift+F12—to display the **Glyphs** palette. Unlike other InDesign palettes, this one comprises a grid of cells, each of which contains a glyph from the active font. If the swash *M* is still highlighted in your document, you will see the *M* surrounded by a bevy of other swash letters, as in Figure 3-54.

Figure 3-54.

The Glyphs palette accommodates standard fonts as well as OpenType. Because it shows each and every glyph—including those that are not available from PC or Mac keyboards—it's especially great for locating characters in non-Roman or symbol fonts. Some things to know about this incredibly useful palette:

- To insert a glyph into the active text block, double-click its cell in the palette.
- To examine a different typeface or style, select it from one of the two pop-up menus in the bottom-left corner of the palette.
- To examine a glyph more closely, click on the big mountain icon in the lower-right corner of the palette. To zoom out, click the little mountain to the right of that.
- Drag the size box in the lower-right corner to expand the palette and see more glyphs at a time.

There's some other stuff, but that's good enough for now.

13. ***Replace the violet* F *with a swash.*** Using the type tool, select the *F* in the word *For* that begins the two lines of violet text. Doing so scrolls up to the top of the character set, where the capital *F* lives. Click and hold the F cell to display a menu of alternatives, which includes an unrelated ornament and a swash F. This little menu shows us not only that a swash exists for this character, but also what it looks like (see Figure 3-55). Choose the swash F to replace the selected letter in the document.

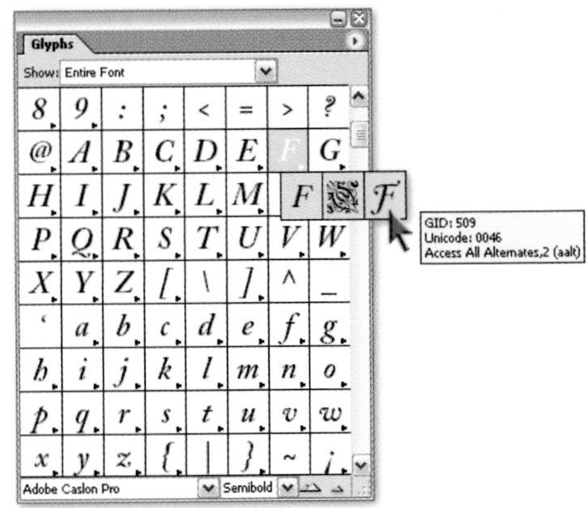

Figure 3-55.

14. ***View just the swashes.*** If you want to go swash crazy—I know I warned you against it, but they're just so darn fun—choosing OpenType→Swash or selecting an alternate from the Glyphs palette cell menus can get old fast. The much faster, slicker way to work is to double-click the swash cell you want to use. But sifting through the cells is its own mind-numbing chore. What is the swash enthusiast to do?

    The solution is to restrict the range of glyphs you see in the palette. Click the **Show** pop-up menu at the top of the palette—the one that currently reads Entire Font—and choose **Swash**. That *should* work, but if you're using the same version of Adobe Caslon Pro that I'm using (Adobe occasionally upgrades its fonts just like any other software), you won't see a thing. This is because the swashes are incorrectly assigned—i.e., we've encountered a little bug—which sometimes happens. Fortunately, there's a backup solution. Click the pop-up menu again and choose **Access All Alternates**, as in Figure 3-56. Then scroll down to the bottom of the palette where the swash characters hang out.

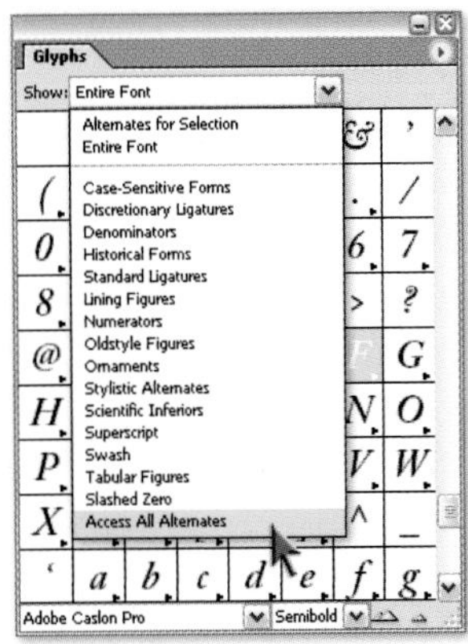

Figure 3-56.

15. ***Make and fill a custom glyph set.*** Because Adobe Caslon Pro doesn't properly separate its swashes, you must separate them for yourself:

    - Click the ▶ arrow in the top-right corner of the palette and choose **New Glyph Set**.
    - Name the set "Caslon Swashes" and click **OK**.
    - Now right-click the cell that contains the swash capital *A* and choose **Add to Glyph→Caslon Swashes**, as I demonstrate in Figure 3-57.
    - If you're so inclined, repeat the last action for each of the other swash characters, from *B* to *Z*. Unfortunately, there's no way to select multiple glyphs simultaneously, so you have to add each glyph independently.

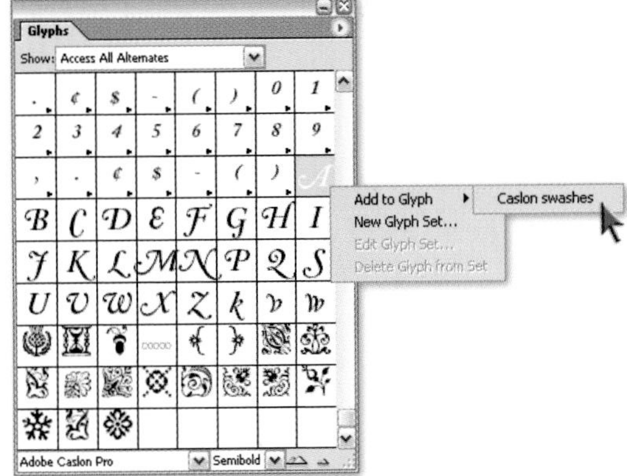

Figure 3-57.

16. ***Display the Caslon Swashes set.*** When you've had enough right-clicking and choosing the Add to Glyph command, click the **Show** pop-up menu and you'll see, there at the top, **Caslon Swashes**. Choose it to display just those swash characters that you added to your custom glyph library.

    From here on, it's just a matter of selecting the character you want to replace in the document and then double-clicking the desired swash in the Glyphs palette. In all, I introduced a total of seven swashes, all highlighted in Figure 3-58. Did I overdo it? Oh come now. Nothing says rough-and-tumble little boy's birthday party like a heaping helping of frilly, ornamental swash characters.

I should mention, nothing says you have to relegate a custom glyph set to a single font. In fact, I use just such a multi-font set to lay out this book. That way, I don't have to hunt through three separate typefaces with several hundred glyphs apiece to find the symbols I use most often; they're all right there in one location.

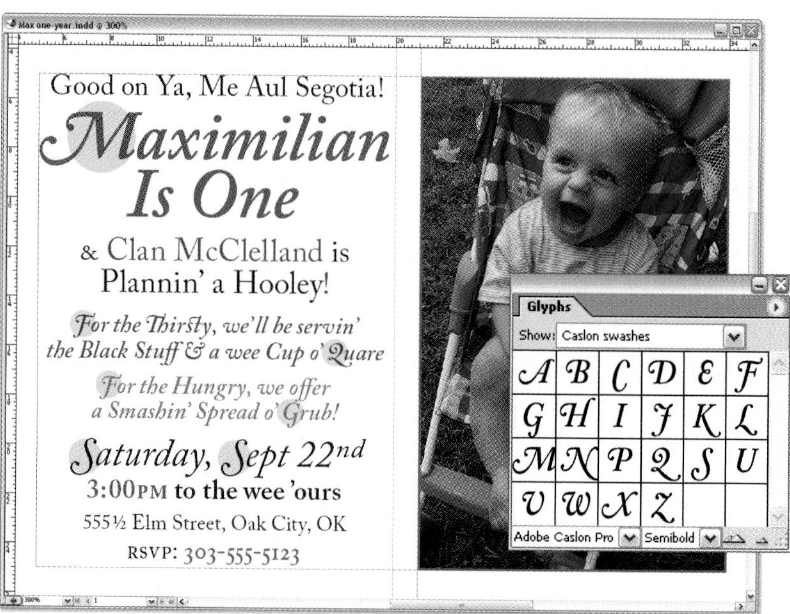

Figure 3-58.

WHAT DID YOU LEARN?

Match the key concept in the numbered list below with the letter of the phrase that best describes it. Answers appear upside-down at the bottom of the page.

Key Concepts

1. Formatting attributes
2. Leading
3. Serif
4. Baseline
5. X-height
6. Kerning
7. Side bearing
8. Widow
9. Stack
10. Paragraph Composer
11. Ligature
12. Ordinal

Descriptions

A. The tapering wedge that appears at the end of a character set in Times or one of many other fonts, including the one you're reading now.

B. The disconnect in the appearance of the last line of a paragraph, whether that line is stranded by itself at the top of a new column or reduced to one or two words at the bottom of a paragraph.

C. The tops of *a*, *c*, *e*, and most lowercase letters (termed medials) reach this horizontal line.

D. The specific physical traits of type, which are divided into character- and paragraph-level properties.

E. A special combination of characters (such as *fi* or *fl*) intended to print as a single character by the creators of a font.

F. A fine adjustment—measured in fractions of an em space—made to the space between two adjacent characters of type.

G. A composition problem in which identical words in consecutive rows of type appear directly on top of each other.

H. The distance from the baseline of the selected line of type to the baseline directly above it.

I. A fixed amount of space on both the left and right sides of a character of type, as defined by the font.

J. The imaginary horizonal axis on which all words and characters on a line of type reside.

K. A variety of numbers that imply order in a sequence (as in *first*, *second*, or *third*), which when expressed as numerals end in a pair of superscripted letters (1st, 2nd, and 3rd).

L. Built into InDesign, Illustrator, and Photoshop, this feature looks at all lines in a paragraph when distributing characters or hyphenating words in any one of them.

Answers

1D, 2H, 3A, 4J, 5C, 6F, 7I, 8B, 9G, 10L, 11E, 12K

LESSON 4

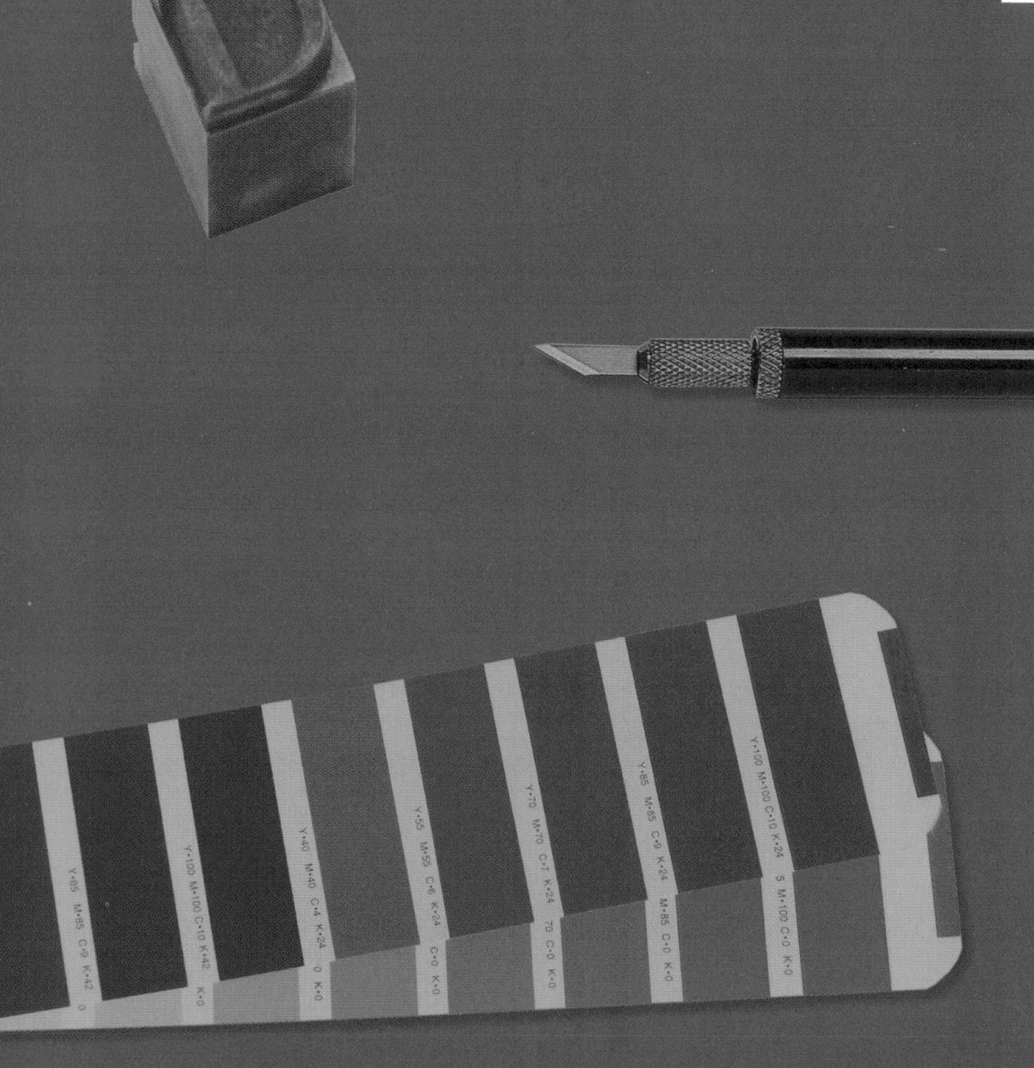

LISTS AND TABLES

FORMATTING TEXT is a monumental discipline. Monks, scribes, and calligraphers have devoted their lives to it. (Well, monks had other duties—prayer, contemplation, making beer—but they made up for it by putting in longer hours.) So it's hardly surprising that we haven't seen the end of formatting. In fact, we're only about a third of the way through the topic. Long as that last lesson was, we still have two more lessons to go.

This time around, we'll look at those varieties of formatting attributes that are specifically applicable to lists and tables. These may be numbered or bulleted lists, short tables of contents, or elaborate, multipage tables of products and prices. You'll learn how to break rows of text into columns of facts and figures, all inside the confines of a single frame, as illustrated in Figure 4-1.

Along the way, we'll be looking at such traditional paragraph-level formatting attributes as indents, drop caps, and tab stops. We'll also look beyond formatting and learn how and when to use an array of invisible characters, including line breaks, tabs, and differently sized spaces. In the final exercise, we'll examine InDesign's full-blown table function, which creates a nested text frame and divides it into a matrix of regular rows and columns. If these sound like daunting prospects, just remember that the monks of old didn't have computers and they still managed to build tables, not to mention chairs, davenports, and fancy curio cabinets. If they could do it with nothing more than years of experience and divine inspiration, you can do it with InDesign.

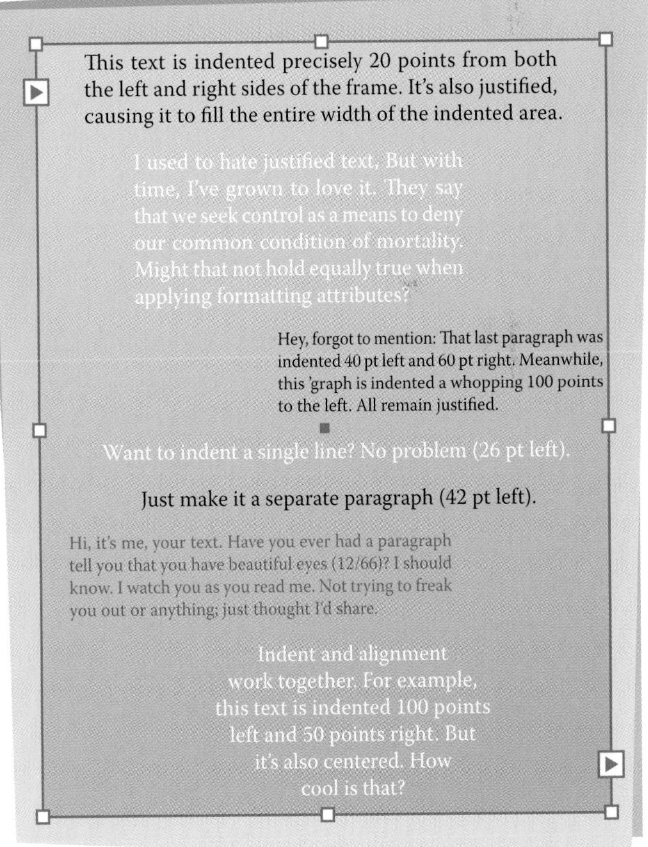

Figure 4-1.

ABOUT THIS LESSON

Project Files

Before beginning the exercises, make sure that you've installed the lesson files from the CD, as explained in Step 5 on page xv of the Preface. This should result in a folder called *Lesson Files-IDcs 1on1* on your desktop. We'll be working with the files inside the *Lesson 04* subfolder.

In this lesson, we'll take a look at the best ways to build lists and tables in InDesign. I'll also introduce you to a handful of specialty characters essential to page layout. You'll learn how to:

- Insert an automatic drop cap at the outset of a paragraph. . . . . page 131
- Format numbered or bulleted lists using hanging indents . . . . page 137
- Shape the appearance of a document using dashes, spaces, and line breaks . . . . page 143
- Create a table by entering tab characters and setting tabs stops . . . . page 153
- Establish and format a spreadsheet-style table complete with repeating headers . . . . page 159

Video Lesson 4: Spaces, Indents, and Tabs

If you spend much time with a word processor, you may have developed the habit of using the spacebar to indent or align text. But in professional publishing, you use the spacebar for one purpose only: to separate one word from another, and *never* by more than one space at a time, not even at the end of sentences. For larger spaces, you use special fixed-width characters and tabs.

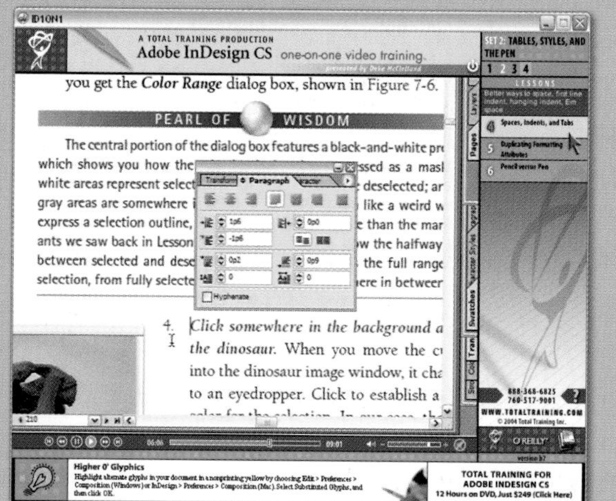

To learn all about separating and aligning text in InDesign, watch the fourth video lesson on the CD. Insert the CD, click the **Start Training** button, click the Set 2 button, and then select **4, Spaces, Indents, and Tabs** from the Lessons list. Clocking in at 9 minutes and 1 second, this movie examines the following operations and shortcuts:

Operation	Windows shortcut	Macintosh shortcut
Display the Paragraph palette	Ctrl+Alt+T	⌘-Option-T
Raise or lower value by 1 point	↑ or ↓	↑ or ↓
Raise or lower value by 1 pica	Shift+↑ or Shift+↓	Shift-↑ or Shift-↓
Access special characters	Right-click with type tool	Right-click (Control-click) with type tool
Insert em space (width of type size)	Ctrl+Shift+M	⌘-Shift-M
Display the Tabs palette	Ctrl+Shift+T	⌘-Shift-T

The Power of the Indent

Everything in this lesson stems from one of the most basic formatting options we've witnessed so far, the indent. Remember how you indented the left and right edges of the quote in the "Paragraph Spacing and Alignment" exercise in Lesson 3 (page 103)? Couldn't have been easier, right? And yet, thanks to this humble attribute, a line of text doesn't have to align precisely with the edges of the frame. As Figure 4-2 shows, each and every paragraph—nay, each and every line—can float inside the frame just as the frame floats on the page.

Now take the simple indent and imagine it repeated multiple times inside a single line of type. Instead of indenting just the beginning or end of a line, you can indent a single word or character. Plus, you can move the type to a specific location, relative either to the edge of the frame or another character. The only thing you can't do is make one character overlap another. If this threatens to happen, InDesign bumps the text to the next indent or wraps it to the next line.

Once you understand that InDesign's indenting capabilities can pop up literally anywhere inside a paragraph, you have the core concept. The next five exercises explain when these specialized indents are useful and how to apply them.

1 Ullam, consequiam, velit am iniatio guh dionullum zzrit, seth volore. Commodolent acil lan velisse veliquam.

2 Feum quat, qui tiedn digna fer faccum iure vercil ing ea feuvruey facilis acilla aliscipit loreja alvaf gherew theinopm.

3 Eui ex euipis alit velit wisl ullum doluptat landio do. Suscillandre dolore feugue del ero odiam, vel eugue faccum.

● Hanjitru lorper simty erciliq uisissequam, quisl irit luptat. Rud modolor summod et augait loreet ex eum.

✯ Dit ulluptate commo loborem dio dolenib ex ent wisci tatummo do dipit ad tis et alit acipit volobore tat.

⚜ Erostrud dolore ame modolobor augaityll velesequat. Uptatitar ure diamet, quat, sed dip ea commodi.

Part	Description	In stock	Price	Unintelligible annotations
AI5	Dionsenim ipexero	yes	$ 16	Very phenwicked ferrets
A34	Ugait wiscipsustrud	yes	$ 79	Mosta facile chipmunk
A37	Pipsit sisissevolesto	no	$ 34	Exer'il lemming ulluptatie
B04	Aacincillan tortilla	yes	$ 12	Autpat nim hungry lab rat
B09	Overt flaptuousity	yes	$ 99	Molorper bunny rabbit
B11	Nonsecon ullafac	no	$ 17	Cumirilla dromedary conu
B12	Mnimnimo dipsust	yes	$ 23	Ruddolore magna squirrel
B45	Feuguer ipisldo	yes	$ 65	Del ipiscip elite rodentia
B67	Banana fantastico	yes	$ 41	Oui, et vullaore magnissi!
C60	Sunk my battleship	no	$ 36	La piggypoo blandreet
C73	Feum dolor aquaslug	yes	$ 51	Magna carta porcupine

Figure 4-2.

Adding a Drop Cap

Let's start things off with the ever-popular drop cap. Contrary to the latter half of its name, a *drop cap* doesn't have to be a capital letter. It can be any character—a lowercase letter, a number, a punctuation mark, or a symbol. But it does have to drop. As illustrated in Figure 4-3 on the next page, the traits that distinguish a drop cap from the rest of the pack are its large size and the way it drops down to consume multiple lines of type.

A drop cap may also comprise multiple characters. But without exception, drop caps appear at the beginning of a paragraph, and typically at the outset of a chapter or story. This explains why InDesign expresses the drop cap as a paragraph-level formatting attribute even though it affects just a few isolated characters.

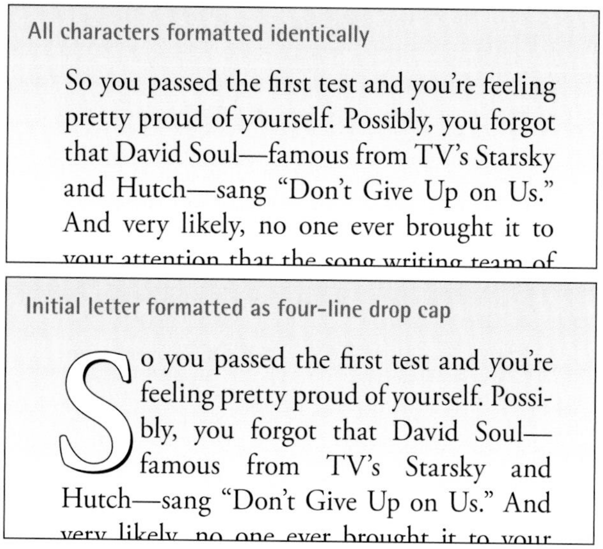

All characters formatted identically

So you passed the first test and you're feeling pretty proud of yourself. Possibly, you forgot that David Soul—famous from TV's Starsky and Hutch—sang "Don't Give Up on Us." And very likely, no one ever brought it to your attention that the song writing team of

Initial letter formatted as four-line drop cap

So you passed the first test and you're feeling pretty proud of yourself. Possibly, you forgot that David Soul—famous from TV's Starsky and Hutch—sang "Don't Give Up on Us." And very likely, no one ever brought it to your

Figure 4-3.

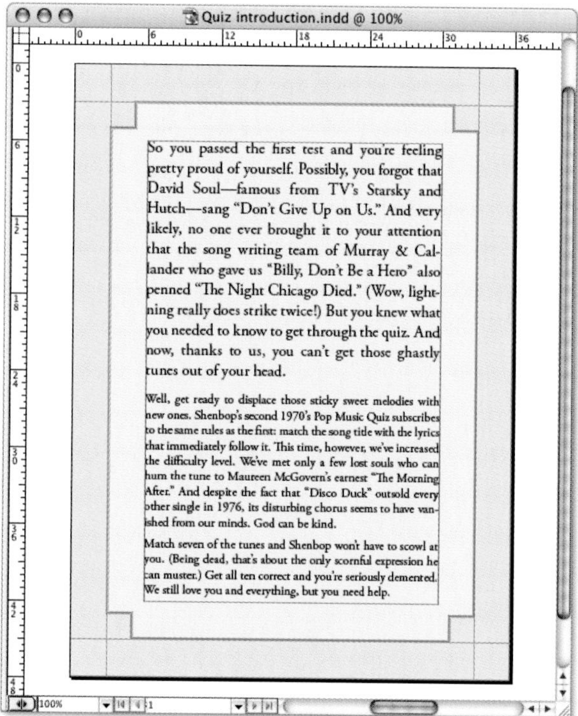

Figure 4-4.

PEARL OF WISDOM

In case you're scratching your head and thinking, "What does a drop cap have to do with lists and tables," take another peek at Figure 4-2 on the preceding page. The numbered list in the upper-left corner is actually a series of paragraphs that begin with drop caps. The enlarged numbers displace several lines of type and shift those lines rightward, exactly as if I had indented them. In this exercise, you'll be applying the drop cap to a single paragraph. But were you to apply just the first four steps to several paragraphs in a row, you'd have yourself a list.

In this exercise, you'll enlarge the first word of a paragraph and drop it down to fill three lines of type. You'll also apply some more specialized formatting attributes that fall outside, but nicely augment, InDesign's limited drop cap capabilities.

1. ***Open a document.*** Go into the *Lesson 04* folder inside *Lesson Files-IDcs 1on1* and open the document *Quiz introduction.indd*. Pictured in Figure 4-4, this small-format document contains three paragraphs of type, the first set larger than the others. This first paragraph will contain our drop word.

2. ***Select the first paragraph.*** Double-click somewhere inside the first paragraph with the black arrow tool to switch to the type tool and insert the blinking insertion marker.

3. ***Bring up the Paragraph palette.*** You may click its tab or press Ctrl+Alt+T (⌘-Option-T on the Mac). If the Paragraph palette is partially collapsed, expand it by clicking the ⇕ next to the word Paragraph once or twice. (Alternatively, you can work inside the Control palette. To do so, click the ¶ in the upper-left corner of your screen to switch to the paragraph options.)

4. ***Change the number of lines to 3.*** Whether you're using the Paragraph or Control palette, click the icon that looks like a drop cap *A* (A≣). This option controls the size of the drop cap as measured in lines of type. Change the value to 3 and press the Tab key.

5. ***Change the number of characters to 2.*** By pressing Tab, you both enlarge the first letter of the paragraph, an *S*, and advance to the Aa≡ option box. Change this value to 2 and press the Enter or Return key. InDesign enlarges both letters in the word *So*, as in Figure 4-5.

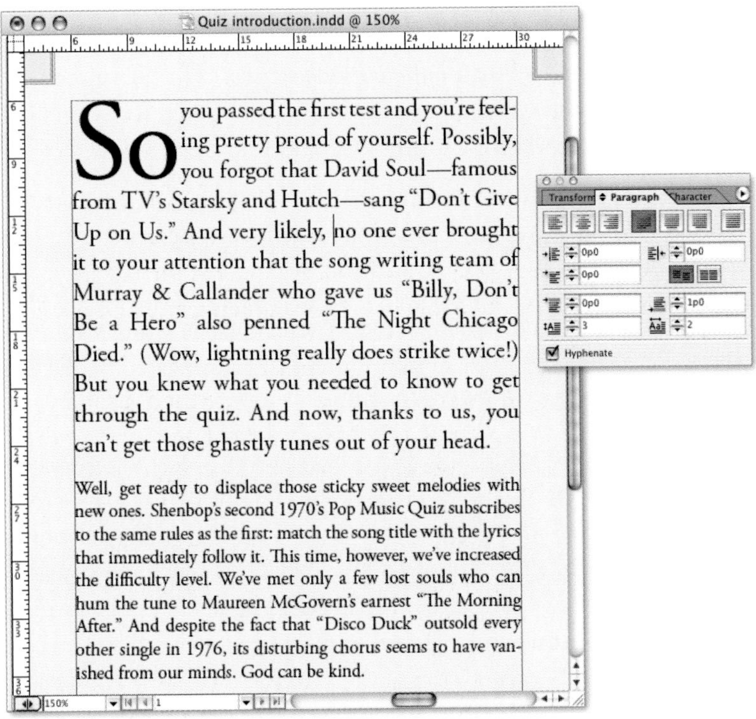

Figure 4-5.

That's really all there is to it. With no more effort than that, you tell InDesign to not only enlarge the first word to fill three lines of type but also indent the first three lines to avoid any overlap. Better yet, the effect is dynamic—if you change your mind, just enter new values and the drop cap updates.

PEARL OF WISDOM

Although InDesign's automated drop cap functions are great, it's unlikely you'll want to stop there. For example, what if you want to assign the characters a different font or color? Or perhaps give them outlines and shadows, as we saw back in Figure 4-3? That requires some additional work.

6. ***Select the drop word.*** Using the type tool, double-click the word *So* to select it. From here on out, we'll modify these characters by applying character-level formatting attributes as well as a handful of graphics functions.

7. ***Change the word to all caps.*** As I mentioned earlier, drop caps can be any characters. But they're called drop *caps* for a reason—whatever they can be, they usually look best when set in capital letters. To change the word *So* to all caps, switch back to the character attributes in the Control palette and click the TT button. Or more simply, press the keyboard shortcut Ctrl+Shift+K (or ⌘-Shift-K).

8. ***Assign a white fill and a black stroke.*** The big round O makes the drop cap appear a bit heavy. To lighten it, we'll fill it with white and give it a thin black outline. Here's how:

   - Display the **Color** palette, by clicking the Color tab (labeled ❶ in Figure 4-6) or by pressing the F6 key.
   - Click the black T in the upper-left corner of the palette (❷) to make the fill active. Then click the white swatch on the far right side of the gradient strip (indicated by the ❸). This makes the fill white.
   - White text against a light background doesn't show up too well, so we need to add an outline. Press the X key or click the bottom of the two T's (labeled ❹ in the figure) to make the stroke active. Then click the black swatch at the end of the gradient strip (❺). The result is a beautiful black outline and a return to visibility for the drop caps.
   - Switch to the **Stroke** palette by clicking the Stroke tab (❻) or pressing F10. Then change the **Weight** value to 0.5 points (labeled ❼ in Figure 4-6).

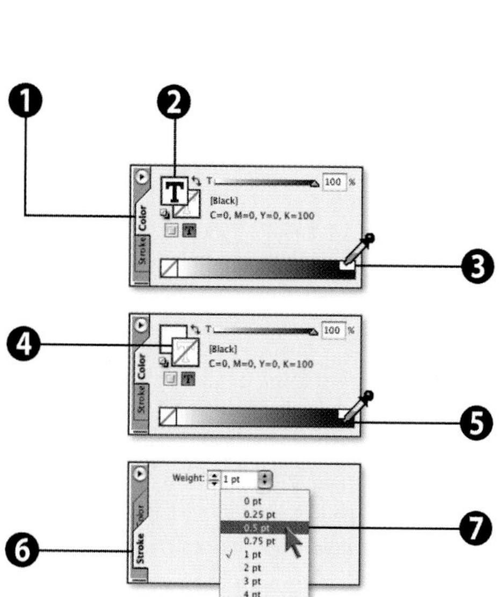

Figure 4-6.

EXTRA CREDIT

You now have two big white letters with very thin black outlines. But let's say you want to go further. Specifically, let's say you want to add a drop shadow. Unfortunately, InDesign doesn't let you add drop shadows to a single word inside a paragraph. But it does let you add a drop shadow to a graphic. So the trick is to first convert the text to a graphic and then add a drop shadow, as in the remaining steps.

9. ***Convert the selected letters to graphic outlines.*** Choose **Type→Convert to Outlines** or press Ctrl+Shift+O (⌘-Shift-O on the Mac). This changes the letters into full-fledged graphics, like those we'll be learning about in Lesson 6, "Drawing inside InDesign." You can no longer edit the type from the keyboard—whether to fix a typo or change the typeface—but you can add a drop shadow.

10. ***Select the* S *with the black arrow tool.*** To manipulate the graphic letters, you must first select them using the black arrow tool. And because they're housed inside a text block, you can select them only one at a time. It's a drag, frankly, but that's the way it is. So here goes: Assuming you loaded Deke Keys as instructed in the Preface (see page xvii), press the Enter key on the keypad to switch to the black arrow tool. Then click on the outline of the *S* to select it.

11. ***Add a drop shadow.*** Choose **Object→Drop Shadow** or press Ctrl+Alt+M (⌘-Option-M). When the **Drop Shadow** dialog box appears, select the settings shown in Figure 4-7, as follows:

    - Turn on the **Preview** check box so you can see what you're doing.
    - Turn on the **Drop Shadow** check box to get the shadow started.
    - Change the **Opacity** value to 100 percent. This results in a shadow that begins solid black and tapers off.
    - Enter a value of 0p1 for both the **X Offset** and **Y Offset** values. This positions the shadow just 1 point down and to the right from the *S*.
    - Blurred shadows don't work well for drop caps. To keep the shadow sharp, reduce the **Blur** value to 0p0.

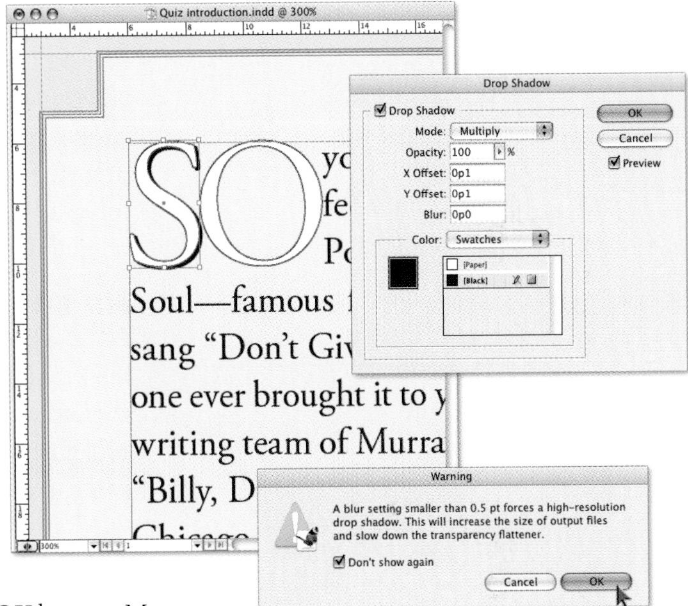

Figure 4-7.

When you finish with those settings, click the **OK** button. Most likely, InDesign will display a warning message, telling you that sharp shadows result in high-resolution output. The implication is that this will slow the printing process, but in fact, because the shadow is fully opaque, it will actually speed up the program. I recommend you turn on the **Don't show again** check box—it really is a silly message—and then click **OK**.

12. ***Select the* O.** That takes care of the *S*, now for the *O*. Click on the outline of the letter with the black arrow to select it.

13. ***Select the eyedropper tool in the toolbox.*** At this point, you could add the same drop shadow to the *O* that you added to the *S* by choosing the **Drop Shadow** command and resetting every single one of the options described in Step 11. But there's a better way: the eyedropper. Click the eyedropper icon (see Figure 4-8) or press the I key to get it.

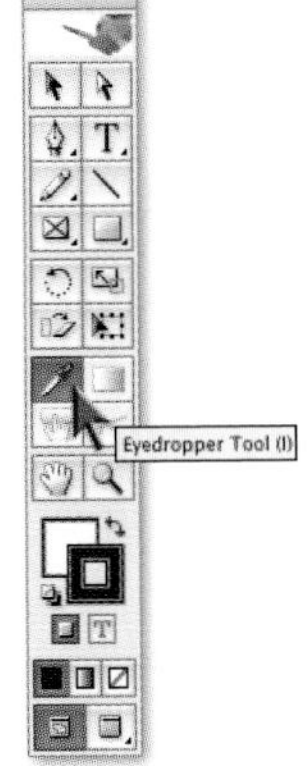

Figure 4-8.

14. ***Click the S to lift its attributes.*** Click anywhere along the outline of the *S* to copy the drop shadow from the first letter to the second. That's all it takes to transfer all those settings from one object to another.

One word of advice: You may notice that clicking with the eyedropper changes the cursor's appearance. This tells you the eyedropper is now loaded with the new settings and ready to apply them over and over to other objects. To load new settings—because you didn't quite click right on the *S*, for example—press the Alt key (or Option on the Mac) and click again. For more information on the eyedropper, see Video Lesson 5, "Duplicating Formatting Attributes" (see page 168).

---

15. ***Switch back to the type tool.*** The only remaining problem is that the type is spaced too closely to the drop caps. We'll remedy this with kerning. Press the T key to select the type tool. Then click on the *y* in *you*, right after *SO*. You should see a short insertion marker, just the height of the word *you*. (If it appears the full height of *SO*, press the → key until the blinking insertion marker becomes shorter.)

16. ***Kern the text away from the drop caps.*** Change the kerning value in the Control palette to 50. Or, assuming you changed the Kerning value in the Preferences dialog box to 5/1000 em (as I recommended in the "Formatting Shortcuts" sidebar on page 100 of Lesson 3), press Ctrl+Alt+→ (⌘-Option-→ on the Mac) twice in a row to kern *you* away from *SO*. Either way, InDesign kerns all three lines away from the drop caps in unison, as shown in Figure 4-9.

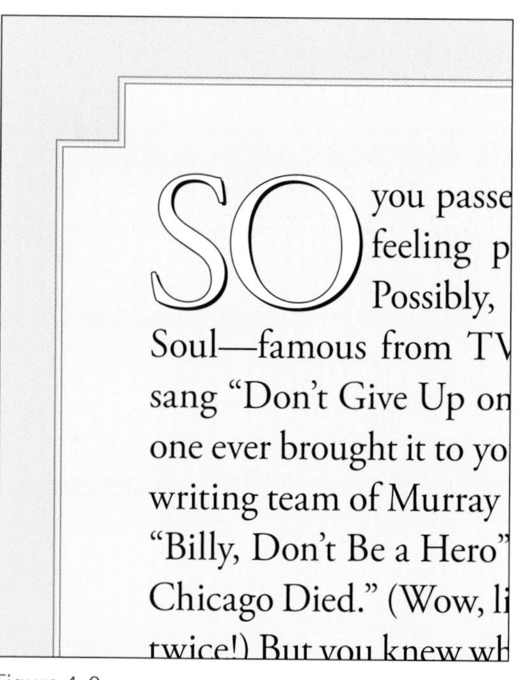

Figure 4-9.

You'll probably also want to increase the spacing between the *S* and the *O*. To do so, press the ← key twice in a row to position the insertion marker between the two graphic letters. Then press Ctrl+Alt+→ (or ⌘-Option-→) to kern them apart.

I'm a big fan of drop caps. But despite my enthusiasm, I don't use them in this particular book. (Hey, different documents call for different solutions.) Instead, each lesson begins with what are termed *initial caps*, which are nothing more than letters set in a larger type size. Initial caps require no special paragraph-level formatting. If you decide you want to make initial caps with drop shadows, however, that takes some extra work. Fortunately, that work is identical to what we did in the Extra Credit portion of the preceding exercise.

Lists and Hanging Indents

As I say, drop caps are a wonderful way to begin list entries. But the more popular method of formatting is the *hanging indent*. Introduced in Video Lesson 4, "Spaces, Indents, and Tabs," a hanging indent occurs when the first line of a paragraph extends to the left of the other lines. Another way to think of it is that all lines except the first line receive an indent. Usually, this means a number or bullet hangs off to the left, as illustrated by the formatting applied to every step in this book.

In this exercise, we'll apply hanging indents to entries in a numbered list. We'll also take a look at a special formatting option available only in InDesign, a character that goes by the name indent-to-here.

1. ***Open a document.*** Open the document *Look&Learn p122.indd*, contained in the *Lesson 04* folder inside *Lesson Files-IDcs 1on1*. As you can see in Figure 4-10, this one-page document features a seven-entry list. The entries begin with blue letters, but they could just as easily start with numbers or bullets, formatted in any typeface, size, and color you like.
2. ***Select the first lettered entry.*** Assuming that the black arrow tool is active, double-click inside the paragraph that leads off with the blue *A* to get the type tool and the blinking insertion marker.
3. ***Display the paragraph options in the Control palette.*** This time, just for variety, we'll work inside the Control palette (though you could just as easily use the Paragraph palette). Indents are a paragraph-level formatting attribute. So if the character attributes are visible, press F4 to bring up the paragraph attributes instead (assuming you loaded the Deke Keys shortcuts, as instructed on page xvii of the Preface).
4. ***Change the left indent value to 1p3.*** Note the orange guideline toward the left side of each of the two columns. If all goes according to plan—which it will, of course—the text will indent in alignment with one of the orange lines. In other words, the lines are there so we can gauge our progress.

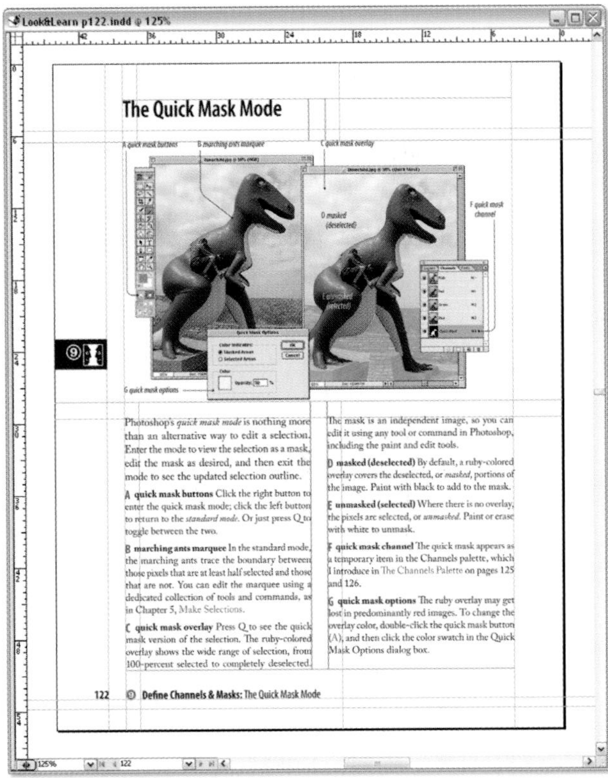

The Quick Mask Mode

Photoshop's *quick mask mode* is nothing more than an alternative way to edit a selection. Enter the mode to view the selection as a mask, edit the mask as desired, and then exit the mode to see the updated selection outline.

A quick mask buttons Click the right button to enter the quick mask mode; click the left button to return to the *standard mode*. Or just press Q to toggle between the two.

B marching ants marquee In the standard mode, the marching ants trace the boundary between those pixels that are at least half selected and those that are not. You can edit the marquee using a dedicated collection of tools and commands, as in Chapter 5, Make Selections.

C quick mask overlay Press Q to see the quick mask version of the selection. The ruby-colored overlay shows the wide range of selection, from 100-percent selected to completely deselected. The mask is an independent image, so you can edit it using any tool or command in Photoshop, including the paint and edit tools.

D masked (deselected) By default, a ruby-colored overlay covers the deselected, or *masked*, portions of the image. Paint with black to add to the mask.

E unmasked (selected) Where there is no overlay, the pixels are selected, or *unmasked*. Paint or erase with white to unmask.

F quick mask channel The quick mask appears as a temporary item in the Channels palette, which I introduce in The Channels Palette on pages 125 and 126.

G quick mask options The ruby overlay may get lost in predominantly red images. To change the overlay color, double-click the quick mask button (A), and then click the color swatch in the Quick Mask Options dialog box.

122 Define Channels & Masks: The Quick Mask Mode

Figure 4-10.

The guides happen to be spaced 15 points in from the left side of the columns. So click the ⇥≡ icon in the Control palette to highlight the left indent value. Enter 15 pt and press Tab. InDesign converts the value to 1p3 and indents the text 15 points to the left, in line with the orange guide.

To highlight the first option box in the Control palette from the keyboard, press Ctrl+6 (⌘-6 on the Mac). It's not the easiest shortcut to remember but, man, is it useful when you're trying to move quickly.

---

5. ***Change the first-line indent value to –1p3.*** Press the Tab key a second time to advance to the first-line indent value, identified by ⁺≡. This option controls the first line in the paragraph independently of all others. A positive value sends the first line rightward, resulting in a standard paragraph indent; a negative value sends the first line leftward. To align the first line with the left edge of the column, the negative first-line indent should exactly offset the left indent. So enter –1p3 and press Enter or Return. The *A* returns to the left margin, as in Figure 4-11.

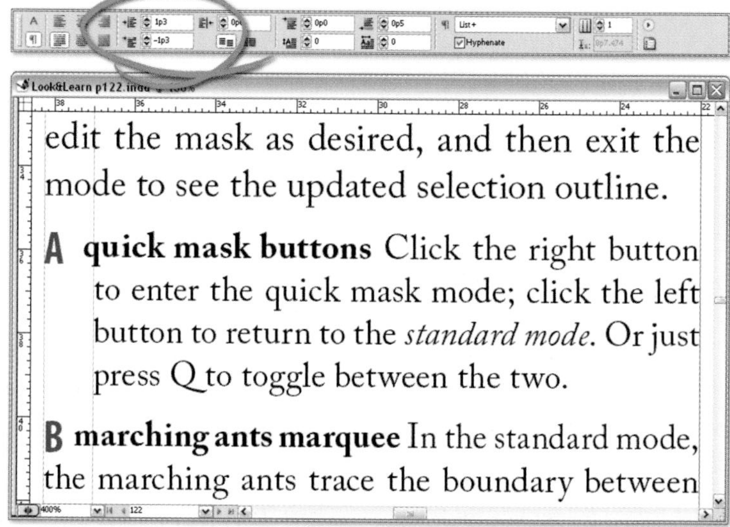

Figure 4-11.

6. ***Update the other paragraphs to match.*** All right, that takes care of one paragraph, but what about the others? Fortunately, this paragraph and most of the others are tagged with a custom style sheet that I designed in advance. I discuss style sheets in detail in Lesson 5, "Using Style Sheets." But for the present, just know this: A style sheet links a group of formatting attributes to a word or a paragraph. This way, if you change one paragraph, you can update the others to match.

To take advantage of this wonderful feature, first make sure the indented paragraph remains active, with the insertion marker blinking away. Then click the ⦿ arrow on the far right side of the Control palette to display the palette menu. Choose the **Redefine Style** command or press Ctrl+Shift+Alt+R (⌘-Shift-Option-R on the Mac). This updates the style sheet definition and changes all other entries to match, as in Figure 4-12. (Only the last entry, *G*, is not updated. We'll fix that one manually in a moment.)

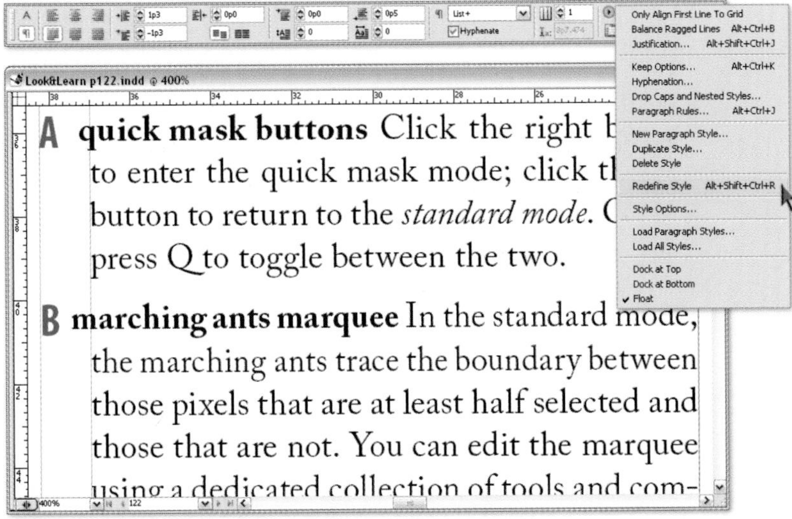

Figure 4-12.

7. ***Show all hidden characters.*** That takes care of the hanging indents, but we have some outstanding alignment problems. Ideally, the words after the big blue letters should align with the lines below them. But not only do they fail in this regard, they don't even align with each other. In Figure 4-12, for example, the bold word *quick* is a bit to the right of *marching*.

   The culprit is the spacing that I used. To see this spacing, choose **Type→Show Hidden Characters** or press Ctrl+Alt+I (⌘-Option-I). InDesign displays a series of orange dots, ¶s, and # symbols. The dots represent spaces, the ¶s are paragraph breaks, the # marks the end of a story. Two spaces follow each blue letter. Space characters can vary in width—especially in justified paragraphs—and are therefore unpredictable spacing tools. They're great for spacing one word from the next, but that's it.

PEARL OF WISDOM

Note that the spaces and ¶'s appear orange in this document because I assigned orange to this specific layer. By default, hidden characters in other documents appear light blue. To learn how to assign colors to layers, read the exercise "Creating and Using Layers" on page 343 in Lesson 9.

8. ***Replace the double spaces with tabs.*** So if spaces aren't the solution, what are? Tabs. You can set the exact width of a tab character. Better yet, tabs automatically provide exactly the proper amount of spacing inside hanging-indent lists. So do this: Select the two spaces that separate the *A* and *quick*. Then press the Tab key. In a flash, InDesign inserts a tab character and fixes the spacing, as in Figure 4-13.

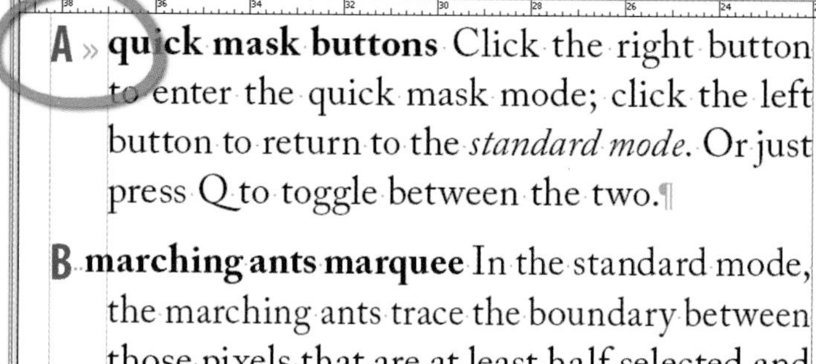

Figure 4-13.

9. ***Choose the Find/Change command.*** Of course, just because you fix one entry doesn't mean you've fixed them all. The other entries still have spaces. You could fix them manually by entering one tab at a time. Or you could search for the offending double spaces and replace them with tabs, thus saving yourself labor and time.

   To begin your search-and-replace operation, choose **Edit→Find/Change** or press the shortcut Ctrl+F (⌘-F on the Mac). InDesign displays the **Find/Change** dialog box (see Figure 4-14 on the facing page), which lets you search for one sequence of characters and replace it with another. You might not think hidden characters like spaces and tabs are searchable, in which case rejoice for I have glad news: they are.

10. ***Fill in the desired search and replace variables.*** Enter two spaces into the **Find what** option box. (The spaces are invisible, but so long as you press the spacebar twice, you'll be fine.) Then press the Tab key to advance to the **Change to** value.

    But wait a second. If pressing the Tab key advances you from one option to another, how are you supposed to enter a tab character? The answer: in code. Like Microsoft Word and other apps, InDesign uses codes to represent many invisible characters. Click the ⊙ arrow to the right of the Change To value and choose the **Tab Character** option. InDesign enters the code *^t* (see Figure 4-15), which stands for the tab character.

11. ***Click the Change All button.*** When you do, InDesign searches for all appearances of two spaces together and replaces them with a tab. A moment later, a message appears telling you that the program made 6 changes. Click **OK** to accept the message; then click the **Done** button to leave the Find/Change dialog box. Now, all the paragraphs in the list use tabs, precisely as they should.

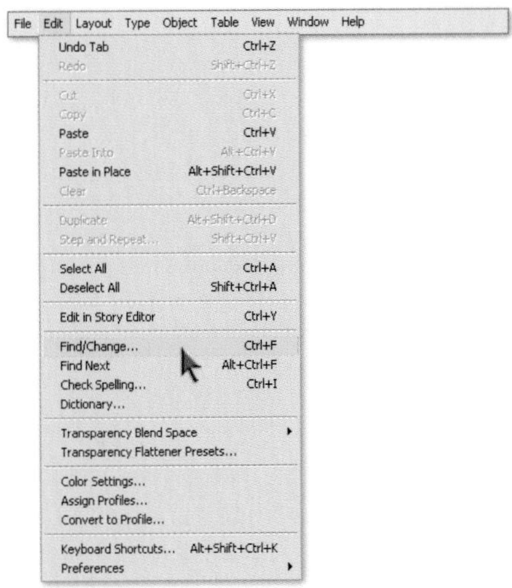

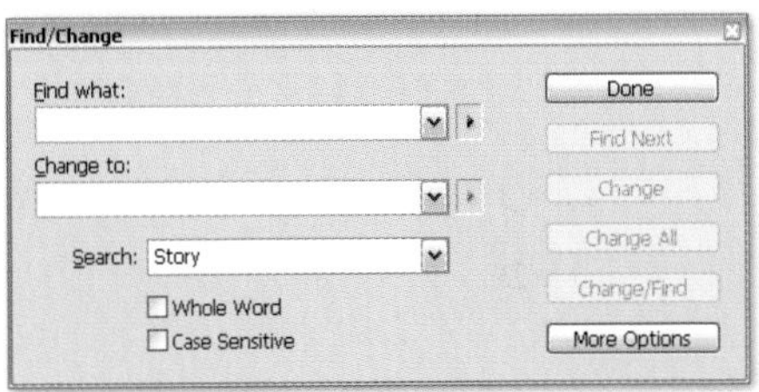

Figure 4-14.

EXTRA CREDIT

Now I want you to scroll to the last paragraph in the list. Either press Alt+spacebar (or Option-spacebar) and drag or use the scroll bars, it's up to you. When you do, you'll notice that the *G* entry remains improperly formatted. The reason: I never tagged it with the style sheet. Why ever not? So we can all enjoy the opportunity to try out that unique indenting character that I mentioned at the outset of the exercise, indent-to-here.

12. ***Click in the last paragraph with the type tool.*** This of course assumes the type tool is still active. This time, I want you to click at a specific location, directly before the *q* in the bold *quick*. This is where we'll eventually place the indent-to-here character.

13. ***Display the Tabs palette.*** In stark contrast to the other paragraphs, the tab for the final paragraph is not even slightly aligned with the orange guide. This is because, without the hanging indent, InDesign defaults to a first tab stop of 3 picas. To fix this problem, choose **Type→Tabs** or press Ctrl+Shift+T (⌘-Shift-T on the Mac) to display the slim **Tabs** palette, often known as the Tabs ruler.

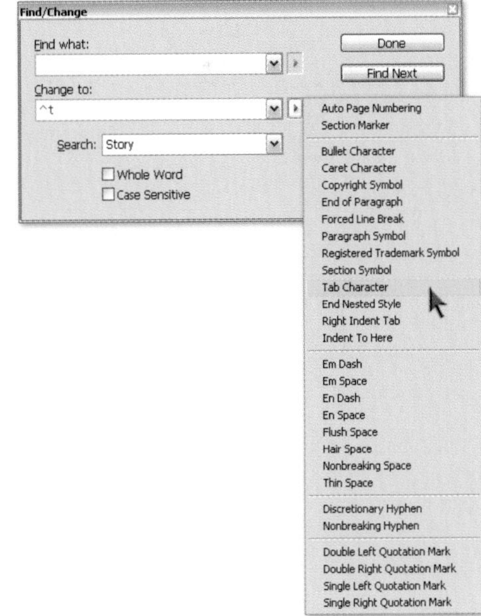

Figure 4-15.

14. ***Set a tab stop at 1p3.*** The Tabs palette lets you set the position of tab stops, which determine the exact width of tab characters. We'll get into this topic in more detail in the exercise "Setting Tabs," which begins on page 153. For now, do this:

    - Click in the strip just above the ruler at a point that looks to be a bit more than a pica in from the left side of the palette. (In all likelihood, the 1 pica mark is not labeled, so just do your best. Even if you're way off, it's fine.)

    - Select the **X** value above the ruler and change it to 1p3. Then press Enter or Return to invoke the tab stop. As shown in Figure 4-16, this exactly aligns the word *quick* with the orange guide.

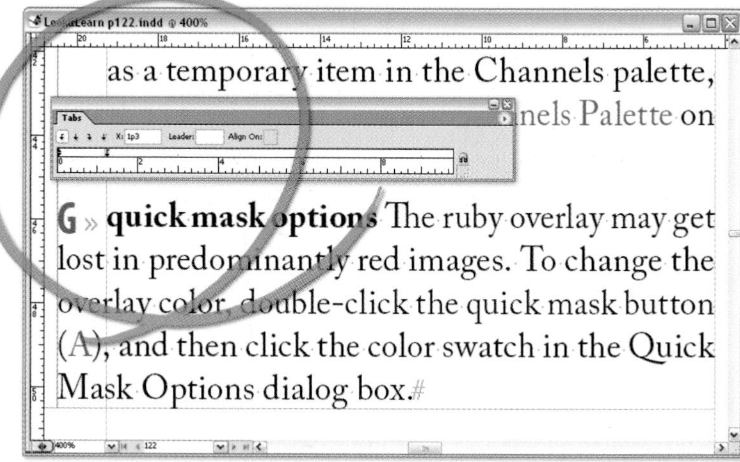

Figure 4-16.

15. ***Insert the indent-to-here character.*** Check to make sure the blinking insertion marker appears just before the *q* in *quick*. Then right-click (or if your Apple mouse offers just one button, press Control and click) to display the shortcut menu and choose **Insert Special Character→Indent to Here**. Alternatively, you can press the keyboard equivalent, Ctrl+\ (or ⌘-\). InDesign creates a new orange character called a dagger; all remaining lines in the paragraph align with that dagger (see Figure 4-17).

The downside of using the indent-to-here marker to create a hanging indent is that you can't replicate it with a style sheet, as you can using the indent options in the Control or Paragraph palette (see Step 6, page 138). The upside is that you can position the indent-to-here character absolutely anywhere and the lines below will match up. Better yet, if you edit the text or change its formatting, the indent-to-here character rolls with the punches, shifting position with the other characters.

Conclusion: Use the indent values to format multiple paragraphs in a list. Use the indent-to-here character to format a single special paragraph, especially when you want the spacing to update as you edit the text.

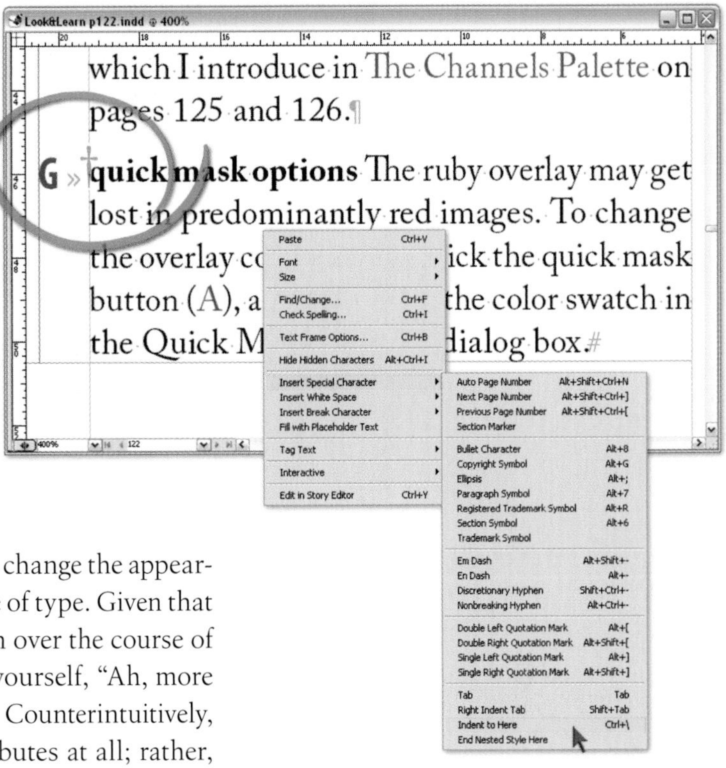

Figure 4-17.

Dashes, Spaces, and Breaks

The next functions we'll examine permit you to change the appearance of a sentence, paragraph, or longer passage of type. Given that the same can be said for everything you've seen over the course of the last lesson and a half, you might think to yourself, "Ah, more formatting attributes." But this topic is different. Counterintuitively, the features that follow aren't formatting attributes at all; rather, they are glyphs, like those I discussed in the preceding lesson.

The length of a dash, the width of a space, even how one line of type breaks to the next—these are all qualities that InDesign expresses as special characters. Some, like dashes, are defined by the typeface. The rest are brought to you by InDesign itself. Strange as it may sound, InDesign ships with its own glyphs, all of which you can use in combination with any typeface, size, or style. And they are, as a group, indispensable.

In the following steps, we'll take a three-page spread and load it up with a veritable top ten collection of dashes, spaces, and breaks. While this may sound like a strange and remote topic, it's actually the very model of practicality. I use some of these characters—em dashes, nonbreaking spaces, and line breaks—more regularly than I use many letters in the alphabet. Rarely have so many invisible characters had such a profound effect on the look of a document.

1. ***Open a multipage document.*** This time, I'd like you to open a revised version of the last document, called *Look&Learn three-pager.indd*, which you'll find in the *Lesson 04* folder inside *Lesson Files-IDcs 1on1*. Most likely, you'll see the first two pages in the document window, as in Figure 4-18 on the next page. The beige page with the dinosaur is the one we created in the previous exercise. It serves as

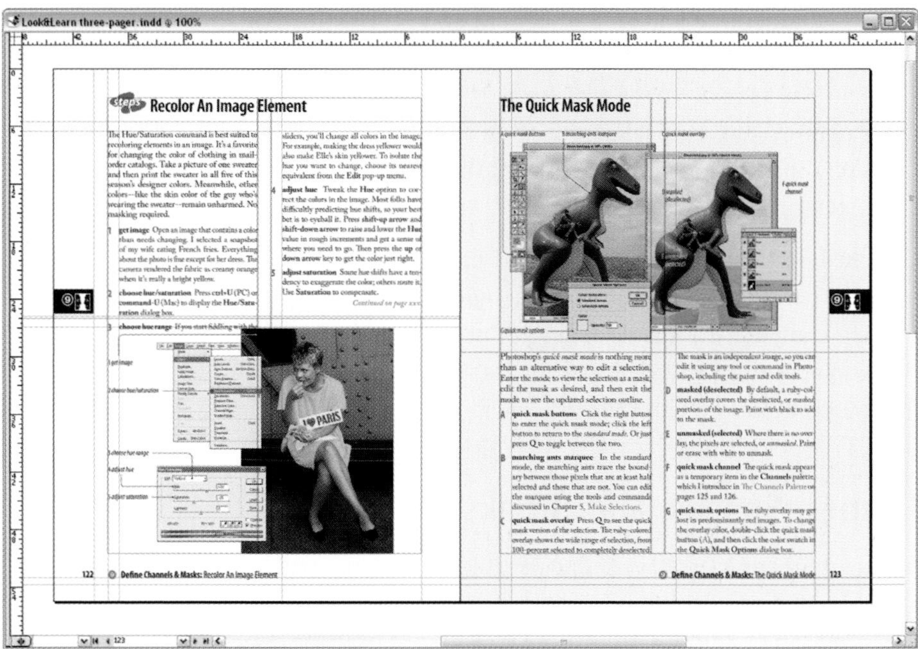

Figure 4-18.

a sidebar, breaking up the content that flows from page 122 to page 124. In examining the document, you may happen to notice a few formatting flubs, including some overlapping text blocks. If so, good eye; we'll remedy all problems in the upcoming steps.

2. ***Select one of the two double hyphen combinations.*** Zoom in on the first paragraph on page 122 (the first page). Notice that the second-to-last sentence—the one that begins *Meanwhile*—contains two pairs of consecutive hyphens, each highlighted in Figure 4-19 on the facing page. These double hyphens are stand-ins for long dashes, commonly used to offset descriptive or parenthetical phrases in a sentence. Were this a piece of plain-text email, I would regard such uses of double hyphens as the height of grammatical decorum. But it ain't, so they ain't either. In the realm of professional typesetting, the better solution is the *em dash*, so-called because it extends the full width of a capital *M*, roughly as long as the type size is tall.

One brief pet peeve: Never, *ever* use a lone hyphen in place of a dash. A lone hyphen is used to hyphenate a word onto separate lines or join multiple words into a compound word. It is never used to separate a phrase from the rest of its sentence.

Now that I've finished haranguing you on the subject of hyphenation etiquette, get the type tool and select one of the hyphen pairs so we can set about replacing it.

3. ***Replace the double hyphens with em dashes.*** Right-click in the document window (or on the Mac, press Control and click) to display the shortcut menu. Then choose **Insert Special Character** to display a submenu. Midway down are four dash and hyphen commands, which work like so:

   - The Em Dash command inserts a long dash, suitable for punctuating inset phrases like ours.
   - The next command, En Dash, creates a slightly narrower dash, ideal for making minus signs.
   - Choose Discretionary Hyphen to change where InDesign breaks a word. As explained in the upcoming Step 6, this character shows up only when it's needed. If you edit the text and the word fits completely on one line, the hyphen disappears.
   - Nonbreaking Hyphen prohibits InDesign from breaking a compound word at the hyphen. We'll see this one in use in the very next step.

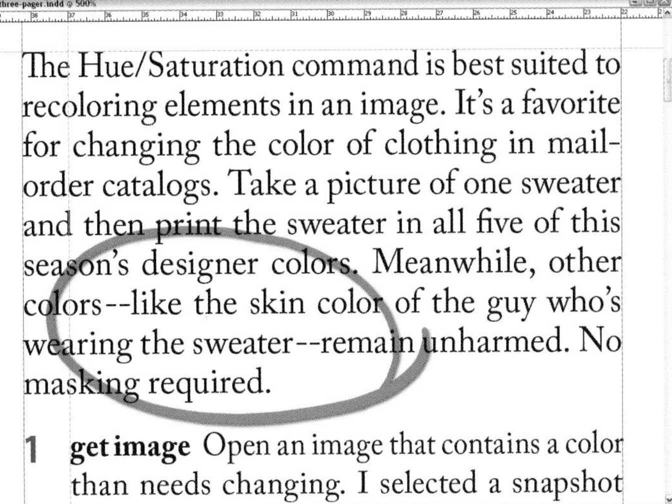

Figure 4-19.

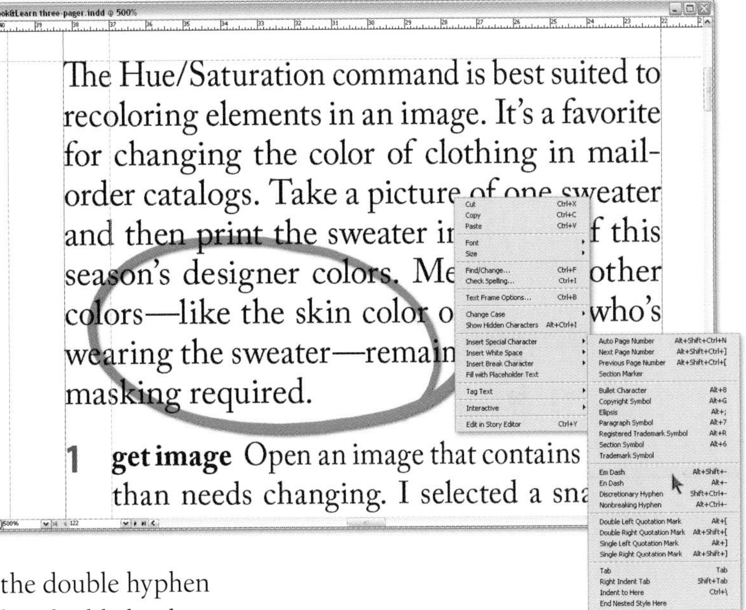

Figure 4-20.

Choose the **Em Dash** command to replace the double hyphen with a proper long dash. Then select the other double hyphen and replace it using the keyboard shortcut, Shift+Alt+⊟ (Shift-Option-⊟ on the Mac). Both methods deliver the em dash defined by the active font, as pictured in Figure 4-20. (You may notice that my em dashes are "closed," or tight to the text that surrounds them. This is the custom of most publications, although some prefer to surround the em dash with spaces.)

4. ***Replace the standard hyphen with a nonbreaking hyphen.*** Toward the top of this very same paragraph—just three lines down on the right—is the compound word *mail-order* broken

onto two lines. Although there's nothing inherently wrong with InDesign busting up a compound word, in this case, I think it interrupts the flow. For example, when I read *mail-* on one line, I don't expect to see *order* pop up on the next. Makes me wonder if I skipped a line, which slows me down and ultimately impairs the legibility of the document. Fortunately, we can tell InDesign to keep both parts of the word together, as follows:

- Select the hyphen after *mail*.
- Right-click to display the shortcut menu. Then choose **Insert Special Character→Nonbreaking Hyphen**.

Or you could press the keyboard shortcut Ctrl+Alt+⊟ (⌘-Option-⊟). InDesign spreads the text and knocks the whole of *mail-order* to the fourth line.

5. ***Break the word* of *to the next line.*** In the previous lesson, I spoke of the wonders of InDesign's Paragraph Composer, which attempts to balance the spacing from one line of type to the next. Usually, it works splendidly. But the nonbreaking hyphen has thrown it for a loop. Now we have four loosely spaced lines followed by rather packed fifth and sixth lines. The solution is to balance the spacing manually.

   With the type tool, click directly in front of the word *of* at the end of the fifth line. Then press the Backspace or Delete key to delete the preceding space, so that *fiveof* runs together. Now try each of the following:

   - Press the Enter or Return key. InDesign invokes a new paragraph, complete with a short fifth line followed by a generous supply of paragraph spacing, as in Figure 4-21. (Note that I've turned on Show Hidden Characters so we can see the paragraph breaks and other invisibles.)
   - This is obviously the wrong solution, so press Ctrl+Z (or ⌘-Z) to undo.
   - Now for the right solution: Right-click to display the shortcut menu and choose **Insert Break Character→Forced Line Break**. InDesign adds a *line break* that knocks the word *of* to the next line without starting a new paragraph. The appearance is therefore one of a single paragraph with more uniform spacing, as in Figure 4-22.

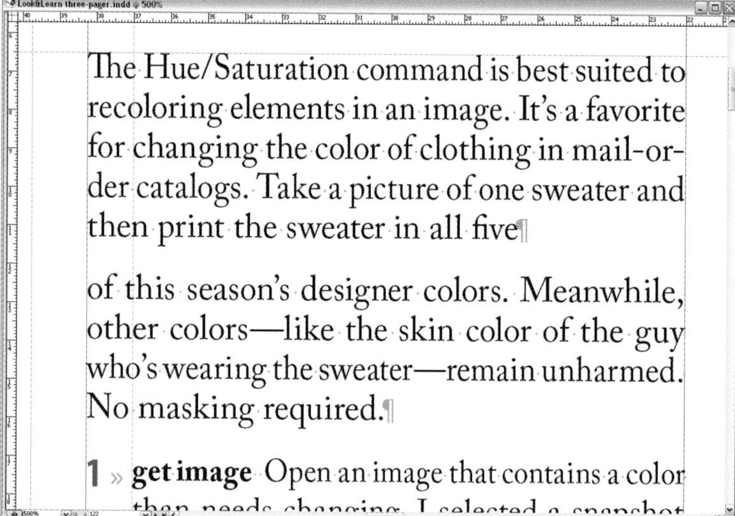

Figure 4-21.

The immensely useful line break character includes its own keyboard shortcut, one common to other page-layout and word-processing programs, and I recommend you assign it to memory. Fortunately, it's easy: Shift+Enter (Shift-Return on the Mac).

6. ***Add a discretionary hyphen.*** Scroll down a few paragraphs to step 2 in the text. Notice the way the bold command name breaks at the end of the second line (*Hue/Satu-ration*). Personally, I'm not too fond of it, so let's move that hyphen to a different spot using a *discretionary hyphen*.

   - Click with the type tool between *ra* and *tion* at the beginning of the third line.
   - Right-click (or Control-click) and choose **Insert Special Character→Discretionary Hyphen**, or press Ctrl+Shift+⊟ (⌘-Shift-⊟ on the Mac). InDesign shifts the hyphen so the word breaks as *Hue/Satura-tion*.

   Now for a bit of hypothetical. Let's say at this point, you decide to modify the sentence. Click immediately after the word *the* that precedes *Hue/Satura-tion*. Then press the spacebar and type the word "familiar." The text now reads *the familiar Hue/Saturation dialog box* without any hyphenation whatsoever. That's the beauty of the discretionary hyphen—it thoughtfully disappears when not needed so as not to leave an extraneous hyphen in the middle of a line of type.

Figure 4-22.

7. ***Break step 3 to the next column.*** Just below these lines, you may notice that step 3 in the text overlaps the graphic below it. Somehow, I've clumsily permitted the text frame to dip too low. Naturally, I could select the frame with the black arrow tool and drag the bottom handle up a bit to force a column break. But so long as we're in the text edit mode, let's try a different solution.

   Click in front of the big blue 3. Right-click (or Control-click) and choose **Insert Break Character**. The commands at the top of this submenu work as follows:

   - The Column Break command forces the text after the blinking insertion marker to the next column in a multicolumn text block, like the master frame that I demonstrated in Video Lesson 2, "Text and Frames" (see page 48).
   - The more useful Frame Break command moves the text to the next frame in the story.
   - To bypass all remaining frames on this page and send the text to the next page, you'd choose the Page Break command. Other commands move the text to the next odd or even page.

   The best way to move step 3 to the top of the next column is to choose the **Frame Break** command. (As it turns out, Column Break delivers the same result, but it could create problems in the unlikely event that you later decided to add columns to the text block.) Or press Shift+Enter on the numerical keypad. Either way, you end up with the results pictured in the zoomed out Figure 4-23.

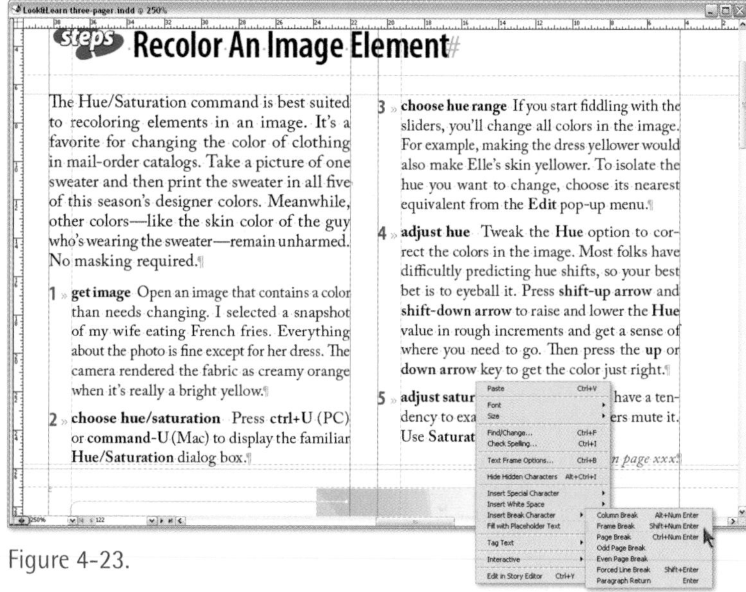

Figure 4-23.

PEARL OF WISDOM

Now we shift our attention from dashes and breaks to spaces. If you peer closely at the bold text at the outset of each step in the sample file, you'll notice it ends with two spaces. As I've intimated, consecutive spaces are bad form, even at the end of sentences. In professional typesetting, just one space character separates a sentence from its successor. The idea is that two spaces result in a gap that impedes legibility. Besides, the sentence ends with a period; what do you need multiple spaces for? But this bold text is different. Termed a *run-in head*, the bold text demands a larger space. And a larger but more predictable space we will give it.

---

8. ***Replace a pair of double spaces with an en space.*** Select any old pair of spaces. For my part, I select the spaces that follow the bold text in step 3. Then right-click (or Control-click) and choose **Insert White Space**. InDesign displays a long list of *fixed-width spaces*, which the program does not alter to suit the alignment or spacing of a paragraph. Here's how the space characters work, in logical order:

    - You can think of an *em space* as being roughly as wide as a capital letter *M*. More precisely, it's exactly as wide as the type size is tall. It also happens to be the space on which many of the other fixed-width spaces are based.
    - An *en space* is ½ as wide as an em space, making it approximately equal in width to a typical lowercase letter.
    - The *figure space* is exactly as wide as a number, making it well suited to spacing numbers in a table. In most fonts, the figure space is nearly equivalent to an en space.
    - The *punctuation space* matches the thickness of an exclamation point in the prevailing typeface.
    - Thinner than the punctuation space is the *thin space*, which is ¼ as wide as an en space, or ⅛ as wide as an em space. Hence, it tends to be about half as wide as a lowercase *i*.
    - If you want to shave a gap even thinner, the *hair space* is just ⅓ as thick as the thin space, or 1/24 an em space. You may find the hair space useful for offsetting punctuation (such as an em dash) that otherwise crowds neighboring characters.
    - The *nonbreaking space* matches the width of a standard space character, and may even vary in width to suit the spacing needs of a justified paragraph. But it will not break from one line to the next.

- The other variable-width space character is the *flush space*, which grows to fill all the excess space in the last line of a justified paragraph. InDesign aligns the word or character that follows the flush space with the right side of the column, helpful when spacing end-of-paragraph ornaments.

I want you to choose the **En Space** command. Or press the keyboard shortcut Ctrl+Shift+N (⌘-Shift-N on the Mac).

9. ***Search and replace the other double space combos.*** Just as you can search and replace tabs, you can search and replace every special character covered in this exercise. Choose **Edit→Find/Change** or press Ctrl+F (⌘-F). Then do the following:

   - Enter two spaces into the **Find what** option box.
   - Press the Tab key to advance to the **Change to** option.
   - Click the ⊙ arrow to the right of the option and choose **En Space**. InDesign enters the cryptic code ^>, as in Figure 4-24.
   - Click the **Change All** button. After InDesign announces that it's made 10 changes, click **OK**.
   - Click the **Done** button to exit the dialog box.

   Every step now features an en space that divides the bold run-in heads from the plain text that follows. In many cases, the en spaces are roughly equivalent to two standard spaces apiece. But because the en spaces are fixed-width characters, they are consistent in width from one step to the next.

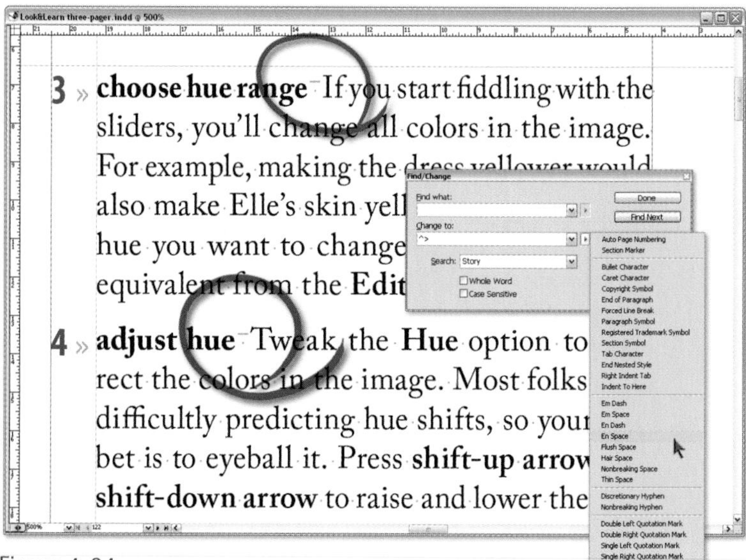

Figure 4-24.

10. ***Prevent one or more words from breaking.*** Moving right along, scroll to the hyphenated word at the end of the first line in step 4, which should read *cor-rect*. This isn't a bad break, but it does result in overly loose spacing in the first line. Fortunately, you can instruct InDesign not to break one or more words. And it's the one time in this exercise that we'll apply a formatting attribute:

    - Double-click on the word *cor-rect* to select it.
    - In the Control palette, make sure the character-level attributes are visible. (If they aren't, click the 🄰 or press F4.)
    - Click the ⊙ arrow on the far right end of the palette to bring up the palette menu. Then choose **No Break**. With that, InDesign deletes the hyphen and squeezes the word *correct* onto the first line. And as fortune would have it, it fits just fine, as you can see in Figure 4-25.

    The No Break command is equally useful for binding together several words. It is so useful, in fact, that I've given it a keyboard shortcut. If you loaded my Deke Keys shortcuts (see page xvii of the Preface), press Ctrl+Alt+N (⌘-Option-N on the Mac).

11. ***Add a page number to the* Continued *reference.*** Scroll farther down the column to the end of step 5 and the italic blue *Continued* item. Note that the reference ends with the placeholder *xxx*, which I routinely use to stand in for page numbers that I fill in after the chapter is laid out. But InDesign is capable of updating some kinds of page number references automatically, and this turns out to be one of them.

    Double-click inside the italic blue *xxx* to select it. Then right-click and choose **Insert Special Character**. The first four commands add page number variables that InDesign forevermore updates automatically:

    - The Auto Page Number command adds the number assigned to the active page. You can use this very handy command to add folios, as I explain in the "Page Numbers and Sections" exercise, which begins on page 327 in Lesson 9.

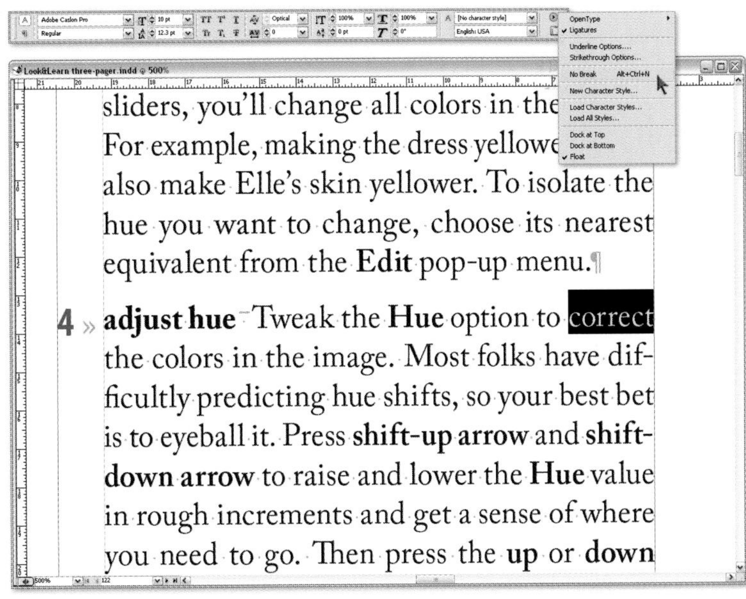

Figure 4-25.

- Choosing Next Page Number or Previous Page Number adds the number of the page that contains the next or previous linked frame in the active story. This may or may not be an adjacent page in the document. These are the commands you use to complete *Continued on* and *Continued from* references.
- The final command, Section Marker, recalls any Section Marker text you may have entered into the Numbering & Section Options dialog box. Again, I explain this in the "Page Numbers and Sections" exercise in Lesson 9.

Therefore, choose **Next Page Number** or press the long shortcut Ctrl+Shift+Alt+] (on the Mac, ⌘-Shift-Option-]). As illustrated in Figure 4-26, InDesign replaces the *xxx* with *124*, which is not the next page number but the one after. Just as it should be, InDesign is smart enough to know which page contains the rest of the story.

Bear in mind, InDesign treats each of these options as very real, if occasionally invisible, characters. (The one exception is the No Break command, which is a formatting attribute.) This means that once created, you can copy the character, paste it in a new location, change its formatting, or even delete it. This goes not only for line breaks, special spaces, and discretionary hyphens, but also for the tab and indent-to-here characters from the previous exercise. Just turn on Type→Show Hidden Characters to see the invisible glyphs, and then edit away.

Figure 4-26.

Setting Tabs

Remember typewriters, those clattering, monitorless contraptions that were all the rage not so very long ago? Although about one-millionth as capable as computers, they had the distinct advantage of being input and output devices all in one. There wasn't much mystery, because what you typed was what you got. Take tables, for example. If you were an adept typist, you knew how to set tab stops on your typewriter, thereby permitting you to exactly align table entries by pressing the Tab key. If you were a complete novice, you could accomplish the same thing with a bit more effort by tapping the spacebar a dozen or so times in a row. It was by no means an exact science—one too many taps would throw your columns out of alignment—but it worked.

Not so in InDesign. Unless you use Courier or some other monospaced font, all characters—including spaces—are slightly different in width. And when text is justified, a space character in one line of type is different than a space character in the next. In other words, using the spacebar to align text is a recipe for disaster. And setting tab stops isn't a best practice; it's the *least* you should do. Tables set in InDesign look a heck of a lot better than tables created on a typewriter, but they require a more deliberate approach as well.

In the following steps, you'll format a table entry by setting and adjusting tab stops in the Tabs palette. Just for fun, you'll also learn how to use paragraph rules to improve the legibility of rows. Suffice it to say, if you've ever even considered aligning columns with spaces, this exercise is for you.

Selection shortcuts 1.indd @ 100%

Selection Shortcuts

Making and manipulating selections rank among Photoshop's most fundamental operations. In addition to the selection-related shortcuts that appear in Menu Command Shortcuts on page 282—including **Select All, Deselect, Reselect,** and **Feather**—Photoshop offers a number of shortcuts dedicated to creating and manipulating selection outlines. Use the shortcuts in the following table to quickly move, combine, modify, and clone selections from the keyboard.

selection task	windows shortcut	macintosh shortcut
draw marquee from center outward	alt-drag	option-drag
constrain marquee to square or circle	shift-drag	shift-drag
move marquee as you draw it	spacebar-drag	spacebar-drag
add corner to straight-sided selection	alt-click with lasso tool	option-click with lasso tool
lock down point in magnetic selection	click with lasso tool	click with lasso tool
delete last point in magnetic selection	backspace	delete
tighten or spread magnetic radius	bracket key, [or]	bracket key, [or]
close lasso outline	enter or double-click	return or double-click
...with straight segment	alt+enter	option-return
cancel polygon lasso outline	escape	escape
add to outline with selection tool	shift-drag/shift-click	shift-drag/shift-click
subtract from outline	alt-drag/alt-click	option-drag/option-click
retain intersection of outlines	shift+alt-drag	shift-option-drag
select move tool	V or ctrl	V or command
move selection outline	drag	drag
move selected pixels (any tool)	ctrl-drag	command-drag
constrain movement	shift-drag	shift-drag
nudge outline	arrow/shift+arrow	arrow/shift-arrow
nudge pixels	ctrl+arrow	command-arrow
clone selected pixels	ctrl+alt-drag	command-option-drag
nudge and clone	ctrl+alt+arrow	command-option-arrow
move outline to other image window	drag & drop	drag & drop
move selected pixels to other image	ctrl+drag & drop	command-drag & drop
paste image into selection	ctrl+shift+V	command-shift-V
paste image behind selection	ctrl+shift+alt+V	command-shift-option-V
change opacity of floating selection	ctrl+shift+F	command-shift-F
hide selection outline	ctrl+H	command-H
insert point into path (pen tool)	click segment	click segment
delete anchor point from selected path	click point	click point
convert anchor point in selected path	alt-click/alt-drag point	opt-click/opt-drag point
convert work path to selection outline	ctrl+enter	command-return

Essential Shortcuts 279

Figure 4-27.

1. ***Open a document that contains a table.*** Open the file called *Selection shortcuts 1.indd*, which you'll find in the *Lesson 04* folder inside *Lesson Files-IDcs 1on1*. Pictured in Figure 4-27, this page shows a bunch of keyboard shortcuts for selecting images in Photoshop. The table looks pretty nice until you get about a third of the way down, where you come to a row that begins *close lasso outline*. For one thing, this row should be blue. For another, it's out of alignment with everything else in the table. Our job is to remedy both of these problems in the most expedient manner possible.

2. ***Show the hidden characters.*** This table is constructed with tabs. But because tabs are invisible, we can't see them. Fortunately, InDesign let's you view tabs as special, non-printing characters. To view the hidden characters lurking inside the table, I first suggest you zoom in on the middle

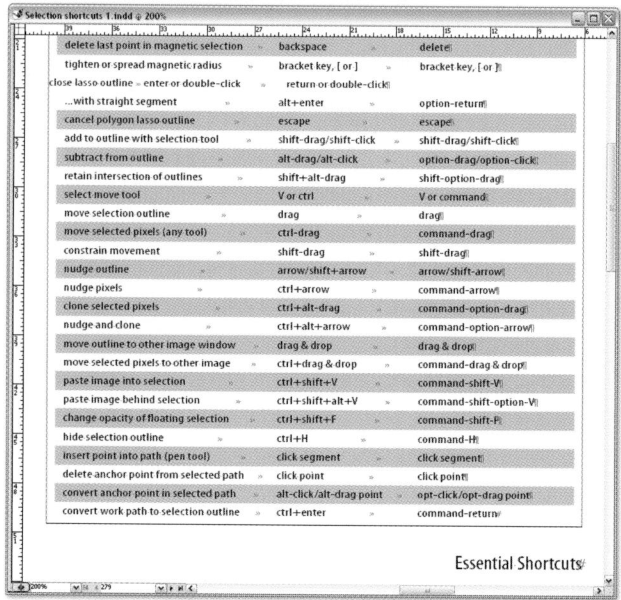

delete last point in magnetic selection	backspace	delete
tighten or spread magnetic radius	bracket key, [or]	bracket key, [or]
close lasso outline » enter or double-click	return or double-click	
...with straight segment	alt+enter	option-return
cancel polygon lasso outline	escape	escape
add to outline with selection tool	shift-drag/shift-click	shift-drag/shift-click
subtract from outline	alt-drag/alt-click	option-drag/option-click
retain intersection of outlines	shift+alt-drag	shift-option-drag
select move tool	V or ctrl	V or command
move selection outline	drag	drag
move selected pixels (any tool)	ctrl-drag	command-drag
constrain movement	shift-drag	shift-drag
nudge outline	arrow/shift+arrow	arrow/shift-arrow
nudge pixels	ctrl+arrow	command-arrow
clone selected pixels	ctrl+alt-drag	command-option-drag
nudge and clone	ctrl+alt+arrow	command-option-arrow
move outline to other image window	drag & drop	drag & drop
move selected pixels to other image	ctrl+drag & drop	command-drag & drop
paste image into selection	ctrl+shift+V	command-shift-V
paste image behind selection	ctrl+shift+alt+V	command-shift-option-V
change opacity of floating selection	ctrl+shift+F	command-shift-F
hide selection outline	ctrl+H	command-H
insert point into path (pen tool)	click segment	click segment
delete anchor point from selected path	click point	click point
convert anchor point in selected path	alt-click/alt-drag point	opt-click/opt-drag point
convert work path to selection outline	ctrl+enter	command-return

Essential Shortcuts

Figure 4-28.

delete last point in magnetic selection	backspace
tighten or spread magnetic radius	bracket key, [or]
close lasso outline » enter or double-click	return or double-click
...with straight segment	alt+enter
cancel polygon lasso outline	escape

Figure 4-29.

delete last point in magnetic selection	backspace
tighten or spread magnetic radius	bracket key, [or]
close lasso outline	enter or double-click
...with straight segment	alt+enter
cancel polygon lasso outline	escape

Figure 4-30.

portion of the table. Then choose **Type→Show Hidden Characters** or press Ctrl+Alt+I (⌘-Option-I on the Mac). As in Figure 4-28, the document becomes peppered with little red symbols that indicate the various invisible characters. The »s are tabs.

3. ***Position the insertion marker after a wayward tab.*** Press T to select the type tool and click between the first tab character and the word *enter* in the misaligned row. Figure 4-29 shows exactly where the insertion marker should be.

4. ***Press the Tab key.*** We want to align the *enter or double-click* entry with the second column, directly below *bracket key, [or]*. Since you can align columns using tab characters, you just need to press Tab a few times to bring the text into alignment, right? So give it a try:

   - Pressing Tab once isn't far enough.
   - Pressing Tab a second time still doesn't do the trick.
   - As Figure 4-30 shows, pressing Tab a third time overshoots the column.

   Why didn't the tabs work? Because a tab character doesn't describe an exact position on the page; it merely moves the text to the next column increment, known as a *tab stop*. Although we can't see these tab stops yet, it's obvious that the neatly aligned rows in this table are obeying a different set of tab stops than the active row. Therefore, to fix the errant row, we need to adjust the tab stops, not heap on more tab characters.

5. ***Delete the three extra tabs.*** As you can see, entering excess tab characters doesn't do any good. So as a rule of thumb, use no more than one tab character in a row. We now have four consecutive tab characters; to delete the excess three, press Backspace or Delete three times in a row. (Don't delete all four tabs; we still need one!)

6. ***Display the Tabs ruler.*** To gain access to the all-important tab stops, we need to bring up the Tabs palette. To do just that, choose **Type→Tabs** or press

Ctrl+Shift+T (⌘-Shift-T on the Mac). Pictured in Figure 4-31, the palette features a small handful of options and a horizontal ruler. This ruler is where you position your tab stops.

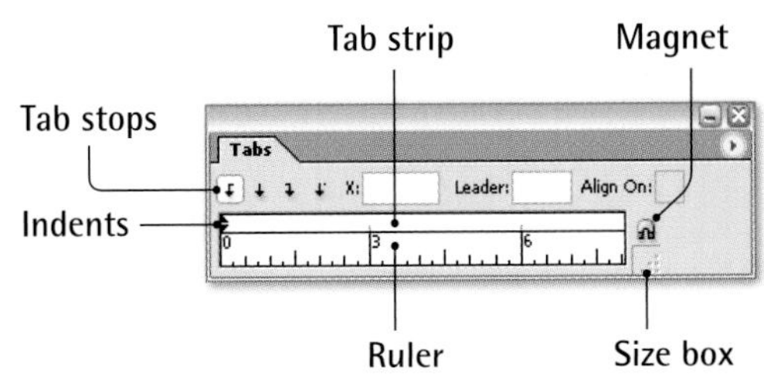

Figure 4-31.

7. ***Align the Tabs ruler to the text that you want to modify.*** Most likely, InDesign centered the Tabs palette on your screen. But to truly be useful, the palette ruler needs to line up with the text that you want to modify. One way to align the ruler to the text is to manually drag the palette to the top of the screen and expand it by dragging the size box in the lower-right corner. Another way is to have InDesign align the palette automatically, which is the purpose of the magnet icon (⋒). Bad news: the magnet is notoriously finicky. Good news: it's great when it works, so here goes:

   - Make sure the ⋒ icon is active. If it isn't, click in the text again with the type tool.
   - Once you have an active ⋒, go ahead and click it. Nothing happens; the Tabs palette just sits there like a slug. That's because the infuriating ⋒ needs to be able to see the top of a text block before it can align to it. Idiotic, frankly, but who can argue with a palette?
   - Turns out, the Tabs palette needs not only to see the top of the text block but also sufficient room above the block to place itself. What a diva! Scroll up so that you can see at least an inch of the document above the top of the table.
   - Click the ⋒ again. As if by magic, the Tabs ruler stretches and snaps to the top of the frame, as in Figure 4-32.

Now that the Tabs palette is properly aligned, you can scroll up or down in the document window all you want. So remember, when auto-aligning the Tabs ruler, make the ⋒ happy, and *then* make yourself happy.

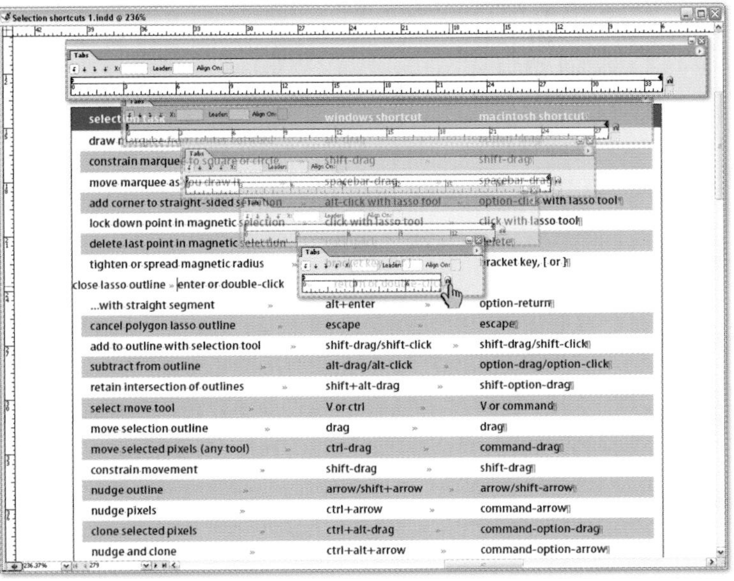

Figure 4-32.

8. ***Indent the row to the left 1 pica.*** Notice the pair of triangles (▸) above the 0 in the Tabs ruler. Of the two, the top triangle sets the first-line indent; the bottom triangle sets the overall left indent. In this table, every row is its own paragraph, so moving either triangle produces the same results.

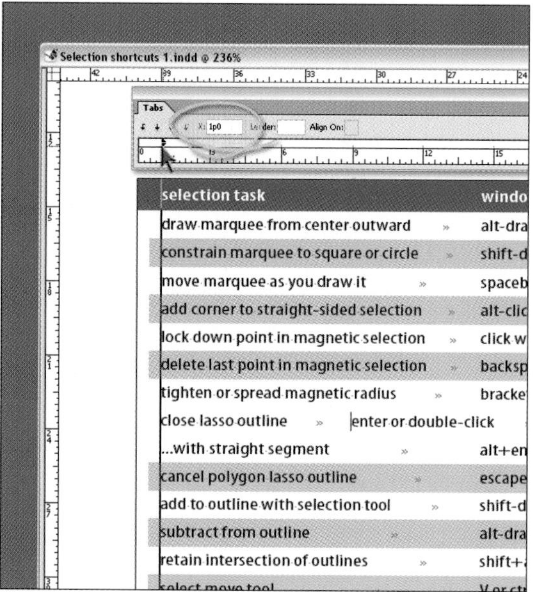

Figure 4-33.

Here's what I want you to do: Drag the bottom triangle to the right exactly 1 pica. You can track the movement on the ruler, with the help of the vertical guideline that drops down into the document window, or by keeping an eye on the **X** value above the ruler in the Tabs palette. Figure 4-33 shows the guideline and X value at work.

When you drag the bottom triangle, the top first-line triangle travels along for the ride. However, you can drag the bottom triangle independently. Just press the Shift key and drag it. The result is a hanging indent, like the one we reviewed earlier in the exercise "Lists and Hanging Indents," which began on page 137.

---

9. ***Set a tab stop at 14p6.*** Now to set some tab stops. Click somewhere near the 12-pica point in the space directly above the ruler. A tab stop appears at this position. This specific variety of tab stop, which looks like ↡, is called a *left-justified tab* because the left side of the entry (in our case, *enter or double-click*) aligns to it. Drag the tab stop so that the entry aligns with the second column in the table; the X value should read 14p6, as in Figure 4-34.

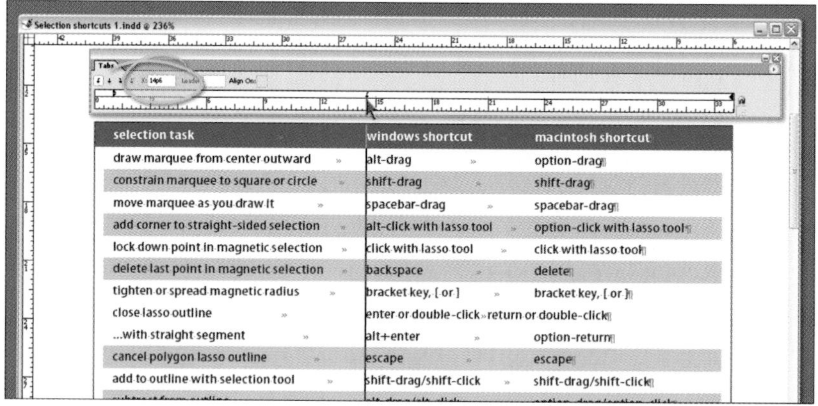

Figure 4-34.

Although we'll be sticking to left-justified tabs in this table, there are other ways to align columns. To apply a different alignment option, click one of the icons in the top-left corner of the palette while a tab stop is active. For your general edification, here's how the icons work:

- The center-justified tab (↓) centers the entry (such as *enter or double-click*) below the tab stop.
- The right-justified tab (↴) aligns the right edge of the entry with the tab.

- The decimal tab (↓) aligns the entry at a character specified in the Align On option box. This setting is most frequently used to align a column of numbers by the decimal point, which is why the default Align On value is a period.

To cycle through the different types of tabs, Alt-click (or Option-click) the tab stop in the strip above the ruler.

---

10. ***Set another tab stop at 23p6.*** Click in the strip above the ruler to the right of the existing tab stop to create another one. The *return or double-click* entry jumps into alignment. Notice that the new stop is surrounded by a gray or colored rectangle; this indicates that the stop selected, which permits you to reposition the stop numerically. Select the **X** value and change it to 23p6. Then press the Enter or Return key. This aligns the entry with the third row, as in Figure 4-35.

As a side tip, you may notice that you can't press Backspace or Delete to delete a tab stop, even if it's selected. Instead, you have to drag the tab stop out of the Tabs palette. To delete all tab stops, choose Clear All from the palette menu.

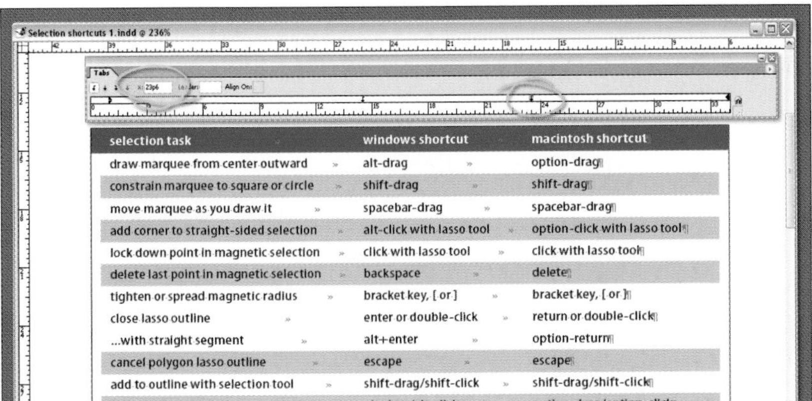

selection task	windows shortcut	macintosh shortcut
draw marquee from center outward	alt-drag	option-drag
constrain marquee to square or circle	shift-drag	shift-drag
move marquee as you draw it	spacebar-drag	spacebar-drag
add corner to straight-sided selection	alt-click with lasso tool	option-click with lasso tool
lock down point in magnetic selection	click with lasso tool	click with lasso tool
delete last point in magnetic selection	backspace	delete
tighten or spread magnetic radius	bracket key, [or]	bracket key, [or]
close lasso outline	enter or double-click	return or double-click
...with straight segment	alt+enter	option-return
cancel polygon lasso outline	escape	escape
add to outline with selection tool	shift-drag/shift-click	shift-drag/shift-click

Figure 4-35.

PEARL OF WISDOM

Before we depart the Tabs palette, you should know about one more option. The Leader option lets you specify a *tab leader*, which is a series of characters that fills the space between the entry before a tab and the entry after a tab. A common example of a tab leader is a series of repeating periods between, say, a chapter name and page number in a table of contents. To create a tab leader, simply select a tab stop, type one or more characters in the Leader option box, and press Enter or Return.

11. ***Choose the Paragraph Rules command.*** Our final task is to create the blue background that should appear in the newly-aligned row. So click the ¶ icon in the Control palette to bring up the paragraph options. Then click the ⊙ arrow on the right side of the palette and choose the **Paragraph Rules** command, or press Ctrl+Alt+J (⌘-Option-J on the Mac). InDesign responds by displaying the **Paragraph Rules** dialog box. Rather than providing a list of rules concerning paragraphs, this dialog box lets you place a straight line (or *rule*) above, below, or even behind the paragraphs in your document.

12. ***Turn on the paragraph rule and adjust the settings.*** Look at Figure 4-36 to see exactly how I want you to set the options in the Paragraph Rules dialog box. Here's the low-down:

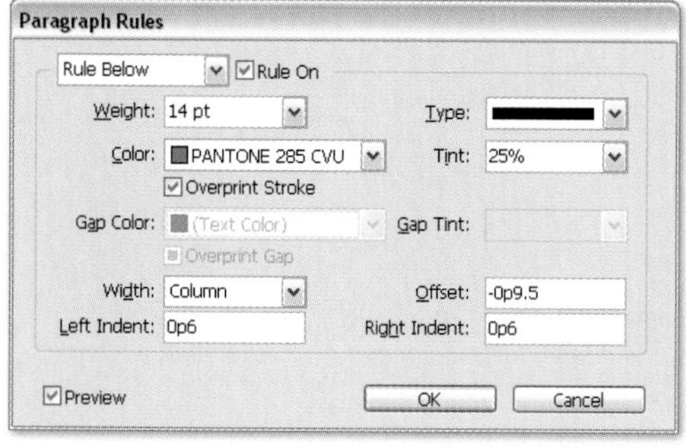

Figure 4-36.

- First turn on the **Preview** check box so you can see what you're doing.
- Select **Rule Below** from the pop-up menu in the upper-left corner of the dialog box. Then turn on the **Rule On** check box. At this point, all the remaining work may be done for you, but it's worth running through the rest of the options to see how they work.
- **Weight** controls how heavy the rule will be; set this value to 14 points.
- The **Type** pop-up lets you select from different line patterns. Choose **Solid** for a plain, unbroken rule.
- From the **Color** pop-up menu, choose **Pantone 285 CVU**, which is a spot color that I added to this document. Reduce the **Tint** value to 25 percent to create a light version of the color that won't interfere with the legibility of the table entries.
- Turn on **Overprint Stroke** to make sure the blue rule and the black text blend together. Technically, this setting is redundant—black is set to overprint by default in InDesign—but if the person printing my document goes and turns black overprinting off, I want to be covered.
- The **Width** option determines how far the rule extends across the row; set this to **Column**.
- **Offset** determines where the rule will appear in relation to the baseline of the text. Counterintuitively, positive values lower the rule and negative values raise it. Enter –0p9.5 to

raise the rule so it appears behind the text rather than below it.

- Set both **Indent** options to 0p6 to scoot the rule 6 points in on the left and right sides.

13. ***Accept the rule and save the document.*** Click the **OK** button to accept the new blue rule. As Figure 4-37 shows, the wayward row has finally joined the fold. We'll continue working on this document in the next exercise, so you might as well take a moment and save your work. Choose **File→Save As**, name your document "My table.indd," and save it in the *Lesson 04* folder.

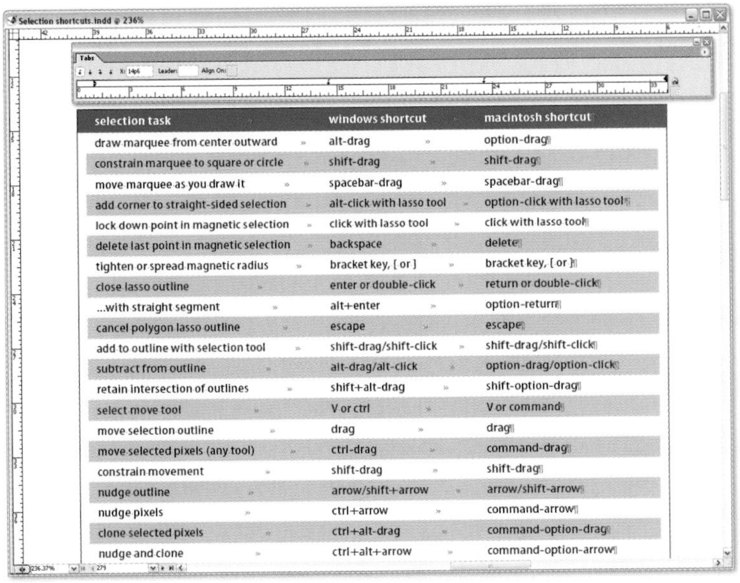

selection task	windows shortcut	macintosh shortcut
draw marquee from center outward	alt-drag	option-drag
constrain marquee to square or circle	shift-drag	shift-drag
move marquee as you draw it	spacebar-drag	spacebar-drag
add corner to straight-sided selection	alt-click with lasso tool	option-click with lasso tool
lock down point in magnetic selection	click with lasso tool	click with lasso tool
delete last point in magnetic selection	backspace	delete
tighten or spread magnetic radius	bracket key, [or]	bracket key, [or]
close lasso outline	enter or double-click	return or double-click
...with straight segment	alt+enter	option-return
cancel polygon lasso outline	escape	escape
add to outline with selection tool	shift-drag/shift-click	shift-drag/shift-click
subtract from outline	alt-drag/alt-click	option-drag/option-click
retain intersection of outlines	shift+alt-drag	shift-option-drag
select move tool	V or ctrl	V or command
move selection outline	drag	drag
move selected pixels (any tool)	ctrl-drag	command-drag
constrain movement	shift-drag	shift-drag
nudge outline	arrow/shift+arrow	arrow/shift-arrow
nudge pixels	ctrl+arrow	command-arrow
clone selected pixels	ctrl+alt-drag	command-option-drag
nudge and clone	ctrl+alt+arrow	command-option-arrow

Figure 4-37.

Creating a Full-Fledged Table

Okay, I didn't want to mention this in the last exercise—you seemed to be having so much fun using tabs to polish up that table—but tabs aren't necessarily the best tools for creating tables. Tabs work well when all the entries in a row fit neatly onto a single line of text, as they do in our shortcuts table. But in my experience, single-line tables are the exception rather than the rule. More often, at least one entry wants to break onto multiple lines, at which point a tabbed table falls apart.

So in this exercise, we're going to upgrade to the better solution, InDesign's full-fledged Table function. Specifically, you'll take the tabbed table from the last exercise and convert it to a spreadsheet-style table, in which each entry is relegated to its own private *cell*. You'll also learn how to style the table to split it over multiple pages.

1. ***Open a document with a tabular table.*** If you still have open the *My table.indd* document that you saved in the preceding exercise, you're all set. If you didn't work through the last exercise or you neglected to save the file, open *Selection shortcuts 2.indd*, located in the *Lesson 04* folder inside *Lesson Files-IDcs 1on1*.

2. ***Hide the tabs and the Tabs palette.*** The red tab characters and Tabs palette are now nothing more than distractions. So press Ctrl+Alt+I (⌘-Option-I on the Mac) to hide the tabs and press Ctrl+Shift+T (⌘-Shift-T) to hide the palette.

3. ***Select all the text in the table.*** Armed with the type tool, click anywhere inside the table. Then choose **Edit→Select All** or press Ctrl+A (⌘-A) to select all the text in the table. Alternatively, you can quintuple-click (that's five clicks) inside the table, but you're a special person if you think that's the easier solution.

4. ***Choose the Convert Text to Table command.*** If you were creating a table from scratch, you would draw a frame with the type tool and choose Table→Insert Table. But because we already have a tabbed table, we can convert it. Choose **Table→Convert Text to Table** to display the **Convert Text to Table** dialog box, which appears in Figure 4-38.

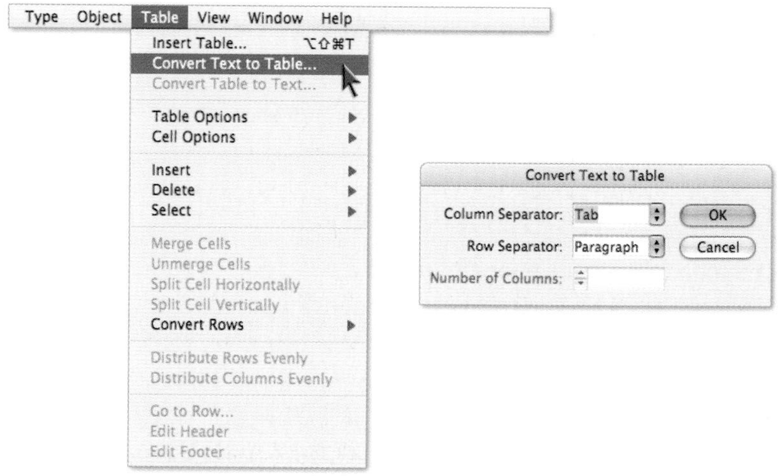

Figure 4-38.

5. ***Click OK.*** We want the columns in our table to be based on tab characters and the rows to be based on paragraph breaks, so the default Convert Text to Table settings are fine. Click the **OK** button to create the table shown in Figure 4-39. Given that it's an automatic conversion, the table doesn't look half bad. But there are some residual problems left over from the paragraph rules we applied in the last exercise. Plus, there are those ugly cell borders. We'll fix all that.

6. ***Click within the text block to the left of the table.*** To the untutored eye, our table appears to fill the text block. But in InDesign, a table is actually an element—like a character of type—inside a text frame. And as things stand now, that element is indented 1 pica, as you specified back in Step 8 of the preceding exercise (see page 155). To remove that indent, click in the vertical white strip to the left of the table. You should see

an extremely tall, table-height blinking insertion marker. Assuming that the paragraph options remain visible in the Control palette, press Ctrl+6 (or ⌘-6) to highlight the very first option box, which controls the left indent. Enter 0 and press Enter or Return. The table now fits squarely within the text frame.

7. ***Select all the text in the table.*** Now we need to set about formatting the table. Click on a word in the table to move the insertion marker into the table text. (Make sure to click when your cursor appears as an I-beam. If you click with some other cursor, you run the risk of moving a row or column boundary.) Then choose **Table→Select→Table** or press Ctrl+Alt+A (⌘-Option-A on the Mac). This selects all text inside the table.

8. ***Turn off the paragraph rules.*** Let's start things off by dismissing the paragraph rules. Press Ctrl+Alt+J (or ⌘-Option-J). Alternatively, you can display the Paragraph palette and choose Paragraph Rules from the palette menu. (You can no longer access the Paragraph Rules command from the Control palette, because the latter now displays table options.) Inside the Paragraph Rules dialog box, make sure the **Rule Below** option remains active. A square or dash appears inside the **Rule On** check box. This indicates that the rule is sometimes on and sometimes off inside the selection. Click once in the check box to change the dash to a checkmark; click again to eliminate the checkmark and the paragraph rules. Then click **OK**.

9. ***Choose the Strokes and Fills command.*** As shown in Figure 4-40, the disjointed blue lines are gone from the table. But the cells (the rectangular intersections of rows and columns) continue to exhibit borders, which I find very obtrusive. I can get rid of the borders by choosing Table→Cell Options→Strokes and Fills, and then working my way through a dialog box, but there's an easier way:

   - Note that the Control palette contains a score of options that let you change the formatting of a table. On the far right is a grid (labeled ❶ in Figure 4-41 on the next page). Make sure all lines in the grid are blue. If they aren't, triple-click on any line in the grid to select them all. This shows you that all borders in the table are active and ready to accept changes.

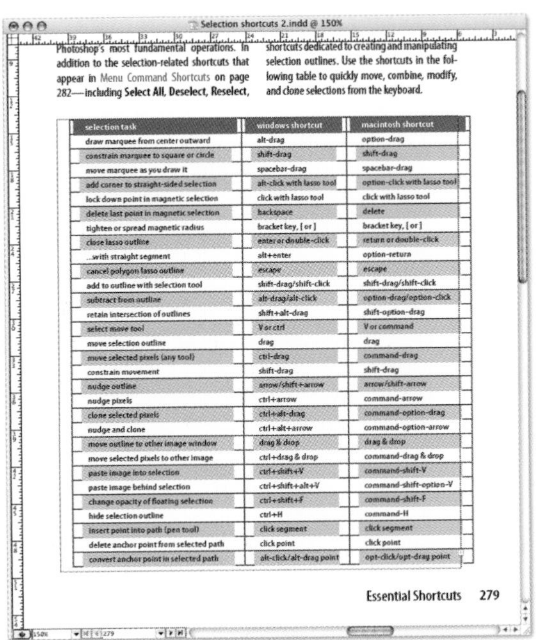

Selection shortcuts 2.indd @ 150%

Photoshop's most fundamental operations. In addition to the selection-related shortcuts that appear in Menu Command Shortcuts on page 282—including **Select All, Deselect, Reselect,** shortcuts dedicated to creating and manipulating selection outlines. Use the shortcuts in the following table to quickly move, combine, modify, and clone selections from the keyboard.

selection task	windows shortcut	macintosh shortcut
draw marquee from center outward	alt-drag	option-drag
constrain marquee to square or circle	shift-drag	shift-drag
move marquee as you draw it	spacebar-drag	spacebar-drag
add corner to straight-sided selection	alt-click with lasso tool	option-click with lasso tool
lock down point in magnetic selection	click with lasso tool	click with lasso tool
delete last point in magnetic selection	backspace	delete
tighten or spread magnetic radius	bracket key, [or]	bracket key, [or]
close lasso outline	enter or double-click	return or double-click
...with straight segment	alt+enter	option-return
cancel polygon lasso outline	escape	escape
add to outline with selection tool	shift-drag/shift-click	shift-drag/shift-click
subtract from outline	alt-drag/alt-click	option-drag/option-click
retain intersection of outlines	shift+alt-drag	shift-option-drag
select move tool	V or ctrl	V or command
move selection outline	drag	drag
move selected pixels (any tool)	ctrl-drag	command-drag
constrain movement	shift-drag	shift-drag
nudge outline	arrow/shift+arrow	arrow/shift-arrow
nudge pixels	ctrl+arrow	command-arrow
clone selected pixels	ctrl+alt-drag	command-option-drag
nudge and clone	ctrl+alt+arrow	command-option-arrow
move outline to other image window	drag & drop	drag & drop
move selected pixels to other image	ctrl+drag & drop	command-drag & drop
paste image into selection	ctrl+shift+V	command-shift-V
paste image behind selection	ctrl+shift+alt+V	command-shift-option-V
change opacity of floating selection	ctrl+shift+F	command-shift-F
hide selection outline	ctrl+H	command-H
insert point into path (pen tool)	click segment	click segment
delete anchor point from selected path	click point	click point
convert anchor point in selected path	alt-click/alt-drag point	opt-click/opt-drag point

Essential Shortcuts 279

Figure 4-39.

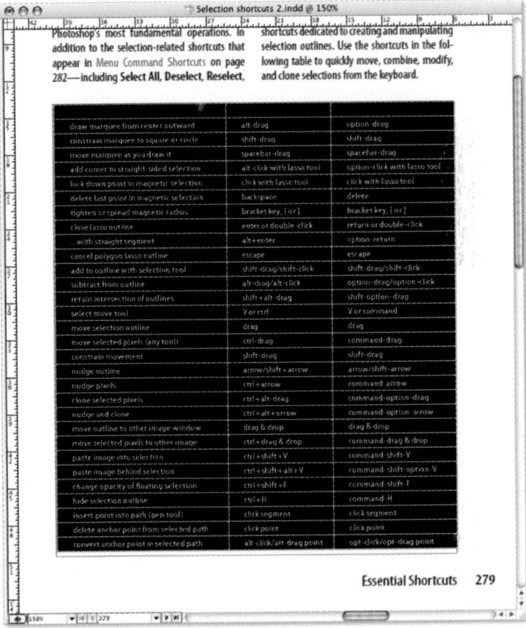

Selection shortcuts 2.indd @ 150%

Photoshop's most fundamental operations. In addition to the selection-related shortcuts that appear in Menu Command Shortcuts on page 282—including **Select All, Deselect, Reselect,** shortcuts dedicated to creating and manipulating selection outlines. Use the shortcuts in the following table to quickly move, combine, modify, and clone selections from the keyboard.

draw marquee from center outward	alt-drag	option-drag
constrain marquee to square or circle	shift-drag	shift-drag
move marquee as you draw it	spacebar-drag	spacebar-drag
add corner to straight-sided selection	alt-click with lasso tool	option-click with lasso tool
lock down point in magnetic selection	click with lasso tool	click with lasso tool
delete last point in magnetic selection	backspace	delete
tighten or spread magnetic radius	bracket key, [or]	bracket key, [or]
close lasso outline	enter or double-click	return or double-click
...with straight segment	alt+enter	option-return
cancel polygon lasso outline	escape	escape
add to outline with selection tool	shift-drag/shift-click	shift-drag/shift-click
subtract from outline	alt-drag/alt-click	option-drag/option-click
retain intersection of outlines	shift+alt-drag	shift-option-drag
select move tool	V or ctrl	V or command
move selection outline	drag	drag
move selected pixels (any tool)	ctrl-drag	command-drag
constrain movement	shift-drag	shift-drag
nudge outline	arrow/shift+arrow	arrow/shift-arrow
nudge pixels	ctrl+arrow	command-arrow
clone selected pixels	ctrl+alt-drag	command-option-drag
nudge and clone	ctrl+alt+arrow	command-option-arrow
move outline to other image window	drag & drop	drag & drop
move selected pixels to other image	ctrl+drag & drop	command-drag & drop
paste image into selection	ctrl+shift+V	command-shift-V
paste image behind selection	ctrl+shift+alt+V	command-shift-option-V
change opacity of floating selection	ctrl+shift+F	command-shift-F
hide selection outline	ctrl+H	command-H
insert point into path (pen tool)	click segment	click segment
delete anchor point from selected path	click point	click point
convert anchor point in selected path	alt-click/alt-drag point	opt-click/opt-drag point

Essential Shortcuts 279

Figure 4-40.

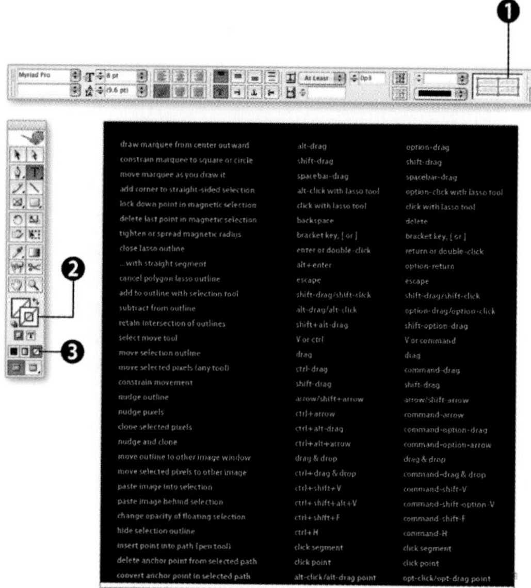

Figure 4-41.

- Now turn your attention to the bottom of the toolbox. Click the stroke icon below the zoom tool (❷) to target the color of the borders. The icon should look like ⧉.
- Click the ⧄ icon near the bottom-right corner of the toolbox (❸), or press the / key. The borders are now invisible, just as they should be.

The one remaining border is a rectangle around the entire table. That happens to be an outline I applied to the text frame itself, and I want to leave that in place.

10. ***Choose the Alternating Fills command.*** You may have noticed that the top row of text has turned invisible on us. This is because we have white text against a white background. To see the text again, we need to restore the alternating pattern of blue and white rows.

Choose **Table→Table Options→Alternating Fills** to bring up the **Fills** section of the **Table Options** dialog box. Then apply the settings shown in Figure 4-42, as follows:

- Turn on the **Preview** check box in the lower-left corner of the dialog box. Why is this option ever off?
- Choose the **Every Other Row** option from the **Alternating Pattern** pop-up menu. This sets every other row as a different color.

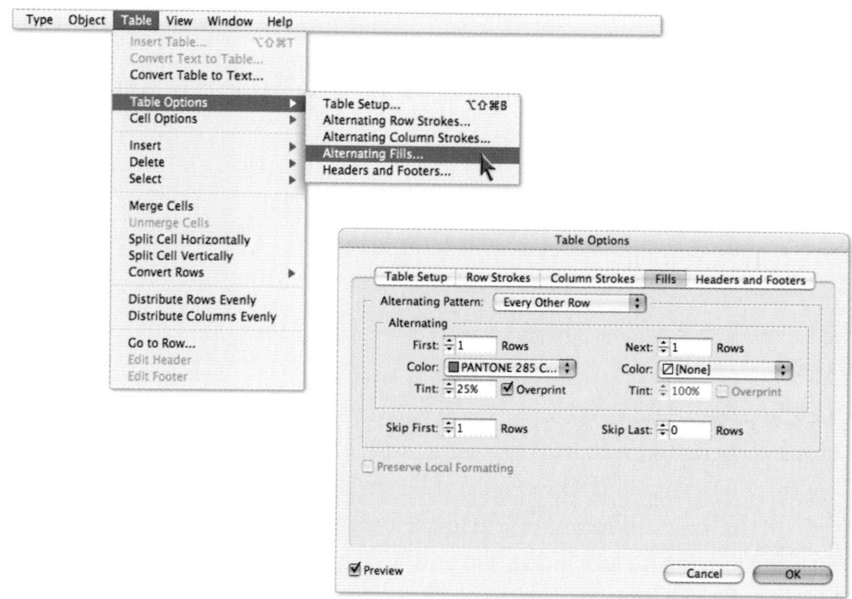

Figure 4-42.

- Choose **Pantone 285 CVU** from the **Color** pop-up menu on the left side of the dialog box. This establishes the color for the first alternating row. Set the left **Tint** value to 25 percent.
- The Color option on the right side of the dialog box sets the color for the next row. Leave it set to **[None]**.
- Turn on the **Overprint** check box. As I mentioned in the last exercise, this is redundant. But backups are redundant, and backups are good.
- Set the **Skip First** value to 1 row. I want the first row of the table to be white. That may not make sense, given that the top row has white text in it. But trust me, the colors will work themselves out in the end.

draw marquee from center outward	alt-drag	option-drag
constrain marquee to square or circle	shift-drag	shift-drag
move marquee as you draw it	spacebar-drag	spacebar-drag
add corner to straight-sided selection	alt-click with lasso tool	option-click with lasso tool
lock down point in magnetic selection	click with lasso tool	click with lasso tool
delete last point in magnetic selection	backspace	delete
tighten or spread magnetic radius	bracket key, [or]	bracket key, [or]
close lasso outline	enter or double-click	return or double-click
...with straight segment	alt+enter	option-return
cancel polygon lasso outline	escape	escape
add to outline with selection tool	shift-drag/shift-click	shift-drag/shift-click
subtract from outline	alt-drag/alt-click	option-drag/option-click
retain intersection of outlines	shift+alt-drag	shift-option-drag
select move tool	V or ctrl	V or command
move selection outline	drag	drag
move selected pixels (any tool)	ctrl-drag	command-drag
constrain movement	shift-drag	shift-drag
nudge outline	arrow/shift+arrow	arrow/shift-arrow
nudge pixels	ctrl+arrow	command-arrow
clone selected pixels	ctrl+alt-drag	command-option-drag
nudge and clone	ctrl+alt+arrow	command-option-arrow
move outline to other image window	drag & drop	drag & drop
move selected pixels to other image	ctrl+drag & drop	command-drag & drop
paste image into selection	ctrl+shift+V	command-shift-V
paste image behind selection	ctrl+shift+alt+V	command-shift-option-V
change opacity of floating selection	ctrl+shift+F	command-shift-F
hide selection outline	ctrl+H	command-H
insert point into path (pen tool)	click segment	click segment
delete anchor point from selected path	click point	click point
convert anchor point in selected path	alt-click/alt-drag point	opt-click/opt-drag point

Figure 4-43.

11. *Click the OK button.* Click **OK** to apply the alternating row colors. You might also want to deselect the table by clicking inside it with the I-beam cursor so you can take in your changes, as shown in Figure 4-43. When I originally created this document in 2000, back before InDesign added its Table feature, I had to color each alternating line independently. This is so much easier, it makes me cry.

12. *Select the top row of the table.* Our next task is to format the top row so that it's no longer invisible. Click in the top row to set the insertion marker. Then choose **Table→Select→Row** or press Ctrl+3 (⌘-3 on the Mac). InDesign selects the entire row.

13. *Fill the cells with blue.* Even selected, you can't see your white-on-white text. So let's set it against a different color:

    - Go to the bottom of the toolbox and click the fill icon (labeled ❶ in Figure 4-44), so it looks like ⧄. Or press the X key. This targets the interior of the selected cells.
    - Choose **Window→Swatches** or press F5 to display the **Swatches** palette.
    - Click the blue swatch named **Pantone 285 CVU** (❷ in the figure).

selection task	windows shortcut	macintosh shortcut
draw marquee from center outward	alt-drag	option-drag
constrain marquee to square or circle	shift-drag	shift-drag
move marquee as you draw it	spacebar-drag	spacebar-drag
add corner to straight-sided selection	alt-click with lasso tool	option-click with lasso tool
lock down point in magnetic selection	click with lasso tool	click with lasso tool
delete last point in magnetic selection	backspace	delete
tighten or spread magnetic radius	bracket key, [or]	bracket key, [or]
close lasso outline	enter or double-click	return or double-click
...with straight segment	alt+enter	option-return
cancel polygon lasso outline	escape	escape
add to outline with selection tool	shift-drag/shift-click	shift-drag/shift-click
subtract from outline	alt-drag/alt-click	option-drag/option-click
retain intersection of outlines	shift+alt-drag	shift-option-drag
select move tool	V or ctrl	V or command
move selection outline	drag	drag
move selected pixels (any tool)	ctrl-drag	command-drag
constrain movement	shift-drag	shift-drag
nudge outline	arrow/shift+arrow	arrow/shift-arrow
nudge pixels	ctrl+arrow	command-arrow
clone selected pixels	ctrl+alt-drag	command-option-drag
nudge and clone	ctrl+alt+arrow	command-option-arrow
move outline to other image window	drag & drop	drag & drop
move selected pixels to other image	ctrl+drag & drop	command-drag & drop
paste image into selection	ctrl+shift+V	command-shift-V
paste image behind selection	ctrl+shift+alt+V	command-shift-option-V
change opacity of floating selection	ctrl+shift+F	command-shift-F
hide selection outline	ctrl+H	command-H
insert point into path (pen tool)	click segment	click segment
delete anchor point from selected path	click point	click point
convert anchor point in selected path	alt-click/alt-drag point	opt-click/opt-drag point

Figure 4-44.

Figure 4-44 shows the top row inverted—black against orange—because the text is highlighted. But really truly, the text is white against a rich cobalt blue.

Figure 4-45.

PEARL OF 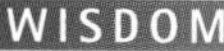 WISDOM

Each of the entries in the first column is a title for the column under it. The first row is therefore known as a *header*, which has special significance in InDesign. To wit, notice the red ⊞ in the bottom-right corner of the text block. When you converted the tabbed text into a table, the rows expanded slightly and created one row of overflow text. You could shorten the rows by choosing Table→Cell Options→Text and reducing the Top or Bottom value. But I'd prefer to flow the table onto a second page. Naturally, if a table is going to spread over two pages, you need the header to repeat at the top of the second page. Thankfully, InDesign's headers can do exactly that.

14. ***Identify the row as a header.*** InDesign doesn't recognize a header automatically; it needs to be told. Make sure the first row of the table is still selected and choose **Table→Convert Rows→To Header**. While no visible change occurs in the first row, the blue and white alternating lines reverse in all subsequent rows. Why? At the end of Step 10, we told InDesign to skip the first row. That first row used to be the top row, but now that you've designated the top row as the header, the first row becomes the one below the header, thus matching the color scheme of the original shortcuts table.

15. ***Deselect the table and show the guides.*** Assuming you loaded my Deke Keys shortcuts (see page xvii), press Enter on the keypad to deselect the table and select the black arrow tool. Or just click the black arrow tool in the toolbox. Then choose **View→Show Guides** or press Ctrl+[;] (⌘-[;] on the Mac) to show all guides.

16. ***Shorten the text block.*** Make sure the frame that contains the table is selected. Then drag the bottom handle of the frame upward until it snaps to the orange guide, as in Figure 4-45. You don't want just one row of overflow text (which is what we have now). By shortening the text block, you force a couple of additional rows to flow onto the second page.

Figure 4-46.

17. ***Flow the table onto the second page.*** Click the red ⊞ out port in the bottom-right corner of the text block. Press Shift+Page Down to advance to the second page. Move your cursor into the empty text frame at the very top of the page (so that the cursor looks like ⁂) and click. InDesign automatically tops off the three rows of overflow text with the header, as in Figure 4-46.

WHAT DID YOU LEARN?

Match the key concept in the numbered list below with the letter of the phrase that best describes it. Answers appear upside-down at the bottom of the page.

Key Concepts

1. Drop cap
2. Hanging indent
3. Hidden characters
4. Tab stop
5. Em dash
6. Forced line break
7. Discretionary hyphen
8. Run-in head
9. Fixed-width space
10. No Break
11. Cell
12. Header

Descriptions

A. This exceedingly useful command prevents the selected text from breaking between lines, even at a hyphen, dash, or space.

B. This top row of a table contains the titles for the columns beneath it.

C. A boldface or italic introduction separated from a caption or list entry by multiple spaces or, better, a fixed-width space.

D. Spaces, paragraph breaks, tabs, line breaks, end-of-story markers, and other nonprinting glyphs that you can display by choosing a command from the Type menu or pressing Ctrl+Alt+I (⌘-Option-I on the Mac).

E. Used in place of a pair of consecutive hyphens to offset descriptive or parenthetical phrases, this specialized punctuation is roughly as long as the type size is tall.

F. One or more large characters at the beginning of a paragraph that descend below the first line of type into the lines below.

G. This intersection of a row and column in a full-fledged table houses a single table entry.

H. This specialized punctuation—which you get by pressing Ctrl+Shift+⊟ (⌘-Shift-⊟ on the Mac)—appears only when needed to break a word to the next line of type.

I. Any of several specialized space characters that InDesign cannot alter to suit the alignment or spacing of a paragraph.

J. An invisible character that knocks all text after it to the next line without starting a new paragraph.

K. A ↓ or other mark on a ruler to which the text after a tab character aligns, whether to the left, right, center, or by a specified character.

L. A common formatting convention in which the first line of a paragraph extends to the left of the other lines, commonly used to set bulleted and numbered lists.

Answers

1F, 2L, 3D, 4K, 5E, 6J, 7H, 8C, 9I, 10A, 11G, 12B

LESSON 5

Y•85 M•85 C•9 K•42
Y•100 M•100 C•10 K•42
Y•40 M•40 C•4 K•24
Y•55 M•55 C•6 K•24
Y•70 M•70 C•7 K•24
Y•85 M•85 C•9 K•24
Y•100 M•100 C•10 K•24

USING STYLE SHEETS

A TYPICAL DOCUMENT is made up of a handful of formatting attributes that you apply over and over and over again. Take this book, for example. The text you're reading right now is set in Birka. The type size is 10.5 points with a leading of 14 (shorthand: 10.5 over 14, or 10.5/14). The kerning is Optical, the alignment is justified, and the paragraph spacing is 6 points. All in all, it's not so bad—just a handful of settings, really. Even so, if I had to apply each and every one of these attributes to each and every paragraph independently, I'd go stark raving bonkers.

Of course, I don't have to. I can select multiple paragraphs before I apply an attribute. And a new paragraph automatically adopts the attributes applied to its predecessor. But if you think about it, that doesn't really do me much good. The normal body copy is interrupted by headlines, subheads, steps, bulleted lists, and so many other variations it makes your head spin. It's rare to find more than a few paragraphs in a row that share the same formatting.

Fortunately, there is another way. The fact is, you never need to apply a specific sequence of formatting attributes more than once. After you establish a group of settings—such as Birka 10.5/14 Optical justified with 6 points of paragraph spacing—you can save them and then reapply them with a single click. Such an attribute group goes by a variety of names, including *style sheet*, *custom style*, and just plain *style*. I and most other designers prefer the first, style sheet. It implies a long list of attributes (only fitting) and helps to distinguish this kind of style from the humble type style, be it plain, italic, or bold. Adobe in its online documentation comes down on the side of plain old style. Those nuts.

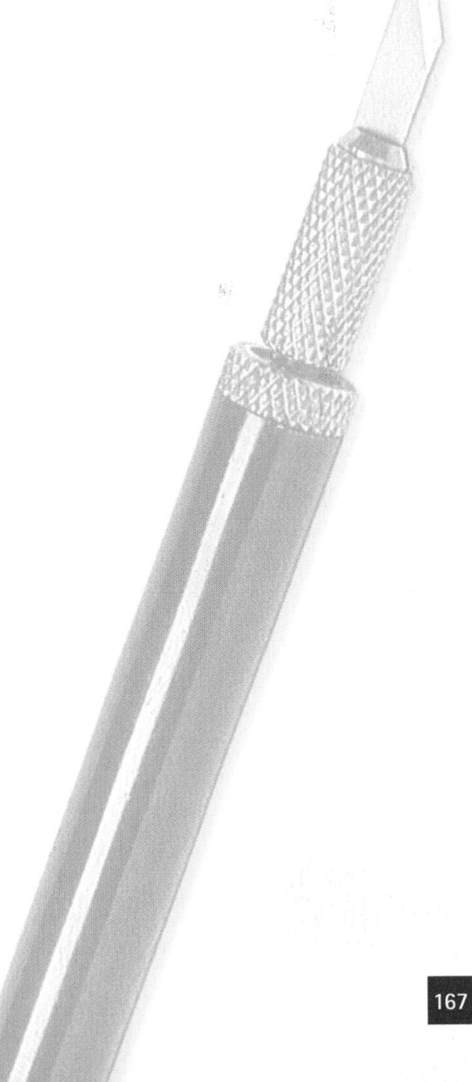

ABOUT THIS LESSON

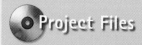

Project Files

Before beginning the exercises, make sure that you've installed the lesson files from the CD, as explained in Step 5 on page xv of the Preface. This should result in a folder called *Lesson Files-IDcs 1on1* on your desktop. We'll be working with the files inside the *Lesson 05* subfolder.

As much as you may like InDesign, I'm guessing you're eager to avoid busy work even if that means spending less time in the program. If so, you'll love style sheets, which allow you to apply and modify dozens of formatting attributes at a time. In this lesson, you'll learn how to:

- Create and edit paragraph styles, and set up relationships between them . . . . page 170
- Modify a paragraph style and automatically update all linked paragraphs to match . . . . page 177
- Use character styles to format individual words and sentences . . . . page 179
- Embed character styles into paragraph style definitions to create nested styles . . . . page 184

Video Lesson 5: Duplicating Formatting Attributes

The simplest tool for copying formatting attributes from one word or paragraph to another is the eyedropper. If you're familiar with other graphics programs, you may associate the eyedropper with lifting colors. But in InDesign, it's much more capable. Sure, it can lift colors—but it can also lift typeface, size, leading, alignment, and scads of other attributes.

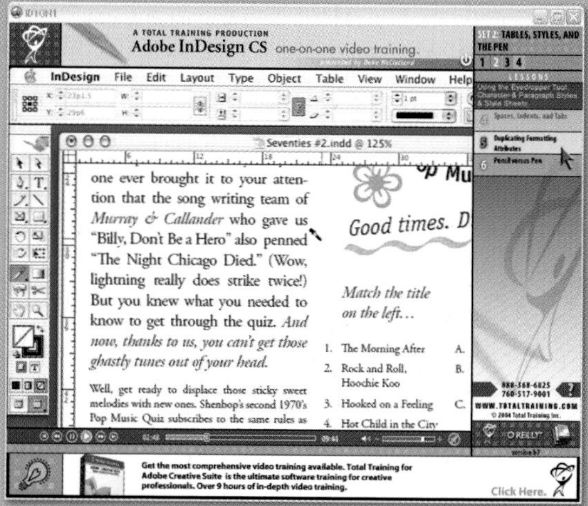

To see the eyedropper in action—as well as a brief introduction to style sheets—watch the fifth video lesson included on the CD. Insert the CD, click the **Start Training** button, click the Set 2 button, and then select **5, Duplicating Formatting Attributes** from the Lessons list. Over the course of this 9-minute 44-second movie, I mention the following operations and shortcuts:

Operation	Windows shortcut	Macintosh shortcut
Load new attributes with the eyedropper	Alt-click	Option-click
Scroll when text and eyedropper are active	Alt+spacebar-drag	Option-spacebar-drag
Change eyedropper settings	Double-click eyedropper icon	Double-click eyedropper icon
Display Paragraph Styles palette	F11	F11
Display Character Styles palette	Shift+F11	Shift-F11
Modify style sheet	Double-click style in palette	Double-click style in palette
Undo and redo (for before-and-after view)	Ctrl+Z, Ctrl+Shift+Z	⌘-Z, ⌘-Shift-Z

Designing Your Own Custom Styles

Like formatting attributes, style sheets break into two camps. *Paragraph styles* affect entire paragraphs at a time; *character styles* affect individual letters or words. And here, as luck would have it, Adobe and the countless designers who rely on its graphics and publishing software use the same terms.

The more common of the two, the paragraph style, may contain all formatting attributes, from font to alignment to tabs. Figure 5-1 shows four paragraph styles applied to a passage from the ever-cheerful *Macbeth*. In each case, the style sheet changes both the character- and paragraph-level attributes, making it useful for formatting all kinds of text, from body copy to captions to headlines. When people talk about style sheets, this is what they mean.

A character style is a subset of paragraph styles that is limited to character-level attributes and may define as many or as few attributes as you like. On the next page, Figure 5-2 shows the result of creating a character style that includes just two attributes—18-point size and italic style—and applying it to each of the four styled paragraphs. The character style changes what little formatting it can and leaves the rest intact.

In addition to facilitating the formatting of a document, style sheets make quick work of changes. Suppose your fickle client decides to use a different typeface. No problem. Just change the style sheet and all styled paragraphs or letters update in kind. You can even create dependent style sheets, so that changing one paragraph style affects many others.

Possibly best of all, InDesign can import and override style sheets from a word processor. This makes it possible for the content provider—that is, the guy or gal who's writing the text—to work independently of the content designer—that is, you—and still have all the pieces fit together seamlessly. For example, I'm writing this text in Microsoft Word. The text is set in a paragraph style that I named Body. In Word, Body is 10-point Verdana, which is easy to read on screen. In InDesign, Body is 10.5-point Birka. Thanks to

Paragraph style 1: Bernhard Modern, 12.5/16, flush left

Out, out brief candle! Life's but a walking shadow, a poor player, that struts and frets his hour upon the stage, and then is heard no more; it is a tale told by an idiot, full of sound and fury, signifying nothing.

Paragraph style 2: Chaparral Light, 11/16, flush left

Out, out brief candle! Life's but a walking shadow, a poor player, that struts and frets his hour upon the stage, and then is heard no more; it is a tale told by an idiot, full of sound and fury, signifying nothing.

Paragraph style 3: Rotis Serif Italic, 11.5/16, justified

Out, out brief candle! Life's but a walking shadow, a poor player, that struts and frets his hour upon the stage, and then is heard no more; it is a tale told by an idiot, full of sound and fury, signifying nothing.

Paragraph style 4: Silentium Roman, 9/13.5, centered

Out, out brief candle!
Life's but a walking shadow, a poor player,
that struts and frets his hour upon the stage,
and then is heard no more; it is a tale told by
an idiot, full of sound and fury,
signifying nothing.

Figure 5-1.

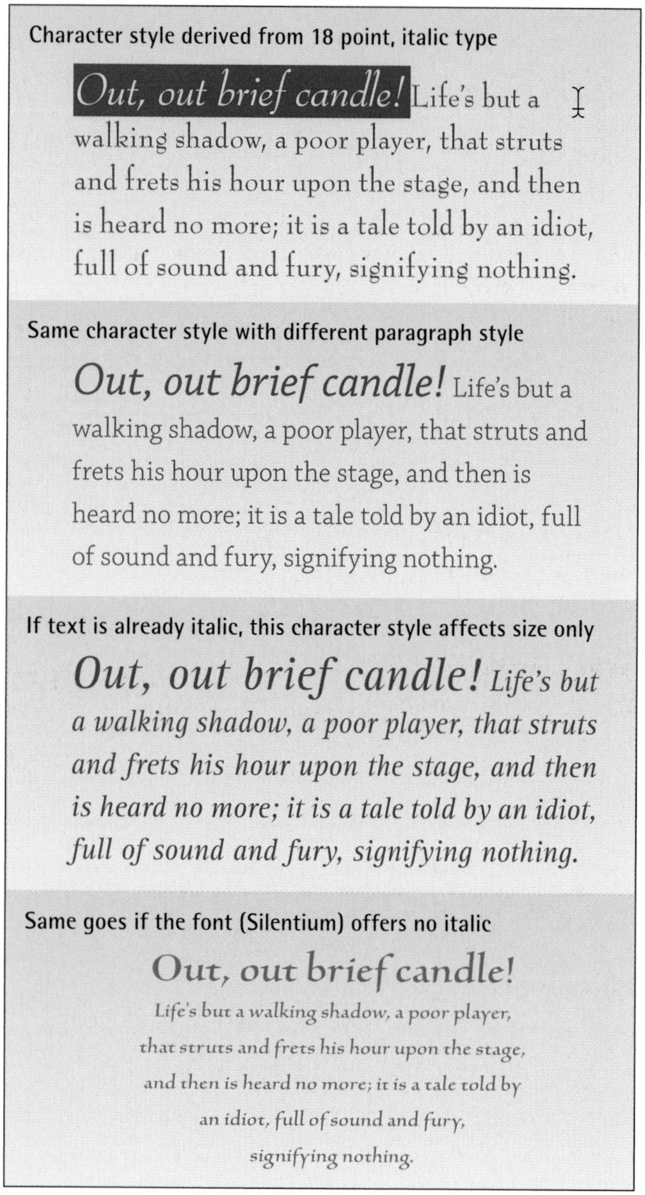

Character style derived from 18 point, italic type

Out, out brief candle! Life's but a walking shadow, a poor player, that struts and frets his hour upon the stage, and then is heard no more; it is a tale told by an idiot, full of sound and fury, signifying nothing.

Same character style with different paragraph style

Out, out brief candle! Life's but a walking shadow, a poor player, that struts and frets his hour upon the stage, and then is heard no more; it is a tale told by an idiot, full of sound and fury, signifying nothing.

If text is already italic, this character style affects size only

Out, out brief candle! Life's but a walking shadow, a poor player, that struts and frets his hour upon the stage, and then is heard no more; it is a tale told by an idiot, full of sound and fury, signifying nothing.

Same goes if the font (Silentium) offers no italic

Out, out brief candle!

Life's but a walking shadow, a poor player, that struts and frets his hour upon the stage, and then is heard no more; it is a tale told by an idiot, full of sound and fury, signifying nothing.

Figure 5-2.

style sheets, InDesign imports the text and converts it automatically, no questions asked. It's all buttoned-down, by the book, and according to Hoyle. Welcome to your first glimpse of automation in InDesign.

Creating a Paragraph Style

We'll begin our exploration of style sheets with the most commonly used variety: paragraph styles. In this exercise, you'll learn how to create paragraph styles based on the formatting of selected text and assign shortcuts to the styles so you can apply them in a flash. You'll even learn how to base one style on another and specify the next style that will be applied when you begin a new paragraph.

1. ***Open a document.*** Open the file named *Buckle my shoe 1.indd* located in the *Lesson 05* folder inside *Lesson Files-IDcs 1on1*. Pictured in Figure 5-3, this is a page intended for a book of nursery rhymes. The illustrations are by Nashville artist Jerry Hunt.

2. ***Open the Paragraph Styles palette.*** Choose **Type→Paragraph Styles** to bring up the **Paragraph Styles** palette shown in Figure 5-4. Alternatively, you can press F11 to display the palette. (Mac users running OS X 10.3 may find that pressing F11 activates Exposé's desktop-revealing trick instead of bringing up the palette. If this happens to you, see page xvii of the Preface to learn how to change Exposé's behavior.)

   Each line in the nursery rhyme is its own paragraph. The first two lines of the long text block in the middle of the page are already formatted, which is fortunate because the easiest way to create a style is to base it on existing text. In fact, that's precisely what we're going to do.

3. ***Select the white line of type.*** Press T to select the type tool and click anywhere in the first line of the middle text block, the one that reads *One, two*. This is enough to tell InDesign which paragraph's formatting we want to employ.

4. ***Create a new style sheet.*** Click the ⧉ icon at the bottom of the Paragraph Styles palette. As Figure 5-5 shows, a new style called Paragraph Style 1 appears in the palette. This style contains all the character and paragraph formatting that has been applied to the active paragraph of text, including the font, color, alignment, and other attributes.

5. ***Apply the new style to the white line of type.*** Although the first paragraph is styled exactly as Paragraph Style 1 dictates, the paragraph doesn't actually have the style applied to it. How do we know this? Because the default [No Paragraph Style] remains selected in the Paragraph Styles palette. So click **Paragraph Style 1** in the Paragraph Styles palette to apply the new style sheet and establish a link between the text and the paragraph style.

This is one of the easiest things to forget when working with style sheets: After you create a style based on a formatted paragraph, you must then turn around and apply that style to the same text. Otherwise, the text won't reflect any changes that you might make to the style later on down the road.

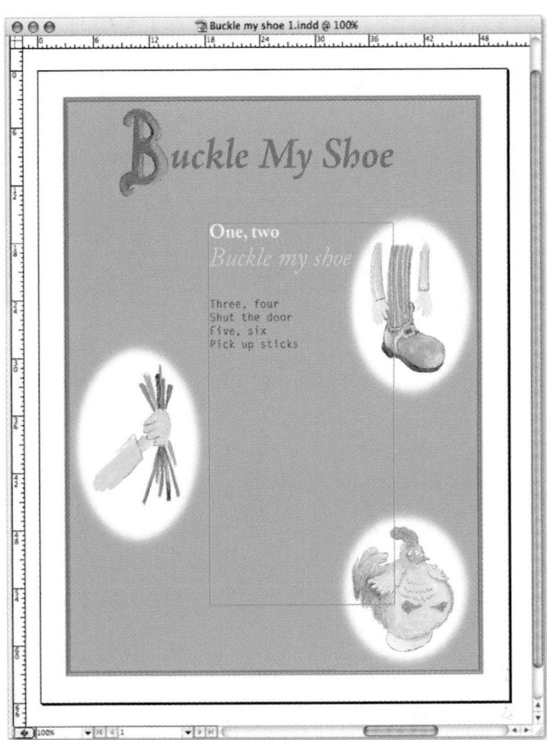

Figure 5-3.

6. ***Edit the new style sheet.*** After you create a style sheet, it is by no means set in stone. You can edit it—and any text linked to it—at any stage in the development of a document. To modify the style sheet you just created:

   • Click the ⊙ in the upper-right corner of the Paragraph Styles palette and choose the **Style Options** command.

   • Or, just double-click the **Paragraph Style 1** item in the palette list.

   InDesign displays the **Paragraph Style Options** dialog box shown in Figure 5-6. Change panels by clicking the options on the far left side of the dialog box, or press Ctrl (⌘ on the Mac) with a number key.

7. ***Name the style Number Lines.*** This dialog box lets you view and edit the various formatting attributes contained in your paragraph style. Our first task is to give this style sheet a more descriptive name. Tab

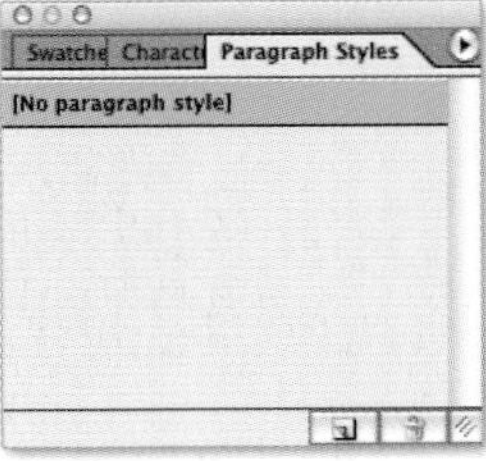

Figure 5-4.

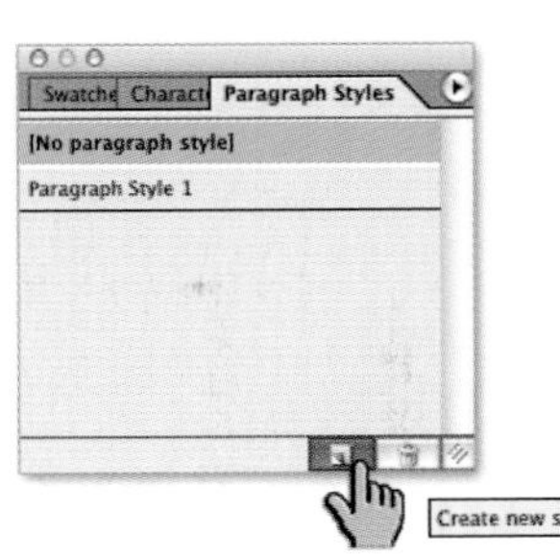

Figure 5-5.

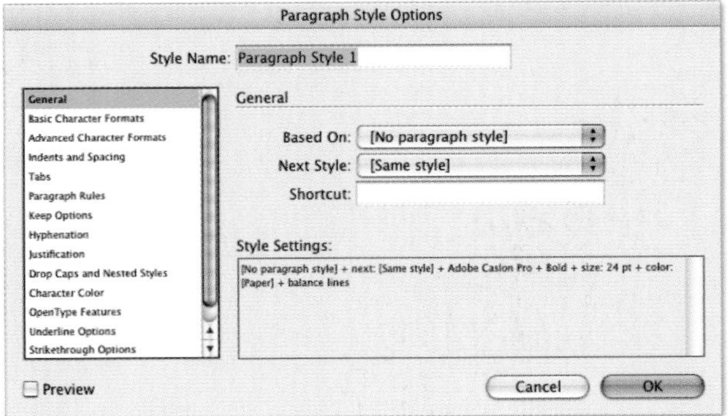

Figure 5-6.

to the **Style Name** option box and type "Number Lines"—that is, lines that have numbers in them. We'll use this style sheet to format the first line in every couplet in the nursery rhyme, such as *Three, four*, and so on.

I cannot stress enough the importance of giving your style sheets descriptive names. Name the style after its function—not its formatting—so that you (or someone working after you) can easily identify what in the heck purpose it serves.

---

8. ***Assign a keyboard shortcut.*** Let's next assign a keyboard shortcut to our paragraph style so that we can apply it without hunting through the Paragraph Styles palette. InDesign requires that style shortcuts include one or more modifier keys—Ctrl, Alt, or Shift (⌘, Option, or Shift on the Mac)—combined with a number on the numeric keypad. That's right, it has to be a number, 0 through 9, on the keypad only, and the Mac's Control key is out of bounds.

PEARL OF WISDOM

The problem with Adobe's idiotic keypad restriction is that not all keyboards have keypads. To activate the keypad equivalents on many laptops—Apple's PowerBooks come to mind—you must press the Num Lock key, which overrides a dozen or so letter keys. After you enter the shortcut, press Num Lock again to turn the function off and continue typing as usual. Frankly, this is an inconvenience of the highest magnitude and there is no workaround. So when using InDesign on a laptop, you may well find it easier to skip style sheet shortcuts and just apply them by clicking the style names in the Paragraph Styles palette as you did in Step 5.

Assuming your keyboard includes a keypad, click in the **Shortcut** option box. Then press Ctrl+Shift+6 on the numeric keypad (⌘-Shift-6 on the Mac). If InDesign beeps at you or does nothing at all, press the Num Lock key and try again. When you are successful, InDesign spells out the sequence of keys in the Shortcut option box. If you don't have access to a keypad, skip this step and shake your fist in frustration.

9. ***View the Indents and Spacing category.*** The Style Settings field at the bottom of the dialog box provides a summary of the attributes conveyed by this paragraph style. We can see that the font used is Adobe Caslon Pro, the style is Bold, and the type size is 24 points. We also see an item that reads *color: [Paper]*, which tells us that the text will be the same color as the paper on which it is printed, presumably white. But what does that last item, *balance lines*, mean?

To find out, click **Indents and Spacing** in the list on the left side of the dialog box or press Ctrl+4 (⌘-4) to switch to the Indents and Spacing panel. As in Figure 5-7, you'll see a check box for **Balance Ragged Lines**. As you learned in Lesson 3 (see Step 10 of the "Paragraph Spacing and Alignment" exercise on page 106), this function balances lines in a headline so one line isn't vastly longer than another. But the paragraphs in the nursery rhyme are exclusively one line apiece. In other words, this option isn't doing any good, so go ahead and turn it off.

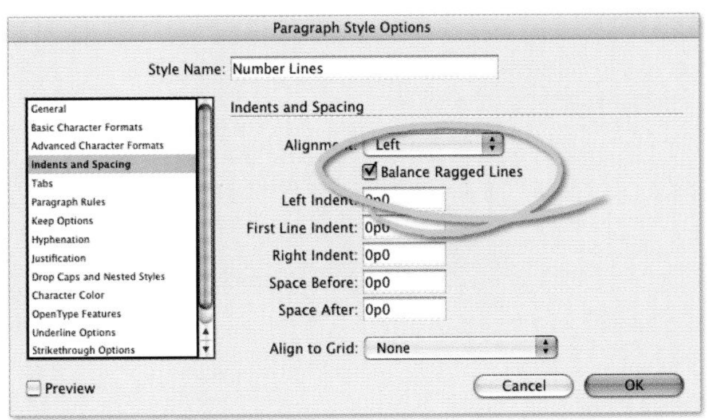

Figure 5-7.

I mention this not because there's anything necessarily wrong with leaving a formatting attribute on that's not serving any purpose. (After all, it wasn't doing any harm, either.) Rather, I want you to see that you can modify the formatting of a style sheet right after making it. And those modifications translate to the linked paragraphs in your document.

10. ***Click OK.*** Click the **OK** button to close the Paragraph Style Options dialog box and accept your changes. As Figure 5-8 shows, the style formerly named Paragraph Style 1 now appears as Number Lines, and with a shortcut to boot.

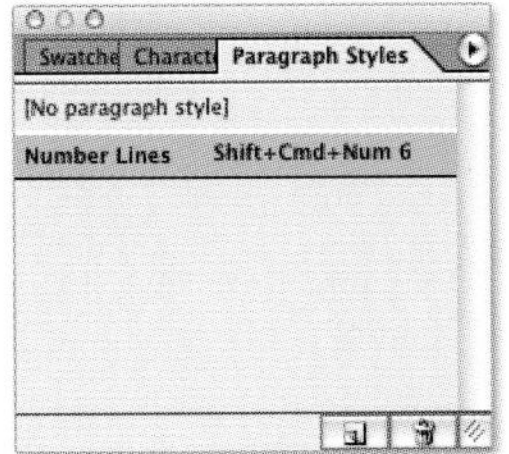

Figure 5-8.

11. ***Select the yellow line of type.*** Press the ↓ key to move the insertion marker to the second line of type. Again, [No Paragraph Style] becomes highlighted in the Paragraph Styles palette, indicating that no style sheet is associated with the active paragraph.

12. ***Create and name a new style sheet.*** Let's create a new style sheet for this paragraph and, in the process, name it as well. Press the Alt key (Option on the Mac) and click the ◲ icon at the bottom of the Paragraph Styles palette. Having the key down displays the **New Paragraph Style** dialog box, which lets you modify a style sheet as you create it. Tab to the **Style Name** option box and enter "Rhyming Lines," so named because the second line of each couplet completes the rhyme.

13. ***Base the style sheet on Number Lines.*** Now turn your attention to the Based On option. This option establishes a parent-child relationship between two

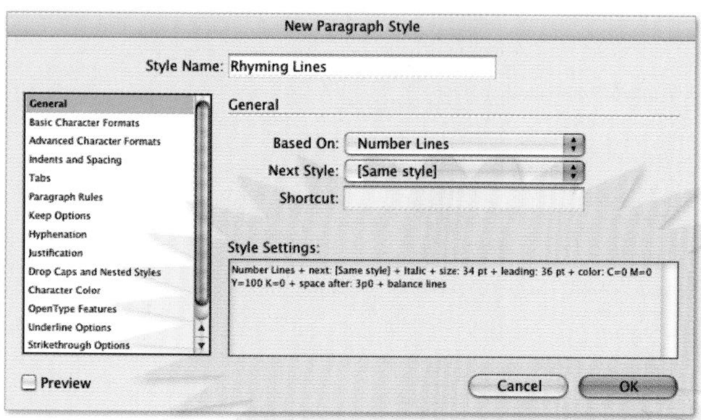

Figure 5-9.

style sheets. Any changes made to the parent style will affect shared formatting attributes in the child style. In other words, the Based On option makes it possible to modify multiple styles at a time.

To see what I mean, choose **Number Lines** from the **Based On** pop-up menu. This may seem like an odd thing to do, since the new style isn't really based on the Number Lines style at all; in fact, the two styles look quite different. But there's a method to my madness. To see what it is, take a look at the Style Settings field at the bottom of the dialog box. As Figure 5-9 shows, the field lists the Number Lines style and then details only the *differences* between that style and the new Rhyming Lines style. A couple of implications:

- Absent from this list is the font. Thus, the font must be a shared attribute. So if I were to change the font for Number Lines, the font for Rhyming Lines would change too. And that's a good thing, because I don't want to mix font families within the nursery rhyme.
- Color is listed in the Style Settings field, so it's not a shared attribute. If I were to change the color of the Number Lines style, the color of Rhyming Lines would remain unchanged.

14. ***Set the Next Style to Number Lines.*** The Next Style option allows you to pick a style sheet that will automatically become active when you begin a new paragraph. For example, when creating a newspaper article, you could set the Body Copy style to follow the Headline style. That way, pressing the Enter or Return key after typing a headline would automatically switch you to the body copy. We want to set up an alternating relationship between our two styles, so choose **Number Lines** from the **Next Style** pop-up menu.

15. ***Assign a keyboard shortcut.*** Click in the **Shortcut** option box, and then press Ctrl+Shift+7 (⌘-Shift-7 on the Mac). Remember that you have to use the number keys on the numeric keypad. Skip this step if you don't have 'em.

16. ***Click OK and assign the style.*** Click the **OK** button to create your new style sheet. And don't forget to click the **Rhyming Lines** style to assign it to the active paragraph, as in Figure 5-10.

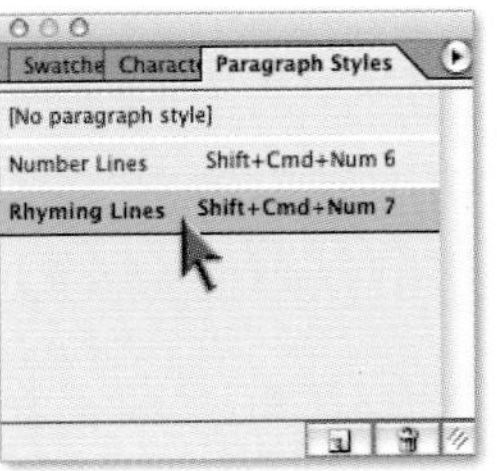

Figure 5-10.

EXTRA CREDIT

Congratulations. You have created and applied two style sheets in InDesign, and even established a relationship between the two. Frankly, that last part makes you more adept at using style sheets than most working designers. But it's not enough. We need to make one slight adjustment to the Number Lines style, and then we need to put our style sheets in play. Join me, won't you? You'll be glad you did. (Or to skip these next tasks, go to "Updating a Paragraph Style" on page 177.)

17. ***Edit the Number Lines style.*** There's a little problem with our alternating-line nursery rhyme formatting scheme. While we established that Number Lines follows Rhyming Lines, we haven't said that Rhyming Lines follows Number Lines. We couldn't do that back in Steps 7 through 10 because there was no Rhyming Lines style. So now's our chance:

    - Press the ↑ key to move the blinking insertion marker to the white text in the document window. (If you don't do this, you run the risk of applying the Number Lines style to another paragraph.)
    - Double-click the **Number Lines** style to display the Paragraph Style Options dialog box
    - Set the **Next Style** pop-up menu to **Rhyming Lines**.
    - Click the **OK** button to accept the change.

    Note that InDesign prohibits you from setting the Based On option to Rhyming Lines and thus creating a recursive, incestuous, time-traveling relationship. We've already established that Number Lines is the parent of Rhyming Lines, so logically we can't say that the opposite is true as well. A style sheet cannot be its own grandparent, just so's you know.

18. ***Apply the style sheets to the other lines of type.*** Now that our styles are complete, let's put them to use:

    - Click in the line that reads *Three, four* and then click the **Number Lines** style in the Paragraph Styles palette. The text assumes the Number Lines formatting attributes.

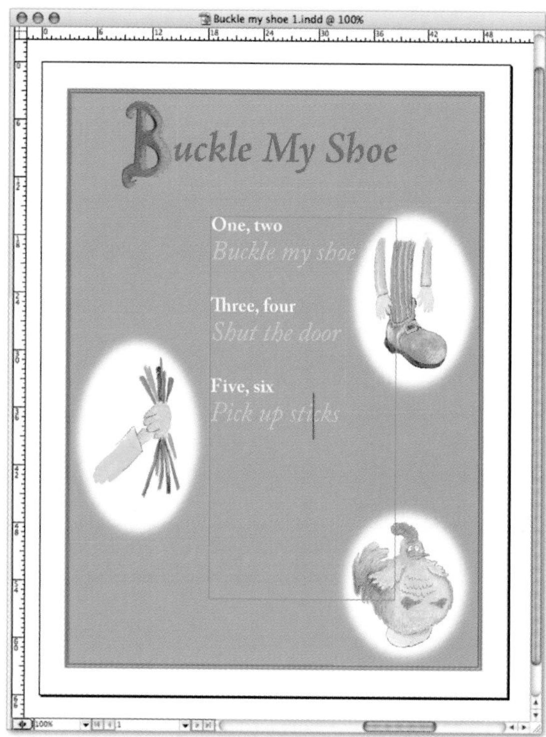

Figure 5-11.

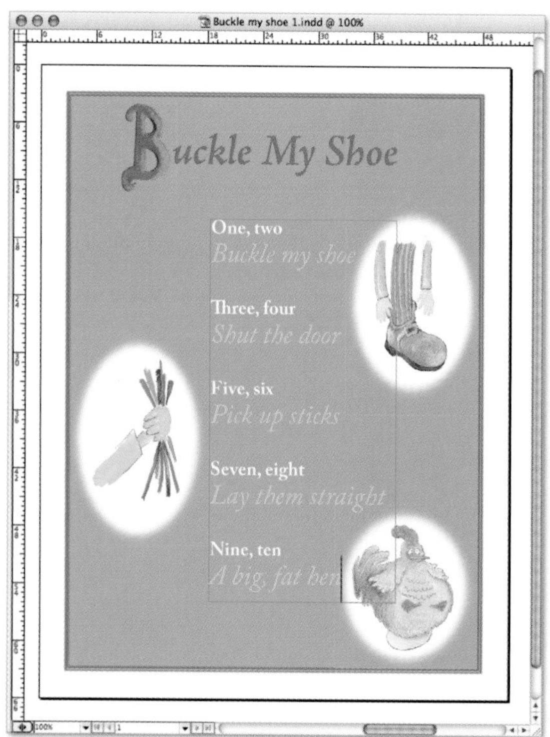

Figure 5-12.

- Press the ↓ key to move the insertion marker to the fourth line of type and click **Rhyming Lines** in the Paragraph Styles palette.
- Press ↓ again, and then press the keyboard shortcut for Number Lines, Ctrl+Shift+6 on the numeric keypad (⌘-Shift-6 on the Mac). If you didn't assign a keystroke, click the Number Lines style in the palette.
- Press ↓ yet again and press Ctrl+Shift+7 on the keypad (⌘-Shift-7). Or click the Rhyming Lines style.

Your text should now look like it does in Figure 5-11. So far, so good. But as I recall, there's more to this nursery rhyme. We have a hen graphic, but no text reference. Looks like we have some typing to do.

19. ***Type the rest of the nursery rhyme.*** There's not much to this poem, so let's go ahead and finish it. Press the End key to advance to the end of the final line, after the word *sticks*. Then do the following:

    - Press the Enter or Return key. Because we set Number Lines to follow Rhyming Lines, pressing Enter or Return automatically switches to the Number Lines style.
    - Type "Seven, eight" and press Enter or Return again. InDesign switches back to the Rhyming Lines style.
    - Type "Lay them straight," and press Enter or Return a third time.
    - Type "Nine, ten," followed by Enter or Return.
    - And now for the stirring if pejorative finale: "A big, fat hen." (As my son tells me every time he hears this poem, "We don't say that word.")

    Figure 5-12 shows the final result.

20. ***Save your work.*** Nicely done, friend. We will continue working on this document in the next exercise, so choose **File→Save As**, name your document "My rhyme.indd," and save it in the *Lesson 05* folder.

Updating a Paragraph Style

In addition to automating the application of many formatting attributes at a time, style sheets are dynamic. InDesign creates a live link between the style and the text to which it's applied. So when you make a change to a style sheet, the text updates to match.

In this brief exercise, we'll make a couple of changes to an existing paragraph style and see firsthand how those changes affect our text. We'll also see exactly how changes to a parent style get passed down to the children.

1. ***Open the nursery rhyme document.*** This exercise picks up where the last one left off. If you still have open the *My rhyme.indd* file that you saved in Step 20 of the preceding exercise, super. If not, open the file named *Buckle my shoe 2.indd* in the *Lesson 05* folder inside *Lesson Files-IDcs 1on1*. You should see the document pictured in Figure 5-12.
2. ***Deselect any active text.*** If you are reading this on the heels of the last section, the insertion marker may still be blinking away at the end of the last line, *A big, fat hen*. I don't want you to run the risk of harming that exquisite line of type, so choose **Edit→Deselect All** or press Ctrl+Shift+A (⌘-Shift-A on the Mac) to deselect any and all text.
3. ***Edit the Number Lines style sheet.*** Double-click the **Number Lines** style in the **Paragraph Styles** palette. InDesign displays the familiar Paragraph Style Options dialog box.
4. ***Turn on the Preview check box.*** When editing a style, it's a good idea to turn on the **Preview** check box so you can observe the results of your changes as you make them.
5. ***Change the typeface.*** Select the **Basic Character Formats** category on the left side of the dialog box, or press Ctrl+2 (⌘-2 on the Mac). Then choose **Adobe Jenson Pro** from the **Font Family** pop-up menu. (The font is listed alphabetically under *J* for *Jenson*.) Alternatively, you can highlight the words *Caslon Pro* inside the Font Family option box and press the J key. Then press Tab to preview the results in the document window.
6. ***Click OK.*** Click the **OK** button to apply your changes. Because Rhyming Lines is the child of Number Lines, and both were set to the same font, all ten lines of the poem in the middle

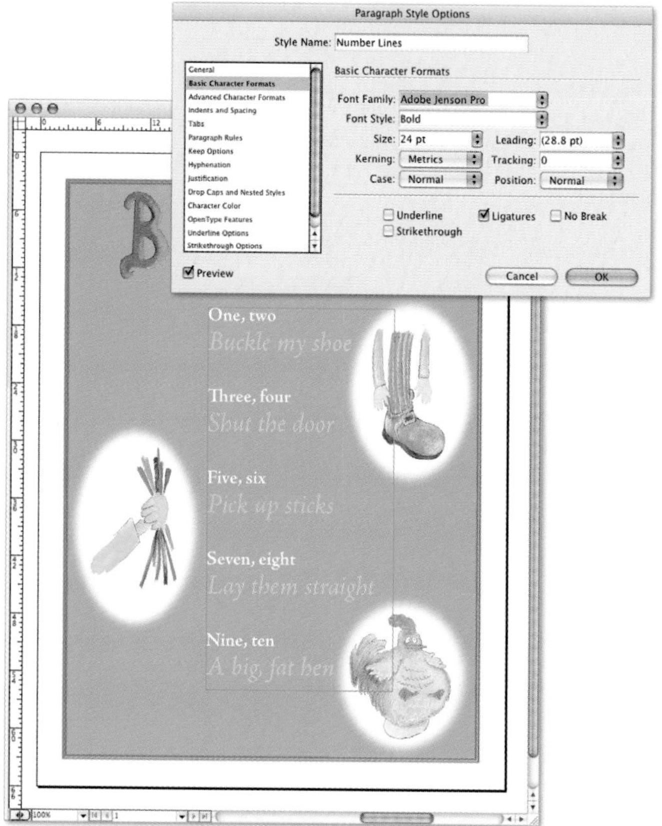
Figure 5-13.

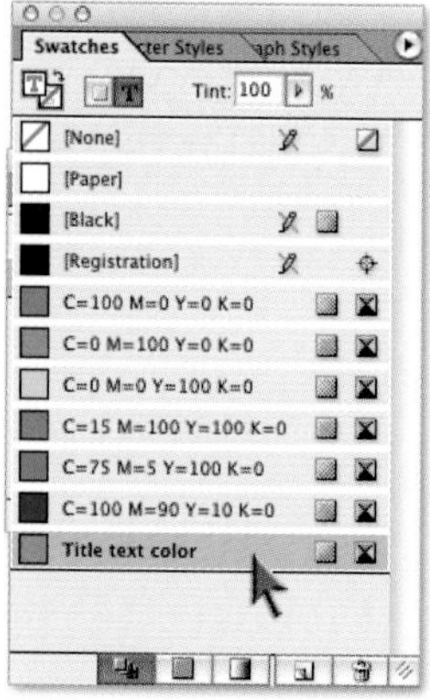
Figure 5-14.

Figure 5-15.

of the document change to Jenson Pro (see Figure 5-13). Note, however, that the two style sheets maintain their individual color, size, and type style settings. The first line of each couplet is white, 24-point, and bold; the second is yellow, 36-point, and italic.

7. ***Select all the text in the first line.*** All right, that was one way to update a style sheet. Now let's look at a potentially easier and certainly more intuitive way. Select all text in the first line of the poem by triple-clicking on *One* or *two* with the type tool.

8. ***Change the color of the text.*** Choose **Window→Swatches** or press F5 to bring up the **Swatches** palette. Then click the swatch called **Title text color**, as shown in Figure 5-14.

9. ***Click anywhere in the first line of type.*** Or press the ↑ key. This deselects the first line so that you can better see its new color, while keeping the paragraph selected. As Figure 5-15, the text in the first line is now a dullish medium red, and the Number Lines style in the Paragraph Styles palette ends in a small plus sign. This is InDesign's way of warning you that changes have been made to this particular paragraph, and it no longer exactly matches the Number Lines style. In other words, the active paragraph enjoys what's called a *local override*. If you were to change the font associated with the Number Lines style, the first line would update in kind. But if you gave Number Lines a new color, the local override—namely red—would remain in place.

10. ***Redefine the Number Lines style.*** Suppose you like the color of the first line of type. You like it so much, in fact, that you want all the number lines to appear in this color. Switch back to the Paragraph Styles palette. Then click the ⊙ arrow in the upper-right corner of the palette and

choose the **Redefine Style** command. Or press the keyboard shortcut, Ctrl+Alt+Shift+R (⌘-Option-Shift-R on the Mac). As shown in Figure 5-16, all paragraphs using the Number Lines style update to reflect the new color. In the Paragraph Styles palette, the plus sign next to the Number Lines item disappears. Meanwhile, the text styled with Rhyming Lines remains unchanged. The child style does not share a common color with its parent, so the child's color is not affected.

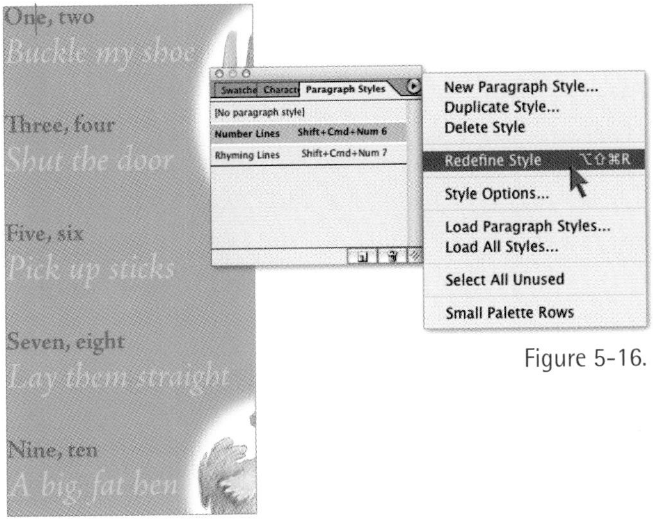

Figure 5-16.

Augmenting Text with Character Styles

Ask a room full of professional designers what they think of style sheets, and they'll tell you that they assign paragraph styles to just about every line of type they create. Formatting a few pages of text is just too tedious and time-consuming without them.

But ask those same designers about character styles, and you'll get a different response. Sure, they use them, just not as much. And with good reason. Paragraph styles permit you to assign dozens of formatting attributes to entire blocks of text with a single click. Character styles typically convey far fewer attributes and affect only a few words or letters at a time. Simply put, applying character styles takes more effort and produces a smaller effect. (For an exception to this—a Great Big Exception, as it just so happens—see "Employing Nested Character Styles" on page 184.)

The primary strength of character styles is editability. When you assign a character style—a process made slightly easier if you add your own keyboard shortcut—you tag the styled text. From that point on, changing the character style updates all tagged text as well. Several pages of underlined words can be changed to italic in a matter of seconds. In the following steps, you'll create a character style and apply it to several sentences, all in different paragraphs. Then you'll update an entirely different style and watch the results cascade up and down the page in the blink of an eye. It's the usual style sheet miracle, just on a more microscopic level.

1. ***Open the sample document.*** This time around, we'll be starting with the document *Page 21.indd*, which is found in the *Lesson 05* folder inside *Lesson Files-IDcs 1on1*. Pictured in Figure 5-17, this excerpt from *Adobe Photoshop CS One-on-One* comprises a total of six paragraphs, all but one of which are styled as steps. The other paragraph, second from the top of the page, is styled as a tip. Feel free to inspect these styles from the Paragraph Styles palette, as explained in the previous exercise.

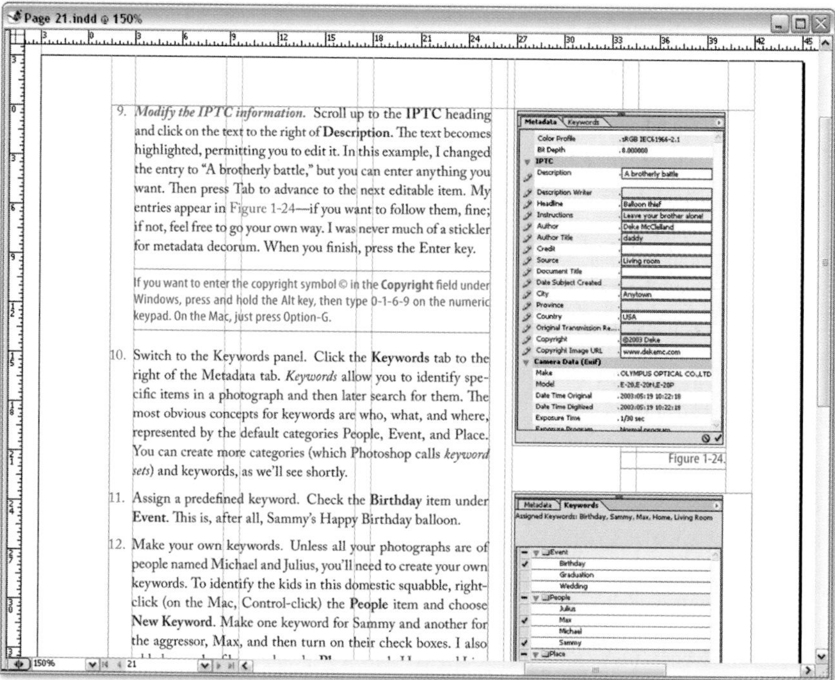

9. *Modify the IPTC information.* Scroll up to the **IPTC** heading and click on the text to the right of **Description.** The text becomes highlighted, permitting you to edit it. In this example, I changed the entry to "A brotherly battle," but you can enter anything you want. Then press Tab to advance to the next editable item. My entries appear in Figure 1-24—if you want to follow them, fine; if not, feel free to go your own way. I was never much of a stickler for metadata decorum. When you finish, press the Enter key.

If you want to enter the copyright symbol © in the **Copyright** field under Windows, press and hold the Alt key, then type 0-1-6-9 on the numeric keypad. On the Mac, just press Option-G.

10. Switch to the Keywords panel. Click the **Keywords** tab to the right of the Metadata tab. *Keywords* allow you to identify specific items in a photograph and then later search for them. The most obvious concepts for keywords are who, what, and where, represented by the default categories People, Event, and Place. You can create more categories (which Photoshop calls *keyword sets*) and keywords, as we'll see shortly.

11. Assign a predefined keyword. Check the **Birthday** item under **Event.** This is, after all, Sammy's Happy Birthday balloon.

12. Make your own keywords. Unless all your photographs are of people named Michael and Julius, you'll need to create your own keywords. To identify the kids in this domestic squabble, right-click (on the Mac, Control-click) the **People** item and choose **New Keyword.** Make one keyword for Sammy and another for the aggressor, Max, and then turn on their check boxes. I also

Figure 5-17.

2. ***Open the Character Styles palette.*** Assuming the Paragraph Styles palette is still open, switching to the Character Styles palette is a simple matter of clicking the **Character Styles** tab. Alternatively you can choose **Window→Type & Tables→Character Styles** (see Figure 5-18 on the opposite page) or press Shift+F11.

   This document happens to include five character styles. Illustrated in Figure 5-19, these styles control the appearance of individual words, such as vocabulary terms and option names. The style sheets are mostly simple, applying as little as a bold or an italic variation. But by relying on a character style instead of a type style, I permit myself to modify the style at a moment's notice, something you'll do in just a few moments.

But first, let's create a style. Among the many specially formatted words in the figure, you may notice that one—the first sentence of the first paragraph—goes unlabeled. This text is not yet tagged with a character style. Nor, it so happens, is its treatment repeated in subsequent steps. We shall remedy these two omissions.

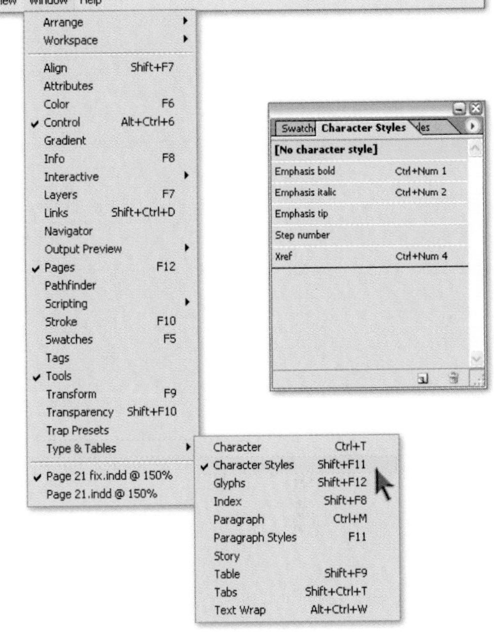

Figure 5-18.

3. ***Select the first sentence on the page.*** Start by selecting the characters on which you intend to base your style—in this case, the turquoise sentence. Among its many selection shortcuts, InDesign lacks a keystroke that selects an entire sentence. Instead, you do so manually by arming yourself with the type tool and employing one of the following methods:

   - Double-click the word *Modify*; on the second click, drag to the end of the sentence. Drag all the way to the *S* in *Scroll* so that you include the period and the en space.
   - Click in front of the *M* in *Modify*. Then press Ctrl+Shift+→ (or ⌘-Shift-→) five times in a row, once for each word plus the punctuation.
   - Don't cotton to such fancy tricks? Select the sentence the old-fashioned way by dragging from one end of the sentence to the other.

Step number   Xref   Emphasis bold

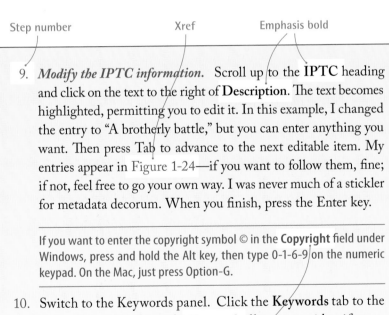

9. ***Modify the IPTC information.*** Scroll up to the **IPTC** heading and click on the text to the right of **Description**. The text becomes highlighted, permitting you to edit it. In this example, I changed the entry to "A brotherly battle," but you can enter anything you want. Then press Tab to advance to the next editable item. My entries appear in Figure 1-24—if you want to follow them, fine; if not, feel free to go your own way. I was never much of a stickler for metadata decorum. When you finish, press the Enter key.

If you want to enter the copyright symbol © in the **Copyright** field under Windows, press and hold the Alt key, then type 0-1-6-9 on the numeric keypad. On the Mac, just press Option-G.

10. Switch to the Keywords panel. Click the **Keywords** tab to the right of the Metadata tab. *Keywords* allow you to identify specific items in a photograph and then later search for them. The

Emphasis italic   Emphasis tip

Figure 5-19.

However you decide to approach it, your selection should appear as it does in Figure 5-20.

4. ***Create a new character style.*** Choose **New Character Style** from the **Character Styles** palette menu. Or press the Alt key (Option on the Mac) and click the icon at the bottom of the palette. InDesign displays the **New Character Style** dialog box, which lists all special formatting attributes applied to the highlighted text, namely *Bold Italic + color: Deep Turquoise*.

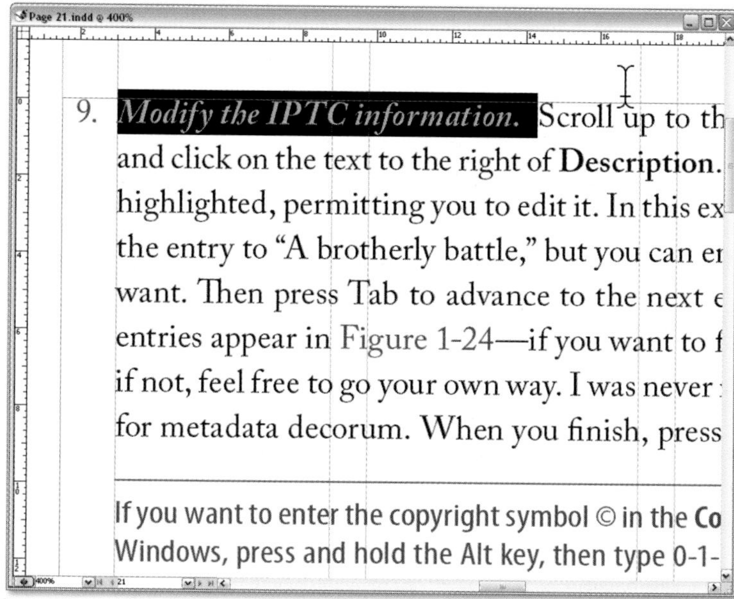

Figure 5-20.

5. ***Name the style and give it a shortcut.*** Change the **Style Name** to "Step leader." Then Tab to the **Shortcut** option and press Ctrl (or ⌘) and 5 on the numeric keypad. The Shortcut option should now read *Ctrl+Num 5* (or *Cmd+Num 5*).

   Remember, if InDesign beeps or ignores you when you try to enter a shortcut, tap the Num Lock key and try again. As I mentioned earlier, not all keyboards have keypads; if yours does not, don't worry about the shortcut.

6. ***Select a Based On style.*** Set the **Based On** option to **Step Number**, as shown in Figure 5-21. This establishes a parent/child relationship between the two style sheets. Any change made to the parent, Step Number, will also affect the shared attributes of the child, Step Leader. I'll show you how this works in Step 9 on the next page.

PEARL OF WISDOM

Style shortcuts are a matter of taste. But for my part, I keep my character styles simple—just Ctrl or ⌘ and a number—and add modifier keys to the paragraph styles. In this document, for example, Ctrl+Alt+1 applies the essential Headline paragraph style; just plain Ctrl+1 applies the discretionary Emphasis Bold character style. If this sounds counterintuitive, consider this: I apply most of my paragraph styles as I write the text in Microsoft Word, so they're already established when I import the text into InDesign. Character styles are finishing effects, so I wait to apply them until I'm well into the layout phase. I spend more time applying character styles, hence they get the quicker shortcuts. You don't have to do as I do, but you should design your shortcuts to suit your working habits.

7. ***Apply the new style sheet to the text.*** Click the **OK** button to create the new character style. Then, with the text still selected in the document window, click the **Step Leader** item in the **Character Styles** palette. Or press the keyboard shortcut, Ctrl+[5] (⌘-[5] on the Mac). Now any changes made to the style will affect the highlighted text in kind.

8. ***Apply the character style to the other first sentences.*** Select the sentence at the outset of step 10, being sure to select the period and the en space. Then apply the **Step Leader** style sheet. Repeat this process for each of the sentences that begin steps 11 through 13. Figure 5-22 shows how the finished styles should look. (Note that I've deselected the text and pressed the W key to hide all guidelines.)

9. ***Deselect the text.*** The remaining steps explain how to modify a character style. Unless you want to apply the style as you edit it (which we don't), you need to first deselect all text. For the sake of variety, here's a new way to do that: Press Ctrl (or ⌘) to temporarily access the arrow tool. Then with the key pressed, click in an empty portion of the document window.

10. ***Edit the Step Number style.*** Now let's say you show your design to a client. The client loves it, except for one thing—she wants the number and lead-in text to be brown. No problem; you can do it all in one operation. Here's how:

    - Double-click the recently established parent style **Step Number** in the Character Styles palette. This displays the **Character Style Options** dialog box, as in Figure 5-23 on the next page.

    - If it's not on already, turn on the **Preview** check box so you can see the effects of your changes.

    - Click the **Character Color** item on the left side of the dialog box. InDesign displays a panel of options that assign color attributes to the active style.

    - Click the fill icon in the center portion of the dialog box so it looks like ■.

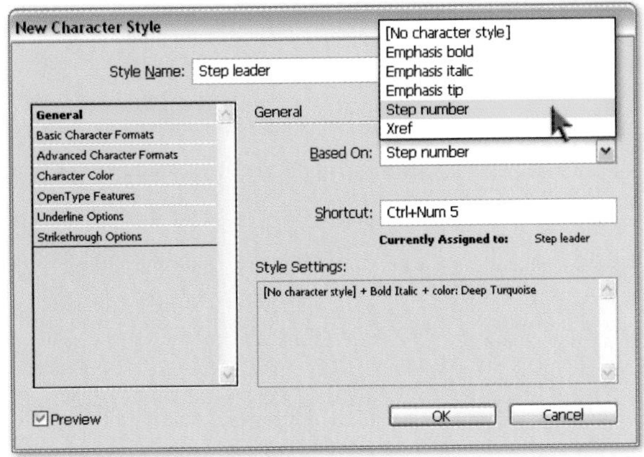

Figure 5-21.

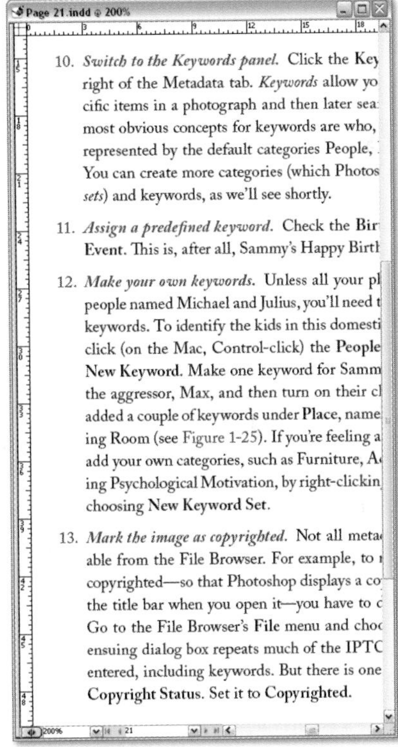

10. *Switch to the Keywords panel.* Click the Key right of the Metadata tab. *Keywords* allow yo cific items in a photograph and then later sea most obvious concepts for keywords are who, represented by the default categories People, You can create more categories (which Photos *sets*) and keywords, as we'll see shortly.

11. *Assign a predefined keyword.* Check the Bir Event. This is, after all, Sammy's Happy Birtl

12. *Make your own keywords.* Unless all your pl people named Michael and Julius, you'll need t keywords. To identify the kids in this domesti click (on the Mac, Control-click) the **People** **New Keyword**. Make one keyword for Samm the aggressor, Max, and then turn on their cl added a couple of keywords under **Place**, name ing Room (see Figure 1-25). If you're feeling a add your own categories, such as Furniture, A ing Psychological Motivation, by right-clickin choosing **New Keyword Set**.

13. *Mark the image as copyrighted.* Not all meta able from the File Browser. For example, to copyrighted—so that Photoshop displays a co the title bar when you open it—you have to c Go to the File Browser's **File** menu and choo ensuing dialog box repeats much of the IPTC entered, including keywords. But there is one **Copyright Status**. Set it to **Copyrighted**.

Figure 5-22.

- The right side of the dialog box features a short list of colors that I created in the Swatches palette. (To learn how to create your own, see the "Fill, Stroke, and Color" exercise, which begins on page 211 in Lesson 6.) Click the final color, **Medium Brown**, to apply it.
- Click the **OK** button to accept your changes and exit the dialog box.

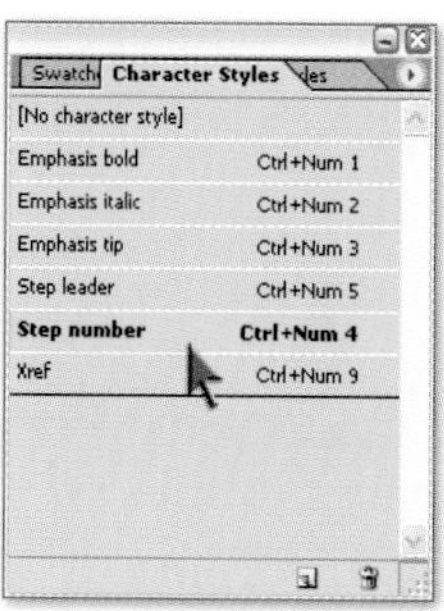

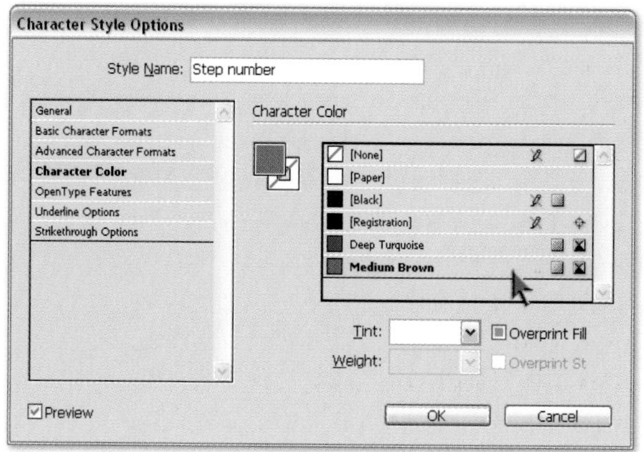

Figure 5-23.

Because color is a shared attribute of Step Number and its progeny Step Leader, both the numbers and the bold-italic sentences change to medium brown. All other attributes remain unchanged. Likewise unchanged are other turquoise words tagged with style sheets that are not children of Step Number, as verified by the figure reference and tip text in Figure 5-24.

Figure 5-24.

Employing Nested Character Styles

When I introduced the preceding exercise, I explained that character styles take a long time to apply. If you apply them traditionally—a few words or characters at a time—that's certainly true. But thanks to a brilliant innovation in InDesign CS, there's a better way. You can embed character styles into paragraph style definitions, resulting in one of the great automation functions in all of InDesign, *nested styles*.

Let's say you find yourself repeating a series of character styles over and over again within a specific kind of styled paragraph. The steps in this book are a perfect example. The number is colored;

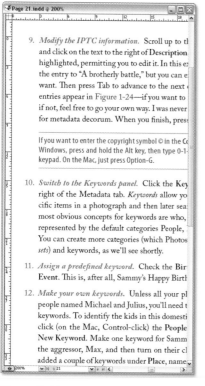

the leading sentence is colored, bold, and italic; the second through last sentences are black and roman. This is exactly the sort of style pattern that nested styles are designed to facilitate. Using spaces, periods, and other delineators, nested styles tell InDesign exactly when to start applying a character style and when to stop.

In this exercise, you'll nest the Step Number and Step Leader character styles inside the Step paragraph style so that InDesign assigns them automatically to all steps in the document. You'll also learn what to do when, contrary to your wishes, nested styles spill over into child style sheets. By the end of this lesson, don't be surprised if your head is spinning with ideas for ways to put nested styles to work in your own documents.

1. ***Open yet another sample document.*** Open *Page 19.indd* from the *Lesson 05* folder inside *Lesson Files-IDcs 1on1*. As shown in Figure 5-25, this is another excerpt lifted from the pages of *Adobe Photoshop CS One-on-One*, with two important differences: First, I saved the document in the preview mode so we can focus on the text without having to sift through the guides and other falderal. Second, the document contains the necessary character styles, Step Number and Step Leader, but I haven't yet applied them.

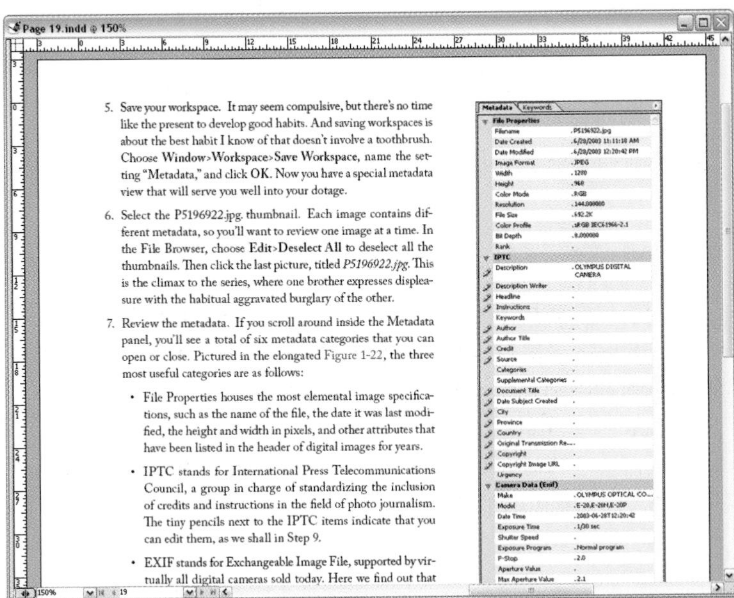

Page 19.indd @ 150%
5. Save your workspace. It may seem compulsive, but there's no time like the present to develop good habits. And saving workspaces is about the best habit I know of that doesn't involve a toothbrush. Choose Window>Workspace>Save Workspace, name the setting "Metadata," and click OK. Now you have a special metadata view that will serve you well into your dotage.
6. Select the P5196922.jpg. thumbnail. Each image contains different metadata, so you'll want to review one image at a time. In the File Browser, choose Edit>Deselect All to deselect all the thumbnails. Then click the last picture, titled P5196922.jpg. This is the climax to the series, where one brother expresses displeasure with the habitual aggravated burglary of the other.
7. Review the metadata. If you scroll around inside the Metadata panel, you'll see a total of six metadata categories that you can open or close. Pictured in the elongated Figure 1-22, the three most useful categories are as follows:
• File Properties houses the most elemental image specifications, such as the name of the file, the date it was last modified, the height and width in pixels, and other attributes that have been listed in the header of digital images for years.
• IPTC stands for International Press Telecommunications Council, a group in charge of standardizing the inclusion of credits and instructions in the field of photo journalism. The tiny pencils next to the IPTC items indicate that you can edit them, as we shall in Step 9.
• EXIF stands for Exchangeable Image File, supported by virtually all digital cameras sold today. Here we find out that
150%
19

Figure 5-25.

PEARL OF WISDOM

Before we go any further, I'd like you to play a quick visualization game with me. After manually applying character styles to page 21 ("Augmenting Text with Character Styles," page 179), you switch to page 19 only to find you have all that work to do over again. And then there's the rest of the book to look forward to—12 lessons in all with roughly 100 steps per lesson. Can you imagine having to apply these character styles 2,400 times (1,200 times each) over the course of a single book-length document? In QuarkXPress and every other layout application prior to InDesign CS, that's what you'd have to do. I just want you to appreciate how much time you're about to save.

2. ***Display the Paragraph Styles palette.*** Although nested styles are technically character styles, you apply them within the context of paragraph styles. So click the **Paragraph Styles** tab or press F11 to bring up the Paragraph Styles palette. Of the eight styles, we are concerned with just the two applied to the body copy, Step and Step Bullet, illustrated in Figure 5-26.

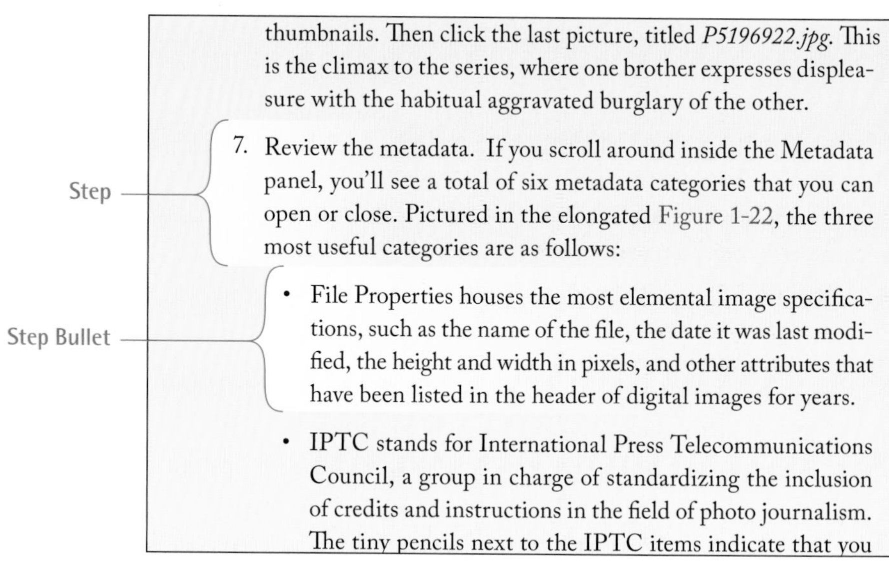

Step
Step Bullet
thumbnails. Then click the last picture, titled *P5196922.jpg*. This is the climax to the series, where one brother expresses displeasure with the habitual aggravated burglary of the other.
7. Review the metadata. If you scroll around inside the Metadata panel, you'll see a total of six metadata categories that you can open or close. Pictured in the elongated Figure 1-22, the three most useful categories are as follows:
• File Properties houses the most elemental image specifications, such as the name of the file, the date it was last modified, the height and width in pixels, and other attributes that have been listed in the header of digital images for years.
• IPTC stands for International Press Telecommunications Council, a group in charge of standardizing the inclusion of credits and instructions in the field of photo journalism. The tiny pencils next to the IPTC items indicate that you

Figure 5-26.

3. ***Open the Nested Styles options for the Step style sheet.*** We'll start by assigning character styles to the Step style sheet. And to do that, we need to open one of InDesign's most well-hidden collections of options, like so:

   - Double-click the **Step** item in the Paragraph Styles palette to display the **Paragraph Style Options** dialog box.
   - Click **Drop Caps and Nested Styles** on the left side of the dialog box.

Why InDesign has chosen to couple its nested styles options with drop caps is anyone's guess. (Okay, they both affect the first few characters in a paragraph, but let's face it, that's a stretch.) Alas, Adobe makes these decisions, we can but follow. Needless to say, we'll be giving drop caps the slip and focusing exclusively on the Nested Styles options, highlighted in Figure 5-27.

4. ***Add the Step Number character style.*** Click the **New Nested Style** button, located bottom-center in the dialog box. This adds an entry to the Nested Styles field, which reads *[No character style] through 1 Words*. While hardly grammatical, this strangely worded entry is editable. Click the ⌄ arrow (⬍ on the Mac) to the right of *[No character style]* and choose the **Step Number** style to make it the first nested style.

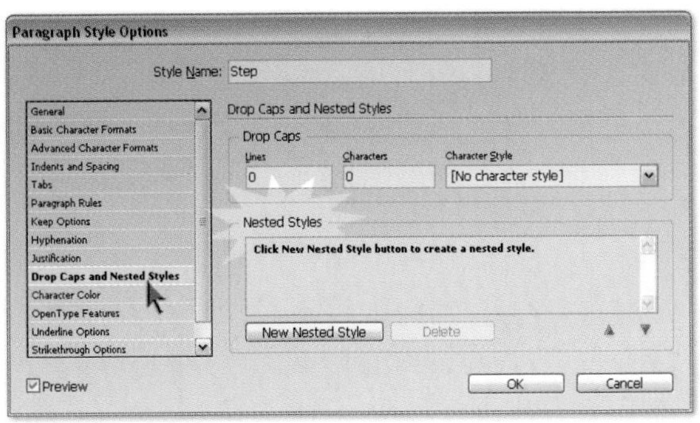

Figure 5-27.

To preview the effect of this addition in the document window, turn on the **Preview** check box. If Preview is already turned on, press Enter or Return, or click an empty portion of the dialog box. Either action deactivates your choice of character style and invokes the preview.

The modified entry, *Step Number through 1 Words*, tells InDesign to apply the Step Number character style to the first word of each tagged paragraph. (Think of *through* as being short for "through and including.") The first word ends at the first space character (in this case, a tab), which means that InDesign styles both the number and its period, as witnessed in Figure 5-28.

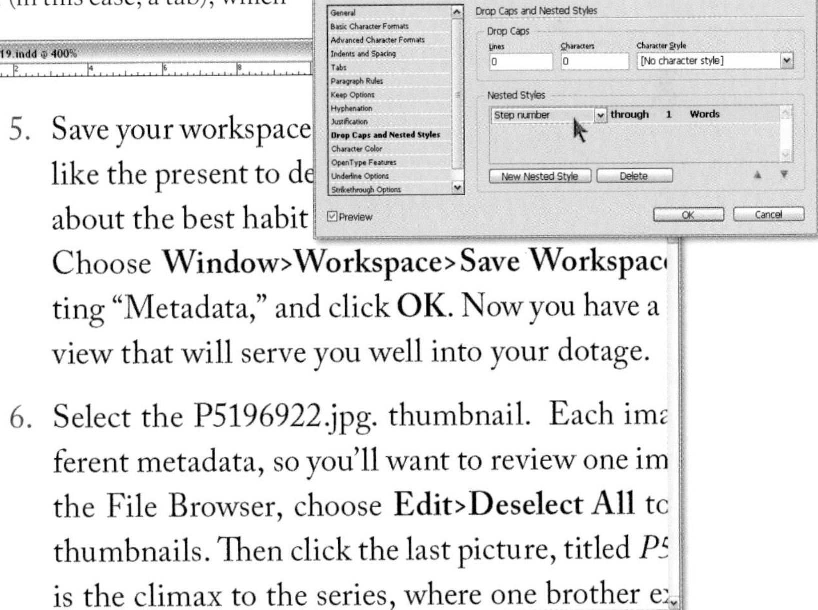

Figure 5-28.

5. ***Add the Step Leader character style.*** The next step is to apply the Step Leader style to the first full sentence in the paragraph. Here's how you do it:

   - Click the **New Nested Style** button. A new entry appears.
   - Click the ▾ arrow (⇕ on the Mac) and choose **Step Leader**.
   - Click on **Words** (the last word in the entry) to activate this option. Then click the ▾ arrow and choose **Sentences**, which changes a full sentence to the Step Leader style.

   Assuming the Preview check box is on, press the Enter or Return key to preview the nested style in the document window. All is well—except for step 6, and here we have a problem. As illustrated in Figure 5-29, the word *thumbnail* (circled in red) is actually part of the lead-in to the step. But a typographic error—namely, a misplaced period—has cut short my sentence.

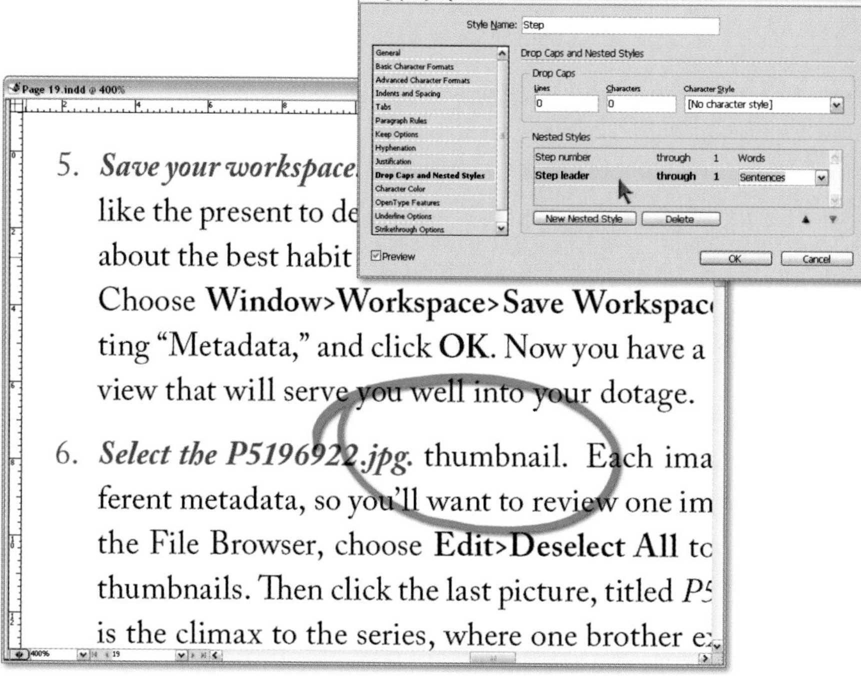

Figure 5-29.

PEARL OF WISDOM

The Sentences option ends the character style at a period, question mark, or exclamation point. But a period goes unnoticed within *P5196922.jpg* (a digital camera file name). The Sentences option is smart enough to demand that a space follow the period. But alas, it is not smart enough to account for human error. We must seek a more foolproof solution.

6. ***Change the ending point for Step Leader.*** I separated the initial sentence from the text that follows with an en space. Fortunately, this is a character that InDesign has chosen to identify:

   - Click on the word **Sentences** to activate the option.
   - Click the ☑ arrow (⊡ on the Mac) next to Sentences and choose **En Spaces** near the bottom of the pop-up menu.
   - Click the word **through**, and then click its ☑ and choose **up to**. This tells InDesign to apply the character style to everything up to (but not including) the en space.

   Press Enter or Return to see the preview in Figure 5-30. When you are satisfied that all is well, click the **OK** button.

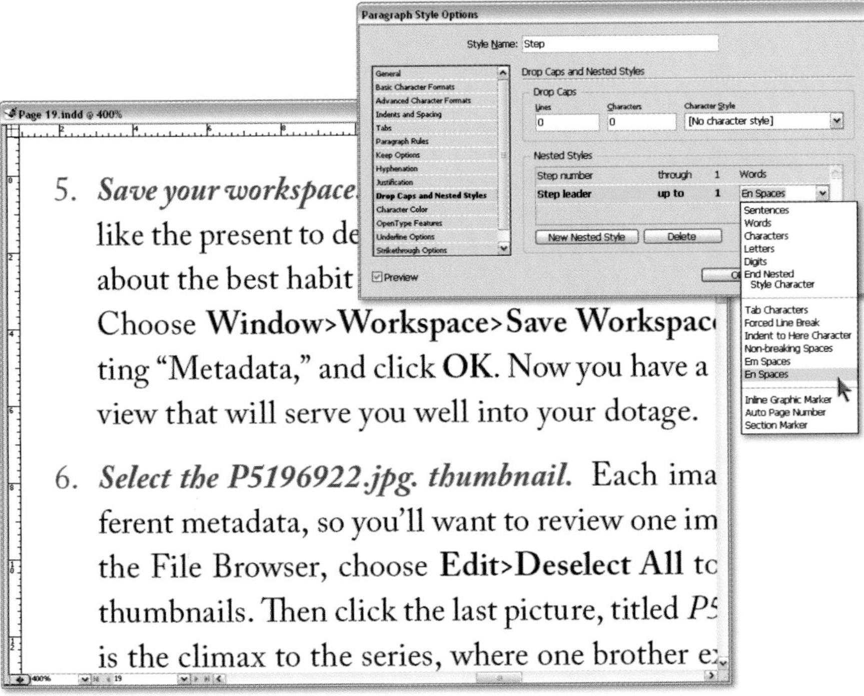

Figure 5-30.

7. ***Scroll to the bullet points.*** If all is going according to plan, your steps and nested character styles are looking fine. But scroll down to the bulleted paragraphs after step 7 and all is far from fine—all is royally bungled. As illustrated in Figure 5-31, the bulleted items are without exception turquoise, bold, and italic. Two reasons for this: 1) the Step Bullet style (which oversees these paragraphs) is a child to the Step style and has therefore adopted its nested styles, and 2) the paragraphs lack en spaces to stop the formatting. Solution: adjust the Step Bullet style.

8. ***Open the Nested Styles options for the Step Bullet style sheet.*** Go to the **Paragraph Styles** palette and double-click the **Step Bullet** item. After the **Paragraph Style Options** dialog box appears, click **Drop Caps and Nested Styles** to display the character styles that you added in Steps 4 through 6.

9. ***Remove any character styles from the first nested style.*** For starters, let's change the bullets to their normal state. Click **Step Number** directly below **Nested Styles** to activate the option. Then click the ▼ arrow (or ⬍) and choose **[No character style]**. Press the Enter or Return key to make the bullets black.

10. ***Change Step Leader to Emphasis Bold.*** Still inside the Paragraph Style Options dialog box, click the **Step Leader** item to make it active. Then click ▼ (or ⬍) and choose **Emphasis**

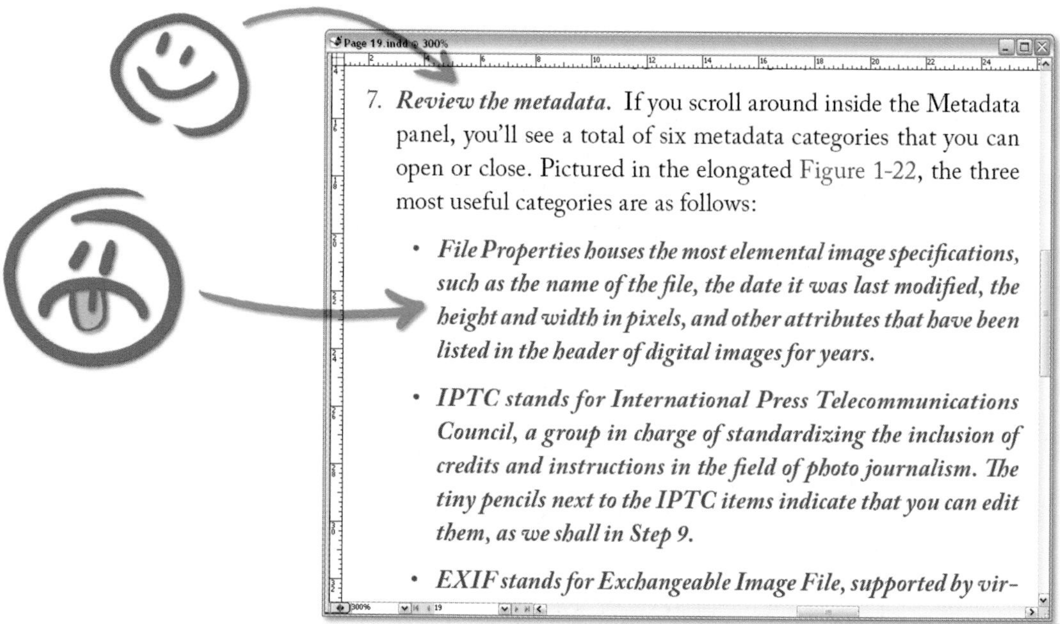

7. ***Review the metadata.*** If you scroll around inside the Metadata panel, you'll see a total of six metadata categories that you can open or close. Pictured in the elongated Figure 1-22, the three most useful categories are as follows:

- ***File Properties houses the most elemental image specifications, such as the name of the file, the date it was last modified, the height and width in pixels, and other attributes that have been listed in the header of digital images for years.***
- ***IPTC stands for International Press Telecommunications Council, a group in charge of standardizing the inclusion of credits and instructions in the field of photo journalism. The tiny pencils next to the IPTC items indicate that you can edit them, as we shall in Step 9.***
- ***EXIF stands for Exchangeable Image File, supported by vir-***

Figure 5-31.

Bold. Previewed inside the document window, InDesign makes all bulleted items bold, but I want only the first one or two words—*File Properties*, *IPTC*, and *EXIF*—to be bold. There is no delimiting character to offset these words, but fortunately, you can add one.

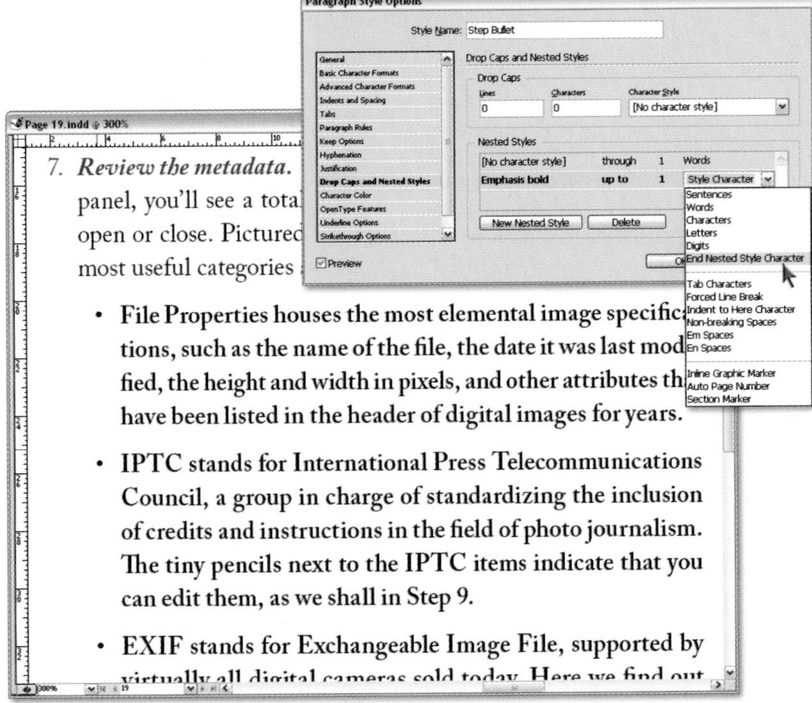

Figure 5-32.

11. *Change En Spaces to End Nested Style Character.* Currently, the style ends at the first en space. To change this, click the **En Spaces** item to make it active. Next click ☑ (or ⬍) and choose **End Nested Style Character**. Initially, this doesn't change anything (see Figure 5-32). It merely calls upon a special character, which we'll insert in the next step.

    Click the **OK** button to exit the dialog box and accept your changes. Believe it or not, the nested styles are working just fine. Now, let's see how to put them in play.

12. *Add an End Nested Style glyph.* The End Nested Style Character option looks for the first occurrence of a special character, called (surprise) the End Nested Style glyph. To enter this glyph, do the following:

    - Press T to get the type tool. (Or select it from the toolbox if you prefer.)

- Click immediately after the words *File Properties*. The blinking insertion marker should appear between the *s* and the space that follows it. If it doesn't, use the ← or → key to nudge the marker into position.

- Right-click to display the shortcut menu. (If your Macintosh mouse has no right mouse button, press the Control key and click.)

- Choose **Insert Special Character→End Nested Style Here**. As shown in Figure 5-33, this ends the nested Emphasis Bold style and resumes normal text.

Congratulations. You now know more than most full-time designers about style sheets and their application inside InDesign CS. Admittedly, you have a few loose ends. If you want to fix them, here's how: First, you have a couple of messed up bullet items. To fix them, click to set the insertion marker after *IPTC*, right-click, and choose **Insert Special Character→End Nested Style Here**. Repeat, this time setting the insertion marker after *EXIF*. Second, there's the typo that I pointed out in Step 5 (page 188). Delete the period after *P5196922.jpg* and the typo is resolved. Well done—I now release you to go about your business.

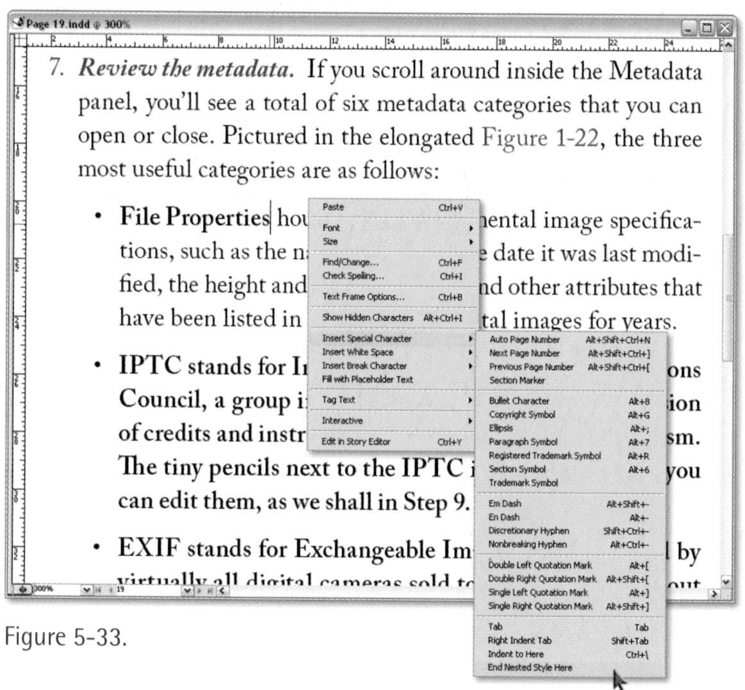

Figure 5-33.

WHAT DID YOU LEARN?

Match the key concept in the numbered list below with the letter of the phrase that best describes it. Answers appear upside-down at the bottom of the page.

Key Concepts

1. Style sheet
2. Paragraph Style palette
3. Num Lock
4. Based On
5. Next Style
6. Local override
7. Redefine Style
8. New Character Style
9. Nested style
10. Through and up to
11. Sentences
12. End Nested Style Character

Descriptions

A. This option looks for a special glyph to signal the termination of an embedded character style.

B. This option allows you to pick a style sheet that will automatically become active when you begin a new paragraph.

C. A collection of formatting attribute settings that you can save, reapply, and even assign a keyboard shortcut.

D. These options in the Drop Caps and Nested Styles panel of the Paragraph Style Options dialog box assign limits to the scope of a nested character style.

E. A formatting change applied to a word or paragraph so that it no longer exactly matches its corresponding style sheet.

F. Your primary means for creating, modifying, and applying style sheets, which you can show and hide by pressing the F11 key.

G. This command creates a special kind of style sheet that affects single words or characters of type at a time.

H. This option establishes a parent-child relationship between two style sheets, after which any changes made to the parent style will affect shared formatting attributes in the child style.

I. This option in the Drop Caps and Nested Styles panel of the Paragraph Style Options dialog box ends the nested character style at a period, question mark, or exclamation point followed by a space.

J. If your laptop or notebook computer lacks a numeric keypad, you must press this key before using a keyboard shortcut to apply a style sheet.

K. This command updates a style sheet to include any local overrides applied to the selected text, and includes the keyboard shortcut Ctrl+Alt+Shift+R (⌘-Option-Shift-R on the Mac).

L. You create this special kind of style sheet by embedding a character style into a paragraph style definition.

Answers

1C, 2F, 3J, 4H, 5B, 6E, 7K, 8G, 9L, 10D, 11I, 12A

LESSON 6

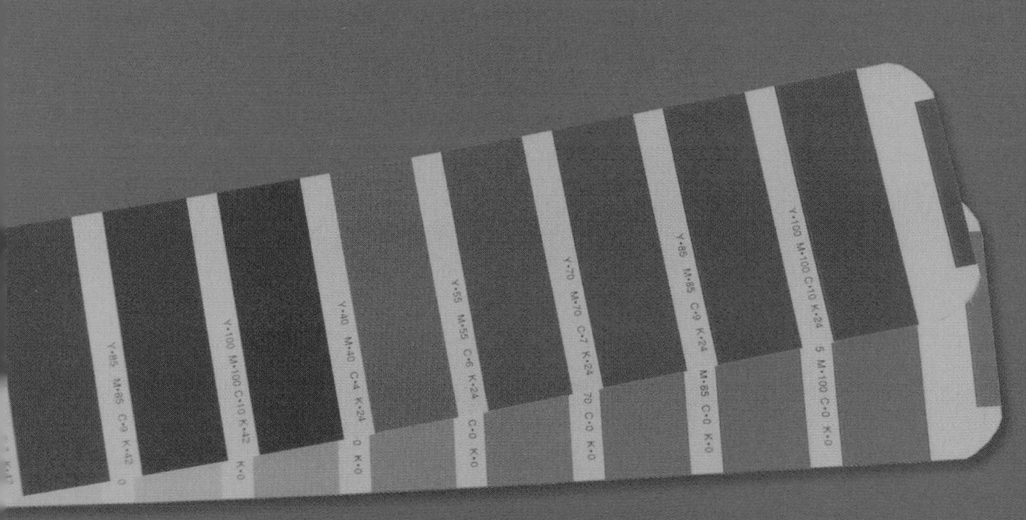

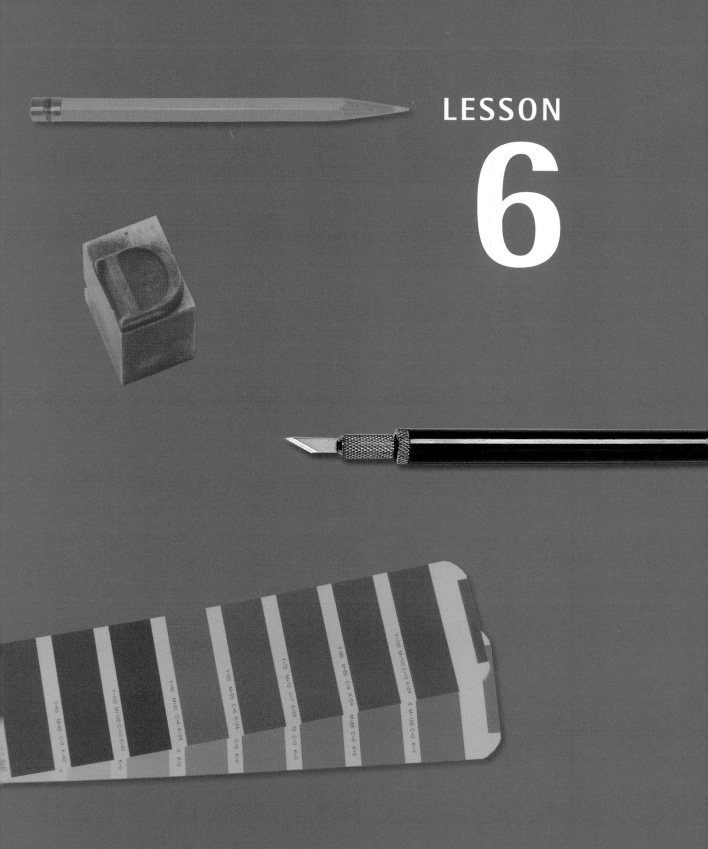

DRAWING INSIDE INDESIGN

BY NOW, WE can all agree that InDesign's text-handling capabilities are the best in the business. If not entirely beyond reproach, they are safely beyond compare. And if you ask me, that's only fitting. Great typography is integral to great design. If the world's best layout program won't provide us with the best tools for manipulating and formatting type, I ask you, then what in the world will?

No, InDesign's text-handling prowess is no surprise. What's truly astounding—what knocks my socks off, tosses them in the oven, and bakes them at 450 degrees (which, were that to really happen, would surprise me)—is how much attention InDesign lavishes on graphics. Here's an application that's intended first and foremost for laying out pages, and yet it provides better illustration tools than most illustration programs. Once upon a time, for example, I might have drawn the line art in Figure 6-1 using a 2-D drawing program. While I still use such programs—Adobe Illustrator in particular is extremely powerful—I drew these particular lines and shapes directly in InDesign.

Figure 6-1.

InDesign's illustration tools are devoted to the creation of *vector-based graphics*. By this, I mean mathematically defined outlines that conform to the highest resolution of your printer, monitor, or other piece of hardware. No matter how far you zoom in or scale the outlines, they appear impeccably smooth (see Figure 6-2 on the next page). Therefore, anything you draw in InDesign is said to be resolution-independent.

ABOUT THIS LESSON

Project Files

Before beginning the exercises, make sure that you've installed the lesson files from the CD, as explained in Step 5 on page xv of the Preface. This should result in a folder called *Lesson Files-IDcs 1on1* on your desktop. We'll be working with the files inside the *Lesson 06* subfolder.

In this lesson, we'll explore InDesign's extensive collection of drawing tools. You can draw paths, edit them, mix colors, select from spot-color libraries, create multicolor gradients, align objects, combine simple shapes to create more complex ones—the list goes on and on. Along the way, you'll learn how to:

- Use the line, pen, rectangle, ellipse, and polygon tools to draw graphic objects . . . . . . page 198
- Apply fill and stroke, specify process and spot colors, and design custom outlines . . . . page 211
- Create linear and radial gradients . . . . page 221
- Align and distribute text and graphic objects . . . . page 228
- Combine shapes using compound paths and Pathfinder operations . . . . page 233

Video Lesson 6: Pencil versus Pen

InDesign lets you draw page ornaments and symbols directly on the page using a wealth of versatile line and shape tools, most of which are lifted right out of Adobe's flagship illustration program, Illustrator. Prominent among these are the pencil and pen tools. Use the pencil to draw freehand lines that follow the path of your drag; use the pen to draw precise outlines one anchor point at a time.

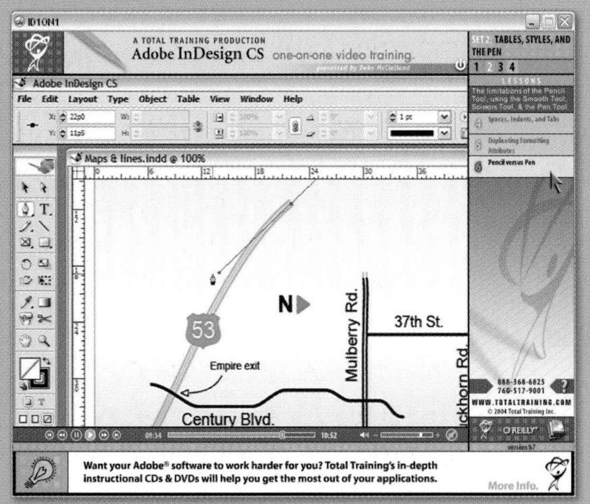

To learn how the pencil and pen tools work—and why the pen is so much better—watch the sixth video lesson on the CD. Insert the CD, click the **Start Training** button, click the Set 2 button, and then select **6, Pencil versus Pen** from the Lessons list. During its 10 minutes and 52 seconds, this movie covers the following operations and shortcuts:

Operation	Windows shortcut	Macintosh shortcut
Select the pencil tool	N	N
Nudge selected object	↑, ↓, ←, or → (arrow keys)	↑, ↓, ←, or → (arrow keys)
Temporarily access the white arrow tool	Ctrl	⌘
Smooth line with pencil tool	Alt-drag over line	Option-drag over line
Select the pen tool	P	P
Send selected object to back	Ctrl+Shift+[(left bracket)	⌘+Shift+[(left bracket)

The technical term for a line or shape in InDesign is *path outline*, or just plain *path*. The idea is that the contour of the shape follows a mathematically defined path from Point A to Point B and so on. We'll be learning a great deal about paths—including how you draw them and how you put them to use—in the upcoming exercises. In fact, paths are what this lesson is all about.

Figure 6-2.

Home-Grown Graphics

As impressed as you might be that you can draw inside a page-layout program, you may wonder why you would want to. After all, isn't drawing a great example of a task that's better handled in another program? Then there's the matter of talent. Just because you're good at designing and assembling pages doesn't mean you're an artist. What good is a bunch of drawing tools if you can't draw?

InDesign provides its drawing tools primarily for your convenience. Rather than making you go to another program to create page ornaments, symbols, maps, diagrams, and other common graphics, InDesign lets you do it right there on the page. In addition to saving you the time and effort otherwise required to swap programs and place artwork, drawing in InDesign means that you can edit in InDesign. So just as you can fix a typo without returning to your word processor, you can adjust the angle of a line without having to open, modify, and save the illustration with a separate application.

Better yet, when you draw inside InDesign, you know exactly how big and what proportions to make your graphic because you can see it interact with text and other elements as you build it. In other words, InDesign's drawing tools eliminate guesswork and make for a more intuitive page-creation experience.

For those of you concerned about your lack of drawing skills—if even the best of your stick figures make you blush with shame—don't despair. I can't promise that InDesign will have you drawing faces like the one in Figure 6-2. But the program's handful of simple line and shape tools will have you drawing, well, simple lines and

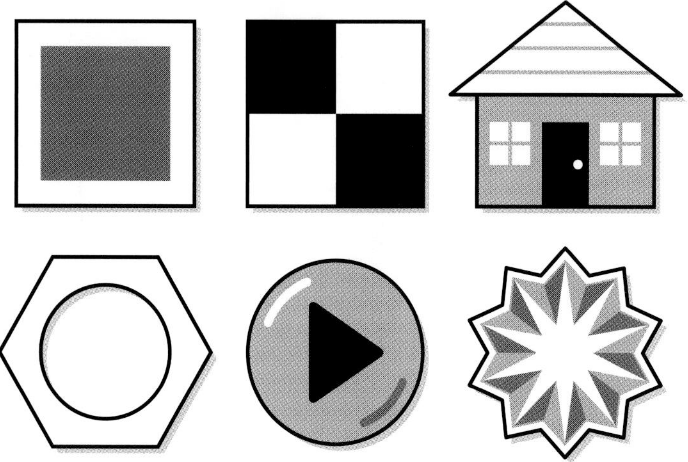

Figure 6-3.

Figure 6-4.

shapes in no time. Figure 6-3 shows a series of basic ornaments crafted entirely using the simplest of the simple shapes: rectangles, ovals, and stars. None of these shapes is the least bit difficult to draw. The success of the ornaments therefore hinges on having a clear idea of what you want to accomplish and divining the proper means to that end. In other words, drawing inside InDesign is less about artistic dexterity and more about creative thinking. Throw in a dash of practice, and I dare say the quality of your stick figures might improve as well (see Figure 6-4).

Drawing Lines and Shapes

You might think of InDesign's drawing tools as being organized into a kind of pyramid, with the pen tool at the top and everything else below. Introduced in Video Lesson 6, "Pencil versus Pen" (see page 196), InDesign's pen tool is so versatile and capable that, truth be told, it can draw *anything*. In comparison, the tools at the bottom of the pyramid are very narrowly focused. For example, the rectangle tool draws rectangles and squares, that's it.

But that doesn't mean you should focus on the pen to the exclusion of all others. Just try drawing a circle with the pen tool and you'll quickly come to appreciate the narrow focus and utter simplicity of the ellipse tool. In fact, as with the food pyramid, the tools at the bottom are your staples, the ones you turn to on a regular basis. The pen tool is dessert, and as such, to be used sparingly.

In this exercise, we'll look at all courses in the drawing tool banquet—line, rectangle, ellipse, polygon, and pen. (The only drawing tool I skip is the pencil tool; I said all there is to say about it in the video.) We'll use these drawing tools to complete a map.

1. *Open the map to the party.* Go to the *Lesson 06* folder inside the *Lesson Files-IDcs 1on1* folder and open the document named *Party map 1.indd*. Pictured in Figure 6-5, this document features a map to Jerry's house. It seems that Jerry is having some friends over after their weekly karaoke night, where he hopes the gang will party like it's 1979. Obviously, Jerry needs help—so let's give him a hand.

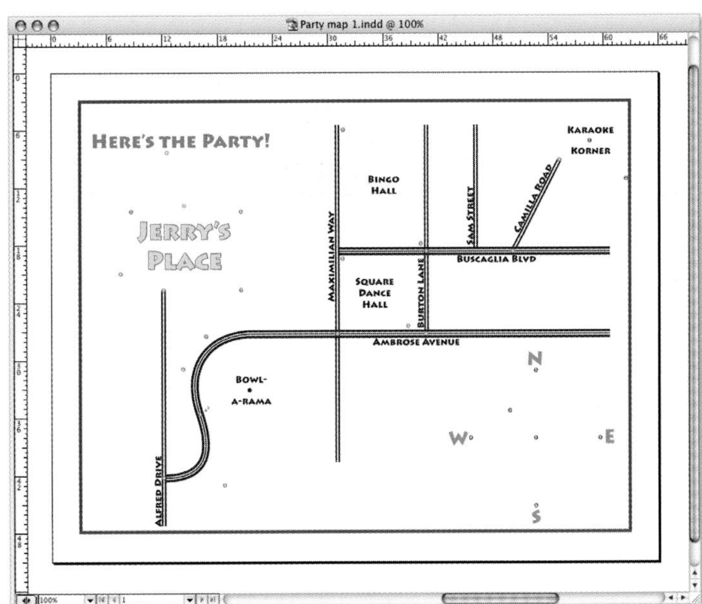

Figure 6-5.

2. *Examine the layers.* To keep the various elements of the map separate from each other, I've assigned this document three layers. If you're unfamiliar with layers, don't fret; I discuss them at length in Lesson 9, "Pages, Layers, and XML." But for now, let's take a look at them:

   - Choose **Window→Layers** or press F7 to display the **Layers** palette shown in Figure 6-6.

   - The bottom layer, Map, contains the lines and street names that make up the map.

   - The middle layer, Guide Dots, contains the color-coded dots you'll be using as guides for drawing. You may have to zoom in to 200 percent or more to clearly see the colors and numbers of the dots.

   - You can turn either of these layers off by clicking the icon in front of the layer name. Click where the eye used to be to turn the layer back on.

   - The icon next to the Map and Guide Dots layers means that these layers are locked and their contents cannot be altered. Please leave them locked.

   - The top layer, Layer 3, is the active layer. This is the layer you'll be drawing on.

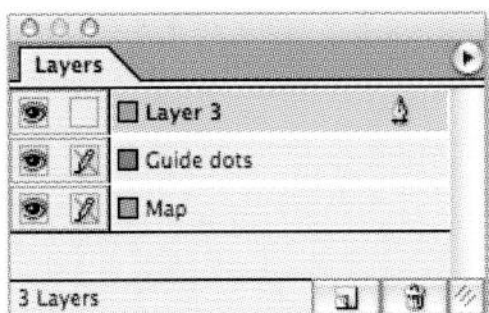

Figure 6-6.

If you are trying to use the drawing tools but your cursor resembles the icon, you've managed to select a locked layer. Click Layer 3 in the Layers palette and all will be well.

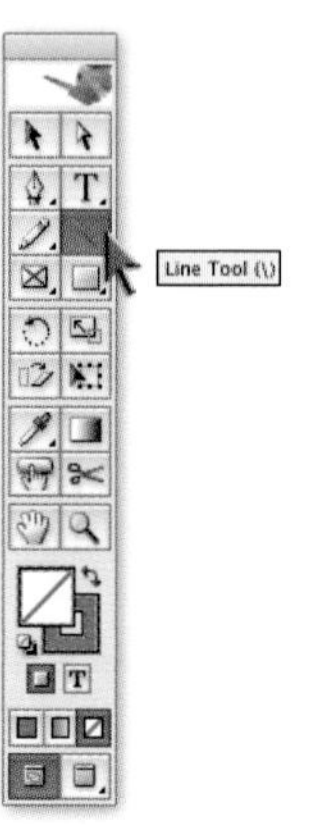

Figure 6-7.

3. *Select the line tool.* The map may appear to be more or less complete, but it's missing a few elements. For example, we need to draw a red line down the streets to show the correct route to Jerry's house. Click the line tool icon in toolbox (see Figure 6-7) or press the \ (backslash) key. This turns out to be one of the easiest shortcuts to remember because the line tool looks like a backslash.

4. *Draw a line on Camilla Road.* We'll start the route from Karaoke Korner in the upper-right corner of the map. Zoom in so that you can read the green numbered guide dots at either end of Camilla Road. Drag from the green ❶ to the green ❷. You should see a 1-point red line inside a bright green bounding box, as in Figure 6-8. Don't stress if your line doesn't lie at *exactly* the same angle as Camilla Road; it won't be noticeable by the time we finish the map.

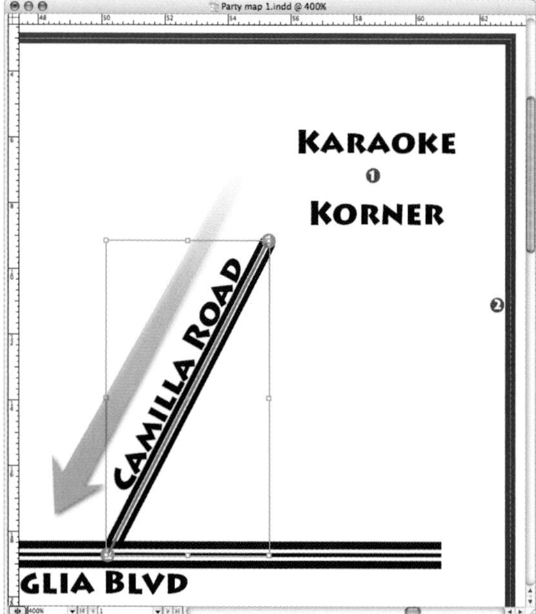

Figure 6-8.

5. *Change the line weight in the Control palette.* The line looks good, but a heavier line would be easier to read. So let's change the thickness of the line, known as the *line weight*. Choose **3 pt** from the weight pop-up menu on the right side of the Control palette. Your red line should now fill the gap between the black lines, as in Figure 6-9.

Figure 6-9.

6. ***Set a new default line weight.*** Press Ctrl+Shift+A (⌘-Shift-A on the Mac) to deselect the line. The bounding box disappears from the thick red line. But also notice that the line weight setting in the Control palette switches back to its default, 1 pt. When you change the value when an object is selected, the change affects that object only. To change the weight of all subsequent lines, you have to change the weight with *no* object is selected. So again choose **3 pt** from the weight pop-up menu on the right side of the Control palette.

7. ***Draw a horizontal line down Buscaglia Blvd.*** Press and hold the Shift key as you drag from the green ❷ to the green ❸. This creates an exactly horizontal line, as in Figure 6-10.

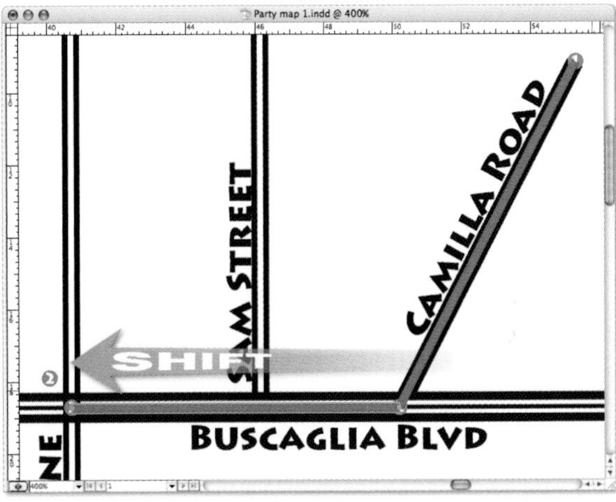

Figure 6-10.

Holding down Shift when drawing with any tool constrains the behavior of that tool. When drawing with the line tool, pressing Shift locks the angle of the line to a multiple of 45 degrees, perfect for drawing horizontal or vertical segments. You can press Shift at the outset of your drag or in the middle. Just make sure you hold the Shift key down until after you release the mouse button.

---

8. ***Draw a vertical line down Burton Lane.*** Drag the green ❸ to the green ❹. Again, hold down Shift as you drag to constrain the angle of the line so it's precisely perpendicular.

Have you ever started drawing a line, only to realize midway that you started in the wrong place? Apparently someone inside Adobe has as well, because there's no need to start over. While drawing, press and hold the spacebar. So long as the spacebar is down, moving your mouse moves the line to a different location. When you've relocated the line to your satisfaction, release the spacebar and finish drawing the line. This techniques works with all drawing tools except the pencil.

---

9. ***Draw a horizontal line up Ambrose Avenue.*** Now for something a little bit different. Press the Shift and Alt keys (Shift and Option on the Mac) and drag from the green ❺ to the green ❹. Notice that you're dragging the opposite way of usual, from the intersection of Maximilian Way back to the intersection of Burton Lane.

Moreover, the line moves in two directions at once, both to the left and the right, as in Figure 6-11. This is because pressing Alt (or Option) draws the line outward from the center.

The Control palette's L value tells you the exact length of the selected line. It even tells you the length of the line as you draw it. So you will do well to keep an eye on it.

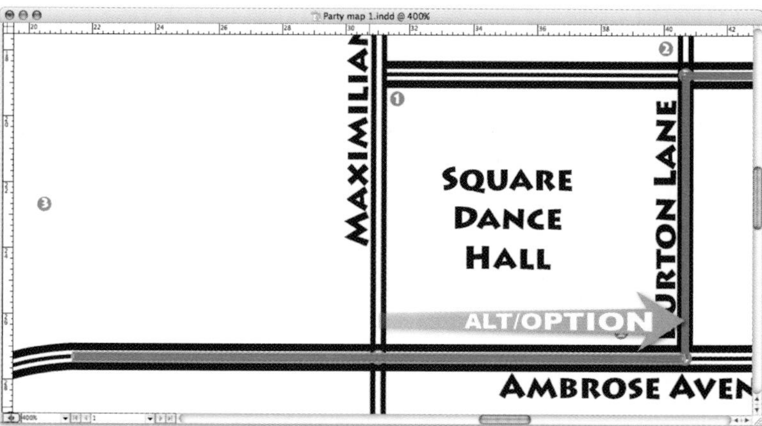

Figure 6-11.

10. ***Draw a line between the two orange guide dots.*** We're done with the line tool; now let's turn our attention to the pen tool. As I demonstrated in the video (see page 196), the pen tool draws paths one point at a time. This means you can create free-form paths that contain lots of lines all linked together. InDesign calls these lines *segments*. The points at which they join are *anchor points*.

    Scroll to the upper-left portion of the document, below the words *Here's the Party*. Click the pen tool icon (below the black arrow in the toolbox), or press the P key to select it. Then draw a straight line between the two orange dots. To do so, click the orange ❶ to set an anchor point at this location. Then click the orange ❷ to set a second point. InDesign automatically connects the dots with a straight segment, as in Figure 6-12.

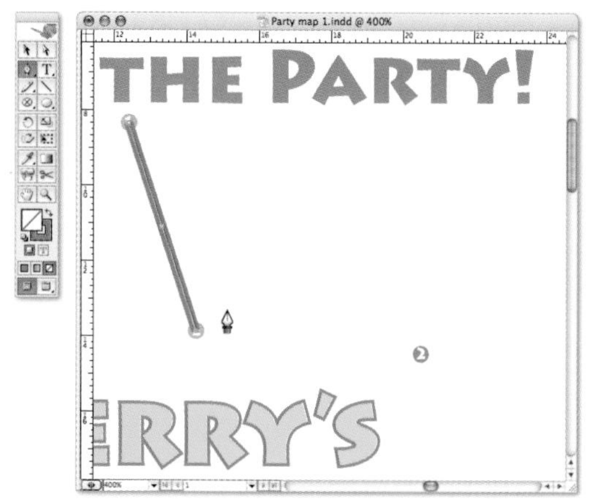

Figure 6-12.

11. ***Deselect the line.*** Next, I want you to use the pen to draw a free-form box by clicking around the words *Jerry's Place*. But don't start clicking yet—if you did, you'd add more segments to the existing line. Before you can start a new path, you must deselect the active one. Press Ctrl+Shift+A (⌘-Shift-A). Or, if

you'd prefer to try something new, press the Ctrl key (⌘ on the Mac) to get the white arrow tool. And with the key pressed, click an empty portion of the document.

12. ***Click or Shift-click each of the four blue guide dots.*** The pen tool is now poised to begin a completely new path. I want you to draw this path as follows:

    - Click the blue ❶ to set the first anchor point. Notice it doesn't connect to the preceding line; it's just a point on its own.
    - Press the Shift key and click the blue ❷. A horizontal line extends from one point to the other. As when drawing with the line tool, the Shift key constrains the angle of a pen segment to the nearest multiple of 45 degrees. The one difference is that you have to press Shift *before* you click. In other words, press and hold Shift, click with the pen tool, and release Shift.
    - Shift-click the blue ❸. InDesign adds a vertical segment to the previous horizontal one.
    - Release the Shift key and click the blue ❹. InDesign appends a skewed segment. The beauty of the pen tool is that you can draw paths in any shape you want.

13. ***Close the path.*** The result is an incomplete, or *open*, shape. To finish the shape, we must draw a segment between the first and last points. Notice that when you hover over the first point in the path (at the blue ❶), a tiny circle appears next to the pen tool cursor, like this: ✒ₒ (see Figure 6-13). This circle signifies that you are about to *close* the path you are drawing. Click when you see the ✒ₒ cursor and the box will be complete.

Figure 6-13.

14. ***Begin drawing a curve on Ambrose Avenue.*** Our next task is to complete the red route that we started drawing with the line tool. In addition to drawing straight segments, the pen tool can draw curved segments. Scroll down to the left end of the line you drew on Ambrose Avenue. Move the pen over the left end of the red horizontal line. If you get the pen

in exactly the right place, you should see a little slash next to the pen cursor, like this: ✒/. This means that you are ready to add on to a previously drawn path. If you see an × instead (as in ✒×), move the cursor until you see the slash.

When you see the slash, click. This activates the red line so that the pen tool can add to it. Now drag from this same point to the red ❶. Rather than drawing a line, the pen draws a nonprinting *control handle*, as in Figure 6-14. This handle will force the next segment you draw to bend.

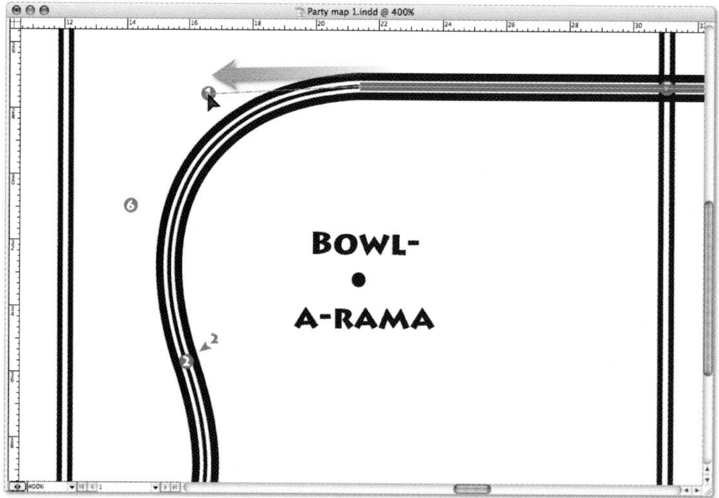

Figure 6-14.

15. ***Draw the first curve.*** Drag from the red ❷ farther along the curve to the red ❸, as illustrated in Figure 6-15. The beginning of the drag decides the location of the anchor point; from there, you draw out a pair of control handles in opposite directions. This is known in the biz as a *smooth point* because it defines a smooth arc in the path. The handle that stretches up and to the left of the smooth point bends the new segment toward it, causing it to curve. (You may note that it diverges pretty radically from the road; we'll fix that in Step 17.) The bottom-right handle will bend the next segment.

16. ***Complete the path.*** To finish off the route to Jerry's house, do the following:

    - Click the red ❹ at the intersection of Alfred Drive. Clicking with the pen tool adds an anchor point with no control handle, known as a *corner point* because it creates a corner in the path. But the new segment curves anyway. It remains under the influence of the lower-right control handle from the preceding smooth point.

- Shift-click the red ❺ near the bottom of the free-form box that represents Jerry's house. A straight segment completes the path.
- Ctrl-click (or ⌘-click) off the path to deselect it.

17. *Fix the errant curve.* Now let's take a moment to fix that overly loopy curve:
    - Press Ctrl (or ⌘) to temporarily get the white arrow tool, and click the smooth point on the red ❷. (Because the ❷ is covered, a red 2 with an arrow points to it.) This selects the smooth point and displays its control handles.
    - With the Ctrl (or ⌘) key still down, drag the top-left handle to the red ❻, as in Figure 6-16. This reduces the bulge of the curve so it better matches the road.

18. *Redraw the vertical line from Step 8.* One of the wonders of the pen tool is that you can use it to augment any path, regardless of which tool you used to draw the path in the first place. For example, scroll up and to the right to find Burton Lane. If you zoom in very tight on either end of the vertical line, you'll see that the corners don't actually line up properly, as shown in Figure 6-17. This is because each line was drawn independently.

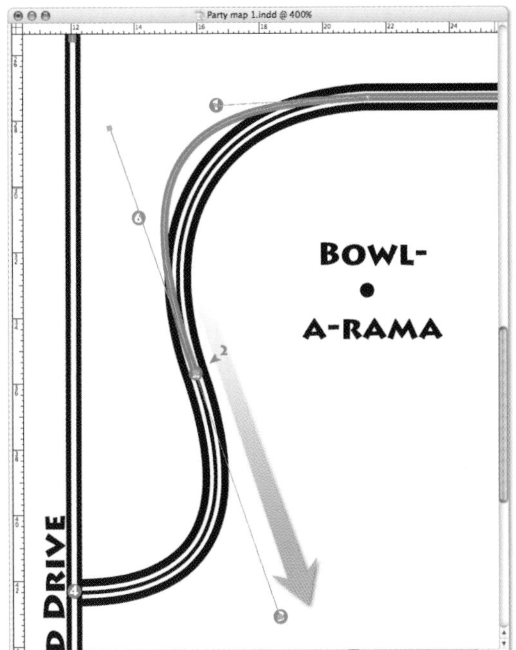

Figure 6-15.

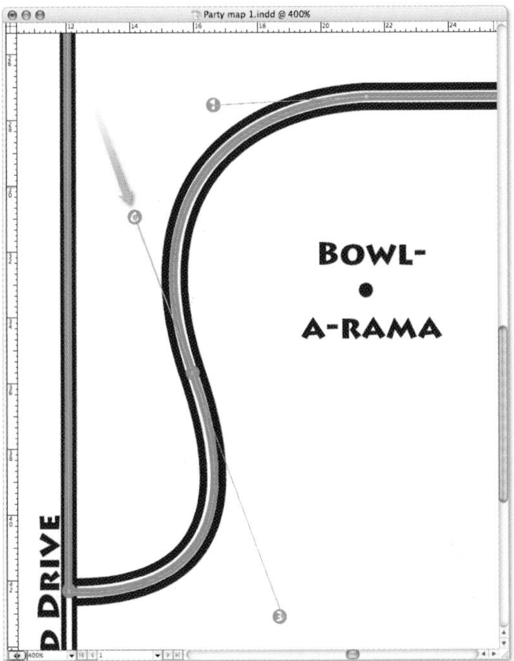

Figure 6-16.

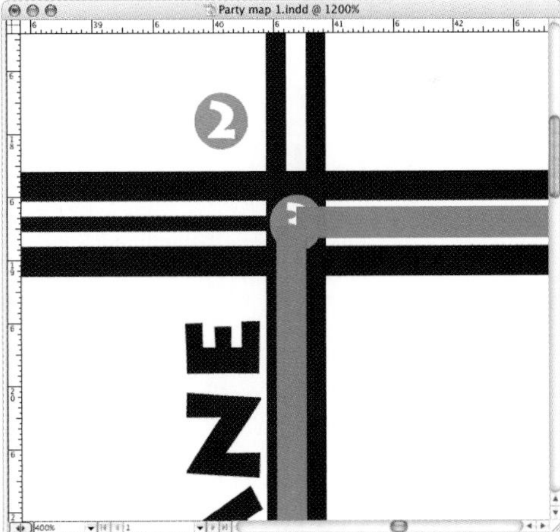

Figure 6-17.

In a dedicated illustration program, you could fuse together the existing lines by joining their anchor points. But InDesign is not so sophisticated. So here's what I want you to do:

- Press the V key to switch to the black arrow tool. (If you loaded the Deke Keys shortcuts, you can press the Enter key instead.)
- Click the vertical line on Burton Lane to select it, and then press the Backspace or Delete key to get rid of it.
- Press the P key to switch back to the pen tool.
- Move your cursor over the green ❸ at the intersection of Buscaglia Blvd. When you see the pen cursor, click to activate the horizontal line.
- Now move your cursor over the green ❹ at Ambrose Avenue. The pen should look like the join pen cursor, which tells you InDesign is ready to join the two lines together. When it does, click.

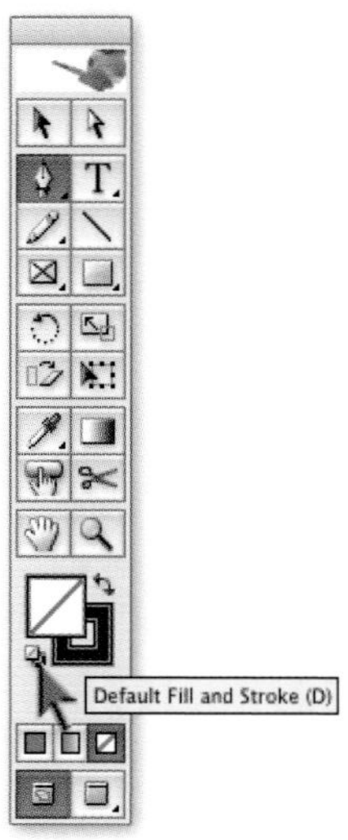

Figure 6-18.

You now have one continuous line from Buscaglia Blvd. to Jerry's Place. The line from Camilla Road remains disconnected. If it bothers you, delete it and redraw it with the pen.

EXTRA CREDIT

At this point, we've traced the entire route from Karaoke Korner to Jerry's Place using the line and pen tools. We now move to the shape tools to draw what are commonly known as *primitives*, which are simple symmetrical shapes like rectangles, squares, ovals, circles, polygons, and stars. We'll use the shape tools to draw a few buildings and a compass rose (the thing that shows what directions are what).

19. ***Reset the colors to their defaults.*** Press Ctrl+Shift+A (⌘-Shift-A) to deselect the active path. This way, your next operation won't affect the path. Now click the tiny default color icon in the lower-left region of the toolbox (see Figure 6-18) or press the D key. InDesign resets the colors so our shapes will have transparent interiors and black outlines.

20. ***Draw a rectangle around Bingo Hall.*** Select the rectangle tool by clicking the fourth icon on the right side of the toolbox or by pressing the M key. (This shortcut comes from Photoshop, where the rectangle tool is called the *marquee*.) Scroll to the words *Bingo Hall* above Buscaglia Blvd. Drag from the magenta ❶ to the magenta ❷. This creates a rectangle that indicates the Bingo Hall building, as in Figure 6-19.

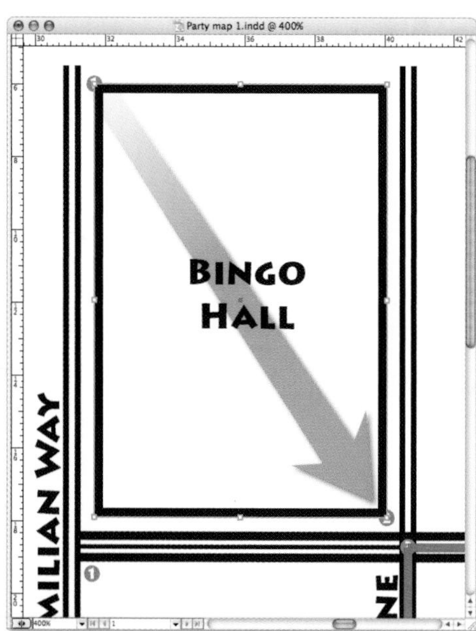

Figure 6-19.

21. ***Draw a square around Square Dance Hall.*** Scroll down and you'll see the words *Square Dance Hall*. Press the Shift key and drag from the gray ❶ to the gray ❷, as in Figure 6-20. Pressing the Shift key constrains the rectangle to a perfect square. You can press the Shift key after beginning your drag, but make sure you have the key down when you release the mouse button.

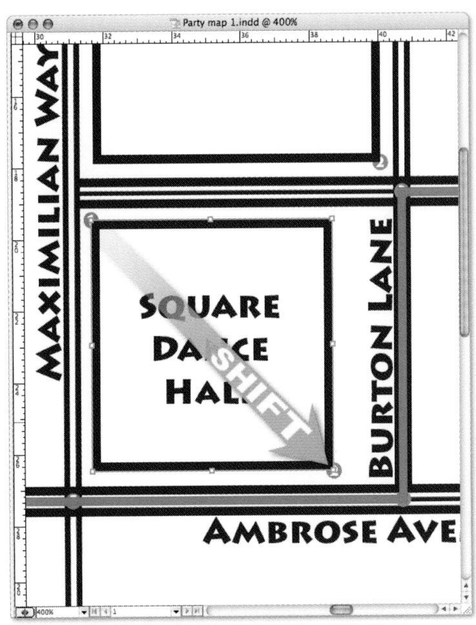

Figure 6-20.

22. ***Select the ellipse tool in the toolbox.*** Scroll down and to the left to the words *Bowl-a-rama*. This happens to be a round building, so we'll draw it with the ellipse tool. Select the ellipse tool in one of the following ways:

    - Click and hold the rectangle tool in the toolbox to display the shape tool flyout menu. Then choose the ellipse tool.
    - Alt-click (Option-click) the rectangle tool icon.
    - Press the L key.

23. ***Bring up the Ellipse dialog box.*** Although you can draw the shape by dragging inside the document window, I'd like to take this opportunity to show you a different technique:

    - Press the Alt key (Option on the Mac) and click the unnumbered black guide dot in the middle of the *Bowl-a-rama* text. This brings up the **Ellipse** dialog box, which allows you to define the width and height of a prospective shape. (Note that the dialog box would have appeared if you had simply clicked. Pressing the key instructs InDesign to center the shape at the click point.)
    - Change both the **Width** and **Height** values to 10. Then click **OK**. The result is a perfect circle with a diameter of 10 picas, as in Figure 6-21.

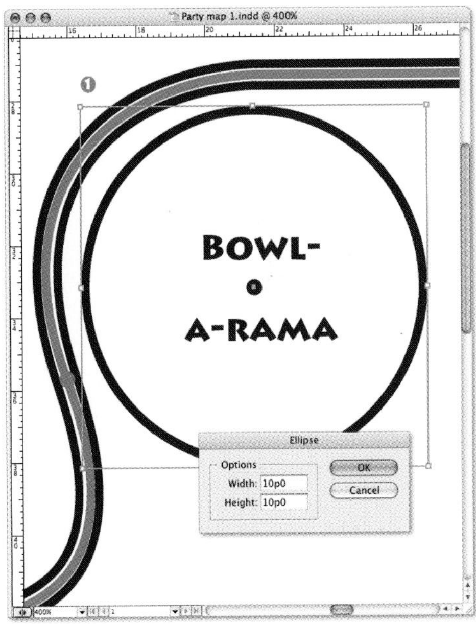

Figure 6-21.

The Ellipse dialog box always lists the dimensions of the last oval or circle you drew, even if you drew it by hand. This means you can repeat shapes over and over again just by clicking with the tool. This technique works with the rectangle tool as well.

---

24. ***Select the polygon tool in the toolbox.*** Scroll to the upper-right corner of the document until you find the words *Karaoke Korner*. Then select the polygon tool, which draws geometric shapes with a specified number of straight and equal sides.

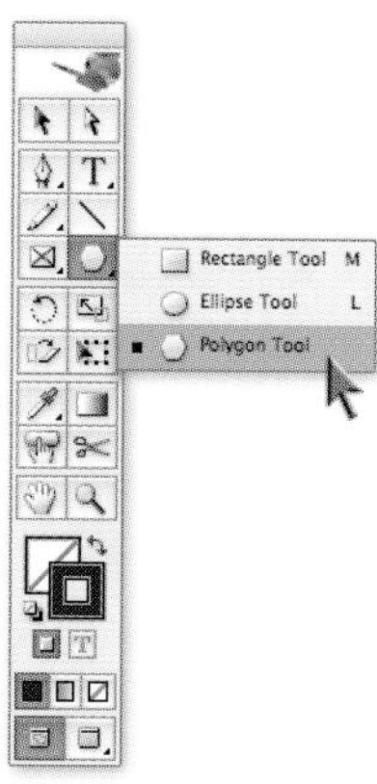

Figure 6-22.

There's no keyboard shortcut for the polygon tool. So select the tool from the shape tool flyout menu, as in Figure 6-22, or Alt-click (Option-click) the ellipse tool icon.

25. ***Draw a pentagon.*** By default, the polygon tool draws a hexagon, which is a shape with six sides. You can change the number of sides in the midst of drawing with the polygon tool by pressing the ↑ or ↓ key. Each press of the key adds or deletes a side. The feature is a little flaky, however, and it only works when your mouse is in motion. So here's what I'd like you to do:

    - Drag from the brown ❶ toward the brown ❷, and keep your mouse button down.
    - Keep dragging toward the ❷ and—while moving the mouse—press the ↓ key once to delete a side and create a pentagon. If it doesn't take, wiggle your mouse and try pressing the key again.
    - When your cursor arrives at the ❷, press and hold the Shift and Alt keys (Shift and Option on the Mac). Shift makes the shape symmetrical; Alt (or Option) causes it to be drawn from the center outward.
    - Release the mouse button. And then release the keys. Figure 6-23 shows the result.

Figure 6-23.

26. ***Set the polygon tool to make stars.*** Scroll to the bottom-right corner of the document until you find letters for the four directions. This is where we'll put that ages-old map element, the compass rose. And we'll draw it using the polygon tool.

    A typical compass rose begins life as a star shape. To set the polygon tool to draw stars, double-click the polygon tool icon in the toolbox. This displays the **Polygon Settings** dialog box, which allows you to adjust the number of sides that the tool draws by default and the "pointiness" of a star:

    - Change the **Number of Sides** value to 8. If we were to draw a polygon, this would result in an octagon. For a star, it means 8 points (16 sides).
    - You create a star by folding the sides of the polygon into the body of the shape. The Star Inset value decides how deeply the sides fold. A higher value results in a spikier star. Set the **Star Inset** value to 50 percent.
    - Click the **OK** button. The next polygon you draw will adopt these settings.

27. ***Draw a star.*** Press Shift+Alt (or Shift-Option) and drag from the navy blue ❶ to the similarly colored ❷. This draws the star from the center out and forces all sides to be equal. Figure 6-24 shows the result.

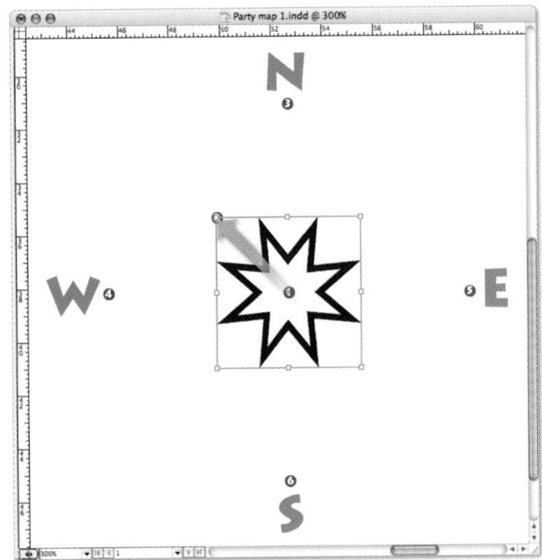

Figure 6-24.

28. ***Rotate the star 22.5 degrees.*** Rather stupidly, in my most humble opinion, InDesign invariably chooses to draw its polygons upright. (The polygon tools in Photoshop and Illustrator draw symmetrical shapes that spin as you draw them, which I venture to say makes much more sense.) This means we have to rotate the star in the proper direction, which is something we can do from the Control palette:

    - See that grid of nine tiny squares on the far left side of the Control palette? That's the *reference point matrix*. Click the center box so it looks like ⠿. This ensures that the star rotates about its center.
    - Now click the △ icon in the right half of the Control palette to highlight the rotation angle value. Type 22.5 and press Enter or Return. The star rotates into the position shown in Figure 6-25.

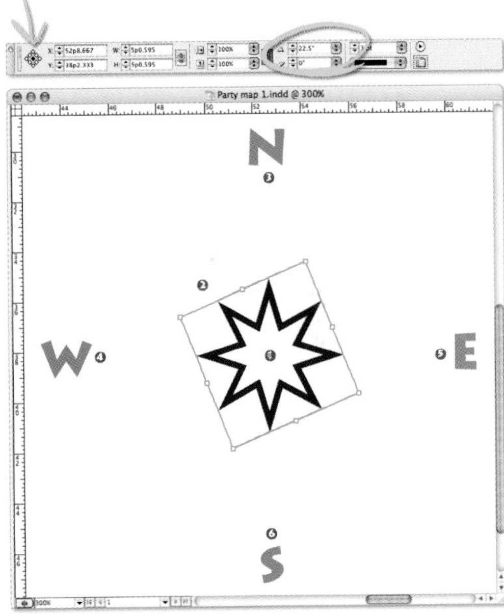

Figure 6-25.

29. ***Shift-drag the top star point upward.*** Our star is currently symmetrical, with every point exactly as long as its neighbor. I want to extend the four points that point toward the letters. And to do that, we need the white arrow tool (which Adobe calls the direct-selection tool). Click the white arrow icon in the toolbox or press the A key.

30. ***Shift-drag the top of the star upward.*** Click the top anchor point in the star to select it. The point changes from a hollow square to a solid one. (It's hard to see in bright green, but that's what's happening.) Press the Shift key and drag the selected anchor point up to the navy blue ❸. Holding down Shift constrains the movement to the closest multiple of 45 degrees—in this case, vertically.

31. ***Extend the left, right, and bottom points.*** You can repeat that same process on the left, right, and bottom points. That is, click the point to select it, and then Shift-drag the point to the nearest navy blue grid dot: ❹, ❺, or ❻. But that's the sucker's way. Better to move all points at once by scaling them. Here's how this wonderful technique works:

    - First, undo the last operation. Press Ctrl+Z (⌘-Z on the Mac) to restore the top point to its previous position.

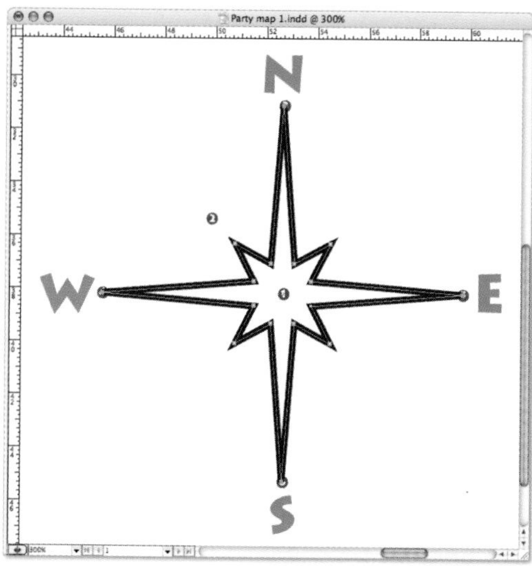

Figure 6-26.

- The top point should still be selected, but click it just to be sure. Then press the Shift key and click on each of the other three points (left, right, and bottom). All four points should now be selected.
- Click the icon in the Control palette to highlight the horizontal scale value. Enter 256 percent and press the Tab key to transform the points.
- If the icon is on, InDesign ought to move all points outward. But thanks to a bug, it moves just the left and right points. No problem. Type 256 percent for the vertical scale value () and press Enter or Return.

Note that unlike the rotate value, InDesign resets the scale values to 100 percent when the operation is complete. Although I've long argued this is not the way it should be, it is standard behavior and nothing to worry about. As long as your compass rose looks like the one in Figure 6-26, all is well.

32. *Turn off the Guide Dots layer.* Congratulations, you're done drawing. That means you don't need to see the guide dots anymore. Inside the **Layers** palette, click the icon in front of the **Guide Dots** layer. The dots disappear.

33. *Select the free-form box.* InDesign's drawing tools are terrific and all, but you may have noticed one missing—the rounded rectangle tool. Sure enough, InDesign lacks a tool for drawing rounded rectangles. Instead, it gives you something better: a command that can round off the corners of *any* shape.

    Scroll up and to the left to the free-form box around the words *Jerry's Place*. Press Ctrl+Tab (Control-Tab on the Mac) to switch from the white arrow to the black arrow. (Just figured you might want yet another shortcut. This one switches between the black and white arrow tools.) Then click on the red box outline to select it.

34. *Apply the Corner Effects command.* Choose **Object→Corner Effects** or press Ctrl+Alt+Shift+R (⌘-Option-Shift-R on the Mac) to display the **Corner Effects** dialog box. Then make the following changes:

    - Turn on the **Preview** check box so you can see what you're doing.
    - Set the **Effect** option to **Rounded**. (Or experiment with one of the others, if you prefer.)

- Change the **Size** value to 1p6, or ¼ inch. InDesign rounds off the corners as in Figure 6-27.
- Click the **OK** button.

Not only can you apply Corner Effects to any line, shape, or frame, the command is dynamic, meaning you can change or remove a corner effect at any time just by choosing Object→Corner Effects. (To remove the effect, select None from the Effect pop-up menu at any time.) Furthermore, I could edit the shape of this box using the white arrow tool and InDesign would adapt the corners to fit.

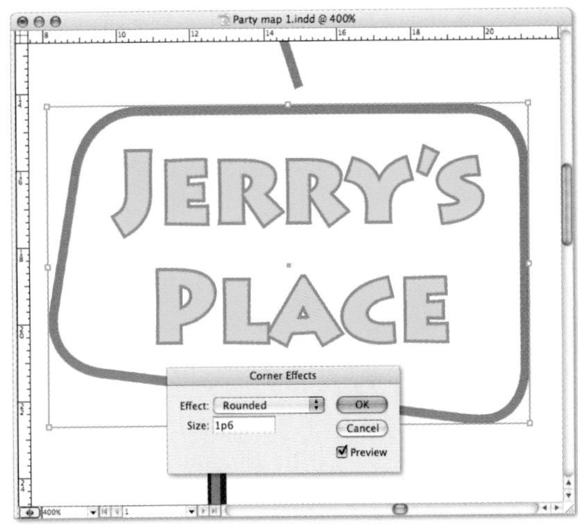

Figure 6-27.

35. *Save the document.* We're going to continue working on this map in the next exercise, so it's a good idea to save your work. Choose **File→Save As**, name your document "My map.indd," and save it in the *Lesson 06* folder.

Fill, Stroke, and Color

One of the beauty's of InDesign's vector-based approach is that lines and shapes remain editable long after you create them. If you draw a path in the wrong color, you don't have to undo the operation or redraw the path, you just apply a new color. In this exercise, we're going to change the color of some elements in our map to Jerry's house. We'll be dealing with the two basic components of objects that you draw in InDesign, fill and stroke. *Fill* affects the interior of a shape; *stroke* affects the outline. Over the course of the following steps, you'll learn how to select colors, apply fill and stroke, and even design a custom stroke pattern.

1. *Open a document.* If you still have open the *My map.indd* file that you saved at the end of the last exercise, then skip to the next step. If not, open my saved file, which is called *Party map 2.indd*. You'll find it in the *Lesson 06* folder inside *Lesson Files-IDcs 1on1*.

2. *Click the fill icon in the toolbox.* Let's start things off by applying a fill to the compass rose in the lower-right corner of the document. Press the V key to select the black arrow tool, and then click on the compass rose to select it. Next, click the fill icon in the toolbox (labeled in Figure 6-28). This activates the fill of the selected object, which is currently set to None, as indicated by the red slash icon. In other words, the area inside the compass rose is transparent.

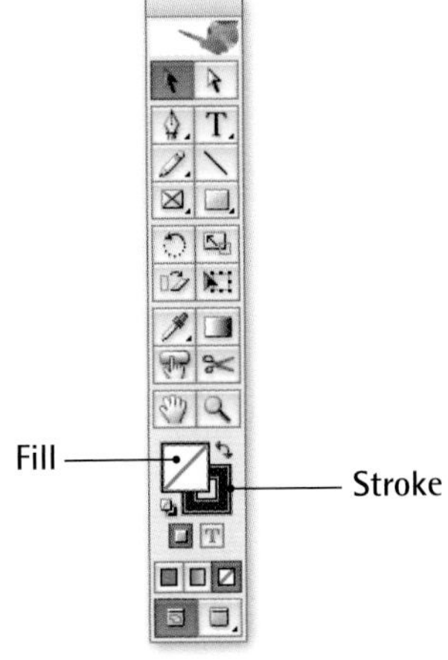

Figure 6-28.

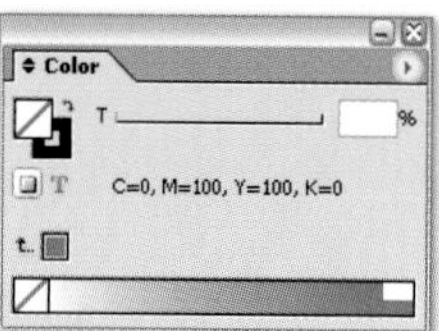

Figure 6-29.

3. ***Display the Color palette.*** Press F6 or choose **Window→Color** to display the **Color** palette, shown in Figure 6-29. The Color palette contains the same fill and stroke icons as the toolbox, plus a couple of options for specifying a color. Choose **Show Options** from the palette menu or click the ♦ next to the palette name if the Color palette doesn't show all the options.

4. ***Click in the middle of the spectrum.*** Move your cursor over the spectrum bar at the bottom of the palette. As Figure 6-30 shows, your cursor turns into an eyedropper. Click in the middle of the spectrum to fill the star shape with a medium shade of the last color applied (red if you're following right on the heels of the last exercise, black if not). InDesign also activates the Tint slider at the top of the Color palette.

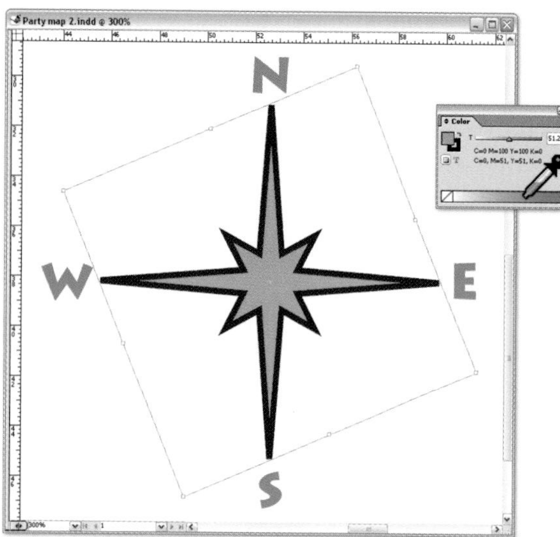

Figure 6-30.

5. ***Choose CMYK from the Color palette menu.*** Whether your star is red or gray, InDesign treats it as a separate ink. This is because both red and black are defined as swatches in the Swatches palette. You can use the Tint slider (simply labeled T) to make the ink lighter or darker. If you want to work with an entirely different color, you first need to select a color model from the palette menu.

InDesign presents you with a choice of three *color models* (which are ways of defining colors):

- Lab is a theoretical color model that seeks to define colors independent of any monitor, printer, or other piece of hardware. However, Lab's implementation is sufficiently abstruse to limit its appeal to only the most gung-ho color geeks.
- CMYK is the color model for printing. As we explore at length in Lesson 12, "Printing and Output," full-color process printing most commonly involves four inks: cyan, magenta, yellow, and black. Hence, they are known as *process colors*. If the final destination for your document is a printing press, then CMYK is the obvious and best choice.
- RGB is the color model of light and is therefore used by devices that display and capture colors, including computer monitors, scanners, and digital cameras. If your document is intended to be viewed on screen—as may be the case when exporting a PDF file—you should define your colors using the RGB model.

Our map is intended for printing, so choose **CMYK** from the palette menu. Or Shift-click in the spectrum bar to switch from one color model to the next. The Color palette now contains four sliders, one for each ink color (including K for black), as in Figure 6-31.

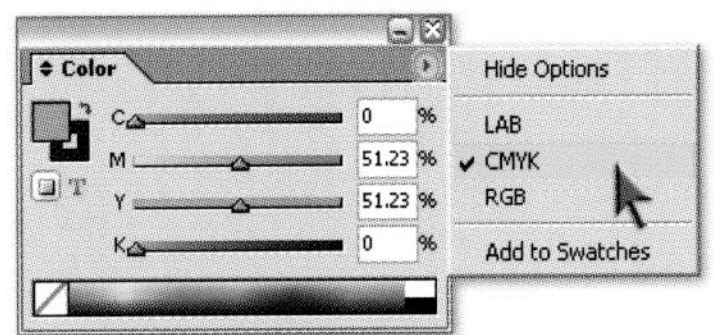

Figure 6-31.

6. ***Dial in an orange color.*** It takes some experience to dial in CMYK colors. To help you out, Figure 6-32 shows a collection of incremental CMYK combinations as they appear when printed in this book. (I mention this because different presses render colors differently. Your experience will surely vary.) Only the last column includes black ink. The role of black is to darken colors, making them less colorful, not more.

   With that in mind, let's say you want to change the star to orange. Bright orange is a combination of 50 to 75 percent magenta and 100 percent yellow. Try entering the following:

   - **C**: 0 percent
   - **M**: 58 percent
   - **Y**: 100 percent
   - **K**: 0 percent

   If you find it tedious to select each value and enter a new one—goodness knows I do—try this: press the F6 key twice to highlight the C value. Then enter a value and press Tab to advance to the next one. When you finish, press Enter or Return to accept the color and escape the Color palette. In any case, your compass rose turns orange.

7. ***Activate the stroke icon.*** Next let's give the compass rose a more colorful stroke. You can click the stroke icon in either the toolbox or the Color palette. Or just press the X key, which toggles activation of the stroke and the fill.

Pressing Shift+X switches the assigned stroke and fill colors. I don't recommend that you do this now, but if you do, you'll get a black star with an orange stroke.

---

8. ***Assign a blue stroke.*** Again, choose **CMYK** from the Color palette menu or Shift-click the spectrum bar twice. This time, instead of dialing in

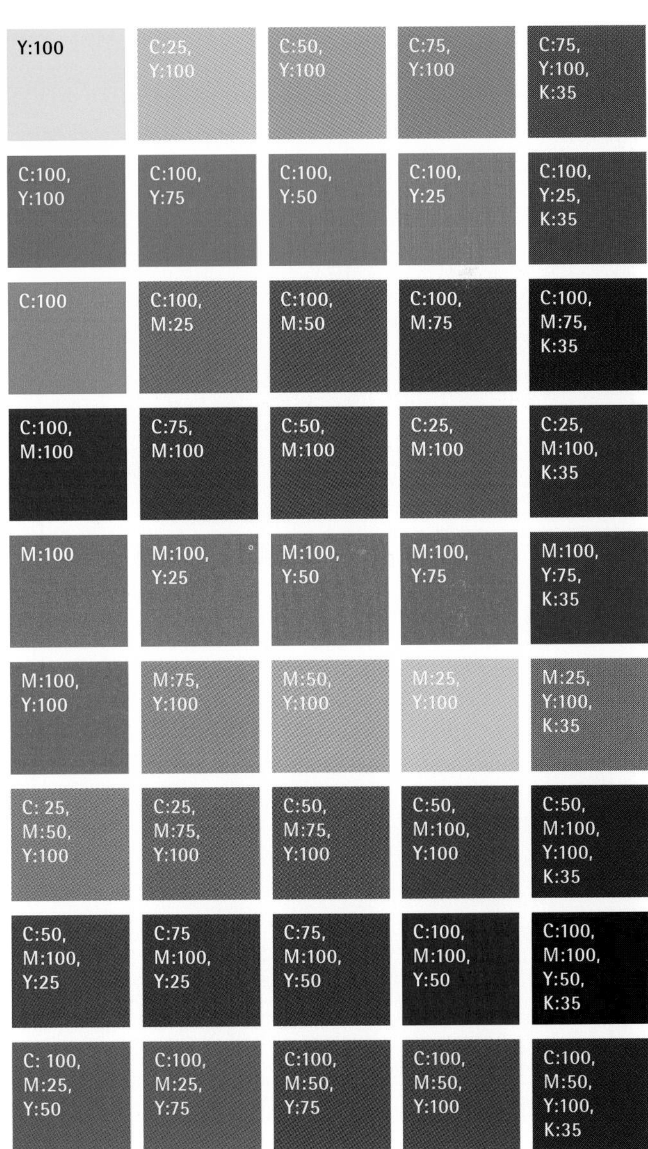

Figure 6-32.

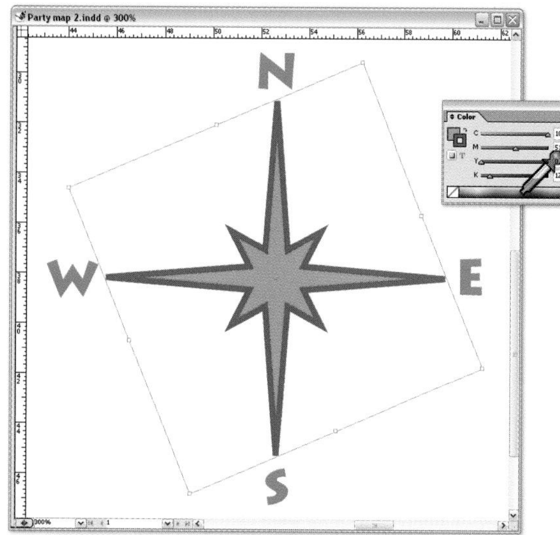

Figure 6-33.

a color, click a shade of blue in the spectrum. Don't worry about getting exactly the same color as I did in Figure 6-33; just pick one that you think works with the orange.

Alt-clicking (or Option-clicking) in the spectrum bar sets the color of the *inactive* attribute. In other words, if the stroke is active, Alt-clicking sets the color of the fill.

9. ***Save the blue as a swatch.*** I like my blue so much that I want to save it for future use. Choose **Window→Swatches** or press F5 to display the **Swatches** palette. Then click the ◰ icon at the bottom of the palette to add the color to the list. Or you can choose **Add to Swatches** from the Color palette menu. The blue appears as the last item in the Swatches palette color list, as in Figure 6-34.

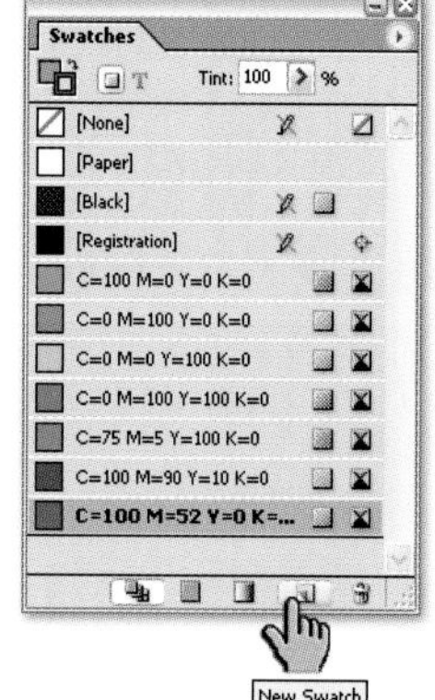

Figure 6-34.

By default, InDesign automatically names a swatch with a close numerical approximation of its CMYK values. If you want to give your swatch a more meaningful name, double-click it, turn off the Name with Color Value check box, enter a new name in the Swatch Name option box, and click OK.

10. ***Create a spot color.*** As long as we're working with the Swatches palette, let's create another swatch using a spot color that we'll put in play a few steps from now. A spot color is not printed from a combination of process inks. Rather, each *spot color* prints as a single, premixed ink. This ensures consistency from print job to print job, and permits you to create colors outside the CMYK range.

    Press Ctrl+Shift+A (⌘-Shift-A on the Mac) to deselect the compass rose. Then Alt-click (or Option-click) the ◰ icon at the bottom of the Swatches palette. This forces InDesign to display the **New Color Swatch** dialog box, where you can mix your own custom color or select from a list of industry-standard presets. Recreate the settings shown in Figure 6-35, as follows:

    - Set the **Color Type** pop-up menu to **Spot** to tell InDesign that you are creating a spot color.
    - Choose **Pantone solid coated** from the **Color Mode** pop-up menu. Pantone is the standard for spot-color

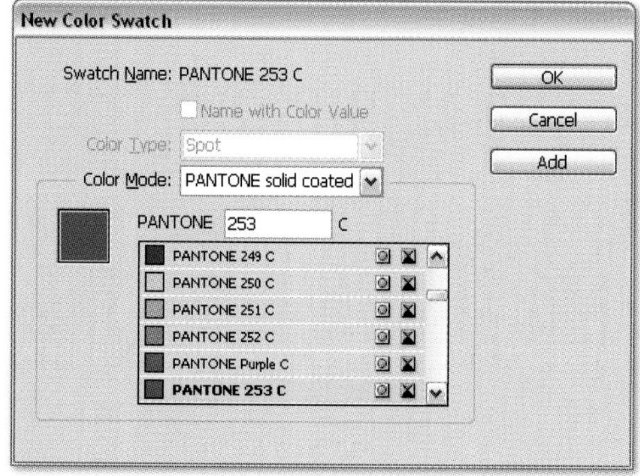

Figure 6-35.

printing in the United States. The word *solid* tells you it's a library of spot colors; *coated* indicates that it's designed for output to glossy paper.

- Click in the **Pantone** option box and enter 253. This selects Pantone color #253, which happens to be a purple, and switches the Swatch Name to Pantone 253 C.
- Click **OK** to create the swatch and close the dialog box. InDesign adds the Pantone spot-color swatch to the bottom of the Swatches palette list.

11. *Display the Stroke palette.* In the last exercise, we changed the thickness of a line from the Control palette (see Step 5 on page 200). But that's just the beginning of what you can do to a stroke. To access all the other stuff, choose **Window→Stroke** or press F10 to bring up the **Stroke** palette (Mac OS X 10.3 users need to change their Exposé settings as I describe on page xvii of the Preface for this keyboard shortcut to work.) If you don't see all the options shown in Figure 6-36, choose **Show Options** from the palette menu or click the ♦ next to the palette name.

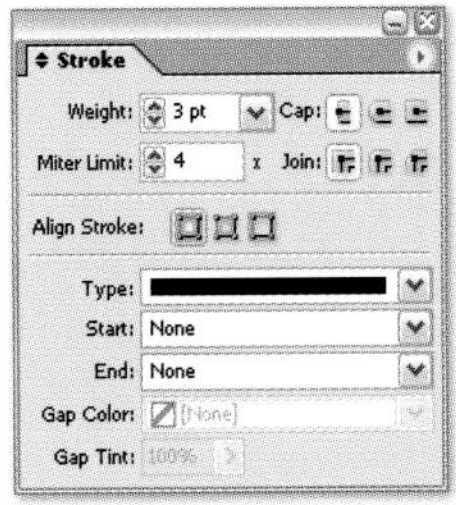

Figure 6-36.

12. *Raise the Miter Limit value.* Click the compass rose with the black arrow tool to select it. We're going to fix a problem that may have been bothering you for some time now: The tips of the long points appear clipped, or *beveled*, rather than coming to a sharp point. The Stroke palette offers three different Join options that determine how the stroke looks at corners in the path:

    - The first option, ⊏, creates a sharp, or *mitered*, tip.
    - The second option, ⊏, rounds off the tips.
    - The final option, ⊏, bevels the tips.

    The miter option is active, and yet the four points are obviously beveled. What gives? Mitered strokes have a habit of extending well beyond their paths, especially at acute (very sharp) corners. To counteract this, InDesign includes a Miter Limit value that keeps moderate corners sharp and bevels acute ones. The value is measured as a ratio between the *miter length* and the line weight, both illustrated in Figure 6-37.

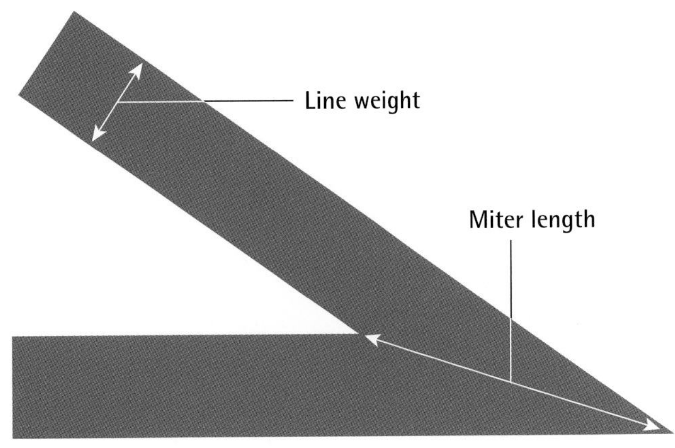

Figure 6-37.

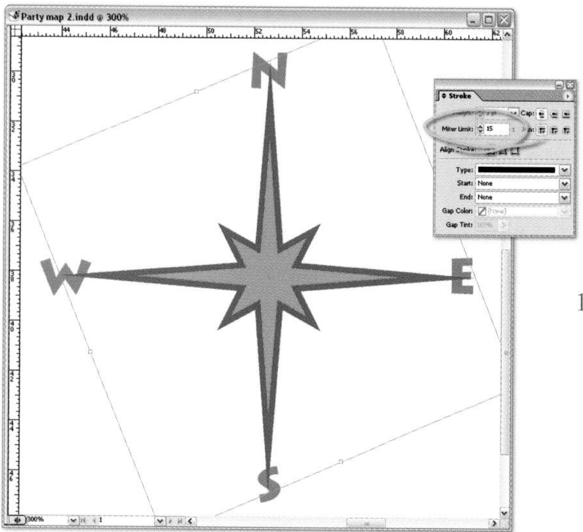

Figure 6-38.

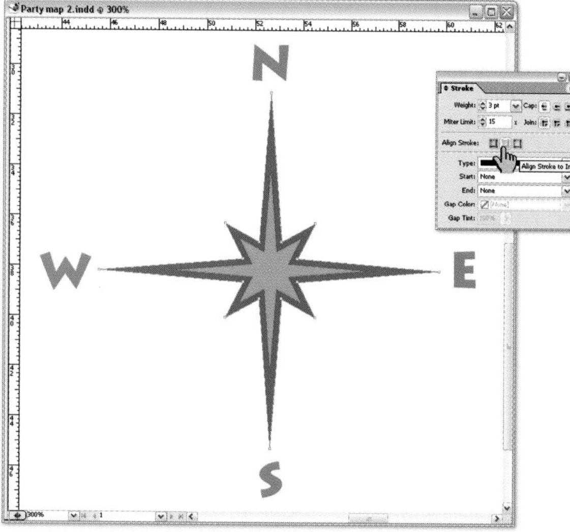

Figure 6-39.

Go ahead and raise the **Miter Limit** to 15. This permits the miter length to grow to 15 times the line weight, or 45 points for our 3-point stroke. The result is that all points in the compass rose become sharp as knives. But now we have a new problem. As you can see in Figure 6-38, the points now intersect with the green directional letters. Something must be done.

13. ***Fix the points so they don't overlap the letters.*** The remedy I favor is to adjust the position of the stroke. In previous versions of InDesign, a stroke was invariably centered on its path. This meant that a 4-point stroke extended 2 points from one side of the path and 2 points in the other. Now, InDesign CS adds the ability to place a stroke either outside or inside a path.

    In our case, we want the stroke to trace the inside of the star. Press Ctrl+Tab (Control-Tab) to switch to the white arrow tool. This isn't an essential step; it merely permits us to see the path running right through the center of the stroke. Then click the middle of the three **Align Stroke** icons (⌑). This moves the stroke inside the path, which shrinks the star and stops it from poking into the green letters, as Figure 6-39 illustrates.

14. ***Apply the spot color to the diagonal line and free-form box.*** Now I want to apply the spot color that we created in Step 10 to the strokes in the upper-left corner of the document. Scroll until you can see the words *Here's the Party*. Then press Ctrl+Tab (Control-Tab) to switch back to the black arrow tool.

    - Click on the red line under *Here's the Party*.
    - Shift-click the free-form box around *Jerry's Place*.

    Now both paths are selected. Click the **Pantone 253 C** swatch in the Swatches palette. As Figure 6-40 shows, the lines take on the purple spot color.

15. ***Round off the line caps.*** Now let's adjust the stroke settings to change the diagonal line into something more dynamic. Inside the Stroke palette, the Cap settings define

the appearance of the stroke at the *endpoints* (that is, the anchor points at the beginning and end of the path):

- Currently the cap is set to my favorite attribute in all of InDesign: the butt cap. (Call me juvenile, but it makes me laugh like a giddy third-grader. Butt I digress.) The butt cap option (⊟) cuts the line abruptly at the ends of the path. It also happens to be the default setting.
- Click the round cap icon (⊟) to end the path with a half circle, which results in a smoother finish.
- The projecting cap (⊟) extends the stroke beyond the endpoints to a distance equal to half the stroke's width. This is a good setting when you want to make sure one stroke overlaps into another.

Click the second **Cap** icon to give the lines gentle round caps.

16. ***Add an arrowhead to the line.*** Actually, I never intended the diagonal line to be a line. All this time, it's been an arrow-in-waiting, and the Stroke palette is here to make it happen. Toward the bottom of the palette, the Start and End options let you add arrowheads and other ornaments to the beginning and end of an open path. Because we created the top point of the path first (see "Drawing Lines and Shapes," Step 10, page 202), the bottom point is the end of the path. The bottom point is where I want the arrow, so select **Simple** from the **End** pop-up menu to append a plain arrowhead to the lowest point in the line, as in Figure 6-41.

Figure 6-40.

Figure 6-41.

As you may have noticed, neither Step 15 nor 16 had any influence on the free-form box. This is because caps and arrowheads affect the endpoints of open paths only. The box is a closed path with no endpoint—like a wedding ring, it never ends—so the caps and arrowheads go unseen. The attributes are there, just in case I ever do open the path, but they lie dormant.

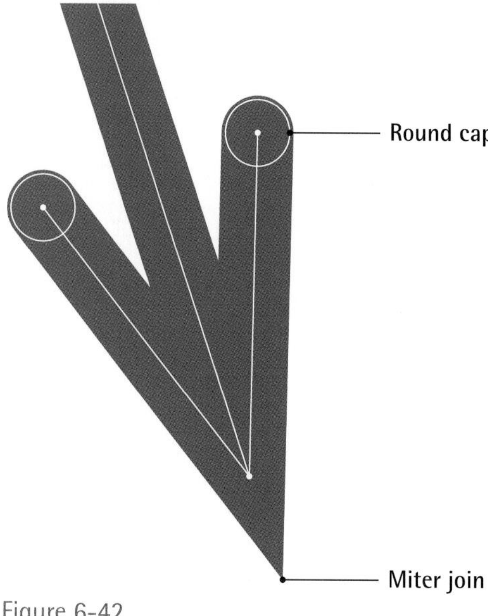

Figure 6-42.

In case you're curious, Figure 6-42 diagrams how the arrowhead and other stroke attributes work together. The round cap setting smoothes off the endpoints; the miter join ensures a nice sharp point. In other words, an arrowhead is just another path—albeit one that InDesign applies in the background—as witnessed by the white outlines in the figure.

EXTRA CREDIT

So you've colored the compass rose and turned your boring line into a helpful arrow. If you're the type who's easily satisfied, you might decide that your map is good enough and skip to "Creating and Using Gradients" on page 221. But be forewarned, you do so at your peril. For if you leave now, you'll miss out on one of InDesign CS's most exciting new features: stroke styles, which let you define elaborate stroke patterns and save them for future use. But that's okay, I understand. Who wants to learn about really cool stuff, lord it over friends and colleagues, probably get promoted and ultimately appointed head of the company, discover the cure for cancer, and bring everlasting peace to the world when you can save a few minutes and skip these last steps? You think I exaggerate? There's only one way to find out...

17. *Select the red line that traces the streets.* Assuming that the black arrow remains active, click the line that traces down Ambrose Avenue and around the Bowl-a-rama. A single click is all it takes to select all but one leg of the long, red route from the karaoke bar to Jerry's house.

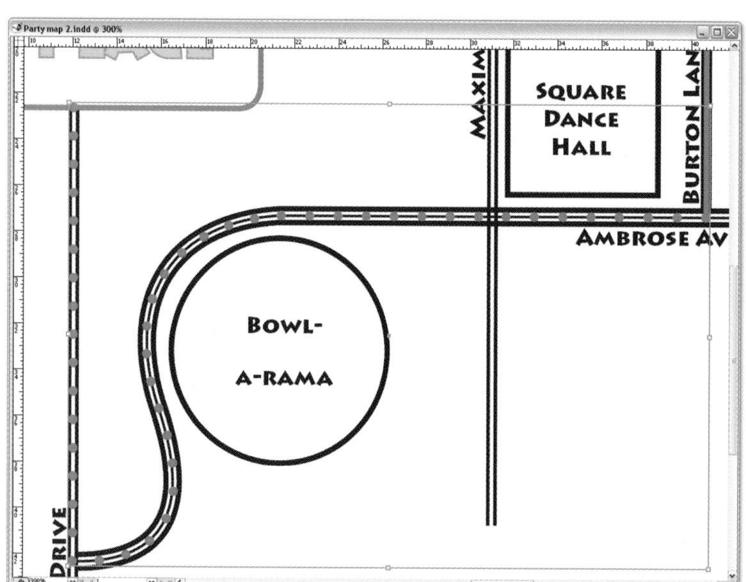

Figure 6-43.

18. *Create a dotted stroke.* Turn your attention to the **Type** pop-up menu in the Stroke palette, which features an assortment of patterned strokes. For what it's worth, I drew the black roads on this map using the Thick–Thin–Thick and Thick–Thick settings. In addition to other multiline variations, the Type menu includes dash patterns, hash patterns, dots, wavy lines, and diamonds. We'll start with the **Dotted** option.

19. *Raise the line weight to 5 pt.* Click the **Weight** option, press the ↑ key twice, and press Enter or Return to increase the size of the dots to 5 points in diameter. Although I like these bigger dots (see Figure 6-43), they're still not quite what I had in mind. I need more control, and InDesign provides it.

20. *Choose the Stroke Styles command.* Click the ⊙ arrow in the upper corner of the Strokes palette and choose **Stroke Styles** from the palette menu. InDesign responds with the **Stroke Styles** dialog box shown in Figure 6-44.

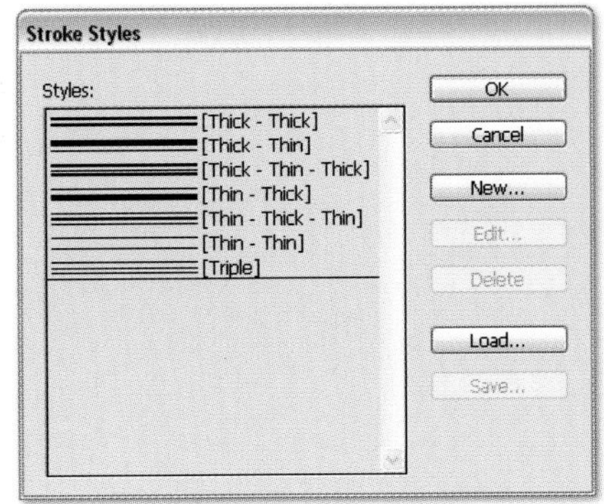

Figure 6-44.

21. *Select a dotted stroke style.* The Styles area lists the seven multiline strokes available from the Stroke palette, but the dashes, hashes, and others are missing. To create a variation on the dotted line, ignore the Styles list and click the **New** button. InDesign displays the **New Stroke Style** dialog box. Near the top, the Type pop-up menu lets you select the kind of stroke you want to create. You have three options:

    - Choose Stripe to create multiline patterns. You define the relative widths of the lines by dragging the edges of the black bars in the Stripe area. Numerical controls are also available.
    - The Dotted option strokes a line with circular dots. Click below the ruler to add dots.
    - Dash results in a repeating sequence of dashes and gaps. Click below the ruler to add a dash. You can even assign the dashes round and square ends and control whether InDesign adjusts dashes or gaps to compensate for corners in a stroked path.

    Choose the **Dotted** option from the **Type** pop-up menu. InDesign produces a horizontal ruler with a single half dot at the 0-pica mark.

22. *Customize the dotted stroke.* Naturally, we don't want to settle for InDesign's default dotted line settings. We want to create something as utterly unique as Jerry is. To that end, let's enter the settings shown in Figure 6-45. They are as follows:

    - To achieve the effect I want, I need a larger playing field. Set the **Pattern Length** option to 2 picas. Then press Tab.
    - Leave the **Corners** option set to **Adjust gaps**. This tells InDesign to align the dots with corners in a path and contract or expand the gaps to compensate.
    - Click at the 6 pica mark below the ruler to add a second dot (as demonstrated in the figure). Drag the new dot until the **Center** value reads 0p6, or enter 0p6 in the Center option box. The result is a pair of closely spaced dots, followed by a long gap.
    - Change the **Name** value to "Double Dots."

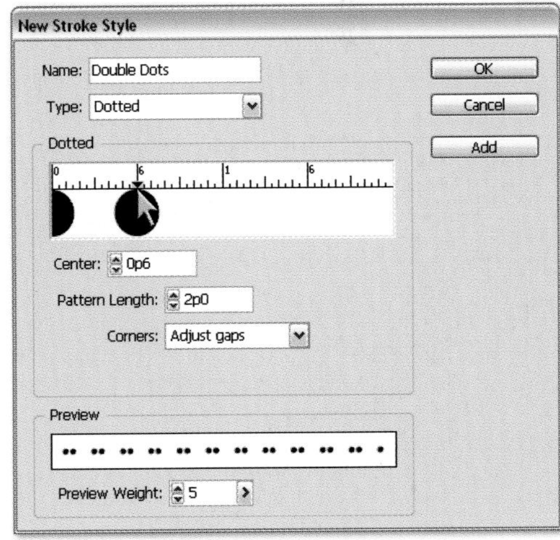

Figure 6-45.

Then click **OK** to return to the Stroke Styles dialog box, where you'll see your new style in the Styles list. Click **OK** again to exit the Stroke Styles dialog box and accept your changes.

Want something besides lines, dashes, and dots? InDesign provides a handful of hidden stroke styles that you can get to only by entering secret codes. Inside the Stroke Styles dialog box, click New. Then change the Name value to "Woof" and click OK. You'll get a repeating pattern of paws. Figure 6-46 shows a few other names you can try. Enter the names exactly as I've written them. Only one of the presets requires an adjustment. After entering "Rainbow," set the Type option to Stripe, and then click OK.

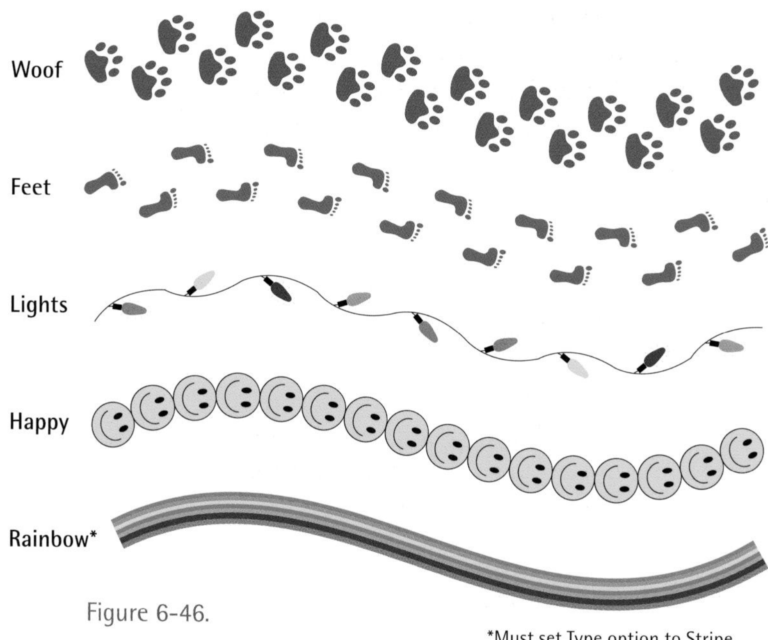

Figure 6-46.

23. *Apply the Double Dots style.* With the route path still selected, choose **Double Dots** from the **Type** pop-up menu in the Stroke or Control palette. InDesign applies the repeating pattern of coupled dots to the path.

24. *Sample the stroke with the eyedropper tool.* I assume that you left Camilla Road a separate line, as it is in the *Party map 2.indd* file. If so, the line remains a solid, 3-point red. The easiest way to apply the new style to the path—with thicker line weight and all—is to use the eyedropper tool. Press the I key to access the eyedropper. Click anywhere along the double-dotted path. The cursor switches from empty and slanted down to the left (🖉) to full and slanting to the right (🖋).

25. *Click the Camilla Road line.* Once the eyedropper is loaded, it remains loaded until you select another tool or Alt-click (or Option-click) to load new attributes. Click once on Camilla Road to transfer the stroke settings to this line and complete the map, as in Figure 6-47.

At this point, you might regard the map as a bit austere. Surely, the buildings would work a little better if they were filled with color. And I think a subtle gradient background might help to set the map off from the white space around it. Although we're done with the map—as long as they can avoid the temptations of the Square Dance Hall, I think Jerry's pals will find their way—we take on the topic of gradients in the very next exercise.

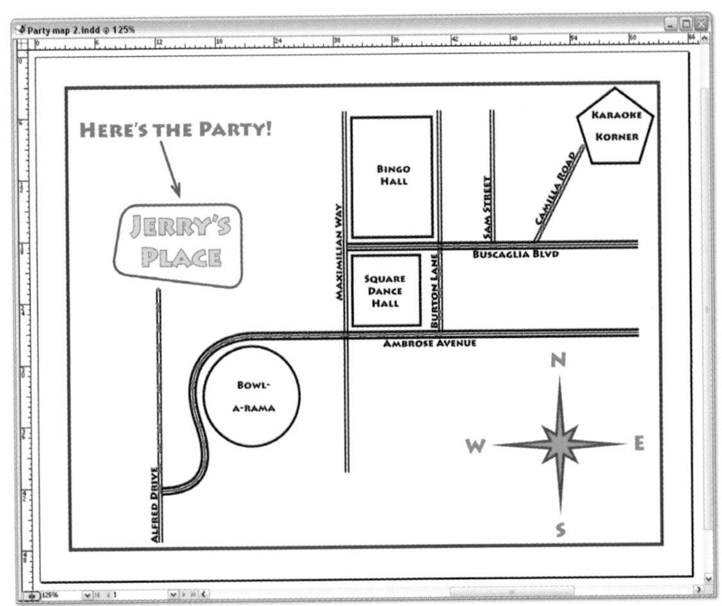

Figure 6-47.

Creating and Using Gradients

A fill or stroke doesn't have to be a single, solid color. Gradients are one of the most powerful tools you can use to add richness to your InDesign illustrations. A *gradient* is a fountain of transitioning colors, moving linearly across an object or radiating outward in concentric circles. InDesign lets you apply gradients to the fill or stroke of an object, whether that object is a path, frame, or character of text.

In this exercise, we'll apply a couple of gradients to spruce up a logo for the fictional Purple Mountains resort. You'll see how easy it is to add depth to an otherwise flat piece of artwork. We'll also experiment with InDesign's Arrange commands, which let you adjust overlapping objects by changing the order in which they're stacked.

1. *Open a document.* Open the file named *Purple mountains.indd*, found in the *Lesson 06* folder inside *Lesson Files-IDcs 1on1*. Pictured in Figure 6-48, our logo is pretty darn basic—two lines of type, three shapes (including the outer rectangle), and that's it. Can you imagine a more perfect subject for gradients?

Figure 6-48.

2. ***Select the large rectangle that frames the logo.*** Click with the black arrow tool anywhere in the large rectangle to select it.

3. ***Apply a gradient fill.*** Make sure the fill icon is active in the toolbox. (If necessary, press the X key to make it so.) Then click the gradient (■) icon at the bottom of the toolbox, or press the G key. As witnessed in Figure 6-49, the entire rectangle fills with a black-to-white gradient, obscuring the text, the logo, and everything else. Apparently, the rectangle is stacked in front of the other objects in the document; we want it to be in back.

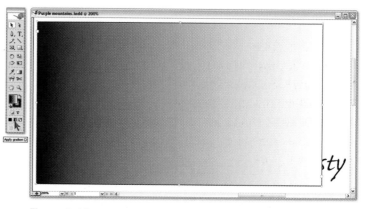

Figure 6-49.

4. ***Move the gradient rectangle behind the other objects.*** Right-click (or Control-click on the Mac) on the rectangle to display the shortcut menu. Choose **Arrange→Send to Back**, which sends the rectangle all the way to the back of the document, as in Figure 6-50.

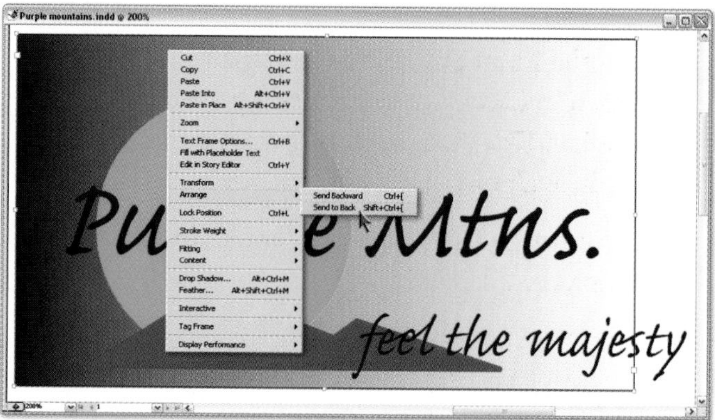

Figure 6-50.

PEARL OF WISDOM

The Arrange commands are available also from the Object menu. You can use the four commands to change the *stacking order* of objects in your document. The Bring Forward and Send Backward commands move the selected object one level up or down in the stack; Bring to Front and Send to Back move the selection to the top or bottom of the stack. You can also access these functions from the keyboard using the bracket keys. Press Ctrl+] (⌘-] on the Mac) for Bring Forward; press Ctrl+[(⌘-[) for Send Backward. Add the Shift key to invoke Bring to Front or Send to Back. If you come from Quark, these shortcuts are downright weird. But I recommend you assign them to memory because they work the same across other Adobe applications, including Photoshop and Illustrator.

---

5. *Bring up the Gradient palette.* While a valiant effort, InDesign's default black-to-white gradient is almost never what you want. To modify the gradient, choose **Window→Gradient** to display the **Gradient** palette. If you don't see all the options pictured in Figure 6-51, choose **Show Options** from the palette menu or click the ♦ arrow next to the palette name. The palette offers the following options:

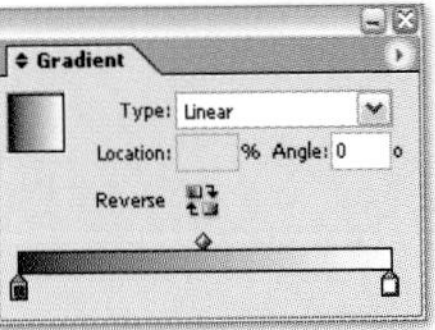

Figure 6-51.

   - Select from two kinds of gradients in the Type pop-up menu. The Linear setting fades colors in a straight line. The Radial setting radiates colors outward in concentric circles.
   - At the bottom of the Gradient palette is a ramp bar that shows the active gradient. At either end of the ramp is a *color stop*, indicated by ▲. The left color stop determines the starting color of the gradient; the right stop determines the ending color. The diamond shape (◇) above the ramp marks the midpoint of the gradient, where the colors mix in equal amounts.
   - Use the Location value to specify the position of a color stop or midpoint measured as a percentage of the overall gradient. The Angle value determines the direction of the gradient along a selected shape.
   - Click the Reverse icon to swap the order of all colors in the gradient.

   You can change the color of a color stop by clicking on it and then choosing another color in the Color palette. But I want to include the exact color of the purple mountains in our gradient, so let's first define that as a swatch.

6. ***Select the mountains and bring up the Swatches palette.*** Select the purple mountains shape with the black arrow tool. Then press F5 or choose **Window→Swatches** to bring up the Swatches palette.

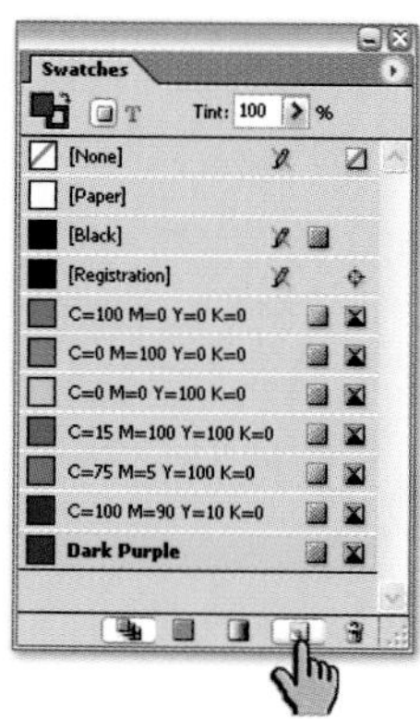

PEARL OF WISDOM

You can see by looking at the icons at the bottom of the toolbox that the mountains have identical fill and stroke colors. Why did I do this? To smoothe the corners. The mountain shape is actually a free-form polygon that I created by clicking with the pen tool. Then I applied a 4-point stroke and set the Join option in the Stroke palette to ⊡. Couldn't I have achieved a similar effect with Object→Corner Effects? Absolutely, it's just a different way to work.

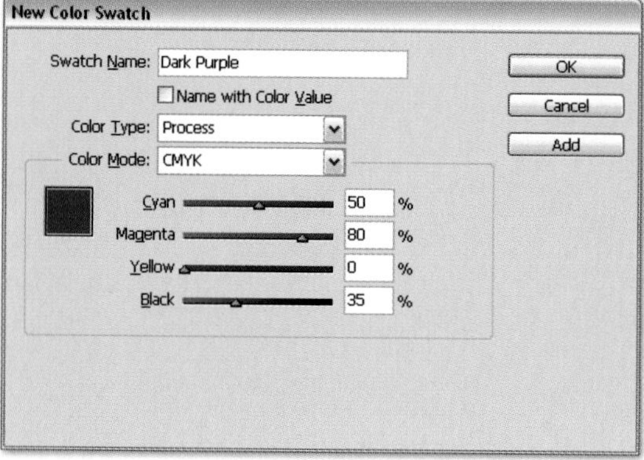

Figure 6-52.

7. ***Create a swatch named Dark Purple.*** Alt-click (or Option-click) the ⊡ icon at the bottom of the Swatches palette. Inside the New Color Swatch dialog box, turn off the **Name with Color Value** check box. Type "Dark Purple" in the **Swatch Name** option box. Then click **OK**. A new swatch appears at the bottom of the Swatches list, as in Figure 6-52.

8. ***Make Dark Purple the first color stop.*** Select the big gray rectangle. Then click the black color stop in the Gradient palette. You can tell that the color stop is selected because the triangular "roof" of the stop turns black (as in ☗). To change the color to purple, press the Alt key (Option on the Mac) and click **Dark Purple** in the Swatches palette.

9. ***Create a vertical gradient with the gradient tool.*** Personally, I like the colors in the gradient, but I don't like the direction in which it flows. I could adjust the direction by changing the Angle value in the Gradient palette. But the more intuitive and more capable solution is the gradient tool.

   To get the tool, click the gradient icon above the scissors in the toolbox, or press the G key. Drag from the base of the mountains to the top edge of the rectangle, as in Figure 6-53 on the facing page. To constrain your drag so it's exactly vertical, press the Shift key before you release the mouse button. Everything below the base of the mountains is now filled with a solid purple. The gradient flows from purple at the base to white at the top of the frame.

Right now the mountains are sort of swallowed up in the gradient. We need to introduce another color in the gradient to provide contrast and make the mountains stand out more.

Figure 6-53.

10. ***Add a color stop at 25 percent.*** Click just below the ramp in the Gradient palette (see Figure 6-54) to create a new color stop. Then drag the color stop until the **Location** value reads 25 percent. Or simply type 25 in the Location option box and press Enter or Return.

11. ***Assign a new color to the stop.*** InDesign automatically sets the new color stop to a lighter shade of the Dark Purple color. But I want to imbue it with a bit more pink. Click the lone **C** in the Color palette to highlight the Cyan value. (Don't press F6 or you'll deactivate the color stop in the Gradient palette!) Then change the values to **C**:10, **M**:50, **Y**:0, and **K**:0. The resulting magenta of the middle color stop becomes part of the background gradient, helping the mountains to stand out more, as in Figure 6-55.

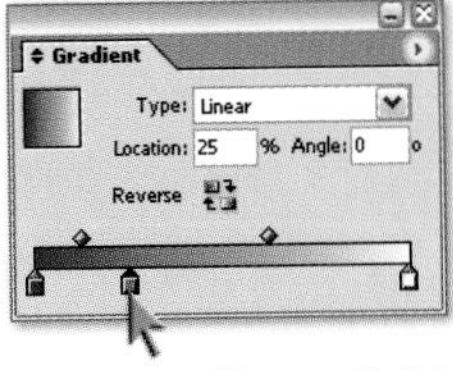

Figure 6-54.

12. ***Set the second midpoint diamond to 25 percent.*** Let's make one last change to this gradient that will introduce a little more white into the sky. Click the second ◇ midpoint control above the gradient ramp. Enter 25 in the **Location** option box and press Enter or Return. The gradient transitions more quickly, leaving a large area of white at the top of the rectangle.

Figure 6-55.

EXTRA CREDIT

Excellent work. You've successfully created and edited a linear gradient in InDesign. The remaining steps show you how to do the same with a radial gradient. You'll also learn some more techniques and experience a few essential options, all in pursuit of a pretty sunset. If that appeals to you, keep stepping. If not, skip to "Aligning and Distributing Objects" on page 228).

13. ***Save the circle color as a swatch.*** I want to fill my sun shape (the circle) with a gradient. But I don't want to lose the color that I've applied to the sun so far. Unfortunately, InDesign doesn't let you add gradient colors to the existing color of an object. You have to assign the last-applied gradient (or a gradient swatch) and then reinstate the original fill color.

Select the circle with the black arrow tool. To save its fill for later use, Alt-click (or Option-click) the ◱ icon at the bottom of the Swatches palette. Turn off **Name with Color Value**, name the swatch "Salmon Sun," and click **OK**.

14. ***Apply a gradient to the sun.*** Now that the fill color is safe, you can apply a gradient to the sun by clicking in the ramp bar at the bottom of the Gradient palette. Or press the [.] key. This applies the last created gradient to the currently selected object. InDesign assigns its new default gradient, which features the familiar colors arranged horizontally, as in Figure 6-56.

15. ***Switch to a radial gradient.*** I rather like the horizontal gradient. But let's try something different. Adjust the settings in the Gradient palette as follows:

    - Delete the middle magenta color stop. To do this, drag the color stop down and away from the palette.
    - Choose **Radial** from the **Type** pop-up menu to apply a radial gradient to the sun. The gradient flows from purple in the center to white along the perimeter.
    - Click the **Reverse** icon. Now the gradient starts off white in the middle and fades outward to purple.

Figure 6-56.

16. ***Move the hot spot.*** As when working with a linear gradient, you can set the beginning and end points of a radial gradient by dragging inside a selected shape with the gradient tool. Plus, you get an extra function: press the G key to switch to the gradient tool. Then click—don't drag, just click—in the upper-right portion of the sun. This relocates the beginning color of the gradient without moving the ending color, thus creating a "hot spot."

    Consider Figure 6-57. I moved the hot spot directly above the letter *l* in *Purple*. By all rights, the hot spot should appear at the precise point where you click. But InDesign CS suffers a little bug in this department. The crosshair cursors in Figure 6-57 indicate the points at which I clicked. The red crosshairs shows where I clicked on the PC; the blue crosshairs shows where I clicked on the

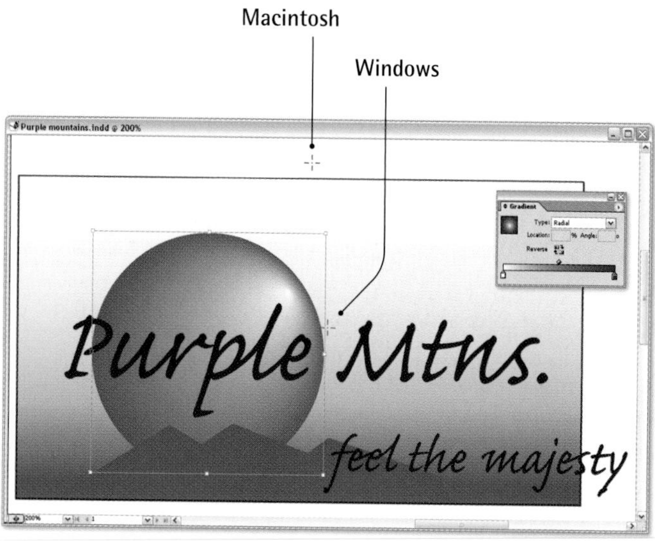

Figure 6-57.

Mac. Moral of the story: If your first click doesn't work, click around and find a point that does.

17. ***Apply the Salmon Sun swatch to the last color stop.*** That hot spot looks pretty cool. But you have to ask yourself, exactly what is casting this intense, shiny highlight? This is the sun after all, the brightest object in our solar system. It's probably not going to lighten up when you shine a flashlight at it. As nifty as the hot spot is, I don't think it makes much sense. Let's try something else:

    - Select the purple color stop in the Gradient palette.
    - Alt-click (or Option-click) the **Salmon Sun** swatch in the Swatches palette.
    - Click the **Reverse** icon. The gradient now runs outward from salmon in the center to white around the perimeter. I want a whole lot less white.
    - Click the midpoint ◇ in the Gradient palette to select it. Change the **Location** value to 84 and press Enter or Return. This is getting closer to my desired effect, but I want a sharper transition still.
    - Select the salmon-colored color stop and change the **Location** value to 78 percent. This means that the first 78 percent of our gradient is solid salmon. Because the ◇ maintains its relative distance from the two color stops, the remaining 22 percent of the gradient moves slowly from salmon to the midpoint color and then very sharply to white. Figure 6-58 shows the result.

Figure 6-58.

18. ***Make the final adjustments.*** So far, so great. But I am bothered by a couple of color transitions in the document. First, I want to get rid of the halo of white around the outside of the sun. Second, the tagline is getting lost in the dark colors at the base of the mountains. Two problems, two solutions:

    - Choose **Window→Transparency** or press Shift+F10 to display the **Transparency** palette. Then choose **Multiply** from the pop-up menu in the upper-left corner of the palette. This drops out the whites and combines the darker colors in the sun with the objects below them.

Figure 6-59.

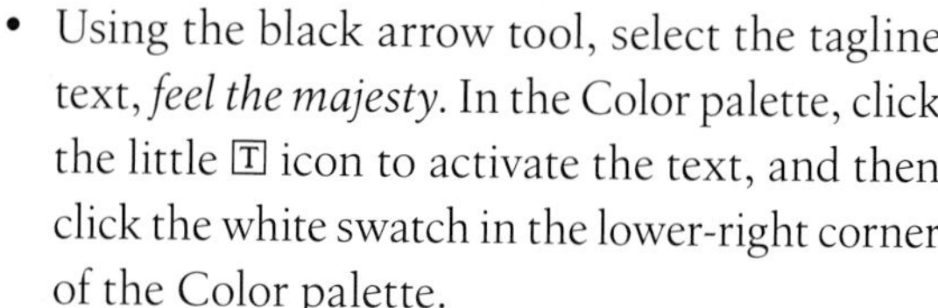

- Using the black arrow tool, select the tagline text, *feel the majesty*. In the Color palette, click the little 🅃 icon to activate the text, and then click the white swatch in the lower-right corner of the Color palette.

I also dragged the text block to the left so it resides completely inside the gradient frame, as we see in Figure 6-59. For a discussion of the Transparency palette and its many options, read Lesson 8, "Transparency and Effects." But for the time being, just sit back and enjoy the sunset.

Aligning and Distributing Objects

If you're arranging a layout in InDesign and you need to bring a bunch of text and graphic objects into alignment, your first move might be to start dragging guides from the rulers to help you position the objects. But why bother when InDesign's Align palette can do the job without a single guide, positioning objects so that their edges or centers are in perfect alignment. The Align palette also can *distribute* a line of selected objects so that the objects are evenly spaced. This exercise shows you how the Align palette's alignment and distribution powers work.

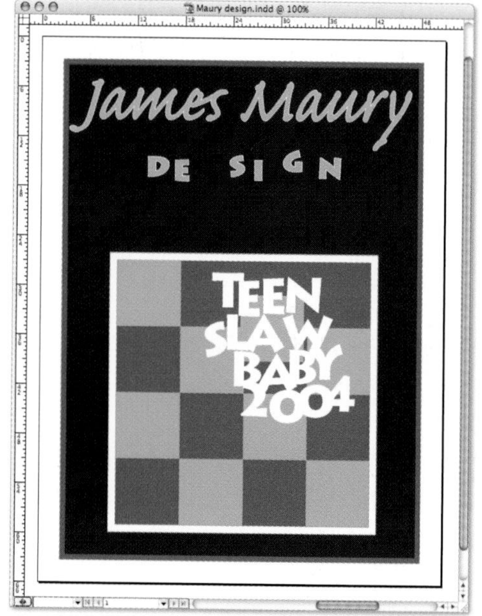

Figure 6-60.

1. *Open a document with objects in need of alignment.* Go to the *Lesson 06* folder inside *Lesson Files-IDcs 1on1* and open the file named *Maury design.indd*. Shown in Figure 6-60, this document features some randomly scattered characters—each housed inside its own frame—over a checkerboard pattern. Each character belongs inside one of the checkerboard squares, which when put in the proper order will spell the street address for our design company. Note that some of the items you won't need to select during this exercise are placed on a locked layer so that you don't move them accidentally.
2. *Select the misplaced beige square.* On closer inspection, one of the beige squares is out of place. Located under the heap of white characters, it should be in the top row of squares. Because the square is so thoroughly buried, you can't select it by simply clicking on it with the black arrow tool. You need to use a special technique that I call "selecting down the stack."

The key to selecting down the stack is the Ctrl key (⌘ on the Mac). Try this: Using the black arrow tool, click on the *A* in *SLAW* to select it. Then press Ctrl (or ⌘) and click on the *A* again.

As Figure 6-61 shows, the bounding box changes to encompass the misplaced square. You selected *through* the *A* to the next lowest item in the stack.

Figure 6-61.

3. ***Add the top-left square to the selection.*** Shift-click on the top-left beige square in the checkerboard to add it to the selection. Except for the misplaced square, all the other squares are locked, meaning that you can select them but you can't move them. As we'll see, locked objects are great for aligning other objects.
4. ***Bring up the Align palette.*** Choose **Window→Align** or press Shift+F7 to display the **Align** palette. The palette contains 12 buttons that let you align and distribute selected objects.
5. ***Top-align the wayward square.*** Click the fourth button in the **Align Objects** section of the palette, which looks like . As Figure 6-62 shows, the misplaced square jumps up so it aligns with the top-left square. There's no chance that the top-left square will move because it's locked. Therefore, it serves as an anchor for the alignment operation.
6. ***Deselect the top-left square and select the sixth beige square.*** Shift-click the first square to deselect it, and then Shift-click the sixth beige square—the one under the *2* and *0* in *2004*—to select it.
7. ***Right-align the wayward square.*** Click the third Align Objects button () to align the right edges of the selected objects. Because the lower of the two squares is locked, the top square moves to the right, precisely aligning to the checkerboard. Figure 6-63 shows the result.

Figure 6-62.

Figure 6-63.

Figure 6-64.

8. ***Lock down the formerly wayward square.*** Now that the errant square has been assimilated into its proper position, it's time to lock it down so it doesn't go moving again. With the squares still selected, choose **Object→Lock Position** or press Ctrl+L (⌘-L on the Mac). One of the selected squares was already locked, but it doesn't hurt anything to lock it again.

9. ***Align the 4 with the top-left square.*** Now we begin the somewhat arduous task of aligning the white letters with their respective squares. We'll start with the *4* in *2004*:
   - Select both the *4* and the top-left beige square by clicking on one and Shift-clicking on the other.
   - Click the second Align Objects button (⊟) to center the two selected objects horizontally. The *4* scoots into the left column.
   - Next, click the fifth alignment button (⊞) to center the objects vertically, as in Figure 6-64.

10. ***Align an* E *to the bottom-right square.*** Click one of the *E*s in *TEEN* and then Shift-click the bottom-right beige square. Again, click the ⊟ and ⊞ buttons to snap the *E* into place with the square.

    We could continue like this, aligning each letter or number to its proper square, but that wouldn't harness the full power of the Align palette. Instead, we'll move more expeditiously to finish the layout.

Figure 6-65.

11. ***Roughly position the other* E *and a* B.** Drag the other *E* and one of the *B*s in *BABY* into the approximate positions shown in Figure 6-65. Then Shift-click to select all four characters along the diagonal—that is, *4*, *E*, *B*, and *E*. We have the *4* and the bottom-right *E* exactly where they need to be, so be careful not to move them when you select them. Now let's distribute the other *E* and the *B* into place.

12. ***Distribute the four selected letters.*** This time, we'll focus on the **Distribute Objects** section of the Align palette. Click the second button (⊟) to vertically distribute the objects so their centers are equally spaced. Next, click the fifth button (⊞) to space the centers of the objects horizontally. Both distribution options move the inside objects only, so the *4* and the *E* remain fixed, as in Figure 6-66.

13. ***Lock the selected letters and position the others.*** Now that we have this diagonal line of letters exactly where we want them, choose **Object→Lock Position** or press Ctrl+L (⌘-L) to secure them in place. You have now positioned and locked a letter in each row and each column of the checkerboard. As you'll see, this will hasten the pace of the remaining alignment operations.

    Now move the 12 other letters into the rough locations shown in Figure 6-67. Don't even attempt to get them centered. As before, we'll have InDesign do this for us.

14. ***Align each of the four rows.*** Starting in the blue area outside the checkerboard, drag with the black arrow tool to draw a marquee through the objects in the first row, as illustrated in Figure 6-68. (Remember, you only want to select the first row; if you select a letter in any other row, click off the objects to deselect them and try again. When done properly, you'll select four letters and a couple of beige squares; since the latter are locked they can't be harmed by the operation.) Click the fifth **Align Objects** button (⊕) to snap the 2 and the two *0*s into vertical alignment with the row.

    Repeat this operation—marqueeing and aligning—for each of the next three rows.

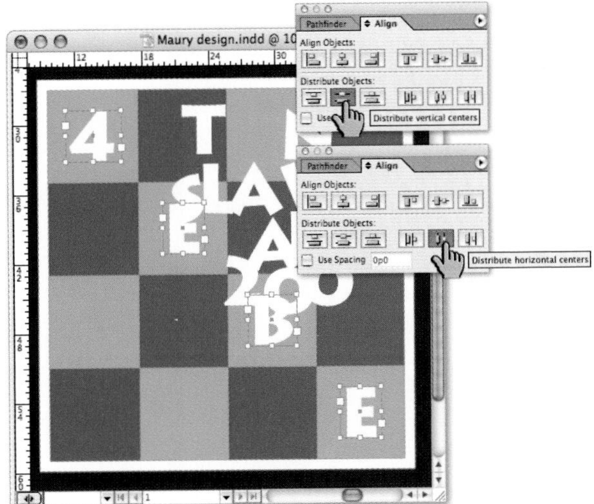

Figure 6-66.

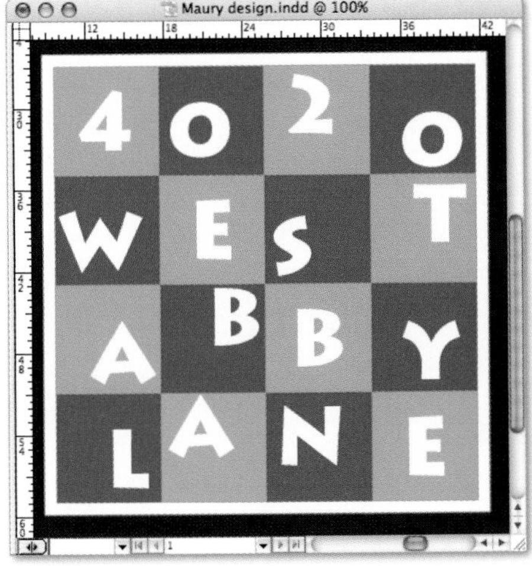

Figure 6-67.

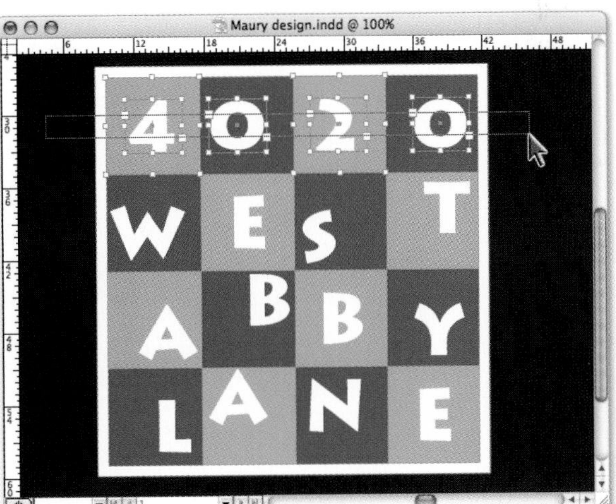

Figure 6-68.

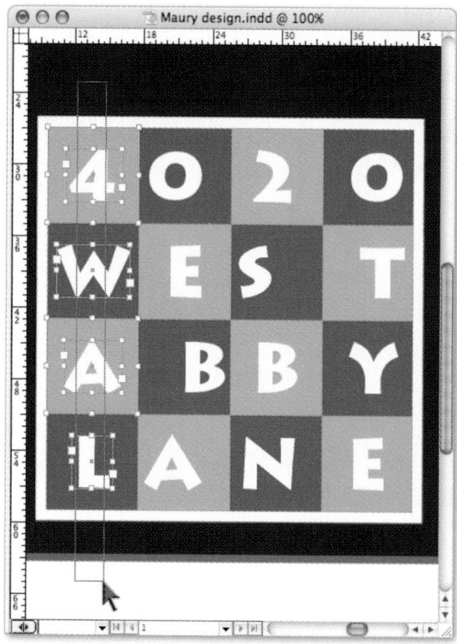

Figure 6-69.

15. *Align each of the four columns.* From rows we move to columns. Draw a slim marquee through the objects in the first column, as in Figure 6-69. Then click the second Align Objects button ( ). This makes the *W*, *A*, and *L* snap into horizontal alignment with the locked *4* above them. You might not see much of a change, but rest assured, the letters are not perfectly aligned. Marquee each of the three remaining columns and align them in a similar fashion.

16. *Align the yellow letters above the checkerboard.* Now that the 16 white letters are precisely aligned, we need to fix the yellow word *DESIGN*. Again, I recommend that you draw a marquee around the letters to select them. Then click the fifth Align Objects button ( ). Note that the *D* is locked so it serves as the anchor. Figure 6-70 shows the result.

17. *Distribute the selected letters.* The letters are now aligned, but the distribution could use some work. Click the fifth Distribute Objects button ( ) to freeze the horizontal placement of the outside letters (the *D* and *N*) and adjusts the intermediate letters so that their centers are an equal horizontal distance apart, as in Figure 6-71. Problem is, that's not really what we want. There's too much space on either side of the *I*, and the *G* and *N* are jammed together. Sadly, the other distribution options don't fair any better. What's a person to do?

18. *Expand the Align palette.* Choose **Show Options** from the palette menu or click twice on the ♦ arrow next to the palette name to reveal the Distribute Spacing options. Rather than moving objects so that there's equal space between their edges or centers, the Distribute Spacing options make sure there's equal space between the neighboring edges of the objects.

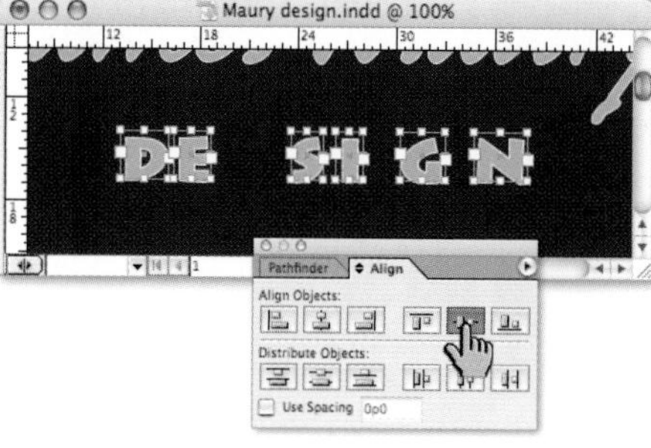

Figure 6-70.

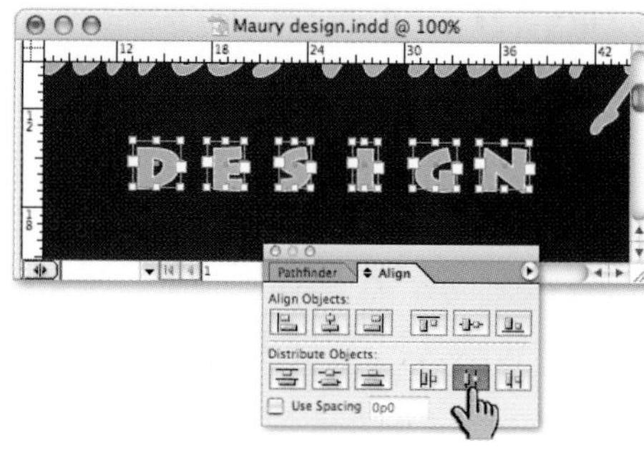

Figure 6-71.

19. ***Even out the space between the letters.*** Click the second **Distribute Spacing** button ( ) to create an equal amount of space between the nearest edges of neighboring letters. As Figure 6-72 shows, there's now an equal amount of space between the *I*, *G*, and *N*, resulting in a more pleasing layout.

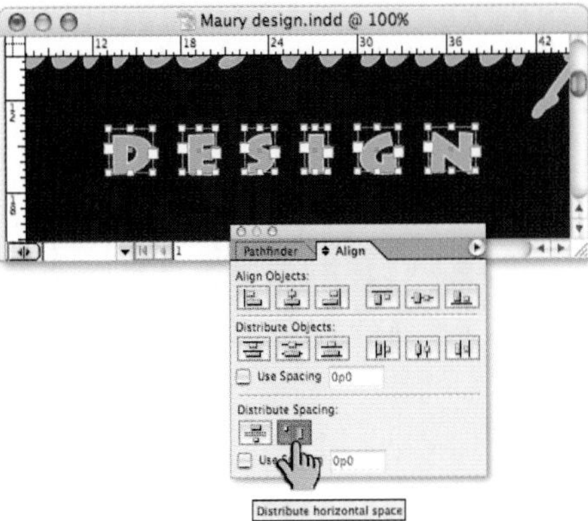

Figure 6-72.

PEARL OF WISDOM

Both the Distribute Objects and Distribute Spacing areas include Use Spacing check boxes. When active, these options permit you to distribute objects by a specified amount of space. One object remains stationary, and the others move with respect to it.

Compound Paths and Pathfinder Operations

As we've seen, InDesign's pen tool is expertly suited to drawing free-form paths. But the pen tool is also difficult to use, so difficult that even veteran designers admit to being intimidated by it. Even if you're one of the few who've taken to it like the proverbial fish takes to water, you have to admit that the pen is hardly quick or convenient. It can be every bit as plodding as it is precise.

Which is why InDesign gives you other options. Instead of drawing an intricate path point-by-point with the pen, you can draw pieces of the path and then assemble those pieces into a composite whole. This not only simplifies the path-drawing ritual but also permits you greater control when creating repeating or symmetrical forms.

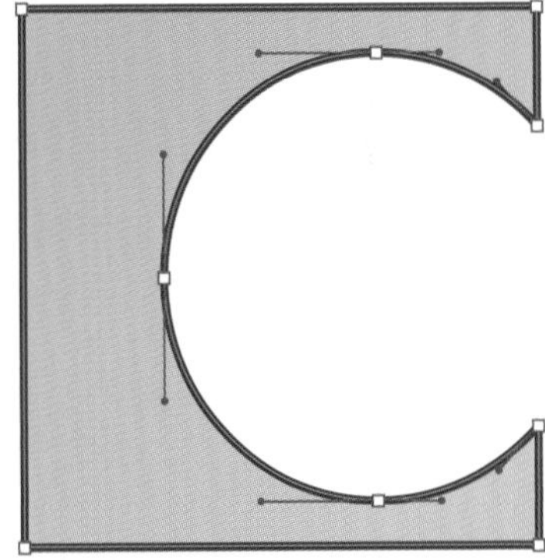

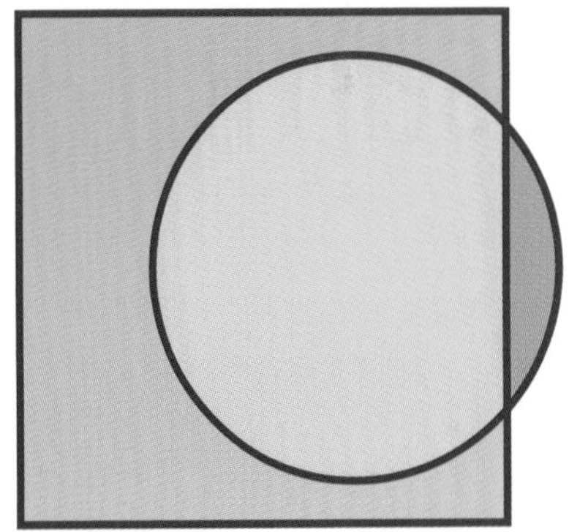

Figure 6-73.

Consider the circle cut from a square pictured at the top of Figure 6-73. Had I attempted to draw the shape with the pen tool, I'd have had to manually position nine points and eight control handles in such a way as to achieve perfect vertical and horizontal symmetry. InDesign offers many constraints (ruler guides, the Shift key, and so on) to help me on my way, but none can guarantee that one arc will be a precise mirror image of another. The better solution is to draw the base shapes using the rectangle and ellipse tools, align them as illustrated at the bottom of Figure 6-73, and finally combine them—in this case, by choosing Object→Pathfinders→Subtract. The approach is simple, the result is symmetrical, and I am happy.

This next exercise shows you how to combine simple paths to create more elaborate ones. You'll use paths to cut holes in one another, add paths together, and even calculate elaborate intersections. Simply put, you'll learn how to do in a few minutes what it would otherwise take hours to do with the pen.

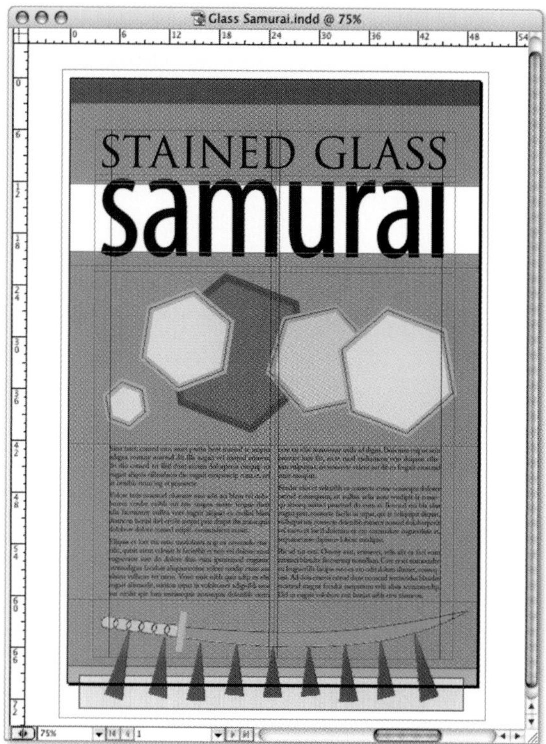

Figure 6-74.

1. ***Open a document that contains some primitive vector art.*** Open the *Glass Samurai.indd* document, which I've included in the *Lesson 06* folder inside *Lesson Files-IDcs 1on1*. Shown in Figure 6-74, this page contains a bevy of basic shapes, including rectangles, ovals, and hexagons. I drew some paths—the triangles at the bottom of the page and the blue blade of the sword—with the pen tool. But even these are limited to three points apiece. Such shapes are commonly called *primitives* because you can use them to build more complex artwork.

2. ***Select the hexagons.*** Using the black arrow tool, draw a marquee across the center of the hexagons to select the five shapes. Figure 6-75 shows me drawing such a marquee. (Note that I've pressed the W key to hide the guides and other nonprinting distractions.) We'll use these shapes to create a stylized stained glass effect.

3. ***Combine the selection into a compound path.*** Choose **Object→Compound Paths→Make** or press the shortcut Ctrl+8 (⌘-8 on the Mac). InDesign converts the hexagons into a special object called a *compound path*. This object possesses the following attributes:

   • A compound path may include just one fill and one stroke. This means all shapes now share the same color scheme, lifted from the lowest shape in the stack.

   • Overlapping areas inside the compound path are treated as holes, and are thus transparent. The number 8 is the quintessential compound path, with two inner circles cutting holes out of a larger shape (hence Ctrl+8 as the keyboard shortcut). For our part, the occasional transparency heightens the stained glass effect.

   Figure 6-76 verifies the first statement and calls the second one into question. All shapes now share the blue fill and stroke originally applied to the rear hexagon. But of the three areas where the shapes intersect, only one is treated as a hole. What gives?

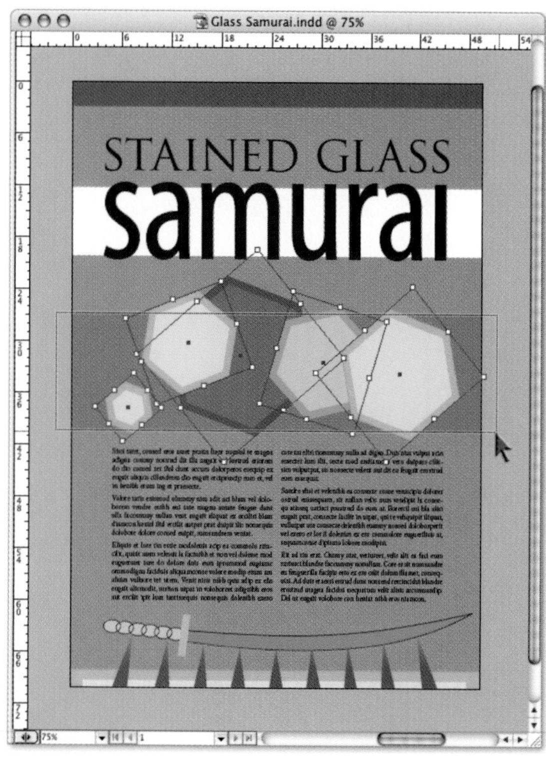

Figure 6-75.

PEARL OF WISDOM

According to an arcane bit of PostScript printing code called the non-zero winding fill rule, shapes cut holes in each other only when they travel in opposite directions. For reasons known only to InDesign, the second hexagon to the left travels in the opposite direction of the other three, so as a result, only it cuts a hole. The specific directions of the shapes are irrelevant. All that matters is that one shape must be reversed.

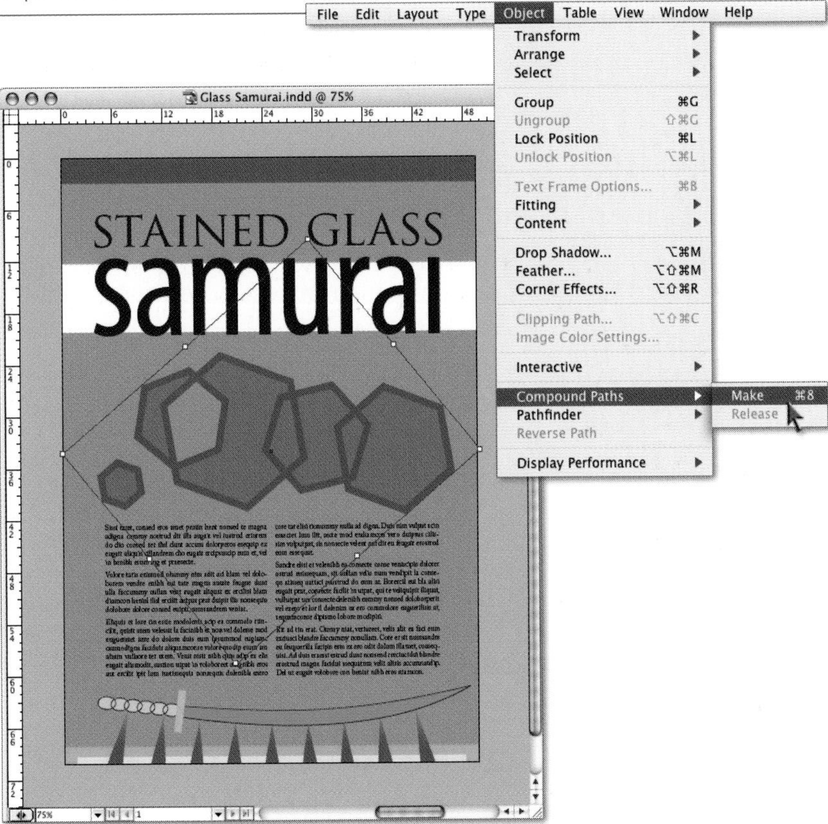

Figure 6-76.

4. ***Reverse the direction of the fourth shape.*** Based on how the hexagons interact, each of the three on the right must travel in the same direction. Therefore, reversing the middle of these—that is, the fourth one from the left—should remedy our problem. Here's how to do it:

   - Switch to the white arrow tool, whether by clicking its icon in the toolbox or by pressing the A key. InDesign selects the individual shape outlines.

   - We only want to select one shape, and the easiest way to do so is to redefine the selection. Press Ctrl+Shift+A (or ⌘-Shift-A) to deselect everything and start again.

- Press the Alt key (Option on the Mac) and click inside the fourth hexagon, the one under the *ur* in *samurai*. InDesign surrounds the shape with solid points to show that it's selected.

- Go to the **Object** menu and choose **Reverse Path**. The redirected shape now cuts holes in its neighbors.

The result is a dynamic interaction of shapes, in which one cuts a hole in its neighbors. If you move or otherwise modify one shape independently of the others, the holes will update dynamically as well. So if InDesign's implementation of compound paths seems a bit weird, take heart that it's exceptionally flexible to boot.

5. ***Select the sword.*** Magnified in Figure 6-77, the sword is a collection of nine shapes. I drew the blade with the pen. Otherwise, it's all rectangles and ellipses that I rotated slightly from the Control palette. (To learn about rotating, see the "Rotating, Slanting, and Flipping" exercise that begins on page 263 of Lesson 7.) In the next step, we'll combine the nine shapes into a single object. But first, we have to select them.

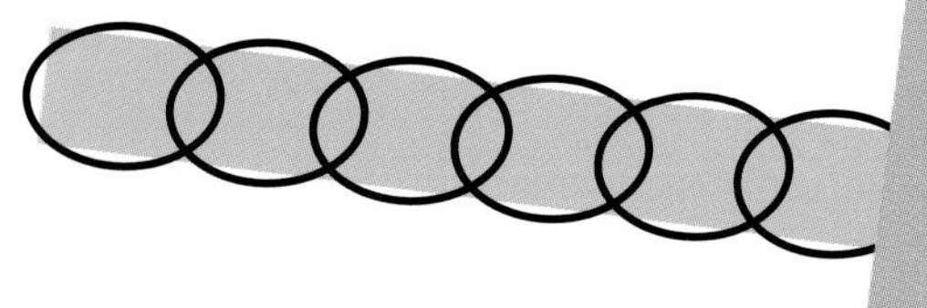

Figure 6-77.

To simplify the task of selecting the various sword elements—and eliminate the chance of selecting the triangles and other shapes that aren't part of the sword—I've relegated the salient shapes to an independent layer. Here's what you should do:

- Choose **Window→Layers** or press F7 to display the **Layers** palette. You should see five layers, from Backdrop at the bottom to Sword at the top.

- Press the Alt (or Option) key and click the word **Sword** at the top of the palette. This wonderful little trick makes the layer active and selects all objects on that layer.

Just like that, the sword is selected. Of course, if you want to hone your manual selection skills, feel free to marquee or Shift-click the individual shapes. But isn't this so much easier?

6. ***Unite the nine paths into one.*** Now that you've selected the shapes, you can combine them using InDesign's foremost Pathfinder operation, Add. *Pathfinder* is Adobe's term for a collection of commands that use one path to manipulate the outline of another. The Add operation takes the selected paths and unites them all together. To apply the Add command, do one of the following:

   - Choose **Object→Pathfinder→Add**.
   - Choose **Window→Pathfinder** to display the diminutive **Pathfinder** palette. Then click the very first button, which looks like ⧉.

   InDesign unites the selected shapes into one continuous path, as in Figure 6-78. The path receives the fill and stroke attributes of the frontmost shape, so it now appears light brown with no stroke.

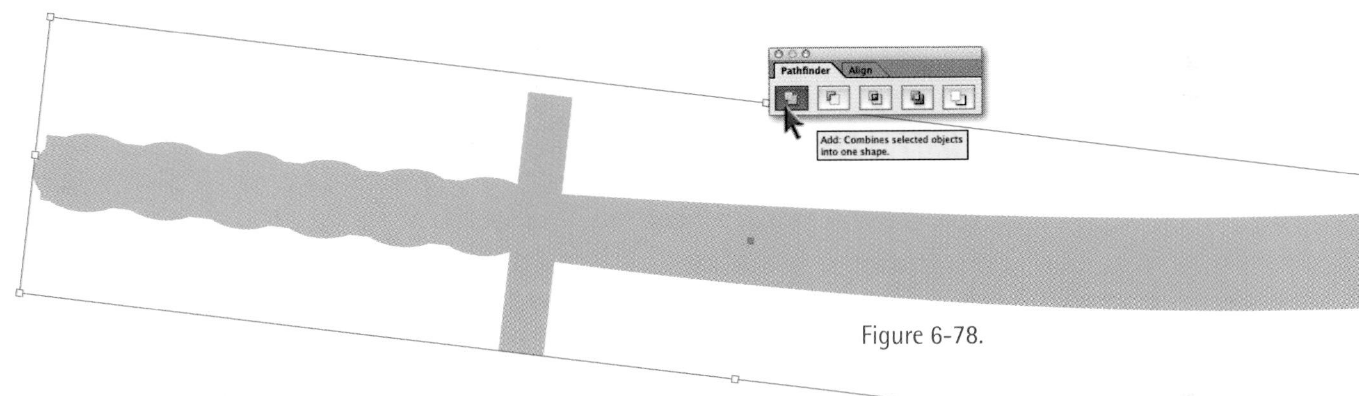

Figure 6-78.

PEARL OF WISDOM

Unlike a compound path, Pathfinders are not dynamic. In other words, InDesign actually redraws the path, point for point and handle for handle. So be sure to get your shapes into their proper position before applying a Pathfinder operation.

7. ***Lock the sword.*** A sword is a dangerous weapon. For example, right now, it interferes with our ability to select other objects. So let's lock it up and keep it safe.

   See that empty box in front of the word Sword in the **Layers** palette? Click inside the box to display the lock icon, which tells you that the active layer is no longer available for editing. We can still see the sword, but we can't touch it, making it much easier to select surrounding elements in the very next step.

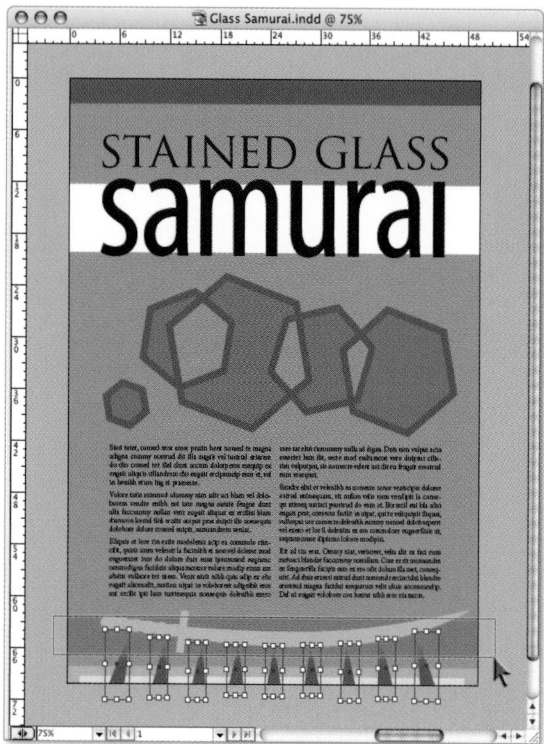

Figure 6-79.

8. *Select the nine triangles.* Press the V key to get the black arrow tool. Then draw a marquee along the tops of the gradient-blue triangles. Be careful not to snag the orange and yellow rectangles along the bottom of the page. But feel free to drag over the sword for all you're worth; it's locked. The result is a dapper row of selected triangles, as in Figure 6-79.

9. *Combine the triangles into a compound path.* The selected triangles are of different heights and all extend beyond the bottom of the page. That's not necessarily a bad thing, but in this case, it offends my keen sense of order. Again, I could have used a ruler guide to align the bottoms of the shapes as I drew them, but that would've involved more work. So instead, I've created a yellow rectangle that we'll use to crop away the bottoms with the help of a Pathfinder operation called Minus Back.

PEARL OF WISDOM

You might therefore expect that we would next: 1) add the yellow rectangle to the selection, and then 2) apply Minus Back. If so, I commend your reasoning; however, InDesign doesn't work that way. Instead of subtracting one shape from the many—the most logical approach, in my opinion—Minus Back subtracts the many from the one. That is, it uses the many rear shapes to crop the foremost shape in the selection. As illustrated in Figure 6-80, only a fraction of the front path would survive the operation.

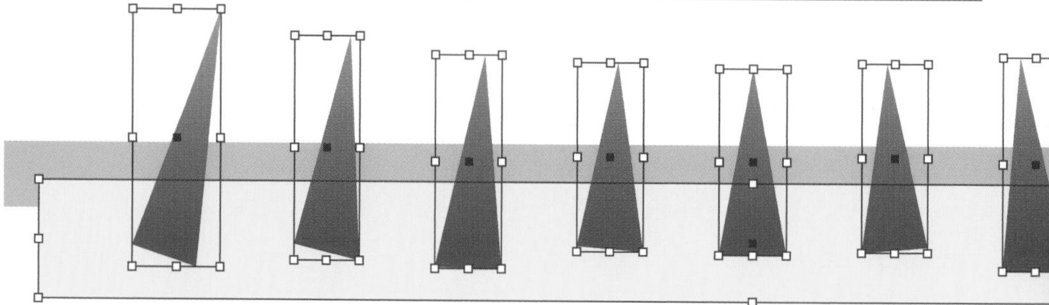

Original gradient triangles and yellow rectangle

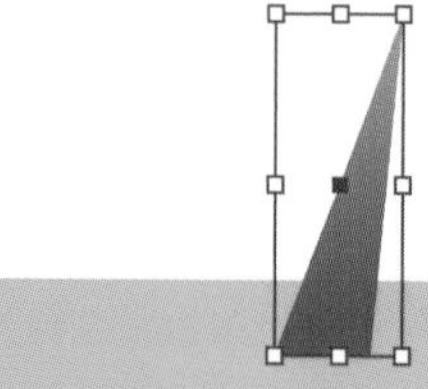

Applying the Minus Back operation leaves a single sliver

Figure 6-80.

The solution? Turn the shapes that you want to crop into a single path. With the nine triangles (and *not* the yellow rectangle) selected, choose **Object→Compound Paths→Make** or press Ctrl+8 (⌘-8). Because the triangles are already colored the same and none overlap, they don't look any different. But InDesign now regards them as a single path, thus setting the stage for Minus Back.

10. ***Subtract the yellow rectangle from the triangles.*** Press the Shift key and click the yellow rectangle to add it to the selection. Then do one of the following:

    - Choose **Object→Pathfinder→Minus Back**.
    - If the **Pathfinder** palette is handy, click the last button, the one that looks like .

    InDesign subtracts the one rear object, the yellow rectangle, from the one foreground object, the compound triangles. The result is a series of precisely aligned spikes, as in Figure 6-81.

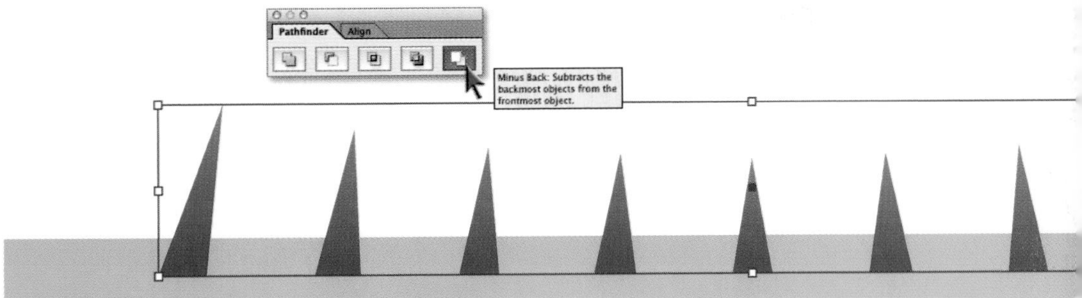

Figure 6-81.

PEARL OF WISDOM

Forgive my proliferation of Pearls, but it's worth mentioning that InDesign offers a very similar Pathfinder operation called Subtract (in the Pathfinder palette). Once termed Minus Front in sibling program Adobe Illustrator, Subtract is Minus Back's opposite, cropping the rearmost object in a selection with those in front of it.

11. ***Unite the modified triangles with the orange rectangle.*** Shift-click the orange rectangle, which exactly aligns to the bottom edges of the page. With triangles and orange rectangle selected, choose **Object→Pathfinder→Add** or click the button in the Pathfinder palette. InDesign unites the shapes and preserves the drab blue-to-brown gradient fill originally assigned to the forward shapes, as in Figure 6-82 on the next page.

EXTRA CREDIT

By now, you have a basic sense of how you can combine simple shapes to create more complex ones. If a basic sense is all the sense you need, I release you to skip ahead to page 243, where you can test your newfound knowledge. But if you have a few minutes to spare, I'd like to show you a few more things. For starters, InDesign offers two additional Pathfinder operations that deserve your fleeting attention. Plus, I'll show you how to combine text outlines with paths to create augmented character shapes. These last steps offer an exciting glimpse into how you can use letterforms as graphic objects.

12. ***Convert the word* samurai *to path outlines.*** Toward the top of the page, you see the word *samurai* set in black against a white rectangle. Hidden behind the white rectangle is a blue rectangle. In the remaining steps, we'll combine *samurai* and the white shape to create cropped letters that fit entirely inside the blue rectangle.

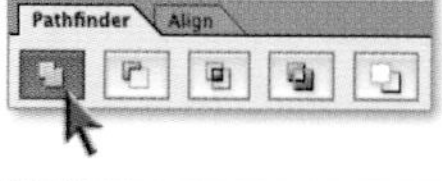

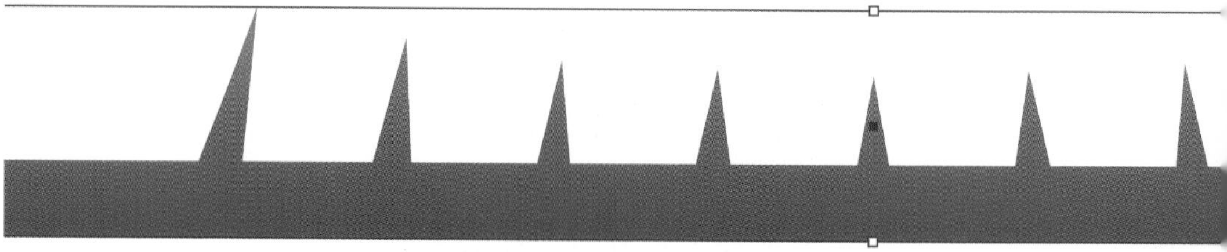

Figure 6-82.

Normally, I would combine the letters and rectangle using a Pathfinder operation. But Pathfinders don't work with text; they work only with graphics. Therefore, before you can combine characters of type, you must first convert the characters to shapes.

Click anywhere on the word *samurai* to select it. Then choose **Type→Create Outlines**, as in Figure 6-83, or press Ctrl+Shift+O (⌘-Shift-O on the Mac). InDesign converts the seven letters to paths. This means you can no longer fix typos or apply formatting attributes. In exchange, you can modify the character outlines just as if the letters were drawn with the pen tool.

13. ***Send the text to the back of the stack.*** Pathfinder operations take on the fill and stroke attributes of the front object. Because I want to fill the text with white, it's better to have the white rectangle in front of the text. With the letters still selected, choose **Object→Arrange→Send to Back** or press Ctrl+Shift+[(⌘-Shift-[on the Mac).

14. ***Find the intersection of the rectangle and the letters.*** Any letter with a hole in it—including the *a*'s in *samurai*—is expressed as a compound path. InDesign then takes the additional precaution of grouping all letters together into a larger compound path. This means the work we had to perform on the triangles in Step 9 has already been done for us. With the word combined into one big path, all that's left for us is to apply our final Pathfinder operation.

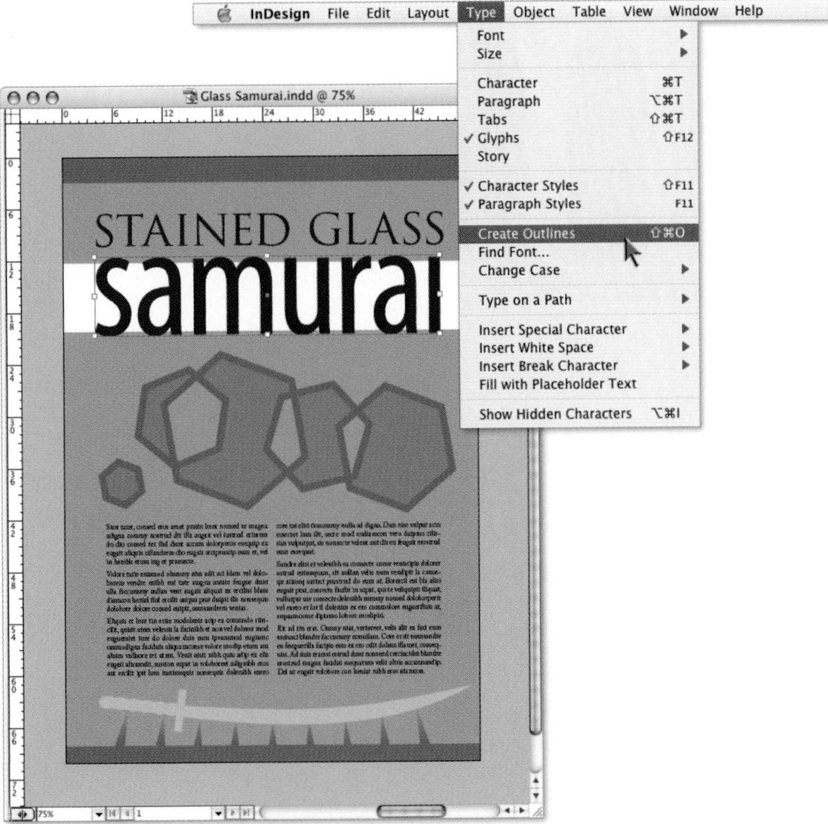

Figure 6-83.

Shift-click on the white rectangle to add it to the selection. Then do either of the following:

- Choose **Object→Pathfinder→Intersect**.
- If you still have the **Pathfinder** palette open, click the middle button, which appears as ⧉.

InDesign keeps only those portions of the letters where they overlap the white rectangle. And because the rectangle was in front, the letter shapes are filled with white, as in Figure 6-84. Furthermore, the letters are cropped so that they exactly fit inside the blue rectangle behind them. For a glimpse of the completed page, see Figure 6-85.

Figure 6-84.

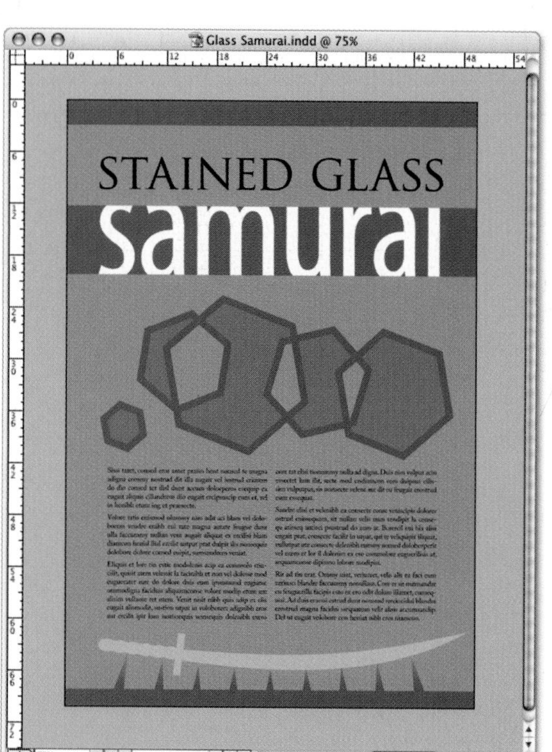

Figure 6-85.

That still leaves one more Pathfinder operation. Termed Exclude Overlap (or ⧉ in button form), it is Intersect's opposite, keeping just those portions of selected shapes that *don't* overlap. In this way, it is much like combining shapes into a compound path, except that the relationship is fixed rather than dynamic. For example, we could have applied Exclude to the hexagons back in Step 3 (page 234), but had we done so, the shapes would have been redrawn to trace around the gaps. Between you and me, I find compound paths to be more useful.

WHAT DID YOU LEARN?

Match the key concept in the numbered list below with the letter of the phrase that best describes it. Answers appear upside-down at the bottom of the page.

Key Concepts

1. Vector-based graphic
2. Path
3. Segment
4. Anchor point
5. Control handle
6. Primitive
7. Stroke
8. Color model
9. Spot color
10. Butt cap
11. Compound path
12. Pathfinder operation

Descriptions

A. An individual line fragment within a path outline, which begins and ends with an anchor point.

B. The color, thickness, roundness, and style of the outline that traces the inside, outside, or center of a path.

C. This prints as a single, premixed ink, ensuring consistency and permitting you to create colors outside the CMYK range.

D. A single object created from the combination of two shapes, one of which cuts a hole into another in the event that the shapes overlap.

E. Artwork made up exclusively of mathematically defined outlines, which conform to the highest resolution of your printer, monitor, or other piece of hardware.

F. A means of defining hues and shades in a computer program; examples include RGB, CMYK, and Lab, among others.

G. Like a dot in a dot-to-dot puzzle, this most essential element of a path outline defines where one segment ends and the next begins.

H. Adobe's term for a collection of commands and palette options that use one path to manipulate the outline of another.

I. This imaginary lever extends from an anchor point, thus curving a segment as it enters or exits the point.

J. The technical term for any line or shape drawn inside InDesign, which comprises anchor points connected by segments.

K. A simple, symmetrical shape such as a rectangle, square, oval, circle, polygon, or star.

L. This option in the Stroke palette ends the stroke abruptly at the first and last anchor points of the path (snicker).

Answers

1E, 2J, 3A, 4G, 5I, 6K, 7B, 8F, 9C, 10L, 11D, 12H

LESSON 7

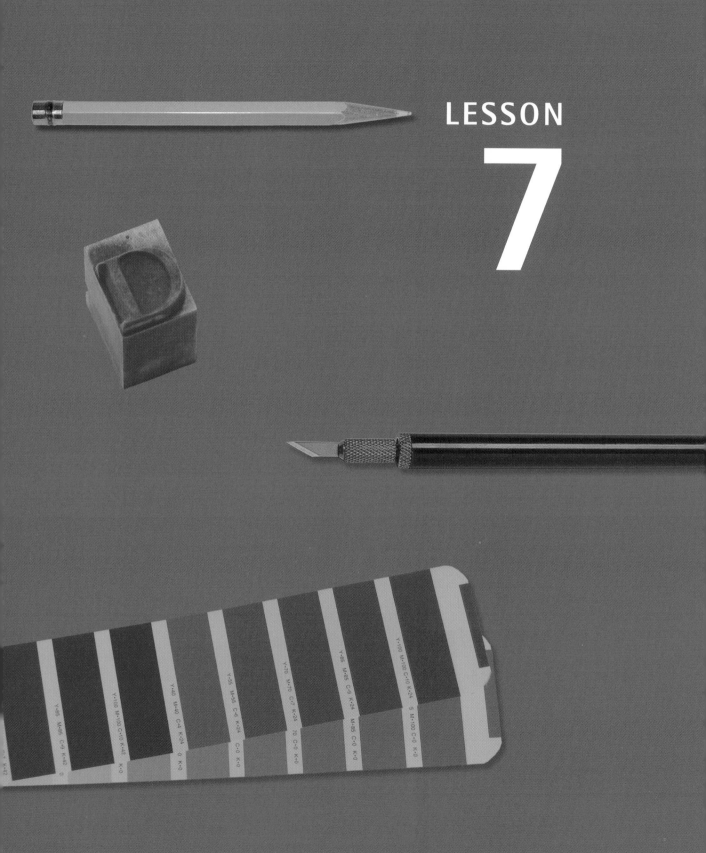

IMPORTING AND MODIFYING ARTWORK

IF YOU COMPLETED the previous lesson, then you know InDesign is an astonishingly capable graphics application. Even so, it can't keep up with a full-blown illustration program like Adobe Illustrator or Macromedia FreeHand, both of which offer scads more options and greater control. If InDesign is sufficient for making little graphics, Illustrator or FreeHand is essential for making big ones.

And lest we forget, vector drawing isn't the only kind of computer art. You have CAD, 3-D, and most importantly, imagery. Every digital snapshot, scanned photograph, 3-D rendering, and computer painting is made up of thousands or millions of tiny colored squares. Called *pixels*, these tiny squares are packed together so tightly and vary in color so gradually that they merge to form a coherent picture, which we in the biz call a *bitmapped image* or just plain *image* for short. One such image graces Figure 7-1. On the right we see a digital photo of the stately Queen Victoria Memorial outside Buckingham Palace; on the left we see a detail from the jolly old monarch's face

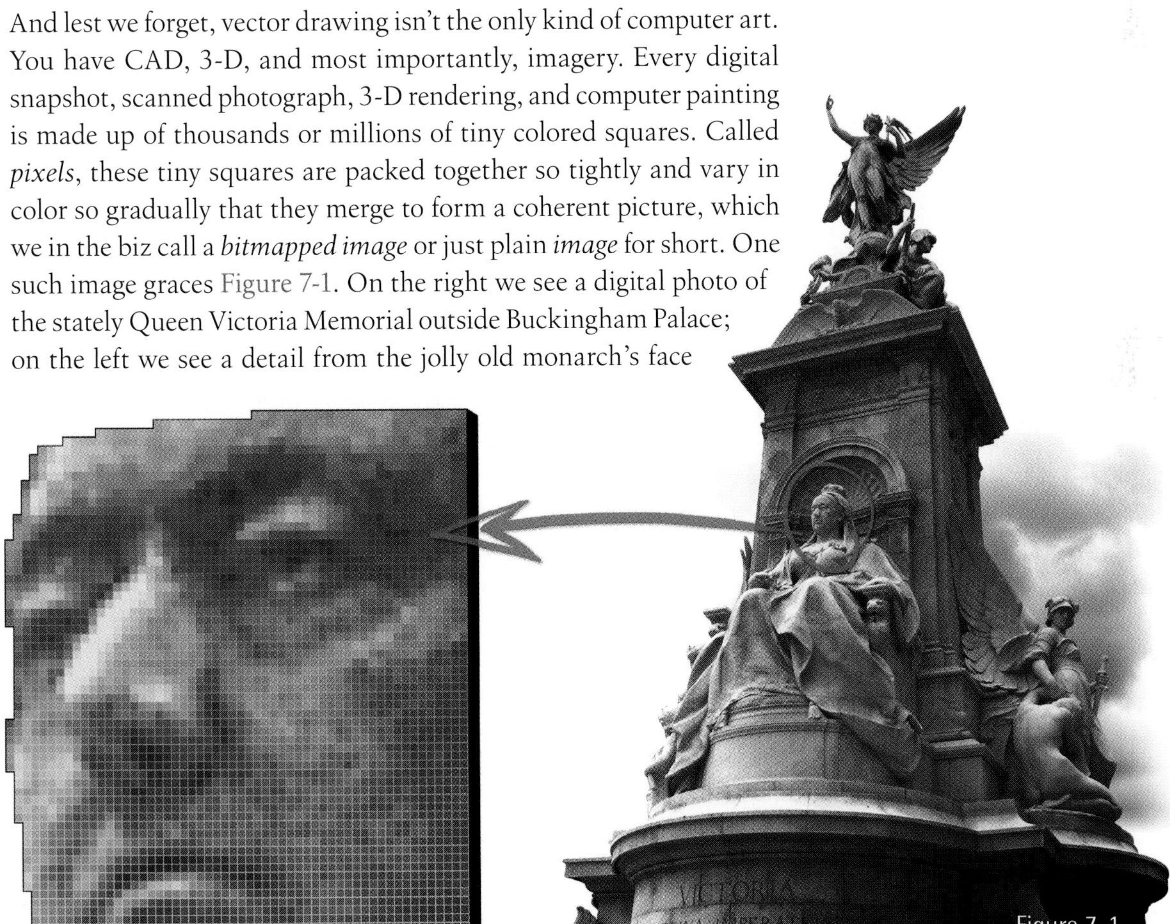

Figure 7-1.

ABOUT THIS LESSON

Project Files

Before beginning the exercises, make sure that you've installed the lesson files from the CD, as explained in Step 5 on page xv of the Preface. This should result in a folder called *Lesson Files-IDcs 1on1* on your desktop. We'll be working with the files inside the *Lesson 07* subfolder.

In this lesson, I explain how to import photographs and artwork created in other programs; apply transformations such as cropping, scaling, and rotating; and combine graphics with text. In particular, you'll learn how to:

Video Lesson 7: Placing and Previewing

After preparing a photograph or vector-based illustration in another program, you can import it into InDesign by choosing File→Place, or by dragging the file from the desktop and dropping it into an open document window. Either way, InDesign places the graphic at the exact size and resolution at which you saved it. Then you can crop the graphic and otherwise transform it to better suit your needs.

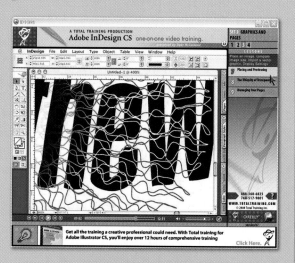

To see how to import graphics, crop them, and view them at full print quality, watch the seventh video lesson on the CD. Insert the CD, click the **Start Training** button, click the Set **3** button, and then select **7, Placing and Previewing** from the Lessons list. Weighing in at 12 minutes and 11 seconds, this movie introduces you to these shortcuts and techniques:

Operation	Windows shortcut	Macintosh shortcut
Import a graphic	Ctrl+D	⌘-D
Move graphic inside frame	Drag graphic with white arrow tool	Drag graphic with white arrow tool
Switch to high-quality display	F3* (or Ctrl+Alt+H)	F3* (or ⌘-Option-H)
Return to typical-quality display	F2* (or Ctrl+Alt+Z)	F2* (or ⌘-Option-Z)
Change display quality preferences	Ctrl+K, Ctrl+0 (zero)	⌘-K, ⌘-0 (zero)

* Works only if you loaded the Deke Keys keyboard shortcuts (as directed on page xvii of Preface).

magnified to 2,400 percent, thus revealing the individual pixels. Statue or flesh, photograph or hand drawing, an image is a mosaic of colored tiles.

InDesign is altogether incapable of creating, correcting, retouching, or otherwise editing the pixels in a bitmapped image. This is the domain of image editors such as Adobe Photoshop, Photoshop Elements, and Jasc Paint Shop Pro, as well as Web-graphics applications Adobe ImageReady and Macromedia Fireworks. Every photographic image has to be prepared outside InDesign and then imported into the program. All the work that went into preparing Figure 7-1 occurred inside Photoshop. The same holds true of all the screen captures in this book.

This lesson explains how to import art into InDesign and, once imported, what you can do with it. Many of the techniques that we'll explore are applicable exclusively to placed artwork. Others work equally well whether you're modifying a foreign-born graphic or one drawn inside InDesign. There are even times when InDesign can't tell the difference. For example, by copying a graphic from Illustrator and pasting it into InDesign, you can convince the latter that the former was never involved.

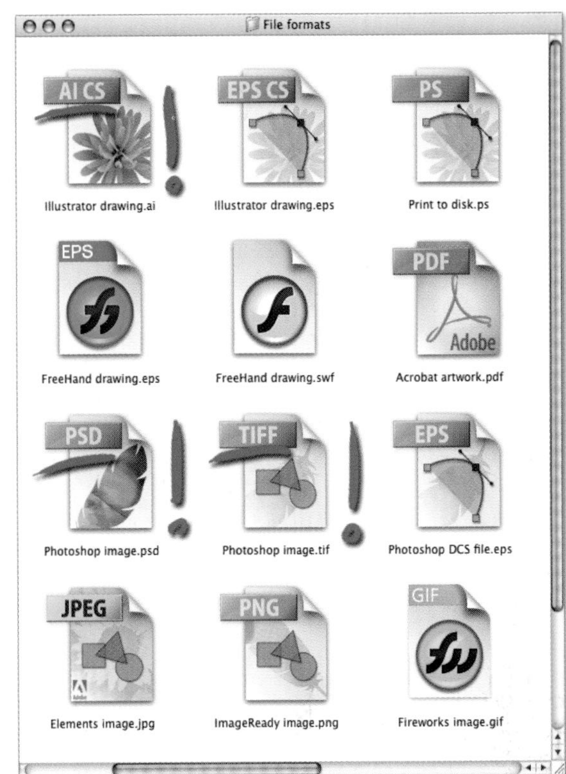

Figure 7-2.

The Anatomy of Import

In its capacity as a page-layout program, InDesign is obliged to support a wide variety of graphic file formats. Like QuarkXPress and PageMaker before it, InDesign can import vector graphics saved as Encapsulated PostScript (EPS) documents or images saved as JPEG, TIFF, or print-ready DCS files. InDesign also permits you to place single-page documents saved in the Portable Document Format (PDF), as well as native Illustrator and Photoshop files (AI and PSD, respectively). InDesign can even import Web graphics saved as PNG, GIF, or Flash (SWF) files. Just for reference, Figure 7-2 shows a sampling of graphic documents saved in the many file formats that InDesign supports. Of the bunch, I recommend the AI, PSD, and TIFF formats, highlighted by blue exclamation points. To learn why, read the sidebar "The Much Ballyhooed All-Adobe Workflow" on page 256.

As a rule, graphic files are large. Really, *really* large. For example, a single, uncompressed pixel in a full-color image consumes 3 bytes of data. Compare that to a character of type—which, depending on the font, consumes 1 or 2 bytes—and you might be tempted to think text and graphics are roughly the same. The difference is one of quantity. Whereas a typical page might contain 2 thousand characters of type, a full-page image routinely contains 5 to 10 *million* pixels. Of the 10GB (10 billion bytes) of files required to create a typical *One-on-One* book (not including video), 8GB are graphics.

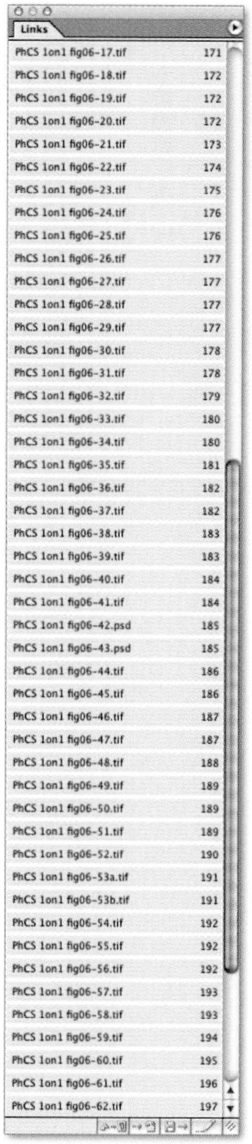

Bear in mind that included in that comparatively scant 2GB of non-graphic data are *all* my InDesign files, including back-up copies and variations. How does InDesign manage to keep its files—which contain plenty of graphics, mind you—from growing into hulking behemoths? By *linking* them. Rather than assimilate a graphic file lock, stock, and barrel, InDesign creates a dynamic link between the page-layout document and the graphic files on disk. Not only does this eliminate the need for InDesign to duplicate large tracts of data, it makes for easy updating. After modifying the graphic in Illustrator or Photoshop, you have only to refresh the link in InDesign and the document is current. It really is the best of all worlds.

You can view, update, and manage links from the aptly named Links palette, which you display by choosing Window→Links or pressing Ctrl+Shift+D (⌘-Shift-D on the Mac). By way of example, Figure 7-3 shows a handful of the links for one of the lessons in a previous *One-on-One* book. To see the Links palette in action, refer back to Steps 9 through 12 of the Lesson 1 exercise "Opening a QuarkXPress Document," which begins on page 10.

Figure 7-3.

The only danger of this otherwise fantastic system is that the linked files may become misplaced or deleted. And so a couple of words of advice:

- First, don't make the mistake of linking to any old graphic located in any old place on your hard drive—or heaven forbid on a CD or other removable media. Do what the pros do and save all graphics associated with a document inside a common folder, preferably not far from the InDesign document itself. That way, when it comes time to copy the InDesign document to another location, you can preserve all links by merely copying the folder of graphic files as well.

- Second, periodically check the Links palette to make sure that all links are up to date. A yellow ⚠ means the linked graphic has been modified and needs to be refreshed, which you can do by clicking the link and choosing the Update Link command from the palette menu. A red ❓ means the linked graphic is missing. Choose Relink from the palette menu to relocate the graphic file on disk.

In other words, plan ahead, stay organized, and you'll be fine. If you have problems organizing your sock drawer, let alone a bunch of links, take heart: Assuming your Links palette is in order—that is, no yellow ⚠ or red ❓ icons—you can instruct InDesign to automatically gather all linked files to a central location by choosing File→Package. To learn how to use this command, read "Preflighting and Packaging" on page 453 of Lesson 12.

Cropping and Scaling Artwork

After you place a photograph or other graphic into an InDesign document (a process that I discuss in appropriate detail in Video Lesson 7, "Placing and Previewing," on the CD), there's a good chance that you'll want to change it. You may not like the size of the graphic. You may want to crop it to better focus on a specific area. Or you may simply want to move it to a different location. Whatever your concerns, InDesign expects change and provides you with the tools you need to make it happen.

In this exercise, you'll learn how to move, crop, and scale graphics as we assemble an ad for a nature retreat. There are so many different ways to perform these transformations that you may feel you never do anything the same way twice. But don't worry, I'll be sure to point out the advantages and disadvantages of the various techniques as we go.

1. ***Open a document.*** Open the file named *Nature retreat 1.indd*, which is located in the *Lesson 07* folder inside *Lesson Files-IDcs 1on1*. As shown in Figure 7-4 on the next page, the document contains several text blocks and a horizontal rule drawn with the line tool. In the pasteboard area on both sides of the page are four images that I have imported in advance. Our task will be to move the images into the document, resizing and cropping where appropriate.

Figure 7-4.

2. ***Shift-drag the pond image into the top of the document.*** As with moving text frames, the most intuitive way to move artwork is to drag it with the black arrow tool. Adding the Shift key as you drag constrains the movement to the nearest 45-degree angle. Try to center the image within the document so that there's more or less equal space on the left and right sides.

   And this highlights a drawback to dragging; it's not terribly precise. Your drag is only accurate to one on-screen pixel, so the amount that an object moves varies greatly according to the zoom ratio. Fortunately, there is a way to position objects with more precision.

3. ***Nudge the image with the arrow keys.*** There are three ways to nudge a selection using the arrow keys. They work as follows, regardless of the zoom setting:

   - Pressing ↑, ↓, ←, or → nudges the selection by precisely 1 point. If you like, you can change the increment by pressing Ctrl+K and then Ctrl+4 (⌘-K, ⌘-4 on the Mac) and changing the Cursor Key value. But for everyday purposes, I suggest you leave this option set to its default, 0p1.
   - Add the Shift key to move the selection by 10 times the standard nudge increment (or 10 points by default).
   - If you need more precision, press Ctrl+Shift (or ⌘-Shift) plus an arrow key. This nudges the select by 1⁄10 the standard increment (1⁄10 point by default).

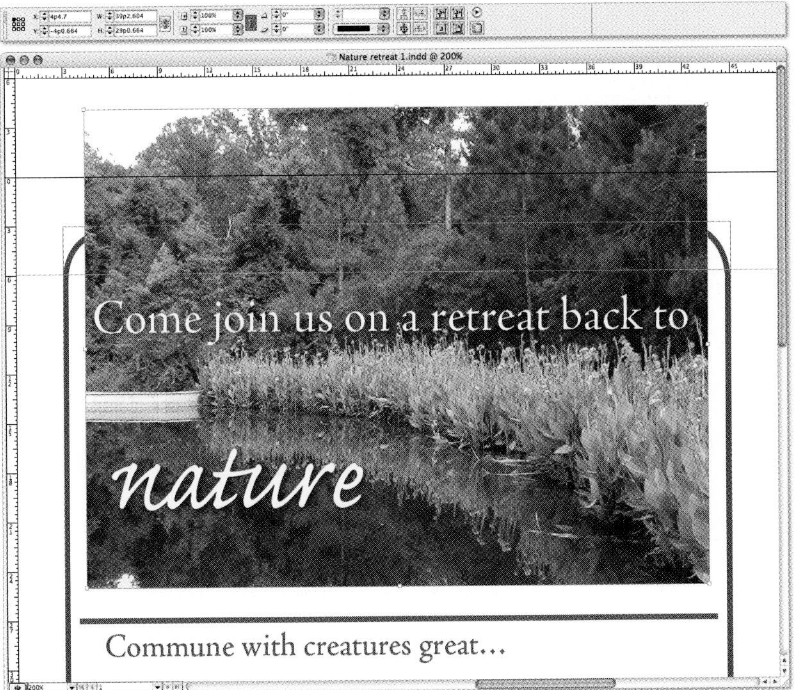

Figure 7-5.

Whatever key combination you decide to use, nudge the pond image to the left or right until it is *precisely* horizontally centered in the page, as in Figure 7-5. According to my calculations, the image is exactly centered when the X value in the Control palette reads 4p4.7. (This assumes that the reference point matrix on the left side of the palette is set to ⊞, in which case the X and Y values list the coordinate position of the upper-left corner of the image.) Note that we're concerned with the horizontal placement only. The image should continue to extend beyond the top of the page, a problem that we will remedy in the very next step.

4. ***Crop the top of the image.*** The selected pond image is surrounded by a frame with eight handles. An imported image and its frame are two different things. While an image is visible only within the boundaries of its frame, the image and frame can be resized and moved independently of each other.

   Using the black arrow tool, click the handle on the top edge of the frame and drag it down until it snaps to the cyan guide, as shown in Figure 7-6 on the next page. You might expect this to squash the pond image. Instead, it changes the size of the frame, which crops the image. The top part of the image is hidden from view, masked by the boundaries of the frame.

Figure 7-6.

5. ***Examine the Control palette.*** The Control palette, pictured in Figure 7-7, offers several options for precisely moving, cropping, and scaling artwork. Here are a few pertinent points in the anatomy of the palette when an imported graphic is selected:

   - The reference point matrix shows the point from which an object's position is measured and around which a transformation occurs. Click a square inside the matrix to relocate the reference point.

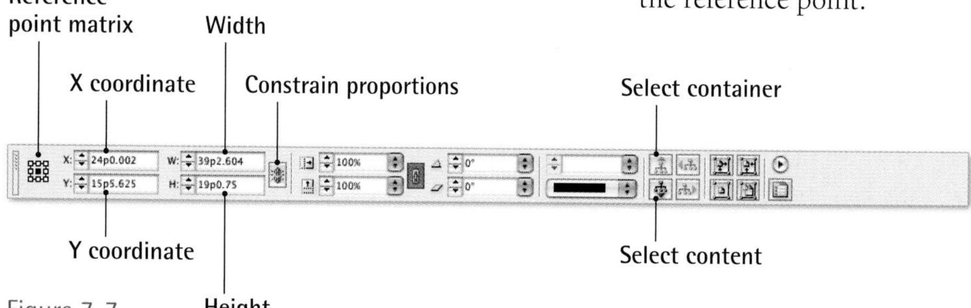

Figure 7-7.

   - The X and Y values display the coordinate position of the selected object's reference point. X lists the horizontal position; Y lists the vertical position.

   - The W and H values display the selected object's width and height, respectively. If you turn on the chain icon, so it looks like 🔗, a change made to the W value changes the H value proportionally, and vice versa.

- The select container icon (⇑) is dimmed, reflecting that the frame for the placed graphic is selected. Clicking the select content icon (⇓) would deselect the frame and select the pond image inside the frame.

Try this: Click the center square in the matrix (⁙) and note that the X and Y values change. As in Figure 7-7, the Y coordinate for the pond image should read 15p5.625, meaning that you cropped the image but you didn't move it. Your X coordinate should be within a bacterium of 24p0. If not, change these values to match those in the figure.

6. ***Locate the left edge of the bottom-right text block.*** Let's now redirect our attention from the pond to the ladybug. I want the left edge of the ladybug image to be in line with the left edge of its caption, which reads *...and super small.* To find out where that left edge is located, scroll down to this text block, click the text block to select it, and then click the upper-left square of the reference point matrix in the Control palette, so it looks like ⁙. The X value now reads 30p0, meaning that the left edge of the text block is 30 picas from the origin point for the rulers, which is aligned to the left edge of the document.

7. ***Position the ladybug image on the page.*** Select the ladybug image located on the pasteboard at the bottom-right corner of the document. Notice that the reference point is still set to ⁙. Enter 30 in the **X** option box and hit Enter or Return. The ladybug image scoots over into the document so that it's flush left with the text. It also obscures the text, which we'll fix next.

8. ***Scale the ladybug image.*** Let's scale the ladybug image so it no longer overlaps the green text:

   - Press Ctrl+Tab (Control-Tab) to switch to the white arrow tool. Move your cursor inside the ladybug. When the cursor changes to a hand, click the ladybug photo. The bounding box turns brown, telling you that the image is now selected independently of its frame. In InDesign, the black arrow tool manipulates a graphic's frame, and the white arrow changes the content.

   - Position the white arrow tool over the bottom-right handle of the brown bounding box. Then press the Shift key and drag the handle toward the center of the image to scale the ladybug proportionally. When the image appears approximately the size shown in Figure 7-8 on the next page, release the mouse button and then release Shift.

- The scale percentage values have updated in the Control palette. They should be somewhere in the neighborhood of 50 percent. Let's make it exact. If it isn't already selected, click the rightmost of the two chain icons to turn it on ( ). Then click the arrow (on the Mac) to the right of either the or value to display a pop-up menu of incremental percentage values. Choose **50%**, as in Figure 7-8. Both scale values update to 50 percent; the size of the ladybug image adjusts accordingly.

If you hold down the Ctrl key (⌘ on the Mac) when choosing a value from the or pop-up menu, the value in the other pop-up menu will change as well, regardless of whether the icon is on or off.

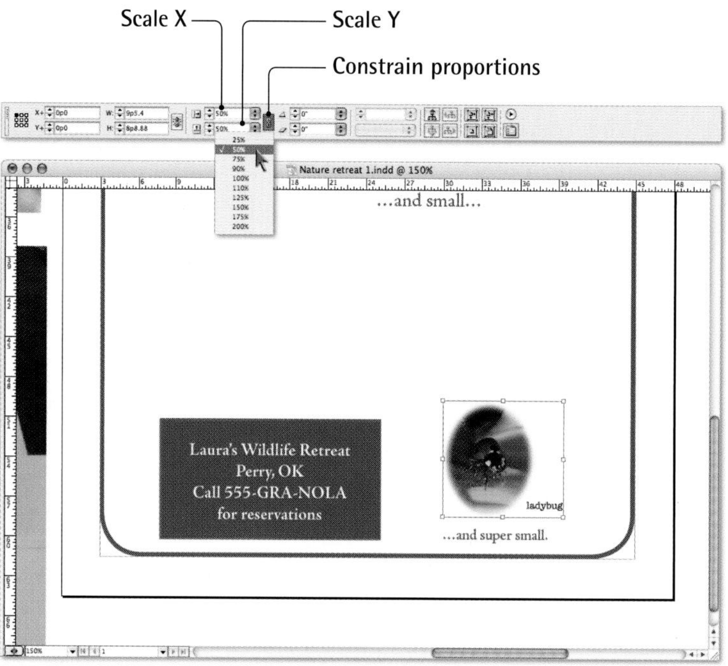

Figure 7-8.

9. ***Fit the ladybug's frame to the image.*** Click the icon in the Control palette to switch the selection from the brown image bounding box to the blue frame, which was not scaled along with the image. This is when the four icons at the right end of the Control palette come into play. Labeled in Figure 7-9, here's how they work:

   - The first icon ( ) scales the image to fit its frame, even if that means scaling the image disproportionately. In our case, it would return the image to its original size.

- The next icon () snaps the frame to precisely match the bounding box of the image.
- The next icon () centers the image inside the frame.
- And finally, the last icon () scales the image to fit its frame while maintaining the artwork's original proportions.

We want to scale the frame. So click the icon or press Ctrl+Alt+C (⌘-Option-C on the Mac). InDesign snaps the frame to the exact boundaries of the scaled ladybug. Despite this, the scale values in the Control palette remain set to 100 percent. In defiance of considerable outcry from its users, InDesign sees fit to forget any and all scaling operations applied to a container. So no matter what you do to a frame, the Control palette invariably regards it as 100 percent.

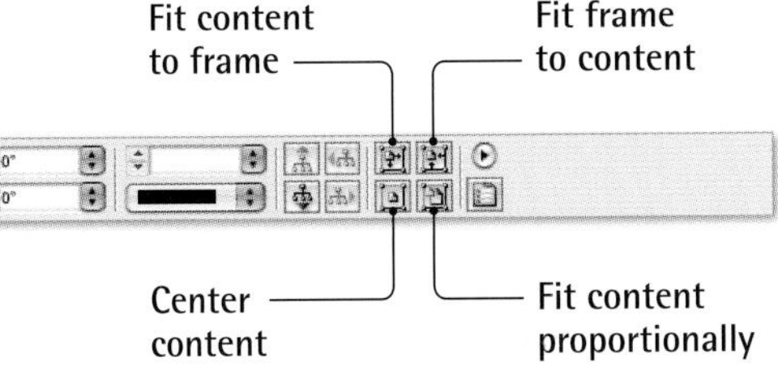

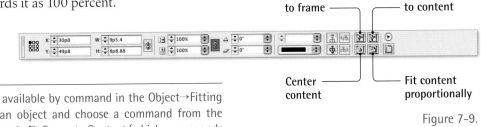

Figure 7-9.

These operations are also available by command in the Object→Fitting submenu. Or right-click an object and choose a command from the Fitting submenu. Of the bunch, Fit Frame to Content (which corresponds to) is by far the most useful. In creating the Nature Retreat document, for example, I used Fit Frame to Content to shrink all the text frames so that they're just big enough to contain their text.

---

10. ***Crop the right side of the ladybug.*** For some reason, someone went and added the word *ladybug* to the image. Generally speaking, it's not a good idea to include text with an image file, because such text is bitmapped (that is, made of pixels) and likely to be fuzzy when compared with InDesign's text. But I have a larger problem with this specific text: I can't imagine a more obvious, recognizable insect than the ladybug. Labeling the animal serves no earthly purpose.

    One way to get rid of the word would be to go back to Photoshop or some other image editor, erase the text, resave the image, and update the link inside InDesign. But why go to all that work when we can crop it out in InDesign?

    - Press Ctrl+Tab (Control-Tab) to switch back to the black arrow tool.
    - Drag the handle on the right side of the frame to the left. Be careful not to crop into the fuzzy edge of the photograph or

The Much Ballyhooed All-Adobe Workflow

For most of the 1990s, the design market was shared by three programs, page-layout software QuarkXPress, image editor Adobe Photoshop, and drawing application Macromedia FreeHand. (Some shops preferred Illustrator, but FreeHand tended to be the more popular page designer's choice.) This benefited users by inspiring fierce competition between the suitors, with each doing its dead-level best to remain on top in its respective market. But because the rivals rarely saw eye-to-eye, it also ensured a certain amount of cross-application friction. There was no such thing as consistent color. And throughout most of the decade, none of the programs supported the others' native file formats. As a result, Photoshop and FreeHand had to export to standardized formats that didn't take advantage of their most recent innovations, and XPress was left bottom-feeding from aging import technology and downright antique graphics-handling functions, many of which had been designed to suit grayscale graphics.

Today's more progressive design market is increasingly dominated by InDesign, Photoshop, and Illustrator, all from a single vendor, Adobe Systems. Time will tell how Adobe handles its monopoly position. Does it innovate in order to keep us buying its products, or does it take us for granted, cut resources from its graphics and design development, and pursue markets that have nothing to do with us (and everything to do with our middle managers)?

It's hard to predict, but for the present, things honestly couldn't be better. InDesign, Photoshop, and Illustrator respect each others' color profiles, so assuming color management is turned on (see "One-on-One Installation and Setup," page xvi), a shape that looks red in Illustrator appears that same shade of red in Photoshop and InDesign. The three programs share common tools and palettes, making it easy to flit from one program to another. And best of all, they recognize and fully support the PSD and AI formats, which are capable of saving every layer, transparency setting, and dynamic effect that Photoshop and Illustrator can dish out. This extraordinary level of support presents us with three practical advantages:

- **Advantage #1**: You no longer need to create two copies of your artwork, one in the native file format that preserves layers and a second in a cross-application standard that can be read by the layout program. Just save one file that supports all features of the program—PSD in the case of Photoshop and AI for Illustrator—and import that file into InDesign.
- **Advantage #2**: InDesign supports all layers and translucent objects inside PSD and AI files. This means you no longer need to trace the opaque boundaries of an imported image with a clipping path, the way you did when importing images into QuarkXPress. Consider the image files pictured at the bottom of this spread. Below is a knife casting a shadow as it appears in Photoshop. Knife and shadow exist on separate layers; the background is transparent. When I place the layered PSD file into InDesign, the transparency remains intact, as on the facing page. The result is a photo-realistic composite with a tapering shadow, something clipping paths cannot come close to matching. For more information on transparency, read Lesson 8, "Transparency and Effects."

Tranparency in Photoshop

- **Advantage #3**: You can share complex artwork between Illustrator and InDesign via the clipboard. For example, just copy a group of paths in Illustrator, switch to InDesign, and paste. If you have the right options turned on, you can even edit the paths in InDesign. To learn more, see Steps 6 through 8 of the exercise "Inserting Inline Graphics," which begins on page 277 of this lesson.

To increase compatibility between the Adobe products, it's essential that you save your artwork properly from the originating application. Some advice:

- When saving a document from Illustrator CS in the Illustrator format, be sure to include the .ai extension at the end of the filename. When asked how to save the file, turn on all available check boxes at the bottom of the dialog box, as pictured above right. The first, Create PDF Compatible File, makes the file readable by InDesign. The third, Embed ICC Profiles, permits InDesign to display the colors just as they appeared in Illustrator.

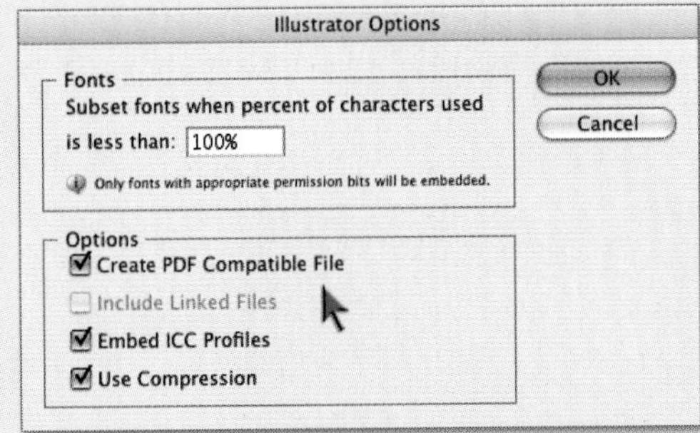

The same image when placed into InDesign

- When creating an opaque Photoshop image—which you can recognize by the appearance of the Background layer at the bottom of the Layers palette—I recommend that you flatten the document by choosing Layer→Flatten Image before importing it into InDesign. This reduces the complexity of the image and helps it print faster. I also recommend that you save the image to the TIFF format. With LZW compression turned on, TIFF usually results in smaller files than PSD, and with no loss in quality.
- If you want to convey transparency to InDesign, as I did when importing my knife image, delete the Background layer in Photoshop and reduce the file to as few layers as possible. Then use the Save As command to save the image under a different name (so as not to harm the original). Either the PSD or TIFF format work fine for this purpose.

So to those of you who've permitted the Creative Suite to swaddle you in the warm embrace of an all-Adobe workflow, rest easy. InDesign, Photoshop, and Illustrator provide you with a degree of cross-application synergy that goes unmatched by any other combination of programs. They really do work like cogs in a great, harmonious wheel. As for Adobe owning all aspects of the design market and, in turn, our very souls, heck, that's nothing to worry about. If sci-fi movies are to be believed, we will come to love our assimilation. Remember when folks used to hate Microsoft? I believe that's a federal crime now.

Figure 7-10.

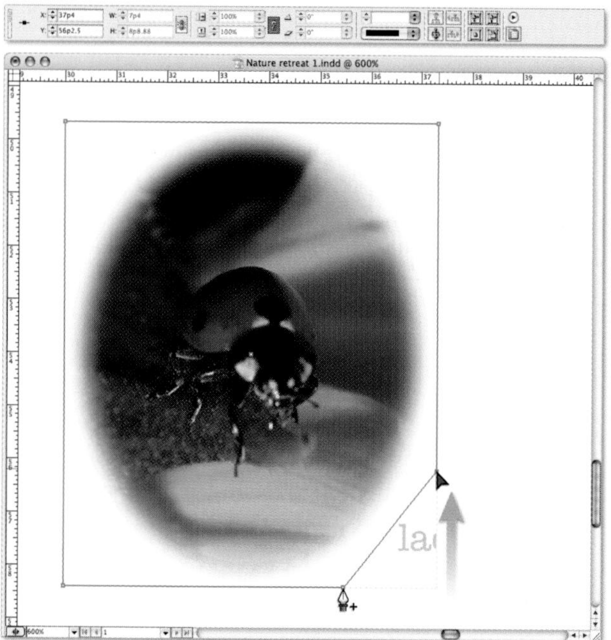

Figure 7-11.

you'll end up with a sharp edge. I recommend that you drag the handle until the W value reads 7p4 (or thereabouts) as in Figure 7-10.

Do *not* type 7p4 into the W option box! This will scale the graphic, not crop it. Just drag the right handle until you get the desired reading. Zoom in if necessary. Multiple drags are entirely acceptable.

11. ***Reshape the frame.*** You may notice that we didn't altogether delete the word. A fraction of the first three letters remains visible. To get rid of these, we need to reshape the frame.

    • Press the P key to access the pen tool.

    • Position the pen cursor over the bottom edge of the frame at the position indicated by the pen tool cursor in Figure 7-11. You should see a plus sign next to the pen cursor. Click to add a point to the frame.

    • Next, hold down the Ctrl key (⌘ on the Mac) to temporarily access the white arrow tool and click the bottom-right point in the frame to select it. Then press Ctrl+Shift (or ⌘-Shift) and drag the point straight up until the word *ladybug* is cropped out, as demonstrated in the figure. As you drag, the X and Y options in the Control palette track the location of the selected point. Release when you get somewhere in the vicinity of X: 37p4, Y: 56p2.5.

The result is a small and rather simple change to the shape of the frame. But armed with the pen and white arrow tools, it's possible to radically reshape any frame if you wish, whether it contains text, an image, or some other kind of graphic.

12. ***Adjust the horizontal scale of the mouse image.*** Our next task is to scale and reposition the mouse photo that's currently located in the upper-left area of the pasteboard.

PEARL OF WISDOM

The mouse photo is actually a frame from a digital video clip. In keeping with the NTSC video standard, the frame measures 720 by 480 pixels. However, video pixels aren't square; they are slightly thinner than they are tall. When video frames are displayed on a computer, the rectangular pixels are usually stretched to fit into the square screen pixels. The result is that the image appears too wide. Such is the case here with our little mouse, who's not actually quite as well-fed as he might look.

A modicum of horizontal scaling will return the image to the proper aspect:

- Press the A key to select the white arrow tool. Then click inside the mouse to select the video image independently of its frame.
- Click the center square in the Control palette's reference point matrix to move the point to . When scaling artwork, the reference point acts sort of like a nail driven through the image into the document. (Mind you, I would never do such a thing to a real mouse, just to a photo.) As the image changes size, the reference point remains stationary.
- To resize this image, we'll use the scale tool. Select the scale tool, which is the fifth tool on the right side of the toolbox, as in Figure 7-12.
- A bullseye (⌖) appears in the center of the mouse image, as directed by the reference point matrix. But you don't have to leave it there. Drag the ⌖ into the mouse's right eye (your left). Now the eye will remain stationary and the rest of the mouse will scale around it.
- Double-click the scale tool in the toolbox. The **Scale** dialog box shown in Figure 7-12 appears. Tab your way to the **Horizontal** option box. Enter 90 percent, which happens to be the exact value needed to restore the proper D1/DV NTSC aspect ratio. (Sounds technical, but it's just the American television standard.) Then click **OK**. The image scales and the mouse loses a little weight.

Figure 7-12.

13. ***Resize the mouse with the scale tool.*** Now let's scale the mouse down to a more appropriate size. We'll accomplish this by dragging with the scale tool. In InDesign, the scale tool resizes a selection with respect to the reference point. Drag toward the reference point to reduce the selection; drag away to enlarge the selection. Here's what I want you to do:

    - Move the cursor to a spot outside the mouse. You don't have to drag on a handle or inside the image to scale it. And starting your drag far away from the reference point gives you more control.
    - Click and hold down the mouse button until your cursor changes to an arrowhead. This permits InDesign to update the image so that 1) the scaling values in the Control palette update on the fly, and 2) InDesign can preview the image as you scale it. It's a heck of a trick, one that I suggest you exploit on a regular basis.
    - With the mouse still down, press and hold the Shift key and drag toward the reference point, as in Figure 7-13.
    - As you drag, keep an eye on the scale values in the Control palette. When reads approximately 27 percent and is close to 30 percent, release the mouse button. (For example, if you hit 26.96 and 29.96 percent, that's fine.) Then release the Shift key.

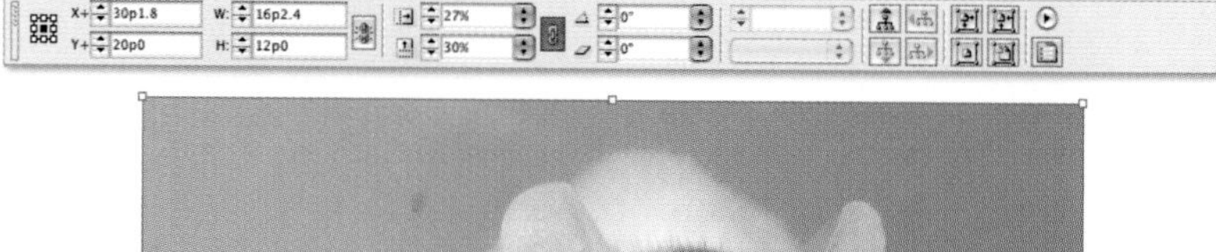

Figure 7-13.

PEARL OF WISDOM

The scale tool ignores the constrain proportions for scaling icon in the Control palette, so it's necessary to hold down Shift to achieve a proportional scaling. Also, the scale tool measures proportionality relative to the last state of the object. This means the tool maintains the proper D1/DV NTSC aspect ratio that we established in the previous step, which is a very good thing. Compare this to entering values into the Control palette. If you were to change the value to 27 percent, would likewise change to 27 percent. To maintain the proper aspect, you'd have to turn off the link icon and enter the two scale values independently.

---

14. ***Move the mouse image using the white arrow tool.*** Now let's move the mouse onto the page. Zoom out so that you can take in the mouse image and the page at once. Press the A key to get the white arrow tool. Then drag the mouse image below the words *and small*. As Figure 7-14 shows, a very odd thing happens. We see the brown bounding box for the image, but the image itself is invisible. What gives? Dragging the image with the white arrow tool moves it independently of its frame. The frame remains in the upper-left area of the pasteboard, so the image is hidden from view.

15. ***Reunite the frame with the image.*** Click the icon in the Control palette or press Ctrl+Alt+C (⌘-Option-C on the Mac). That's all it takes to reunite the frame with the image so that the mouse is once again visible.

16. ***Align the mouse to the text block.*** Press Ctrl+Tab (Control-Tab) to get the black arrow tool. Click the *and small* text block to select it. Then click the bottom-left square in the reference point matrix (as in) in the Control palette. Note that the X and Y values read 24p10 and 35p0, respectively. We'll set the upper-left corner of the mouse image to be in this exact same place and then offset it slightly:

    - Select the mouse image with the black arrow tool.

    - Set its reference point to the upper-left corner, or .

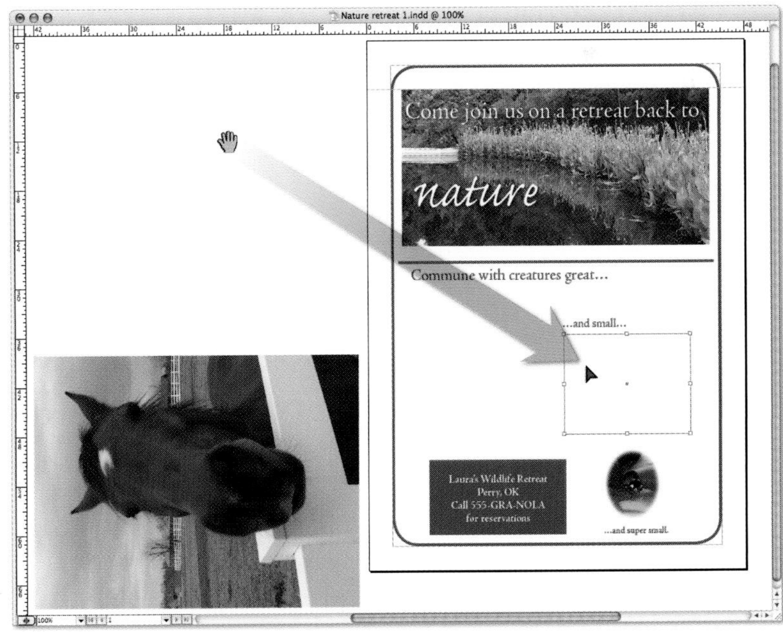

Figure 7-14.

- Click the **X** to highlight the value. Or press the keyboard shortcut Ctrl+6 (⌘-6). Then type in 24p10, press the Tab key to advance to the **Y** option box, and enter 35.

- Press the Enter or Return key. The top of the image snaps to the bottom of the text block.

17. ***Move the mouse down half a pica.*** We actually want a bit of space between the text and the image. To accomplish this we'll use yet another technique for moving objects. Double-click the black arrow icon in the toolbox to display the **Move** dialog box. Alternatively, you can choose Object→Transform→Move, or press Ctrl+Shift+M (⌘-Shift-M on the Mac). I want a gap of 6 points between the caption and image, so Tab to the **Vertical** option box and enter 0p6. Press Tab again and notice that the Distance and Angle values update to 0p6 and –90 degrees, which is the direct distance and angle of the move—that is, 6 points straight down. Turn on the **Preview** check box to see the movement, as in Figure 7-15. Then click the **OK** button to make it happen.

18. ***Save your document.*** Obviously we have a little more work to do before this document is complete, so we'll finish things up in the next exercise. Choose **File→Save As**, name your document "My retreat.indd," and save it in the *Lesson 07* folder.

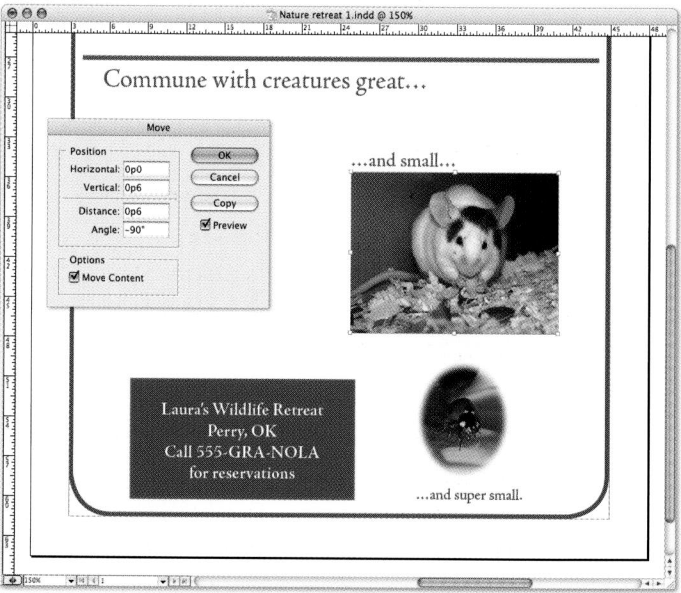

Figure 7-15.

Rotating, Slanting, and Flipping

Moving, cropping, and scaling are the most common kinds of transformations you'll apply in InDesign, but they're not the only ones. In this exercise, we'll explore the secondary transformations, which include rotating, slanting, and flipping. As with the last exercise, there are gobs of ways to apply these operations. I'll show you several different techniques and point out advantages and disadvantages as we go.

1. ***Open the sample document.*** If the *My retreat.indd* file that you saved in the previous exercise is close at hand, open it. If not, you can use the file named *Nature retreat 2.indd*, which is located in the *Lesson 07* folder inside *Lesson Files-IDcs 1on1*. In the last exercise, we positioned, cropped, and scaled three of four images. The last image we need to work on is the horse. This is a portrait shot, which means it required turning the camera sideways to capture it. Some digital cameras are smart enough to rotate portrait photos upright, but most just leave them on their sides. So obviously, the horse is in need of rotation. But first, let's position the image on the page.

2. ***Open the Transform palette.*** In the last exercise we focused much of our attention on the Control palette. As it turns out, many of the options we used first appeared in an older feature: the Transform palette. For the sake of variety—and so you can better judge your options—we'll switch to the Transform palette for this exercise. Choose **Window→Transform** or press F9 to access the palette. (If F9 invokes one of the Mac's Exposé functions, follow my advice on page xvii of the Preface.)

3. ***Note the location of the text block.*** Get the black arrow tool and select the text that begins *Commune with creatures*. Go to the Transform palette and click the bottom-left square in the reference point matrix, so it looks like . Make note of the X and Y positions, 5p6 and 29p2, as pictured in Figure 7-16.

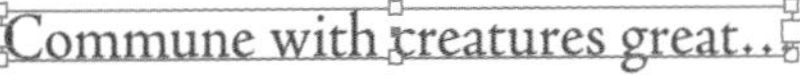

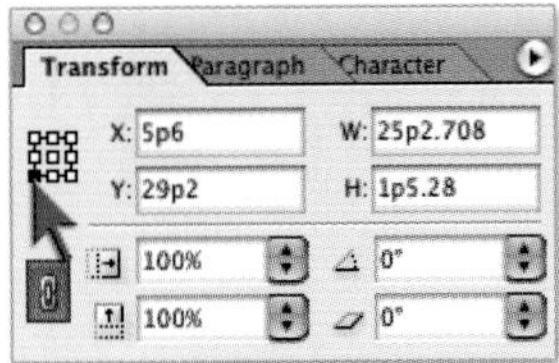

Figure 7-16.

4. ***Position the horse image.*** Next, scroll to the lower-left section of the pasteboard and select the horse image. I want the horse's upper-left corner to align with the text block's lower-left corner, but since the horse image still needs to be rotated, that prospective upper-left corner is currently the lower-left corner. So leave the reference point matrix set to . Then do the following:

   - Click the **X** value to activate it. Or press the F9 key twice, once to hide the palette and again to display the palette and highlight the X value.

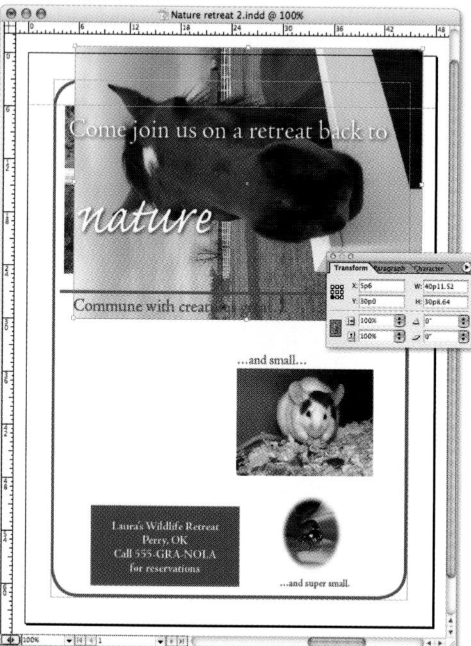

Figure 7-17.

- Enter 5p6 and press the Tab key to advance to the **Y** value. The sideways horse photo moves inside the page.
- I want to create a 10-point gap between the text block and the horse. To that end, we'll take advantage of InDesign's little-known calculator capabilities. For the **Y** value, enter this: 29p2+0p10. Then press the Enter or Return key to accept your changes.

As shown in Figure 7-17, InDesign adds the numbers, returns the sum 30p0, and spaces the bottom edge of the horse photo 10 points below the bottom edge of the text block.

Don't think InDesign is limited to addition. You can use other mathematical symbols as well. Enter – for subtraction, * for multiplication, and / for division. You can even combine different units of measure. For example, I could have just as easily expressed the vertical position of the horse as "29p2+10pt." The one limitation is that you can use only one operand (+, –, *, or /) per option box.

Figure 7-18.

5. ***Rotate the horse image.*** The lower-left corner of the horse image is exactly where we need it to be. As a result, it'll serve as a wonderful fulcrum for our rotation. So keep the reference point set to . Then click the arrow (on the Mac) to the right of the rotation value () to display a pop-up menu of common angles. In InDesign, a positive value rotates the selection in a counterclockwise direction; a negative value applies a clockwise rotation. We want the horse image to rotate 90 degrees clockwise, so choose **–90 degrees**. As Figure 7-18 shows, the horse dutifully swings into place.

Take a look at the reference point matrix and notice that it's changed from to . In other words, the matrix actually rotated along with the selected object, thereby maintaining a consistent reference point for future transformations. The matrix will even turn into a diamond configuration () when an object is rotated in the neighborhood of 45 degrees.

---

6. ***Scale the horse image.*** After all the ways we scaled images in the last exercise, you'd think we had pretty much exhausted the topic. But there's one more technique I'd like to share with you. It isn't particularly precise, but what it lacks in precision, it makes up for in convenience.

With the black arrow tool is selected, press the Ctrl key (⌘ on the Mac) and drag the lower-right handle of the horse's frame.

InDesign scales the image and frame together. Midway into the drag, press and hold the Shift key to scale the height and width of the image proportionally. When the horse reaches the size shown in Figure 7-19, release the mouse button and then release the keys.

Frankly, I'm not an enormous fan of this technique. For starters, InDesign provides you with insufficient feedback. While the X, Y, W, and H values update on the fly, the and values remain inexplicably fixed at 100 percent. (For an exception to this, see Step 10.) Plus, InDesign invariably uses the opposite corner as a reference point, regardless of the setting of the reference point matrix. You can't even scale with respect to the object's center.

But you can't beat the convenience—no need to switch tools or anything. And there are two silver linings. First, this trick works with any object, including text. That is to say, if you Ctrl-drag (or ⌘-drag) the handle on a text block, you scale both the frame and the characters inside it. Second, InDesign provides a secret way to judge the percentage by which you've scaled an object:

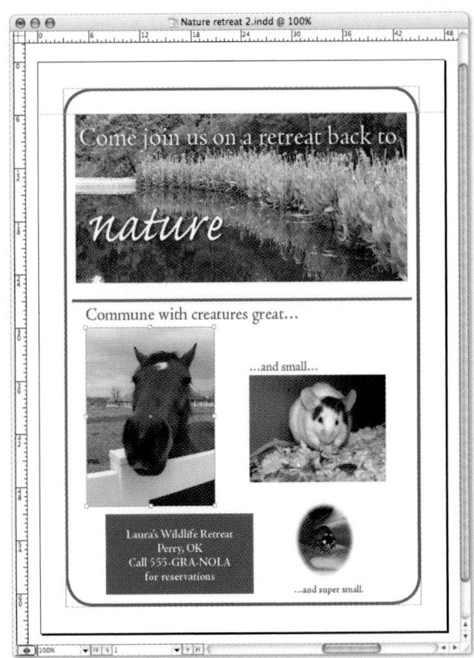

Figure 7-19.

After scaling the horse by Ctrl-dragging (or ⌘-dragging) with the black arrow tool, click the icon in the Control palette. Or press Ctrl+Tab (Control-Tab) to switch to the white arrow tool and then click in the image. The and options now list the exact percentage by which the image has been scaled. Somewhere around 50 percent is perfectly acceptable. If you decide to edit the values, press Ctrl+Alt+C (⌘-Option-C) to fit the frame when you're through.

---

7. ***Select the free transform tool.*** Now that all the images are in place, I want to add one more effect. The text block that reads *nature* is set in the font Caflisch Script Pro, which ships with InDesign. Although I like the natural, handwritten effect, I don't care for the italic slant. Every one of InDesign's transformation capabilities works equally well on text and graphics, so we'll skew the text to straighten it.

   Click the *nature* text block with the black arrow to select it. You can now adjust the slant of the text in one of four ways:

   - Enter a value in the option box in either the Control or Transform palette.
   - Press the O key to get the shear tool. Then drag with the tool to skew the text.

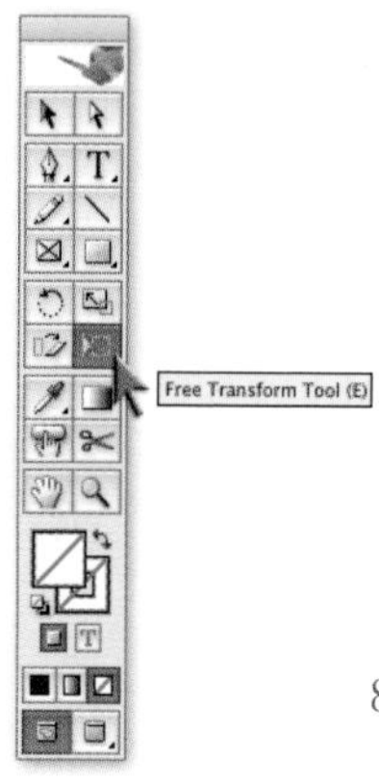

Figure 7-20.

- Double-click the shear tool icon in the toolbox or choose Object→Transform→Shear to access the Shear dialog box. Then enter the desired values and click OK.
- Use the free transform tool, which lets you scale, rotate, and skew objects in one operation.

Naturally, I want you to avail yourself of the most powerful option. So click the free transform icon in the toolbox, as in Figure 7-20. Or press the E key.

8. ***Skew the* nature *text.*** When armed with the free transform tool, your options are as follows:
   - Drag inside a selected object to move it.
   - Drag a handle to scale the object.
   - Drag outside the selected frame to rotate the object.
   - To skew the object, well, that's a bit more involved.

   Here's what I want you to do: Click and hold the handle at the top of the text block. With the mouse button still down, press and hold the Ctrl key (⌘ on the Mac) and then drag to the left. To constrain the skew and make it a bit easier to control, press and hold the Shift key as well. Keep an eye on the ▱ value in the Transform palette. When it gets close to –20 degrees, release the mouse button. Then release the keys. The text updates as shown in Figure 7-21.

9. ***Clone and flip the text.*** Part of the reason I've placed the *nature* text in front of the pond image is that I want the letters to reflect into the water. To accomplish this, we need to create a copy of the letters and flip them horizontally, as follows:
   - Press the V key to switch from the free transform tool to the black arrow tool.
   - Confirm that the bottom-left square is active in the reference point matrix, as in ▦.
   - Click the ⊙ arrow in the upper corner of the Transform palette to display the palette menu.
   - Press the Alt (or Option) key and choose **Flip Vertical**. Having the key pressed creates a copy of the text, known as a *clone*. The command reflects the text downward, as in Figure 7-22.

Figure 7-21.

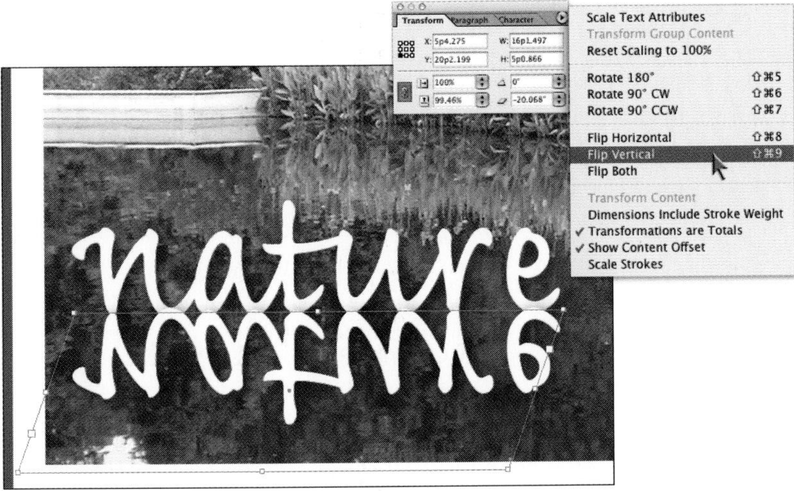

Figure 7-22.

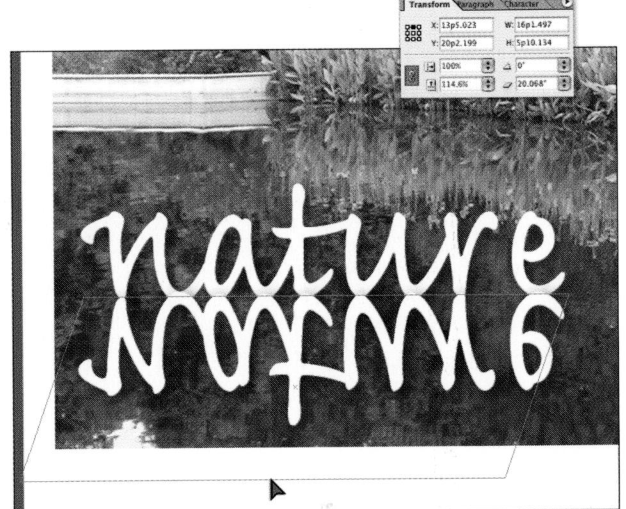

Figure 7-23.

10. ***Scale the cloned text vertically.*** To make the text look a little more like a reflection, press the Ctrl (or ⌘) key and click and hold on the bottom handle. After waiting for the arrowhead cursor to display, drag downward. The text should update on the fly and, this time, the scale values in the Transform palette update to reflect the percentage change. (To what do we owe the fact that InDesign is now tracking the scale operation? The program behaves differently when scaling text.) When the value nears 115 percent, as in Figure 7-23, release the mouse button and the Ctrl (or ⌘) key.

11. ***Lower the opacity of the clone.*** No reflection is complete without a little translucency. Choose **Window→Transparency** or press Shift+F10 to open the **Transparency** palette. Change the **Opacity** value to 50 percent and press Enter or Return. The translucent reflection appears in Figure 7-24. Our nature retreat ad is complete.

Figure 7-24.

Wrapping Text around Graphics

Regardless of how you introduce graphics into InDesign—whether you import them or create them inside the program—you face the challenge of weaving the graphics into the fabric of text. Many publications relegate graphics to their own columns; others separate words and pictures into independent rectangular blocks. But often you need a more free-form solution, in which the text wraps around the contours of the artwork, as demonstrated in Figure 7-25.

If you have worked with QuarkXPress, you know this as a *runaround*. InDesign calls it a *text wrap*. But as in Quark, InDesign applies the effect to the graphic object. The contour of the wrap (termed the *offset boundary*) acts as an invisible force field beyond which the text cannot pass. When a word hits the boundary, it wraps to the next line.

In this exercise, you'll learn how to create two kinds of text wrap, one manual and the other automatic. You'll also learn how to use basic shapes to simplify the text wrap process so you don't have to draw the offset boundary point by ponderous point.

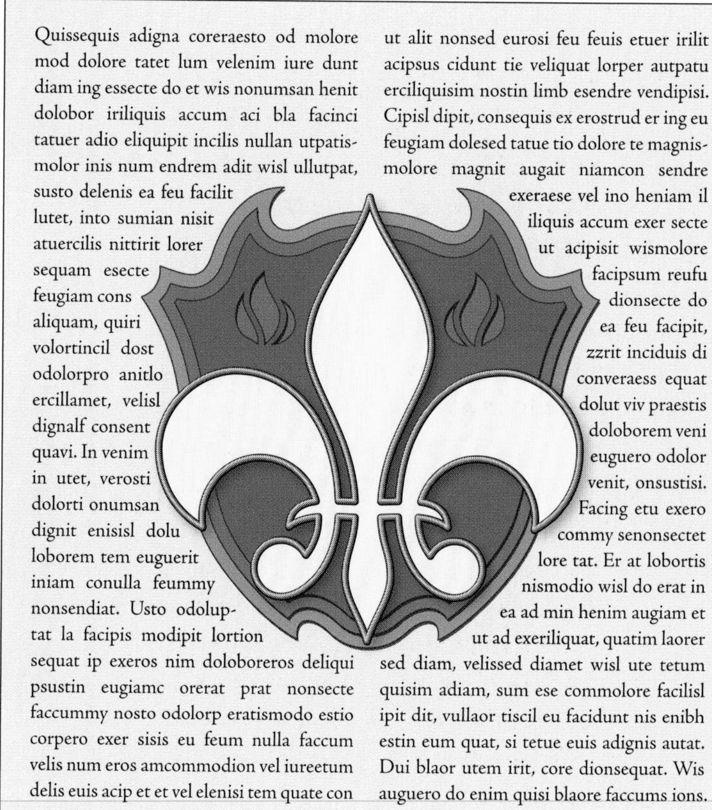

Figure 7-25.

1. ***Open a page with a text wrap object.*** The document in question is *Seventies quiz #3.indd*, which you'll find in the *Lesson 07* folder inside *Lesson Files-IDcs 1on1*. Pictured in Figure 7-26, this page features a vector cartoon surrounded by a text wrap. I drew the cartoon directly in InDesign, but it could just as easily be a graphic piece of artwork brought in from Photoshop, Illustrator, or some other graphics program.

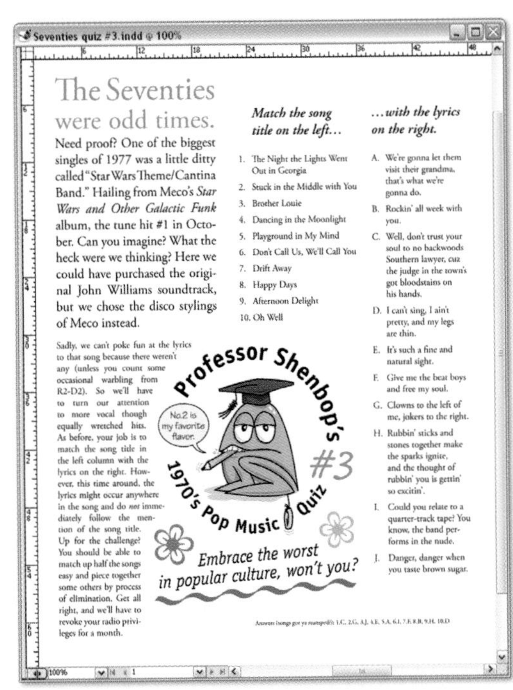

Figure 7-26.

2. ***Select the graphic.*** To see the text wrap, select the graphic by clicking on it with the black arrow tool. You'll see two boundaries, one dark and one light. The dark rectangle is the bounding box of the artwork. The light free-form outline (which appears yellowish in Figure 7-27 but is actually light green on your screen) is the offset boundary. Notice that the two are very different from each other. As luck and good product design would have it, you can draw offset boundaries in any shape you like.

3. ***Ungroup and regroup the graphic.*** Now that we know what a text wrap looks like, let's destroy this one and draw one of our own. The selected cartoon happens to be a grouped object (that is, a collection of text and paths that I combined into a single item using Object→Group). If we break the group apart, the text wrap will go with it. So here's what you do:

   - Go to the **Object** menu and choose **Ungroup**. Or press Ctrl+Shift+G (⌘-Shift-G on the Mac). The object busts into pieces and the text wrap evaporates, as in Figure 7-28 on the next page.

   - Choose **Object→Group** or press Ctrl+G (⌘-G) to put the group back together. Now it is once again one item that we can edit as a whole.

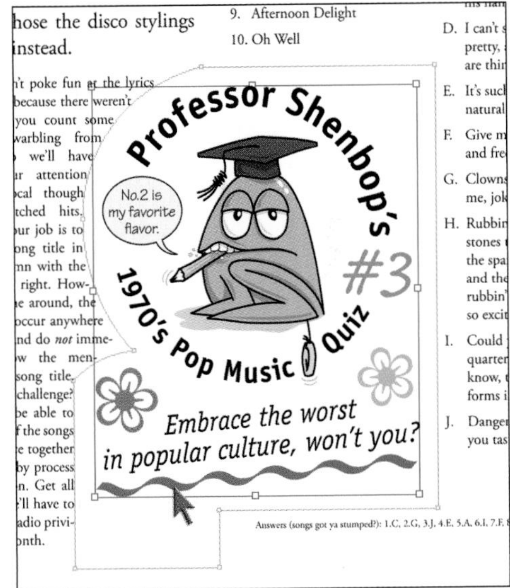

Figure 7-27.

4. ***Bring up the Text Wrap palette.*** Text wrap may win my vote for the hardest feature to locate in InDesign. First, instead of implementing it as a command, the way it is in QuarkXPress, InDesign gives you a palette. Second, even though you apply text wrap to an object—and typically a graphic object—InDesign groups the feature with the type palettes. The net result is this: Choose **Window→Type & Tables→Text Wrap**—or press the somewhat memorable keyboard shortcut, Ctrl+Alt+W (⌘-Option-W on the Mac)—and up comes the **Text Wrap** palette.

Figure 7-28.

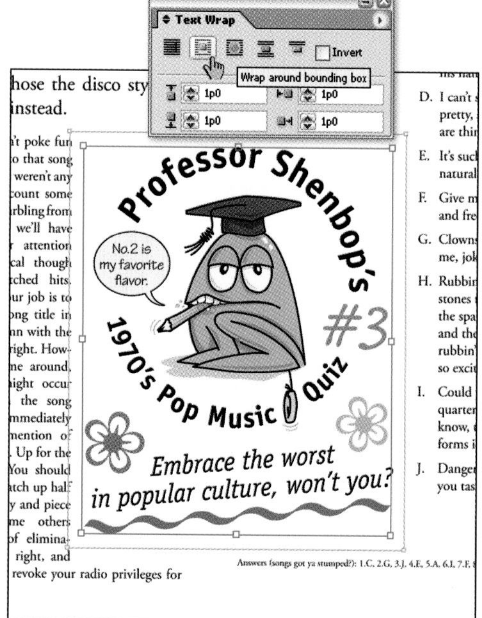

Figure 7-29.

PEARL OF WISDOM

Notice that I said text wrap *typically* applies to a graphic object. Although you'll usually wrap type around graphics, you can just as easily wrap the type in one text block around the frame of another. In other words, any kind of frame—text or graphic—can serve as the starting point for a text wrap.

5. ***Turn on the text wrap and establish base offset values.*** The top row of icons in the Text Wrap palette establish what style of wrap you want to apply. They work as follows:

   - The first icon, , turns the wrap off, as it is now.
   - The second icon, , creates a rectangular wrap with top, bottom, left, and right offsets.
   - Click to trace a free-form offset boundary around the perimeter of the selection. If InDesign can't find a perimeter—as it can't for this grouped graphic—the result is a rectangular wrap.
   - The icon causes the text to skip over the graphic, so type appears above and below the graphic but not on either side of it. Strictly speaking, this is not a text wrap function; it's a *jump*.
   - And finally, click to jump the graphic and break the text to the next frame or column.

   Because doesn't recognize grouped objects, click the second icon, . Then enter 1p0 (or just 1) for each of the four numerical values in the palette. This creates a rectangular offset boundary spaced 1 pica from each of the four sides of the cartoon, as shown in Figure 7-29.

PEARL OF WISDOM

Why 1 pica? First, it's easy to enter (just 1-Tab-1-Tab-1-Tab-1). Second, it separates the offset boundary from the group's bounding box so that you can easily access the offset and edit it.

6. ***Add points to the offset boundary.*** InDesign treats the offset boundary in much the same way as it treats a path. That is, you can add points, delete points, and move them into other locations. You can even add and reposition control handles if you have a mind to.

For our purposes, let's keep things moderately simple and just add and move a few points.

- Press the P key to select the pen tool. Suddenly, InDesign shows you all the points in the paths that make up the cartoon.
- Position the pen cursor over the left side of the offset boundary. Notice that the pen gets a + sign, showing you that it's poised to add points. Click to add points at each of the five locations illustrated in Figure 7-30.
- Press the A key to switch to the white arrow tool, your pal when moving individual points in an offset boundary.
- Drag the points to the right to trace the boundary of the graphic. Assuming you positioned the points properly when creating them, you should be able to leave point ❺ alone. But you'll have to move the upper-left corner point, which I labeled ⓿ in Figure 7-31. If you're feeling fussy, press the Shift key while dragging the points to constrain your movements to exactly horizontal.

The net result is a pretty good wrap. My one problem with it is that the straight segments don't exactly follow the circular shape of the top half of the cartoon. Your only option for making the segments curve is a special tool in the pen tool flyout menu called the convert direction point tool. But I'm here to tell you, it's not worth the effort. Assuming you managed to gain some semblance of comfort with the tool—most designers find it pretty unwieldy—it'd take you five to ten minutes to get the points and control handles in their proper positions.

Figure 7-30.

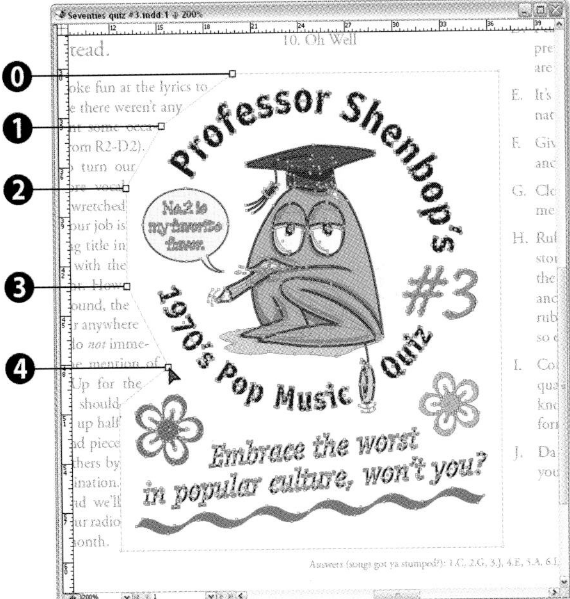

Figure 7-31.

PEARL OF WISDOM

And why bother when there's a better way? What is that better way? Draw more accurate and infinitely more intuitive outlines with the shape tools and use these outlines to generate offset boundaries. The only drawback is that it involves throwing away what we've done so far and starting over. I know, it's a shame, but I wanted you to have those first six steps of experience under your belt. For one thing, it's the typical way to work. For another, it'll help you better appreciate the nonstandard but more elegant approach to come.

Figure 7-32.

Figure 7-33.

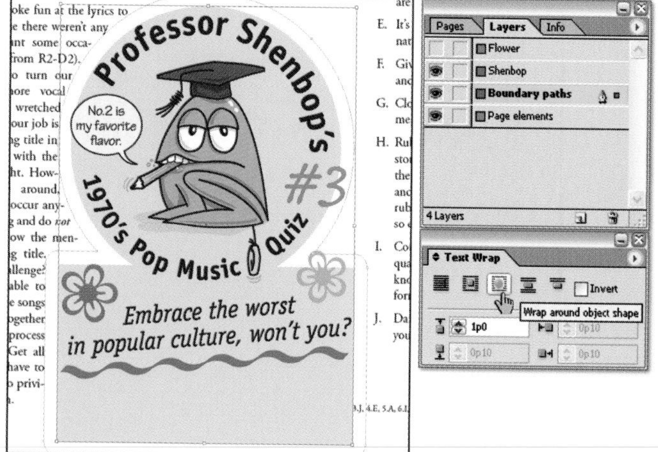

Figure 7-34.

7. ***Turn off the text wrap.*** Die old approach, die die die. To that end, press the V key to switch to the black arrow tool. Click Shenbop to make sure the graphic is selected. Then click the icon in the upper-left corner of the Text Wrap palette.

8. ***Turn on the Boundary Paths layer.*** Choose **Window→Layers** (or press the F7 key) to display the **Layers** palette. Then click in the column of s to the left of the **Boundary Paths** layer to show the icon and view the contents of the layer. You'll see two overlapping light cyan shapes—one a circle and the other a rectangle. These two incredibly simple shapes very precisely trace the outline of the graphic.

9. ***Select the cyan shapes.*** Press the Alt key (Option on the Mac) and click on the **Boundary Paths** layer name. InDesign selects all the objects on the layer. In this case, all the objects amount to just two, the circle and rectangle, which appear selected in Figure 7-32.

10. ***Combine the two shapes into one.*** The Text Wrap palette is best suited to wrapping a single shape at a time. Technically, you *can* wrap multiple shapes at once, but it complicates the document and creates problems with the offset values. So I recommend that you combine the two shapes into one. To do so, choose **Window→Pathfinder** to display the **Pathfinder** palette. Then click the button, as illustrated in Figure 7-33.

11. ***Wrap the text around the contours of the shape.*** Click the third icon, , at the top of the Text Wrap palette. This wraps the text around the exact contours of the selected shape. Then change the first offset value to 1p0 to achieve the text wrap pictured in Figure 7-34.

    (If you neglected to combine the circle and square in the preceding step, the first offset value appears dimmed. Click the button in the Pathfinder palette to make the value available.)

12. ***Hide the Boundary Paths layer.*** The cyan shape has served its purpose. So return to the **Layers** palette and click the 👁 in front of **Boundary Paths** to turn the layer off. The shape disappears, but remarkably, its text wrap remains in play, as Figure 7-35 attests. In fact, a text wrap is the only function that remains in force even when the layer that contains the function is turned off. It's like a planet that disappears but somehow leaves its gravitational effects behind. I'm not sure this feature makes a lot of sense, but it can be very useful when properly exploited.

    Now take a look at the document. If you have a keen eye, you may notice that all text around the hidden shape wraps. This includes not only the paragraph to the left of the shape, but also the small *Answers* line in the lower-right corner of the document. The latter is a problem—I want it to remain on a single line, just the way I had it. I could edit the circle-and-rectangle shape to avoid overlap with the *Answers* line, but there's a better way, as you'll see next.

Figure 7-35.

13. ***Deactivate wrapping for the line of type.*** Using the black arrow tool, click on the *Answers* text to select it. Choose **Object→Text Frame Options**, or press Ctrl+B (⌘-B on the Mac). When the **Text Frame Options** dialog box appears, turn on the **Ignore Text Wrap** check box. If you turn on **Preview** as well, you'll see the *Answers* text return to its previous unwrapped state, as in Figure 7-36 on the next page. Click the **OK** button to accept the change.

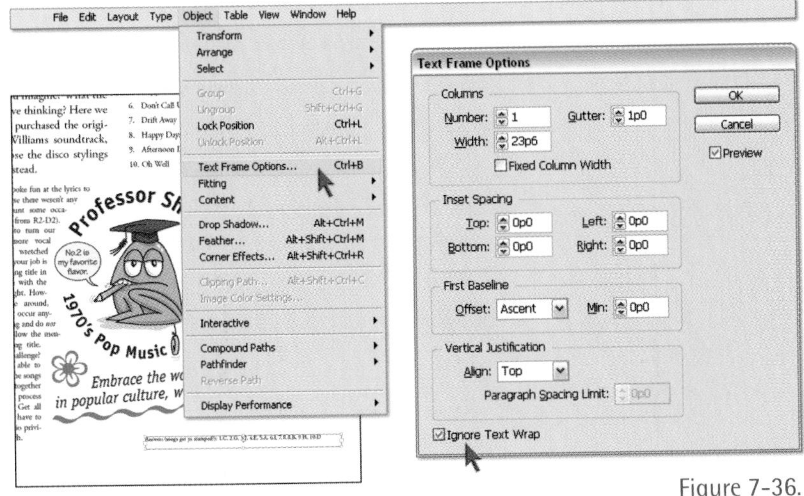

Figure 7-36.

EXTRA CREDIT

At the risk of beating a dead horse—or in this case, a dead frog—I want to show you one more way to wrap text around an object. The auto-wrapping technique we employed in Step 11 works beautifully when working with home-grown shapes and paths, but it requires a bit of additional tweaking when working with artwork imported from Photoshop or Illustrator. If you'd like to learn about this tweaking, then join me as I resume the exercise with the riveting Step 14. If not, skip to the next section, "Inserting Inline Graphics," which begins on page 277.

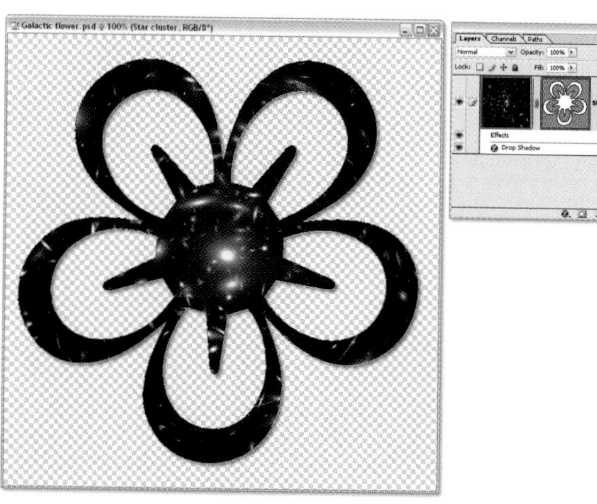

Figure 7-37.

14. ***Turn off the Shenbop layer and turn on the Flower.*** Let's imagine that we show this page to a client, and he hates the Shenbop art. "What does a dead frog have to do with 70's music?" he asks. My answer—"Honestly, I hadn't really thought about that"—turns out not to be very compelling, and so the cartoon goes. In its place, the client wants an "outer-space-looking flower." Ever eager to please, I whip up some artwork in Photoshop. Shown in Figure 7-37, it features a star cluster clipped into the shape of a flower by a vector-based shape layer. (If you have Photoshop CS, you can check out this artwork for yourself by opening *Galactic flower.psd* in the *Links graphics* folder inside *Lesson 07*.) After saving the image, I placed it into InDesign.

    To swap the frog for the flower, go to InDesign's **Layers** palette. Click the 👁 in front of **Shenbop** to hide the cartoon; then click in front of the word **Flower** to turn that layer on. You should now see the *Galactic flower* art in place of Shenbop, as in Figure 7-38.

15. ***Turn off the existing text wrap.*** The only problem with my new art is that it no longer matches the text wrap. I need to turn off the existing wrap and create a new one. One way to turn the wrap off is to throw away the Boundary Paths layer, but then we lose all that work.

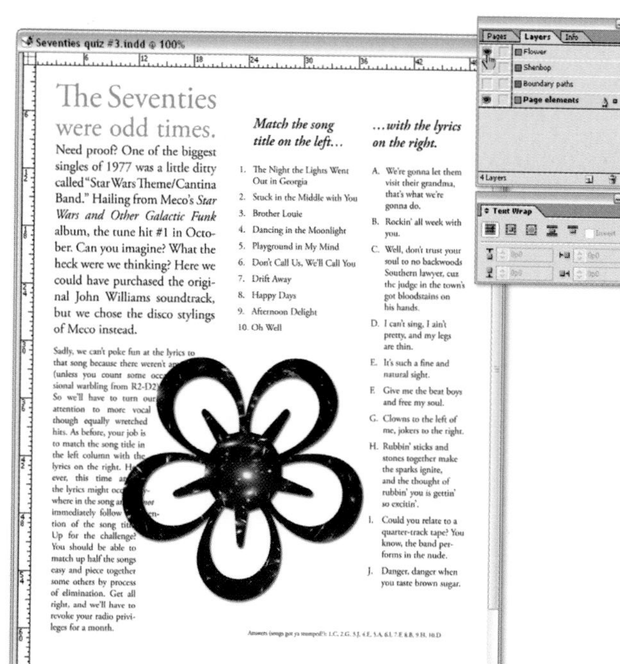

Figure 7-38.

That's why I prefer to do the following:

- Double-click the **Boundary Paths** item in the Layers palette. This displays the **Layer Options** dialog box.
- Turn on the **Suppress Text Wrap When Layer Is Hidden** check box. Then click the **OK** button.

That's all there is to it. As Figure 7-39 illustrates, InDesign deactivates the text wrap and returns the wrapped paragraph to its normal appearance.

16. ***Wrap the text around the flower.*** Armed with the black arrow tool, click on the flower to select it. Then click the third icon (▣) in the **Text Wrap** palette. Also change the first offset value to 1p0. This time, rather than wrapping the text around the exact outlines of the selected shape, InDesign aligns the offset boundary with the square bounding box, as in Figure 7-40. The culprit is a misreading of the contours of the imported image, one that we shall correct in the next step.

17. ***Set the Contour Type to Detect Edges.*** If necessary, expand the Text Wrap palette, either by clicking the ⊙ arrow and choosing **Show Options** or by clicking the ♦ in the palette tab twice. This displays the **Contour Options** settings. The **Type** option is currently set to Same As Clipping. But because the selected image lacks a clipping path, the setting produces no effect. To make InDesign sense the outline of the flower shape, click the pop-up menu and choose **Detect Edges** instead. As shown in Figure 7-41 on the next page, the wrap isn't entirely symmetrical—there's a bit more of a gap at the bottom than at the top—but it's mighty good for something so automatic.

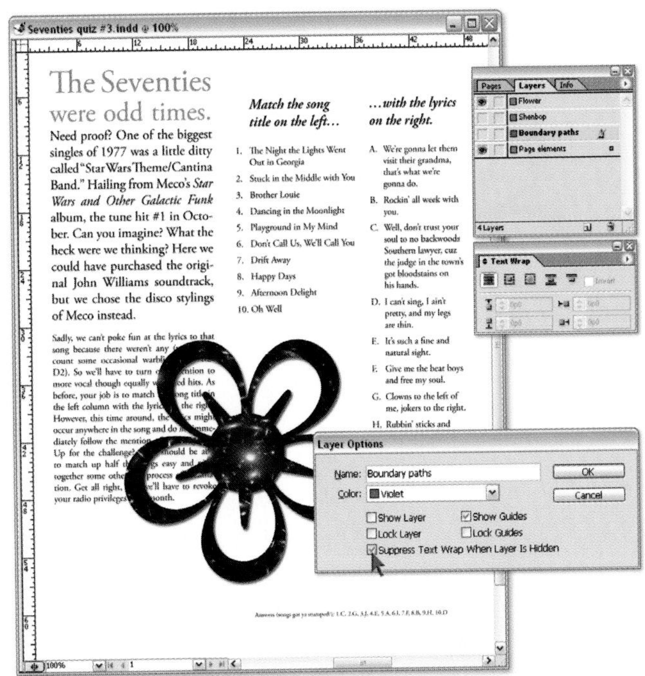

Figure 7-39.

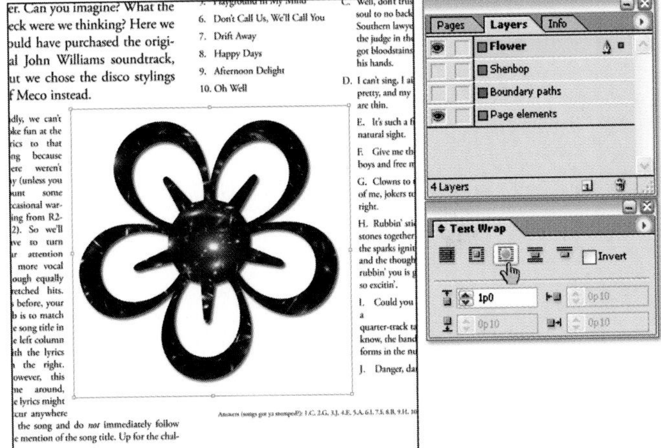

Figure 7-40.

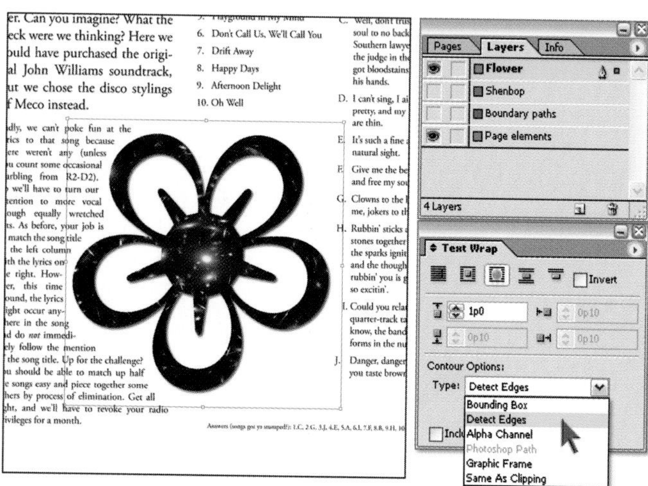

Figure 7-41.

For a tighter wrap, try selecting Alpha Channel instead. This traces the offset boundary around the so-called *opacity mask*, which defines the exact boundaries of the layer. Technically, it's a more accurate wrap. But in this specific case, I don't care as much for the results.

18. ***Turn off wrapping for the third column of text.*** The flower extends slightly into the third column, nudging over the *I* in the second-to-last paragraph. Click the column with the black arrow tool. Then choose **Object→Text Frame Options** or press Ctrl+B (⌘-B). Turn on **Ignore Text Wrap** and click the **OK** button. The completed page appears in Figure 7-42.

If you find yourself wanting to edit one of InDesign's contour boundaries, choose **Object→Select→Content** or just click on the object with the white arrow tool. Figure 7-43 shows the page before and after I modified the boundary below the left petal to bring in another line of type and close up the gap. InDesign's contour paths tend to be obscenely complex, but moving a few points here and there is often all it takes to work your necessary wonders.

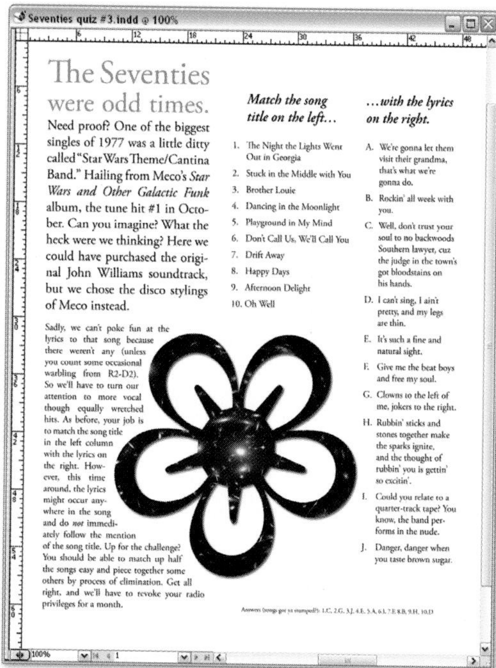

Figure 7-42.

Figure 7-43.

Inserting Inline Graphics

Most of the text you create in InDesign is made up of letters, numbers, and punctuation. But symbols are becoming increasingly common. Some symbols—$, %, •, #—are so routine that they show up in even the leanest of typefaces. Others require you to seek out specialty dingbat or "pi" fonts. And still others aren't characters of text at all. In fact, they're graphics.

Consider the icons peppered throughout this very book—things like , , , and . While I find these symbols very useful for calling attention to elements of the InDesign interface, I could not locate any of them in a readily available typeface. By that I mean, I really didn't search that hard because I decided it was easier to draw the symbols myself. And that's what I did; I drew the symbols in Illustrator and pasted them directly into my text blocks as *inline graphics*—that is, graphics that InDesign treats as characters of type.

In this exercise, you'll introduce and edit three inline graphics, each time employing a different technique. All three graphics are Illustrator files, but they could just as easily be bitmapped images prepared in Photoshop or some other image editor. And best of all, the graphics flow with the type and even respond to certain formatting attributes. Here, let me show you.

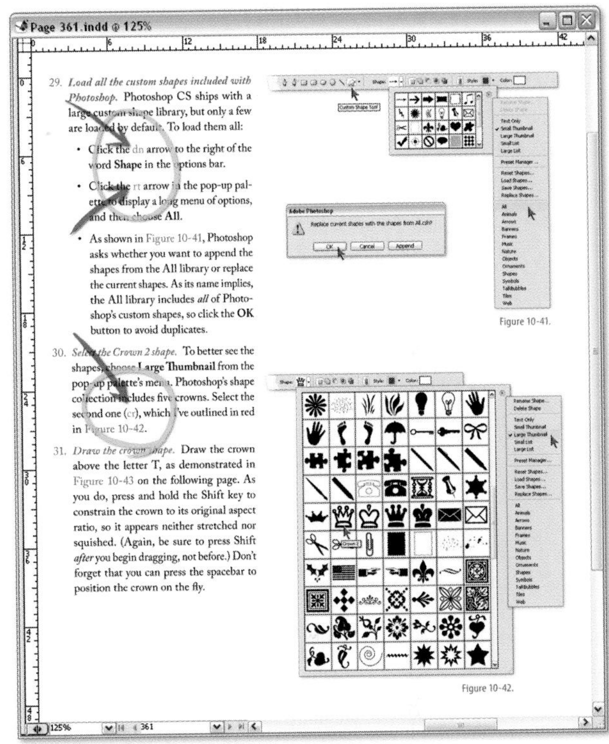
Page 361.indd @ 125%

29. *Load all the custom shapes included with Photoshop.* Photoshop CS ships with a large custom shape library, but only a few are loaded by default. To load them all:
    - Click the dn arrow to the right of the word Shape in the options bar.
    - Click the rt arrow in the pop-up palette to display a long menu of options, and then choose **All**.
    - As shown in Figure 10-41, Photoshop asks whether you want to append the shapes from the All library or replace the current shapes. As its name implies, the All library includes *all* of Photoshop's custom shapes, so click the **OK** button to avoid duplicates.

30. *Select the Crown 2 shape.* To better see the shapes, choose **Large Thumbnail** from the pop-up palette's menu. Photoshop's shape collection includes five crowns. Select the second one (cr), which I've outlined in red in Figure 10-42.

31. *Draw the crown shape.* Draw the crown above the letter T, as demonstrated in Figure 10-43 on the following page. As you do, press and hold the Shift key to constrain the crown to its original aspect ratio, so it appears neither stretched nor squished. (Again, be sure to press Shift *after* you begin dragging, not before.) Don't forget that you can press the spacebar to position the crown on the fly.

Figure 10-41.

Figure 10-42.

Figure 7-44.

1. *Open a document.* This one's called *Page 361.indd*, which you'll find in the *Lesson 07* folder inside *Lesson Files-IDcs 1on1*. Another excerpt from *Adobe Photoshop CS One-on-One*, this single-page document contains placeholders for three inline graphics. Highlighted with arrows in Figure 7-44, each placeholder appears in red, tagged with a character style called Symbol. This makes the placeholders easy to find so I remember to replace them with the proper inline graphics.

   Each placeholder is a two-letter abbreviation for the vector-based illustration I intend to use. Figure 7-45 shows a key to the three placeholders used on this particular page, in the order in which they appear. Each symbol corresponds to an element of the Photoshop interface featured in the figures.

dn = down = ▼

rt = right = ▶

cr = crown = ♛

Figure 7-45.

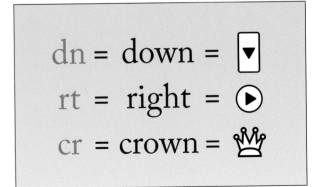

2. ***Select the first placeholder.*** We'll start by replacing the first placeholder, *dn*. Press the T key to get the type tool. Then double-click on the red word *dn* to select it.

3. ***Place the corresponding vector art.*** Choose the **Place** command from the **File** menu or press Ctrl+D (⌘-D on the Mac). Make your way to the *Symbols* folder in the *Lesson 07* folder inside *Lesson Files-IDcs 1on1*. There you'll find four AI files. Click the one that reads *dn-Down arrow.ai*. Make certain that the **Replace Selected Item** check box is turned on (as circled in Figure 7-46). Then click the **Open** button or press Enter or Return. InDesign replaces the selected text with the graphic.

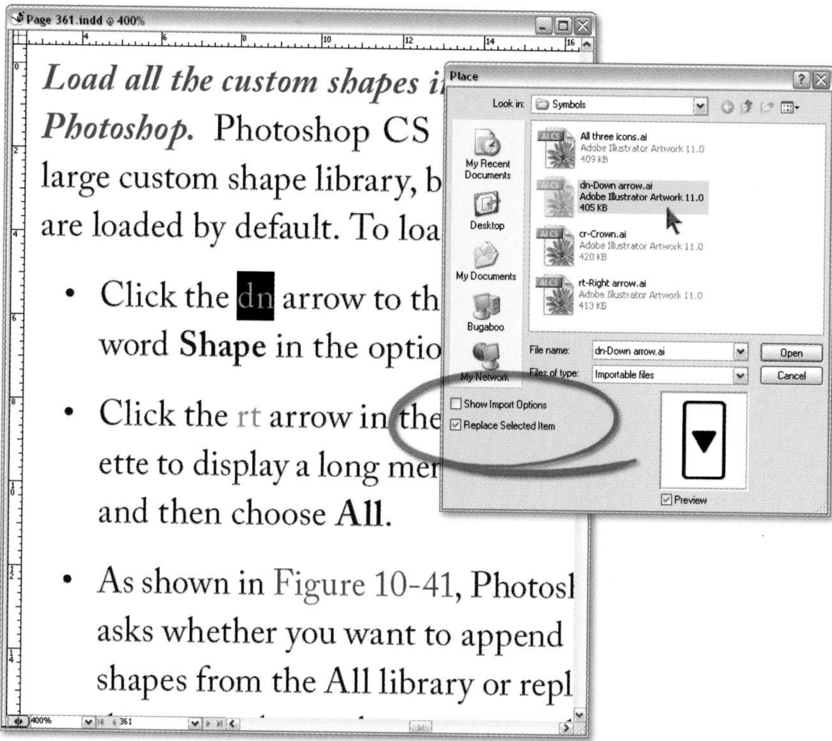

Figure 7-46.

4. ***Insert some text.*** You now have a graphic that floats inside the text block like a character of type. Try inserting some text. Figure 7-47 on the facing page shows the result of adding the preposition *on* after *Click*, which nudges the inline graphic to the right along with the other letters. You can likewise wrap inline graphics to other lines, select them with the type tool, and copy and paste them into new locations.

5. ***Nudge the graphic down.*** But while an inline graphic behaves like character of type, it remains first and foremost an imported

graphic. Get the black arrow tool and click the imported artwork to select it (see Figure 7-47). You can now crop the graphic by dragging a corner handle or transform it using any of the techniques discussed in the earlier exercises "Cropping and Scaling Artwork" and "Rotating, Slanting, and Flipping" (pages 249 and 263, respectively).

Perhaps surprisingly, you can also move the graphic inside the text. The one caveat is that you can drag it exclusively vertically, and even then only a limited distance. (I'll show you how to move the artwork horizontally in the final Step 11.) To do so, either drag the artwork or, better yet, use the ↑ and ↓ arrow keys to nudge it.

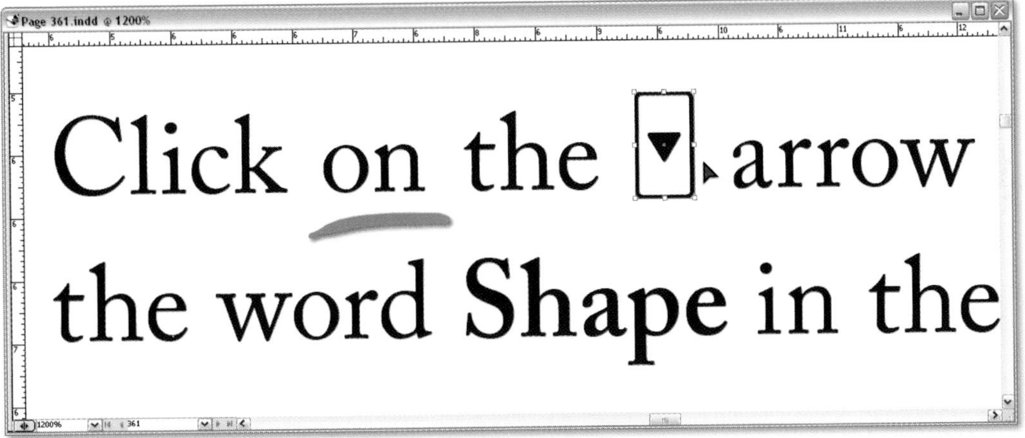

Figure 7-47.

In our case, the artwork is a bit high compared with the text around it. So press the ↓ key once to nudge the graphic down 1 point. (This assumes that the Cursor Key value in the Units & Increments panel of the Preferences dialog box is set to 0p1, as it is by default.) Figure 7-47 shows the result.

To nudge an inline graphic by smaller increments, which tends to be useful when working inside lines of type, remember that you can add Ctrl (or ⌘) and Shift to the mix. For example, Ctrl+Shift+↓ nudges the artwork down by 1/10 point.

Note that InDesign restricts how far you can nudge an inline graphic up or down. You can't drag the top of the frame below the baseline or the bottom above the leading boundary (where the next baseline would be, if there were a higher line in this same paragraph).

PEARL OF WISDOM

Bear in mind that dragging a graphic up and down can mess up the line spacing of text governed by auto leading. This becomes even more evident if the graphic is larger than its surrounding type. To make sure the line spacing remains constant, set the leading value in the Control palette to a specific value, anything other than Auto. The leading of this paragraph is 14 pt, so the distance from one baseline to the next is 14 points regardless of the size of any artwork the text may contain.

---

6. ***Copy a graphic in Adobe Illustrator CS.*** This time, we're going to try a different way to import a graphic, by copying and pasting it directly from Illustrator CS. Obviously this means you'll need Illustrator CS to perform this step. If you own the Creative Suite (either the Standard or Premium edition), you have Illustrator. Otherwise, you likely don't. If you don't, no worries. I'll give you an opportunity to catch up in Step 8A.

   For those of you who do have access to Illustrator CS, launch the program and open the file called *All three icons.ai* in the *Symbols* folder inside *Lesson 07*. Then do the following:

   - Choose **Edit→Preferences→File Handling & Clipboard** (on the Mac, choose **Illustrator→Preferences→File Handling & Clipboard**). See the **Copy on Quit** options near the bottom of the dialog box? Turn on the second check box, **AICB (no transparency support)**, which conveys editable paths. Then turn on **Preserve Paths**. Finally, click **OK** to accept your changes.
   - Using Illustrator's black arrow tool (which serves the same function as it does in InDesign), click the central icon, ⦿, to select it.
   - Choose **Edit→Copy** or press Ctrl+C (⌘-C on the Mac) to transfer a copy of the icon to the application-level clipboard, as in Figure 7-48 on the facing page.

7. ***Inside InDesign, select the second placeholder.*** Switch back to InDesign CS. As you do, Illustrator secretly slips the contents of its clipboard to the operating system, and then the operating system slips it to InDesign. Only it all happens so fast, you don't even notice.

   Now let's prepare the new home. Get the type tool and double-click the red word *rt* to select it.

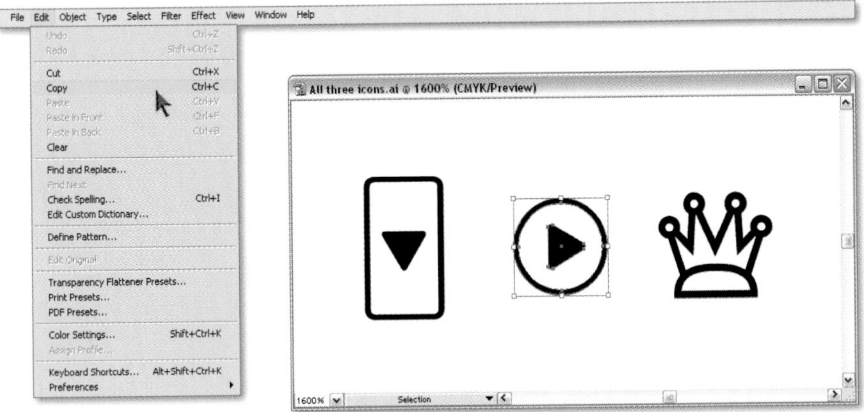

Figure 7-48.

8. ***Paste the corresponding vector art.*** Choose **Edit→Paste** or press Ctrl+V (⌘-V on the Mac). InDesign should insert the ⦿ icon into the text, as in Figure 7-49. If it does not, as it very well may not on the Mac, you have to jump through a few additional hoops:

   - Press the Enter key on the keypad to switch back to the black arrow tool. (This assumes you switched to the Deke Keys shortcuts as directed on page xvii of the Preface.)
   - Again choose **Edit→Paste** or press Ctrl+V (⌘-V). The ⦿ should appear in the middle of the document window.
   - Choose **Edit→Cut** or press Ctrl+X (⌘-X). This replaces the ⦿ in the clipboard with the exact same graphic. Admittedly, it seems like a pretty silly thing to do. But it forces InDesign to reevaluate the artwork, which often works wonders.
   - Reselect the red *rt* with the type tool and choose **Edit→Paste**. You should now see the result shown in Figure 7-49.

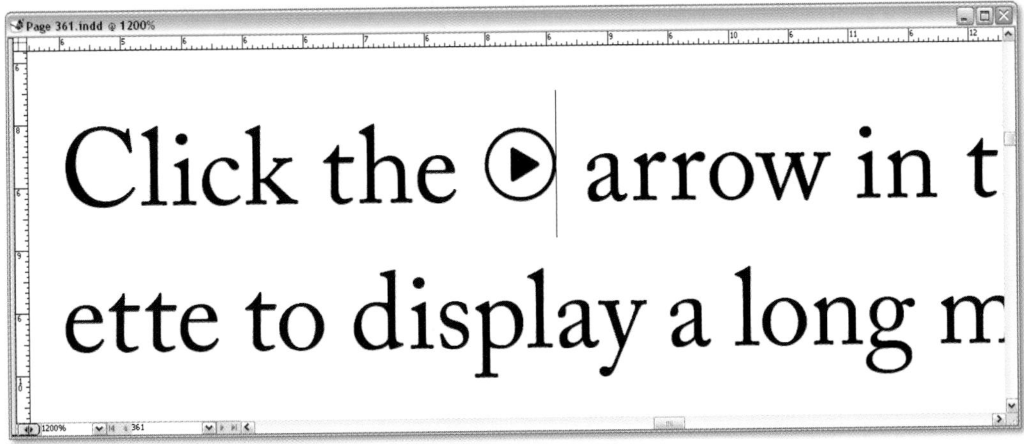

Figure 7-49.

If you have successfully pasted the graphic, skip to Step 9. Otherwise, perform the following extra-special Step 8A.

8A. ***Or, if you don't have Illustrator...*** You can place the graphic traditionally. Here's how to go about that:

- Select the red *rt* with the type tool.
- Choose **File→Place** or press Ctrl+D (⌘-D).
- Select the file called *rt-Right arrow.ai* in the *Symbols* folder inside *Lesson 07*. Then click the **OK** button. InDesign replaces the selected text with the Illustrator art.

PEARL OF WISDOM

At this point, you might wonder why in the world you'd copy and paste a graphic from Illustrator when it seems so much easier to place it from disk. First, copying and pasting actually goes very quickly once you come to terms with it. Second, a placed graphic is not editable in InDesign; a pasted graphic is, provided that AICB is on (see Step 6) and the artwork does not include text. This means I can take the artwork shown in Figure 7-49 and reshape or augment it, just as if it were drawn directly inside InDesign. I can also recolor the icon, which is essential when matching a symbol to differently colored text, as I often have to do in this book.

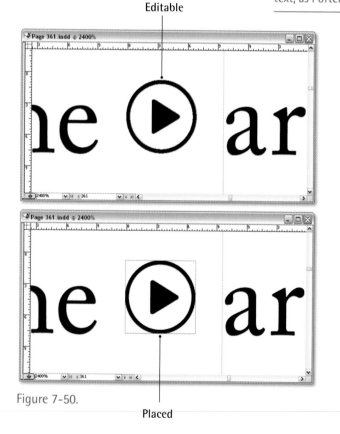

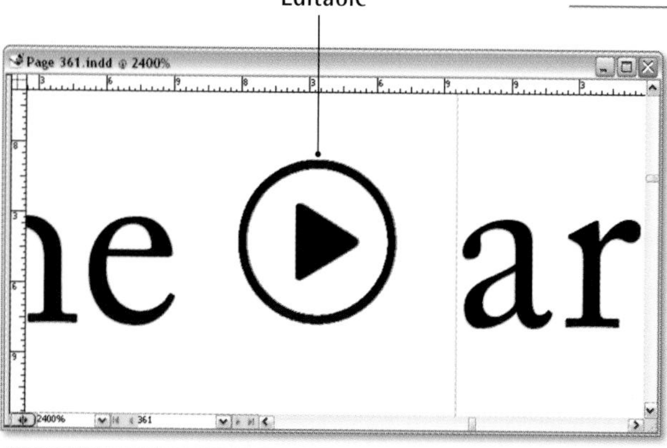

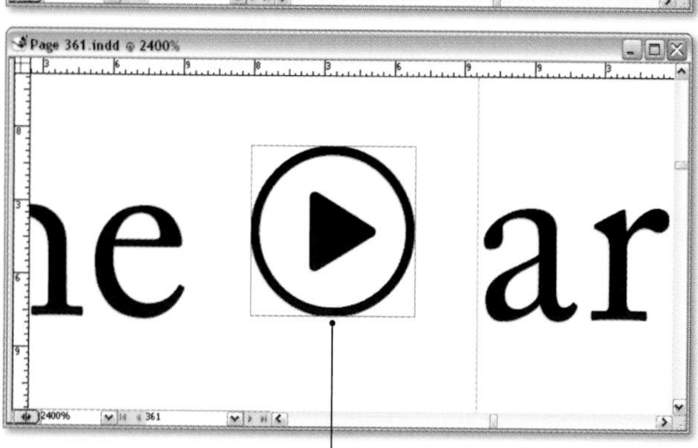

Figure 7-50.

And how can you tell whether a graphic is editable or not? If you switch out of the preview mode—either by clicking the icon in the lower-left corner of the toolbox or pressing the W key—you see the graphic frame. A colored frame that exactly traces the perimeter of the artwork means the graphic is editable; a rectangular frame means it's not. Figure 7-50 shows examples.

9. ***Replace the third placeholder with the crown art.*** Scroll down to the final red placeholder, *cr*. This time, you can replace it by either copying and pasting or placing, whichever you prefer. If in doubt, do like so:
   - Select the red *cr* with the type tool.
   - Choose **File→Place** or press Ctrl+D (⌘-D).
   - Select the file called *cr-Crown.ai* in the *Symbols* folder inside *Lesson 07*.
   - Click **OK** to import the crown graphic.

PEARL OF WISDOM

Parentheses are designed to be used with lowercase letters. Therefore, the crown appears off-center vertically (i.e., too high). The parentheses are also a bit too tight to the crown for my taste. I want to adjust both the vertical and horizontal placement of the crown. And the best way to do that is to treat the graphic as a character of type.

10. ***Adjust the baseline shift.*** Select the crown with the type tool by dragging over it. Or press Shift+→ to select one character to the right (presuming of course that your blinking insertion marker is immediately to the left of the crown). Then do one of the following:

    - Press Shift+Alt+↓ (Shift-Option-↓ on the Mac). In creating this document, I set the Baseline Shift value in the Units & Increments panel of the Preferences dialog box to 0.5 point. So Shift+Alt+↓ scoots the crown ½ point below the baseline.
    - Alternatively, you can enter –0.5 for the A↕a value in the Control palette and press Enter or Return.

    InDesign shifts the crown down a mere 1/144 inch. But it's enough to center it vertically inside the parentheses.

11. ***Spread out the tracking.*** Press Shift+← to expand the selection to include the "open" parenthesis, which is the one on the left. Then track the selected text using one of these two methods:

    - Press Ctrl+Alt+→ (or ⌘-Option-→). I set the Kerning value in the Units & Increments panel of the Preferences dialog box to 5/1000 em space. Therefore, pressing Ctrl+Alt+→ spreads the characters by 5 times that increment, or 25/1000 em space.
    - Not so fond of shortcuts? Change the tracking value (AV) in the Control palette to 25 and press Enter or Return.

    Either way, InDesign spaces the two selected characters with respect to the ones immediately following them. This spreads the crown ever so slightly away from both parentheses, as in Figure 7-51 on the next page.

Figure 7-51.

PEARL OF WISDOM

In addition to letting you move inline graphics both vertically and horizontally, employing a combination of baseline shift and tracking permits you to record your settings and repeat them using a character style. I find this particularly helpful when I plan on using a certain symbol multiple times. After creating the character style, I have only to select the symbol with the type tool and apply the character style to repeat all horizontal and vertical spacing information.

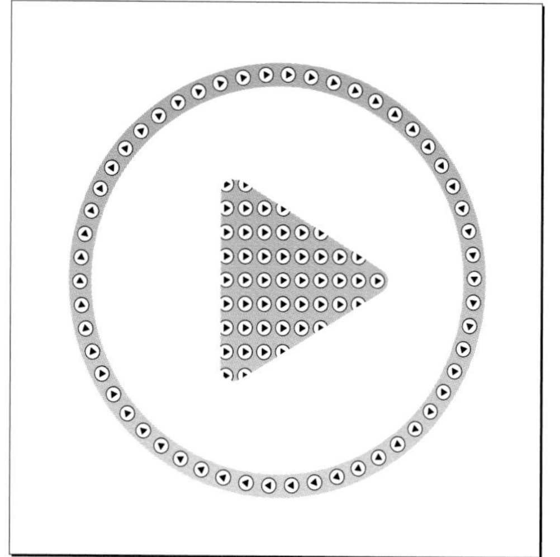

Figure 7-52.

For an unusual but (I think) highly entertaining use of inline graphics, open the document *Paths on Paths.indd* contained in the *Lesson 07* folder. Pictured in Figure 7-52, this file features a series of small right-pointing arrowheads inset within a large one. Throughout, the small arrowheads are inline graphics.

- The central arrowheads are set as normal type—albeit with relatively tight leading and tracking—inside a rectangular text block. I then drew a series of white paths in front of the text block. These paths cover portions of the little arrowheads and carve them into the shape of a big arrowhead. (Press the W key to make the path outlines visible. They will appear in red.)
- I created the outer ring of arrowheads by pasting graphics into path type that traces the outline of a circle. (To learn about path type, see "Joining Type to a Curve," which begins on page 72 of Lesson 2.) In other words, using inline graphics, you can create artwork that follows the outline of a path.

If you're feeling adventurous, try your hand at selecting some of the characters using the type tool. You can even edit them if you like. Otherwise, just remember this: Just about anything you can do with characters of text you can likewise do with inline graphics.

WHAT DID YOU LEARN?

Match the key concept in the numbered list below with the letter of the phrase that best describes it. Answers appear upside-down at the bottom of the page.

Key Concepts

1. Pixel
2. Bitmapped image
3. Links palette
4. Reference point matrix
5. X and Y coordinates
6. Constrain proportions
7. Select content
8. Fit frame to content
9. White arrow
10. Offset boundary
11. Text Frame Options
12. Inline graphic

Descriptions

A. Click the in the Control palette or press Ctrl+Alt+C (⌘-Option-C on the Mac) to resize a container so it exactly matches the graphic inside.

B. This feature—which you can hide or show by pressing Ctrl+Shift+D (⌘-Shift-D on the Mac)—allows you to keep track of every piece of artwork that you import into an InDesign document.

C. When pasted into a text block, InDesign treats this kind of artwork as a character of type.

D. The horizontal and vertical positions of a specific point in an object, as defined by the reference point matrix.

E. Also known as the direct selection tool, this tool lets you move and scale an image independently of its frame.

F. Click the in the Control palette to burrow inside a frame and gain access to the imported graphic inside.

G. A single square of color in a digital photograph or other image that you might prepare in Photoshop and import into InDesign.

H. This command grants you access to the Ignore Text Wrap check box, which makes a selected text block immune to any text wrap settings.

I. A picture captured by a digital camera or scanner that comprises thousands or millions of pixels.

J. Click the in the Control palette to link either the W and H values or the and values so that InDesign scales a selected object uniformly.

K. The contour of a text wrap, which acts as an invisible force field beyond which neighboring text cannot pass.

L. This controls the point from which an object's position is measured and around which a transformation occurs.

Answers

1G, 2I, 3B, 4L, 5D, 6J, 7F, 8A, 9E, 10K, 11H, 12C

LESSON 8

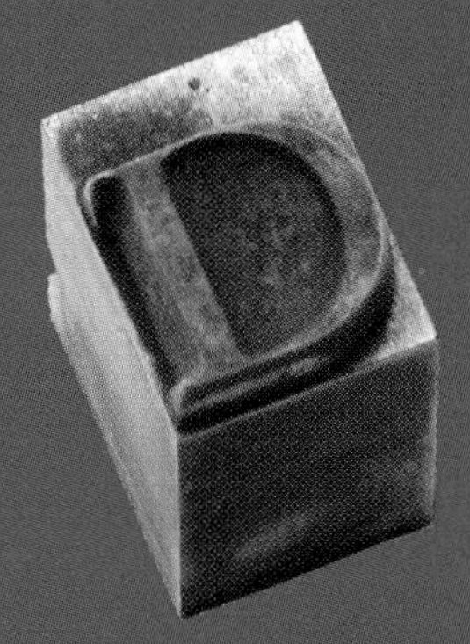

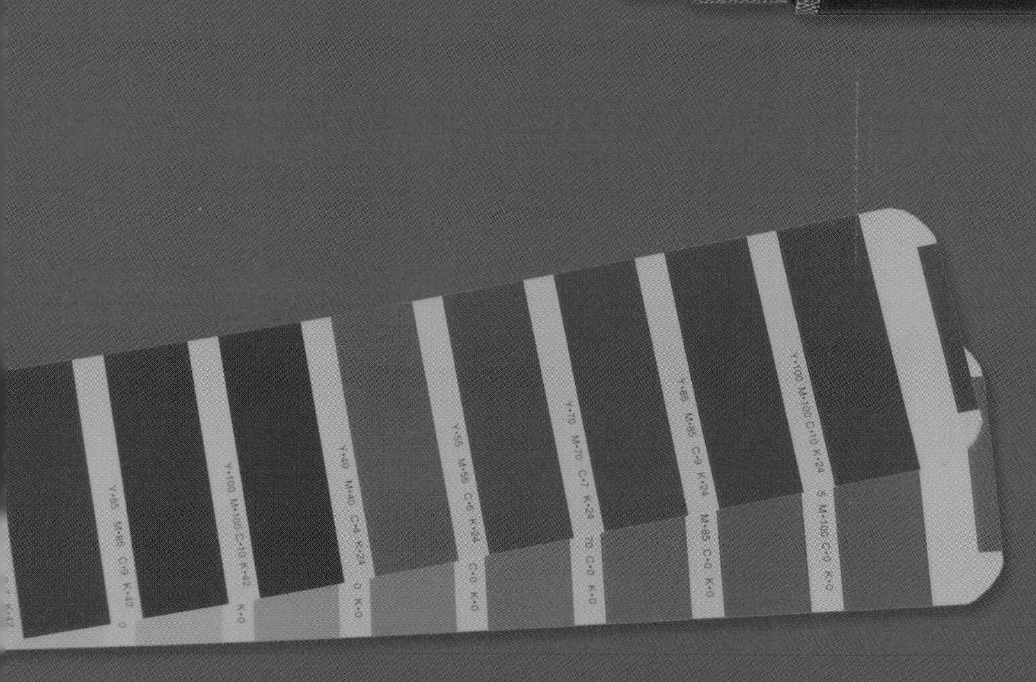

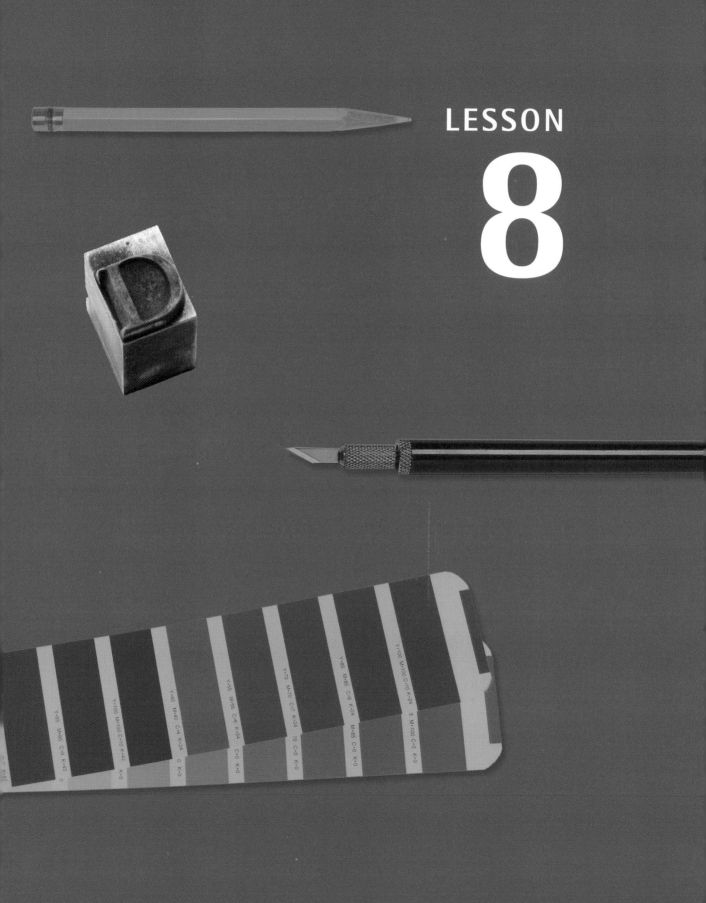

TRANSPARENCY AND EFFECTS

ONCE UPON a time, your options for transparency inside a vector-based application like InDesign numbered two: fully opaque or altogether transparent. An object could have an opaque fill or stroke, but it was invariably transparent on the outside. And the transition between these two extremes was abrupt. You could create the appearance of soft transitions using, say, a gradient. But under the hood, the gradient was rendered as a sequence of objects, each characterized by an opaque fill and a transparent exterior. Figure 8-1 offers some examples. The checkerboard represents transparency.

In those dark old days—just a few years ago, come to think of it—a vector program did not permit partial transparency. This meant you couldn't blend the colors of, say, one graphic object into another. And an imported photograph was always rectangular or cut by a sharp-edged vector mask. To give you a sense of what this means, consider the image file pictured in Figure 8-2 on page 289. Once upon a time, if I were to import that image into a page-layout program, it would invariably appear as an opaque rectangle, as witnessed on the left. If you wanted to introduce transparency into that rectangle, your one and only option was to place the image into a vector shape, as demonstrated on the right side of the figure.

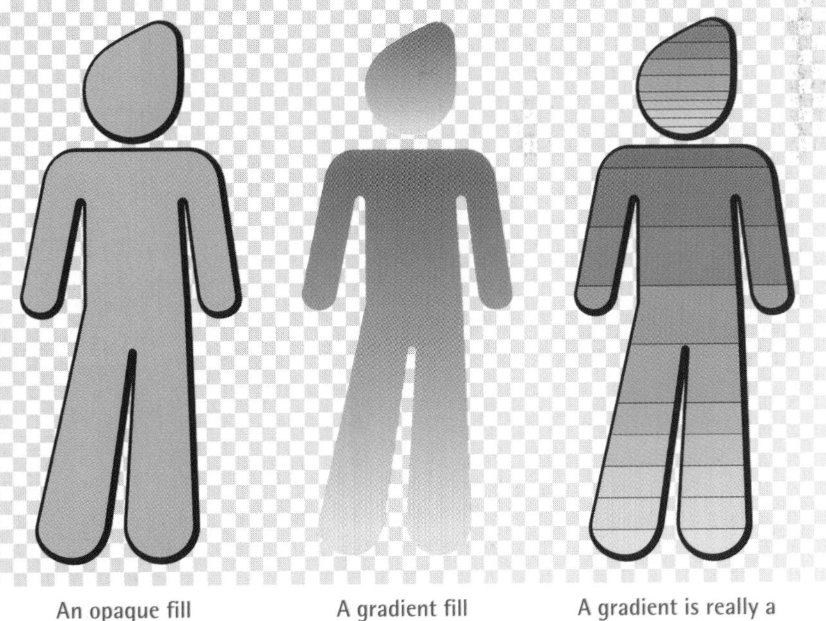

An opaque fill and stroke against a transparent background
A gradient fill and no stroke helps to soften the edges
A gradient is really a sequence of separate, opaque objects

Figure 8-1.

ABOUT THIS LESSON

Project Files

Before beginning the exercises, make sure that you've installed the lesson files from the CD, as explained in Step 5 on page xv of the Preface. This should result in a folder called *Lesson Files-IDcs 1on1* on your desktop. We'll be working with the files inside the *Lesson 08* subfolder.

This lesson examines the many ways you can apply transparency to text blocks, paths, and imported images inside InDesign. Over the course of these exercises, you'll learn how to:

Video Lesson 8: The Ubiquity of Transparency

Although transparency is relatively new to InDesign, Adobe has managed to weave the function into virtually all aspects of the software. You can apply transparency to both graphics and type. You can set the transparency of shadows and glows. You can even import a layered Photoshop or Illustrator file with all transparency intact. You might say InDesign offers transparency as far as the eye can see.

To take "opaque" at this exciting feature, watch the eighth video lesson on the CD. Insert the CD, click the **Start Training** button, click the Set 3 button, and then select **8, The Ubiquity of Transparency** from the Lessons list. In this 9-minute 54-second movie, I explain the following operations and shortcuts:

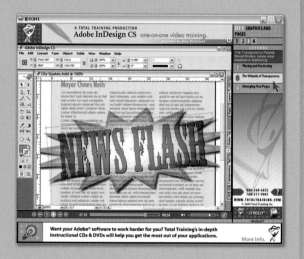

Operation	Windows shortcut	Macintosh shortcut
Show or hide the Transparency palette	Shift+F10	Shift+F10
Display the Drop Shadow dialog box	Ctrl+Alt+M	⌘-Option-M
Nudge numerical value	↑ or ↓	↑ or ↓
Display the Feather dialog box	Ctrl+Shift+Alt+M*	⌘-Shift-Option-M*
Place a Photoshop file	Ctrl+D	⌘-D

* Works only if you loaded the Deke Keys keyboard shortcuts (as directed on page xvii of the Preface).

Did I imply this was all in the past? How silly of me, I forgot. This is *still* the way transparency is handled by PageMaker, QuarkXPress, and the PostScript printing language—the latter being the industry standard for printing reports, mailers, magazines, and other mass-market documents. These remain the dominant tools used to produce the pages that cross our desks, mail boxes, and breakfast tables on a daily basis. But thanks to InDesign, there's a better way. Among page-layout applications, only InDesign dares to operate outside the PostScript box and deliver partial transparency, cross-fades, drop shadows, and other translucency effects. If you come from Quark or one of the other traditional design programs, it may all seems like a trendy grab bag of impractical tricks and gimmicks. But in time, I guarantee you, it will change the way you work.

A bitmapped image imports as a rectangle

You can then carve it into shapes using vector masks

Figure 8-2.

Gradations in Translucency

Transparency is the name Adobe gives to a group of functions that permit you to see through one object to the objects behind it. Every one of these functions is a live effect, so you can always change your mind without degrading an object or in any way modifying the original version of a placed graphic.

For example, let's say I want to make a text block or graphic translucent, so that it appears to be ghosted. Translucency is expressed as a percentage value called Opacity, with 100 percent being opaque and 0 percent, transparent. Every one of the orange-and-violet shapes in Figure 8-3 on the next page is a copy of the very same Illustrator artwork set to a different Opacity value. This value can be especially useful when setting dimmed graphics in front of text, as in the case of the first three shapes, or behind it, as in the last one. If I decide the artwork is too light or too dark, there's no need to go back to Illustrator, adjust the fill and stroke, and replace the graphic (as I'd have to do in Quark). I have only to change one value in InDesign and the fix is made.

An Opacity setting is constant over the course of an object. But other transparency effects may vary. InDesign's drop shadows are perfect examples. The first strange humanoid in Figure 8-4 casts a shadow onto the checkerboard pattern behind it. The shadow starts off dark and fades into nothingness a pica beyond the image. This particular shadow was created inside InDesign, but I could have just as easily imported it as part of the original artwork. InDesign preserves translucent effects created in Illustrator and Photoshop. It evens goes so far as to recognize and correctly interpret the translucency of each and every pixel on each and every Photoshop layer, essential for maintaining custom blurs and articulated edges like those featured in the right-hand image in Figure 8-4.

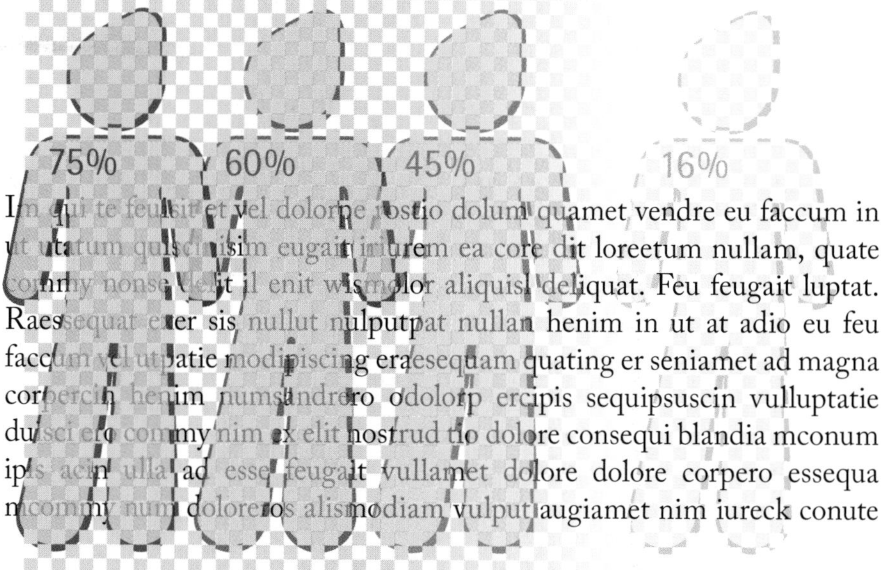

InDesign lets you make any object translucent . . . ideal for dimming graphics in front of and behind text.

Figure 8-3.

As a professional-level page-layout program, InDesign can't merely equip you with everything you need to create translucent objects and incremental fades; it also has to print them. This means translating every single Opacity value, drop shadow, and imported Photoshop layer to the PostScript printing language—no small feat given that translucency is strictly outside PostScript's ability to render. But translate InDesign does. Personally, I have yet to encounter a problem printing translucent objects directly from InDesign—and you may notice, this book is full of them. But if you do hit a wall, trust InDesign to give you the tools you need to make things right again. And trust me to help you learn how these and other transparency functions work over the course of this lesson.

Adjusting Opacity and Blending Colors

In this first exercise, we'll take a look at the most obvious expression of transparency inside InDesign, the Transparency palette. In addition to the Opacity value I mentioned a moment ago, the Transparency palette provides you with a pop-up menu of *blend modes*, which are ways of mixing the colors of overlapping objects using prescribed mathematical equations. For instance, the Multiply blend mode multiplies the color values of overlapping objects. Turns out, this makes the colors darker, which is why Multiply is most often used to create shadows.

In the following steps, you'll learn how to use the Opacity value along with blend modes to combine the colors of overlapping objects. Rather than teach you all the blend modes—there are 16 in all—I'll focus on the few that you're likely to need on a regular basis, and leave you to explore the rest (which vary dramatically in practicality) on your own. You'll be applying these functions to vector graphics that I copied from Illustrator and pasted into InDesign. But bear in mind that everything you see can be applied just as easily to homegrown lines and shapes, imported Photoshop images, and text.

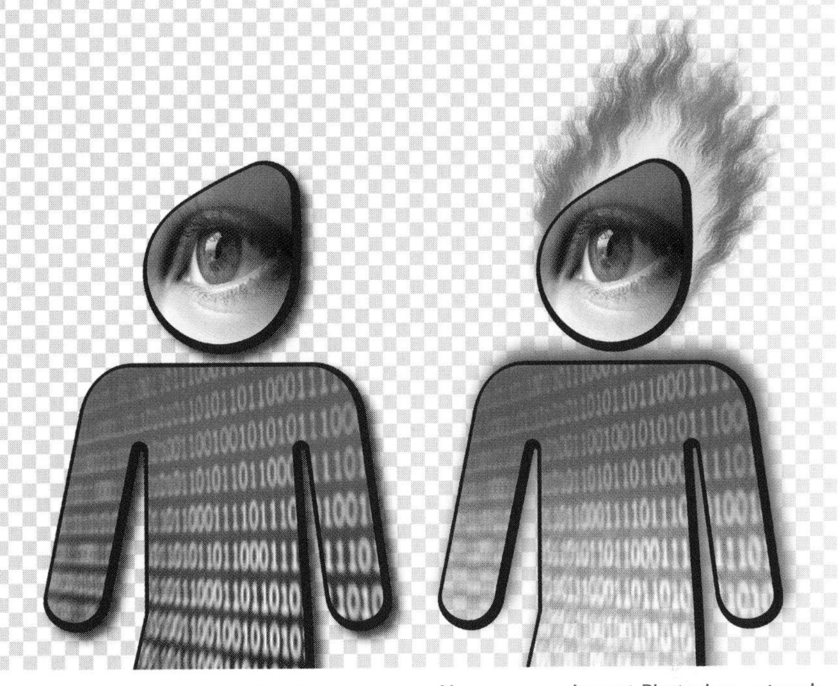

InDesign lets you add soft drop shadows to any object

You can even import Photoshop artwork with translucent layer effects

Figure 8-4.

1. ***Open a document.*** Open *Seventies quiz #2.indd*, located in the *Lesson 08* folder inside *Lesson Files-IDcs 1on1*. As Figure 8-5 on the next page shows, the file includes a two-page spread, with text and artwork on the right page and a big purple rectangle on the left. We'll use this rectangle as a backdrop for our translucent, blended artwork.

2. ***Turn on the Big Bopper layer.*** Press F7 or choose **Window→Layers** to display the **Layers** palette. Then click in the box to the far left of **Big Bopper** to display the icon and reveal the enormous visage of Shenbop the cartoon frog. Although slightly different than the illustration on the facing page, it's ultimately a repeat graphic. But thanks to transparency, it will receive a very different treatment.

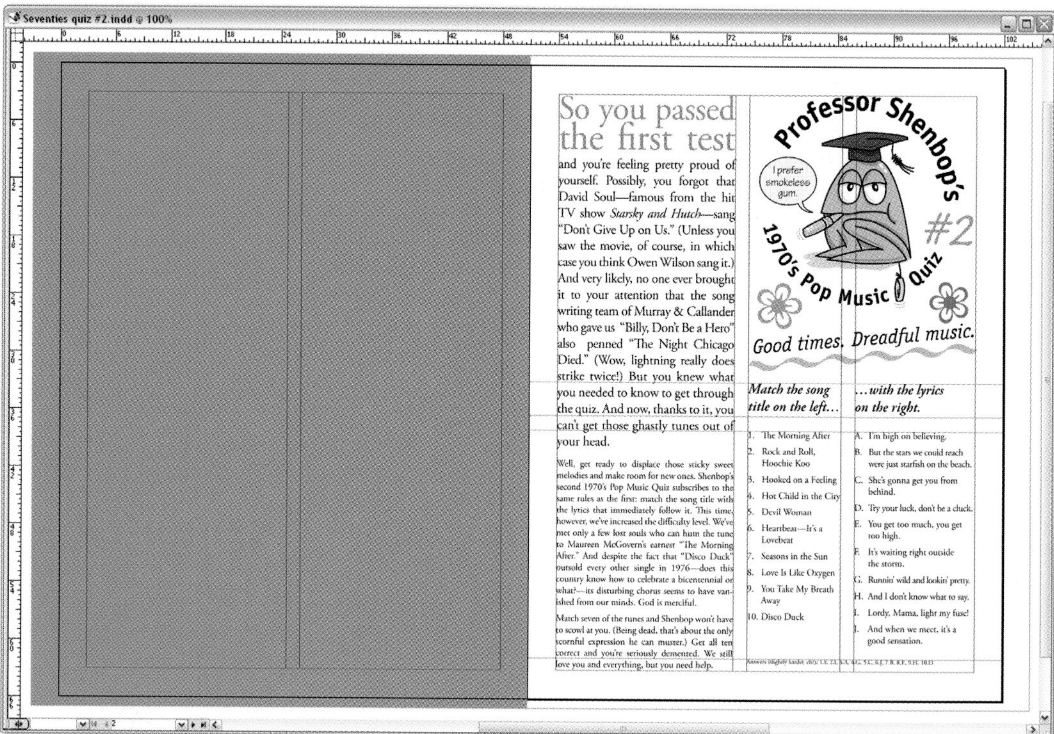

Figure 8-5.

3. ***Reduce the Opacity of the large cartoon to 25 percent.*** Select the graphic by clicking inside it with the black arrow tool. Then choose **Window→Transparency** or press Shift+F10 to display the slim **Transparency** palette. You can then change the Opacity value in one of two ways:

   - Click the word **Opacity** to highlight the value. Enter 25 and press Enter or Return.
   - Click the ▶ to the right of the Opacity value to display a slider bar. Drag the slider triangle to the left to reduce the value to 25 percent.

   Either action results in a dimmed version of the graphic. Set to 25 percent Opacity, the artwork is nearing transparency with 75 percent of the background showing through, as in Figure 8-6.

4. ***Apply the Luminosity blend mode.*** Although the frog is ghosted, you can see a lot of color. And quite frankly, I don't like it. The green mixes with the purple to create a murky gray. (Shenbop looks greenish, but that's because he's set against purple and our brains are trained to see relative colors rather than absolute. If you separate his colors from the background, as I have in the

three swatches on the right side of Figure 8-6, you can see that the frog flesh is actually purplish gray. Believe it or not.) It looks terrible, so better to just trash the green entirely. To accomplish this, we'll apply the first of our blend modes, Luminosity.

Click the ⊻ arrow (⬍ on the Mac) to the right of the word **Normal**. (Selected by default, Normal applies no special math to an object and is therefore equivalent to turning off the blend mode.) InDesign displays a pop-up menu of the 16 blend modes. Select the last mode, **Luminosity**. InDesign tosses out the colors in the frog and keeps only its lights and darks—termed *luminosity values*—as in Figure 8-7.

Figure 8-6.

PEARL OF WISDOM

Luminosity is one of the two great color blending modes. The other is Color. As we've just seen, Luminosity maintains the lights and darks of the selected objects and lets the background colors show through. Color does the opposite: It keeps the colors of the selected object and lets the lights and darks show through. Apply the Color blend mode to an object to colorize the objects behind it; use Luminosity to abandon color.

5. *Turn on the Flower Logo layer.* Click in the box to the far left of **Flower Logo** to turn on its 👁 and display a few more objects. Among these is a gray pad-like shape under Shenbop's feet. This is intended to be a shadow. Like the shadow in the illustration on the right-hand page of the Seventies quiz, I created this one for use against a white background. Now that we have a purple background, it's way too light. Let's fix that.

Figure 8-7.

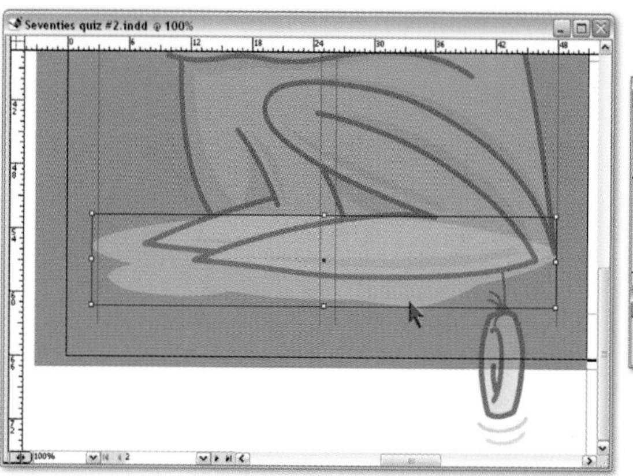

Figure 8-8.

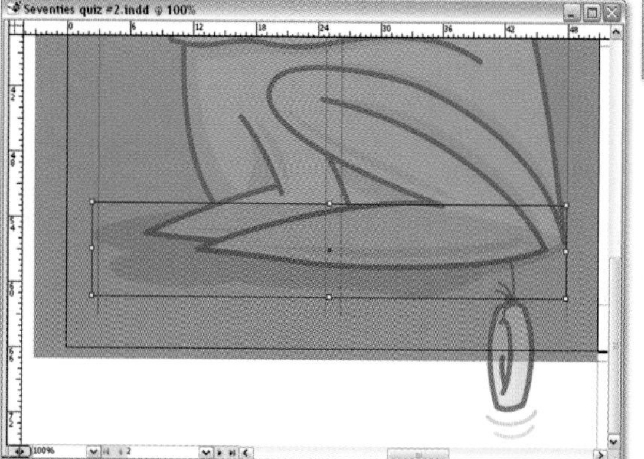

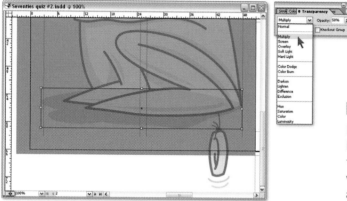

Figure 8-9.

6. ***Reduce the Opacity of the shadow.*** Click the shadow to select it, and then click the **Opacity** option and change the value to 50 percent. The shadow blends in better, but it's still not right. The object remains substantially lighter than its background (see Figure 8-8), something that cannot be said of a shadow. No Opacity value can remedy this problem, so it's time to bring in another blend mode.

7. ***Apply the Multiply blend mode.*** As I mentioned earlier, Multiply is the mode of shadows. It drops out the whites and burns in the other colors. To see for yourself, click the option to display the blend mode pop-up menu, and then choose the **Multiply** option, as in Figure 8-9. The object darkens the purple beneath it, transforming the selected shape into a deep, rich, credible cartoon shadow.

PEARL OF WISDOM

Personally, I like math, so sometimes I find it helpful to know how InDesign calculates a blend mode. If you feel the same, then read on; if not, skip to Step 8. Let's say you place one 50 percent cyan circle in front of another and set the top circle to Multiply. InDesign multiplies 50 times 50 to get 75 percent cyan where the two shapes intersect. How does 50 times 50 get you 75? InDesign converts the percentage values to decimals (which means dividing the percent by 100) and then *normalizes* the decimal by subtracting it from 1. So 0% becomes 1.0, 25% becomes 0.75, 50% becomes 0.5, 75% becomes 0.25, and 100% becomes 0, just to name a few. Thus, the resulting equation looks like the one at the top of Figure 8-10. The math for Multiply's opposite, Screen, looks more complicated in the figure, but it's actually very similar, with InDesign subtracting everything from 1. (In other words, Screen is Multiply without the normalization.) This results in lighter overlapping colors, making it great for creating highlights.

8. ***Reduce the Opacity of the logo.*** Now to attack the logo elements in the upper-left corner of the page. Click inside the flower to select it

and the surrounding type on a circle. Then lower the **Opacity** value for this group to 75 percent. This fades the logo, but only slightly, as Figure 8-11 confirms. We need a more powerful solution—such as yet another blend mode.

9. ***Apply the Screen blend mode.*** See how the radial gradient in the flower transitions from medium violet in the center to very dark violet at the outside? I want to drop out those dark colors so the flower appears to gradually fade away. And no blend mode is better for dropping out darks than Screen. Click the pop-up menu in the upper-left corner of the Transparency palette and choose the third blend mode in the list, **Screen**. The Screen mode drops out the darkest colors and uses all others to brighten the document. As seen in Figure 8-12, the letters appear light; the flower starts light in the center and fades outward toward transparency. It's precisely the effect I want, and I didn't have to redraw or recolor a thing. (To learn more about creating custom gradient effects with Screen, read the sidebar, "How Color Space Affects Blend Mode," on the next page.)

   You may notice that the Screen mode lightens colors only until it exceeds the boundaries of the rear purple rectangle. This is because InDesign can blend objects only so long as there are objects to blend. When a blend mode arrives at an empty portion of a page or a pasteboard, the object returns to its normal appearance. But not to worry; our problem transition is well outside the document, outside even the bleed. Press the W key to enter the Preview mode and the wonky details disappear from view.

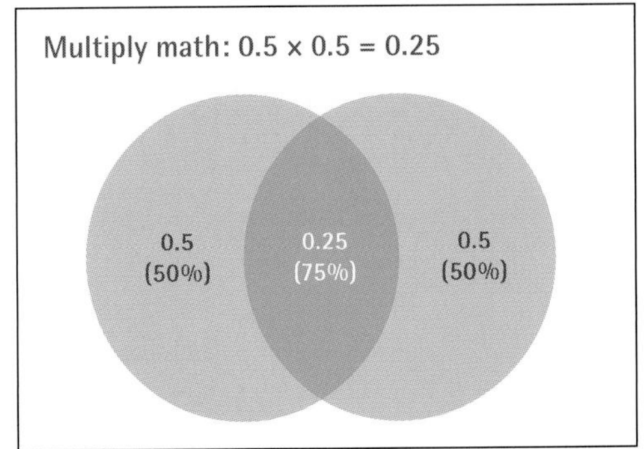

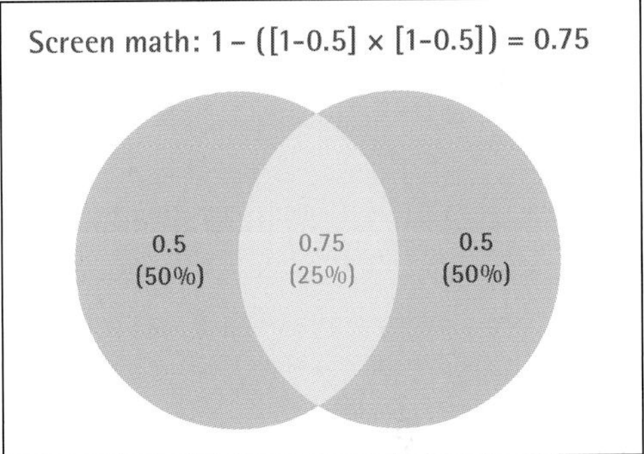

Figure 8-10.

Figure 8-11.

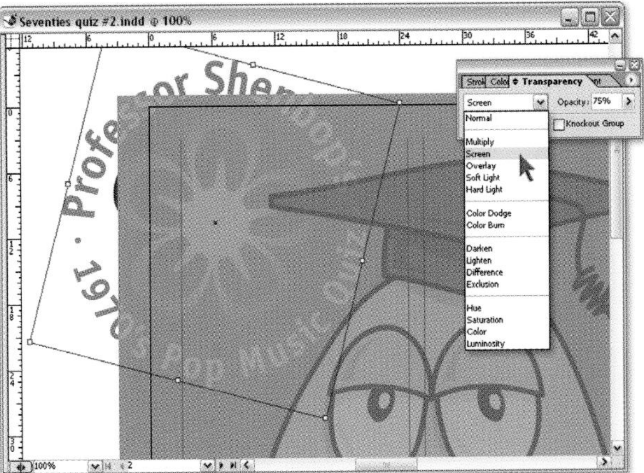

Figure 8-12.

How Color Space Affects Blend Mode

Like other varieties of transparency, blend modes—Multiply, Screen, Overlay, and the rest—grew up inside Photoshop. In fact, for an entire decade, they existed *only* in Photoshop. So it's hardly a coincidence that blend modes were specifically designed to suit digital photographs, scanned artwork, and other images stored in the RGB color space. When Adobe ported its blend modes over to InDesign, they met with a different default color space, CMYK. As a result, many blend modes behave differently in InDesign than they do in Photoshop.

To understand why this is, we have to take on a little color theory. Red, green, and blue are the primary colors of light. Cyan, magenta, and yellow are inks that absorb those lights. In this regard, the two color spaces are opposites. That turns out not to be a problem; because of the way InDesign normalizes color values, blend modes behave the same in RGB and CMY. Unfortunately, CMY*K* contains a pesky fourth ink, black. The black ink is great for filling in shadows and enhancing contrast, but it can create problems for blend modes.

By way of example, let's consider one of my favorite uses for blend modes in InDesign, creating custom gradients. I'll start by taking a rectangle and filling it with a linear gradient from bright red (C:0, M:100, Y:100, K:0) to deep blue (C:100, M:100, Y:0, K:50), as indicated by figure ❶. (The exact colors aren't important; these just happen to pop nicely on the page.) Now let's say I want to add a glow of light color to the lower-left corner of the shape. InDesign doesn't let me add colors to specific points in a filled shape, so I have to float another gradient on top. Ideally, this would be a light-to-transparent gradient—so the glow would be visible in the lower-left corner and that's it—but InDesign doesn't let me add transparency to gradients either. So my only option is to combine the floated gradient with a blend mode.

❶

Here's what I do: I draw another rectangle on top, precisely aligned to the first but a bit shorter (because I'm only trying to lighten the bottom of the first shape). I fill this one with a white-to-black gradient and use the gradient tool to angle it up and to the right, as in figure ❷. Note that there's a wealth of solid black at the top of the forward shape; this ensures that the top of the shape will turn transparent when I drop out the blacks.

❷

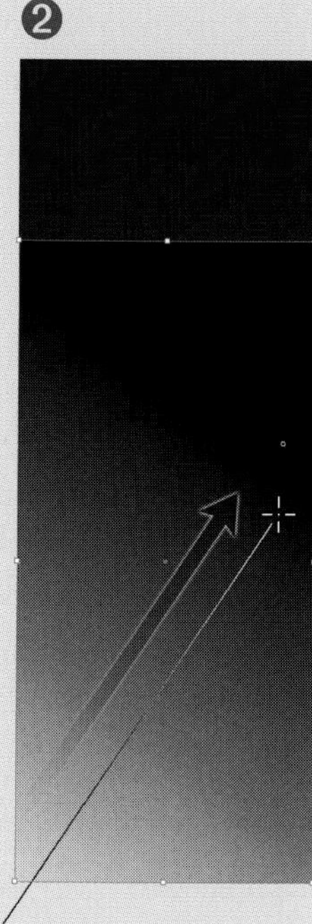

I go to the Transparency palette and choose the blend mode that keeps the whites and tosses out the blacks, Screen. If I were working on an RGB image in Photoshop, the blacks would completely drop out, leaving just a light highlight. But in the CMYK environment of InDesign, I'm left with a white-to-light gray gradient that doesn't even mildly resemble what I want, as in figure ❸.

The culprit is the way black is represented in CMYK, which is not as the absence of all light, as in RGB, but as solid black ink. The Screen mode doesn't expect that, and so it fails. One possible solution is to ask InDesign to calculate blend modes in RGB instead of CMYK. I do this by choosing Edit→Transparency Blend Space→Document RGB. Depending on the specifics of your color management settings, this may actually solve the problem. But more likely, you'll end up with a more colorful but still wrong gradient, like the one shown in figure ❹.

The more foolproof solution is to redefine black in the white-to-black gradient as a *rich black*, filled with all four inks. With the front rectangle still selected, I bring up the Gradient palette and click the color stop for black. Then I switch to the Color palette. By default, black is defined as C:0, M:0, Y:0, K:100—that is, solid black ink, but no cyan, magenta, or yellow. The Screen mode therefore reads the front gradient as bright in the CMY space and leeches all colors but gray from the red-to-blue gradient. To remedy this, I need to crank up the CMY values to their maximums. I choose CMYK from the palette menu to see all inks. Then I change the values to read C:100, M:100, Y:100, K:100 (100 percent across the board). The blacks in the front rectangle now drop off to complete transparency, thus producing the gorgeous multidirectional gradient pictured in figure ❺.

The moral of the story? When a blend mode fails you, try choosing Edit→Transparency Blend Space→Document RGB. This solution is acceptable even when your document is ultimately bound for CMYK output. (If in doubt, consult the Separations palette, which I introduce in Video Lesson 12, "Previewing Color Separations.") Note, however, that this command affects all blend modes in a document, not just the one you're having problems with. If changing the blend space doesn't work—or you're just worried about the print-worthiness of your document—try redefining the CMYK ingredients of your blacks.

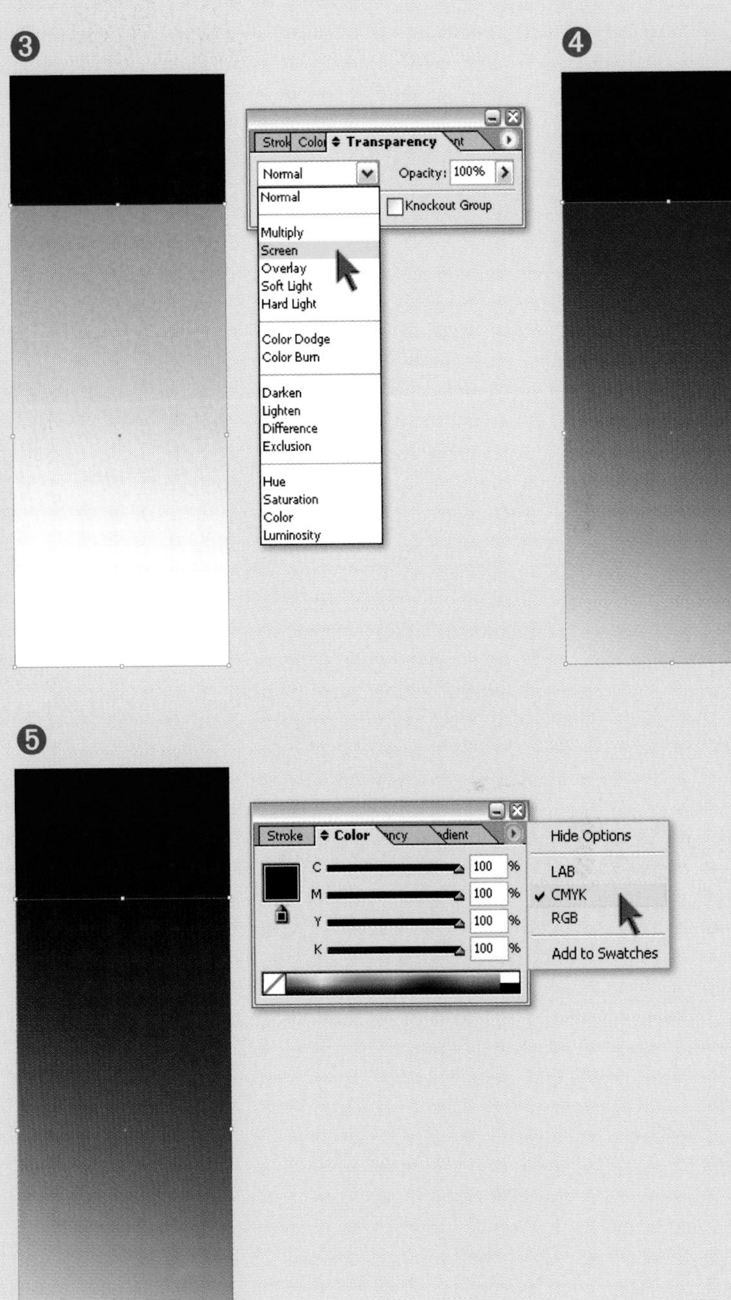

10. ***Assemble the artwork into a knockout group.*** The last remaining problem is to resolve the odd interactions between our blended graphics. If you look closely, you can see the edge of an *s* and a small bullet intersecting the left side of Shenbop's mortar board. Worse, we can see through the poor frog's translucent feet to his shadow. That's no good, so here's what you do:

    - Select all three graphics—the logo, the shadow, and Shenbop. It's probably easiest if you click on one of the items and Shift-click the other two.
    - Choose **Object→Group** or press Ctrl+G (⌘-G on the Mac) to group them all together.
    - With the massive group selected, go to the **Transparency** palette and turn on the **Knockout Group** check box.

    Just like that, the various objects inside the group no longer show through each other. As shown in Figure 8-13, Shenbop's feet and mortar board hide the shadow and text behind them, and our facing page graphics are complete.

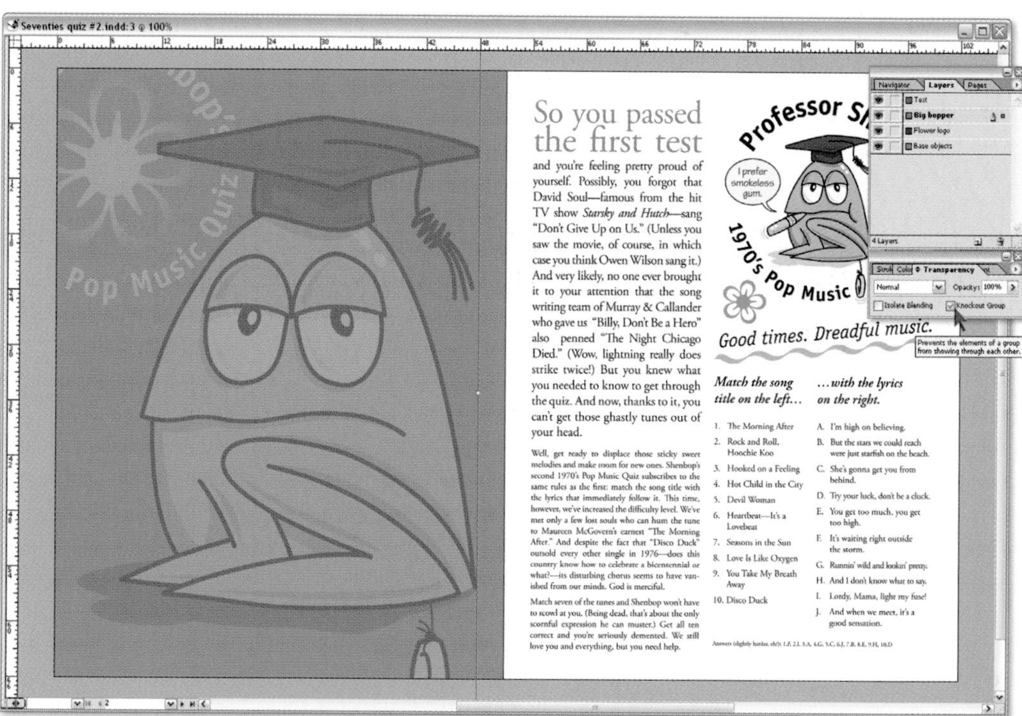

Figure 8-13.

The Transparency palette contains one more check box, Isolate Blending. Like Knockout Group, this check box controls blending inside a group. But instead of preventing blending inside the group, it prevents the group from blending with anything outside it, turning off blend modes but leaving translucency intact. If that sounds pretty obscure, it's because it is. My recommendation is to have fun experimenting with Opacity adjustments and blend modes and not worry too much about the check boxes. If a pesky problem arises, group your blended objects and fiddle with turning the check boxes on and off. If the problem goes away, great; if not, no harm done.

Drop Shadows and Feathers

This next exercise is about just two commands: Drop Shadow and Feather. The Drop Shadow command creates a translucent shadow behind an object. The Feather command blurs the object's edges, so that it fades gradually into the background. Although the two commands have different purposes, they are actually very similar functions. Both employ InDesign's transparency capabilities. Both are live effects, meaning that you can edit them long after applying them. Both are equally applicable to both type and graphics. And both are more capable than you might imagine.

In the following steps, we'll use the Drop Shadow and Feather commands to add a bit of depth to a document. Along the way, we'll explore some unorthodox but highly rewarding uses for these effects.

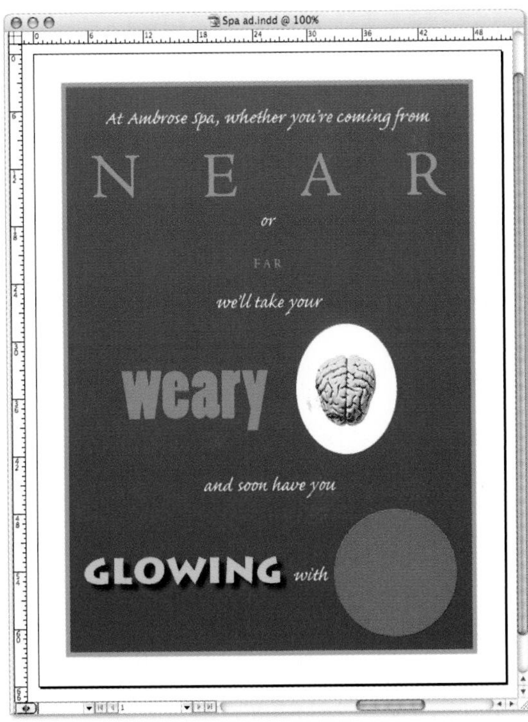

Figure 8-14.

1. *Open a file in need of shadows and feathering.* Open the file named *Spa ad.indd*, which is located in the *Lesson 08* folder inside *Lesson Files-IDcs 1on1*. Shown in Figure 8-14, this single-page document contains a series of independent text blocks and graphics relegated to different layers. The layers don't affect the Drop Shadow or Feather command; they merely make the objects easier to select.

2. *Choose the Drop Shadow command.* We'll start by applying a drop shadow to the word *NEAR* at the top of the page. Click on the word *NEAR* with the black arrow tool and choose **Object→Drop Shadow** or press Ctrl+Alt+M (⌘-Option-M on the Mac) to bring up the **Drop Shadow**

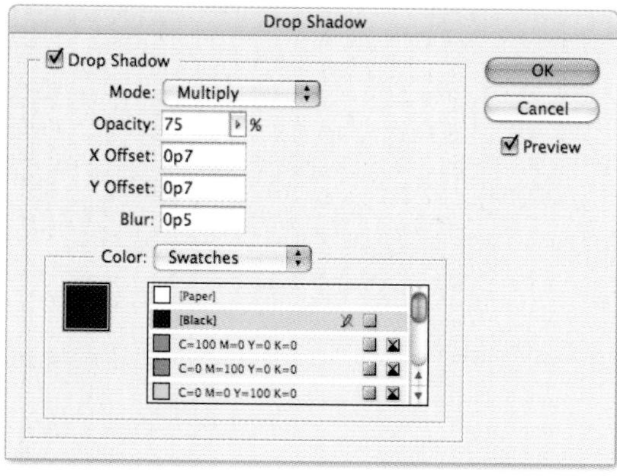

Figure 8-15.

dialog box, shown in Figure 8-15. As usual, I recommend that you turn on the **Preview** check box so you can see what you're doing. Then turn on the **Drop Shadow** check box to create a dark shadow behind the text (assuming you use the default settings).

Here's a quick rundown of the options at your disposal:

- The Mode pop-up menu lets you select a blend mode. Multiply is the best choice for creating a shadow because it ensures that the shadow darkens everything behind it. But there are plenty of other options for experimenting with soft glows and other effects, as you'll see in Step 6.
- Lower the Opacity value to create increasingly translucent shadows.
- The X and Y Offset values position the shadow with respect to the object that is casting it. Positive values move the shadow down and to the right. Negative values move the shadow up and to the left.
- Blur determines the sharpness of the shadow. A value of 0p0 creates a razor-sharp shadow; higher values increase the blurriness.
- The Color option lets you choose a method for setting the color of the shadow. The default setting of Swatches gives you access to colors defined in the Swatches palette. You can also choose RGB, CMYK, or Lab to display sliders and dial in custom color values.

3. *Specify the Drop Shadow settings.* We want the word *NEAR* to appear far from the page and near to the reader. So we'll create a drop shadow that's a good distance from the text:

   - Click the **X Offset** value to select it, then enter –1p6 and press the Tab key. The shadow moves 18 points to the left of the text.
   - Change the **Y Offset** value to 3 and press Tab. The shadow moves 3 picas down.
   - If the text is supposed to be far away from the surface that's catching its shadow, then that shadow should be blurry. Enter a full pica for the **Blur** value.

   The values should appear as they do in Figure 8-16. When they do, click **OK**. The word *NEAR* hovers high above the page.

4. ***Apply a drop shadow to the word* FAR.** If we want the word *NEAR* to hover closer to the read, then the word *FAR* should be farther back—that is, close to the page. Select the text block for the word *FAR* and choose **Object→Drop Shadow** once again. Then do like so:

   - Turn on the **Drop Shadow** check box.
   - Close text makes for a dark shadow. So raise the **Opacity** value to 100 percent.
   - I want the word *FAR* to observe the same light source as the word *NEAR*, which means a negative X Offset and a positive Y Offset value twice as large. Tab to the **X Offset** value and change it to –1pt.
   - Press Tab to advance to **Y Offset** and change it to 2pt.
   - Again press Tab and lower the **Blur** value all the way to 0. Note that you can nudge these values with the ↑ and ↓ arrow keys if you like.

   When the values look like those in Figure 8-17, click the **OK** button.

5. ***Dismiss the warning message.*** InDesign displays an alert message, which claims that the shadow you're about to create is likely to increase the complexity of the file and slow down the print process (see Figure 8-17). Like people, some error messages are full of baloney. A drop shadow with a Blur value of 0 is nothing more than a direct copy of the object that is casting it. Meanwhile, the shadow is 100 percent opaque, so InDesign's transparency function doesn't even enter into the picture. Select the **Don't show again** check box and click **OK** to move along.

6. ***Adjust the drop shadow for the word* GLOWING.** Scroll down to the yellow word *GLOWING* and select it. This text already has a drop shadow applied. But the shadow isn't really glowing, is it? Let's see if we can't come up with something a little more appropriate.

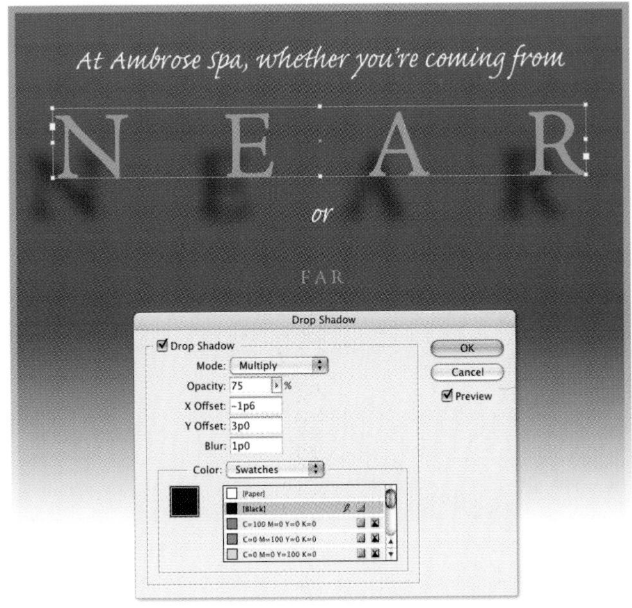

Figure 8-16.

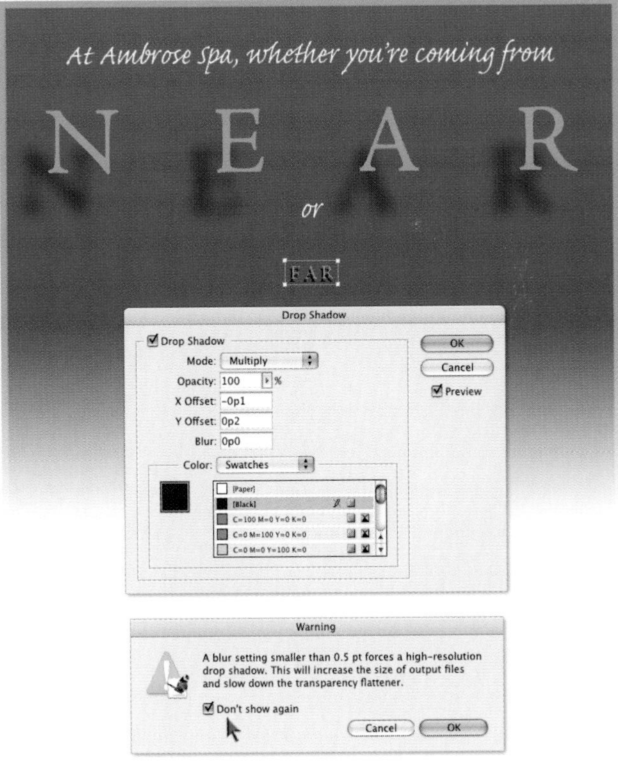

Figure 8-17.

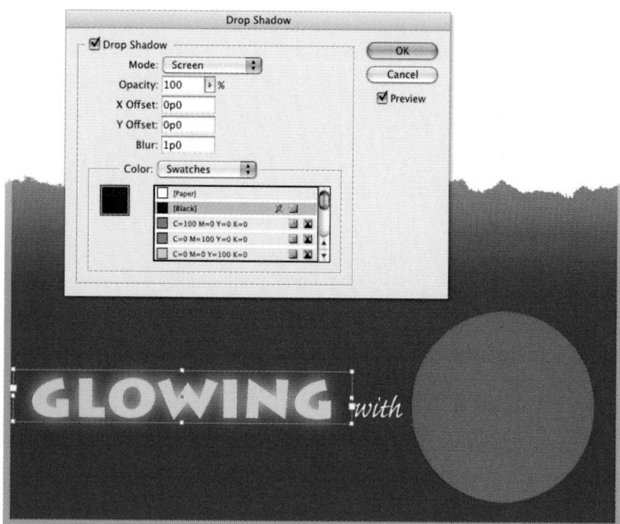

Figure 8-18.

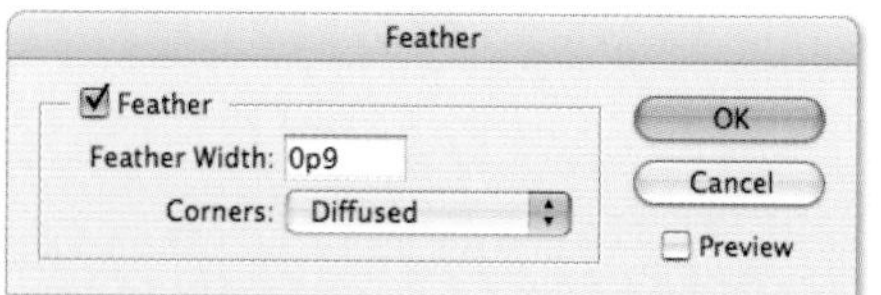

Figure 8-19.

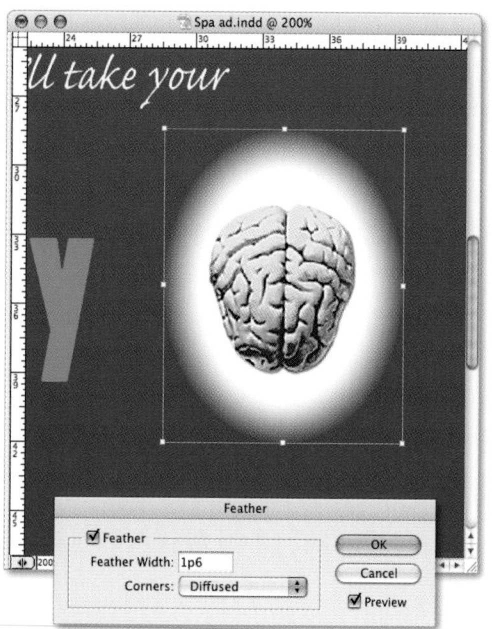

Figure 8-20.

To edit the existing shadow, choose **Object→Drop Shadow** or press Ctrl+Alt+M (⌘-Option-M). Then change the settings as follows:

- Change the **Opacity** value to 100 percent.
- I want the text to glow evenly in all directions, so change both the **X Offset** and **Y Offset** values to 0.
- Raise the **Blur** value to 1 pica.
- To get a glowing effect, click the **Mode** option to unfurl the pop-up menu. Then choose **Screen**. Oddly, applying the Screen mode to the Black color swatch results in a bright glow. Because the Black swatch contains only black ink, the other colors brighten. (See the sidebar "How Color Space Affects Blend Mode" on page 296 for more info.)

Click the **OK** button to make the text emit a soft glow, as in Figure 8-18.

7. ***Feather the brain.*** Now let's move on to the Feather command. Select the brain image and choose **Object→Feather**. If you loaded Deke Keys as directed on page xvii of the Preface, you can also press Ctrl+Shift+Alt+M (⌘-Shift-Option-M on the Mac). Either way, you get the **Feather** dialog box (see Figure 8-19). Turn on the **Feather** and **Preview** check boxes to bring the function to life. The remaining two options work as follows:

   - Use the Feather Width value to define the amount by which you want to blur the perimeter of the selected object. A bigger value means more blur.
   - The Corners pop-up menu offers three options. The first, Diffused, blurs away any corners in the selected shape. To bolster the corners, select Rounded to smooth them off or Sharp to keep them crisp. We'll see examples of all these in the upcoming steps.

8. ***Specify the Feather settings.*** For our part, we want to blur the perimeter of the brain to create a *vignette* effect. So leave **Corners** set to **Diffused**. Then raise the **Feather Width** value to 1p6 and click **OK**. Our lovely brain now possesses a soft, flattering vignette, which I think goes a long way toward masking those unsightly wrinkles. But why take my word for it when Figure 8-20 permits you to judge for yourself?

9. ***Feather the word* weary.** The Feather command produces a decidedly strange effect when applied to text, giving the letters a gooey, stencil-like look. To see what I mean, click the word *weary* and choose **Object→Feather**. Turn on the **Feather** check box. To make the letters appear less ghostly and more worn, set the **Corners** option to **Rounded**. Then tab to the **Feather Width** value and use the ↓ key to nudge down the effect until the text appears barely legible, which happens at about 0p7. When you're done, click **OK**. The word *weary* should appear suitably beaten, as in Figure 8-21.

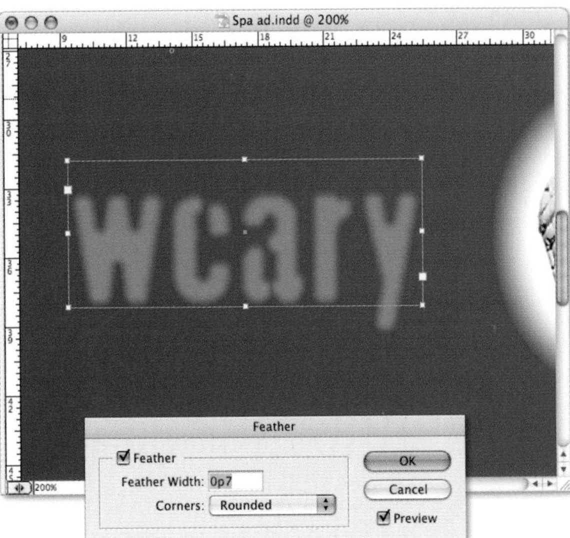

Figure 8-21.

If you're familiar with feathering images in Photoshop, it may strike you that the perimeters of the letters look pretty awful. Truth be told, InDesign's feathering never manages to equal Photoshop's—InDesign employs a simpler, "flat" algorithm—but it shouldn't look this bad. To make it look better, right-click on the text. (Or if your Apple mouse lacks a right mouse button, press the Control key and click.) Then choose **Display Performance→High Quality Display**. Even though you may already have your screen set to the high-quality display setting, applying the feature directly to a drop shadow or feather effect makes it look better on screen. Go figure.

EXTRA CREDIT

For our final act, we'll turn the large red circle in the lower-right corner of the document into an embossed disk with a tangible sense of depth. We'll accomplish this by adding a beveled edge effect using a clever combination of the Drop Shadow and Feather commands (even if I do say so myself). If you aren't interested, skip to the next exercise, "Using Clipping Paths and Alpha Channels," which begins on page 306. Or suspend your disinterest and continue on to Step 10.

10. ***Examine the various layers.*** Press F7 or choose **Window→Layers** to bring up the **Layers** palette, which contains the items pictured in Figure 8-22. The bottom layer, Locked Layer, contains the blue background and white text in the document. The next one up, Text and Graphic, contains all the text you've worked with so far as well as the brain. The rest is all red circle. You'd hardly know it to look at it, but the red circle is actually a pile of many red objects—three circles and two text blocks. I've broken the shapes and text blocks onto five layers so that we can more easily select them.

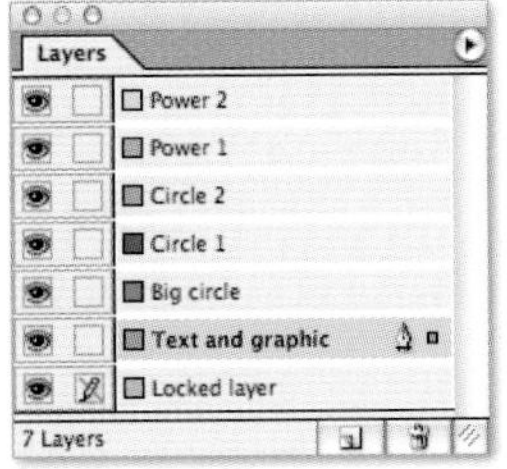

Figure 8-22.

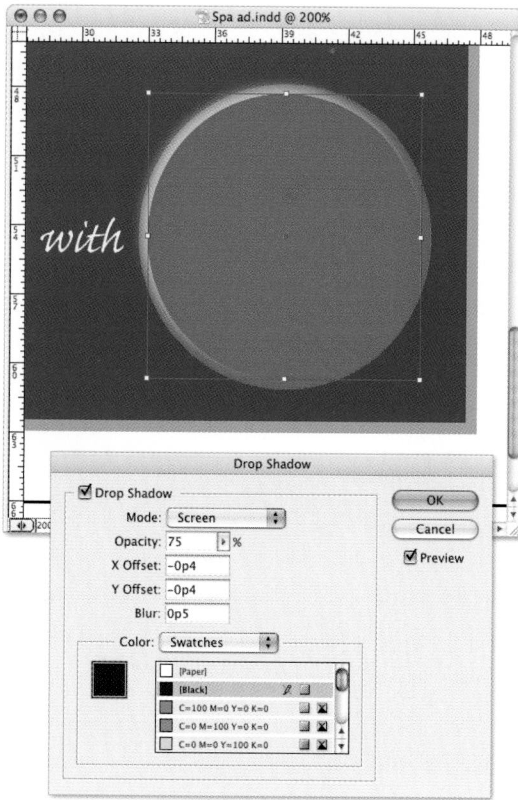

Figure 8-23.

11. *Add a drop glow to the Circle 1 layer.* Start by Alt-clicking (or Option clicking) the **Circle 1** layer in the Layers palette. This selects the content of the layer, which just so happens to be one of two identical inset red circles.

    Now to add a highlight that simulates a light source hitting the edge of an embossed shape:

    - Choose **Object→Drop Shadow** and turn on the **Drop Shadow** check box.
    - Set the **Mode** option to **Screen**.
    - Change both the **X Offset** and **Y Offset** values to –0p4 and click **OK**. Things should now appear as they do in Figure 8-23.

12. *Feather the Circle 1 layer.* Now to soften the circle slightly. Choose **Object→Feather** and turn on the **Feather** check box. Leave **Corners** set to **Diffused**, set the **Feather Width** to 0p2, and click **OK**. You won't see any difference at this point because there's an identical shape in back of this one. But have patience, the softening will come through in the next step.

13. *Shade and feather the Circle 2 layer.* Next, let's repeat the process with a slight twist on the other twin inset circle. Alt-click (or Option-click) the **Circle 2** layer in the Layers palette to select the shape. Then do the following:

    - Choose **Object→Drop Shadow**, turn on the **Drop Shadow** check box, set both the **X Offset** and **Y Offset** values to 0p4, and click **OK**. Rather than getting a glow, we get a shadow progressing in the opposite direction.
    - Choose **Object→Feather**, turn on the **Feather** check box, set the **Feather Width** value to 0p2, and click **OK**.

    As Figure 8-24 shows, the three red circles—the two we edited and the one in the background—now resemble a raised disk.

14. ***Add a drop shadow to the Power 1 layer.*** Alt-click (or Option-click) the **Power 1** layer to select what appears to be an empty frame. This is actually a text block that contains the word *POWER*, set in red. I want the word to appear recessed into the disk. Here's how:

    - Choose **Object→Drop Shadow** and turn on the **Drop Shadow** check box.
    - Set the **Mode** option to **Screen** to achieve a highlight.
    - Change both **Offset** values to 0p1.
    - Set the **Blur** value to 0. And click **OK**. The button text should now appear to have a subtle highlight.

15. ***Shade and feather the Power 2 layer.*** We are now ready for the top and final object. Alt-click (or Option-click) the **Power 2** layer in the Layers palette. This selects the front text block, which contains another copy of the red word *POWER*. We'll use this text block to create the shading around and inside the letters:

    - Choose **Object→Drop Shadow**, turn on the **Drop Shadow** check box, change both **Offset** values to –0p1, set the **Blur** to 0, and click **OK**.
    - Choose **Object→Feather**, turn on the **Feather** check box, change the **Feather Width** to 0p3, set the **Corners** option to **Sharp**, and click **OK**.
    - The Feather command has the effect of offsetting the text slightly. So press the ↓ key and then the → key to nudge the text block into better alignment.

As illustrated in Figure 8-25 on the next page, the Drop Shadow and Feather commands can be combined to impart the illusion of depth in an otherwise flat document. Remember, to make the effect look better, right-click on the selected text and choose **Display Performance→High Quality Display**. The *POWER* disk is now complete, and so is our ad.

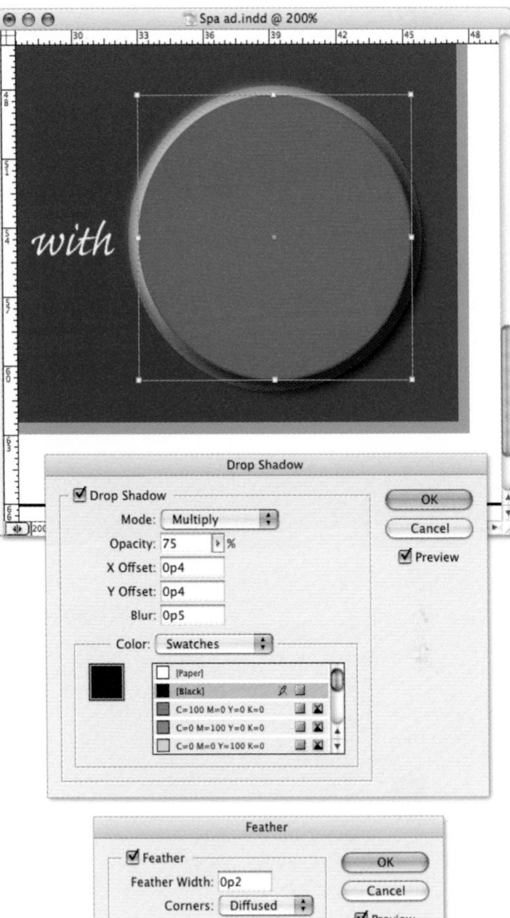

Figure 8-24.

Using Clipping Paths and Alpha Channels

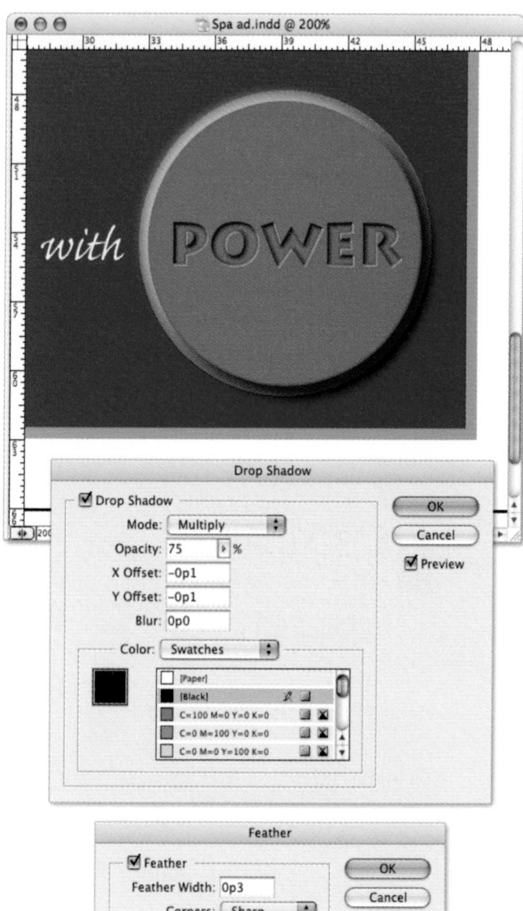

Figure 8-25.

According to the rules of the PostScript printing language, vectors may convey transparency but images may not. For example, suppose you take a circle drawn in FreeHand and place it into QuarkXPress. Because the circle is a vector, Quark knows to treat everything inside the circle as opaque and everything outside as transparent. But draw that same circle in Photoshop, and Quark sees it very differently. According to the sacred text of PostScript, every pixel must be opaque. So what appears as a layered circle set against a transparent background in Photoshop looks like a circle inside an opaque white rectangle in Quark.

Thankfully, the designers of PostScript came up with a clever solution: If an image can't be transparent, why not place it inside a vector, which can? To create a circular photograph, for example, you would place a flat image file inside a circular vector-based frame. The portion of the photo inside the frame is opaque; the portion outside is transparent. Such a frame is called a *clipping path* because it's a path outline that clips an image into a custom shape.

The illustrious Photoshop first introduced support for clipping paths in 1993, more than a year before it added layers. And yet, almost a dozen years later, clipping paths remain the only way to carve images into non-rectangular artwork in QuarkXPress, PageMaker, and most other vector programs. Fortunately, InDesign is the exception. Like the sophisticated drawing programs Illustrator and FreeHand, InDesign can import a native Photoshop document, complete with layers, and recognize the exact amount of translucency applied to each and every pixel. As a result, you can import soft-edged images, something QuarkXPress and its contemporaries cannot do.

In this exercise, you'll experiment with two varieties of transparency. First, you'll import an image that contains a clipping path. Then, you'll swap the hard-edged clipping path for a soft-edged alpha channel. To perform these steps in their entirety, you'll need to have Adobe Photoshop (included with InDesign if you purchased the Creative Suite) running on your computer. If you don't have Photoshop CS, you should be able to get by okay with an older version of Photoshop. If you don't own any version of Photoshop, *c'est la vie*. With a few very minor adjustments (which I'll explain as we go), you'll still be able to complete the project just fine.

1. ***Launch Photoshop.*** Make sure Photoshop is running. If you have Photoshop CS, launch that. But Photoshop 6 or 7 should work just as well.

   If you do not own Photoshop, continue reading for now. (In other words, no skipping—I have a couple of things to show you.) I'll switch back to InDesign in Step 7 (page 309), at which point you can take up mouse and rejoin our elaborate game of Simon Says.

2. ***Open an image that contains one or more paths.*** Using File→Open or Photoshop's File Browser, open the image called *Bird with paths.tif*, included in the *Lesson 08* folder inside *Lesson Files-IDcs 1on1*. Pictured in Figure 8-26, this vibrant composition features a pelican-shaped trash can against an oddly colored, aqueous background.

   (If you read *Adobe Photoshop CS One-on-One*, you may recognize this pelican trash can as part of a project we created using Photoshop's pen tool and Paths palette. This time around, we'll be experiencing those same paths in a large, cross-application context.)

Figure 8-26.

3. ***Display the Paths palette.*** Choose **Window→Paths** (or click the **Paths** tab in the Layers palette) to display the **Paths** palette. This palette contains vector-based path outlines that you can convert to selections inside Photoshop or employ as clipping paths outside the program. We'll be doing the latter.

4. ***Select a clipping path.*** In all, I've added three paths to this image. The first exactly traces the outline of the cartoon trash can; the second is a sun pattern; the third adds some bubbles to the trash can outline. The thumbnail icon next to each path name preview shows how the clipping path will work. The white areas are inside the path and thus opaque; the gray areas are outside the path and transparent. As you'll see in Step 10 (page 311), you can access from inside InDesign any path outline saved

with an image. But it's typically a good idea to identify one as a clipping path before leaving Photoshop, if only to establish a preferred setting.

Click the **Peli Can** path in the Paths palette. The path appears in the image window. Then click the ⊙ arrow to display the palette menu and choose the **Clipping Path** command, as in Figure 8-27. Make sure the **Path** option in the Clipping Path dialog box is set to Peli Can and then click **OK**.

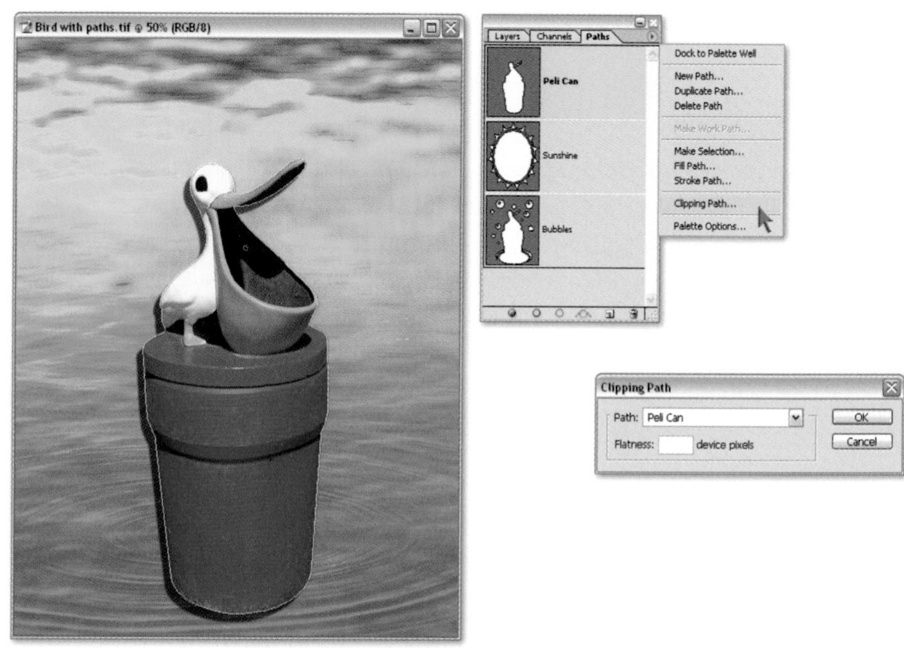

Figure 8-27.

Now press the Shift key and click **Peli Can** in the Paths palette to turn the path off. On the PC, the path name remains bold. On the Mac, it appears bold and outlined. Either way, you know it is now the clipping path that will be used to frame the image when you import it into InDesign, QuarkXPress, or some other page-layout program.

5. ***Take a look at the alpha channels.*** Another way to specify transparency in a Photoshop image is to add an *alpha channel*. Also known as *masks*, alpha channels distinguish opaque from transparent areas using pixels instead of vectors. To see the alpha channels that I've added to this image, click the **Channels** tab at the top of the Paths palette or choose **Window→Channels**. Photoshop displays the **Channels** palette. The palette begins

with the composite RGB image followed by the independent Red, Green, and Blue channels. The remaining channels, Silhouette through Final Mask, are the alpha channels.

The thumbnails next to each channel name preview the mask. White indicates opacity; black means transparency. You can also view the mask and image together. Click in the box to the left of the last channel, **Final Mask**, to show the 👁 icon and make the channel visible. As demonstrated in Figure 8-28, Photoshop displays the mask as a cyan overlay. Any place you see cyan will turn transparent. The cyan overlay gradually fades away toward the center of the image, suggesting that under the right circumstances, this alpha channel might result in soft transitions.

6. ***Save your changes to the image.*** That's enough in Photoshop. But before you leave, you need to save your clipping path designation. Choose **File→Save** or press Ctrl+S (⌘-S on the Mac). In a flash, Photoshop updates the file on disk.

7. ***Open the InDesign document.*** Switch back to InDesign CS. (Those of you who've been waiting for the Photoshop steps to end, it's time to get back to work.) Then open the document called *Pelican page.indd* from the *Lesson 08* folder inside *Lesson Files-IDcs 1on1*. Pictured in Figure 8-29, this single-page news story includes a handful of blended gradients, several text blocks, and a large empty frame ready to accept the Photoshop image.

8. ***Place the trash can image.*** With black arrow tool in hand, click the big frame with the X through it to select it. Then choose **File→Place** or press Ctrl+D (or ⌘-D). Select the *Bird with paths.tif* file in the *Lesson 08* folder. Make sure the **Replace Selected Item** check box is turned on, and then click **Open**. If you successfully completed Steps 1 through 6, the pelican trash can appears separated from its background inside the selected frame, as in Figure 8-30 on the next page. If not, you see the entire image, complete with its toxic yellow-orange background. Either way is okay for now—we'll all end up with the same result in just a few steps.

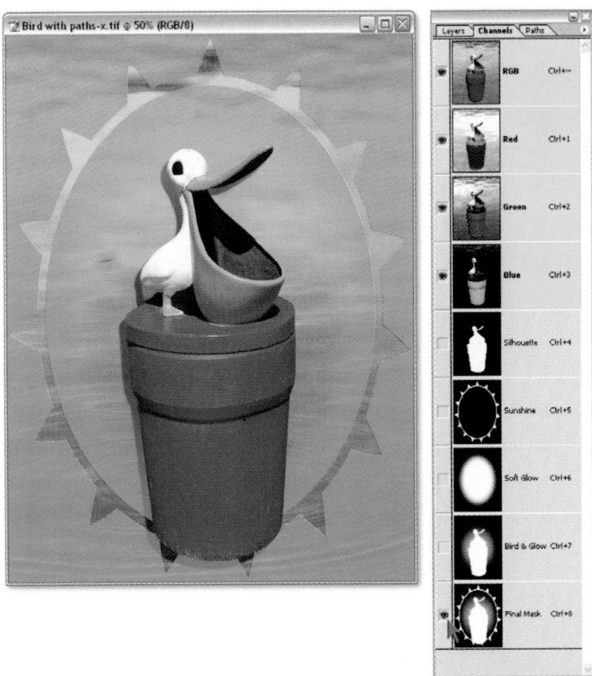

Figure 8-28.

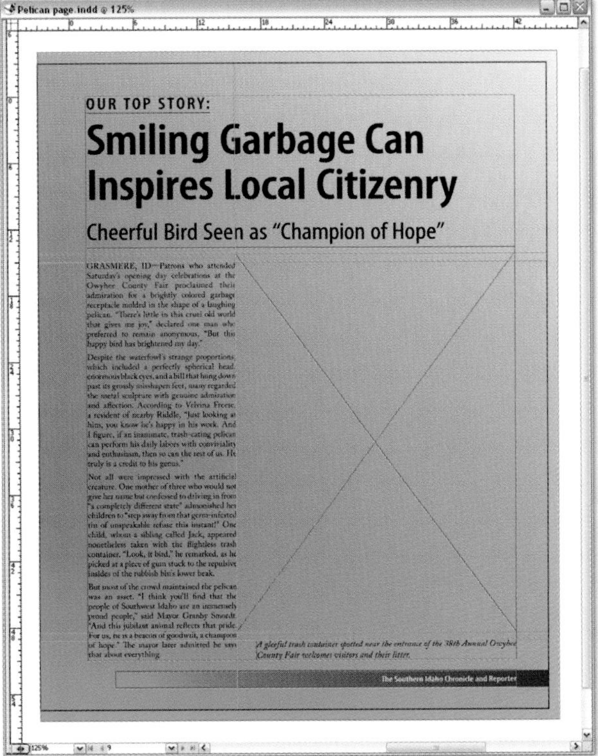

OUR TOP STORY:

Smiling Garbage Can Inspires Local Citizenry

Cheerful Bird Seen as "Champion of Hope"

GRASMERE, ID—Patrons who attended Saturday's opening day celebrations at the Owyhee County Fair proclaimed their admiration for a brightly colored garbage receptacle molded in the shape of a laughing pelican. "There's little in this cruel old world that gives me joy," declared one man who preferred to remain anonymous. "But this happy bird has brightened my day."

Despite the waterfowl's strange proportions, which included a perfectly spherical head, enormous black eyes, and a bill that hung down past its grossly misshapen feet, many regarded the metal sculpture with genuine admiration and affection. According to Velvina Freese, a resident of nearby Riddle, "Just looking at him, you know he's happy in his work. And I figure, if an inanimate, trash-eating pelican can perform his daily labors with conviviality and enthusiasm, then so can the rest of us. He truly is a credit to his genus."

Not all were impressed with the artificial creature. One mother of three who would not give her name but confessed to driving in from "a completely different state" admonished her children to "step away from that germ-infested tin of unspeakable refuse this instant!" One child, whom a sibling called Jack, appeared nonetheless taken with the flightless trash container. "Look, it bird," he remarked, as he picked at a piece of gum stuck to the repulsive insides of the rubbish bin's lower beak.

But most of the crowd maintained the pelican was an asset. "I think you'll find that the people of Southwest Idaho are an immensely proud people," said Mayor Granby Smoot. "And this jubilant animal reflects that pride. For us, he is a beacon of goodwill, a champion of hope." The mayor later admitted he says that about everything.

A gleeful trash container spotted near the entrance of the 38th Annual Owyhee County Fair welcomes visitors and their litter.

The Southern Idaho Chronicle and Reporter

Figure 8-29.

9. ***Add a slim drop shadow.*** To provide the pelican with some additional definition, choose **Object→Drop Shadow** or press Ctrl+Alt+M (⌘-Option-M). Then do the following:

   - Turn on the **Drop Shadow** check box.
   - Leave the **Mode** option set to **Multiply**. Raise the **Opacity** value to 100 percent.
   - Set the **X Offset** to –0p2 and the **Y Offset** to 0p2. This nudges the shadow down and to the left.
   - Reduce the **Blur** to 0p2 to match the Offset values.

   Assuming the **Preview** check box is on, you'll see the shadow in the document window. If it looks like the one shown in Figure 8-31, click the **OK** button to apply it. (If you see the entire Photoshop image, your shadow overlaps slightly into the text. We'll fix that shortly.)

Figure 8-30.

Figure 8-31.

PEARL OF WISDOM

As a result of the active clipping path, the pelican is too small to fill the space I've allotted it. Therefore, the active clipping path might strike you as a bad idea. Fortunately, InDesign gives you ample opportunity to change your mind. Just because you import an image with a clipping path doesn't mean you have to use that clipping path. You can turn off the clipping path, turn on a different path, or even generate one from an alpha channel.

---

10. ***Swap one clipping path with another.*** To exercise any of these options, choose **Object→Clipping Path**. If you loaded Deke Keys back on page xvii of the Preface, you can take advantage of the keyboard equivalent Ctrl+Shift+Alt+C (or ⌘-Shift-Option-C). InDesign loads the **Clipping Path** dialog box, which lets you extract a clipping path from an image.

    Here are a few tricks you might like to try:

    - To turn off the active clipping path, choose **None** from the **Type** pop-up menu. Then turn on the **Preview** check box to see the restored background.
    - If you do not own Photoshop and therefore have yet to see the original clipping path in play, set Type to **Photoshop Path**. And then choose **Peli Can** from the **Path** pop-up menu.
    - To try out other paths saved with the image, make sure Type is set to Photoshop Path. Then select either **Sunshine** or **Bubbles** from the Path menu. Figure 8-32 shows the effect each setting has on the placed graphic.
    - If you prefer to work from one of the soft masks saved with this image (those that we saw in Step 5), choose **Alpha Channel** from the Type menu. Then select the mask name from the **Alpha** pop-up menu, which lists every single one of the five alpha channels pictured back in Figure 8-28 (see page 309).

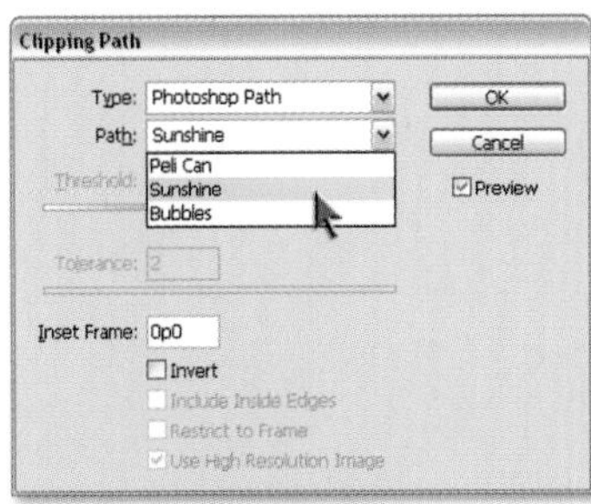

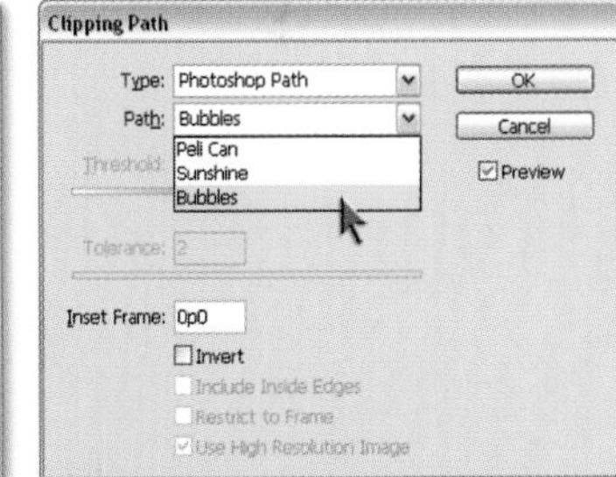

Figure 8-32.

- Choose **Final Mask** from the Alpha menu to load the most elaborate of the masks, which I created by combining elements of the four previous masks. Surprisingly, InDesign ends up displaying only its outer perimeter, as witnessed by the first example in Figure 8-33. To remedy this oversight, turn on the **Include Inside Edges** check box. This carves out the inner portion of the sunshine shape. Then raise the **Threshold** value to 160, which expands the size of the inner ellipse, as shown on the right side of the figure.

PEARL OF WISDOM

If you've been following events closely, you might notice a tiny disconnect. Back in Step 5, I said alpha channels permit soft transitions. And yet the edges in Figure 8-33 are every bit as sharp those associated with clipping paths. That's because these *are* clipping paths. The Clipping Path dialog box cannot load a mask with its softness intact; instead, it traces a clipping path around the mask. The Threshold value determines where along the softness that trace occurs; raising the value spreads the path outward, lowering the value chokes it inward. (You can also use the Tolerance value to smooth over rough edges, though I generally leave this value unchanged.)

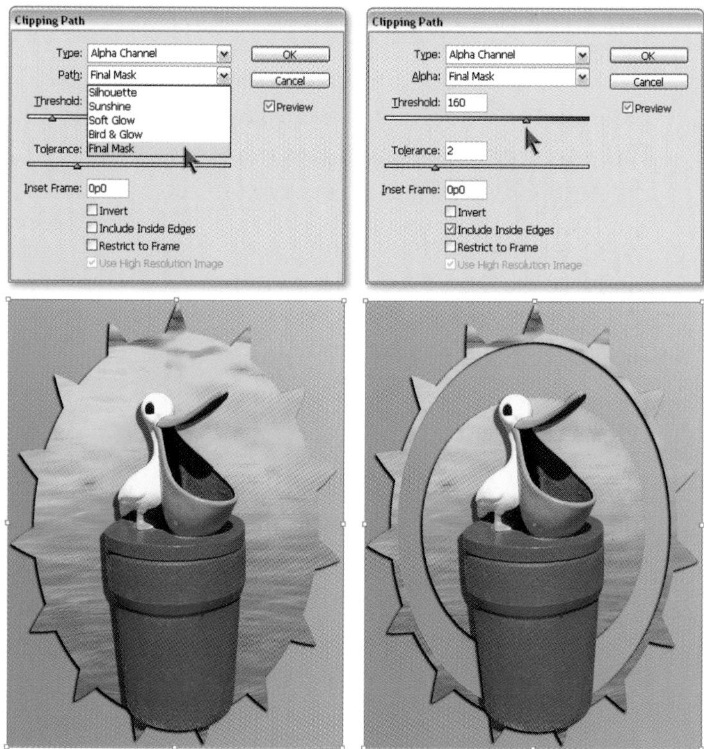

Figure 8-33.

In the final analysis, the Clipping Path dialog box is the cat's meow when it comes to loading predefined clipping paths and something of a hairball when tracing alpha channels. If the alpha channel is really what you want, you're better off reimporting the image, as I discuss in Step 13.

11. ***Set the clipping path to Bubbles.*** That last step was essentially a minute or two of educational play time. Now, let's make a choice. Set the two pop-up menus at the top of the dialog box to **Photoshop Path** and **Bubbles**, respectively. Then click **OK**. Figure 8-34 shows the resulting graphic replete with surrounding text.

12. ***Edit the clipping path.*** Let's say you're not quite happy with the clipping path. No problem, you can edit it right here inside InDesign. Press the A key to switch to the white arrow tool. Then click anywhere on the pelican. InDesign displays all the anchor points and segments that make up the clipping path. You can make whatever adjustments you like, but here's what I recommend:

   - Press the Alt key (Option on the Mac) and click the outline for the bubble directly to the left of the pelican's fanny. This selects the entire circle, as in the left example of Figure 8-35.

Figure 8-34.

Figure 8-35.

- Press Shift and Alt (or Shift and Option) and click the outline of the inset circle to select it as well.
- Drag the two circles up and slightly to the right to fill in the gap toward the top of the image, as illustrated on the right side of Figure 8-35.

If you see other things you want to change, by all means, soldier on. Clipping paths behave like paths drawn with InDesign's pen tool, so feel free to apply any of the path-editing techniques you learned in Lesson 6, "Drawing inside InDesign." For example, you can move independent anchor points, drag control handles, and even add or subtract points using the pen tool. When you finish, press the V key (or Enter on the keypad) to exit the path edit mode and return to the black arrow tool.

Figure 8-36.

EXTRA CREDIT

At this point, you've seen just about everything there is to see on the topic of creating, importing, and modifying clipping paths. But that's just one method for assigning transparency to an image, and a relatively narrow method at that. The remaining steps in this exercise document another means of communicating transparency from Photoshop to InDesign: alpha channels. Rather than converting an alpha channel to clipping paths, as illustrated back in Figure 8-33, we'll instruct InDesign to ignore clipping paths altogether and respect all levels of translucency in the mask, something QuarkXPress and others can't do.

13. *Replace the trash can image.* The only time you can tell InDesign to lift an alpha channel from an image file is when you import it. In other words, we have to reimport the pelican trash can art. Make sure the black arrow tool is active and the image remains selected. Choose **File→Place** or press Ctrl+D (⌘-D) and again select the file *Bird with paths.tif* in the *Lesson 08* folder. However, this time, I want you to turn on the **Show Import Options** check box (highlighted in Figure 8-36), which is your doorway to InDesign's support for alpha channels. Then click the **Open** button to proceed.
14. *Select the desired alpha channel.* Because you selected Show Import Options, InDesign displays the **Image Import Options** dialog box, which permits you to modify clipping path and mask settings. We

won't be needing a clipping path this time around. So turn off the **Apply Photoshop Clipping Path** check box to ignore the Peli Can path that you assigned back in Step 4 (see page 307). Select **Final Mask** from the **Alpha Channel** option. Click the **OK** button to replace the previous version of the pelican graphic with the new one.

Unfortunately, as shown in Figure 8-37, the artwork looks terrible. If you're thinking that it looks like some sick, twisted combination of both an alpha channel and a clipping path, you're absolutely right. Even though you specifically requested that InDesign lay off the clipping path, the previous path, our customized variation on Bubbles, remains in force. I'm afraid it's up to you to manually eliminate it.

15. *Turn off the clipping path.* Choose **Object→Clipping Path**. Select **None** from the **Type** pop-up menu. Then click **OK**. InDesign shows the image masked only by the alpha channel, complete with gradual transitions between opacity and transparency, thus imparting the hundreds of incremental levels of translucency that we see on display in Figure 8-38.

Figure 8-37.

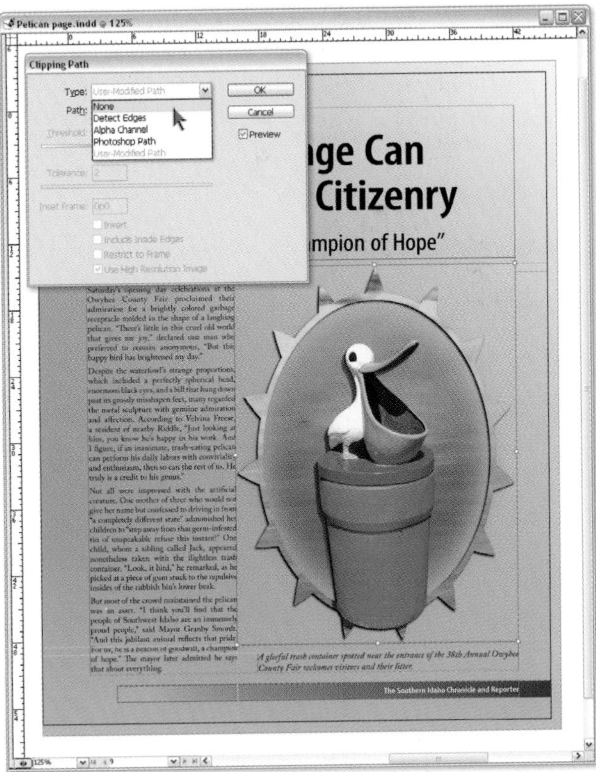

Figure 8-38.

Compare Figure 8-38 to the likes of Figure 8-33 and earlier, and you may notice a general darkening of the happy pelican graphic, especially toward the center of the image. This is a function of the drop shadow you applied in Step 9. Although very slight—just 2 points of offset and blur—it has a pronounced effect on the soft transitions. Because every semi-opaque pixel casts a shadow, and every semi-transparent pixel lets you see through it to the shadow below, translucent pixels actually magnify a drop shadow. If you don't care for the darkening, turn off the effect by choosing Object→Drop Shadow and clicking the Drop Shadow check box. Purely for the sake of reference, Figure 8-39 compares the placed pelican with a drop shadow to the same image without.

With drop shadow

Without

Figure 8-39.

Importing Layered Photoshop Artwork

There's no denying that clipping paths and alpha channels are powerful tools, ones that remain in prevalent use to this day. But neither is the best way to convey transparency from Photoshop to InDesign. Clipping paths are too circumscribed, alpha channels are too obscure, and both are too much work. They are decade-old answers to a thoroughly modern question.

The best solution is the simplest. Create the desired combination of translucent layers and effects in Photoshop, save your artwork in Photoshop's native PSD format, and then import that very same layered image into InDesign. We'll explore these steps using a variation on the pelican image and newspaper article from the previous exercise. This time, the trash can composition is more elaborate, involving a degree of transparency that would be impossible to achieve with clipping paths and exceedingly difficult (if not likewise impossible) with alpha channels. And yet, the procedure involves less work and fewer steps.

Again, we'll start inside Photoshop. Follow along if you can; hang in there if you can't.

Figure 8-40.

1. ***Open a layered image in Photoshop.*** If Photoshop is still open, switch to it; otherwise, launch the application. Then open *Bird with layers.psd* in the *Lesson 08* folder inside *Lesson Files-IDcs 1on1*. Pictured in all its trashy avian glory in Figure 8-40, this PSD file contains a total of four layers, which you can see by choosing **Window→Layers** or pressing F7 to display the **Layers** palette.

2. ***Hide all but the bottom layer.*** Just so you're clear on exactly what you'll be placing inside Photoshop, let's take a moment to walk through the layers and change the composition to bring in some transparency. For starters, press the Alt key (Option on the Mac) and click the 👁 in front of the last layer, **Tide**. This hides all but the bottom layer, which is nothing more than a photo of some water.

3. ***Mask the bottom layer.*** See the white-on-black oval with a red X through it to the left of the word *Tide* in the Layers palette? That's a kind of alpha channel that controls the opacity of a single layer, called a *layer mask*. Currently, it is off, hence the red X. To turn it on, press the Shift key and click on the oval. The layer becomes transparent where the layer mask is black—that is, outside the oval—as shown in Figure 8-41.

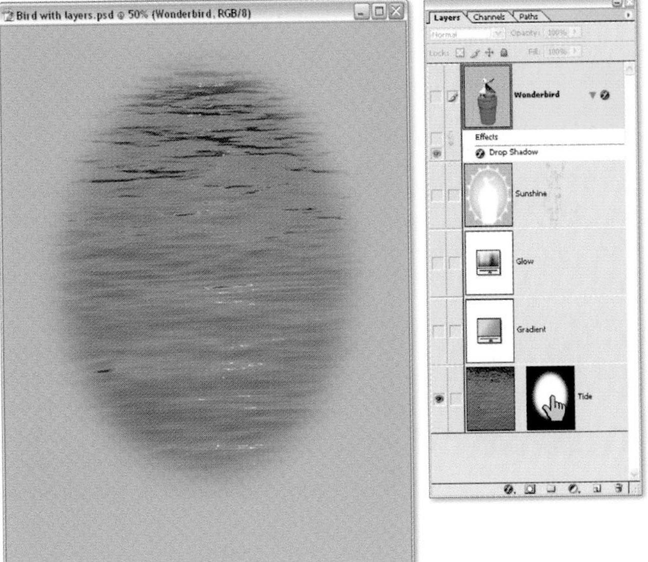

Figure 8-41.

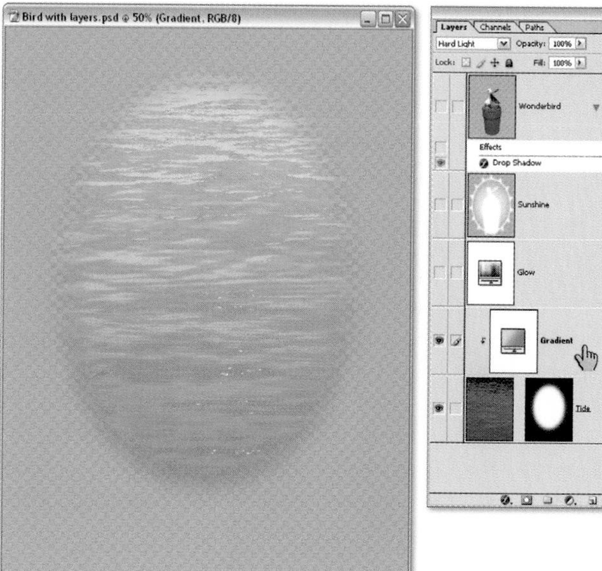

Figure 8-42.

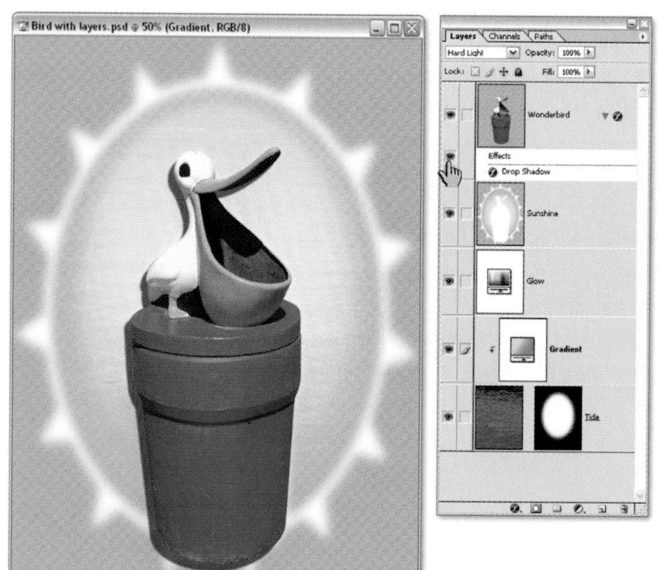

Figure 8-43.

The checkerboard pattern behind the oval water layer represents the void of transparency. Your checkerboard is probably gray and white, as it is by default. I've edited mine to give me a better sense of what the image will look like against the blue-green background in InDesign. To make your checkerboard match mine, press Ctrl+K and Ctrl+4 (⌘-K, ⌘-4) to display the **Transparency & Gamut** options. Click the white square under ▩ Light to display the **Color Picker** dialog box; change the H, S, and B values to 220, 30, and 90, respectively; and click **OK**. Then click the gray square; change its H, S, and B values to 160, 30, and 85, respectively; and click **OK**. Click **OK** again to exit the dialog box. Mind you, this has no effect on the final appearance of the image; it merely helps you to better gauge the results of your edits.

4. ***Group the Gradient and Tide layers.*** Click the word **Gradient** in the Layers palette. This displays the layer and makes it active. This yellow-to-red gradient should appear only inside the oval. To mask the gradient with the layer behind it, choose **Layer→Create Clipping Mask** or press Ctrl+G (⌘-G on the Mac). Photoshop groups the two layers to create a *clipping mask*, in which the bottom layer in a group masks those above it. A clipped layer appears indented in the Layers palette, as in Figure 8-42.

5. ***Turn on the other layers.*** Click in the box to the far left of each of the **Glow**, **Sunshine**, and **Wonderbird** layers. This brings back their 👁 icons and shows the layers in the document window. The Glow layer brightens the colors; Sunshine contains a silhouette of white pixels; and Wonderbird gives us the bird. Lastly, click the box to the left of the word **Effects** to unveil the drop shadow. The finished composition appears as shown in Figure 8-43. If it looks a little pale, don't worry; it'll pop nicely on the InDesign page.

6. ***Turn on Maximum File Compatibility.*** Before saving the revised composition, we have to visit a special saving preference that helps InDesign

interpret layered Photoshop files. Choose **Edit→Preferences→File Handling** (**Photoshop→Preferences→File Handling** on the Mac) or press Ctrl+K followed by Ctrl+2 (⌘-K, ⌘-2). Midway down, you'll see a **Maximize PSD File Compatibility** pop-up menu. Set it to **Ask** (see Figure 8-44) and click the **OK** button.

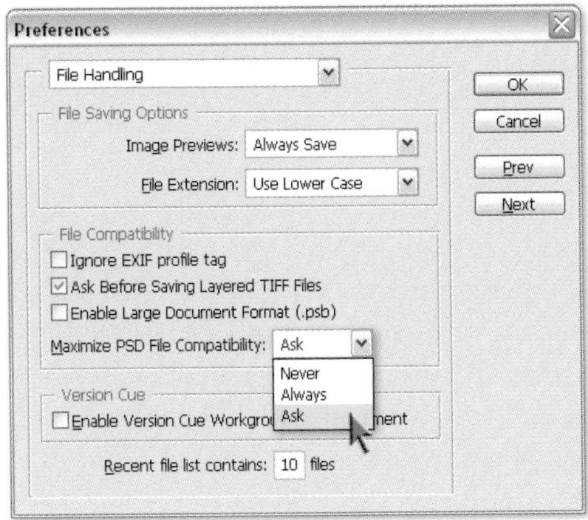

Figure 8-44.

7. *Save the image under a new name.* Choose **File→Save As** or press Ctrl+Shift+S (⌘-Shift-S). Change the filename to "Bird with MFC.psd" and make sure the **Save in** option is trained on the **Lesson 08** folder. Turn on the **Layers** and **ICC Profile** check boxes (see Figure 8-45) and then click the **Save** button. Photoshop displays a slim alert message, asking how you'd like to save the image. Make sure the **Maximize Compatibility** check box is turned on and click **OK**. Thanks to this option, Photoshop creates two versions of the image together inside a single file: The first version contains all layers so that you can open and edit them in Photoshop; the second one collapses the layers to reduce InDesign's overhead when printing and exporting the image.

8. *Open the InDesign document.* Switch back to InDesign CS and open the same document we worked on in the previous exercise, *Pelican page.indd* in the *Lesson 08* folder inside *Lesson Files-IDcs 1on1*. If you recently completed the last exercise and still have the document open, choose **File→Revert** to restore the saved version of the file.

9. *Place the layered trash can image.* Select the empty frame with the X through it with the black arrow tool. Choose **File→Place** or press Ctrl+D (⌘-D on the Mac). Select the *Bird with MFC.psd* file in the *Lesson 08* folder. (If you don't own Photoshop, select the image that I built ahead of time for you, *Built bird.psd*, also in the *Lesson 08* folder.)

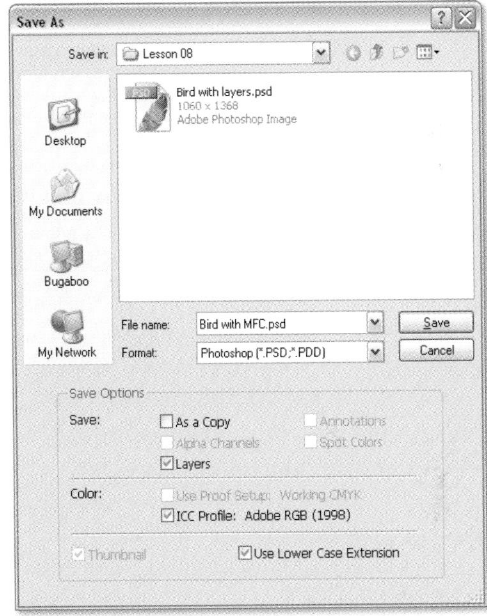

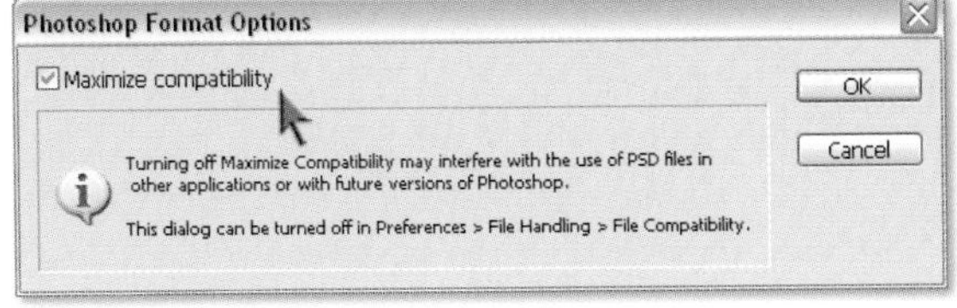

Figure 8-45.

Rasterization and the Flattener Preview Palette

InDesign's wealth of transparency and effects functions are a marvel to behold. But as beautiful as your pages may look on screen, there's always the nagging issue of output. Given that the industry-standard PostScript printing language doesn't support a single one of InDesign's transparency functions—including Opacity settings, blend modes, drop shadows, and imported Photoshop layers—how can we have any confidence whatsoever that this stuff is going to print?

The answer lies in InDesign's ability to translate something that PostScript can't possibly understand into something that it can. Consider that every line, shape, and character of text eventually gets converted to printer dots. These dots are tiny, densely packed squares—in other words, pixels. So a printed page is ultimately just another bitmapped image, albeit one that contains 100 times as many pixels as a typical digital photograph. For example, the page spread you're looking at now contains more than a billion printer dots.

The act of converting vectors to pixels is called *rasterization*. When printing to a PostScript printer, the rasterization is performed by a *raster image processor*, or *RIP* (pronounced *rip*) for short. The RIP may be a piece of hardware or software, the latter being easier to update. In the normal course of printing, InDesign conveys its text and graphics as mathematical objects and lets the RIP convert them to pixels. But when InDesign comes across something that the RIP won't understand, like a translucent or blended object, it simplifies the objects by *flattening* them. When expedient, InDesign flattens objects by breaking them into lots of little vector objects (as when rendering a gradient to a few hundred bands of color). Otherwise, it converts the objects into a high-resolution image. In this regard, InDesign is capable of serving as its own software RIP.

By way of example, take a look at the modified pelican article on the right. (To inspect this page more closely, open the file *Flattener sample.indd* in the *Lesson 08* folder.) The background is a single rectangle filled with a gradient. Among the translucent objects:

- The footer in the lower-right corner of the page features another gradient set to the Multiply blend mode.
- The white headline includes a drop shadow.
- The graphic is a layered Photoshop image.

To see how InDesign plans to flatten the document, choose Window→Output Preview→Flattener to display the Flattener palette. Then choose an option from the Highlight pop-up menu. Any setting but None grays out the document and adds red to call attention to areas that require special treatment. The Highlight menu contains lots of options, but you need to concern yourself with only two:

- Choose All Affected Objects to see all the objects that are slated for flattening. Because the background contains a gradient—which has to be broken into smaller vectors—all but the opaque text turns red.
- To see just those areas InDesign intends to rasterize, choose All Rasterized Regions. As illustrated on the facing page, only the three translucent areas—the drop shadow, the placed Photoshop art, and the multiplied footer gradient—turn red.

Lest you regard the red highlights as rough approximations, rest assured that you are seeing the precise boundaries between vector and raster art. PostScript requires images to be rectangular, so InDesign rasterizes in rectangles. In the case of the pelican page, InDesign is showing us that it means to put the gradient at the bottom of the stack, the three raster rectangles above that, and the vector-based text on top.

Although InDesign rasterizes portions of a page to assist the printer, it doesn't do so at the full resolution of the printer. That would lead to long print times or possibly print failure. Instead, InDesign rasterizes paths and text at about half the resolution of a high-end PostScript device and sets drop shadows and gradients to 300 pixels per inch (ppi). These are good settings; if you decide to change them, I recommend doing so only slightly. For example, in printing this book, I adjusted the path and text resolution a bit higher and the drop shadow and gradient resolution a bit lower. Here's how I did it:

- I chose Transparency Flattener Presets from the palette menu (as indicated by ❶ in the figure below right).
- Inside the Transparency Flattener Presets dialog box, I selected the best of the flattener settings, High Resolution, as a base for my changes and then clicked the New button (❷ in the figure) to display the Transparency Flattener Preset Options dialog box.
- I named my new preset "Best Resolution" and then Tabbed down to the Line Art and Text Resolution value (❸).
- While the resolutions of professional-level PostScript imagesetters vary, one of the more prevalent standards is 2,540 dots per inch (dpi). So I increased the Line Art and Text Resolution value from 1200 ppi to precisely half the printer resolution, 1270 ppi. It's unlikely anyone will notice the difference, but the higher value can smooth out the appearance of very high-contrast raster edges.
- Drop shadows and rasterized gradients (like the one behind the footer) are so soft that the resolution makes little difference. So you might as well lower the value a bit. I reduced my Gradient and Mesh Resolution value to 254 ppi (❹), or 1/10 the printer resolution.
- I clicked OK in each of the two dialog boxes to accept my changes and create the new preset. Then I chose Best Resolution from the Preset pop-up menu in the Flattener Preview palette. And I clicked Apply Settings to Print to make my new preferences the default settings when printing the document.
- Finally, I clicked the Refresh button to confirm that my rasterized areas remained intact, which they had.

When you're satisfied that you understand what will flatten during output, choose None from the Highlight pop-up menu to return the document to its normal appearance. Then close the Flattener Preview palette, safe in the knowledge that InDesign is fully capable of converting your bold experiments in transparency to the buttoned-down world of PostScript.

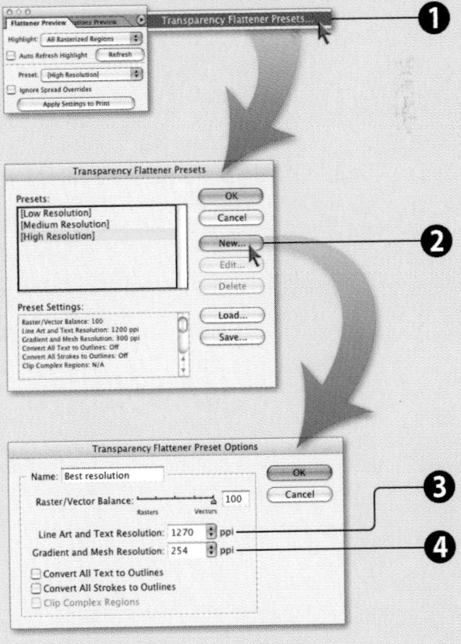

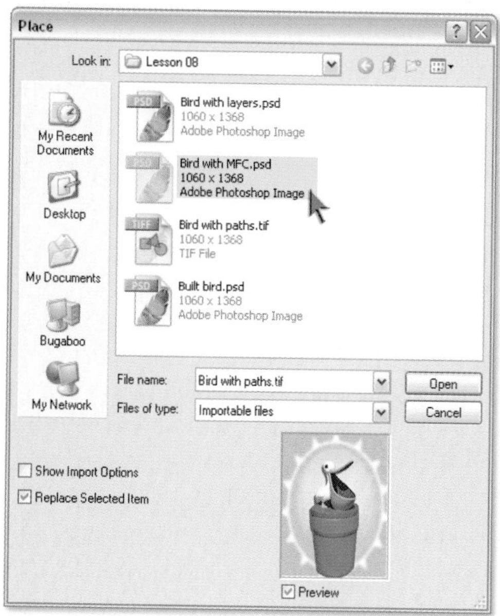

Figure 8-46.

Make sure the **Replace Selected Item** check box is turned on and **Show Import Options** is off, as in Figure 8-46. Then click **Open**. The Photoshop image fills the selected frame, with all layers, effects, and relationships intact.

The layered Photoshop image looks great in its new home, but not perfect. Specifically, the image hugs the body copy to the left of it too closely, and it doesn't appear centered over its caption. To fix this, I pressed Shift+→ six times to nudge the image and its frame 60 points to the right. Figure 8-47 shows the final page in the preview mode, with the image in position, deselected, and blending ever so seamlessly with its gradient background. If ever there was a better looking bird, I haven't seen it. And forgive me while I stress: This awe-inspiring merging of imagery and page layout is in no way, shape, or form possible in QuarkXPress.

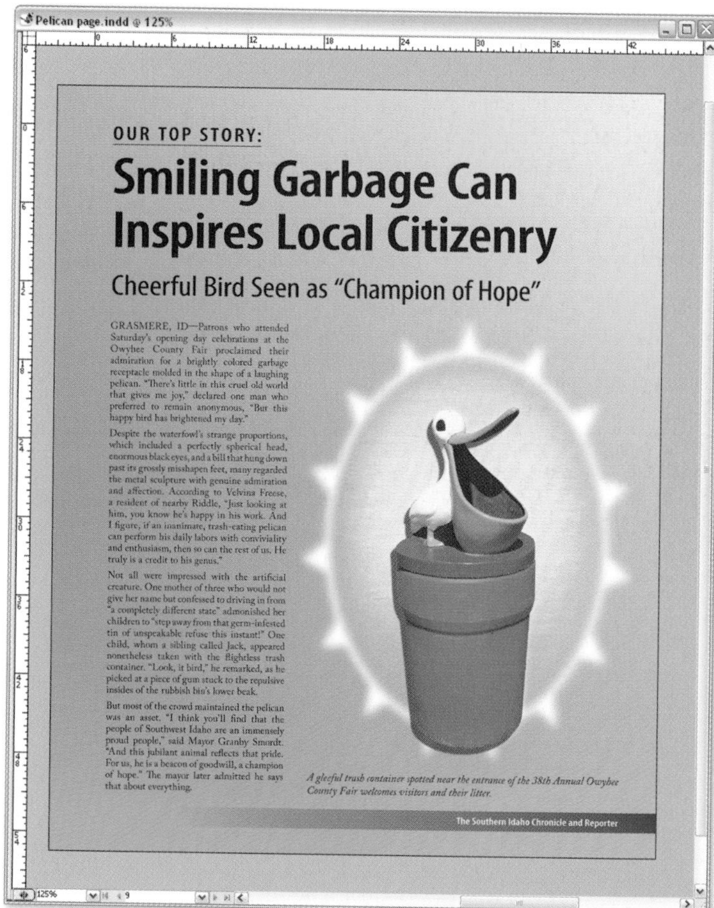

OUR TOP STORY:

Smiling Garbage Can Inspires Local Citizenry

Cheerful Bird Seen as "Champion of Hope"

GRASMERE, ID—Patrons who attended Saturday's opening day celebrations at the Owyhee County Fair proclaimed their admiration for a brightly colored garbage receptacle molded in the shape of a laughing pelican. "There's little in this cruel old world that gives me joy," declared one man who preferred to remain anonymous, "But this happy bird has brightened my day."

Despite the waterfowl's strange proportions, which included a perfectly spherical head, enormous black eyes, and a bill that hung down past its grossly misshapen feet, many regarded the metal sculpture with genuine admiration and affection. According to Velvina Freese, a resident of nearby Riddle, "Just looking at him, you know he's happy in his work. And I figure, if an inanimate, trash-eating pelican can perform his daily labors with conviviality and enthusiasm, then so can the rest of us. He truly is a credit to his genus."

Not all were impressed with the artificial creature. One mother of three who would not give her name but confessed to driving in from "a completely different state" admonished her children to "step away from that germ-infested tin of unspeakable refuse this instant!" One child, whom a sibling called Jack, appeared nonetheless taken with the flightless trash container. "Look, it bird," he remarked, as he picked at a piece of gum stuck to the repulsive insides of the rubbish bin's lower beak.

But most of the crowd maintained the pelican was an asset. "I think you'll find that the people of Southwest Idaho are an immensely proud people," said Mayor Granby Smordt. "And this jubilant animal reflects that pride. For us, he is a beacon of goodwill, a champion of hope." The mayor later admitted he says that about everything.

A gleeful trash container spotted near the entrance of the 38th Annual Owyhee County Fair welcomes visitors and their litter.

The Southern Idaho Chronicle and Reporter

Figure 8-47.

WHAT DID YOU LEARN?

Match the key concept in the numbered list below with the letter of the phrase that best describes it. Answers appear upside-down at the bottom of the page.

Key Concepts

1. Transparency
2. Opacity
3. Blend mode
4. Luminosity
5. Multiply
6. Rich black
7. Knockout group
8. Live effect
9. Clipping path
10. Alpha channel
11. Layered image
12. Rasterization

Descriptions

A. This blend mode maintains the lights and darks of the selected object and lets the background colors show through.

B. The name Adobe gives to a group of live effects that permit you to see through all or part of an object to the objects behind it.

C. Usually saved as a PSD file, this special kind of photographic composition conveys predefined areas of translucency, eliminating the need for clipping paths or alpha channels.

D. A vector-based frame that carves a photograph or other imported image into a custom shape.

E. A method for mixing the colors of overlapping objects using prescribed mathematical equations.

F. Also called a mask, this special image element distinguishes opaque from transparent areas using pixels instead of vectors, thus permitting soft or gradual transitions.

G. Useful for creating shadows, this blend mode drops out the whites in the selected object and burns in the blacks and other colors to create a darkening effect.

H. This Transparency palette option prevents different objects in a group from interacting with each other.

I. The act of converting paths, text, and other vector-based objects to pixels, as performed by either InDesign or a PostScript RIP during the printing process.

J. A selected object becomes translucent when this Transparency palette value dips below 100 percent.

K. You can modify this sort of operation long after applying it; examples include blend modes and the Drop Shadow command.

L. A color created by mixing generous quantities of all four CMYK inks.

Answers

1B, 2J, 3E, 4A, 5G, 6L, 7H, 8K, 9D, 10F, 11C, 12I

LESSON 9

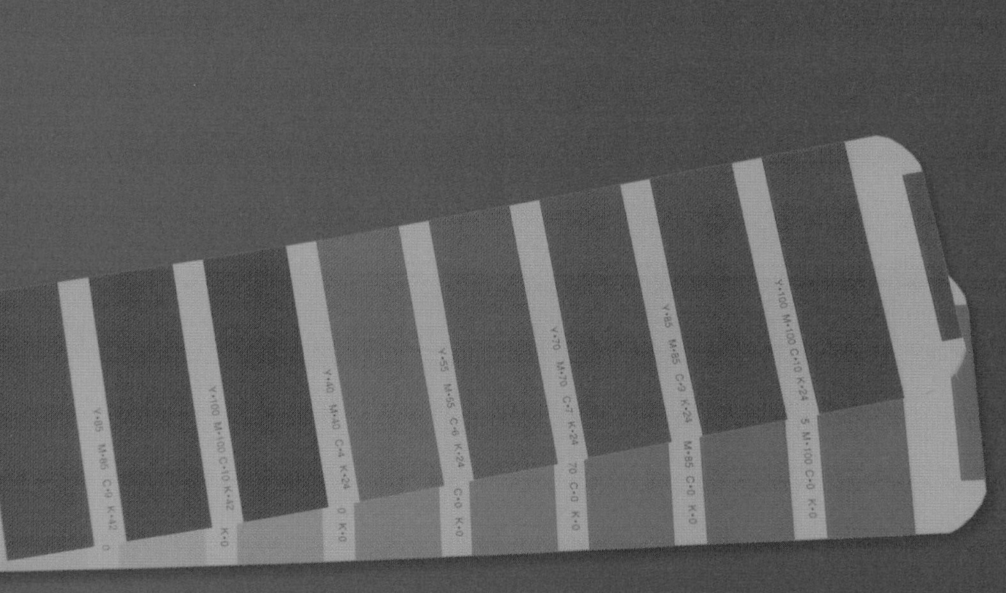

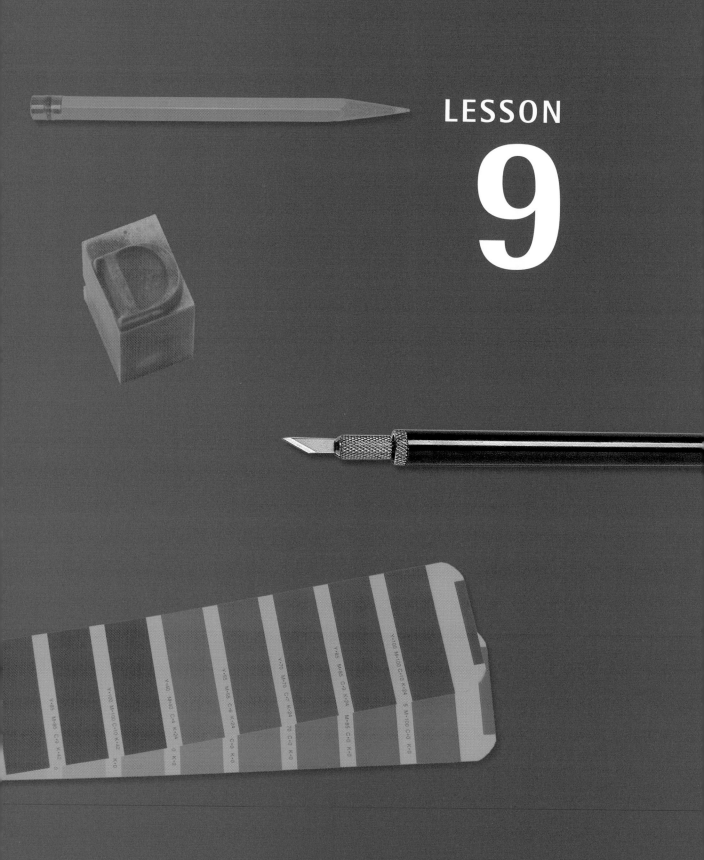

PAGES, LAYERS, AND XML

The bulk of what we've discussed so far has centered on creating, importing, and modifying the content of your documents. In other words, we've spent a whole lot of time with type and graphics. But with the exception of the exercises in Lesson 1, we've given precious little attention to the document itself. This paragraph marks the point at which we shift our collective focus. From here on out, it's all document all the time.

In this lesson, I introduce you to the big S word in the realm of page design, *structure*. If content is the heart, lungs, and brains of a document, the stuff that makes it work and gives it life, structure is the skeleton, the part that gives it form and holds it all together. It is structure's job to arrange, organize, and prioritize information (see Figure 9-1). Structure confines content, so that it's easier for you to edit and your reader to interpret. And it can aid in the assembly of a document, bringing pieces together and even automating repetitive tasks. Blessed with structure, your document becomes a walking, talking thing of beauty.

Content

Structured content

Figure 9-1.

Structure, Structure, Structure

In InDesign, structure takes three forms. First there are the pages, the physical containers that hold everything. Pages may correspond to real, tangible pieces of paper emitted from a printer. Or they may translate to virtual pages displayed on screen in a PDF document (as we'll explore at great length in Lesson 11, "Hyperlinks, Bookmarks, and PDF"). But they always result in rectangular

ABOUT THIS LESSON

Project Files

Before beginning the exercises, make sure that you've installed the lesson files from the CD, as explained in Step 5 on page xv of the Preface. This should result in a folder called *Lesson Files-IDcs 1on1* on your desktop. We'll be working with the files inside the *Lesson 09* subfolder.

In this lesson, we look at the three structures of a document: pages, master pages and layers, and XML. You'll learn how to:

Video Lesson 9: Managing Your Pages

Before you can successfully create a multipage document in InDesign, you must come to grips with the Pages palette. This humble collection of page icons lets you navigate between pages; add, move, duplicate, and delete pages; decide page numbering preferences; assign relationships between document and master pages—in short, it lets you manage the fundamental holding cells for the elements of your publication.

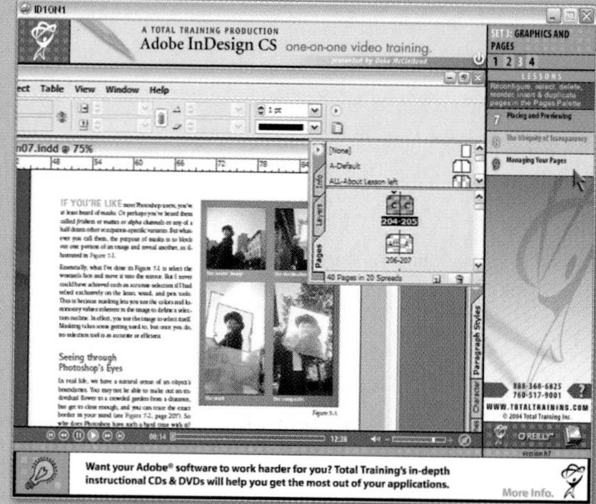

To acquaint yourself with this deceptively powerful feature, watch the ninth video lesson on the CD. Insert the CD, click the **Start Training** button, click the Set 3 button, and then select **9, Managing Your Pages** from the Lessons list. Lasting 12 minutes and 28 seconds, this movie introduces you to the following shortcuts and techniques:

Operation	Windows shortcut	Macintosh shortcut
Show or hide the Pages palette	F12	F12
Select a range of pages	Click one page, Shift-click another	Click one page, Shift-click another
Select multiple nonsequential pages	Ctrl-click page icon	⌘-click page icon
Delete selected pages and bypass alert	Alt-click trash can icon	Option-click trash can icon
Center page in document window	Double-click page icon	Double-click page icon
Add multiple pages at specific location	Alt-click ⊡ icon	Option-click ⊡ icon

collections of text and artwork, modeled after pages in those old-fashioned content containers with which we've communicated for hundreds of years, books.

Next come master pages and layers. These are virtual containers that let you separate and organize key elements of your document. A master page supplies the base elements for a group of pages, much as a piece of stationery provides the base elements for a series of letters or memos. Layers let you group and separate objects so that you can more easily select, lock, hide, edit, stack, and just plain keep track of them. And because InDesign makes a given layer available to all pages and master pages, you can use layers to send objects forward or backward throughout an entire document.

InDesign's third and final structural cohort is XML, the *Extensible Markup Language* developed by the World Wide Web Consortium (W3C). InDesign's support for XML is twofold: First, you can create and assign XML tags, which identify bits and pieces of your content according to the functions that they serve. Second, you can partition a page into XML elements and pair XML tags with style sheets. The result is an intelligent template that enables InDesign to import, position, and format all varieties of content—from individual characters of text to entire text blocks and graphics—in one breathtaking operation.

Conceptually, each form of structure is more challenging than the one before it. Pages are straightforward; XML is at best intimidating. Very likely, each seems progressively more discretionary as well. You can hardly lay out the simplest of documents without pages; meanwhile, most designers don't know what XML is, let alone how to put it to use inside InDesign. But if you take the time to learn how each feature works. InDesign will reward you several times over, saving you time, effort, and a whole lot of busy work. And what better way to learn than to actually create structured documents for yourself with the help of a series of practical hands-on exercises? Seriously, right now, I wouldn't blame you if the very idea of taking on XML makes you break out in a cold sweat. If it helps, I recall feeling the same way myself. But once you finish this lesson, you'll be busting your buttons over all XML—and in turn, you—can do. And you won't just have read about it, you will have actually *done* it.

Page Numbers and Sections

Some types of documents, such as books, manuals, and newspapers, are typically divided into *sections*, which are groups of pages that have their own page numbering schemes. For example, in this book, the table of contents and Preface employ lowercase roman numerals while the rest of the book uses more typical arabic numbers. Meanwhile, technical documents such as owner's manuals and contracts may be divided into lettered or numbered sections that are paginated independently, perhaps beginning A-1, 1-1, or what have you.

In this exercise, we'll put the finishing touches on a brief excerpt from my late lamented *Look & Learn Photoshop 6*. The file contains a handful of replacement pages for a second printing of the book. Our job is to ensure that the pages are correctly numbered and include the proper title information where appropriate. In doing so, you'll learn how to implement multiple sections in an InDesign document and specify unique numbering options for each one. You'll also learn how to use a *section marker* to make the title of a section automatically appear in a chapter opener or footer.

1. ***Open a multipage document.*** Open the file named *Look&Learn 7 pages.indd*, which is located in the *Lesson 09* folder inside *Lesson Files-IDcs 1on1*. The document should open to the page spread shown in Figure 9-2, which consists of the final page of the table of contents and the first page of chapter 1. The large black rectangle below the billiard ball is intended to frame the chapter title, which we will insert later in the exercise.

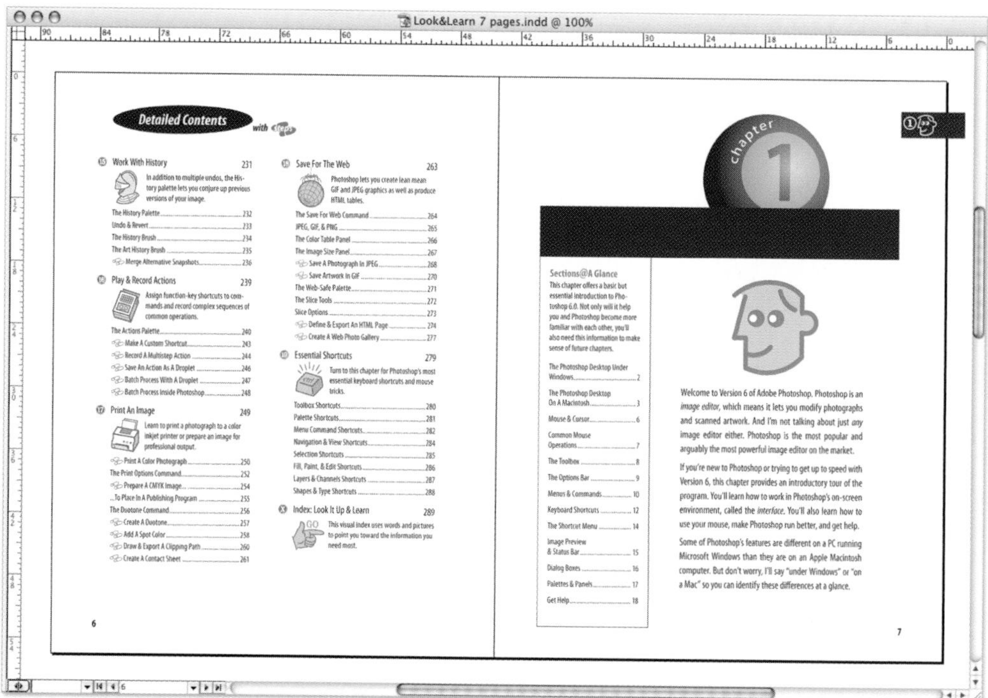

Figure 9-2.

PEARL OF WISDOM

If InDesign greets you with a warning about "hyphenation exceptions," click the Document button to acknowledge the message and move on. This is InDesign's way of telling you that the document contains a list of words that differs from your custom spell check dictionary. To see these words, choose Edit→Dictionary. Then select Look&Learn 7 pages.indd from the Target pop-up menu. When you finish, click the Done button.

---

2. ***Open the Pages palette.*** Choose **Window→Pages** or press F12 to display the **Pages** palette, shown in Figure 9-3. I have my palette options set to show the pages on top and master pages on bottom, as I recommend in Video Lesson 9, "Managing Your Pages" (see page 326). But feel free to use any configuration that suits your extra special needs. The letters in the page icons indicate master pages, which we cover in the next exercise, "Setting Up Master Pages."

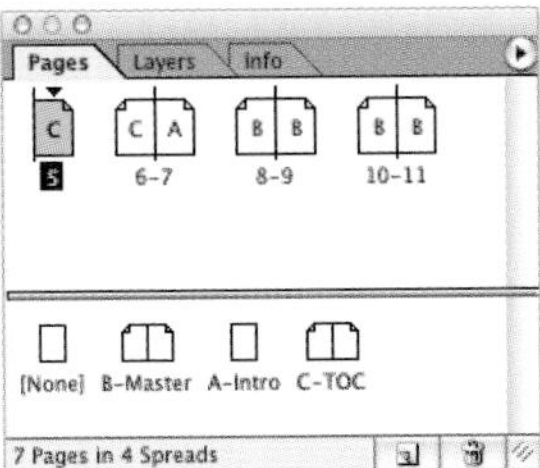

Figure 9-3.

3. ***Switch the active page.*** Notice that page 5 is highlighted in the Pages palette. Meanwhile, we see pages 6 and 7 in the document window. Also notice that the vertical ruler along the left side of the document window is dimmed. These are all tell tale signs that we are not viewing the active page in the document window. And the active page is the only place where things happen in InDesign. I make a special case of mentioning this because it can (and if my experience is any indication, *will*) throw you at times.

If you ever try to do something in the pages that you see on screen—such as, say, dragging a guide from the horizontal ruler—and that something refuses to happen, it may well be that the page or spread that you're looking at is inactive. To remedy the situation, just click in the document window.

Click anywhere in page 6 or 7 in the document window. You'll see both the vertical ruler and the Pages palette change. Now the page spread that you see also happens to be active.

4. ***View pages 8 and 9.*** Double-click the numbers **8-9** below the B|B in the top half of the Pages palette to view the very next page spread in the document, as in Figure 9-4 on the next page. At the bottom of these and subsequent pages in the document is a small graphic featuring the number 1 in a blue circle. This is part of the *footer*, which is recurring information that runs at

the bottom of most pages. We eventually want the name of the chapter to be part of the footer, a task we will have completed by the end of the exercise.

5. ***Open the Numbering & Section Options dialog box.*** As is customary with books, the pages from the table of contents should be numbered using lowercase roman numerals. Then the numbering should switch to regular arabic numerals starting with the first page of the first chapter. We'll start by applying roman numerals to the table of contents:

   - Select page 5 by clicking its page icon (▢) in the **Pages** palette. Although pages 8 through 9 remain active in the document window (as indicated by the black-on-white vertical ruler), page 5 is now active in the Pages palette. This permits you to modify one set of pages in the document window and another in the Pages palette.

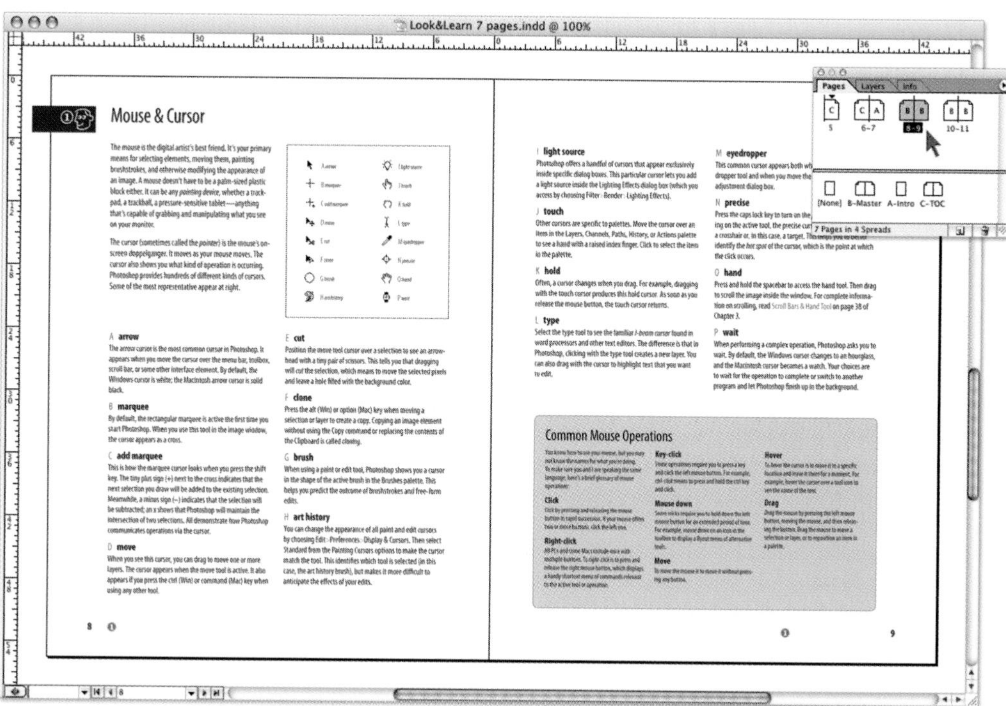

Figure 9-4.

   - Choose **Numbering & Section Options** from either the Pages palette menu or the **Layout** menu. Alternatively, you can double-click the tiny black triangle (▼) above page 5 in the Pages palette. That triangle indicates the beginning of a section—in this case the only section in the document thus far. InDesign responds with the **Numbering & Section Options** dialog box.

6. ***Set the numbering to start at page xxi.*** As I mentioned earlier, imagine that we are preparing a handful of pages for a reprint of the book. A total of 20 pages precede what is currently page 5, so we need to change the page numbering to start at roman numeral xxi (that is, 21). Enter 21 in the **Start Page Numbering at** option box. Then from the **Style** pop-up menu, choose the third option, **i, ii, iii, iv...**, and click **OK**. As Figure 9-5 shows, the first page in the document is now number xxi.

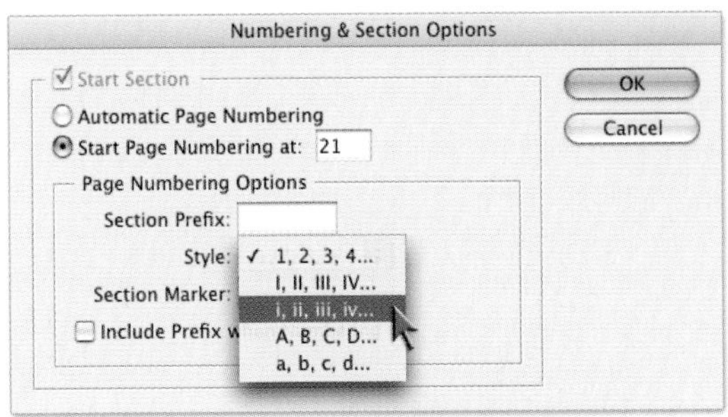

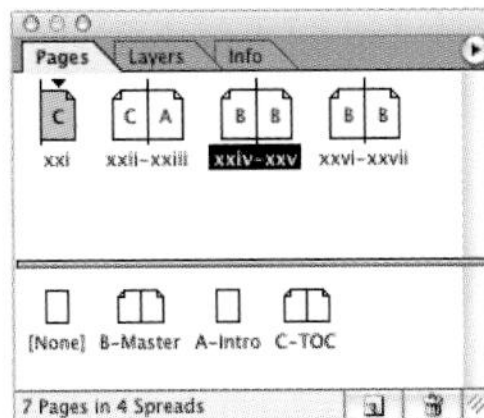

Figure 9-5.

7. ***Create a new section.*** The two pages from the table of contents are now numbered correctly, but we've created another problem: The roman numerals continue into the first chapter, which is no good. We need to create a new section in the document, starting with what is currently page xxiii.

   Click the icon for page **xxiii** in the Pages palette. (Be sure to click just that one page, not the spread.) Then choose **Numbering & Section Options** from the Pages palette menu. If you loaded Deke Keys as directed in the Preface, you also have a shortcut, Ctrl+Shift+Alt+N (⌘-Shift-Option-N on the Mac). Either way, you get the **New Section** dialog box. Here's a rundown of the changes you should make (all of which I feature in Figure 9-6):

   - We want to start a new section, so keep the **Start Section** check box turned on.
   - Select the **Start Page Numbering at** option, which allows you to start the new section at a unique page number. Then enter 1 in the associated option box.
   - In the Page Numbering Options section, the Section Prefix option is useful primarily for creating technical documents. We don't want a prefix, so click the words **Section Prefix** and press the Backspace or Delete key to make the option box blank.
   - Click the **Style** pop-up menu and choose the first option, **1, 2, 3, 4...**, to restore arabic numerals.
   - The **Section Marker** option lets you enter text that you can easily recall and insert automatically within the pages of the section. Section markers frequently accompany page numbers, but that's not the only way you can use them. To see what I mean, press the Tab key and enter the title of this chapter, "Get to Know Photoshop," into the Section Marker option box.

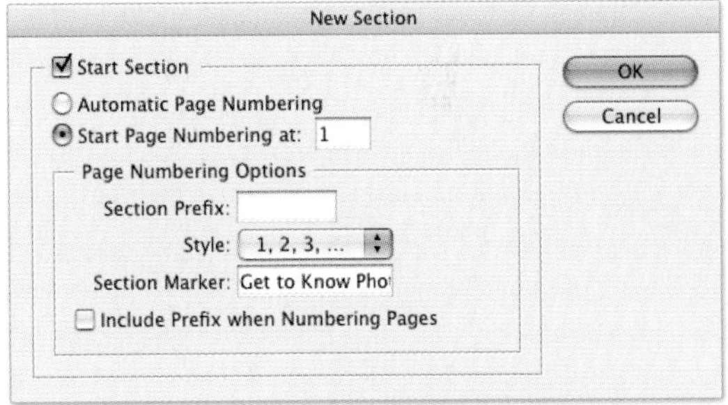

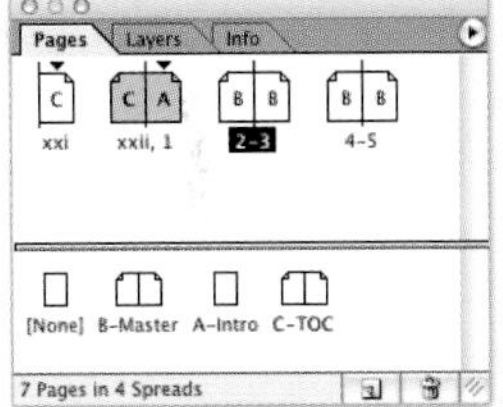

Figure 9-6.

After you specify these settings, click **OK**. You should notice a few changes at the bottom of the page spread in the document window. First, the page numbers have changed from xxiv and xxv to 2 and 3, respectively. Also, the chapter title that we typed in the Section Marker option box now appears in the footer at the bottom of each page, as in Figure 9-7. I'll show you how this works in the remaining two steps.

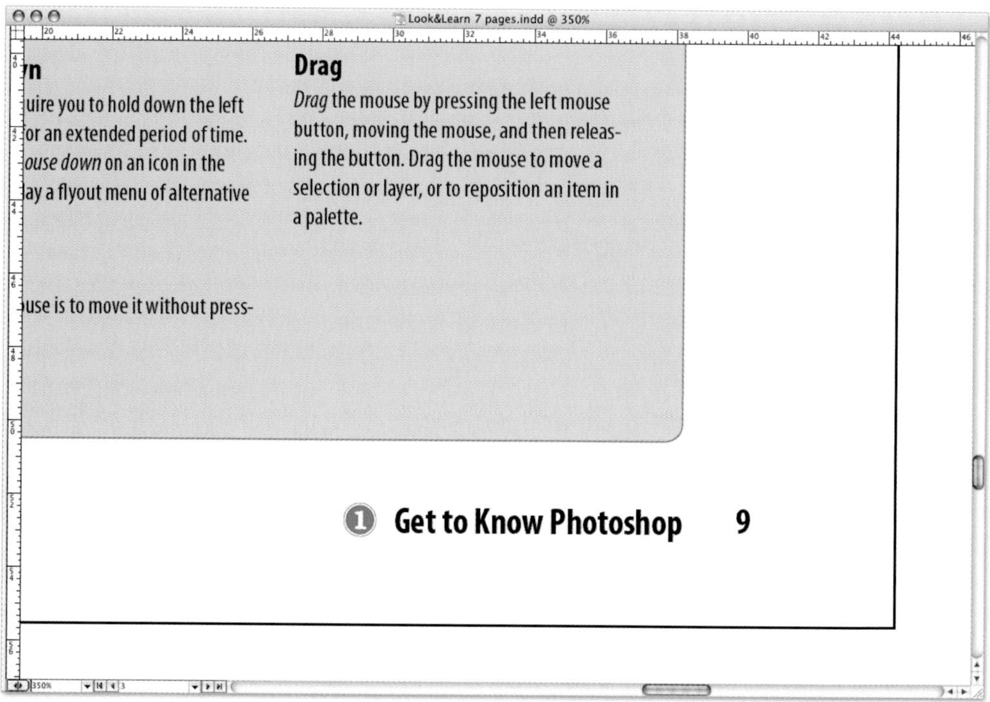

Figure 9-7.

8. ***Place the chapter title on page 1.*** Our last task is to insert the chapter title on the first page of the chapter:

    - Double-click the 🄰 for page 1 in the Pages palette. This activates the page and centers it in the document window.
    - Click with the black arrow tool inside the horizontal black rectangle that appears in front of the blue billiard ball. A cyan text frame (which I created in advance) appears in front of the rectangle.
    - Double-click the text frame to switch to the type tool. The text is formatted flush right, so the insertion marker blinks on the right side.

- Finally, right-click (or Control-click on the Mac) inside the text frame to display the shortcut menu. Choose **Insert Special Character→Section Marker**. The section marker that you entered in the preceding step appears in the black rectangle, as in Figure 9-8.

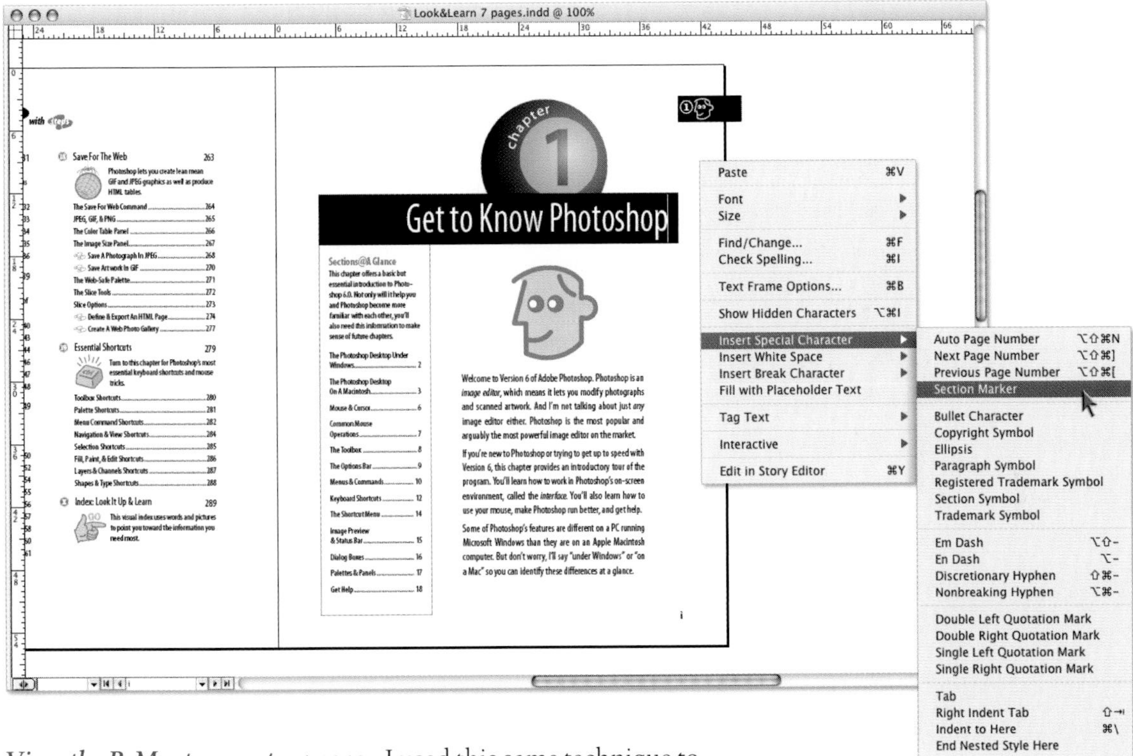

Figure 9-8.

9. *View the B-Master master pages.* I used this same technique to add the chapter name to the footers. The only difference is that I added the section marker to the master page spread instead of to the title page. To see for yourself, double-click **B-Master** below the ▭ in the bottom portion of the Pages palette. The word *Section* marks the spots where the section marker text will appear. Try selecting the word *Section* with the type tool; you'll see that the word is actually a single, special character, as in the magnified view in Figure 9-9.

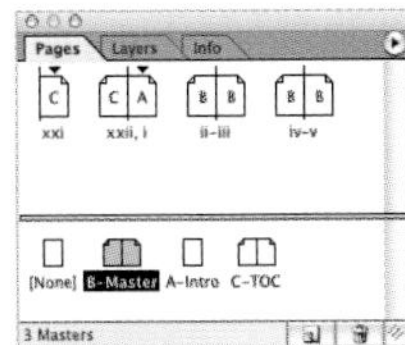

Figure 9-9.

PEARL OF WISDOM

The letter *B* at the bottom of each master page is an automatic page number character. You insert such a character by creating a text block and choosing Type→Insert Special Character→Auto Page Number or pressing Ctrl+Shift+Alt+N (⌘-Shift-Option-N on the Mac). Any pages that have this master page applied to them will automatically display the correct page number. For more information on master pages, keep reading.

Setting Up Master Pages

Master pages are one of the seminal efficiency functions of page-layout software. Like a puppet master who directs the behavior of a stage full of marionettes, the master page dictates the content of many pages at a time. A change made to an object on a master page affects how that object looks and prints on all linked pages. But between you and me, the term *master* and, by association, my analogy are a bit overwrought. Without the puppet master, the marionette would lie in a silent and inert heap; without its master page, a given page of your document might be missing an object or two. Out of all the stuff on the page you're reading now, for example, only the elements at the bottom of the page—the page number (or *folio*) and footer text—hail from the master page. The body copy, headlines, figures, captions, and sundry icons appear on this page and this page only.

But while a master page is less master than servant, it is nonetheless an exceedingly helpful one. As a rule, publications are rife with repeating page elements: headers, footers, folios, borders, copyright statements, logos, contact information, and everything else that tells you where you are in a document and who brought it to you. Even single-page documents such as flyers, transparencies, and handouts contain objects that repeat from one file to the next. Rather than constructing these objects manually for each and every page, you create the object once, place it on a master page, and forget about it. This avoids tedium, minimizes the potential for inconsistencies and errors, and even reduces file size. Master pages may also contain nonprinting elements, such as frames and guides, which help you size and align non-repeating objects.

In this exercise, you'll use master pages to repeat a pair of footers over the course of multiple pages. You'll make a master page, assign that master to a sequence of document pages, base one master page on another, and replace a master-page placeholder with a headline that is unique to the active document page. In other words, you'll learn everything there is to know about master pages and, in doing so, discover the identity of the *real* master in this relationship: you.

1. ***Open a document that contains repeating elements.*** Locate and open *Pages 62 through 67.indd* in the *Lesson 09* folder inside *Lesson Files-IDcs 1on1*. Upon opening, you should land in the middle of the 6-page document, with a distant elephant on the left page and cookies on the right, as in

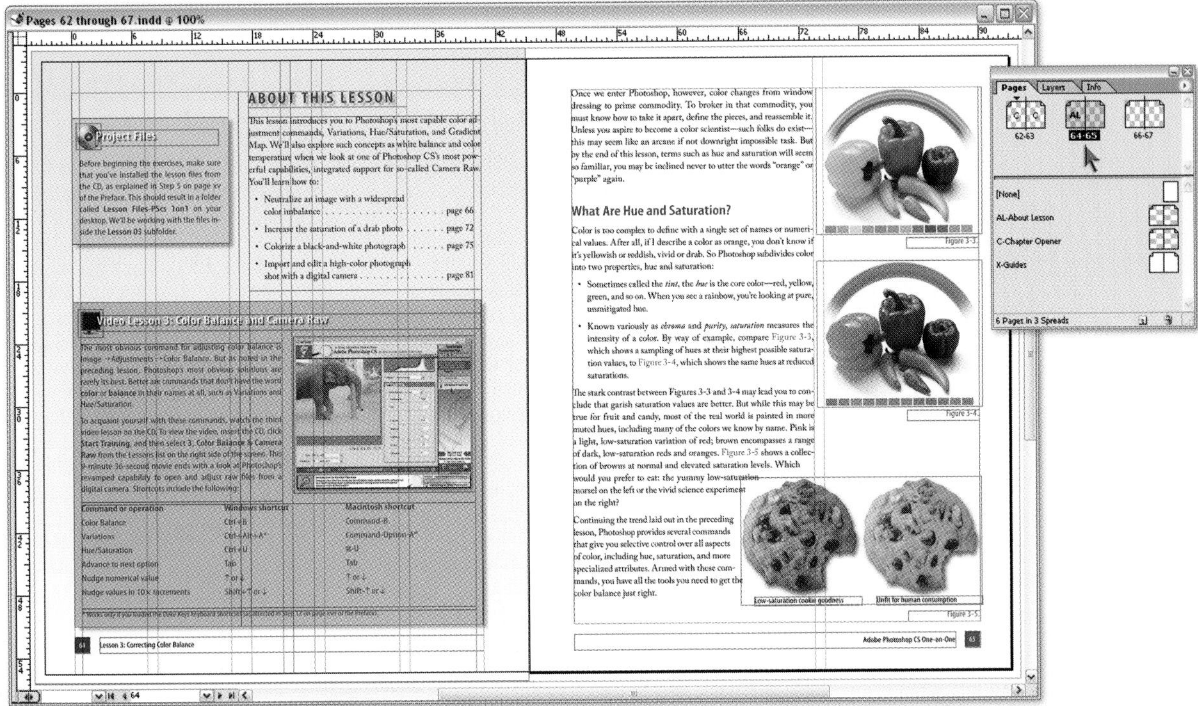

Figure 9-10.

Figure 9-10. If you find yourself someplace else, double-click **64–65** below the [AL] in the **Pages** palette.

2. ***Inspect the Pages palette.*** You create and manage master pages from the Pages palette. So if the palette is not already on screen, choose **Window→Pages** or press F12 to make it available. Expand the palette so that you can see the six document page icons and seven master page icons. (If you followed my advice in Video Lesson 9, "Managing Your Pages," the pages will appear on top; by default, they're on bottom.) Enhanced in Figure 9-11, the Pages palette tells you the following:

    - The document contains six pages, 62 through 67.
    - It also contains six master pages, organized into three spreads. (The [None] icon is not a master page, but is rather provided to disable links to master pages.)
    - The label for each master spread begins with one or two letters. Any page to which a master has been applied displays those letters, which I've colored red in the figure. So pages 62 and 63 link to the C–Chapter Opener master, page 64 uses AL–About Lesson, and the others use none. X-Guides is not yet associated with any page.

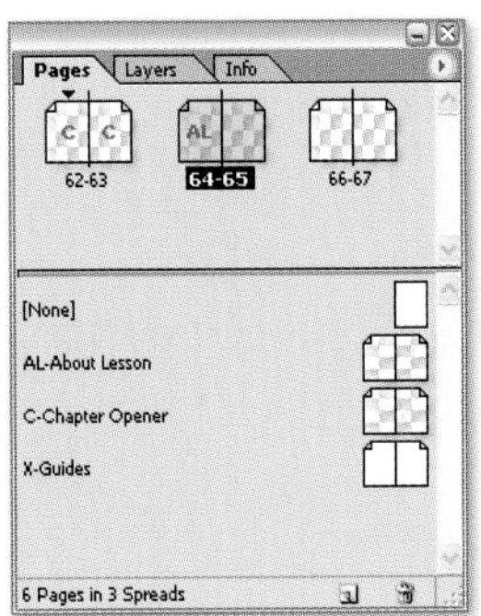

Figure 9-11.

3. ***Select the footers.*** Setting up a master page is first and foremost a matter of deciding what portions of the page you want to repeat. Zoom out to take in the entire spread (see Figure 9-10), and you'll see that the only elements these two pages share in common are the footers and folios. Presumably, you want these to appear on other pages as well, so you should relocate them to a master page.

   I've grouped each footer in advance to make it easier to select. Using the black arrow tool, click the left footer and then Shift-click the right one to select them both.

4. ***Cut the footers to the clipboard.*** The easiest way to move items to a master page is to cut and paste them. (You can also duplicate one or more pages as masters, but that copies *all* elements on the page, which is not what we need.) So go to the **Edit** menu and choose the **Cut** command or press Ctrl+X (⌘-X on the Mac). This deletes the footers and transfers them to InDesign's clipboard.

5. ***Create a new master spread.*** Click the ▶ arrow in the upper-right corner of the **Pages** palette to display the palette menu and choose **New Master**. When the dialog box comes up, click **OK** to accept the default settings and generate the new master spread, which is shown in Figure 9-12.

To bypass the command and dialog box, press the Ctrl key (⌘ on the Mac) and click the icon. Just like that, a new master spread with default settings appears in the Pages palette.

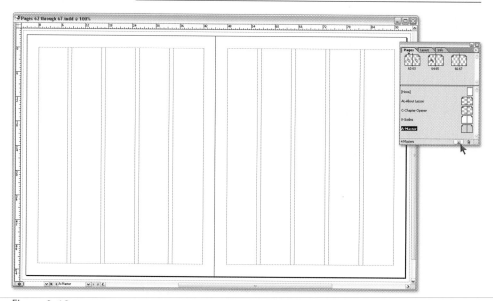

Figure 9-12.

6. ***Apply the X-Guides master.*** One of the irritating things about new master pages is that they subscribe to the settings you entered in the New Document dialog box when you first conceived the file. This particular document is based on a design that began to take shape more than a year ago, and I've changed my mind a lot since then. As a result, the narrow inside margins, glut of columns, and complete absence of ruler guides are all wrong.

   Fortunately, I have us covered. Because I'm so unhappily familiar with this issue, I created the X–Guides master, which is based on the settings we applied in the "Adjusting Margins and Guides" exercise way back in Lesson 1 (see page 26). Thanks to this bit of planning, you can apply the X–Guides settings to the new master spread using one of the following techniques:

   - Choose **Master Options for "A–Master"** from the palette menu. Then select **X-Guides** from the **Based on Master** pop-up menu and click **OK**.
   - In the Pages palette, drag the master named **X–Guides** and drop it on **A–Master**.
   - Make sure the A–Master spread is active. (Its icons in the Pages palette should appear highlighted; if they don't, double-click **A–Master**.) Then press the Alt key (Option on the Mac) and click the name **X–Guides**.

   However you do it, you will have applied a master page to another master page, something that QuarkXPress and earlier publishing programs cannot do. A pair of Xs appear inside the icons to show that the X-Guides master holds sway. Even better, the margins, column guides, and ruler guides are restored to X–Guides perfection, as in Figure 9-13.

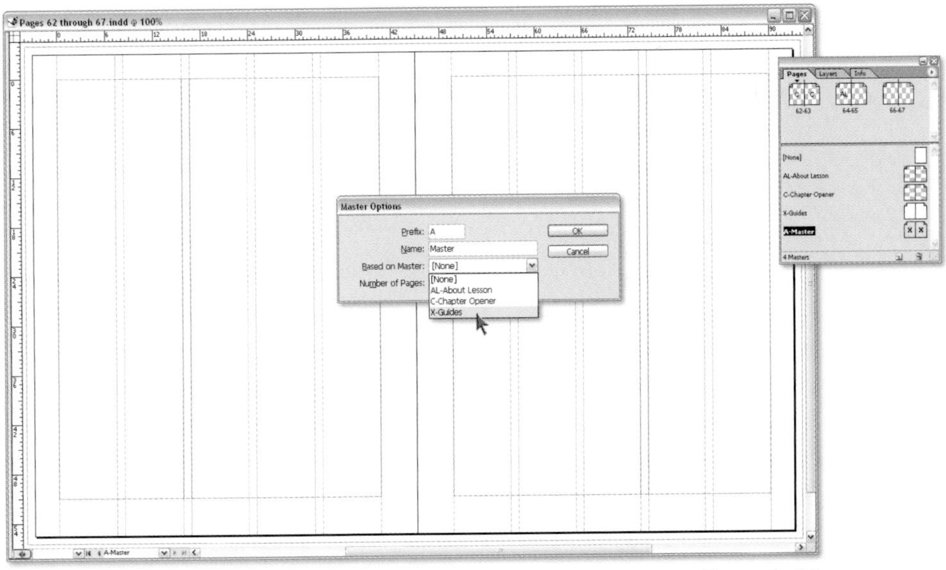

Figure 9-13.

7. ***Paste the footers in place.*** Now it's time to paste the footers and folios you copied in Step 4. If you choose Edit→Paste, InDesign drops the objects in the center of the document. To put them back right where you found them, choose **Edit→Paste in Place** or press Ctrl+Shift+Alt+V (⌘-Shift-Option-V).

   As shown in Figure 9-14, InDesign replaces the automatic page number character in the folio with an *A*. (As you may recall from the preceding exercise, you create this character by choosing Type→Insert Special Character→Auto Page Number.) This tells us we're on the A–Master page. When you return to the document pages, the *A* will update to reflect the page number.

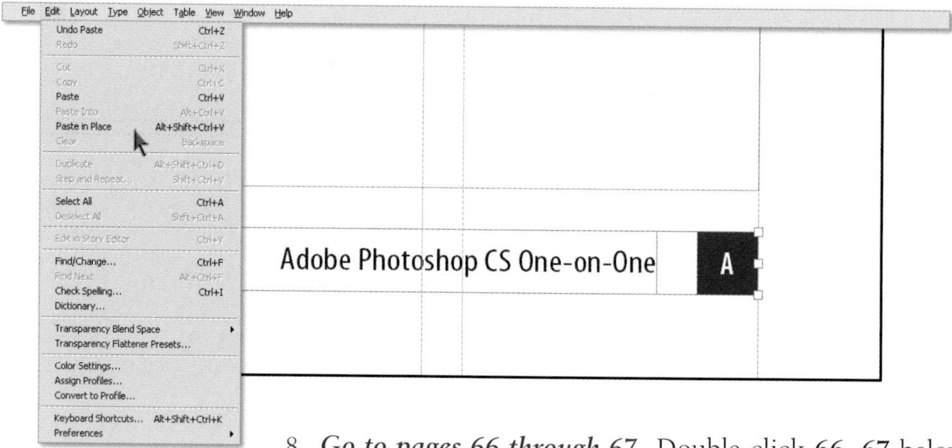

Figure 9-14.

8. ***Go to pages 66 through 67.*** Double-click **66–67** below the ◫ in the Pages palette to display the final page spread. Then zoom out so you can take in both pages. You may notice that the pages lack footers and folios, which is only fitting since we haven't applied the A–Master pages yet.

9. ***Apply A–Master to pages 65 through 67.*** Still inside the Pages palette, Shift-click the 🗋 for page 65. Pages 65 through 67 should now be active. Next, Alt-click (or Option-click) **A-Master**. An *A* appears in each of the highlighted page icons, which tells us that InDesign has applied the associated footers, folios, and guides to the active pages, all witnessed in Figure 9-15.

PEARL OF WISDOM

At this point, A-Master is the master page for pages 65 through 67, and X-Guides is the master page for A-Master. This makes X-Guides a kind of master^2 to pages 65 through 67. Rather than calling it something nutty like "grand master" or "master once removed," InDesign terms X-Guides the *parent* master and A-Master the *child*. As it so happens, X-Guides could be based on another master, resulting in a grandparent master. But for the sake of sanity, most designers limit their discussions to parent and child.

10. ***Advance to the first page spread.*** Double-click **62–63** below the C|C in the palette to go to the first pair of pages in the document. As shown in Figure 9-16, these pages use a different master spread, C–Chapter Opener, which features a full-page opening graphic on the left and a folio on the right. The right master also includes a placeholder for the lesson name, which reads *Chapter Title*. In the last exercise, we added a chapter title using a section marker. This time, we'll try a different way.

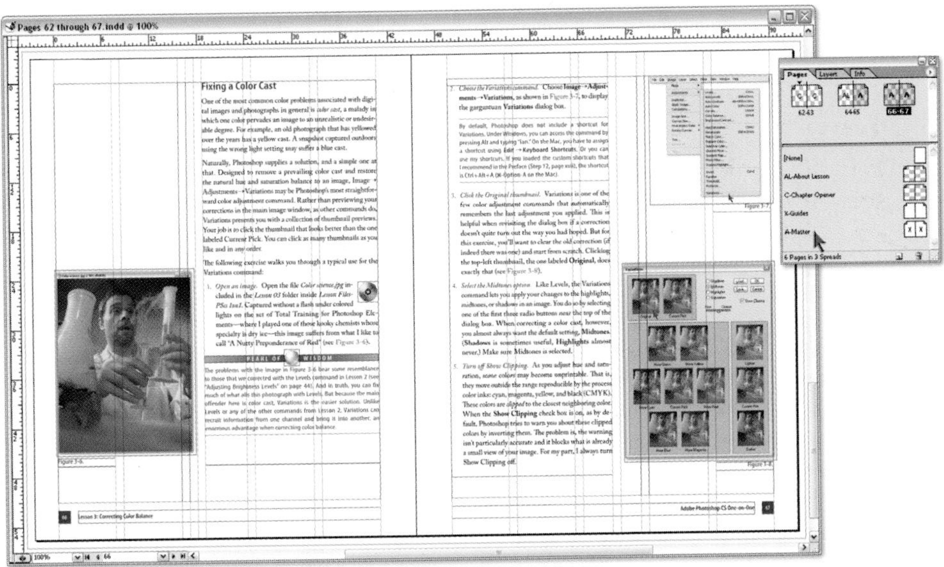

Figure 9-15.

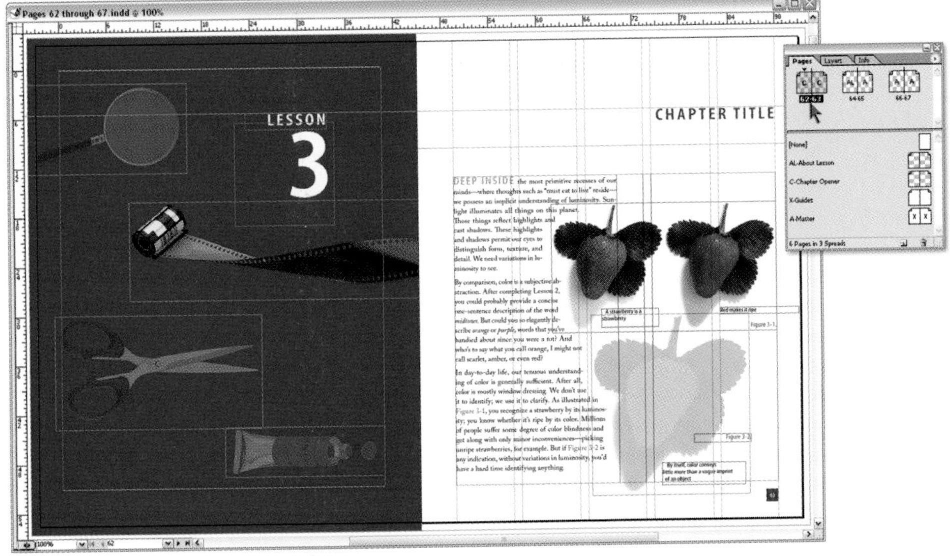

Figure 9-16.

11. ***Enter the proper lesson name.*** By default, InDesign prevents you from accessing master page elements while working on a document page. This protects the master page and ensures that you don't end up moving objects, editing text, and otherwise making a mess of things by complete accident. To override this protection, you perform this top-secret, shortcut-only action:

To edit a master-page object from a document page, press Ctrl and Shift (or ⌘ and Shift on the Mac) and click the object. InDesign copies the master object to the document page and hides the master object so you don't end up with two overlapping items. You can now edit the object.

Using the black arrow tool, Ctrl+Shift-click (or ⌘-Shift-click) the *Chapter Title* text block. InDesign transfers the text block from the master page and selects it. Double-click inside the text block to activate it. Then press Ctrl+A (⌘-A) and change the text to "Correcting Color Balance," the proper name for Lesson 3 of *Adobe Photoshop CS One-on-One*. Then (assuming you loaded my Deke Keys shortcuts) press Enter on the keypad to complete your edit. The revised text appears in Figure 9-17.

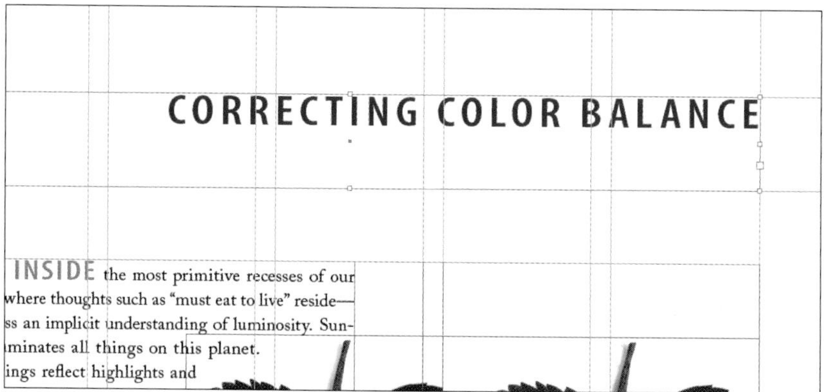

Figure 9-17.

Be aware that Ctrl+Shift-clicking overrides the text inside a master object, but the frames remain attached. In other words, if you were to move or scale the *Chapter Title* frame on the C–Chapter Opener master, the *Correcting Color Balance* frame on page 63 would move or scale as well. Only by selecting the object and choosing Detach Selection From Master from the Pages palette menu do you entirely break the link. To restore overridden master objects to their original condition, choose Remove All Local Overrides.

EXTRA CREDIT

That pretty much covers how master pages work. You've seen how to create master pages, apply them to document pages or other masters, transfer objects between pages and masters using the Paste in Place command, and modify a master-page placeholder. That leaves just one more thing: how to use layers to share items between master pages. For further information on layers—as well as their effects on master pages—read the very next exercise, "Creating and Using Layers," which begins on page 343. But in the meantime, stick with me here and learn how to create a layer that transfers a folio from one master page to another.

---

12. ***Return to pages 64 and 65.*** Double-click **64–65** below [AL|A] in the Pages palette. Notice that page 65 is blessed by both footer and folio, but page 64 contains neither. This is because page 64 relies on the master page AL–About Lesson, which does not yet include a footer. There are three ways to solve this problem:

    - Apply A–Master to page 64 instead. This would solve the footer problem, but we'd lose all the elements specific to the About This Lesson page, like the background gradient, light violet box, and more. Very bad idea; let's not do it.
    - Copy the left footer and folio from A–Master and paste them in place in the AL–About Lesson master page. The problem with this approach is that if I ever want to change the even-page footer—as when laying out Lesson 4, for example—I'd have to update the info twice, both on A–Master and AL–About Lesson, increasing my labor and the odds of introducing typos or other errors.
    - Make A–Master the parent of AL–About Lesson. With any luck, this will carry over the footer text while permitting you to edit it from a single location.

    Having weighed the pros and cons, let's give the third method a try and see whether it works.

13. ***Base the AL–About Lesson master on A–Master.*** Double-click **AL–About Lesson** in the Pages palette to go to that master spread. Then press the Alt (or Option) key and click **A–Master**. This shifts the column guides and copies the footer elements to the right page. But the footer remains absent on the left page. All things being equal, an object from a master or parent master appears below any objects on the document page or child master. Thus the footer is hidden by the big gradient rectangle that covers the left page, and no combination of Bring to Front or Send to Back is going to fix the problem.

14. ***Switch to the A–Master spread.*** Note that I prefaced my preceding remarks with, "all things being equal." In other words, equality is our enemy. To bring the footer forward, we need to jimmy the playing field.

    Double-click **A–Master** in the Pages palette to go the parent master. This is the spread that contains the footers, so this is the spread you need to edit.

15. ***Go to the Layers palette.*** Click the **Layers** tab or press F7 to display the **Layers** palette. It contains two layers: The active one is called Main Layer; the one above it is Top Objects. As you'll learn in the next exercise, all layers exist across all pages and master pages. And the front layer is the front layer throughout all pages. Therefore, moving the footers and folios to the top layer moves them to the front of the stack on all pages.

16. ***Move the footer elements to the Top Objects layer.*** Here's what I want you to do:

    - The ✗ icon in front of **Top Objects** shows that the layer is locked. Click the ✗ to make the icon go away and unlock the layer.
    - Select the footers on both pages of the spread. Because these are the only objects on the spread, you can press Ctrl+A (or ⌘-A) to select them. (If that doesn't work, press Enter and then press Ctrl+A again.)
    - Notice that a tiny blue square (■) appears on the right side of the Layers palette. This ■ represents the selected objects. Drag the square up, so it's even with **Top Objects**, and release. As shown in Figure 9-18, the square turns red, showing that the selection now rests on the frontmost layer.

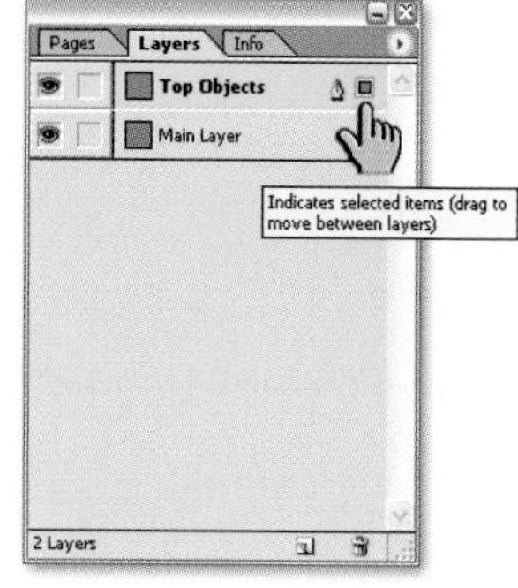

Figure 9-18.

17. ***Return one last time to pages 64 through 65.*** Click the **Pages** tab or press F12 to switch back to the Pages palette. Then double-click **64–65** below the [AL|A] to display the two-page spread at which we began this exercise. As celebrated in Figure 9-19 on the facing page, the footers and folios appear on both pages and all is well in the world.

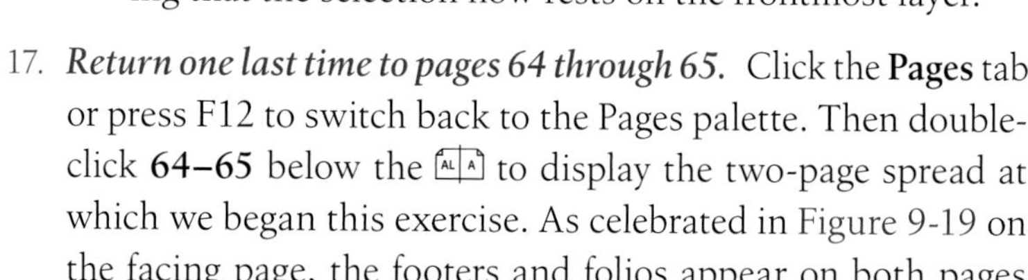

Incidentally, if you're ever curious about which objects are part of the current document page and which objects hail from the master page, choose View→Hide Master Items. Choose View→Show Master Items to bring the master objects back.

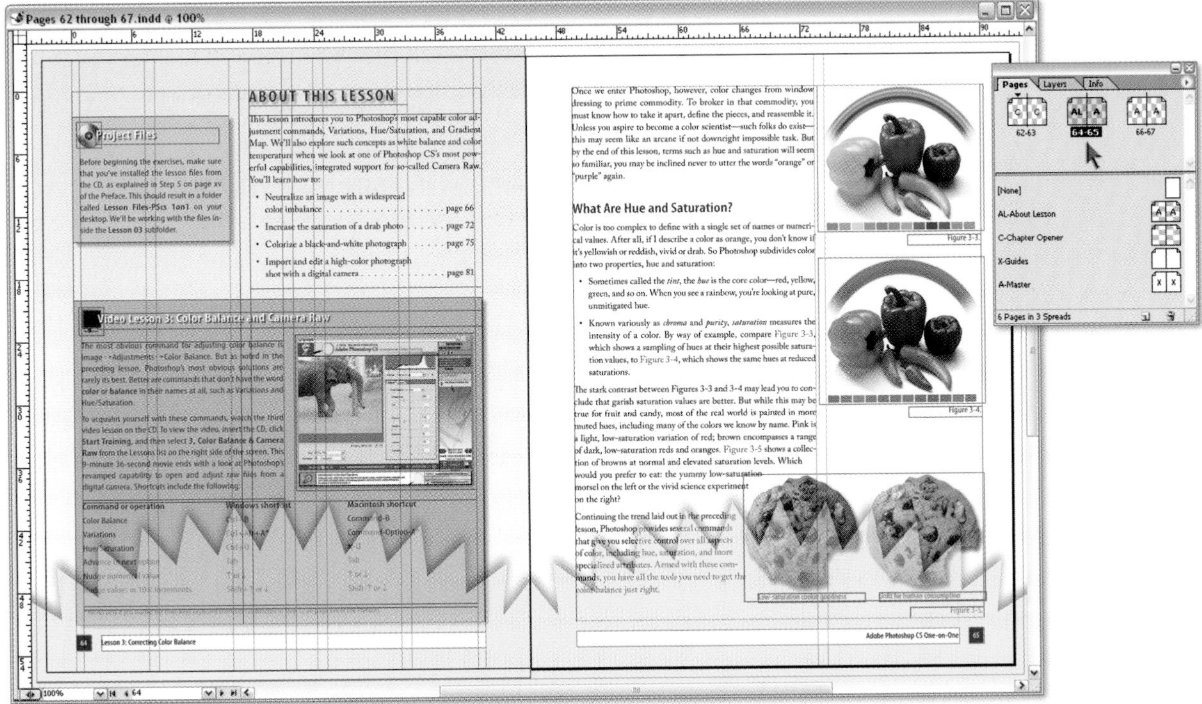

Figure 9-19.

Creating and Using Layers

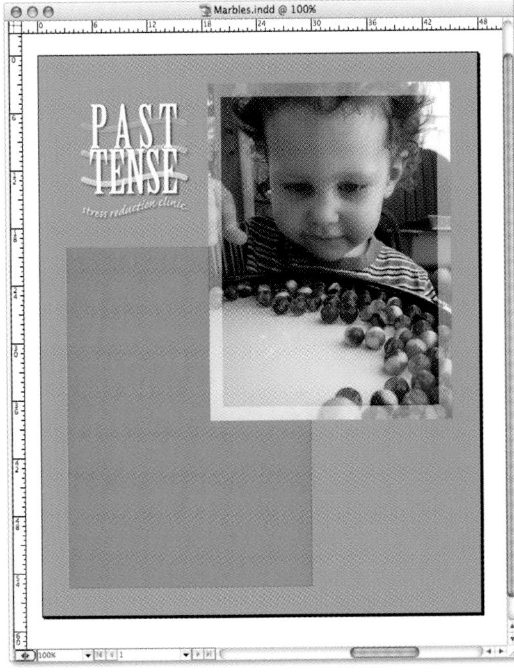

Figure 9-20.

If you use other Adobe products, you're probably well aware of the power and flexibility that layers can bring to your work. Separating the various elements in your document onto layers gives you the ability to select, hide, lock, and arrange those elements with enormous freedom. But in InDesign, layers are even more pervasive than they are in other Adobe apps. For starters, layers can hold *anything*, including text, images, drawn objects, and even guides. Furthermore, layers extend not just to the page you're currently working on, but to every page in the entire document, including master pages.

In this exercise, you're going to assemble the first page of an ad for a fictional stress reduction clinic. In the process, you'll learn a few different ways to create layers and experience firsthand how they can speed your progress as you develop a design. You'll also see how you can use layers to organize guides and minimize on-screen clutter.

1. ***Open a document.*** Open the file named *Marbles.indd*, which is located in the *Lesson 09* folder inside *Lesson Files-IDcs 1on1*. Shown in Figure 9-20, the document includes four visible elements: a blue

background, a photo, a red rectangle, and the logo for the clinic. If you try to select any of these elements, you'll find that you can't. You'll see why in the next step.

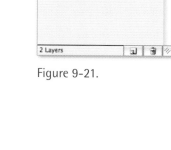

2. *Open the Layers palette.* Choose **Window→Layers** or press F7 to bring up the **Layers** palette. As shown in Figure 9-21, this document consists of just two layers. The visible elements in the document are all placed on the layer named Background, as indicated by the 👁 icon in front of the layer name. Here's some other stuff to note:
   - The Background layer sports a ✗ icon, which tells you that the layer is locked and its contents can't be selected.
   - Meanwhile, you can tell that the Background layer is active because of the highlight and the ✎ icon. The red slash through the ✎ reminds us that the layer is locked.
   - The colored swatch to the left of each layer name shows the color assigned to the layer. Select a frame on that layer and it will appear in this color.

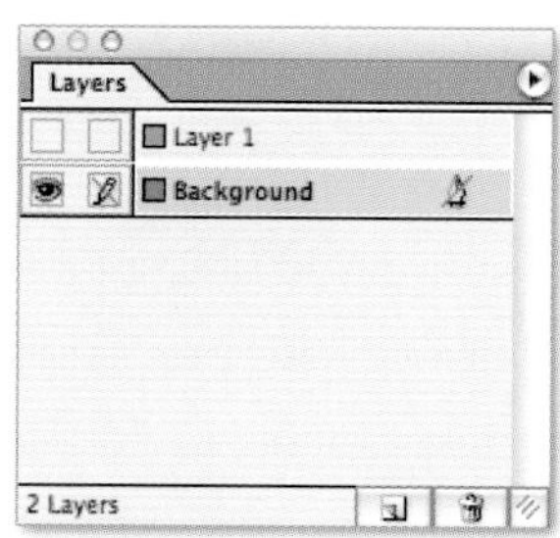

Figure 9-21.

3. *View Layer 1.* Click in the first box to the left of **Layer 1** to bring up the 👁 and display all objects on that layer in the document window (see Figure 9-22). There are a couple of text blocks, a bunch of marbles emanating from the boy's head, and a large black rectangle set to 50 percent opacity. The document is a bit of a mess in its current state, with objects piled on top of each other in a way that makes it difficult to select them. On our way to finishing up this document, we'll separate the various objects on discrete layers so that we can select items more easily.

Figure 9-22.

4. *Create a new layer for the translucent rectangle.* The translucent rectangle will eventually serve as the background for a text block, but right now it's covering the marbles, making it difficult to select them. We could Ctrl-click (or ⌘-click) objects to select the marbles through the rectangle, as described in "Aligning and Distributing Objects" in Lesson 6 (Step 2, page 228), but then we could select only one object at a time. By far the better plan is to put the rectangle on its own layer so we can get to the marbles:
   - Get the black arrow tool and click the rectangle to select it. As Figure 9-23 shows, Layer 1 becomes active, and a tiny blue ■ appears to the right of the ✎ icon. As I mentioned in the preceding exercise, this ■ represents any and all selected objects in the document window.

- Press the Alt (or Option) key and click the icon at the bottom of the **Layers** palette. Pressing the key forces the display of the **New Layer** dialog box.
- Notice that the **Color** for the layer is set to a vivid neon green, telling us that objects on this layer will exhibit a green frame when selected. Leave this setting as is.
- Type "Translucent rectangle" in the **Name** option box, as in Figure 9-24, and click **OK**.

5. ***Move the translucent rectangle to the new layer.*** Notice that the bounding box for the translucent rectangle is still light blue. That's because we still have to move the rectangle to the new layer. To do so, go to the Layers palette and drag the tiny blue ■ to the right of **Layer 1** up to the **Translucent Rectangle** layer. When you release the mouse button, the rectangle's bounding box turns green, as in Figure 9-25, indicating that the shape now resides on its self-named layer.

Figure 9-23.

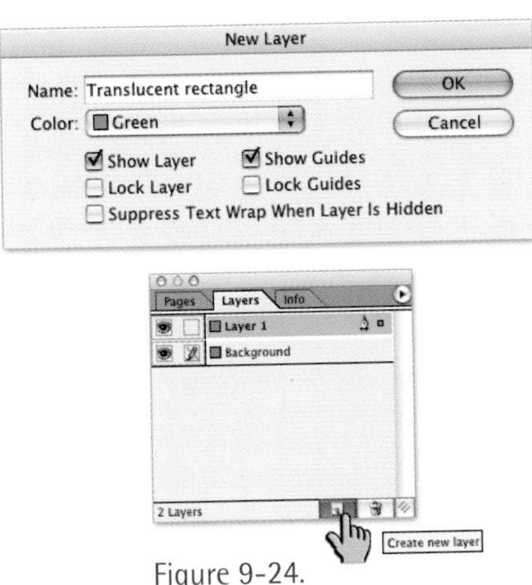

Figure 9-24.

Figure 9-25.

Figure 9-26.

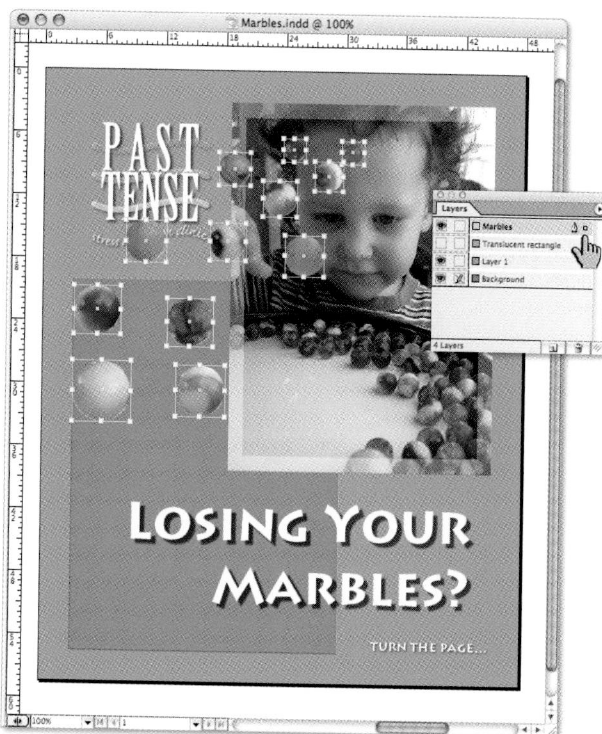

Figure 9-27.

To duplicate one or more selected objects from one layer to another, press the Alt (or Option) key as you drag the tiny selection ■ to a different layer. The clone moves to the new layer; the original stays put.

6. ***Hide the new layer.*** Click the 👁 icon for the **Translucent Rectangle** layer to hide the object in the document window so that we can get to the marbles. Notice the layer's ✎ icon in the Layers palette. InDesign prevents you from making changes to a layer that you can't see.

7. ***Marquee the marbles.*** Select all the imported marble images, twelve in all. Because the objects behind the marbles are on a locked layer, you can marquee the marbles without worry of selecting anything else. Just drag with the black arrow tool to at least partially surround the dozen marbles, as in Figure 9-26.

8. ***Isolate the marbles on their own layer.*** Now let's assign the marbles to a new layer:

   - Alt-click (or Option-click) the ◲ icon at the bottom of the Layers palette to again display the New Layer dialog box.
   - Type "Marbles" in the **Name** option box.
   - InDesign suggests we use Blue as the layer color, but let's pick a color that will show up better against the light blue background. Choose **Yellow** from the **Color** pop-up menu, and click **OK**.
   - Next, drag the tiny blue ■ from **Layer 1** up to the new **Marbles** layer at the top of the palette. As Figure 9-27 shows, the dozen marbles—complete with spiffy yellow bounding boxes—now reside on the Marbles layer.

Clicking the ◲ icon creates a new layer at the very top of the stack. To create a layer directly above the active layer, press Ctrl (or ⌘) and click the ◲ icon. To create a layer below the active layer, Ctrl+Alt-click (or ⌘-Option-click) the ◲ icon. To display the New Layer dialog box during either operation, press Ctrl (⌘) or Ctrl+Alt (⌘-Option) and click the ⊙ arrow in the top corner of the Layers palette. The first command in the palette menu will change to New Layer Above or New Layer Below depending on the keys pressed.

9. ***Rename Layer 1 and change its color.*** The two text blocks are the only items left on Layer 1. Let's give the layer an appropriate name and a selection color that will contrast with the light blue background. Double-click **Layer 1** in the Layers palette to access the **Layer Options** dialog box. Type "Text" in the **Name** option box, choose **Magenta** from the **Color** pop-up menu, and click **OK**. Your Layers palette should look like the one in Figure 9-28.

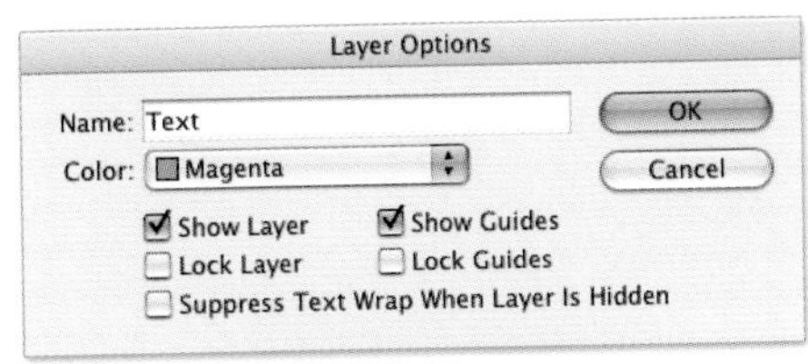

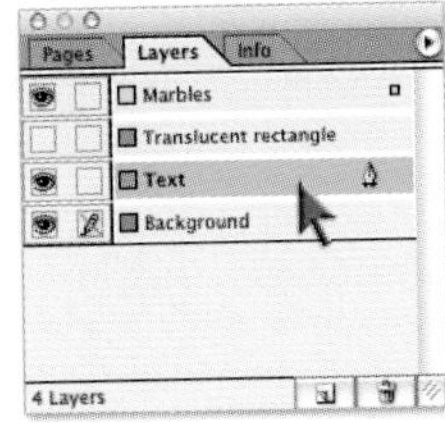

Figure 9-28.

10. ***Show the guides.*** Now that we have the objects separated onto named layers, let's work on the layout. The first thing we'll do is move and resize the translucent rectangle according to some guides that I've already placed. Choose **View→Show Guides** or press Ctrl+; (⌘-; on the Mac) to display the margin guides, along with some cyan and purple ruler guides. All guides reside on the Text layer; the purple guides reside on the master page and are therefore out of reach.

11. ***Reposition and resize the translucent rectangle.*** Make the Translucent Rectangle layer visible once more by clicking the one empty 👁 box in the Layers palette. Then Alt-click (Option-click) the **Translucent Rectangle** layer name to select the translucent rectangle. Returning to the document window, drag the rectangle's bottom-right handle until it snaps to the guide intersection indicated by the violet ⊕ in Figure 9-29. Then drag the top-left handle so it snaps to the yellow ⊕ in the figure.

12. ***Isolate the ruler guides on their own layer.*** Let's position the marbles so that they flow from the marble tin rather than out of the boy's head. We want to align the bottom-left edge of the largest marble with the lower-left intersection of the margin guides. But the document contains so many guides that it's easy to get confused. If you press Ctrl+; (⌘-;) to hide the ruler guides, you'll also hide the margin guides, which you need to position the marbles. The solution is to move the ruler guides to their own layer, and then hide that layer.

    - Press Ctrl+Alt+G (⌘-Option-G on the Mac) to select all the guides.
    - Alt-click (or Option-click) the ⧉ in the Layers palette, type "Guides" in the **Name** option box, set the **Color** to **Brown**, and click **OK**.

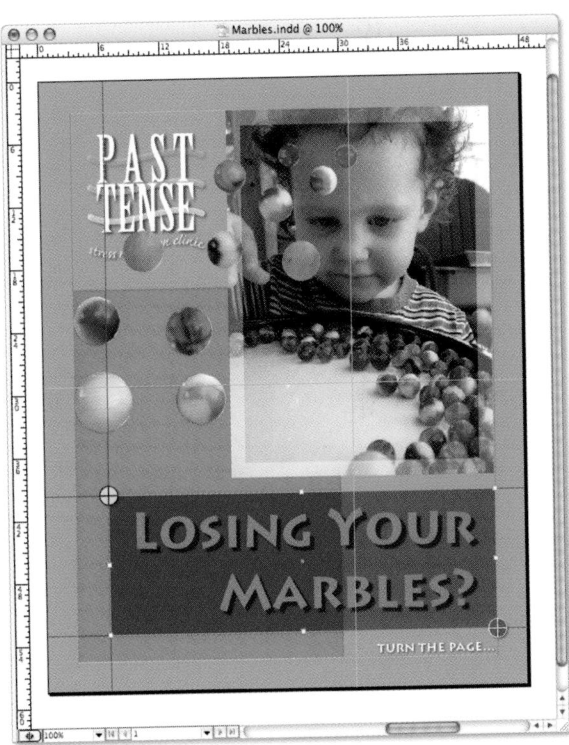

Figure 9-29.

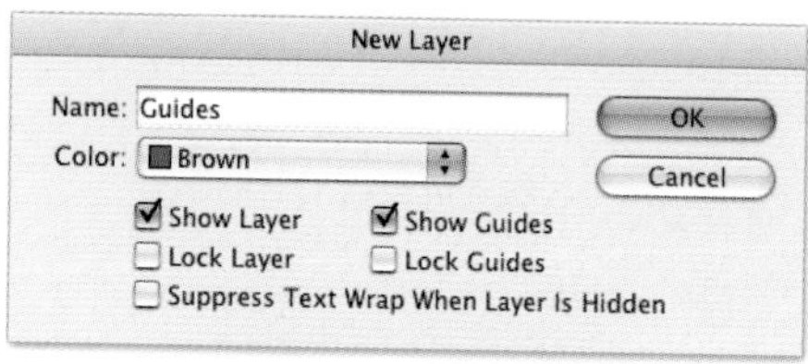

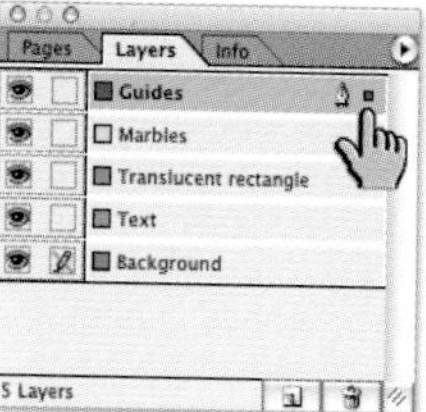

Figure 9-30.

- Drag the tiny magenta ■ to the right of the **Text** layer up to the Guides layer, as shown in Figure 9-30.
- Click the 👁 in front of **Guides** to hide the new layer.

Unfortunately, we were only partially successful in hiding the ruler guides; the cyan guides are gone, but the purple guides are still there. As I mentioned earlier, the purple guides reside on the master page, so we'll have to add these guides to the Guides layer from there.

13. ***View the master page.*** Click the **Pages** tab or press F12 to access the **Pages** palette. Double-click the right-hand 🗋 of the **A-Master** spread. The master page appears, complete with three purple ruler guides.

14. ***Move the master page ruler guides to the Guides layer.*** Here's what you do:

    - Press Ctrl+Alt+G (⌘-Option-G on the Mac) to select the ruler guides.
    - If the Layers palette is not visible (it's grouped with the Pages palette by default), press F7 to call it up. Then click the empty 👁 box to turn on the **Guides** layer. You can modify visible guides only.
    - Again drag the magenta ■ for the **Text** layer up to the Guides layer to move the selected guides. The guides turn brown, indicating that they now reside on the Guides layer.
    - Click the 👁 icon for the **Guides** layer to hide all the ruler guides, whether they're on the page or master page.

15. ***Return to page 1.*** Choose **Layout→Go Back** to return to page 1 of the document. You can also press the keyboard shortcut Ctrl+Page Up (⌘-Page Up on the Mac).

Similarly, you can press Ctrl+Page Down (or ⌘-Page Down) to bounce back to the master page. You might think of Ctrl+Page Up and Ctrl+Page Down (⌘-Page Up and ⌘-Page Down) as the equivalents of the Back and Forward buttons in a Web browser. Bear them in mind when you need to flit back and forth between pages in a document.

---

16. ***Reposition the marbles.*** To select all the marbles, Alt-click (or Option-click) the **Marbles** layer in the Layers palette. Next, drag the largest of the marbles—the bottom-left of the bunch—until it snaps to the lower-left corner of the margin guides, as in Figure 9-31. The other marbles follow suit, giving the rough

appearance that they are streaming out of the picture and into the document.

17. ***Relocate the Marbles layer in the Layers palette.*** The edges of the marbles are pretty rough. I could fix them in Photoshop or fudge them in InDesign. The latter is quicker, so let's fudge away:

    - Choose **Object→Drop Shadow** or press Ctrl+Alt+M (⌘-Option-M on the Mac). A drop shadow is a great way to hide bad edges. It doesn't fix them, mind you; it just distracts attention.
    - Turn on the **Drop Shadow** check box and change the **Opacity** value to 50 percent.
    - Enter −0p4 for the **X Offset** value and 0p4 for the **Y Offset**.
    - Change the **Blur** value to 0p5 and click **OK**.

    Then press Ctrl+Shift+A (or ⌘-Shift-A) to deselect the marbles. The outlines of the marbles should appear a bit more credible, as in Figure 9-32.

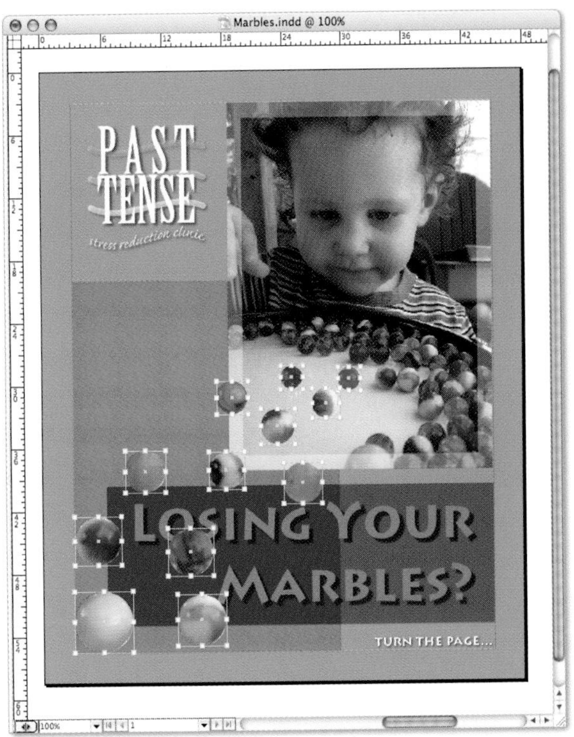

Figure 9-31.

Figure 9-32.

18. ***Reorder the layers.*** We want the marbles to appear behind the text, and we want the text in front of the translucent rectangle. Inside the Layers palette, do the following:

   - Drag the **Marbles** layer below the **Text** layer. You can track the movement of the layers by observing the thick black bar, as demonstrated on the left side of Figure 9-33.

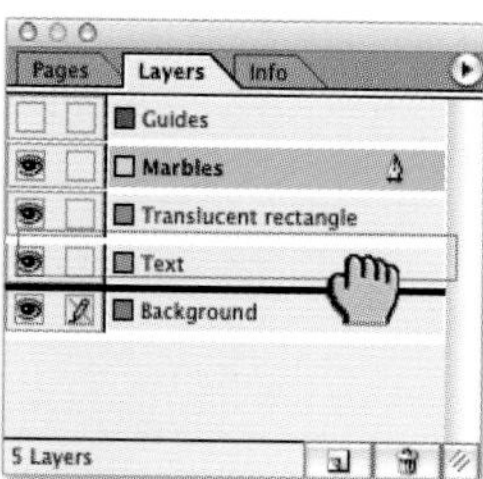

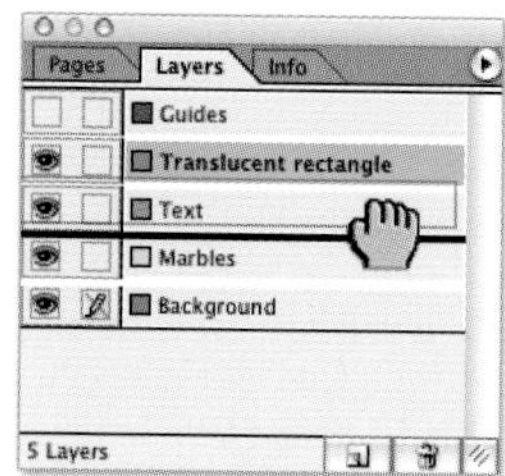

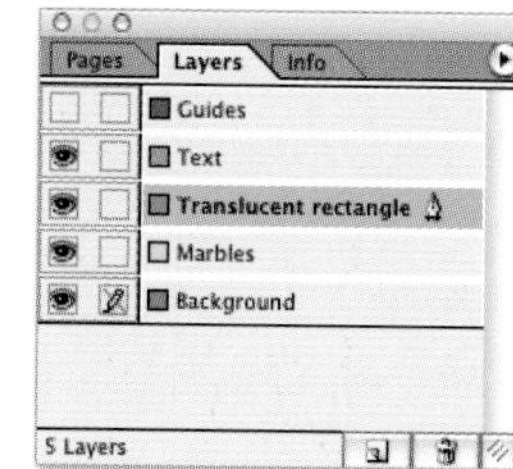

Figure 9-33.

   - Also drag the **Translucent Rectangle** layer below the **Text** layer, as in the middle example in the figure. The last example shows the final palette configuration.

Nice work. The completed layout with reordered layers appears in Figure 9-34 on the facing page.

Assigning XML Tags and Structure

Assembling documents using sections, master pages, layers, and the like is exciting stuff. But it's not what I would call speedy. It takes a lot of time, patience, vigor, fortitude, sweat, tears, and good old-fashioned designer stamina to assemble a document from beginning to end. That's fine, of course. Art is effort, and the manual approach is invariably the best approach. But it's not always feasible. Sometimes time is short, sometimes the budget is a factor, and other times your client is just plain cheap. That's when it's time to automate the design process with the help of those three powerful little letters, XML.

Like its close cousin, HTML (the language used to describe Web pages), XML is a *document processing language*, meaning that it enables you to create and format documents by writing relatively simple computer code. The difference is that XML is *extensible*, allowing you to create your own code words, or *tags*, and define them as you see fit.

If you've never written a line of computer code, rest assured that I'm not about to change that. InDesign reads and writes XML without sharing any of the unpleasantness with you. For those of you who have some coding experience, let me say that InDesign generates efficient, straightforward, and comprehensible XML. You can edit InDesign's code just as easily as you might edit your own.

InDesign employs XML for two purposes:

- First, XML automates the layout of regular documents that contain a consistent collection of elements. For example, suppose that you publish a newsletter that is always 12 pages long. Every month, Page 1 carries the masthead, an article, and a photograph; Page 2 contains a member roster and a list of upcoming events; and so on, just like clockwork. Using a text editor, you can prepare an XML file that contains all text for the upcoming newsletter and lists the locations of this month's graphics. Import that file into InDesign and, within a matter of seconds, every object is in its proper place. A few tweaks and the layout is complete.
- Second, XML lets you separate the content from the design. Then you can place the content into different templates to achieve different results. Placing the newsletter XML file into one template makes it a printed newsletter. Another template turns it into an online PDF file. And a third excerpts a single story and adds it to the annual report. XML facilitates the repurposing of material and permits you to better appeal to the changing needs of your target audience.

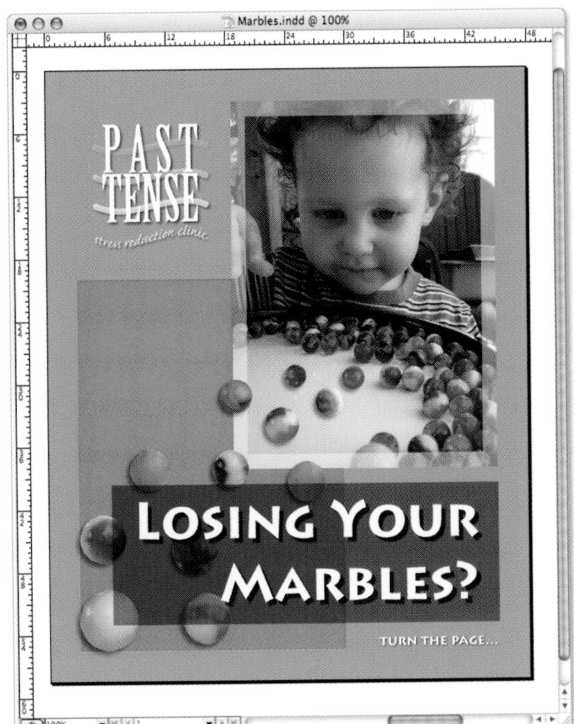

Figure 9-34.

In return for its long-term promise of time-saving automation, XML demands that you spend a hefty amount of time in the up-front planning phase. As a result, I devote a total of three exercises to this topic. In this first exercise, you'll assemble a collection of tags, assign those tags to everything from entire frames to individual words of text, and define the structure of your XML-savvy document. In the second exercise, you'll export your text and graphic links to an XML file and then strip out all content until you're left with a bare-bones, XML-structured template. And finally, you'll overhaul your XML content and place it into the structured template. Then all you have to do is sit back and watch the fireworks.

1. ***Open a file that will serve as a template for future documents.*** Our model document is yet another in the Shenbop-the-dead-frog series, *Seventies Quiz #4.indd* in the *Lesson 09* folder inside *Lesson Files-IDcs 1on1*. Pictured in Figure 9-35, this single-page document sports a thick column of narrative text up top, a flanking piece of imported line art, and three columns of hanging indents below. XML can be a daunting topic, so I've purposely selected a short, simple, goofy design. But bear in mind, everything we'll be doing throughout the remainder of this lesson works just as well for long, complex documents, including newspapers, magazines, and books.

Seventies quiz #4.indd @ 100%

You know, it's really not fair to stigmatize an entire generation of music because of a few awful songs. In our last test, The Rockets' "Oh Well," Sugarloaf's "Don't Call Us, We'll Call You," and Dobie Gray's "Drift Away" are all respectable pop tunes, each a modest classic in its own right.

But the rest of the songs range from lackluster to excruciatingly awful. "The Night the Lights Went Out in Georgia" tells the story of a girl who murders two people, gets a third hung, and yet reckons it's all the fault of ignorant law enforcement officials. "Afternoon Delight" draws a frisky analogy between lovemaking and fish baiting. And "Playground in My Mind" is the stupidest song ever.

Which brings us back to the quiz. As before, match the song title with the lyrics, which might occur at any point in the song. This is the hardest test yet—with 5 more songs than usual!—so prepare to dig back into the darkest recesses of your memory.

Professor Shenbop's #4 1970's Pop Music Quiz

The scars fade, but the pain continues.

Answers: 1.L, 2.E, 3.O, 4.H, 5.D, 6.I, 7.M, 8.J, 9.C, 10.G, 11.B, 12.F, 13.A, 14.K, 15.N

Match these song titles…

1. Rock On
2. Undercover Angel
3. Heaven on the 7th Floor
4. Couldn't Get It Right
5. Radar Love
6. Moonlight Feels Right
7. I'd Really Love to See You Tonight
8. The Night Chicago Died
9. One Tin Soldier
10. Saturday Night
11. Rock Me Gently
12. Brand New Key
13. Come and Get Your Love
14. The Cover of the Rolling Stone
15. You Sexy Thing

…with the lyrics below.

A. Cuz you're fine in your mind and you look so divine.
B. Don't you know that I have never been loved like this before?
C. Turned the stone and looked beneath it. "Peace on Earth," was all it said.
D. No more speed, I'm almost there. Gotta be cool, now, I gotta take care.
E. I never had a dream that made sweet love to me.
F. Some people say I done all right for a girl.
G. We're gonna rock it up, roll it up, do it all, have a ball.
H. I kept on lookin' for a sign in the middle of the night.
I. I play the radio on Southern stations, cuz Southern belles are hell at night.
J. In the heat of the Summer night, in the land of the dollar bill.
K. We sing about beauty and we sing about truth at $10,000 a show.
L. Jump up and down in blue suede shoes.
M. Hello. Yeah, it's been a while. Not much. How 'bout you?
N. I believe in miracles. Where ya from?
O. I thought I was out of luck, and ten seconds later, somehow we got stuck in the elevator.

Figure 9-35.

2. ***Open the Structure bay.*** Click the ◂▸ icon in the lower-left corner of the document window to open the **Structure** bay. Alternatively, you can choose **View→Structure→Show Structure** or press Ctrl+Alt+1 (or ⌘-Option-1 on the Mac). Shown on the left side of Figure 9-36, this clandestine subwindow permits you to manage the underlying structure of the XML document that you'll eventually export from InDesign.

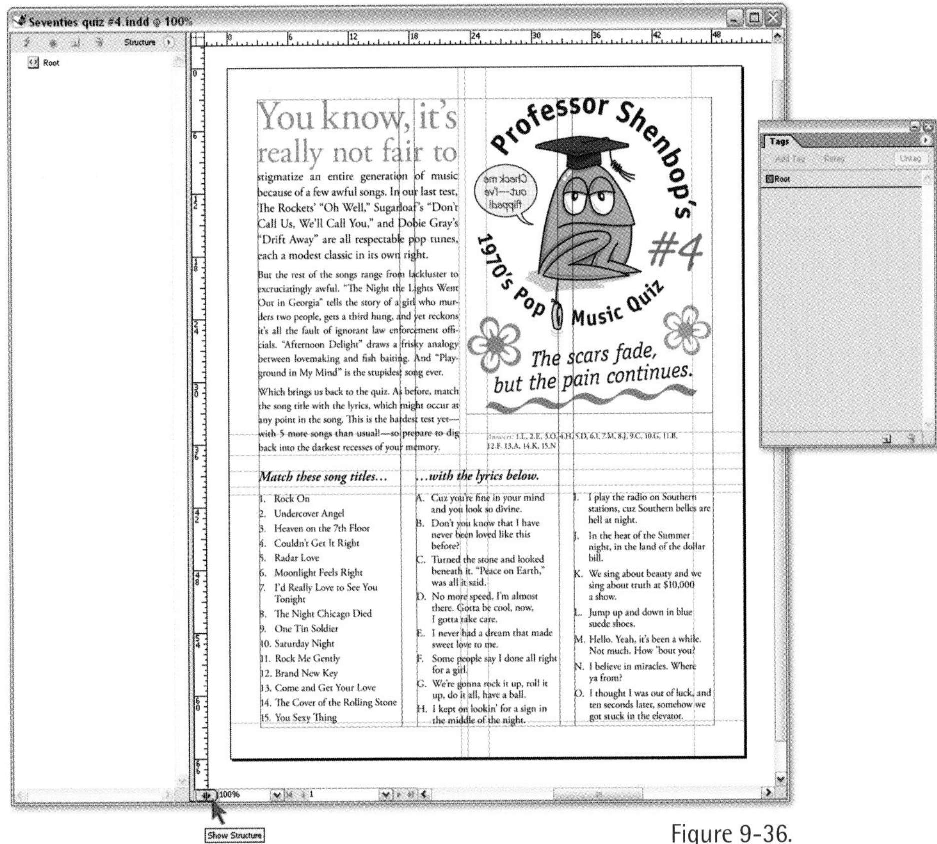

Figure 9-36.

Although this may be the first time you've stumbled across it, the Structure bay is lying in wait inside every document you create. Drag the vertical bar to the left of the ruler to adjust the width of the bay. If you ever find yourself wanting to get rid of it, again click the ◂▸ or press Ctrl+Alt+1 (⌘-Option-1).

---

3. *Open the Tags palette.* Choose **Window→Tags** to display the **Tags** palette, which lets you create and apply XML tags. Although it lacks a keyboard shortcut, the Tags palette is every bit as important as the Structure bay. The fact is, you need both to create an XML-formatted document in InDesign.

PEARL OF WISDOM

Like style sheets, *tags* identify paragraphs and words so that you can format them automatically. You can even apply tags to entire text blocks and graphics to control the placement of imported objects. Unlike style sheets, tags do not by themselves convey formatting attributes. They merely label objects; you then use InDesign to define what those labels mean. For more information on tags, read the sidebar "XML, Tags, and Elements," which begins on page 360. Or just hang in there and all will become clear.

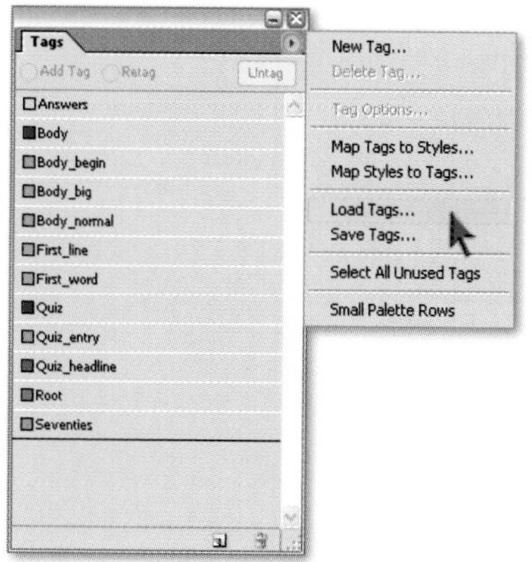

Figure 9-37.

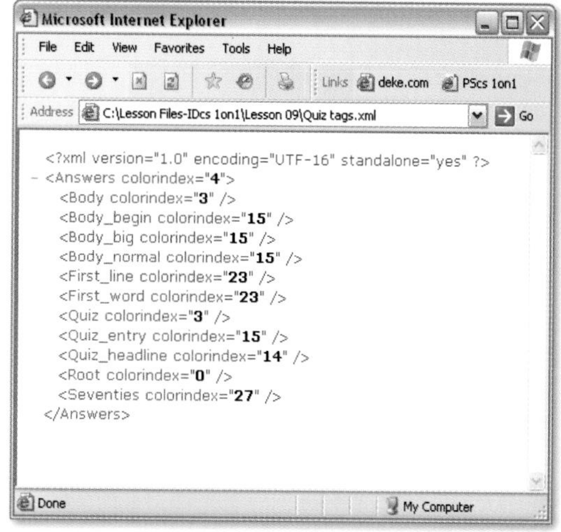


```
<?xml version="1.0" encoding="UTF-16" standalone="yes" ?>
- <Answers colorindex="4">
    <Body colorindex="3" />
    <Body_begin colorindex="15" />
    <Body_big colorindex="15" />
    <Body_normal colorindex="15" />
    <First_line colorindex="23" />
    <First_word colorindex="23" />
    <Quiz colorindex="3" />
    <Quiz_entry colorindex="15" />
    <Quiz_headline colorindex="14" />
    <Root colorindex="0" />
    <Seventies colorindex="27" />
  </Answers>
```

Figure 9-38.

By default, both the Structure bay and Tags palette contain one tag apiece, Root, which represents the base level of XML content. You need do nothing with Root; unless you know better, just leave it as is and everything will work fine.

4. ***Load a file of predefined tags.*** The Tags palette let's you create single tags at a time or import a group of previously saved tags from disk. To cut down on the tedium, we'll start with the latter and then try out the former. Click the ▶ icon in the top-right corner of the Tags palette and choose **Load Tags** from the palette menu. Select the file *Quiz tags.xml* in the *Lesson 09* folder and click the **Open** button. Eleven new tags appear in the Tags palette, as in Figure 9-37.

At this point, you may have some questions: For example, how did I create the *Quiz tags.xml* file that we just loaded? What's with the underscores in the newly imported tag names? And what made me choose *these* particular tag names? My answers:

- To generate *Quiz tags.xml*, I started by manually creating each one of the eleven tags in the Tags palette. Then I chose the Save Tags command from the palette menu and named the file *Quiz tags.xml*. InDesign stored all tags (including Root) to disk. You can likewise load XML documents scripted inside a text editor. For reference, the contents of *Quiz tags.xml* appear in Figure 9-38. (The red and blue coloring is imposed automatically by Internet Explorer, which I used to view the code. The actual file is composed of plain, unformatted text.)
- Your XML tags can be as long or short as you want, but by the laws of XML, they should contain only letters and numbers. Slashes, colons, quotes, and most other punctuation are illegal. Also stear clear of spaces. If you need a space, use one of the sanctioned dashes, an underscore (_) or a hyphen (-).
- Beyond that, you can name your tags anything you want. Just bear in mind that you'll have to reference them again, which may involve entering the tag names with all underscores and capitalization precisely intact. For the most part, I rely on tags that match the names of my style sheets. We'll see why in Step 8 (page 356).

5. ***Create a Cartoon tag.*** As we'll see, the tags comprise all but one element of the page, namely the imported Shenbop graphic. So we need to create a tag for the graphic manually. To do so:

   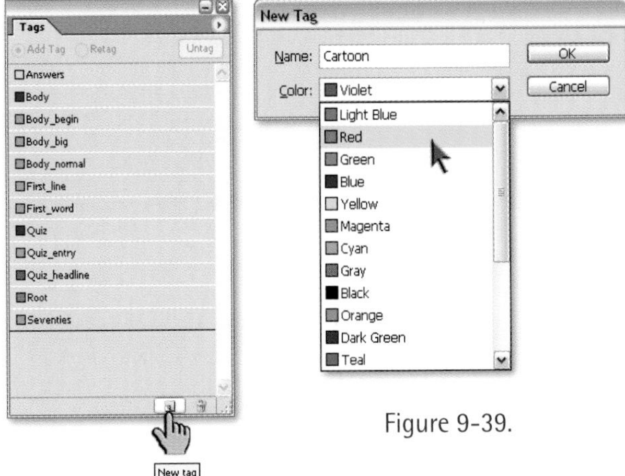

   Figure 9-39.

   - Press the Alt key (Option on the Mac) and click the ◱ icon at the bottom of the Tags palette. Pressing the key forces the display of the **New Tag** dialog box, shown in Figure 9-39.
   - Enter "Cartoon" into the **Name** option box. Be careful to spell the word correctly, start it with a capital C, and make the word singular. Proper naming of this item will affect the success of future steps.
   - Change the **Color** to **Red**. (It's okay to use another color if you like, but your screen will look different than mine.)
   - Click the **OK** button to accept the new tag.

   The word *Cartoon* preceded by a red box appears in alphabetical order inside the Tags palette.

6. ***Apply the Cartoon tag to the graphic.*** Now to put the tags in play. Let's begin with the tag you just created. Select the Shenbop graphic with the black arrow tool and click **Cartoon** in the Tags palette.

   To highlight tagged objects so that you can keep them straight, choose **View→Structure→Show Tagged Frames.** The selected graphic will appear red, as in Figure 9-40 on the next page. This command is merely a display function; it does not represent how the document will print, nor does it affect the export or execution of XML.

   Notice that the Structure bay now contains a Cartoon entry. In XML lingo, this entry is called an *element*. An XML element may in turn contain an *attribute*, which often defines the content of the tagged object. Because the selection is an imported graphic, the Cartoon element contains the attribute *href*, which specifies the location of the linked Illustrator file on disk.

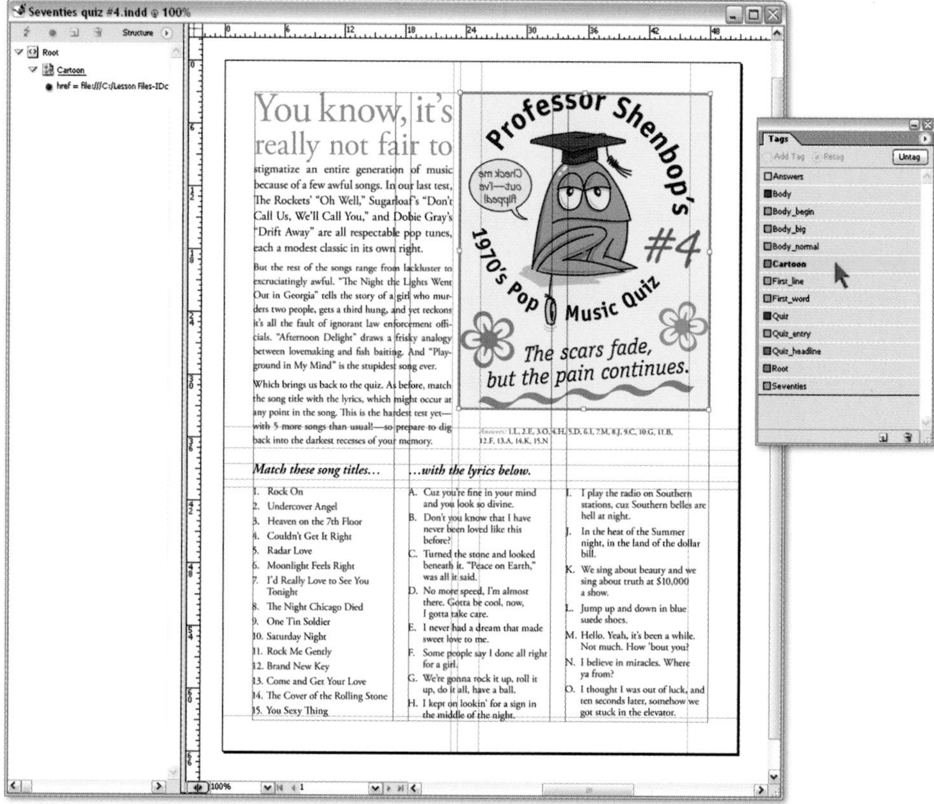

Figure 9-40.

7. ***Apply tags to the text elements.*** All told, this document contains seven text blocks. Here's how I want you to tag them, and in this order:

   - Select the large upper-left frame with the black arrow tool, and then click the blue **Body** tag in the Tags palette.
   - Select the two bold-italic subheads and apply the violet **Quiz_headline** tag.
   - Select all three columns of the hanging-indent list. Then click the **Quiz_entry** tag.
   - Click the small text block below the graphic—the one that begins with the red word *Answers*—and apply the yellow **Answers** tag.

   Assuming you turned on Show Tagged Frames, you should see a fully color-coded document like the one in Figure 9-41.

8. ***Compare the tags to the style sheets.*** It's very important to tag all frames in a document so that InDesign knows where to position imported XML text and referenced graphics. But while that addresses placement, it does nothing for formatting. To

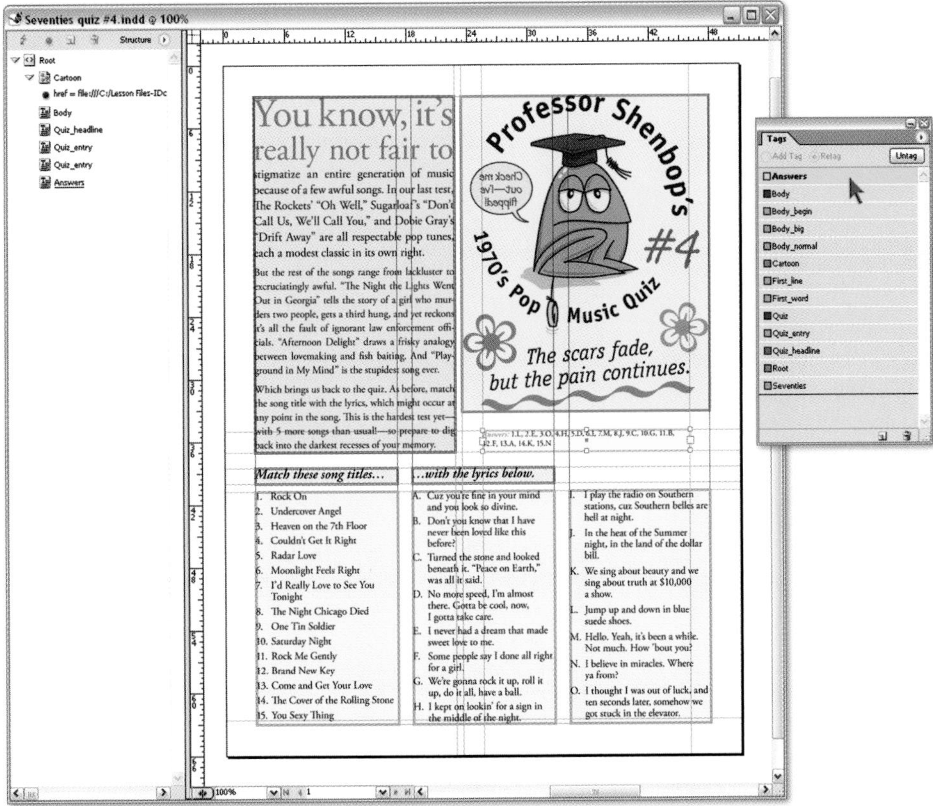

Figure 9-41.

preserve the formatting of individual characters and paragraphs, you have to select and tag text with the type tool, a potentially long and dull process. Fortunately, there's a better way. If you first take the time to apply style sheets to all formatting distinctions, you can map those styles to tags lickety-split.

To see the styles assigned to this document, bring up both the **Paragraph Styles** and **Character Styles** palettes (F11 and Shift+F11, respectively). As illustrated in Figure 9-42, every style sheet corresponds to an identically named tag. This goes for paragraph and character styles alike. Naturally, I did this on purpose. I defined the style sheets first and then created tag names to match, just as I recommend you do when building your own XML-savvy documents.

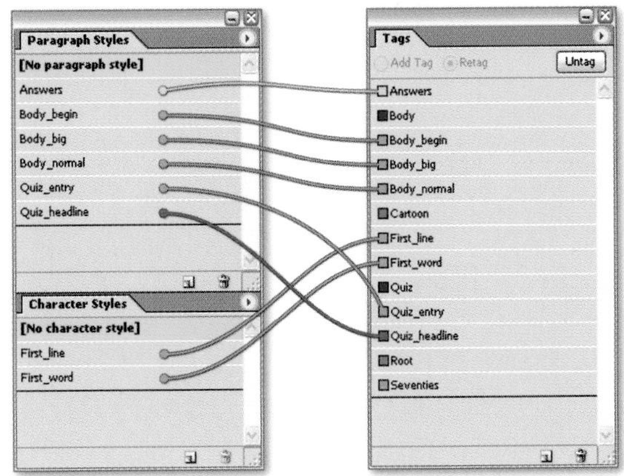

Figure 9-42.

9. *Map the style sheets to tags.* To assign the remaining formatting tags, choose **Map Styles to Tags** from the **Tags** palette menu. (You can also get to the command from the Structure bay menu.) The ensuing dialog box lists every style sheet in the document, both paragraph and character,

followed by a corresponding tag (most likely [Not Mapped] since no style has yet been mapped). Click the tag name to display a pop-up menu of available tags, as shown in Figure 9-43.

Here are your options:

- Because the style sheets and tags share names, you can automate things by clicking the **Map By Name** button, which sets each style to its corresponding tag. The only problem is that you already assigned three of these tags—Answers, Quiz_entry, and Quiz_headline—to text frames. Mapping them to every paragraph of text inside the styled frames would merely duplicate the tags and clutter the code. It might not hurt anything, but it's sloppy and pointless.

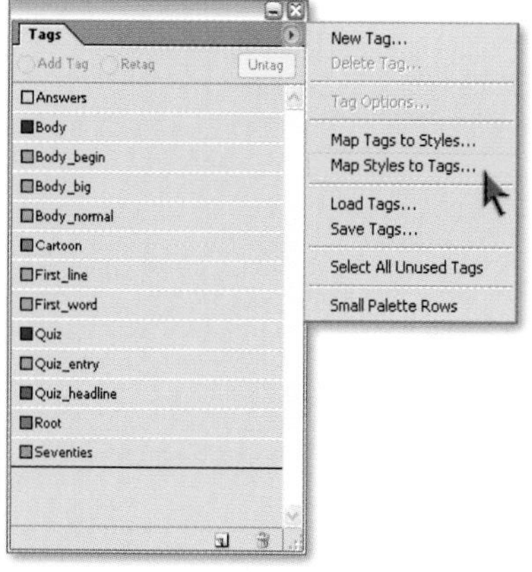

Figure 9-43.

- The better solution is to figure out which tags you haven't applied and select them manually from the pop-up menus. In our case, these amount to five tags in all: those that correspond to the character styles, First_line and First_word, and the three Body variations. To make the tags easier to find, I colored them red in Figure 9-43.

Select the proper tags for the red items in the figure. Then click the **OK** button. InDesign highlights the formatting tags with very subtle colored brackets. The orange brackets in the blue text block are the easiest to see, but you can spot green ones in the blue and yellow blocks if you look carefully.

10. ***Fully expand the element tree.*** The hierarchy of entries in the Structure bay is the *element tree*, so termed because it branches into elements and subelements. To expand the tree so you can see all subelements, do like so: First, click the ▼ triangle to the

left of the word **Root** to collapse the tree and hide all elements. Now, press the Alt key (Option on the Mac) and click the ▶ to expand the tree, this time revealing all elements.

Pictured in Figure 9-44, the expanded tree reveals how elements are grouped. The character tags—First_line and First_word—are nested inside their paragraphs. The Body text tags—the ones with the underscores—are nested inside the Body text block. That's all great, but it's not enough. For one thing, I'd like to see the Quiz subelements grouped together. And then I'd like to shuffle the elements into a more logical order. We'll do both in the next steps.

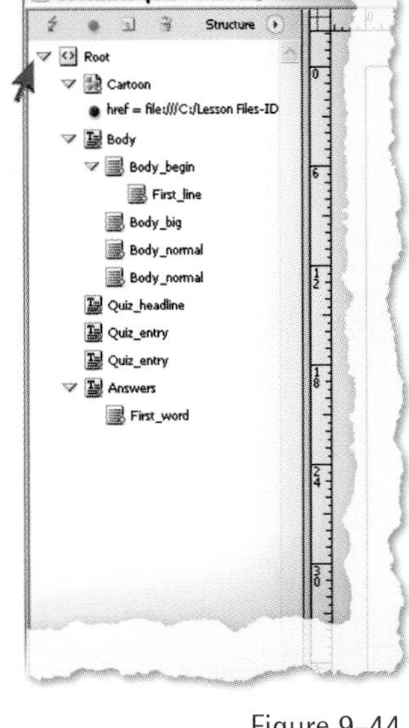

Figure 9-44.

11. ***Create a new Quiz element.*** Click **Root** to select it. Then click the icon to create a new element inside Root. InDesign displays the **Select Tag for Element** dialog box, which lets you assign a tag to the element. Choose **Quiz** from the **Tag** pop-up menu (see Figure 9-45) and click **OK**. A new Quiz element appears at the bottom of the tree.

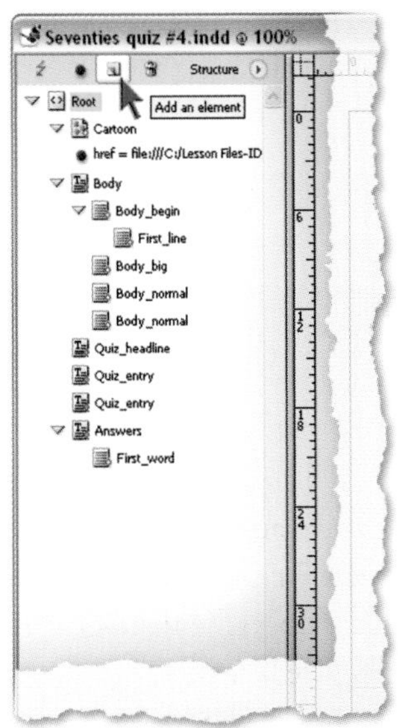

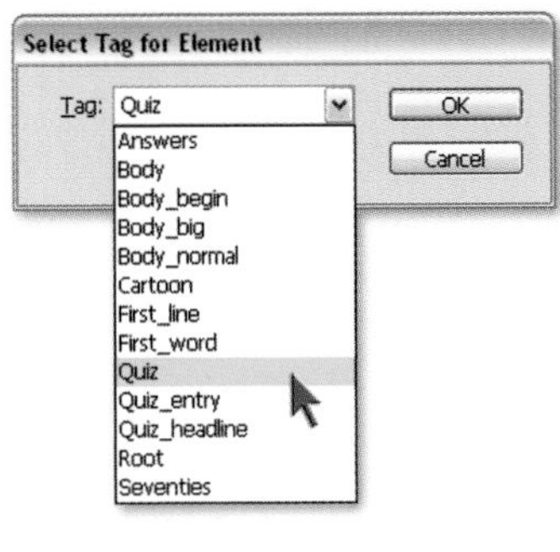

Figure 9-45.

12. ***Reorganize and group elements.*** Now to change how the elements are ordered and grouped:

- Drag the new **Quiz** element above and slightly to the left of Quiz_headline. (This ensures that Quiz is even with Body, not nested inside it.) Wait until you see a long horizontal bar before releasing the mouse button.

- Click **Quiz_headline** and Shift-click the second of the two **Quiz_entry** elements to select all three items. Then drag them onto the **Quiz** icon and release. This makes

XML, Tags, and Elements

Computer languages are a foreign concept to most designers. So when I say that you can use a computer language, XML, to automate page layout, most designers conjure up images of a scripting language, in which one line of code says *put Item A here* and another says *put Item B there*. The script explains a sequence of operations to the application—in our case, InDesign—and the application does as it's told.

Scripting can be an intimidating prospect. To be a successful scripter, you have to understand the syntax, plan a logical approach, verify whether your script works, and troubleshoot when it fails. It's a unique discipline, and it takes time to master.

Thankfully, XML is not a scripting language. As its last two initials suggest, XML is a *markup language*, which means that it uses *tags* to identify elements in a document. InDesign uses these tags to decide where the elements should go and how they should look. I wouldn't go so far as to characterize XML as easy—it's a complex language with its own syntax, standards, and oversight committee. But happily, InDesign doesn't require you to know anything about that stuff. So far as InDesign is concerned, XML is a method for assigning tags and nothing more.

The X in XML stands for *extensible*, which for our purposes means that you can name your tags anything you want. You can call one line of type *Headline*, another *Subhead*, and a third *Caption*. Or you can call them *head-1*, *head-2*, and *cutline*. As long as you subscribe to XML's naming conventions—start with a letter; stick with letters, numbers, and hyphens; and use underscores instead of spaces—then you can call them *Tom*, *Dick*, and *Hermione* for all anyone cares.

To give you a sense of how tags work, the figure on the right shows a few lines of XML code. The red labels encased by blue angle brackets (called *delimiters*) are the tags. An opening tag begins an *element*, a closing tag (which starts with a slash) ends it. An element usually contains text, but it may also contain other elements. For example, in the figure, the *headlines* element includes both the *mainhead* and *subhead* elements. The black text inside the *mainhead* and *subhead* elements and elsewhere is the actual text that will appear in the laid out InDesign document.

If XML's tags remind you of style sheets, it's no coincidence. After all, both tags and style sheets define passages of text, and you can assign them custom names. The big difference is that styles convey formatting attributes, but tags do not. In fact, tags have no intrinsic meaning at all; they are merely labels waiting for definitions, the very definitions that style sheets are eager to supply. Thus, to format the *mainhead* tag in the figure, you have only to create a corresponding *mainhead* style sheet. It's a match made in heaven.

You can also associate tags with InDesign's frames. For example, I might assign the *headlines* tag from the figure to a text frame that's large enough to contain both the *mainhead* and *subhead* text. Assuming that I've defined *mainhead* and *subhead* style sheets, the layout and formatting operations become automatic. As illustrated at the top of the facing page, the *headlines* tags tell the text where to go; the *mainhead* and *subhead* tags define how the text should look. Thus with the help of XML, you can place, position, and format text in one operation, using no more coding than a few simple tags.

You can use XML tags to place and position graphics as well. To do so, you create what's called an *empty element* that contains no text and no closing tag. The opening tag ends with slash, making it self-closing. The tag, which I've named

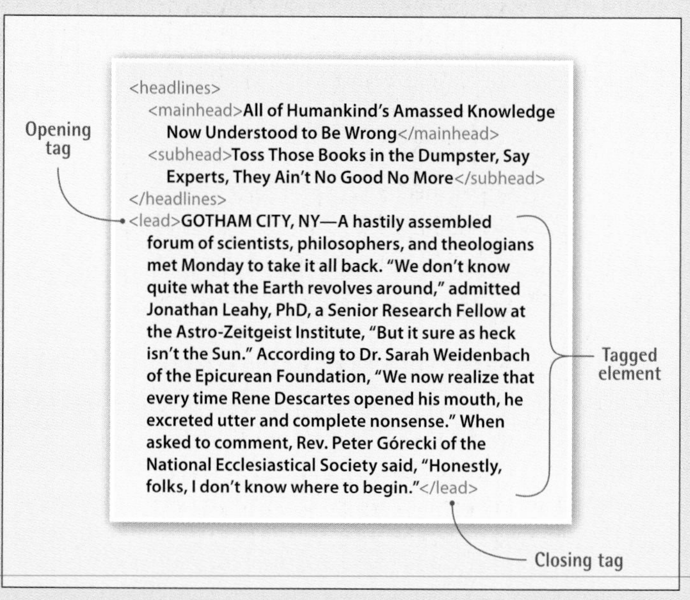

scientist_photo in the illustration at the bottom of the page, is immediately followed by *href*, an attribute borrowed from the Web-page language HTML that's commonly used to reference external graphics. The *href* attribute is followed by an equal sign, *file:///*, and the location and name of the graphic on disk.

This is all a lot to remember, which is why it's fortunate you don't have to. Based on the line of code pictured at the bottom of this page, do as follows:

- Replace the red text with your own tag name.
- Replace the black text with the location and name of the graphic file.
- Enter the blue text exactly as shown, including spaces around the *href*, around the equal sign, and before the slash.

In InDesign, assign your tag to a frame large enough to hold the graphic. If the frame is not large enough, the graphic will be cropped along the right and bottom edges. In other words, InDesign aligns the graphic to the upper-left corner of its frame. InDesign offers no means to include scaling or other transformation data in an XML document, so the graphic comes in at the full size and resolution specified in the originating graphics application. (If only we had graphic style sheets, you could create a style that specified custom cropping, scaling, and rotating info. But for the present, you have to perform these operations by hand after importing the XML content.)

One last note: When specifying the location of a graphic on disk, you should enter all folders relative to the location of the XML file separated by slashes. In the example to the right, the XML file and the *Links* folder must reside together in the same folder or volume, and the file *Nutty Guy.tif* must reside in the *Links* folder. This is not the only way to specify file locations, but it is usually the best way because it permits you to move the XML file and all associated graphic links to another hard drive or shared volume without confusing the *href* attribute.

<headlines>
<mainhead>All of Humankind's Amassed Knowledge Now Understood to Be Wrong</mainhead>
<subhead>Toss Those Books in the Dumpster, Say Experts, They Ain't No Good No More</subhead>
</headlines>
All of Humankind's Amassed Knowledge Now Understood to Be Wrong
Toss Those Books in the Dumpster, Say Experts, They Ain't No Good No More

<scientist_photo href = "file:///Links/Nutty Guy.tif" />
WHAT WERE WE THINKING?

photo by Brian Maffitt

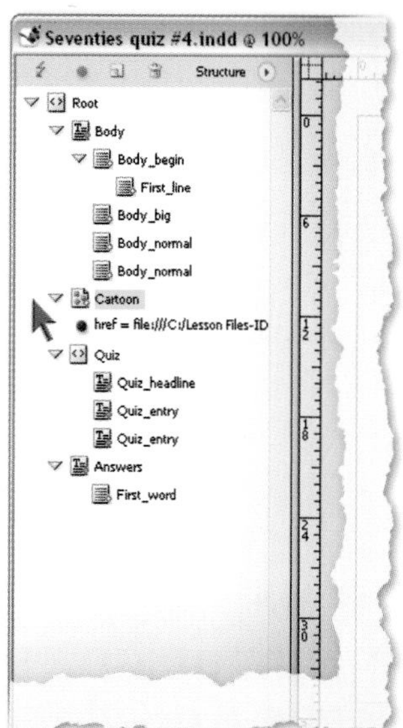

Figure 9-46.

Quiz_headline and Quiz_entry subelements of Quiz. Click the ▶ triangle next to **Quiz** to expand the element and see its contents.

- Drag the **Cartoon** item to just above and slightly to the left of Quiz. (Again, we're trying to ensure that Cartoon is even with Body, not inside it.) The resulting list of four elements and nine subelements should appear as shown in Figure 9-46.

13. ***Add a document-level element.*** This step is not absolutely necessary, but it's a good habit to get into. Currently, we have a series of elements organized under the banner of Root, the XML base. But what's to distinguish these tags—with common names like Body and Cartoon—from similarly named tags in different documents? As it currently stands, someone could import this XML content into the wrong template and have it go completely haywire.

PEARL OF WISDOM

The solution is to gather all elements (except Root) into a document-level element that serves as a project identifier. If a template doesn't include the document element, then the XML content is ignored and no harm is done. If the template does include the element, then the template is confirmed as a match and the import goes forward.

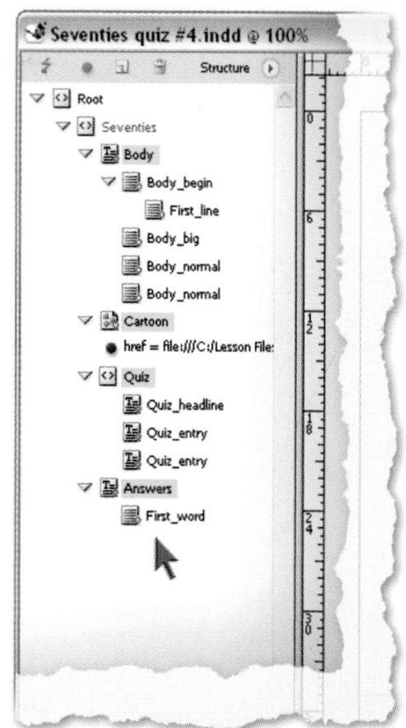

Figure 9-47.

I know, it all sounds dense. Fortunately, it's easy to pull off:

- Select the **Root** item and click the ◱ icon.
- Inside the **Select Tag for Element** dialog box, select **Seventies** from the **Tag** pop-up menu and click **OK**.
- Click **Body** and Shift-click **First_word** (below Answers) to select all elements except Root and Seventies. Then drag the selected elements onto **Seventies** and release.
- Click the ▶ in front of **Seventies** to expand it. As pictured in Figure 9-47, it now comprises every element—not to mention, every word of text and link information for every imported graphic—in the document.

14. ***Save your structured document.*** Choose **File→Save As.** Name your XML-savvy document "Seventies quiz #4-xml.indd" and save it in the same *Lesson 09* folder inside the directory *Lesson Files-IDcs 1on1*. Your saved file will serve as the starting point for the next exercise.

Separating XML Content and Design

Having arrived at a highly organized, XML-savvy InDesign document, our next task is to separate the content from the design. In these steps, you'll export the text from the Shenbop quiz as a tagged XML file. This file will also contain information about the linked Illustrator graphic. Next you'll strip out all text and graphics while leaving the style sheets, tags, and XML elements intact. Then you'll save the result as a super-powerful structured template.

1. ***Open the document you saved in the last exercise.*** If the file is still open, super. If not, open the *Seventies quiz #4-xml.indd* file that you saved to the *Lesson 09* folder inside *Lesson Files-IDcs 1on1*. If you neglected to save the file, you can open my version of the file, *Structured Shenbop.indd*, also inside *Lesson 09*.

   Whichever file you use, make sure that the **Structure** bay is available. If it isn't, click the ◂▸ icon or press Ctrl+Alt+1 (⌘-Option-1 on the Mac). Then Alt-click (or Option-click) the ▶ triangle next to **Root** to expand the entire element tree.

2. ***Add an attribute.*** In addition to elements, the Structure bay may contain *attributes*, which qualify an element. As I mentioned earlier, the Cartoon element includes an href attribute that tells the location of the graphic on disk. While href has a specific meaning in InDesign—if you add an href to a XML element, InDesign will attempt to load a linked graphic—the meaning of other attributes is entirely up to you.

   While custom attributes do not change the behavior of an XML file, they are useful for imparting background information. For example, you can create an attribute to credit the document's author, add a copyright statement, or report the date the document was last updated. I'd like you to credit the author, which in this case is you:

   - To make it easy to locate, you'll most likely want to assign basic information like author credit to the document element. So select the **Seventies** element in the Structure bay.
   - Click the ● icon at the top-left corner of the window to display the **New Attribute** dialog box, as in Figure 9-48.

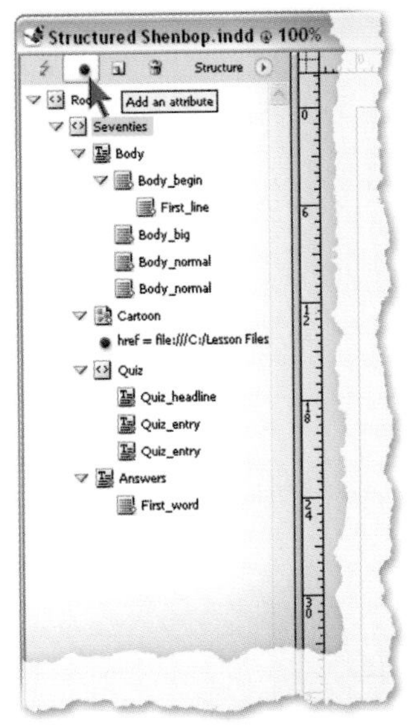

Figure 9-48.

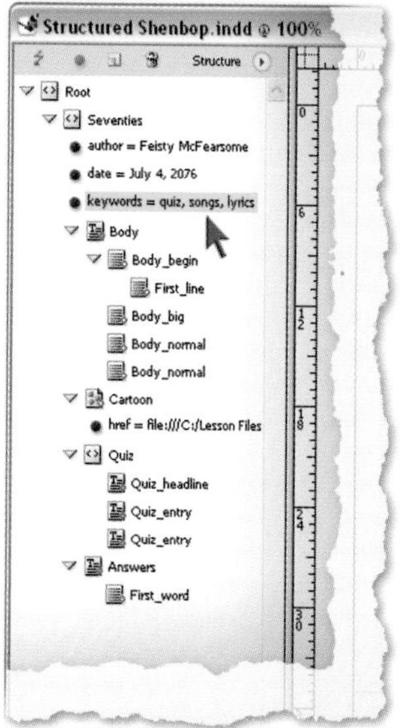

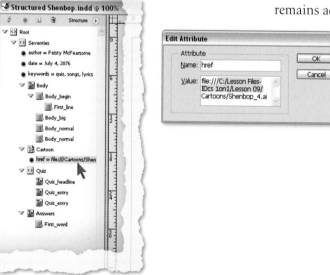

Figure 9-49.

- Type "author" for the **Name**. For the **Value**, type your name (complete with capital and lowercase letters, periods, and whatever else you got going). Then click **OK**.

InDesign adds the attribute as a bullet point below the word *Seventies* that reads *author* = you.

PEARL OF WISDOM

A few words of advice about attributes: First, you can add multiple attributes to an element, but they must all have different names, like the three attributes I added to Seventies in Figure 9-49. If you want to assign multiple values to an attribute—as when crediting multiple authors—go for it. Customarily, values are separated by commas or spaces, but you can use any punctuation you like. In the figure, I added a *keywords* attribute that includes three values, each separated by a comma. But I also used a comma in my *date* attribute, so it's entirely up to you.

3. ***Change the href value to a relative pathname.*** Take a look at the href attribute for the Cartoon element. Most likely, it reads *href = file:///* followed by an *absolute pathname*, meaning that it explains every hard disk, folder, and subfolder that you have to open to get to the linked graphic. The problem with an absolute pathname is that it doesn't work when you transfer the graphic to another computer. Assuming that all your files are collected in a central folder—in our case, the *Lesson 09* folder—you're better off using a *relative pathname*, which explains the location of the graphic relative to that of the XML file. Copy the central folder to a different computer and the relative pathname remains accurate.

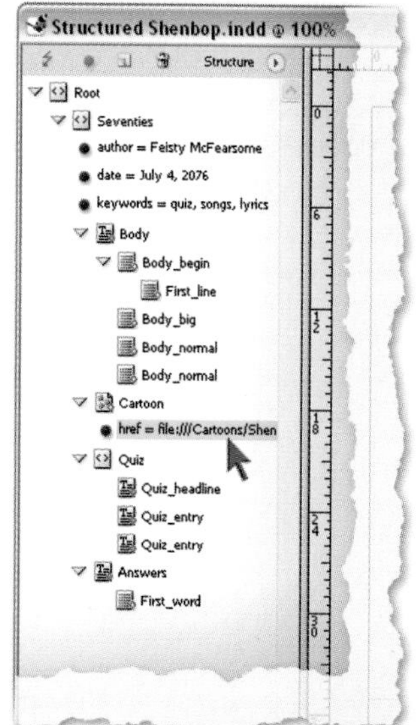

Figure 9-50.

Here's how to change the absolute pathname for the Shenbop cartoon to a relative one:

- Double-click the **href** item to display the **Edit Attribute** dialog box.
- In the **Value** option, delete everything from the hard drive through and including the *Lesson 09* folder (shown highlighted in Figure 9-50). The Value string should now read *file:///Cartoons/Shenbop_4.ai*. (Note that the word *file*, the colon, and the triple-slash must remain intact.)
- Click **OK** to accept your changes.

4. ***Export the XML data.*** Having fixed the graphic attribute, we are ready to export the content of this structured document as an XML data file:

- Choose **File→Export** or press Ctrl+E (or ⌘-E).
- Inside the **Export** dialog box, set the **Save As Type** pop-up menu (which goes by the name **Format** on the Mac) to **XML**. Make sure *Lesson 09* is the active folder. Name the file "Structured Shenbop.xml" and click **Save**.
- Next the **Export XML** dialog box appears. Turn on the **View XML Using** check box and choose **Internet Explorer** (or **iexplore.exe** on the PC, as in Figure 9-51). The other options—including Encoding, which by default is set to UTF-8 (the widely supported 8-bit-per-character Unicode Transformation Format)—are fine as is. Click **Export** to save the XML file.

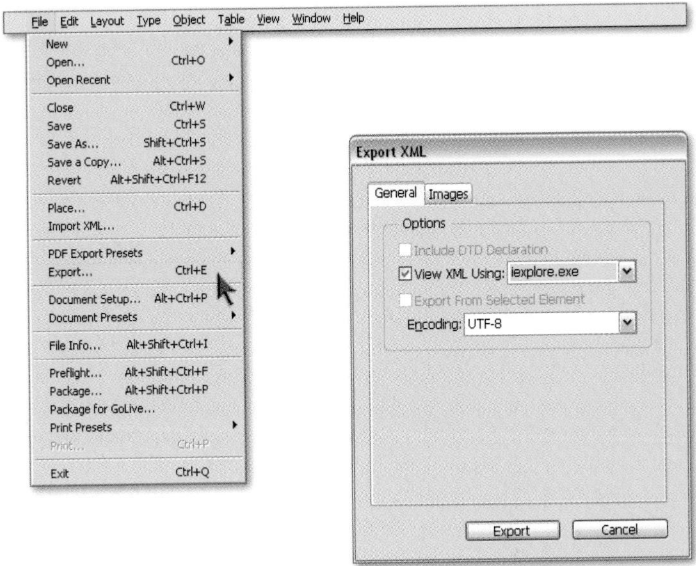

Figure 9-51.

In roughly the blink of an eye, InDesign writes the XML data and opens it up in the cross-platform Web browser, Internet Explorer. The result appears in all its color-coded glory in Figure 9-52. Explorer formats the tags and attribute names in red, special scripting in blue, and all document text and attribute values in black.

PEARL OF WISDOM

If you're a Macintosh user, you may wonder why I don't use Apple's Safari. As I write this, the most recent version of Safari (1.2.2) lacks the ability to color-code and indent XML tags. As a result, all the text runs together, making it darn near impossible to read. Meanwhile, you PC users may wonder what's up with all the hollow squares floating around inside Figure 9-52. Regardless of your platform, InDesign exports XML with Macintosh-style line breaks. Explorer on the PC doesn't understand Mac line breaks, and thus shows them as squares. Fortunately, it's not much of a problem. InDesign imports Mac line breaks just fine. And if you later edit the file and decide to enter PC line breaks instead (by pressing the Enter key), InDesign reads those, too.

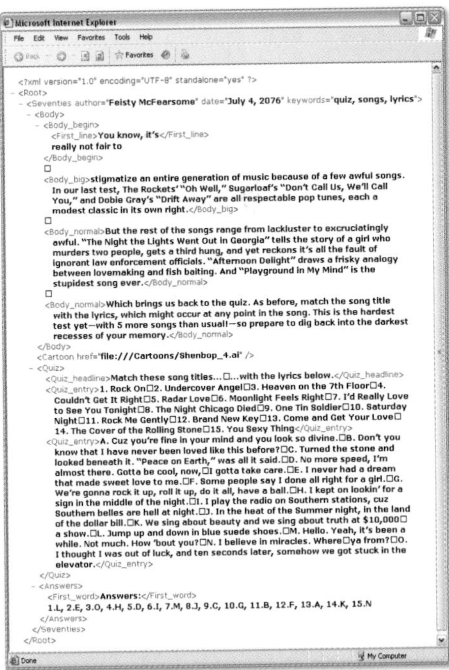

Figure 9-52.

5. ***Switch back to InDesign.*** Thanks to the Export command, the XML content has been set free from the clutches of its design. With the content thus safe and sound, we are free to convert the InDesign document into a template. Return to InDesign so we can get started.

6. ***Delete the cartoon from the graphic frame.*** To successfully convert an XML-savvy document into an XML-savvy template, you must delete the content without removing the frames or the structure. The best way to accomplish this varies depending on whether you're removing an imported graphic or text.

   We'll start with the graphic. First, select the white arrow tool. (Assuming no text is active, you can do this by pressing the A key.) Then click inside the Shenbop cartoon to select the imported graphic independently of its frame. Press the Backspace or Delete key. The cartoon goes away but the frame remains.

7. ***Delete the href attribute.*** InDesign is an astute application. But every once in a while, even it misses a beat. In this case, InDesign has succeeded in deleting the graphic, but it forgot to delete the href attribute, which could create problems when placing other graphics into this container. Click **href** in the **Structure** bay to select it; then press Backspace or Delete.

8. ***Delete all type from the text frames.*** To extract text from its frame, you have to first select the text with the type tool. With seven frames to choose from, this might take a while. So it's fortunate that InDesign provides a slight shortcut.

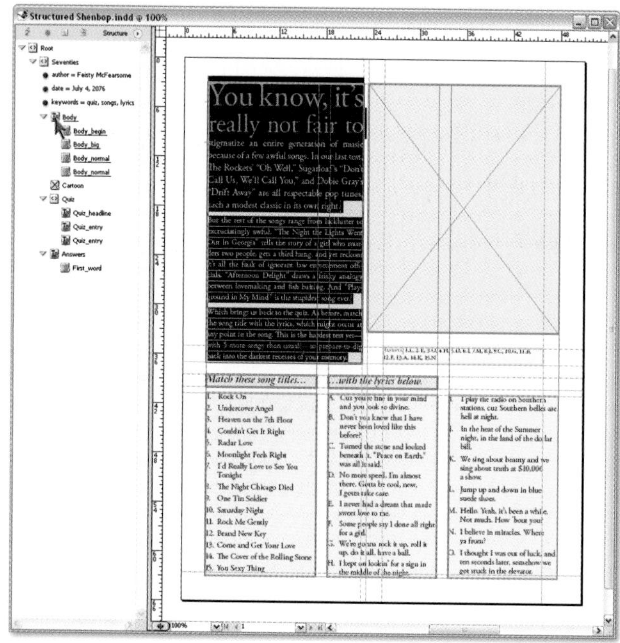

Figure 9-53.

To select the contents of a tagged text frame, double-click its element in the Structure bay. For example, double-clicking the top-level **Body** element selects all text in the upper-left frame, as demonstrated in Figure 9-53. Then press Backspace or Delete to get rid of it.

Repeat this process for the other text elements:

- Double-click the **Answers** element to select the text below the graphic frame. Then press the Backspace or Delete key.
- The Quiz tag is not assigned to a specific frame, so we have to address the Quiz subelements independently. Double-click **Quiz_headline** to select the text inside the violet frames, and then press the Delete key. Next, double-click a **Quiz_entry** element and press Delete. Repeat for the other **Quiz_entry** element.

When the text frames are empty, press Enter on the keypad to deactivate the frames and return control to the black arrow tool. (If you did not load my Deke Keys shortcuts, click the black arrow icon in the toolbox.)

9. ***Detach all character-level style sheets.*** A couple of tiny, subtle formatting problems remain. The blue and yellow text frames each begin with a character-level style sheet. If we neglect to turn off these style sheets, they will haunt us when we import the XML data in the next exercise. Here's the fix:

   - Press Ctrl+A (or ⌘-A) to select all frames in the document.
   - Display the **Character Styles** palette (by pressing Shift+F11, if necessary). Then click the **[No character style]** option, as you see me doing in Figure 9-54. This deactivates the character styles but leaves all paragraph styles intact.

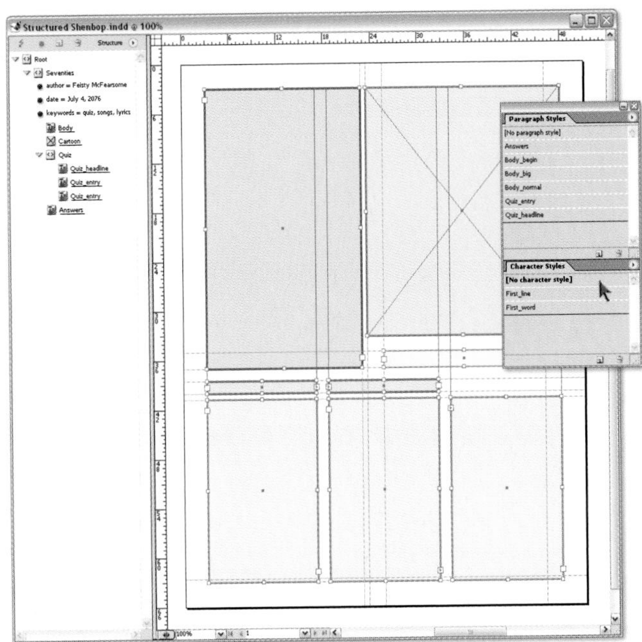

Figure 9-54.

10. ***Save the document as a template.*** Choose **File→Save As**, or press Ctrl+Shift+S (⌘-Shift-S), and navigate to the *Lesson 09* folder. As demonstrated in Figure 9-55, change the **Save as Type** setting (**Format** on the Mac) to **InDesign CS template**. Rename the file "Structured template.indt" and click the **Save** button.

Figure 9-55.

Importing XML-Formatted Text

Congratulations, you have successfully accomplished a feat that precious few professional designers have dared attempt: You have created an XML-compatible template. In this final exercise, you'll see how this one magical document enables InDesign to assemble a complete page design—one that originally took me more than an hour to create—in a few minutes.

1. ***Close all open InDesign documents.*** In particular, be sure to close the document that you saved as a template in Step 10 of the preceding exercise. This prevents you from accidentally overwriting your template document.

2. ***Open your XML-savvy template.*** If you successfully completed the last exercise, open the document you saved in Step 10, *Structured template.indt*, presumably found in the *Lesson 09* folder inside *Lesson Files-IDcs 1on1*. Otherwise, open my version of the template, *My template.indt*, also inside *Lesson 09*.

(Before leaving the **Open a File** dialog box, make sure the **Normal** option (on the Mac, **Open Normal**) in the lower-left corner is turned on, as highlighted in Figure 9-56. This opens the template as an untitled document.)

As always, make sure that the Structure bay is visible. Then Alt-click (or Option-click) the ▶ triangle next to **Root** to expand the entire element tree.

3. ***Import an XML file.*** With the template open, the moment of truth is upon us. Choose **File→Import XML**, which is designed specifically to implement XML code. (By comparison, the Place command would merely flow all text from the XML file—content and tags alike—into columns.) Navigate to the *Lesson 09* folder and select the *Structured Shenbop.xml* file that you saved in Step 4 of the preceding exercise (see page 365). If you can't find it, you can use my version of the file, *Seventies quiz #4.xml*. Click **Open** to import the file. A heartbeat later, InDesign has placed the entire document, arranged all text as well as the imported graphic into their allotted frames, and even attempted to apply the appropriate style sheets. As witnessed by the blue text block in Figure 9-57, not all the styles came out right. But we can fix that in a flash.

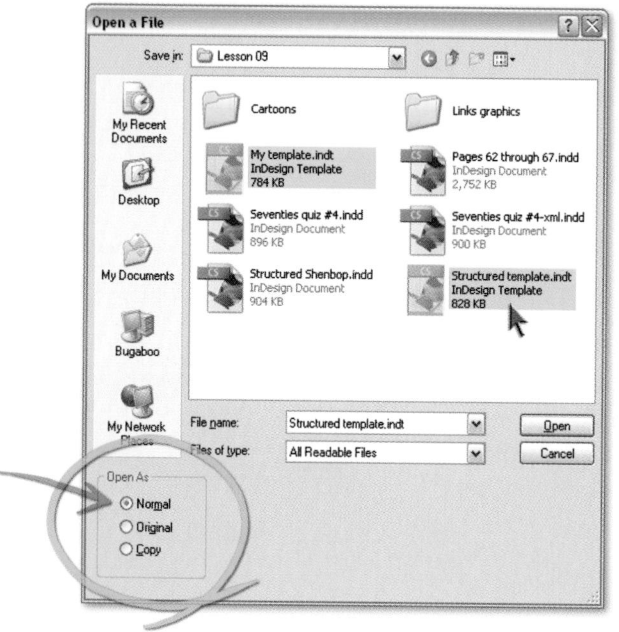

Figure 9-56.

PEARL OF WISDOM

If the Shenbop cartoon appears out of frame or cropped incorrectly, it's because your graphic import options are messed up. To fix them, here's what you do: Press Ctrl+Z (or ⌘-Z) to undo the XML import. Then choose File→Place, locate the *Shenbop_4.ai* file inside the *Cartoons* folder in *Lesson 09*. Turn on the Show Import Options check box and click the Open button. In the Place PDF dialog box, set the Crop To option to Bounding Box. Make sure Transparent Background is on, and then click OK. Now instead of clicking with the place cursor, press Ctrl+Z (or ⌘-Z) again to discontinue the operation. The preference is reset and you are ready to go. Once again choose File→XML Import and place the *Seventies quiz #4.xml* file. Your document should match the one in Figure 9-57 on the facing page.

4. ***Map the tags to style sheets.*** To properly format the imported text, choose **Map Tags to Styles** from either the **Tags** palette or the Structure bay menu. Modeled after the Map Styles to Tags command that we chose back in Step 4 of "Assigning XML Tags and Struc-

ture" (see page 354), this command uses XML tags to select style sheet definitions. And this time, we can do it entirely automatically. Click the **Map By Name** button to assign a style sheet to every applicable tag (highlighted red in Figure 9-58), and then click **OK**. Just like that, InDesign applies all style sheets exactly as we had them before.

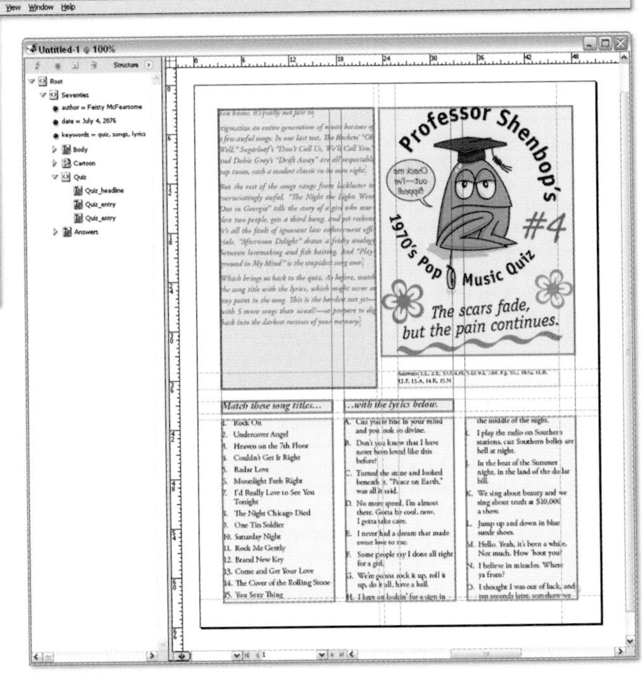

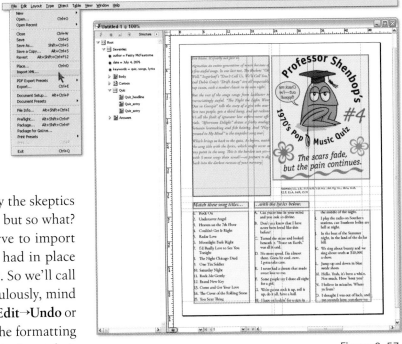

Figure 9-57.

5. ***Choose Undo twice.*** "All right," say the skeptics among you. "That's all hunky dory, but so what? What possible purpose does it serve to import text and graphics that we already had in place two exercises ago?" Ah, good point. So we'll call that a test—one that went over fabulously, mind you, but a test nonetheless. Choose **Edit→Undo** or press Ctrl+Z (⌘-Z) twice to undo the formatting and placement of the XML content. And now, let's replay these steps with a different XML document that contains completely new content.

6. ***Open the XML document for Quiz #5.*** Go to the desktop level of your computer and open the *Lesson 09* folder inside *Lesson Files-IDcs 1on1*. Then double-click the file called *Seventies quiz #5.xml*, which is the next edition of the Shenbop song quiz. With any luck, it'll open inside Internet Explorer. (If not, switch to Internet Explorer, choose **File→Open**, and then click the **Browse** button and locate the file on disk. On the Mac, choose **File→Open File**.)

   This XML document is largely different than the one we saw back in Figure 9-52 (page 365), but it uses the same tags and conforms to the same structure. In Figure 9-59 on the next page, I've highlighted the modified portions of the document in yellow. Notice that only the black text—i.e., the content— has changed, and not quite all of that. The quiz headlines and the word *Answer* are the same. And the only change made to the href attribute is the number at the end of the filename. I was careful not to modify a single red tag, nor did I change the sequence of the tags in the document.

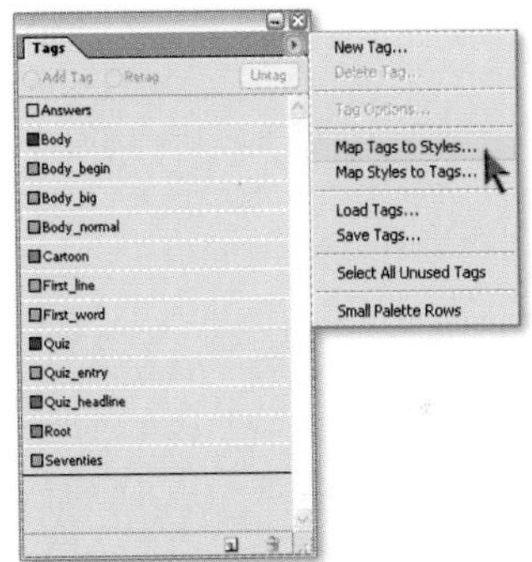

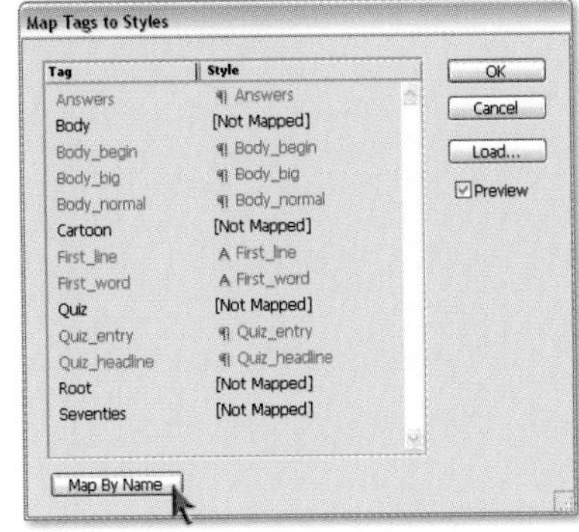

Figure 9-58.

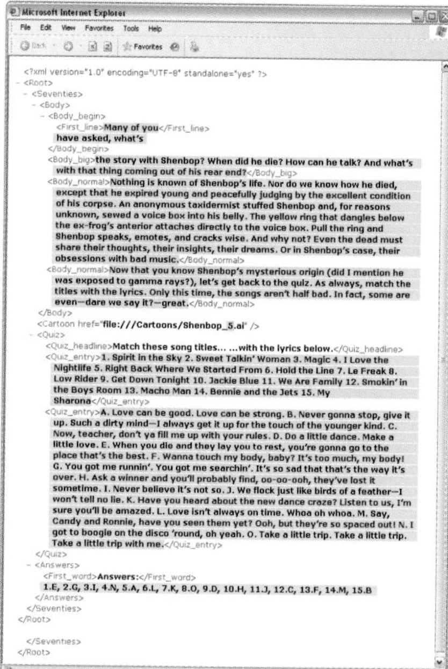

Figure 9-59.

PEARL OF WISDOM

You may wonder what program I used to make my edits. If you own the Premium edition of the Creative Suite, you can edit an XML document in Adobe GoLive. But I prefer to use a run-of-the-mill text editor. On the PC, you can use Notepad, which ships with Windows. I advise against using WordPad, which doesn't properly handle UTF-8 encoding (applied back in the preceding exercise in Step 4 on page 365). To keep your text inside the boundaries of the Notepad window, turn on Format→Word Wrap. On the Mac, I use TextEdit, included with OS X. Figure 9-60 shows the two programs side-by-side, Notepad on the left and TextEdit on the right; the *Seventies quiz #5.xml* document appears open in each. Unlike Internet Explorer, neither program highlights the XML code, so you have to keep an eye out for the angle brackets, < and >, which surround all tags.

7. ***Return to InDesign and import the revised XML file.*** Back inside InDesign, again choose **File→Import XML**. Select *Seventies quiz #5.xml* in the *Lesson 09* folder and click **Open**. InDesign automatically lays out the fifth of the Seventies music quizzes, filling each of the colored frames according to the rules described in the template and the XML file, as shown in Figure 9-61. As before, the text in the blue frame needs work.

8. ***Map the tags to style sheets.*** Choose **Map Tags to Styles** from the **Tags** palette or the Structure bay menu. Click the **Map By Name** button, and then click **OK**. This applies all the proper style sheets to the document, but the blue text block is by no

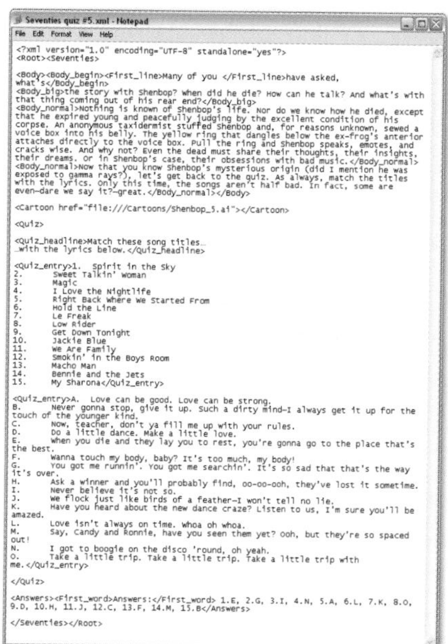

Figure 9-60.

means perfect, exhibiting enormous gaps in the first three lines, as illustrated on the left side of Figure 9-62. This is a common problem when placing XML content. Despite my best efforts to anticipate how much text I needed to fit the space, manual adjustments must be made.

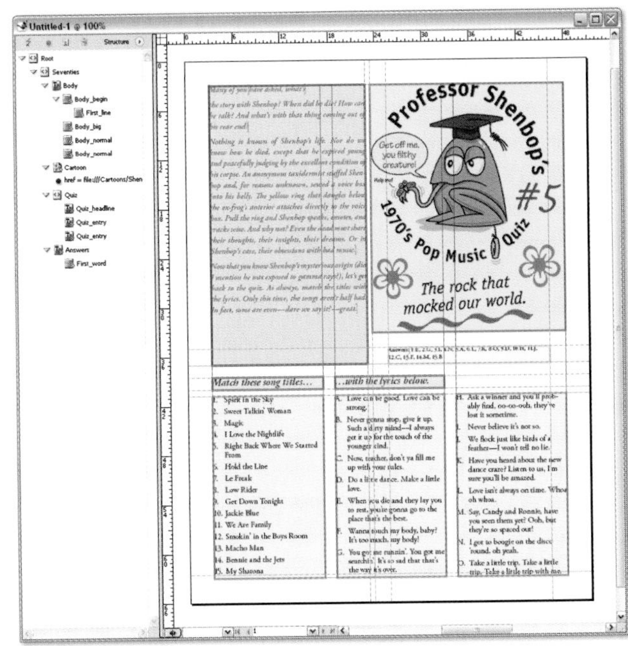

Figure 9-61.

9. ***Adjust the type size for the Body_begin style.*** The paragraph of large, crimson type is governed by the Body_begin style sheet. I'd like you to edit the style as follows:

   - Double-click **Body_begin** in the **Paragraph Styles** palette to display the **Paragraph Style Options** dialog box.
   - Press Ctrl+2 (⌘-2) or click **Basic Character Formats** in the left-hand list to switch to the second panel of options.
   - Click the word **Size** to highlight the type size value. Then press the ↓ key four times to reduce the type size to 34 pt.
   - Click the **OK** button. The crimson type now fits on two lines, as pictured on the right side of Figure 9-62.

10. ***Add some paragraph spacing to the Quiz_entry style.*** The other slight problem with the text is the unevenness of the orange columns in the quiz, and the way the *H* entry splits between the second and third columns. Again, this can be remedied by adjusting a style sheet:

    - Double-click **Quiz_entry** in the Paragraph Styles palette.
    - Press Ctrl+4 (⌘-4) or click **Indents and Spacing** in the left-hand list to switch to the fourth panel.
    - Tab to **Space After** and raise it to 0p4.
    - Click **OK** to accept your changes.

This adjustment fills the orange frames and nudges answer *H* to the third column, as in Figure 9-63 on the next page.

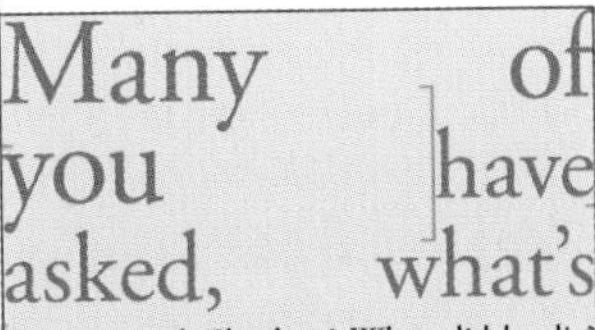

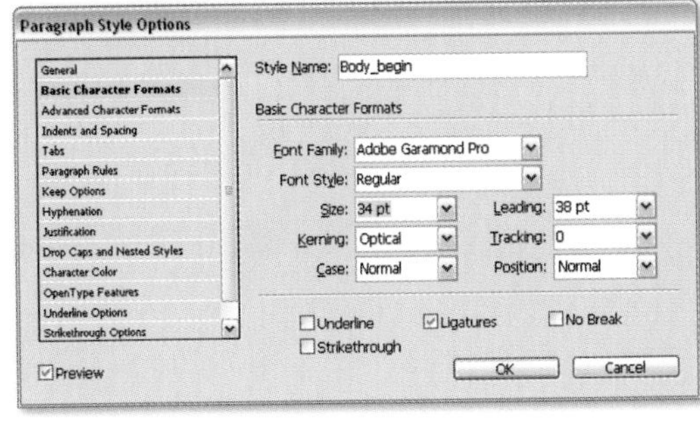

Figure 9-62.

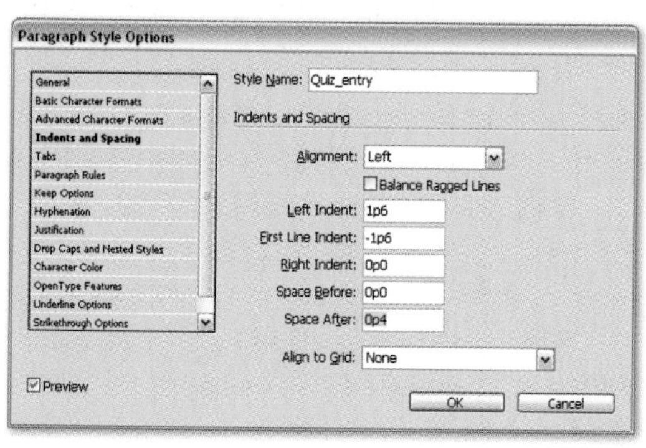

1. Spirit in the Sky
2. Sweet Talkin' Woman
3. Magic
4. I Love the Nightlife
5. Right Back Where We Started From
6. Hold the Line
7. Le Freak
8. Low Rider
9. Get Down Tonight
10. Jackie Blue
11. We Are Family
12. Smokin' in the Boys Room
13. Macho Man
14. Bennie and the Jets
15. My Sharona

A. Love can be good. Love can be strong.
B. Never gonna stop, give it up. Such a dirty mind—I always get it up for the touch of the younger kind.
C. Now, teacher, don't ya fill me up with your rules.
D. Do a little dance. Make a little love.
E. When you die and they lay you to rest, you're gonna go to the place that's the best.
F. Wanna touch my body, baby? It's too much, my body!
G. You got me runnin'. You got me searchin'. It's so sad that that's the way it's over.

H. Ask a winner and you'll probably find, oo-oo-ooh, they've lost it sometime.
I. Never believe it's not so.
J. We flock just like birds of a feather—I won't tell no lie.
K. Have you heard about the new dance craze? Listen to us, I'm sure you'll be amazed.
L. Love isn't always on time. Whoa oh whoa.
M. Say, Candy and Ronnie, have you seen them yet? Ooh, but they're so spaced out!
N. I got to boogie on the disco 'round, oh yeah.
O. Take a little trip. Take a little trip. Take a little trip with me.

Figure 9-63.

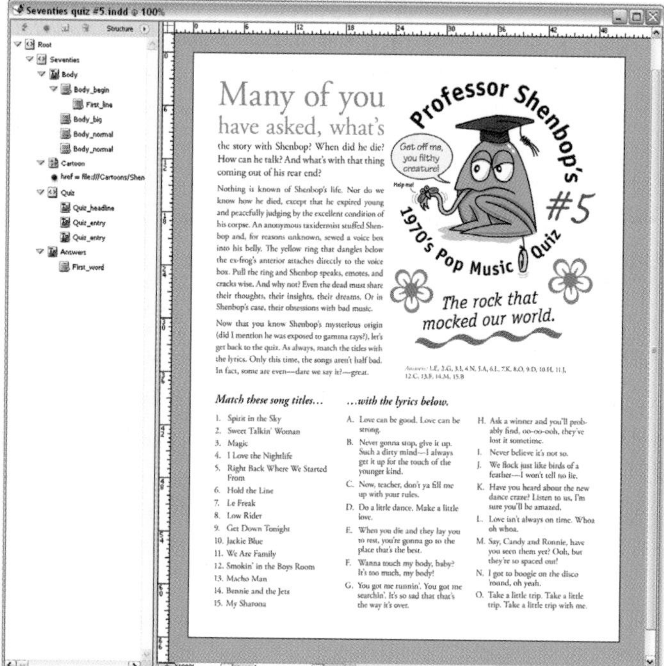

Figure 9-64.

11. ***Save the finished document.*** In the last four steps, you've managed to lay out a page that comprises eight frames, eight style sheets, and dozens of formatting variations. It was a cakewalk, but that's no reason not to save your changes. Choose **File→Save** or press Ctrl+S (⌘-S on the Mac). Then name the file "Seventies Quiz #5.indd" and click the **Save** button.

Between you and me, I made a couple of additional adjustments. The middle column in the quiz struck me as a bit short, so I selected paragraphs *A* through *G* with the type tool and raised the -≡ value in the Paragraph palette from 0p4 to 0p5. I also changed the size of the first crimson line of text in the upper-left corner of the page from 47 pt to 48 pt.

I mention this because I'm one of those designers who tends to fuss over a document long after I should probably let it go. But in this case, there's just not much for me to fuss over. Pictured in the preview mode in Figure 9-64, my final document is every bit as clean and polished as the one we saw way back in Figure 9-35 (see page 352). The difference is that I laid out that document manually, while this one laid out itself. With a little planning, you too can automate your way out of a whole lot of work.

WHAT DID YOU LEARN?

Match the key concept in the numbered list below with the letter of the phrase that best describes it. Answers appear upside-down at the bottom of the page.

Key Concepts

1. XML
2. Section
3. Automatic page number
4. Master page
5. Footer
6. Folio
7. Tag
8. Structure bay
9. href
10. Delimiter
11. Relative pathname
12. Map Tags to Styles

Descriptions

A. Recurring information that runs along the bottom of most pages, such as the lesson names and section titles in this book.

B. This subwindow permits you to manage elements and attributes in an XML document or template.

C. A collection of pages that subscribe to their own independent page-numbering scheme.

D. A code word that identifies a passage of text, a frame, or an imported graphic so that it can be positioned and formatted automatically.

E. The location of a linked graphic or other file on disk, as expressed in relation to the location of an XML or InDesign file.

F. This provides the base elements for a series of pages, much as a piece of stationery provides the base elements for a series of memos.

G. An extensible document processing language that enables you to create and format pages by writing relatively simple computer code.

H. An angle bracket, < or >, used to separate a tag from its contents in an XML document.

I. A fancy name for the printed page number, usually added to the top or bottom of a document.

J. Borrowed from the Web-page language HTML, this attribute specifies the location of a linked illustration or image file on disk.

K. A special character that tracks and records the order of pages in a document, which you can insert from the keyboard by pressing Ctrl+Shift+Alt+N (⌘-Shift-Option-N on the Mac).

L. This command automatically assigns style sheets according to the element specifications in an imported XML document.

Answers

1G, 2C, 3K, 4F, 5A, 6I, 7D, 8B, 9J, 10H, 11E, 12L

LESSON 10

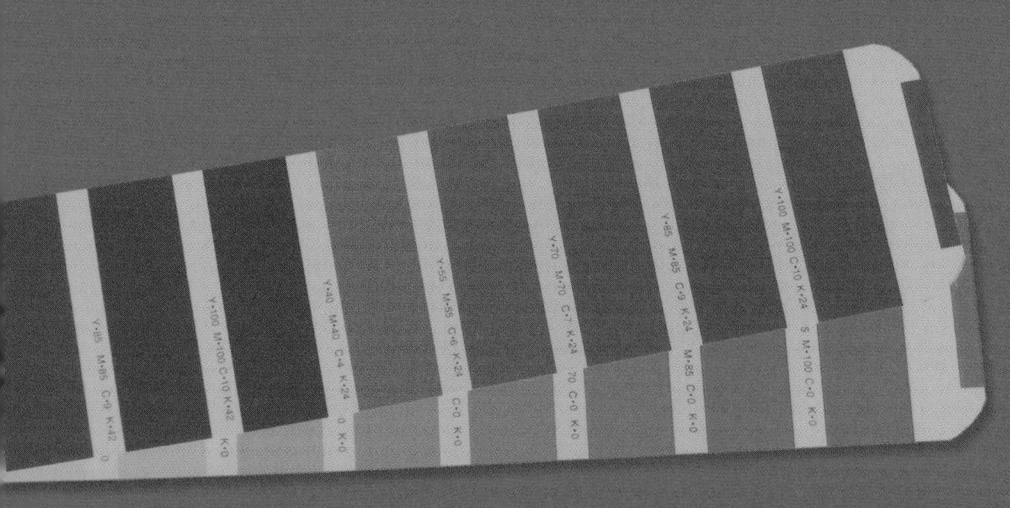
Y•100 M•100 C•10 K•24
Y•85 M•85 C•9 K•24
Y•70 M•70 C•7 K•24
Y•55 M•55 C•6 K•24
Y•40 M•40 C•4 K•24
Y•100 M•100 C•10 K•42
Y•85 M•85 C•9 K•42

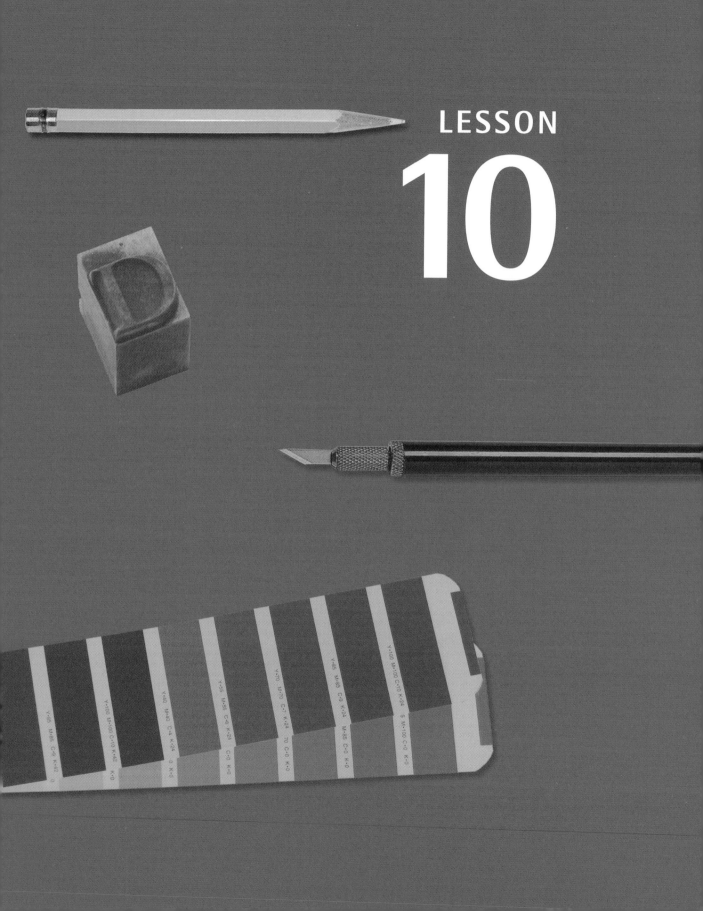

WORKING WITH LONG DOCUMENTS

THIS LESSON, as well as the 11 other lessons in this book, started out as a single InDesign CS document. It was written, illustrated, and edited as its own individual entity, separate from its 11 siblings. But to bring all these documents together into the completed work you hold in your hands, I had to import the lessons into an InDesign *book file*, as symbolically illustrated in Figure 10-1.

Despite its name, a book file isn't restricted to building a book. You can use book files to assemble any type of long document, including catalogs, manuals, reports, and the like. In short, if the easiest way to work on a publication is to break it up into separate documents, then by all means do it. You can always use a book file to assembles the pieces into a unified whole.

An InDesign book file manifests itself as a palette, into which you add the documents that you need to bring together. Of course, you can add new documents to a book at any time, delete documents you don't need anymore, and drag documents around in the palette until you have them in the perfect order. (And by the way, a single document can belong to more than one book.) But essential as the book palette is, it only scratches the surface of InDesign's bookmaking capabilities.

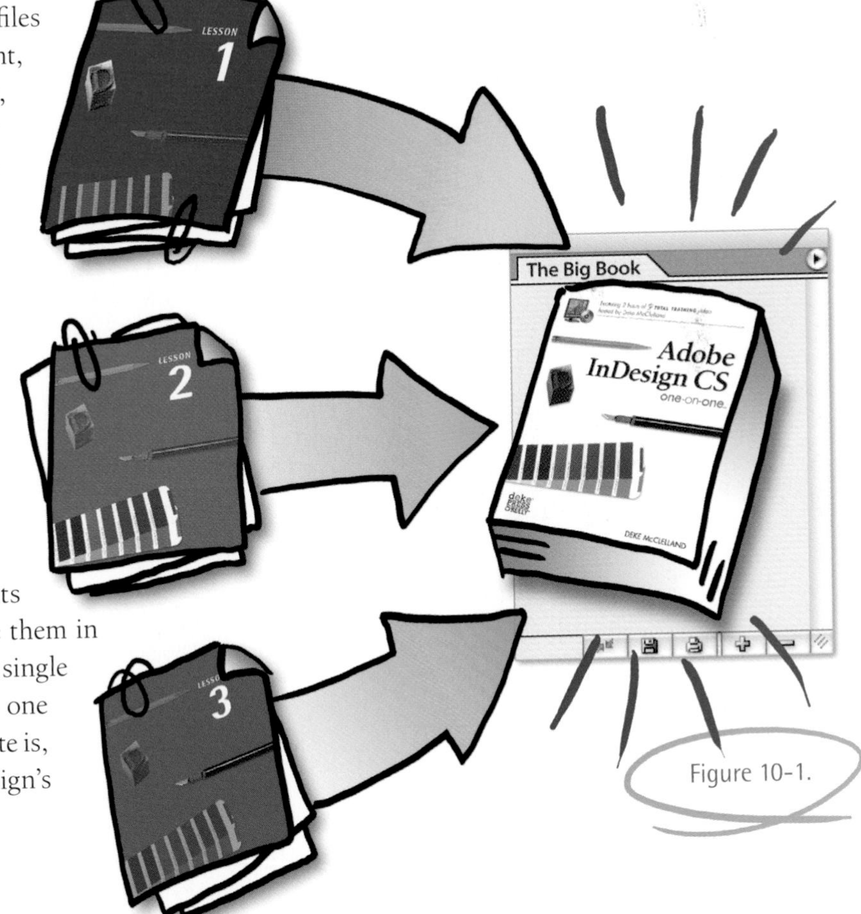

Figure 10-1.

ABOUT THIS LESSON

Project Files

Before beginning the exercises, make sure that you've installed the lesson files from the CD, as explained in Step 5 on page xv of the Preface. This should result in a folder called *Lesson Files-InDncs 1on1* on your desktop. We'll be working with the files inside the *Lesson 10* subfolder.

This lesson examines InDesign's long-document functions, which help you collect multiple files, synchronize style sheets and swatches, and create navigational aids such as a table of content and an index. In these exercises, you'll learn how to:

Video Lesson 10: Making a Book

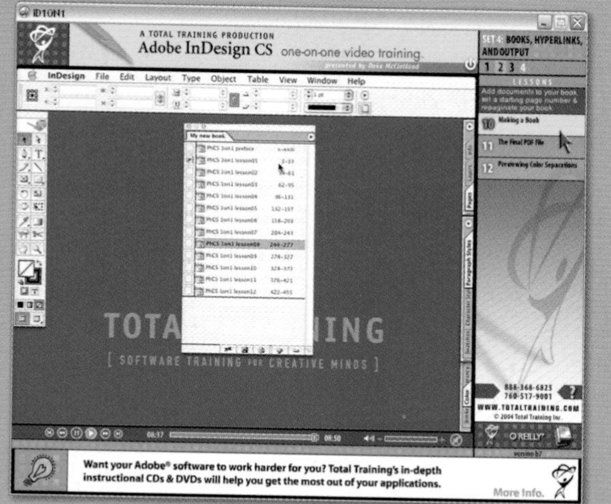

You might reckon that you need InDesign's book palette only when editing, say, a book. But in fact, I recommend that you use it anytime you opt to divide a publication across more than one file. The book palette lets you automatically number pages across multiple documents, as well as synchronize style sheet definitions and generally keep things in order. And it's a great leaping off point for opening files.

For a brief introduction to the book palette, watch the tenth video lesson on the CD. Insert the CD, click the **Start Training** button, click the Set 4 button, and watch me gas on about this and that. When I'm done, select **10, Making a Book** from the Lessons list. As you watch this 8-minute 50-second movie, bear in mind the following shortcuts:

Operation	Windows shortcut	Macintosh shortcut
Select a range of documents	Click one, Shift-click another	Click one, Shift-click another
Open a document from the book palette	Double-click document name	Double-click document name
Change page number options	Double-click page number	Double-click page number
Close a document	Ctrl+W or Ctrl+F4	⌘-W
Save a document when prompted	Y (for the Yes button)	S (for the Save button)
Close a document without saving it	N (for the No button)	D (for the Don't Save button)

Binding, Synchronizing, and Indexing

Regardless of the individual page-numbering schemes your documents may employ, a book file lets you coordinate or even override them to make one group of pages flow evenly into the next. You think that chapter in the middle of the book might work better as an appendix? No problem—a book file's page numbers will adjust on the fly to accommodate any last-minute adjustments.

As you develop the various documents that make up a publication, your style sheets, color swatches, and other presets are likely to evolve and change. Once again, InDesign has the answer. After you've imported all the documents into a book file, just designate one document as the style source. Then you can synchronize the style sheets and swatches of all the other documents to match the style source, creating a cohesive, consistent look from one page of a publication to the next.

If your documents happen to combine into a lengthy work—say, 50 pages or more—your readers might reasonably hope for a little guidance so they can find their way around. InDesign's book function includes tools for generating the most common kinds of publication maps: tables of contents and indexes. Creating a table of contents is largely automatic, a function of properly defining style sheets and assigning them to headlines and subheads. Creating a quality index, on the other hand, requires some effort. InDesign's Index palette does a fine job of making the process as painless as possible, but expect to put in a few hours or even days of work. The good news is that once you have a table of contents or index established, it is a simple matter to update. You define the entries; InDesign keeps track of the page numbers and sorting.

The four exercises in this lesson take you step by step through creating a book file, importing documents, synchronizing styles, generating a table of contents, and creating an index. It's essential that you work straight through this lesson starting with the first exercise. There's a lot to know about assembling a book, but stick with me and you're bound to succeed.

Assembling Documents into a Book

If you watched Video Lesson 10, "Making a Book," then you saw how to assemble documents into a book file and put InDesign in charge of the pagination. Now's your chance to try it out for yourself. In this exercise, you'll assemble three chapters and the table of contents from an old book of mine into an InDesign book file.

You'll see how simple it is to import and arrange the various documents. And you'll witness how, regardless of your previous page-numbering settings, the book palette lets you bring the numbering for all your documents in sync.

1. *Create a book file.* Choose **File→New→Book** to display the **New Book** dialog box. Navigate to the *Lesson 10* folder inside *Lesson Files-IDcs 1on1*. Name the file "Look&Learn book 1.indb," and click **Save**. The palette shown in the bottom-right corner of Figure 10-2 appears.

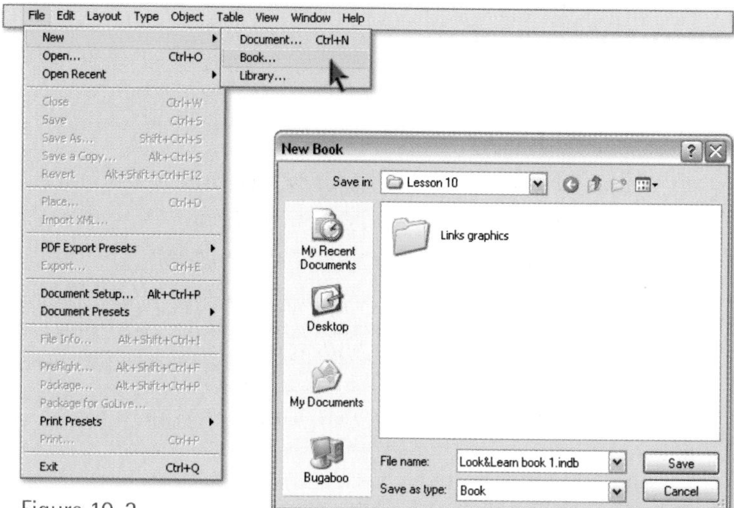

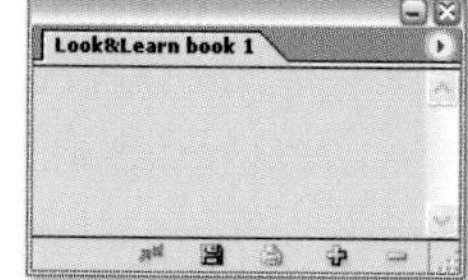

Figure 10-2.

2. *Add documents to the book.* Click the ✚ icon at the bottom of the palette to bring up the **Add Documents** dialog box, as in Figure 10-3. Navigate to the *Lesson 10* folder, if it doesn't come up automatically. We want to bring the four files with names that begin with "Look&Learn" into the book. Click *Look&Learn Ch01.indd*, Shift-click *Look&Learn TOC vii.indd*, and then click **Add** (**Open** on the Mac).

   InDesign confronts you with the warning message shown at the bottom of Figure 10-3. This warning notifies you that there are missing fonts in the *Look&Learn Ch09.indd* document, but it also conveys a larger message: Importing these chapter files into the book has prompted InDesign to begin applying a page numbering scheme to the documents. I've already corrected the font problems in Chapter 1, but Chapters 9 and 11 do indeed have missing fonts. We'll use the book palette to take care of this problem in the next exercise, and everything will work out fine. For now, just click the **Don't show again** check box, and then click **OK**.

3. *Rearrange the order of the documents.* The book palette now displays four imported documents. The documents in the book palette need to be arranged in the order in which they will appear in the book. The TOC file, which stands for Table of Contents, came in last but it should be first. Drag the **Look&Learn TOC vii** item in the palette to the top of the stack. When a thick black line appears above the top item, as in Figure 10-4, release the mouse button. The Look&Learn TOC vii item moves to the top of the palette where it belongs. Note that it may take InDesign several seconds to complete the operation.

4. *Set the page numbering for Chapter 1.* Now let's take a look at the page numbering. The one-page table of contents file is numbered vii, which is fine. But Chapter 1 starts on page 8, which is no good. Chapter 1 should start on page 1, so we need to change that:

   - Click the **Look&Learn Ch01** item in the book palette, and choose **Document Page Numbering Options** from the palette menu, as in Figure 10-5. Or better yet, just double-click the page numbers, **8–25**, in the book palette.

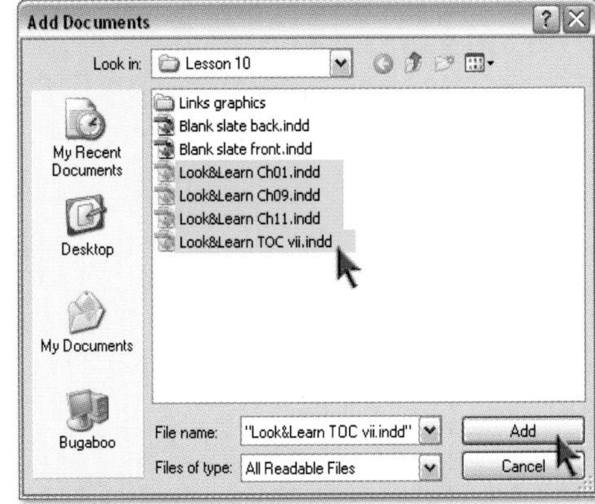

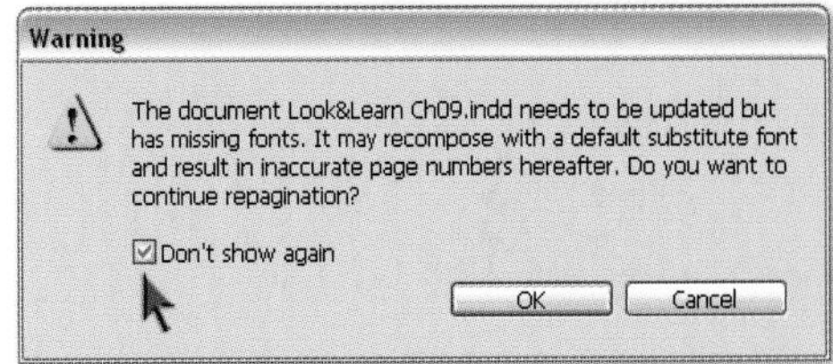

Figure 10-3.

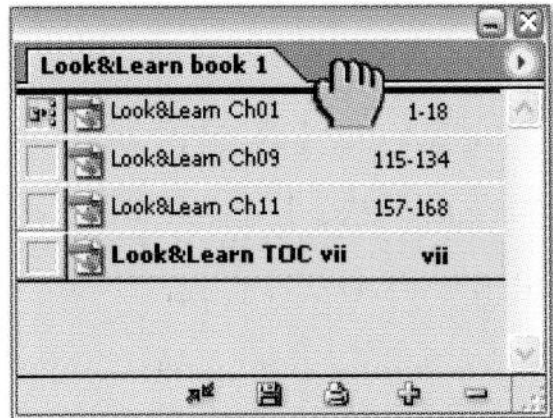

Figure 10-4.

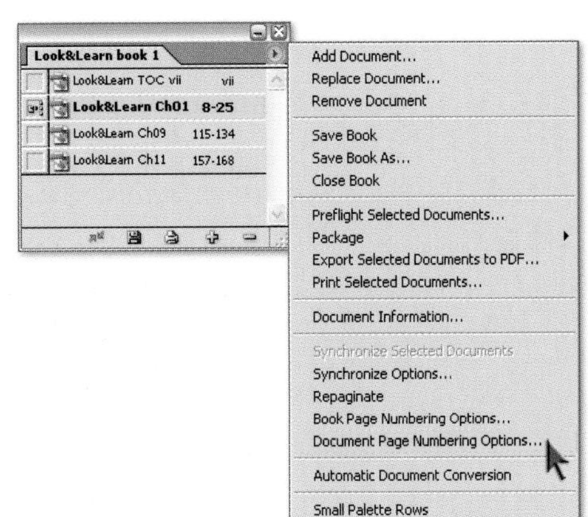

Figure 10-5.

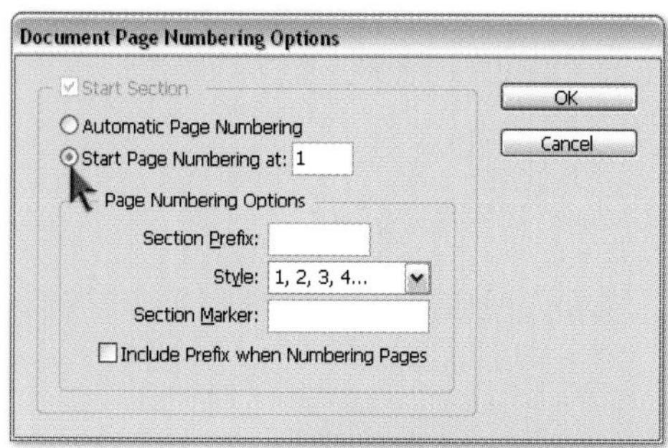

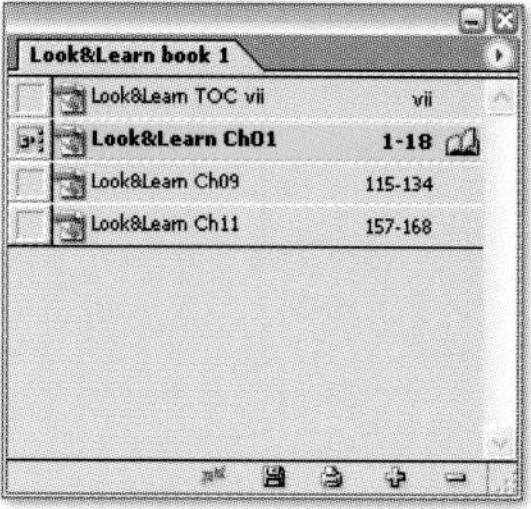

Figure 10-6.

- If you get a hyphenation warning, click the **User Dictionary** button. If you get a missing links error, click **Fix Links Automatically**. Next, InDesign opens the Chapter 1 document. And after that, you are greeted by the Document Page Numbering Options dialog box.
- Here's why Chapter 1 was starting at page 8: Automatic Page Numbering is turned on, which numbers the document immediately after the preceding file in the book palette, which is the TOC. Click the **Start Page Numbering at** radio button, enter 1 in the option box, and click **OK**. As Figure 10-6 shows, Chapter 1 now starts on page 1.

5. *Automatically number Chapter 9.* Let's say, for whatever kooky reason, that we want the page numbering for Chapter 9 to begin where Chapter 1 leaves off. (Okay, I confess. Every so often I have to bend logic for the sake of demonstration.)
   - Select the **Look&Learn Ch09** item in the book palette. Again choose Document Page Numbering Options from the palette menu or double-click the item's page numbers.
   - As the Chapter 9 file opens, InDesign may or may not deliver a hyphenation complaint. If it does, click **User Dictionary**.
   - InDesign will then deliver a warning message about missing fonts. (No matter what, you will see this one.) We'll take care of this problem in the next exercise, "Synchronizing Booked Documents." For now, click **OK** to close the Missing Fonts dialog box.
   - If you get a message about missing links, click **Fix Links Automatically**.
   - Finally the Document Page Numbering Options dialog box appears. Chapter 9 starts on page 115 because that's what its numbering settings are telling it to do. Select the **Automatic Page Numbering** option and click **OK**. The book palette now shows Chapter 9 as starting on page 19, immediately after Chapter 1.
6. *Automatically number Chapter 11.* Now we need to bring Chapter 11 in line. Again, for the sake of demonstration, I want it to follow directly on the heels of Chapter 9:
   - Click the **Look&Learn Ch11** item and double-click its page numbers, **157–168**.

- If InDesign bugs you about hyphenation, click **User Dictionary**. When it bugs you about missing fonts, click **OK**. And if you get the missing links message, click **Fix Links Automatically**. So many alert messages, so little patience.
- Turn on **Automatic Page Numbering** and click **OK**.

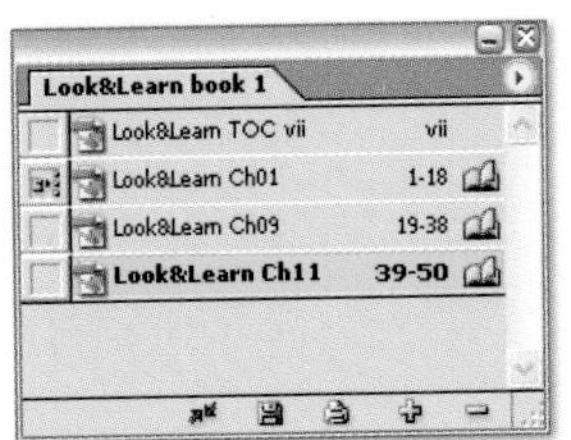

Figure 10-7.

As Figure 10-7 shows, Chapters 1, 9, and 11 are all numbered sequentially. At last, the documents are in the right order, and their page numbering is correct.

7. *Save and close the open documents.* See those open book icons (📖) next to each chapter name in the book palette? They indicate that the corresponding documents are open. By changing the pagination options, we've made changes to the documents themselves. Naturally, we need to save those changes. So for each document, press Ctrl+S to save it and Ctrl+W to close it (⌘-S and ⌘-W on the Mac).
8. *Save the book.* Choose **Save Book As** from the book palette menu, name the file "Look&Learn book 2.indb," and save it in the *Lesson 10* folder. You'll need the current version of this file in the next exercise.

Synchronizing Booked Documents

By assembling documents into a book file and adjusting their pagination, you can combine multiple documents into a single unit. But the book palette provides other ways to connect disparate documents. In this short exercise, we'll synchronize the style sheets between the documents in the book file from the preceding exercise so that all three chapters share a common set of formatting attributes.

As you discovered in the preceding steps, Chapters 9 and 11 contain fonts that are missing from our systems. Chapter 1, however, has no missing fonts; I modified its styles to contain only those fonts that are automatically installed with InDesign. By synchronizing the style sheets from Chapters 9 and 11 to match those in Chapter 1, we'll fix the missing fonts problem and unify the formatting attributes throughout the book.

1. *Open the book file.* If you're reading in a steady stream from the previous exercise, the file is already open. If not, use **File→Open** to open the *Look&Learn book 2.indb* file that you saved in Step 8 of the last exercise. You should find the file in the *Lesson 10* folder inside *Lesson Files-IDcs 1on1*.

2. *Designate Chapter 1 as the style source.* The icon to the immediate left of a document name in the book palette identifies the source document to which all other files will sync. As I mentioned, I fixed the font problems in Chapter 1, so click in the box to the left of **Look&Learn Ch01** in the book palette to set it as the style source.

3. *Specify the style sheets that you want to synchronize.* Before we synchronize the other documents with Chapter 1, we need to specify exactly what it is we want to synchronize. Choose **Synchronize Options** from the book palette menu to bring up the Synchronize Options dialog box, as in Figure 10-8. Chapter 1 has no table of contents styles or trapping presets (see "Trapping and Overprinting," Lesson 12, page 443), and there's nothing worth preserving about its color swatches. So deselect the **TOC Styles**, **Trap Presets**, and **Swatches** check boxes.

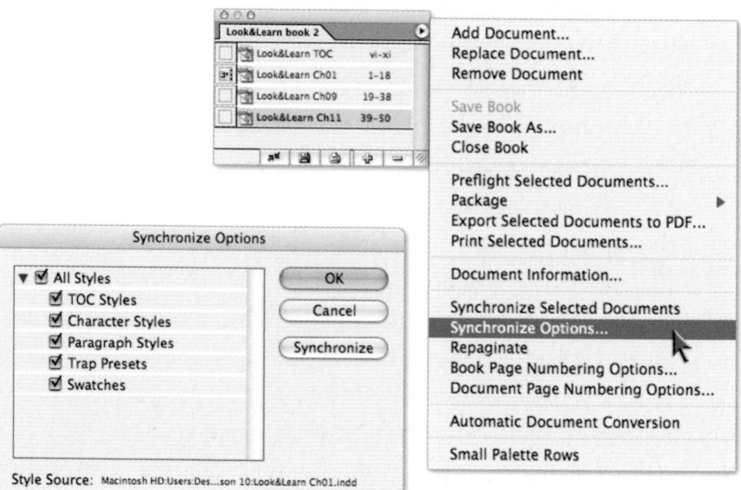

Figure 10-8.

Clicking the Synchronize button synchronizes any selected documents with the designated style source. If no document is selected, the synchronization applies to all files in the book, which is what we want. Given that you might have a document selected (as I do in Figure 10-8), the best course of action is to click the **OK** button to save your sync preferences without actually applying them. We'll sync the files in the next step.

4. *Synchronize all documents with Chapter 1.* Click in the blank space below the last document in the book palette to deselect all files. Then, with no document selected, choose **Synchronize Book** from the book palette menu.

5. *Address the missing fonts warning.* InDesign's first response is to deliver the cautionary missive shown in Figure 10-9. As the message warns, "these documents *may* be recomposed using a default substitute font" (my emphasis). But in our case, they won't. This is because we're recomposing the documents using very specific fonts that are installed on your computer, not some random and patently awful default substitutions. Trust me and click **OK**.

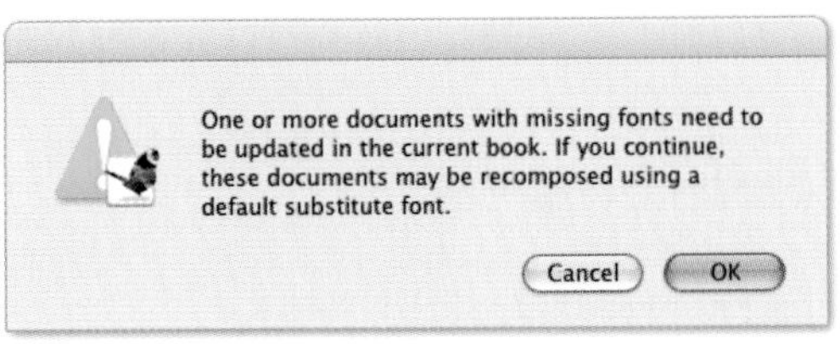

Figure 10-9.

6. *Address the overset text warning.* After displaying a progress bar for a few moments, another warning appears (see Figure 10-10), this time alerting you to the dangers of "overset text" becoming "non-overset." It's classic computer gobbledygook, so here's the skinny: Overset text is what I call overflow text—that is, text that doesn't fit inside its frame. In other words, the text may shrink and actually fit inside the four walls of the document. That sounds like a good thing, but frankly, it's all highly speculative. Furthermore, there's not a darn thing we can do about it. So whatever's going on, click **OK**.

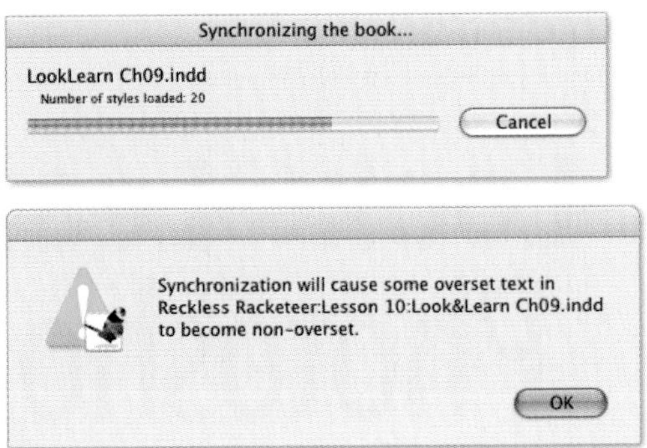

Figure 10-10.

7. *Dismiss the final message.* Next, you are presented with the alert message shown in Figure 10-11. As if InDesign hadn't been perfectly clear during its previous barrage of warnings, this message notifies you that your documents may have changed. Specifically, the synchronization has solved the missing fonts problems in Chapters 9 and 11. This truly is a good thing, so smile as you click **OK**.

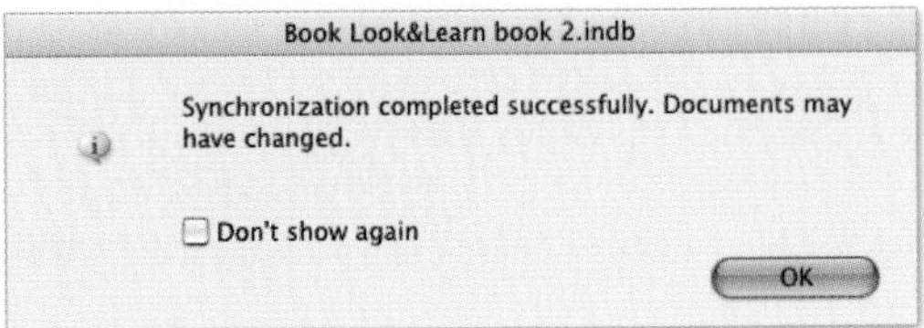

Figure 10-11.

8. *Open a synchronized document.* According to InDesign, the documents are synced. But we humans need confirmation. Double-click on **Look&Learn Ch09** to open the Chapter 9 file. No font warning—in fact, if you've been following along faithfully, no warnings whatsoever. That's a good sign, but perhaps we should dig deeper, just to be safe.

9. *Inspect the fonts.* To check out exactly which fonts are used in the document, choose **Type→Find Font**. InDesign displays the **Find Font** dialog box, with a total of seven fonts. The first three are OpenType fonts that ship with InDesign. The remaining four are crazy fonts like *MyriadMM-It_480_wt_500_wd*. I assure you, these numbered typefaces (all multiple master fonts, varieties of yesterday's cutting-edge technology) are not included on your system. And yet InDesign does not complain. What gives? To see, select the first of the numbered fonts in the list. Note that the standard Find First button changes to **Find Graphic**. Give this button a click. InDesign scrolls to the

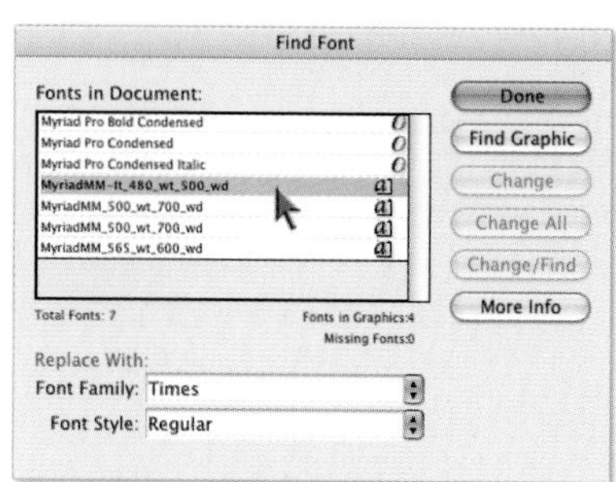

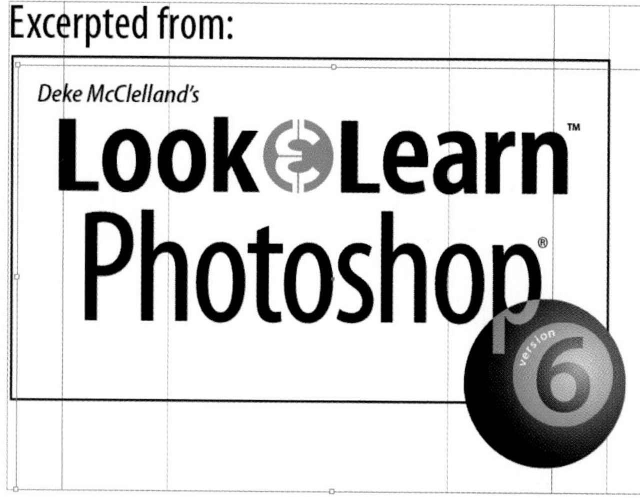

Excerpted from:
Deke McClelland's
Look&Learn™
Photoshop®
version
6

Figure 10-12.

graphic pictured in Figure 10-12. And therein lies your answer. The numbered fonts are not part of the InDesign text, but rather part of the imported Illustrator graphics. It is Illustrator's habit to embed font definitions when saving files, therefore the fact that your system doesn't include these fonts is no problem whatsoever. Click the **Done** button, safe in the knowledge that you are covered.

10. *Save the book.* Press Ctrl+W (or ⌘-W) to close the Chapter 9 file. If InDesign asks you to save your changes, press the N key (D on the Mac) to decline. Then go to the book palette and choose **Save Book As** from the palette menu. Target the *Lesson 10* folder, name the file "Look&Learn book 3.indb," and click **Save**. You'll need this file in the next exercise, so if you're on a roll keep it open.

Creating a Table of Contents

After you've assembled various documents into a book, InDesign can examine those documents and automatically generate a table of contents based on how you set up your style sheets. In this exercise, you'll create a table of contents for the three chapters in the book file we've created so far. You'll tell the program exactly which styles to look for, and you'll set paragraph styles for the table of contents itself.

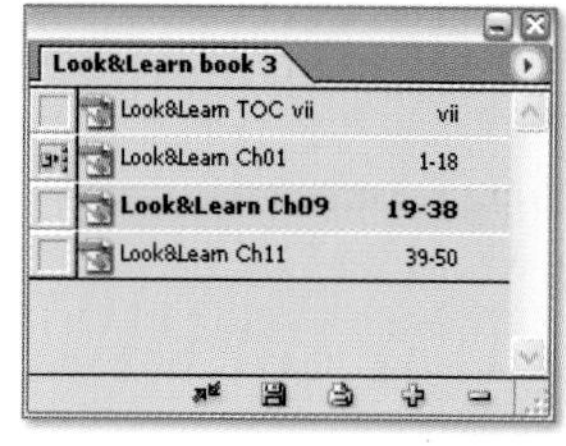

Figure 10-13.

1. *Open the book file.* If you're continuing on from the last exercise, the book file is already open in the book palette. If not, open the *Look&Learn book 3.indb* file that you saved in the *Lesson 10* folder at the end of the last exercise. Your book palette should look like the one in Figure 10-13.

2. *Open the table of contents document.* As you may recall from the previous exercises, this book file already includes a table of contents. To open this document, double-click the **Look&Learn TOC vii** item in the book palette. As shown in Figure 10-14, this is but a single page from the full table of contents for the book. I include it simply so you can see the styles I used to create the document. Note that

the file contains certain elements—such as the one-sentence summaries of each chapter—that InDesign CS's automatic table of contents function can't generate. But that's okay, we don't need them. The table of contents we're going to generate will include the name of each chapter, the sections therein, and the page number on which each chapter and section begins.

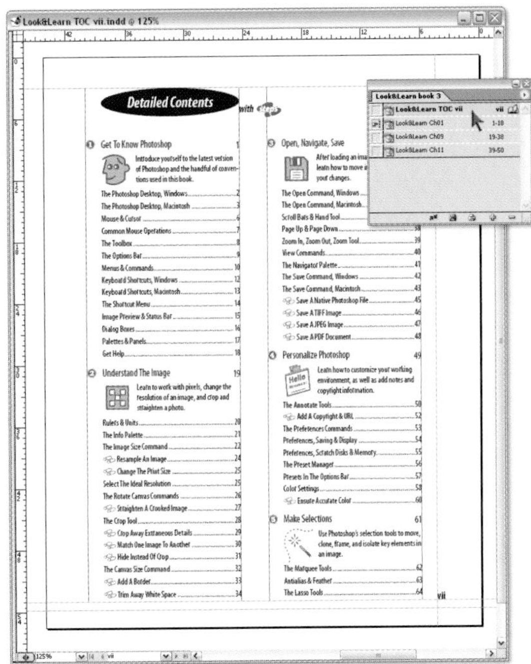

Figure 10-14.

3. *Examine the paragraph styles.* Press the F11 key or choose **Type→Paragraph Styles** to access the **Paragraph Styles** palette. Select the type tool and click to place the insertion marker somewhere in the first chapter title, *Get To Know Photoshop*. A glance at the Paragraph Styles palette reveals that this title was formatted using the TofC Chap Name style (see Figure 10-15).

   Now click to set the insertion marker in the first section name, *The Photoshop Desktop, Windows*. Another glance at the Paragraph Styles palette tells us that this line was formatted using the TofC Section style. (The style includes a + because I adjusted the leading to make the text fit better.) The upshot: I gave each of the two main elements—the chapter name and the section name—a unique paragraph style. These styles will come in handy in future steps.

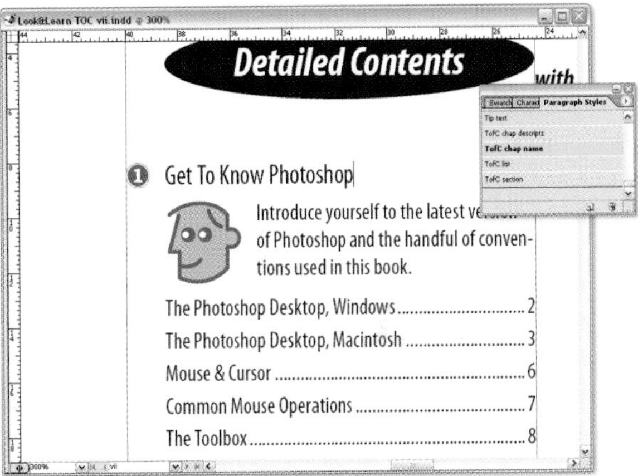

Figure 10-15.

4. *Close the file and remove the TOC from the book.* Press Ctrl+W (or ⌘-W) to close the table of contents file. If InDesign asks to save changes, click **No** (**Don't Save** on the Mac). Now delete the TOC file from the book. Sounds weird, but it's necessary so InDesign doesn't reference the TOC file along with the chapter documents when we generate the new table of contents. Make sure **Look&Learn TOC vii** is selected. Then click the ▭ icon at the bottom of the palette, as in Figure 10-16. You are left with just the three chapter documents.

5. *Add a blank document to the book.* It's good that we deleted the old table of contents. But we need some sort of reservoir for our new table of contents. Click the ✚ at the bottom of the book palette to bring up the Add Documents dialog box. Navigate to the *Lesson 10* folder, select the file named *Blank slate front.indd*, and click the **Add** button (**Open** on the Mac). The new document appears as the last file in the palette.

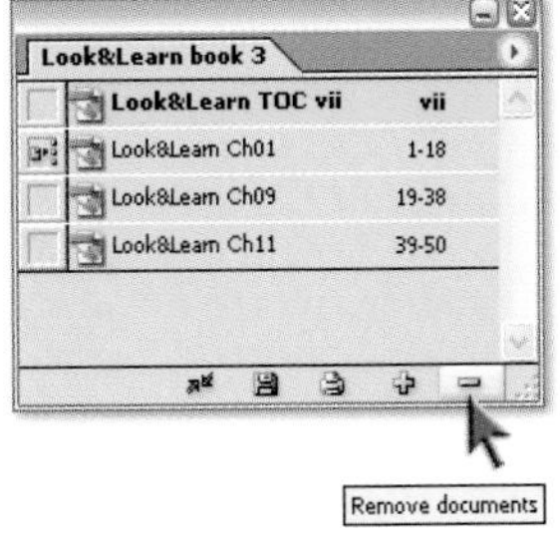

Figure 10-16.

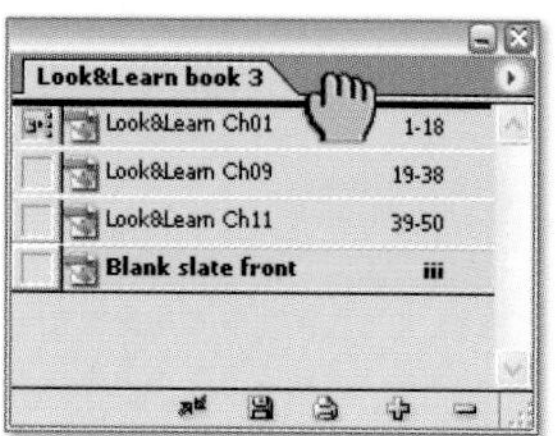

Figure 10-17.

6. *Move the newly added file to the top of the palette.* This document will serve as our new table of contents, so it needs to be placed at the top of the stack. Drag the **Blank slate front** item to the top of the book palette, as in Figure 10-17. Since Chapter 1 is set to begin on page 1, and Chapters 9 and 11 have automatic page numbering turned on, no pagination shifts occur.

7. *Examine the paragraph styles in the blank document.* In the book palette, double-click the **Blank slate front** item to open the document. It's entirely empty, but as Figure 10-18 shows, it includes two paragraph styles similar to the ones we examined in Step 3: TofC Chapter and TofC Section. You'll use these styles to format the new table of contents.

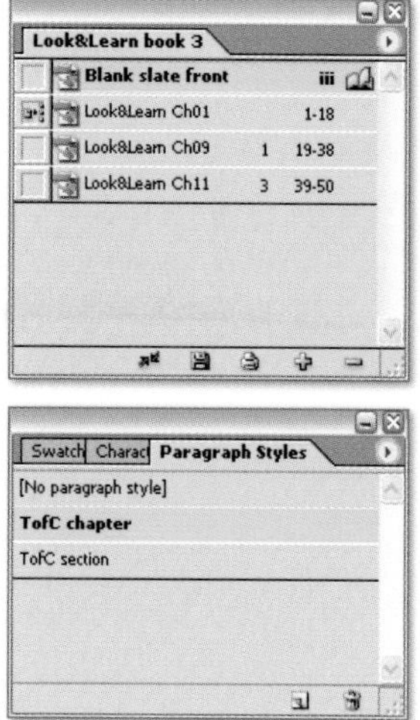

Figure 10-18.

8. *Create a new table of contents style.* Now it's time to decide which portions of the chapters are included in the table of contents, based on how they're styled. Choose **Layout→Table of Contents Styles** to display the dialog box shown at the top of Figure 10-19. Click the **New** button to bring up the **New Table of Contents Style** dialog box, also pictured in the figure below.

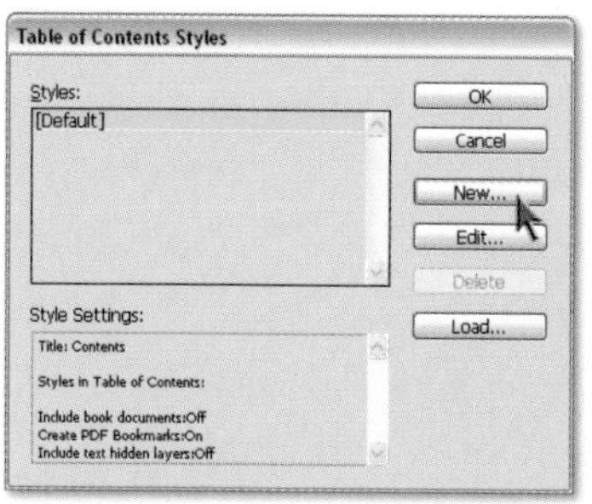

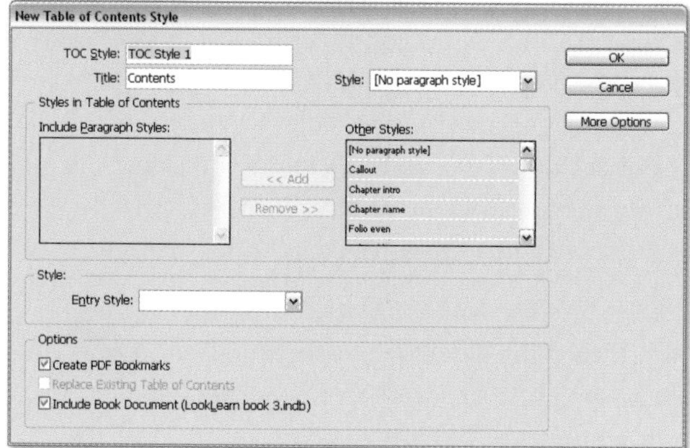

Figure 10-19.

9. *Specify a title for your table of contents.* Change the first few options in the dialog box as follows:

   - Type "L&L TOC style" in the **TOC Style** option box. This is the name that will appear in the Styles list in the Table of Contents Styles dialog box.
   - The next option, **Title**, designates the title that will appear at the outset of the finished table of contents document. Press Tab to advance to this option and type "Detailed Contents."
   - The **Style** setting allows you to apply a style sheet to the title. The options include the two styles currently contained in the document plus a third style that InDesign has created specifically for this purpose. Choose this last option, **TOC title**.

10. *Select the styles you want to include in the table of contents.* InDesign generates a table of contents by looking at the documents in your book file and lifting text formatted with the style sheets that you specify. Select the style sheets that you want InDesign to draw upon from the middle section of the dialog box (the part labeled Styles in Table of Contents). Here's what I want you to do:

    - In the **Other Styles** list on the right, select **Chapter Name**, which is the style applied to the chapter title in each document, and click the **Add** button. The Chapter Name style appears in the Include Paragraph Styles list on the left.
    - You also need to include the subheads, or section names, in the table of contents. These are assigned the Heading 1 and Heading 2 styles. So select **Heading 1** in the Other Styles list and then Shift-click on **Heading 2**. Then click the **Add** button to add both styles to the Include Paragraph Styles list.

11. *Select styles to be applied to the table of contents entries.* Now InDesign knows which style sheets to search for inside the book's documents in order to generate the table of contents. But after the table of contents is generated, what will it look like? To answer that question, do like so:

    - Select **Chapter Name** in the Include Paragraph Styles list, and choose **TofC Chapter** from the Entry Style pop-up menu, lower in the dialog box.

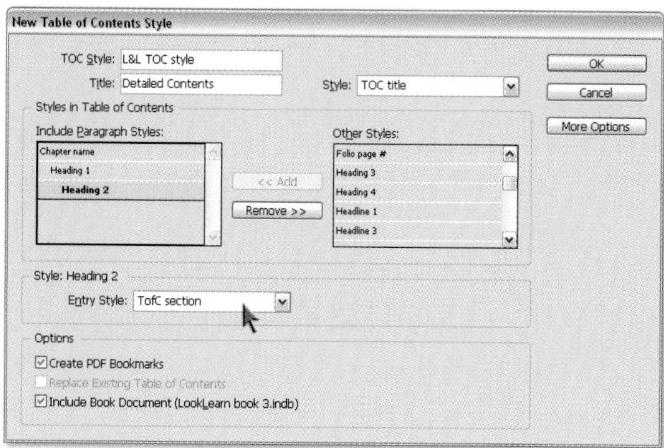

Figure 10-20.

- Next, select **Heading 1** in the Include Paragraph Styles list, and then choose **TofC Section** from the Entry Style option.
- Then select **Heading 2** in the left-hand list, and again choose **TofC Section** as the Entry Style.

The options in the New Table of Contents Style dialog box should now appear as shown in Figure 10-20.

12. *Close the two open dialog boxes.* Make sure that the last check box (**Include Book Document**) is selected so that InDesign includes all documents within your book file in the table of contents. Then click **OK**. As Figure 10-21 shows, the newly-created L&L TOC Style is now selected in the Table of Contents Styles dialog box. Click **OK** to accept it.

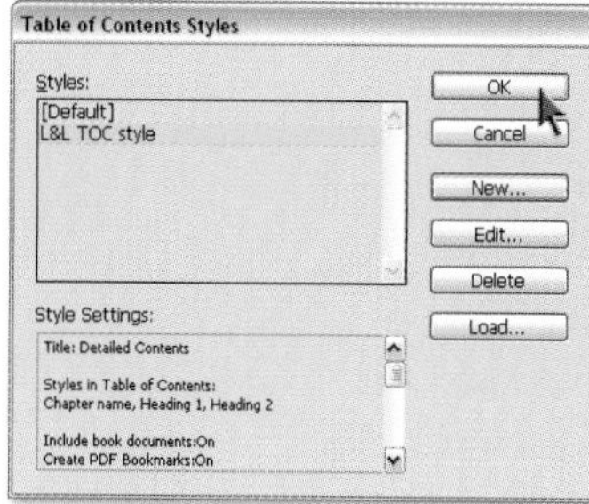

Figure 10-21.

13. *Generate the table of contents.* Now to generate the table of contents. Choose **Layout→Table of Contents** to display the **Table of Contents** dialog box shown in Figure 10-22. Weren't we just here? Well, no. While this dialog box is virtually identical to the one we saw a couple of steps back, there is a difference: You can select and edit any table of contents styles you've created. Make sure the first option is set to **L&L TOC style** and then click the **OK** button. InDesign starts to create a table of contents and then presents you with a loaded text cursor.

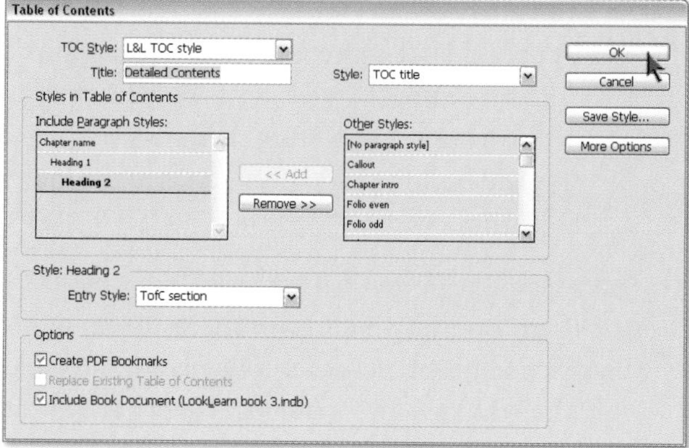

Figure 10-22.

14. *Place the table of contents.* Press the Shift key and click at the top of the first column in the *Blank slate front.indd* document. This places all table of contents entries in one fell swoop. And there it is, a table of contents, automatically extracted from our three-chapter excerpt, as in Figure 10-23.

15. *Eliminate the inline graphics.* All in all, InDesign did a great job of extracting the chosen paragraph styles from the chapter files and compiling them in one document, replete with page numbers. But InDesign also included the inline graphics embedded in some of the section names, and frankly, it just doesn't look right. Let's get rid of them:

    - Choose **Edit→Find/Change** or press Ctrl+F (⌘-F on the Mac) to bring up the **Find/Change** dialog box.
    - To tell InDesign what you want it to find, click the ▶ arrow to the far right of the **Find what** option box and choose **Inline Graphic Marker** (eighth option down) from the pop-up menu. A ^g appears in the option box, which is InDesign's code for an inline graphic.
    - Not only do we want to eliminate each inline graphic, but we also want to delete the space after the graphic. Press the spacebar once to enter a space after the ^g.
    - Leave the **Change to** option box blank so that InDesign replaces everything it finds with nothing. When your settings look like those in Figure 10-24, click **Change All**.

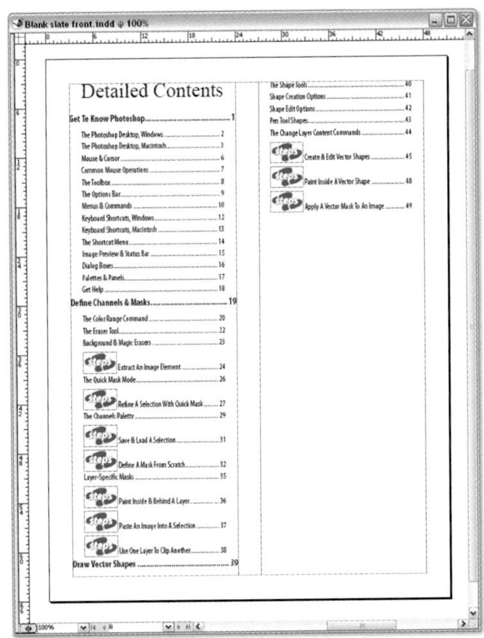

Figure 10-23.

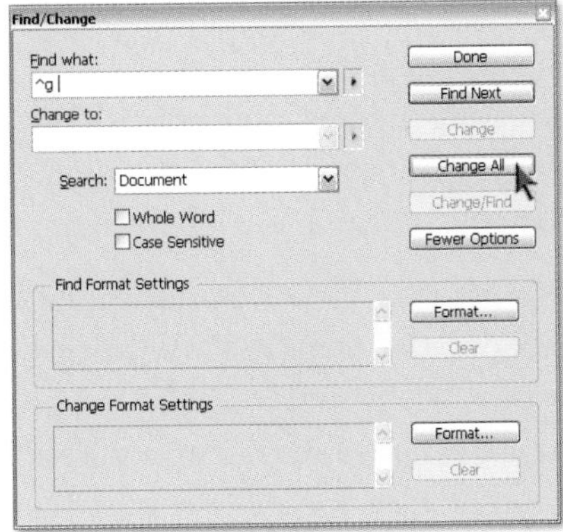

Figure 10-24.

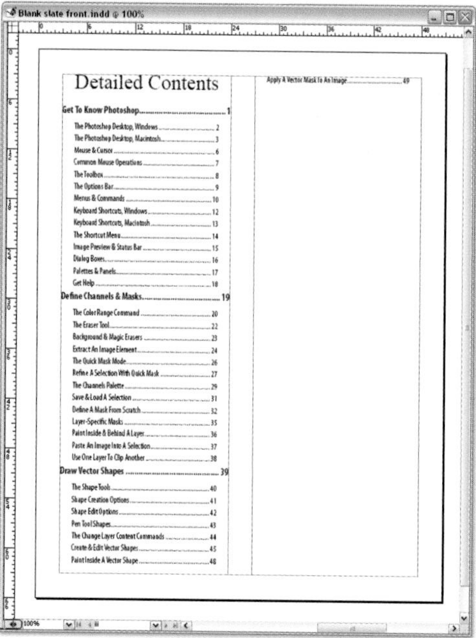

Figure 10-25.

An alert appears to tell you that InDesign deleted 10 inline graphic markers. Click **OK** to dismiss it. Next, click **Done** to close the Find/Change dialog box.

16. *Save your work.* The modified table of contents appears as shown in Figure 10-25. If we were going to publish this document, we'd want to adjust the text frames to eliminate the widow at the top of the second column, but otherwise things look great.

PEARL OF WISDOM

Should you ever need to update a table of contents to account for changes made to the documents in your book file, just select all the text in the table of contents and choose Layout→Update Table of Contents. Note, however, that you would lose any manual changes you may have made. This means you would have to repeat the deletion of the inline graphics that you performed in the last step.

Press Ctrl+S and Ctrl+W (⌘-S and ⌘-W) to save and close your newly created table of contents. Then click the ⊙ in the book palette, choose **Save Book As** from the palette menu, name the file "Look&Learn book 4.indb," and click **Save**.

Generating an Index

When generating a table of contents, you can count on InDesign to do most of the heavy lifting. But when it comes time to make an index, InDesign puts a 500-pound barbell in front of you and says, "Go get 'em, Tiger!" That's why indexing books isn't really a task; it's a profession. There are people who make a living solely out of creating indexes, and while they regard InDesign as a useful tool, it provides only slim automation. Given the current state of technology, indexing is a job for humans, not machines.

Rather than create a complete index—a process that would take about 1,000 steps, 980 of which would bring new meaning to the words "staggeringly dull"—the goal of this exercise is to give you a sense of how indexing works. You'll create a handful of entries and address a few special-case scenarios like cross-references and proper names. In the end, you'll place the partial index—complete with page numbers (InDesign's most helpful automatic contribution)—into a new document. I can't promise you a roller coaster ride, but with some luck we might have a smidgen of fun along the way.

1. *Open the book file.* If the most recent version of the book file is open, advance to the next step. If not, open the *Look&Learn book 4.indb* file that you saved in the *Lesson 10* folder at the end of the last exercise. You should see the palette shown in Figure 10-26.

2. *Open the Chapter 1 document.* Double-click the **Look&Learn Ch01** file in the book palette. InDesign opens the Chapter 1 file, as shown in Figure 10-27. Our rollicking adventure in indexing will begin with this chapter.

3. *Open the Index palette.* Choose **Window→Type & Tables→Index** or Press Shift+F8 to display the **Index** palette. Pictured in Figure 10-28, this sparse palette is the central headquarters for indexing in InDesign. Make sure the **Reference** option is selected, as it is default. This permits us to see all index entries as well as the page numbers on which these entries are found. Then turn on the **Book** check box. We want our index to cover all the documents in the book palette, not just a single chapter.

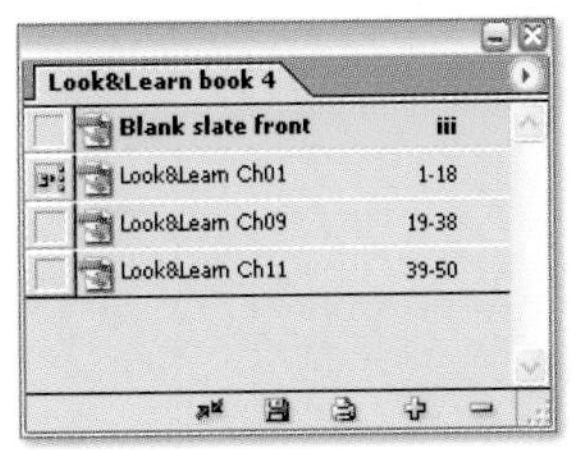

Figure 10-26.

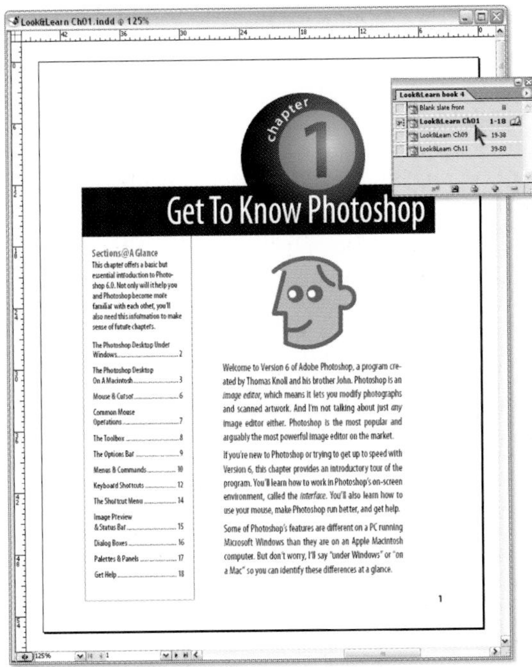

Figure 10-27.

Figure 10-28.

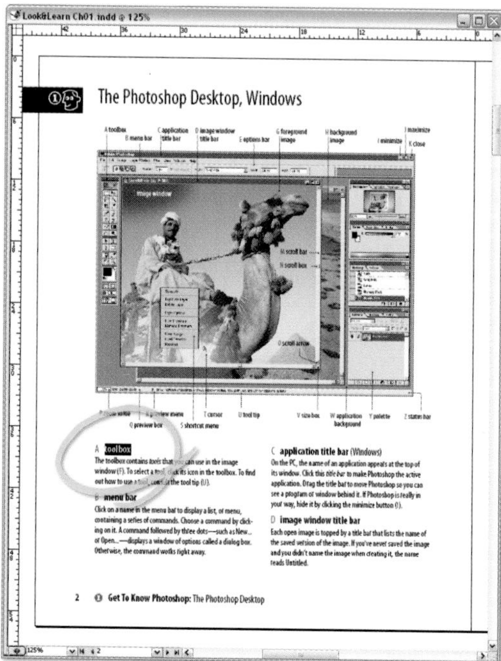

Figure 10-29.

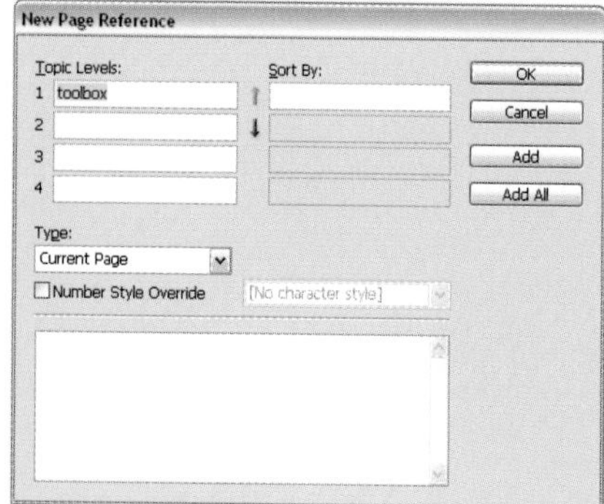

Figure 10-30.

4. *Go to page 2.* At present, you should see some portion of page 1, which is featured in Figure 10-27. Assuming you do, press Shift+Page Down to advance to page 2, which appears in Figure 10-29. We'll create our first index entry here.

5. *Begin an index entry for the word* toolbox. Press T to get the type tool and then double-click the word *toolbox*, circled in Figure 10-29. Then click the icon at the bottom of the Index palette. The **New Page Reference** dialog box appears with the word *toolbox* thoughtfully entered in the first **Topic Levels** option box, as in Figure 10-30.

6. *Specify the topic level.* Numbered 1 through 4, the **Topic Levels** option boxes let you determine where within the index you want the entry to appear. Here we have a few options:

   - Were we to keep *toolbox* as a top-level topic—as it is by default—InDesign would alphabetize it with the *T*s.
   - However, it's conceivable that you might want to make *toolbox* subordinate to another entry, perhaps one for *interface*. In this case, *interface* would be alphabetized under *I*, and *toolbox* would be listed as a subcategory. To make this happen, click the ↓ arrow icon to move *toolbox* to option box 2, then type *interface* in option box 1.
   - InDesign lets you build entries four levels deep, so you could conceivably categorize the entry as, for example, *applications→Photoshop→interface→toolbox*.

   But why make things complicated? I much prefer to stick with first- and second-level entries and keep most entries at the top level. So let's leave *toolbox* as is, as a first-level entry.

PEARL OF WISDOM

It's not necessary to fill out the Sort By option boxes. They exist so you can sort an entry by something other than its first letter. For instance, if you were writing a book on movies and wanted the entry *The Great Muppet Caper* to appear as written but have it alphabetized under the letter *G*, you would enter *The Great Muppet Caper* in the Topic Levels option box and *Great Muppet Caper* in the associated Sort By option box.

7. *Choose a page range option.* Next you need to choose a page range option for your entry. Midway down the dialog box, the **Type** pop-up menu gives you a plethora of choices, all of which determine the range of pages that will be indexed for the entry. We'll stick with the default option, **Current Page**, which references page 2 and page 2 alone.

PEARL OF WISDOM

In addition to indexing a single page, you can choose to index a range of pages that extend to a change in style sheet styles or until the next use of a matching style sheet. You can even extend a range until the end of the story, section, or document. But I recommend you use these options sparingly. Put yourself in the reader's position: When you look up a word in an index, you want to find the exact page on which that entry is discussed, not some nebulous page range. Specific is always better.

8. *Leave Number Style Override off.* The **Number Style Override** check box lets you apply a different style sheet than the default to the page number that follows an index entry. For instance, references that include illustrations are sometimes set in bold type, in which case you might want to employ a specific character style that you created for this purpose. Our entry doesn't require any special styling, so leave this option turned off.

9. *Add the entry to the index.* To add the entry to the index, click the **Add** button. Suddenly, the entire alphabet appears in the large field at the bottom of the dialog box. Scroll down to the *T*'s and click the ▶ to reveal the *toolbox* entry, as in Figure 10-31.

PEARL OF WISDOM

Alternatively, you could click Add All, which would cause InDesign to search all open documents for occurrences of the selected term. This may sound like a great time saving idea, but it rarely is. In truth, you don't want *every* instance of a term indexed, especially for a common term like *toolbox*. Furthermore, if the term appears multiple times on a single page, Add All will usually give each instance its own page reference, rendering your index bloated and useless. That's what I meant when I said that creating an index is a job for humans, not computers. You need to decide which occurrences of the term are worthy of inclusion in the index on a case-by-case basis.

10. *View the index entry.* Click the **Done** button to exit the dialog box. The Index palette now contains an alphabetized index. If you scroll down, you'll see the page 2 reference for *toolbox*, as in Figure 10-32.

11. *Show hidden characters.* InDesign tracks an index entry by inserting an invisible character into the text. To see this character, first deselect the text by pressing Ctrl+Shift+A (⌘-Shift-A on the Mac). Then choose **Type→Show Hidden Characters** or press Ctrl+Alt+I (⌘-Option-I).

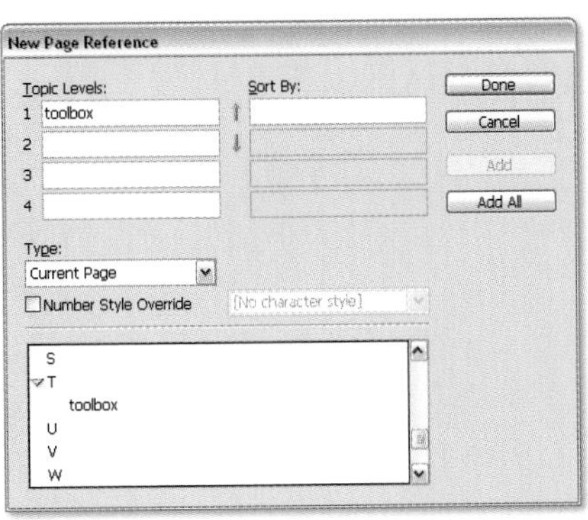

Figure 10-31.

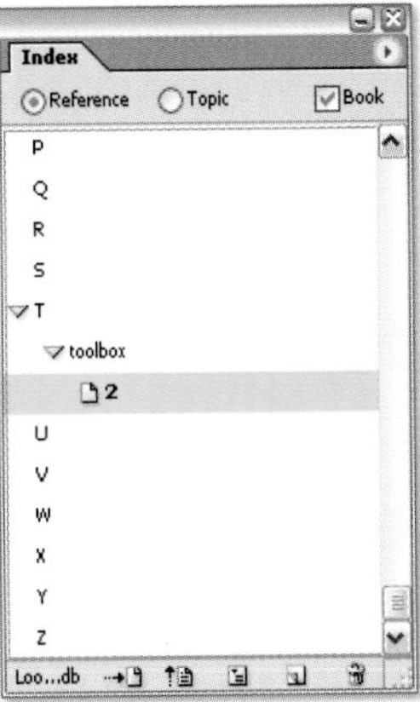

Figure 10-32.

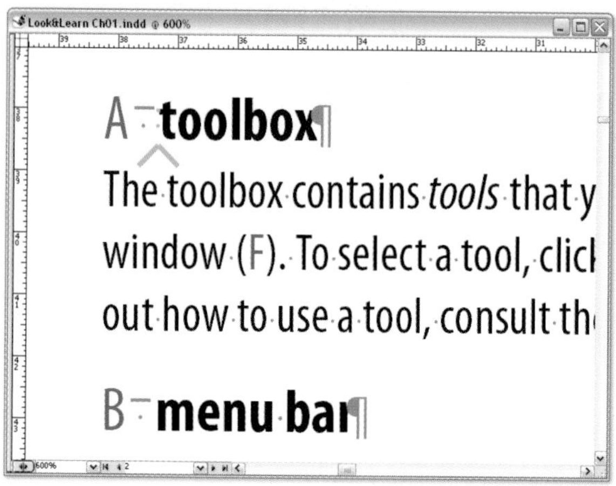

Figure 10-33.

The ‸ character, which I've colored orange in Figure 10-33, indicates the occurrence of an *index marker*, which tracks the location of the word *toolbox*. If you bump the word to a different page, the index marker moves with it and updates the entry in the Index palette. (In case you're curious, that ⁻ character before the ‸ is an en space.)

12. ***Add another entry to the index.*** Press Shift+Page Down to go to page 3. Select the words *options bar* as in Figure 10-34. Then instead of clicking the ◱ icon in the Index palette, press Ctrl+Alt+U (⌘-Option-U on the Mac). InDesign adds the entry *options bar* to the index preview in the Index palette according to the default settings, which make the entry a first-level topic that references the current page only.

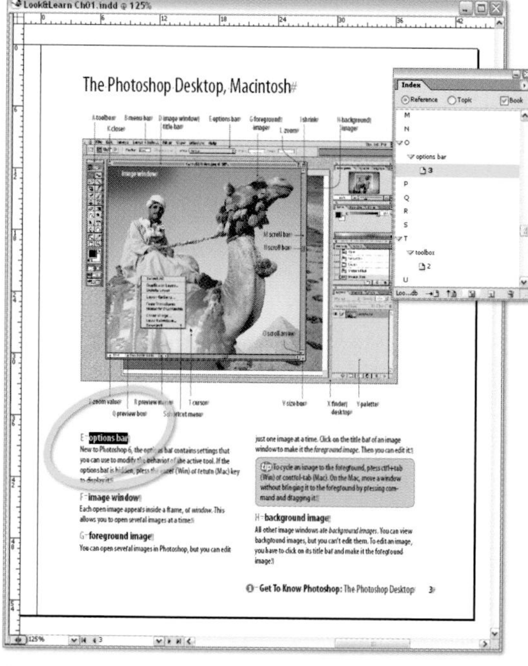

Figure 10-34.

EXTRA CREDIT

By now, you have a pretty good idea of how you add index entries to an InDesign document. But there's so much more—page ranges, subentries, cross-references, and name sorting, just to mention a few. Plus, we really haven't seen the fruits of our indexing, have we? To experience these many options for yourself, I strongly urge you to complete the remaining steps in this exercise. If you prefer to suffer a life of index ignorance, skip to the "What Did You Learn?" quiz on page 399.

13. ***Add another* toolbox *reference.*** Press Shift+Page Down five times in a row—or press Ctrl+J (⌘-J), enter 8, and press Enter or Return—to advance to page 8, which begins a two-page spread devoted to the toolbox. We really owe it to our readers to add the spread to our index. You might be tempted to select the word *Toolbox* in the heading at the top of the page, but don't. By default, doing so would create a new entry for *Toolbox* with a capital *T*, and that's hardly what we want. Instead, do the following:

    - Double-click to select the word *toolbox* in the first full sentence on page 8, circled in Figure 10-35.
    - We need to create a reference that's longer than the current page. So click the ◱ icon at the bottom of the Index palette to bring up the New Page Reference dialog box.

- Choose **To End of Story** from the **Type** pop-up menu, and click **OK**. InDesign adds the page range to our existing *toolbox* entry, as shown in the Index palette in Figure 10-35.

14. *Add a subentry to the index.* Next let's add a reference to the words *quick mask* at the top of page 9:

    - Select the words *quick mask* (circled in Figure 10-36) and click the ⧉ icon at the bottom of the Index palette.

    - Since Photoshop's quick mask control resides in the toolbox, it makes sense to make *quick mask* a subentry under *toolbox*. Inside the New Page Reference dialog box, click the ↓ arrow to the right of Topic Levels option box 2 to send *quick mask* down a level.

    - Next, find the *T* in the index preview at the bottom of the dialog box and click the ▶ to twirl the letter open. Then click in option box 1 at the top of the dialog box and double-click the word *toolbox* in the preview area. (You could also type the word "toolbox," but double-clicking the existing entry eliminates the chance of typos.)

    - Click **Add** to add *quick mask* as a subentry under *toolbox* Then click the ▶ in front of *toolbox* to see the subentry, as in Figure 10-37.

15. *Create a cross-reference.* Before we leave this dialog box, I reckon we ought to create a cross-reference so that anyone looking up *quick mask* under the letter Q will be directed to the *toolbox* entry:

    - Click in the *quick mask* topic level entry, and then click the ↑ arrow to the right of option box 1. The *quick mask* and *toolbox* entries switch places.

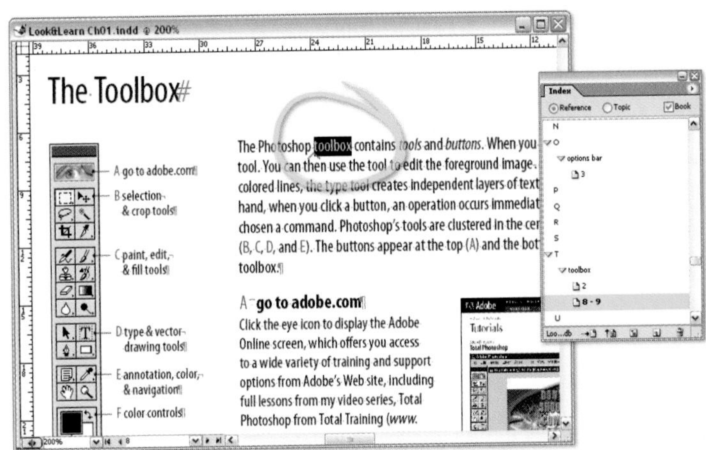

Figure 10-35.

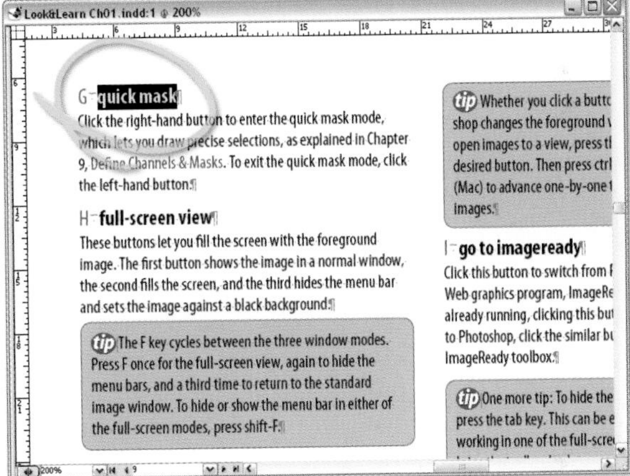

Figure 10-36.

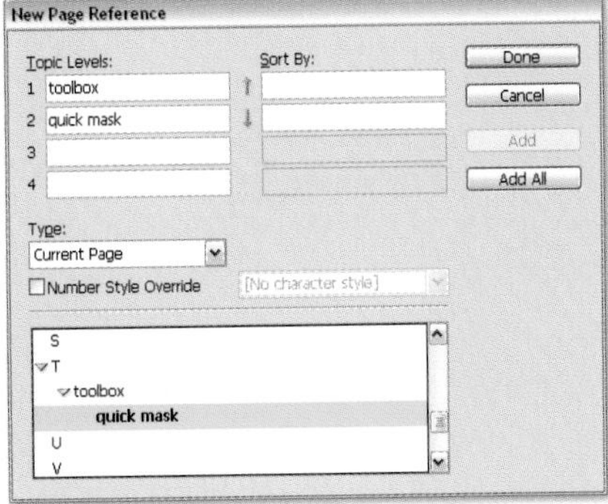

Figure 10-37.

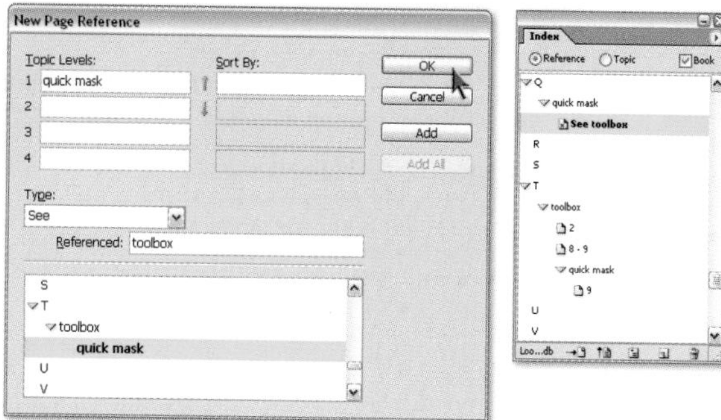

Figure 10-38.

- Select the *toolbox* subtopic level entry and delete it.
- Choose **See** from the **Type** pop-up menu. Then type "toolbox" in the neighboring **Referenced** option box. (You have to type it manually—no double-clicking this time around.)
- Finally, click the **OK** button. As you can see in Figure 10-38, InDesign adds the *quick mask* cross-reference to the Index palette. Clicking the OK button both adds the word and exits the dialog box.

16. *Add a* quick mask *entry from Chapter 9.* Double-click the **Look&Learn Ch09** item in the book palette to open the Chapter 9 file. Then press Ctrl+J (⌘-J on the Mac), enter 26, and press Enter or Return to advance to page 26 of the document, which contains a one-page introduction to the quick mask mode. The page is followed by a two-page step-by-step exercise on this very same feature. We could list these different treatments as two separate entries, but to streamline the index, I suggest we create a single entry for all three pages instead:

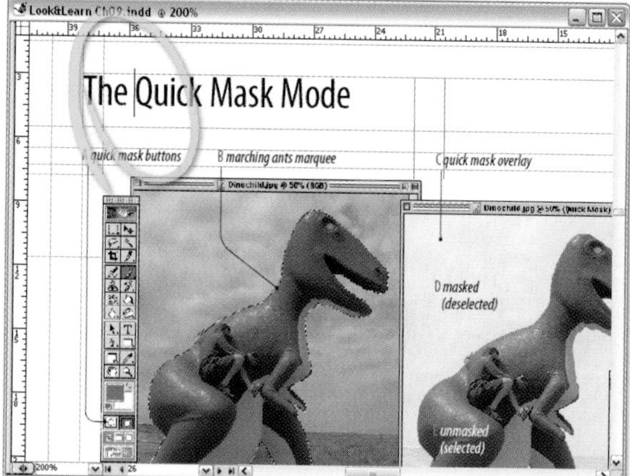

Figure 10-39.

   - Click with the type tool to place the insertion marker immediately in front of the word *Quick* in the headline, which I circled in Figure 10-39.
   - Then click the icon at the bottom of the Index palette. Scroll the index preview at the bottom of the dialog box until you come to the *T*, then twirl it and the *toolbox* entry open by clicking the ▶s so you can see the *quick mask* entry.
   - Double-click the words *quick mask* in the preview area to display *toolbox* and *quick mask*, in that order, in the Topic Levels list.
   - Choose **For Next # of Pages** from the **Type** pop-up menu, and enter 3 in the **Number** option box, as shown in Figure 10-40. Then click **OK**. The Index palette updates to include the new three-page reference.

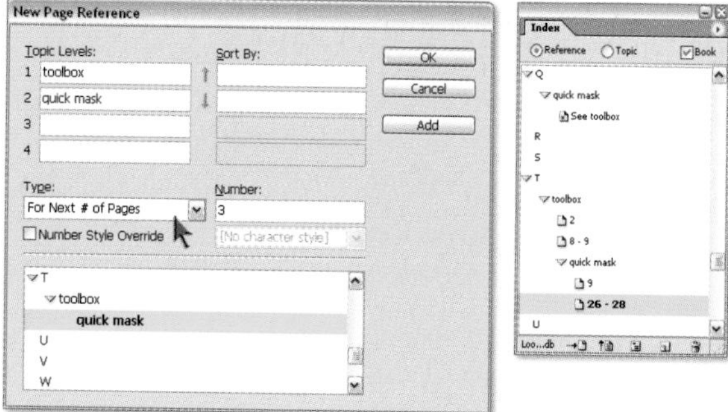

Figure 10-40.

17. *Add a final entry from Chapter 1.* Switch back to Chapter 1, which should still be open. Press Ctrl+Shift+Page Up (⌘-Shift-Page Up) to retreat to the first page in the document, page 1. I want to show you one other keyboard shortcut, which involves indexing names of people. Select the

name *Thomas Knoll* in the second line of the text (circled in Figure 10-41). Because it's a proper name, an index entry for this person should be alphabetized under *K*. While you could do this by creating a new entry and manually replacing the topic entry with *Knoll, Thomas*, there's a quicker way.

Press Ctrl+Shift+F8 (⌘-Shift-F8). Just like that, InDesign adds an entry under K in the Index palette. Thanks to this spiffy keyboard shortcut, InDesign created the entry from the last selected word, *Knoll*, rather than the first.

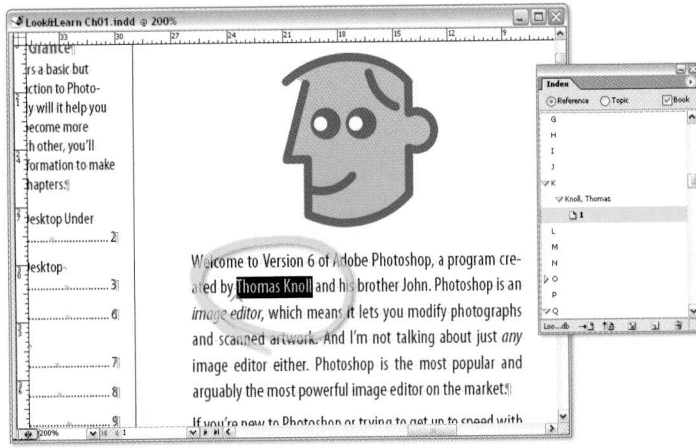

Figure 10-41.

If a proper name ends with a *Jr.* or other suffix, you don't want to create the entry from the last selected word. Fortunately, there's a workaround: Enter a nonbreaking space between the last name and the *Jr.* by choosing Type→Insert White Space→Nonbreaking Space or by pressing Ctrl+Alt+X (⌘-Option-X). This forces InDesign to read the word before the nonbreaking space as the last name.

18. *Save and close the two open documents.* Close Chapter 1 and Chapter 9. Make sure to save your changes when prompted so you preserve the special index markers that InDesign has placed in the documents. After you close the documents, do not be alarmed that the Index palette is now blank. The palette displays the index markers for the open documents only.

19. *Add a document to the book.* Click the ✚ icon at the bottom of the book palette. In the **Add Documents** dialog box, navigate to the *Lesson 10* folder and select the file *Blank slate back.indd*. Then click **Add** (**Open** on the Mac). Drag the document to the bottom of the stack so that your book palette looks like the one in Figure 10-42.

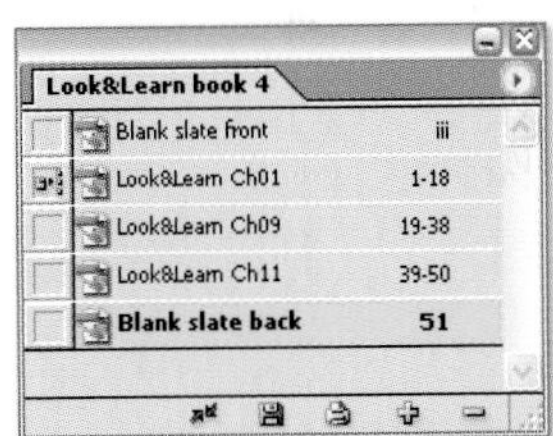

Figure 10-42.

20. *Prepare to generate the index.* Double-click the **Blank slate back** item in the book palette to open this empty document. A book's index can be generated only in a document that's already part of that book; that's why we had to import this blank document into the palette.

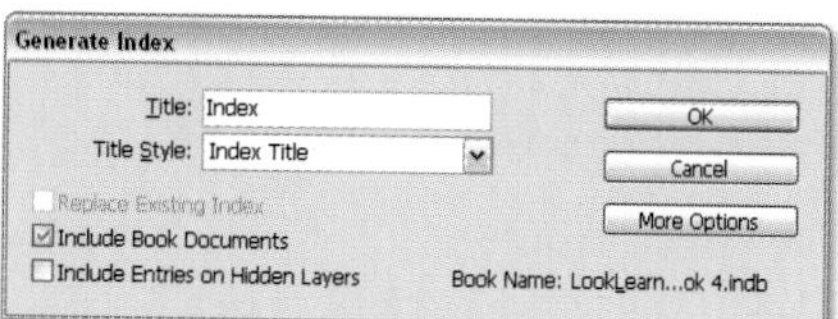

Figure 10-43.

21. *Specify index options.* Click the ▤ icon at the bottom of the **Index** palette to bring up the **Generate Index** dialog box, as in Figure 10-43.

    - The **Title** option lets you specify the title that will appear at the top of the index. The default title, *Index*, is fine for our purposes.
    - The **Title Style** option lets you choose a style to apply to the title. I haven't created any styles for this document, so accept the default **Index Title** style.
    - Turn on the **Include Book Documents** check box to instruct InDesign to search every document in the book palette for index entries.
    - The documents in this book have no hidden layers, so leave the **Include Entries on Hidden Layers** check box turned off.

22. *Generate the index.* Click the **OK** button to dismiss the Generate Index dialog box. Moments later, you are presented with the ▤ cursor. Click at the top of the left column in the *Blank slate back.indd* document to place the index, as in Figure 10-44.

And here's a great feature: Even though this document didn't have any style sheets before you created the index, it has style sheets now. A glance at the Paragraph Styles palette (shown in Figure 10-44) reveals that InDesign has automatically created paragraph styles for the topic levels in the index. If you want to adjust the formatting attributes, simply change the paragraph styles and the index updates. So while building an index is a lot of work, laying out and formatting the index goes very quickly.

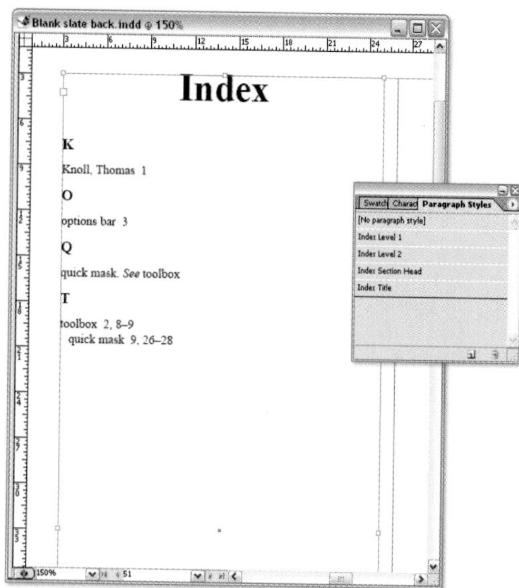

Figure 10-44.

WHAT DID YOU LEARN?

Match the key concept in the numbered list below with the letter of the phrase that best describes it. Answers appear upside-down at the bottom of the page.

Key Concepts

1. Book file
2. Automatic Page Numbering
3. Open book icon
4. Synchronize Options
5. Style source
6. Table of contents
7. Find/Change
8. Index entry
9. Number Style Override
10. Add All
11. Cross-reference
12. Sort By

Descriptions

A. Use this command to specify exactly which attributes you want to match to those in the style source document.

B. When you create one of these, InDesign inserts a hidden character ( ) to monitor the item and its page number.

C. InDesign can generate one of these automatically by examining the style sheets used throughout the documents in a book.

D. Use this option to alphabetize an index entry by something other than its initial letter.

E. If you see this next to a document's name in the book palette, you know that the document is open and ready to accept changes.

F. This command lets you search for a string of characters or inline graphics and either replace them with a different string or delete them entirely.

G. This option lets you apply a character style other than the default setting to the page number for a specific index entry.

H. Marked with a , a document with this designation becomes the model according to which InDesign synchronizes all other documents in the book palette.

I. This option numbers the pages in a document starting at the point where the preceding document in the book palette leaves off.

J. An index entry that begins with the words *See* or *See also* and points you to a different entry in the index.

K. This button instructs InDesign to reference every occurrence of a term within every open document.

L. This function tracks multiple InDesign documents so that you can evaluate and modify them as a group.

Answers

1L, 2I, 3E, 4A, 5H, 6C, 7F, 8B, 9G, 10K, 11J, 12D

LESSON 11

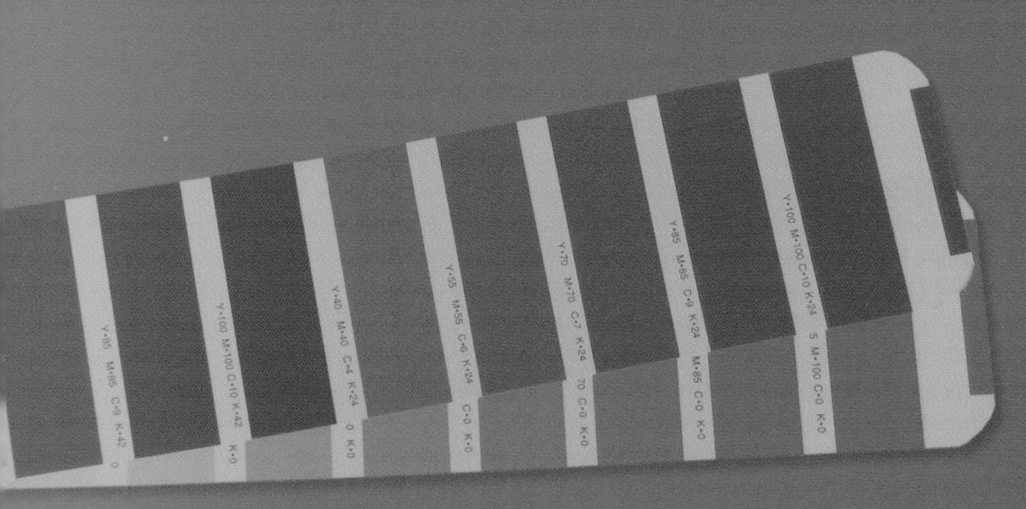

HYPERLINKS, BOOKMARKS, AND PDF

BOOKS AND OTHER printed documents can be many things. They can be instructive. They can be entertaining. They can be thought-provoking. They've even been known to shape events. But one thing printed documents can't be is interactive. Whatever you can say in their defense—and certainly a lot comes to mind—printed pages are static. If you're searching for a particular topic, you might find aid in the form of an index or a table of contents, but you have to thumb through the document to locate the page yourself.

If you're in the mood for an interactive reading experience, you might turn to the World Wide Web, where the document is expressed as a dynamic and nonlinear site. There, you can click links that define or explain a topic, take you to a related topic, or search for an entirely new one. If you have a mind to convert an InDesign document to a Web site, you can export the document to a collection of files that can be read by GoLive, the Web-site-creation application that Adobe includes with the Premium edition of the Creative Suite. Exporting to GoLive is an interesting and powerful solution, but it requires you to learn yet another application and is rarely what I would call quick or easy.

The better medium for expressing an InDesign document is the Portable Document Format, or *PDF* for short. A PDF file is self-contained, with no chance of broken links. It can be viewed on screen or printed, either with or without Internet access. Some operating systems, such as Apple's OS X, can view PDF files without additional software. Otherwise, you need a utility called Adobe Reader, which you can download for free (*www.acrobat.com*) and without registering any personal information. And finally, a PDF file can be static like a book document or interactive like a Web site, or even an amalgam of the two. It all depends on the kinds of elements you add to your document.

Project Files

Before beginning the exercises, make sure that you've installed the lesson files from the CD, as explained in Step 5 on page xv of the Preface. This should result in a folder called *Lesson Files-IDcs 1on1* on your desktop. We'll be working with the files inside the *Lesson 11* subfolder.

ABOUT THIS LESSON

This lesson explores InDesign's little-known multimedia capabilities. You can compose a fully interactive document—with bookmarks, hyperlinks, buttons, sounds, and movies—and export your creation to a PDF file that can be played on any modern computer. In the following exercises, you'll learn how to:

- Generate bookmarks automatically from a table of contents . . . . page 404
- Create hyperlinks that take the reader to other pages within a document or to entirely different documents . . . . page 408
- Design graphic buttons that animate when the reader moves the cursor over the button or clicks . . . . page 413
- Import and define the appearance of sound and movie files . . . . page 418
- Output your bookmarks, hyperlinks, buttons, sounds, and movies to an interactive PDF document . . . . page 422

Video Lesson 11: The Final PDF File

Before you learn how to create an interactive PDF document, you might want to see what you're getting yourself into. Hence, the following guided tour: In this video, I imagine what a book in the *One-on-One* series might look like if it were presented as an interactive PDF eBook, with bookmarks instead of a table of contents, hyperlinks and rollover buttons instead of index markers, and movie files embedded directly into the document. Call me a silly dreamer, but perhaps one day, such a book might even exist.

To join me in my exciting interactive PDF tour, watch the eleventh video lesson included on the CD. Insert the CD, bring up the Launchpad, click the **Start Training** button, click the Set 4 button in the upper-right corner of the player window, and then select **11, The Final PDF File** from the Lessons list. The video lasts 8 minutes and 4 seconds. And for once I don't mention a single shortcut.

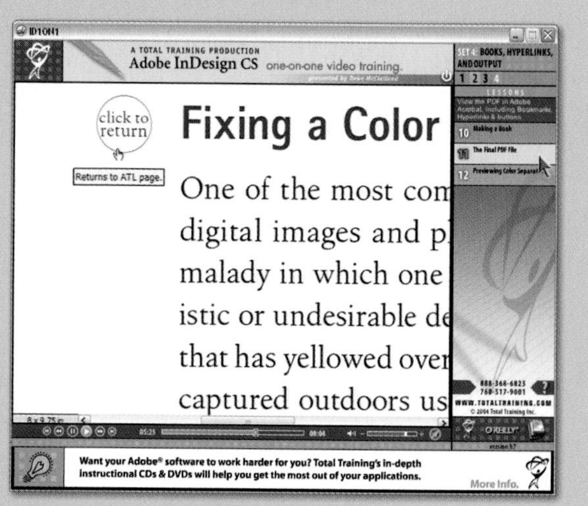

Tools for Interactivity

What varieties of interactivity does InDesign support? For starters, you can create a series of *bookmarks*, which behave like a live table of contents. Click a bookmark and you're whisked away to the corresponding headline. You can also create *hyperlinks*, which are hot spots built into the pages of a document. A hyperlink can be any text or graphic object, including a single word or character of type. Clicking the hyperlink might take you somewhere inside the same PDF file or transport you to a different file, including one posted on the Internet. To lend a hyperlink more visual impact, you can upgrade it to an animated *rollover button* that changes appearance when the reader's cursor passes over it. Buttons can trigger the same actions as bookmarks and hyperlinks, plus perform tasks like opening and closing files, quitting the Adobe Reader, and playing embedded sounds and movies.

Did I say "sounds and movies?" Why, yes I did. Although InDesign hardly qualifies as a full-fledged multimedia program, it does let you implant audio and video files into a PDF document. As long as you're creating a publication for the screen, you might as well take full advantage of all the benefits the screen has to offer (see Figure 11-1). The truth is, InDesign lets you create PDF documents with so many bells and whistles—literally—that your audience will swear the initials PDF stand for "Pretty Darn Fun."

Figure 11-1.

You've made it through these opening credits, and you'll be sitting next to me for the duration of this feature. So relax, turn off your cell phone, and don't kick the seat in front of you.

PEARL OF  WISDOM

As in the last lesson, you'll want to work your way through each exercise in sequence. Sadly, I can't provide you with intermediate documents—if I did, some links would not perform as advertised.

Before you settle in for the feature presentation, I invite you to watch the short subject, Video Lesson 11, "The Final PDF File," which gives you a sense of how your bookmarks, hyperlinks, rollover buttons, and embedded movies will work when exported to an interactive PDF document. Otherwise, prepare yourself to delay an awful lot of gratification before arriving at the stirring conclusion in the final exercise, "Exporting to PDF," which begins on page 422.

Creating Bookmarks

Adobe's use of the word "bookmark" is a little misleading. In the real world, a bookmark is placed at the reader's discretion to indicate where he or she stopped reading. In a PDF document, bookmarks are placed by the document's creator to aid in navigation and to point out sections that the creator thinks are important. It's like going to the bookstore to buy Stephen King's latest thriller and finding it laced with bookmarks put there by Mr. King himself.

In this exercise, you'll start with a formatted version of a document we created back in Lesson 2 and add bookmarks that will make the document easier to navigate when we export it as a PDF file. You'll see that if you're careful and consistent in your use of style sheets, adding PDF bookmarks is as easy as making a table of contents (see "Creating a Table of Contents," Lesson 10, page 384). In fact, generating a table of contents is one of the first things we'll do.

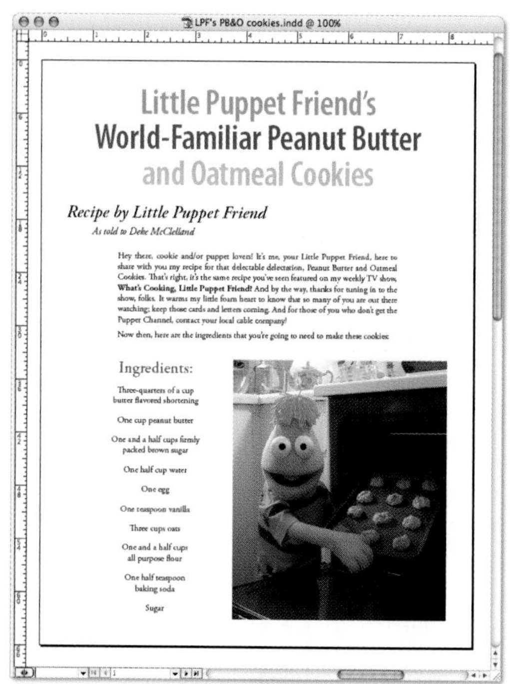

Figure 11-2.

1. *Open a document in need of bookmarks.* Open the file named *LPF's PB&O cookies.indd*, which is located in the *Lesson 11* folder inside *Lesson Files-IDcs 1on1*. As in Lesson 2, we are greeted by LPF and his oven-fresh cookies (see Figure 11-2). Lest you think I'm shamelessly repurposing a sample file, let me assure you, I have plenty of new stuff in store to keep the weary InDesign student entertained. In fact, at the risk of subjecting you to a pun, you're in for a treat.

2. ***Examine the styles used in the document.*** Choose **Type→Paragraph Styles** or press F11 to access the **Paragraph Styles** palette. Press the T key to get the type tool. In turn, click in the multicolored headline and the *Ingredients* subhead (both circled in Figure 11-3) and check out their style sheets in the Paragraph Styles palette. You'll see that the headline uses modified variations of the Title style and the subhead uses Ingredients.

   Repeat the process for the subheads on pages 2 and 3. You'll find that the *Reviewing the Ingredients*, *Making the Cookies*, and *Finishing the Cookies* subheads are formatted with the Headings style. I've also added a subhead called *The Joke* on page 3, but I neglected to assign a paragraph style to it.

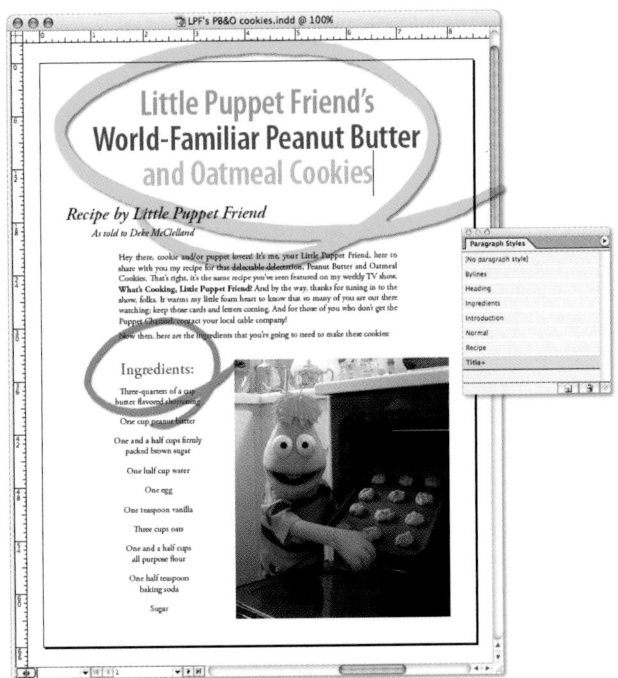

Figure 11-3.

3. ***Open the Bookmarks palette.*** Choose **Window→Interactive→Bookmarks** to open the **Bookmarks** palette. At this point, the palette is empty, but it won't be for long.

4. ***Generate a table of contents.*** Just as InDesign can create a table of contents using paragraph styles, it can create PDF bookmarks from a table of contents. In fact—and I think somewhat bizarrely—that's the *only* way to automate the creation of bookmarks. So choose **Layout→Table of Contents** to summon the **Table of Contents** dialog box. We want to include the title and all subheads in our TOC.

   - Click **Title** in the **Other Styles** list. Then click the **Add** button. Title becomes the first-level head.
   - Click **Ingredients** and then Shift-click **Heading**. Next click the **Add** button. The three styles appear in the left-hand list in the order shown in Figure 11-4.
   - We don't really care what this table of contents looks like, so you can ignore all the formatting options.
   - Turn on the **Create PDF Bookmarks** check box at the bottom of the dialog box. This tells InDesign to automatically make bookmarks for each of the items in the TOC.

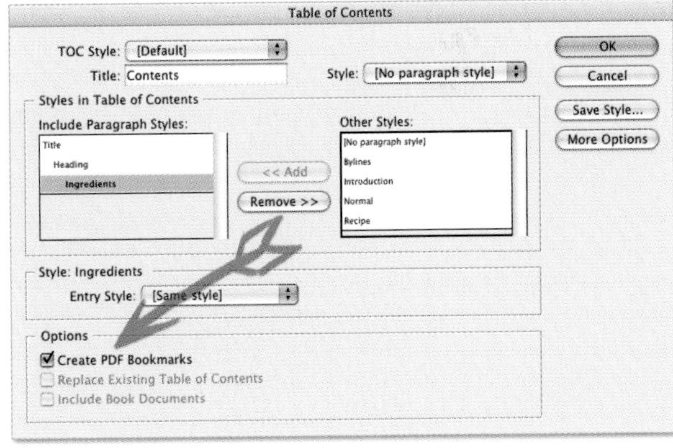

Figure 11-4.

- Click **OK**. You'll notice that the Bookmarks palette is no longer empty and that the cursor is ready to place text.

Figure 11-5.

5. ***Examine the bookmarks.*** Before you click with the cursor, take a look at the Bookmarks palette, which now contains bookmarks for the title and headings, as in Figure 11-5. (If you see only one item in the Bookmarks palette, click the ▶ arrow to the left of the item to reveal the others.)

6. ***Place the table of contents.*** Now to place the table of contents. The question is, where do you put it? We don't want to print the darn thing—what do we need with a TOC for a three-page document, for crying out loud?—so I recommend you throw it on the pasteboard. Armed with the cursor, draw a text frame in the pasteboard next to page 1, as indicated by the text block on the left side of Figure 11-6. The formatting looks pretty ugly, but we don't care. We're keeping it around only to retain the PDF bookmarks. And out there in the pasteboard, it won't print or export to a PDF file, so nobody but you is going to see it.

PEARL OF WISDOM

Even after you place the table of contents, it remains inextricably linked to the bookmarks. In other words, if you were to delete the table of contents at this point, the bookmarks would be deleted as well. It's exceedingly weird—there's no bookmark marker in the TOC text and the relationship between TOC and bookmarks is largely static—but that's the way it works.

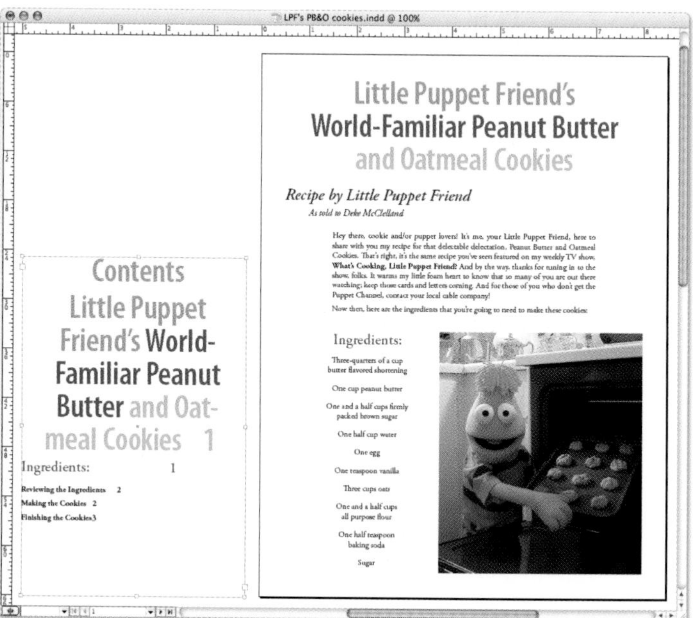

Figure 11-6.

7. ***Test a couple of bookmarks.*** Let's preview some bookmarks to make sure they work. You can test a bookmark by double-clicking it in the Bookmarks palette. Double-click the **Making the Cookies** bookmark to advance to page 2. Then double-click **Finishing the Cookies** to jump to page 3.

Should you be so inclined, you can rearrange bookmarks by dragging them up and down in the Bookmarks palette. Drag a bookmark on top of another bookmark to create a subcategory bookmark. To rename a bookmark, select it and choose Rename Bookmark from the palette menu. Or just click on a bookmark that you've already selected and wait a second. (Think of it as a very slow double-click, as when renaming a file at the desktop level.)

8. ***Create a new bookmark.*** I'd like you to add one more bookmark, this time for the subhead that reads *The Joke* in the first column of page 3. This paragraph doesn't have a style sheet applied so it wasn't included in the table of contents. But no worries, you can add bookmarks manually any time you like:

   - Get the type tool and select the heading *The Joke*. Be sure to select the entire line of text so that InDesign names the bookmark properly.
   - Click the **Making the Cookies** bookmark in the Bookmarks palette so that the next bookmark you create appears below it as a subcategory.
   - Click the ◲ icon at the bottom of the Bookmarks palette. As Figure 11-7 shows, InDesign automatically adds the bookmark and names it after the selected text. Press the Enter or Return key to accept the name.

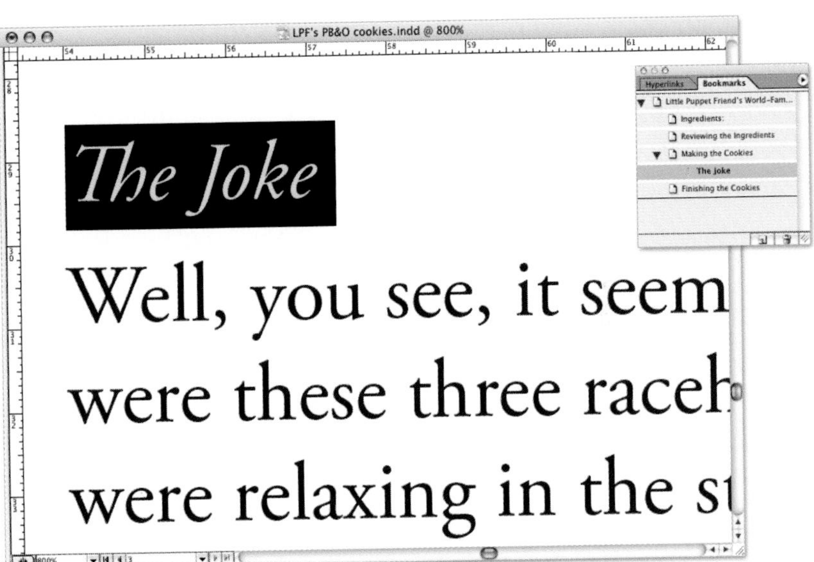

Figure 11-7.

Notice that the new bookmark name has a ⚓ icon beside it in the Bookmarks palette. This indicates a *hyperlink anchor*, or just plain *anchor*, embedded into the text of the document. You'll learn more about hyperlink anchors in the next exercise.

PEARL OF WISDOM

There are a few more things you should know about creating bookmarks manually: If you want a bookmark to take the reader to the top of a page (rather than to a specific anchor on a page), double-click the page in the Pages palette to select it, and then create a new bookmark. You can also bookmark a graphic by selecting it and then clicking the ◱ icon. InDesign will suggest the name *Bookmark*, but you can (and, what the heck, should) give it a more descriptive name.

---

9. ***Save your work.*** If you're going to continue on to the next exercise, you'll need this document in its current state, so it's a good idea to save your work. Choose **File→Save As**, name the document "LPF's PB&O cookies 2.indd," and click **Save**.

Setting Up Hyperlinks

Bookmarks are terrific for helping readers get around inside a document, but hyperlinks offer more flexibility. InDesign lets you create hyperlinks that take readers to different locations within a document or to external documents including other PDF files and Web pages. Put it this way: If bookmarks are the table of contents, then hyperlinks are the index.

In this exercise, you'll add three hyperlinks to the cookie recipe document that you saved at the end of the last exercise. First, you'll create a hyperlink that jumps to a different section of the document. Next, you'll create a hyperlink that leaps to a Web page available only if you have an Internet connection. And finally, you'll create a hyperlink that opens a *future* PDF file, one that won't exist until the end of the final exercise in this lesson.

1. ***Open the cookie recipe document.*** If it's not already up on screen, open the *LPF's PB&O cookies 2.indd* file that you saved in the last step of the last exercise. If you didn't work through the last exercise, please go back and do so now. These exercises must be performed in order.

2. ***Open the Hyperlinks palette.*** If the palette is not already visible, choose **Window→Interactive→Hyperlinks** to display the **Hyperlinks** palette.

3. ***Create a hyperlink destination.*** Let's turn one of the ingredients in the list on the first page into a hyperlink that takes readers to the paragraph description of that ingredient. First, we need to define the destination of the link by adding a hyperlink anchor. Then we can create the link.

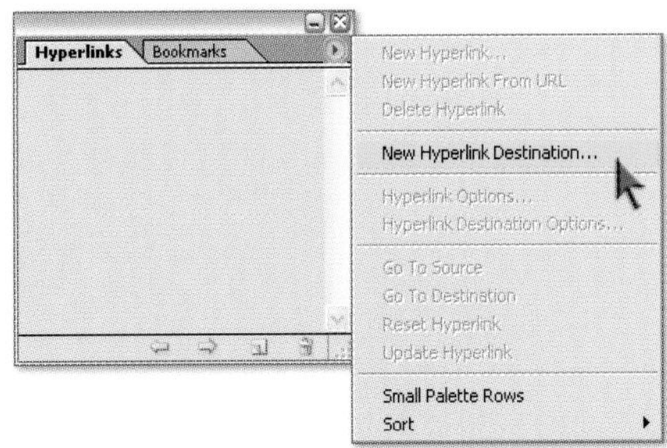

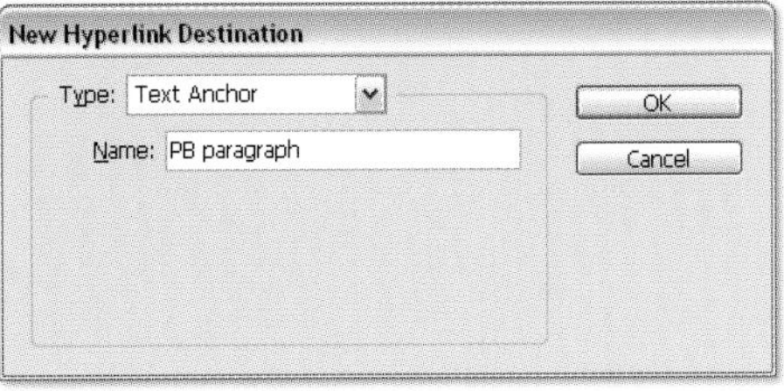

Figure 11-8.

- Go to the second page of the document and locate the second paragraph under the heading *Reviewing the Ingredients* in the first column (the one that begins *Then you're going to need one cup of peanut butter.*) Click in front of the first letter in this paragraph with the type tool to set the blinking insertion marker.
- Next, click the ⊙ in the upper corner of the Hyperlinks palette and choose **New Hyperlink Destination** to bring up the dialog box shown in Figure 11-8.
- The Type option lets you specify whether you want to create a link to a specific page in the document (Page), a hyperlink anchor (Text Anchor), or a Web page (URL). We've already determined that we want to use an anchor, so choose **Text Anchor** from the **Type** pop-up menu.
- Enter "PB paragraph" in the **Name** option box and click **OK** to close the New Hyperlink Destination dialog box.

Nothing appears in the Hyperlinks palette yet, because so far we've created only the destination for the hyperlink, not the hyperlink itself. The only way to confirm that anything whatsoever has happened is to choose Type→Show Hidden Characters or press Ctrl+Alt+I (⌘-Option-I). A light blue colon (:) appears in front of the first letter in the paragraph. That is your new hyperlink anchor.

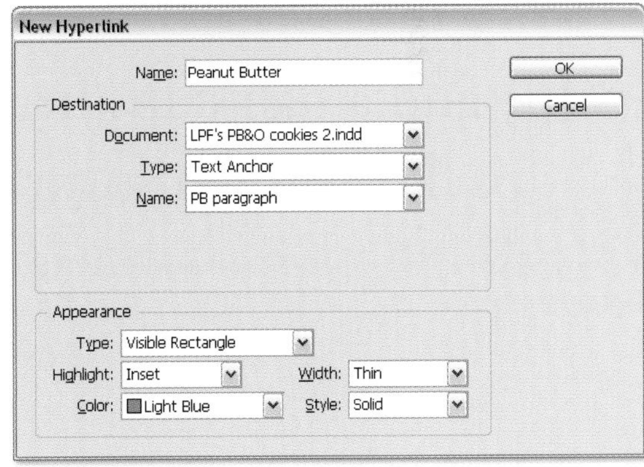

Figure 11-9.

4. ***Create a hyperlink.*** Go to the first page and triple-click on the second ingredient in the ingredients list, *One cup peanut butter*, to select the entire line of text. Then click the ◫ icon at the bottom of the Hyperlinks palette to display the **New Hyperlink** dialog box. Enter "Peanut Butter" in the **Name** option box. Then set the Destination options as shown in Figure 11-9:
   - Leave **Document** set to the default, **LPF's PB&O cookies 2.indd**, which is the document that contains the link destination. Note that when we update this document and save it under different names, InDesign will update this reference.
   - Choose **Text Anchor** from the **Type** pop-up menu.
   - Leave the **Name** option set to **PB paragraph**, which is the destination we set up in the preceding step.

- A hyperlink is useless if no one knows to click on it, so it's best to visually distinguish it from other text. The options in the Appearance section of the New Hyperlink dialog box let you do just that. A rectangle is the only visual clue available for hyperlinks, so choose **Visible Rectangle** from the **Type** pop-up menu (if it's not set that way already).
- The Highlight option determines what a link looks like when it's being clicked. None makes no change in the link's appearance. Invert creates an inverted rectangle, Outline draws a hollow rectangle, and Inset adds a shadowed effect like a button being pushed. Choose **Inset** from the **Highlight** pop-up menu.
- Set the **Color** pop-up menu to **Light Blue**.
- The **Width** setting determines the thickness of the rectangle outline. Stick with the default option of **Thin**.
- The **Style** option lets you choose between a solid or dashed outline; choose **Solid**.

When you're through, click **OK**. Then press Ctrl+Shift+A (or ⌘-Shift-A) to deselect the hyperlink so you can see what it looks like. As Figure 11-10 shows, a blue rectangle now appears around the link, and a hyperlink named Peanut Butter appears in the Hyperlinks palette with a little ⚓ to the right of it.

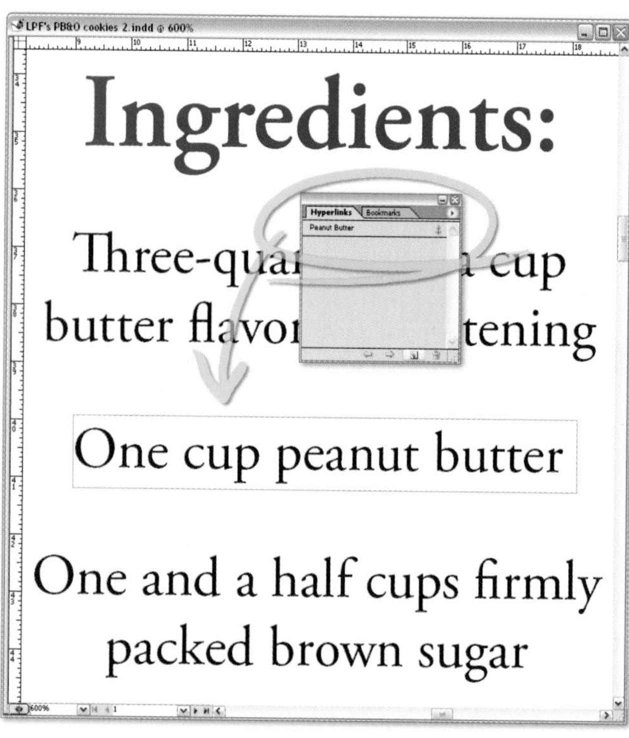

Figure 11-10.

If you wish InDesign would imbue a hyperlink with some visual identifier other than a rectangle, keep in mind that you can format the link text however you want. For instance, say you want *One cup peanut butter* to appear blue and underlined, which would make it look more like a standard hyperlink on the Web. Double-click the link in the Hyperlinks palette and change the Type option in the Appearance area to Invisible Rectangle. (You might also want to change the Highlight option to Invert or None.) Click OK to leave the dialog box. Then use the type tool to select the link text in the document window, and color the text blue and underline it using InDesign's character-level formatting controls.

---

5. *Test the hyperlink.* To test a bookmark, all you had to do was double-click on it in the Bookmarks palette. Not so with hyperlinks; double-clicking a hyperlink opens the Hyperlink Options dialog box, where you can edit the settings for the link. To test the hyperlink, select it in the Hyperlinks palette, and then click the ⇨ arrow at the bottom of the palette. In our case, the document jumps to page 2, and the insertion marker is set at the beginning of the peanut butter paragraph.

Select the link name again and click the ⇦ arrow at the bottom of the Hyperlinks palette to go back to the link, in this case the peanut butter ingredient on page 1.

6. *Create a URL hyperlink.* Let's now create a hyperlink to a Web site. We'll do this by entering a URL (Uniform Resource Locater), which is the address of the Web page. Note that a URL can just as easily point to a file on your hard drive, an image or movie file, or any of a number of other documents. And that's just fine by InDesign. So long as you enter a valid URL, the PDF file can link to it.

   There's no need to specify a destination because the URL *is* the destination. So we'll just make the hyperlink:

   - Navigate to the final paragraph in the lower-right corner of page 3 and select the entire italicized book title, *Baking Cookies One-on-One*.
   - Next, click the icon at the bottom of the Hyperlinks palette to bring up the New Hyperlink dialog box. InDesign names the link after the book title, so you can leave the **Name** option as is.
   - Choose **URL** from the **Type** pop-up menu. Then enter "http://oneonone.oreilly.com" in the **URL** option box. (Note that there's no "www" in the URL.) This is the URL for information on my *One-on-One* books.
   - Ignore the Document and second Name options, neither of which apply. Also ignore the Appearance settings; we'll use the same ones we applied last time.

   Your settings in the New Hyperlink dialog box should match those in Figure 11-11. When they do, click **OK**, and then press Ctrl+Shift+A (⌘-Shift-A) to deselect the text and view the new hyperlink.

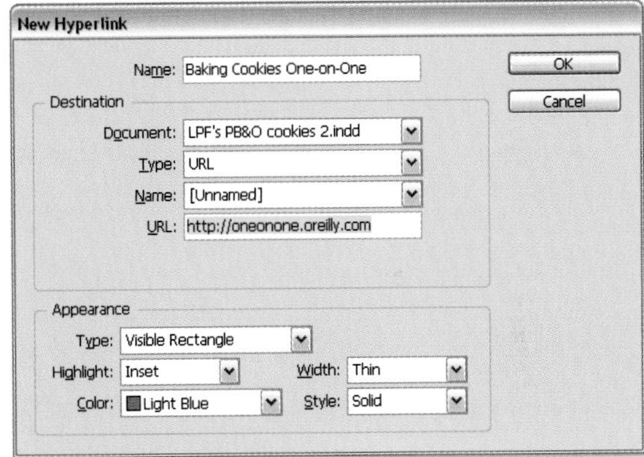

Figure 11-11.

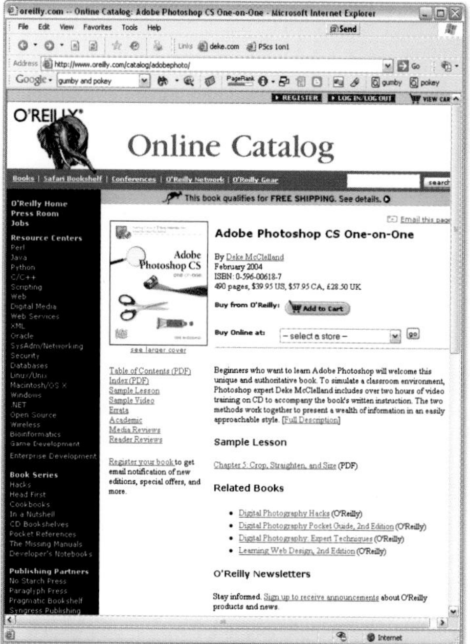

Figure 11-12.

7. ***Test the URL.*** To preview the hyperlink and make sure it works, select the link name and click the ⇨ arrow at the bottom of the palette. This time InDesign launches your default Web browser and then loads the *One-on-One* Web site, pictured in Figure 11-12. Note that you'll need an active Internet connection. If the site looks different than it does in the figure, then the site has been updated. If the link fails, it's probably because you entered it incorrectly. Double-click on the link in the Hyperlinks palette and confirm the URL.

8. ***Create yet another hyperlink.*** We have one last hyperlink to add. This time we'll create a link that opens another document. Go to page 1, and select the boldface *What's Cooking, Little Puppet Friend?* (including the question mark) in the main text. Oh, and as long as we're making a new hyperlink, let's try our hands at a new technique:

   - Right-click in the document window to display the shortcut menu. (If your Mac mouse has just one button, press Control and click.) Then choose **Interactive→New Hyperlink**. This brings up the familiar New Hyperlink dialog box, shown in Figure 11-13 with the settings I want you to enter.

   - Go ahead and accept the default name, which is derived from the selected text.

   - Choose **Browse** from the **Document** pop-up menu to bring up the **Locate InDesign File** dialog box. Navigate to the *Lesson 11* folder inside *Lesson Files-IDcs 1on1*, select the file named *What's cooking.indd*, and click **Open**. Back in the New Hyperlink dialog box, the Document pop-up menu now lists What's cooking.indd.

   - Next, choose **Page** from the **Type** pop-up menu. The Name option is irrelevant for our purposes. The Page option is set to 1 and can't be changed, because *What's cooking.indd* is a single-page document. For the **Zoom Setting** option, choose **Inherit Zoom**, which will open the linked file at the viewer's current zoom setting.

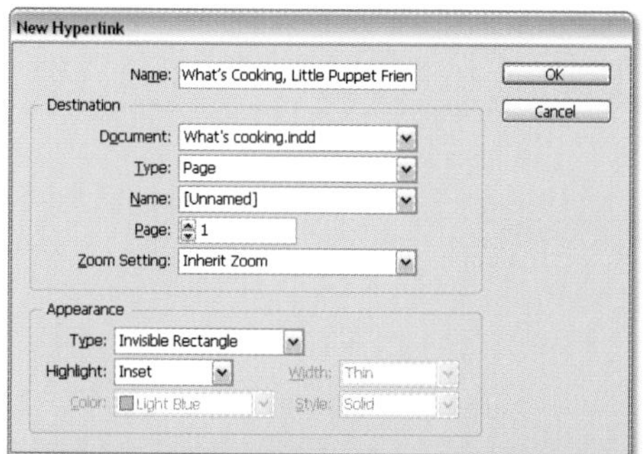

What's Cooking, Little Puppet Friend?

Figure 11-13.

Under Appearance, change the **Type** option to **Invisible Rectangle**. The link text is already bold, so including a rectangle seems like overkill. Besides, we'll create a more compelling way to launch the *What's cooking* document in the next exercise; this link is just a backup. When your settings look like those in Figure 11-13, click **OK**. Then press Ctrl+Shift+A (⌘-Shift-A) to deselect your text. This time, no rectangle. Nice.

9. ***Test the latest hyperlink.*** Click the newest link item in the Hyperlinks palette, and then click the ⇨ arrow at the bottom of the palette. (If you get a dialog box notifying you that links are missing or modified, click Fix Links Automatically.) The *What's cooking.indd* document window opens as shown in Figure 11-14. If the page appears magnified, press Ctrl+1 (or ⌘-1) to zoom out to 100 percent.

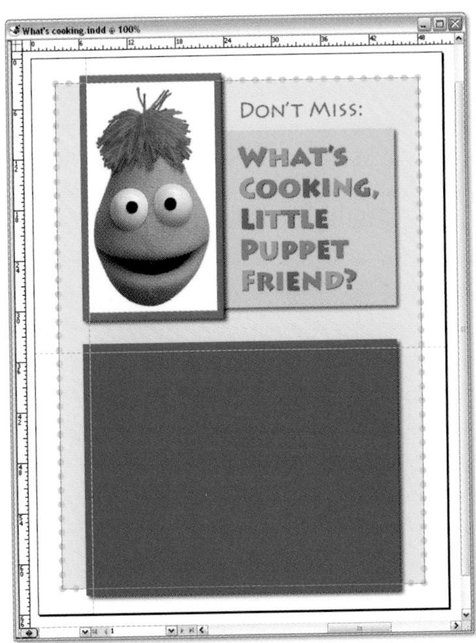

Figure 11-14.

PEARL OF WISDOM

When we export *LPF's PB&O cookies.indd* to a PDF file in the final exercise, this hyperlink will automatically update to look for a file named *What's cooking.pdf*. This means we'll need to export *What's cooking.indd* as a PDF file as well. If we didn't, the link wouldn't work.

10. ***Close one document and save the other.*** Go ahead and close *What's cooking.indd*. If InDesign asks whether you want to save changes, click **Yes** (or **Save** on the Mac). We'll see this document again in a couple of exercises.

    We're not done with the cookie recipe, so keep it open. Choose **File→Save As**, name the document "LPF's PB&O cookies 3.indd," and click **Save**. You'll need this version of the document in the next exercise.

Making Buttons

Our next task is to create a rollover button. A button can link to an anchor, a URL, or another PDF file, just like a hyperlink. It can also exhibit different visual states when you click it or roll over it. In addition to offering a Convert to Button command (which we put to use in the next exercise), InDesign even goes so far as to provide you with a dedicated button tool. In this exercise, you'll learn how to create a button using the button tool, trigger a change in the button's appearance relative to a mouse action, and set up a behavior for the button so that it performs an action.

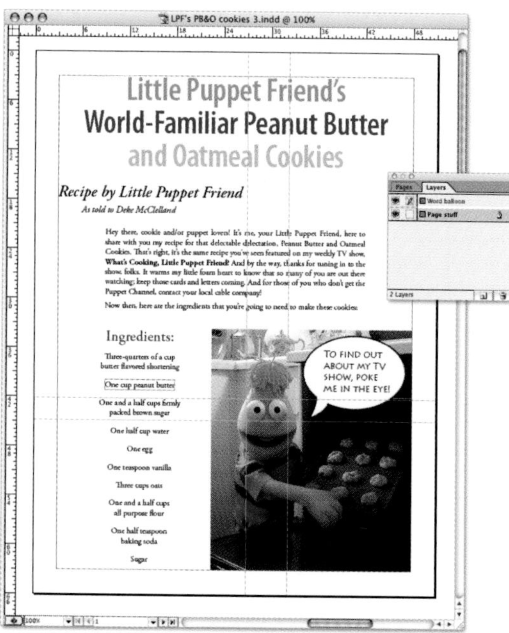

Figure 11-15.

1. ***Open the cookie recipe document.*** If it's not already smack dab in front of you, open the *LPF's PB&O cookies 3.indd* file that you saved in the *Lesson 11* folder in Step 10 of the last exercise.

2. ***Turn on the hidden layer.*** Press F7 or choose **Window→Layers** to open the **Layers** palette. There you'll find a layer called Word Balloon that's been hidden until now. Click in the empty box to the left of the **Word Balloon** layer to show its 👁 icon and display a cartoon word balloon in the document window. The message in the word balloon directs the reader to click a link that we haven't yet created. To make this link, we'll need a little guidance.

3. ***Show the guides.*** Choose **View→Show Guides** or press Ctrl+; (⌘-; on the Mac) to turn on the guides. As Figure 11-15 shows, four gray guides intersect to create a rectangle around Little Puppet Friend's eyes. We'll use these guides to help in drawing the button.

4. ***Draw a button.*** Before drawing a button, you need to make sure that both the fill and stroke icons in the toolbox are set to none, as in . Then select the button tool, the one right above the hand tool on the left side of the toolbox. Or you can press the B key. See that rectangle around the eyes created by the four gray guides? Drag from the upper-left corner of that rectangle to the lower-right corner, as in Figure 11-16. The corners of the button should snap into alignment with the guides. If you don't get the button exactly aligned, use the black arrow tool to adjust the corner handles.

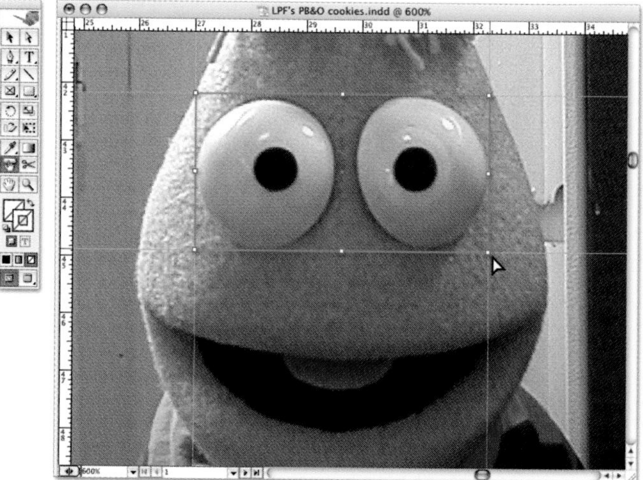

Figure 11-16.

5. ***Name the button.*** Choose **Window→Interactive→States** to open the **States** palette. In the **Name** option box at the top of the palette, type "Button Eyes," and press Enter or Return. This button currently has one state, labeled **Up** in the States palette (see Figure 11-17). This indicates how the button will look when the mouse button is not pressed, or "up." We'll see how to add other states in just a moment. The States palette also offers an Appearance pop-up menu, which offers access to a few prefab effects, useful for creating raised or glowing buttons. But LPF would look weird with raised or glowing eyes, so we'll create our rollover button manually.

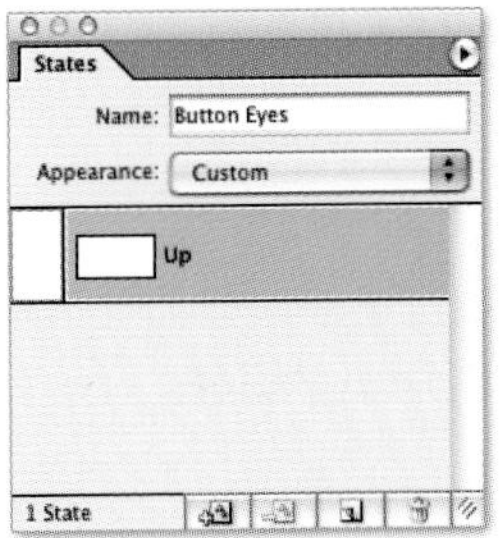

Figure 11-17.

6. ***Create two additional states.*** Click the icon at the bottom of the States palette twice to create two new states, **Rollover** and **Down**. The Rollover state defines how the button looks when you move your move over it; the Down state defines how it looks when the mouse button is down, which happens when you click. You might notice that you can't click the icon more than twice; a button is limited to a maximum of three states.

7. ***Assign the button a Rollover appearance.*** Click the **Rollover** state and then click the first icon at the bottom of the States palette. In the **Place** dialog box, go to the *Links* folder in the *Lesson 11* folder inside *Lesson Files-IDcs 1on1*. Then select the file named *Puppet-eyes-rollover.jpg* and click **Open**. As Figure 11-18 shows, the JPEG image loads into the button's Rollover state, giving Little Puppet Friend a startled appearance. (My guess is you'd look that way, too, if someone was about to poke you in the eye.)

Figure 11-18.

8. ***Give the button a Down appearance.*** Now we need to load an image for the button's Down state. Click the **Down** state in the States palette and again click the icon. In the Place dialog box, select the file called *Puppet-eyes-down.jpg* located in the same *Links* folder as in the last step, and click **Open**. Figure 11-19 shows how LPF looks when the Down state is active.

Figure 11-19.

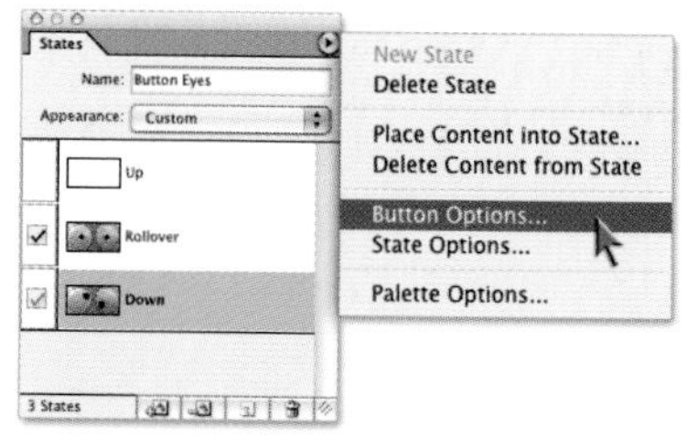

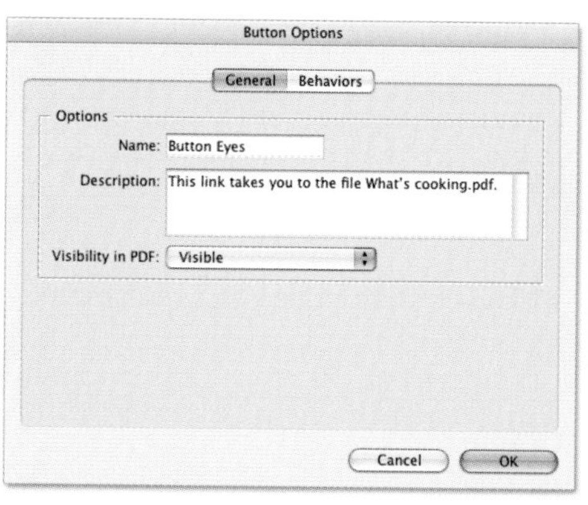

Figure 11-20.

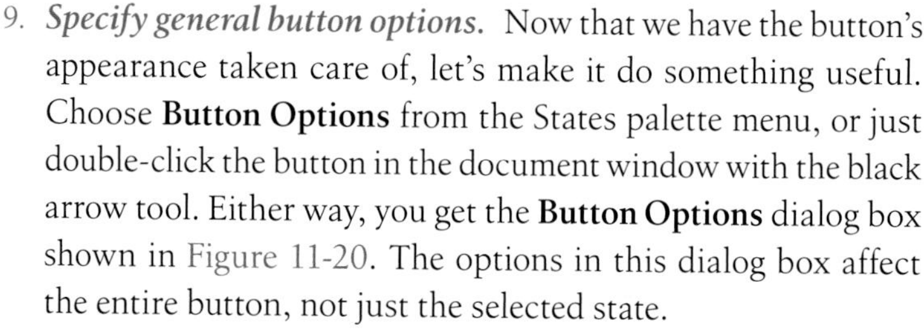

9. ***Specify general button options.*** Now that we have the button's appearance taken care of, let's make it do something useful. Choose **Button Options** from the States palette menu, or just double-click the button in the document window with the black arrow tool. Either way, you get the **Button Options** dialog box shown in Figure 11-20. The options in this dialog box affect the entire button, not just the selected state.

   In the **Description** area, enter the following: "This link takes you to the file What's cooking.pdf." This text will appear when a cursor passes over the button. It may also be read by text-to-speech software used by the visually impaired. The **Visibility in PDF** pop-up menu lets you specify whether the button will be visible in the PDF file on screen and when the PDF document is printed. You can leave the option set to **Visible**.

10. ***Assign an event and a behavior.*** Click the **Behaviors** button at the top of the dialog box to switch to a second panel of op-

tions. This is where we'll assign an action to our button and specify the event that triggers it:

- The Event pop-up menu lists the various things a reader can do to activate the button. The beginning of a click is Mouse Down, the end of the click is Mouse Up. A cursor moving over a button is Mouse Enter, a cursor moving out of the button is Mouse Exit. The final two options, On Focus and On Blur, apply when a button is selected (focused) or deselected (blurred) by pressing the Tab key. We want to initiate the event *after* the reader clicks the button, as is standard, so leave the **Event** option set to **Mouse Up**.
- The Behavior pop-up menu lets you select whether a button jumps you to an anchor or a page, opens or closes a document, or triggers a movie or a sound file. We want this button to open *What's cooking.pdf*. So choose **Go To Anchor** from the **Behavior** pop-up menu. Then click the **Browse** button to bring up the **InDesign Format File** dialog box. Select the file named *What's cooking.indd*, and click **Open**.
- I've created a hyperlink anchor called **What's Cooking, Little Puppet Friend?**, which should appear by default in the **Anchor** pop-up menu. If not, choose it.
- Set the **Zoom** option to **Inherit Zoom** so that the viewer's current zoom factor will be maintained.

11. ***Put the button options into play.*** Assuming that you have all your Behavior options set as in Figure 11-21, click the **Add** button in the lower-right portion of the dialog box. This adds a new event and behavior in the left-hand list. Click **OK** to accept your changes and dismiss the dialog box. The button is now complete. Unfortunately, we can't preview it until we actually export the PDF document in the last exercise. The good news is, that's just one more exercise from now. So hang in there.

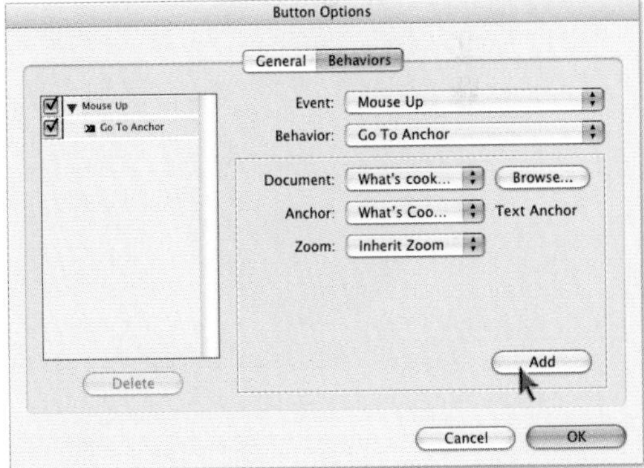

Figure 11-21.

12. ***Uncross LPF's eyes and save your work.*** I can't bear to leave LPF with his eyes crossed. And besides, it's a bad starting point for future endeavors. So click the **Up** state in the **States** palette to restore his eyes to their normal appearance. Then choose **File→Save As**, name the document "LPF's PB&O cookies 4.indd," and click **Save**. We'll revisit this file in the last exercise of this lesson.

Embedding Sounds and Movies

InDesign CS lets you embed audio and video files inside your PDF documents to enhance the reader's experience. You can import audio clips stored in the WAV or AIFF format, as well as videos saved as MOV or AVI files. In this exercise, we'll use WAV for our audio and MOV for our video. You can play a WAV file with just about any sound or music software, including Windows Media Player and Apple's iTunes. To watch the MOV file, you'll need to have Apple's QuickTime installed on your computer. All versions of Macintosh OS X come with QuickTime installed; it's also relatively common on the PC. However, if you don't have QuickTime, please take a moment to download and install it from *www.apple.com/quicktime/download*.

In the following steps, you'll embed sound and movie files into a document. You'll set various options that determine when the files play and how they are displayed in the document. You'll also build upon the skills you learned in the last exercise by creating a button that triggers the embedded files to play.

Figure 11-22.

1. ***Open a document.*** Go to the *Lesson 11* folder inside *Lesson Files-IDcs 1on1* and open *What's cooking.indd*. (If you get a modified links warning, be sure to click the Fix Links Automatically button; otherwise you'll get an error message when you export this document to PDF in the next exercise.) First witnessed back in Figure 11-14 (see page 413), this document is the target of the button we created in the preceding exercise as well as one of the hyperlinks we created in the exercise before that.

2. ***Place a sound file.*** Choose **File→Place** or press Ctrl+D (⌘-D on the Mac). In the **Place** dialog box, select the file named *Hi folks.wav*, located in the *Links* folder inside the *Lesson 11* folder, and click **Open**. Your cursor changes to a little speaker, as in . Click in the top-left corner of the document to place the audio file, as shown in Figure 11-22. This audio file contains an introductory message from LPF. Now we need to set options for playing and displaying the file.

3. ***Set the placed file to play when the document opens.*** Choose **Object→Interactive→Sound Options** or, much easier, just double-click the placed audio file with the black arrow tool.

In either case, the upshot of your efforts is the **Sound Options** dialog box. When it appears, here's what I want you to do:

- Midway down the dialog box, the Poster option determines what the audio file looks like in the PDF file. The default setting of Standard displays a speaker icon. You can also assign an independent image file. But we want our sound file to be heard and not seen, so choose **None** from the **Poster** pop-up menu.
- Turn on the **Play on Page Turn** check box to play the sound file when the document first appears on screen. This way, LPF will greet visitors when they open the document.

Leave the Description field empty; otherwise, a message might spring to life when the reader hovers a cursor over the invisible sound file. When your dialog box is set like the one in Figure 11-23, click the **OK** button. The speaker icon will disappear from the upper-left corner of the document.

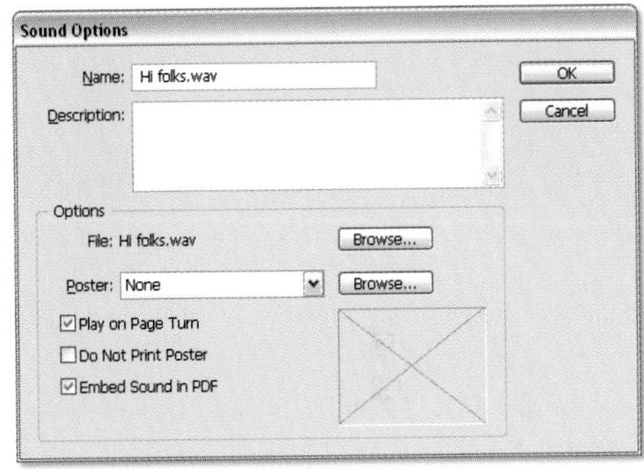

Figure 11-23.

4. ***Place another sound file.*** Press Ctrl+Shift+A (⌘-Shift-A) to deselect the sound file so you don't run the risk of replacing it. Then once again choose **File→Place**. This time, select the file named *Click me.wav* inside the *Links* folder in *Lesson 11*, which features a brief instruction from LPF. Click the **Open** button and then click with the cursor to place the sound file in the upper-right corner of the document. If necessary, drag the file until it snaps into alignment with the corner, as in Figure 11-24.

Figure 11-24.

5. ***Make the sound file invisible.*** Double-click the sound file to open the Sound Options dialog box. Choose **None** from the **Poster** pop-up menu. You can enter a **Description**, but otherwise leave the options as is. (For example, do *not* turn on the Play on Page Turn check box). Then click **OK**.

6. ***Place the movie file.*** Once again press Ctrl+Shift+A (⌘-Shift-A) to deselect the sound file. Then choose **File→Place**, select the file named *WCLPF promo.mov* inside the *Links* folder, and click **Open**. InDesign equips you with the cursor. Click with it at the intersection of the cyan guides on the left side of the page below the photo of LPF. As Figure 11-25 on the next page shows, this centers the now-black movie against the blue background at the bottom of the page.

Figure 11-25.

7. ***Set the options for the movie file.*** Double-click the movie file with the black arrow tool to open the **Movie Options** dialog box. Here's how you should set the options:

   - Tab to the **Description** area and enter the text pictured in Figure 11-26 (or words to that effect). This description will appear in a pop-up when the reader hovers his or her cursor over the movie.

   - The **Source** options let you select a different movie or play an online movie by entering its URL. We already have a movie, so you should leave most of these options alone. However, I do want you to turn on the **Embed Movie in PDF** check box, which saves the movie as part of the PDF file. This makes the PDF file larger, but it also ensures that the link between document and movie is never broken.

   - The **Poster** pop-up menu lets you choose the image that will display in the document when the movie isn't playing. The Default Poster setting displays the first frame of the movie, which—being completely black—serves as a poor representative. Instead, click the **Browse** button just to the right of the pop-up menu. Then select the file named *TPC logo.psd* in the *Links* folder inside *Lesson 11* and click **Open**. The selected image appears in the preview window.

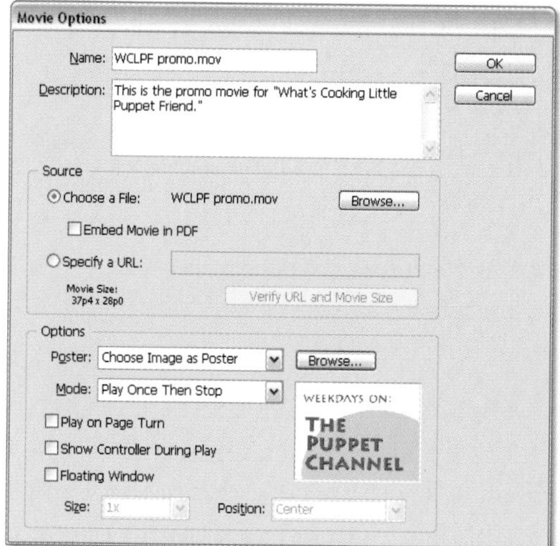

Figure 11-26.

- The Mode pop-up menu lets you choose options for playing the movie. Play Once Then Stop plays the movie once through, and then goes back to displaying the poster frame. Play Once Stay Open is a viable option if you activate the Show Controller During Play or Floating Window options below; rather than displaying the poster frame after the movie has played, the movie controls or floating window (or both) will stick around so that the viewer can watch the movie again. Repeat Play makes the movie loop. Keep this option set to Play Once Then Stop.

Leave all check boxes turned off. When your settings look like those in Figure 11-26, click **OK**. The specified poster image appears at the bottom of the document window, as in Figure 11-27.

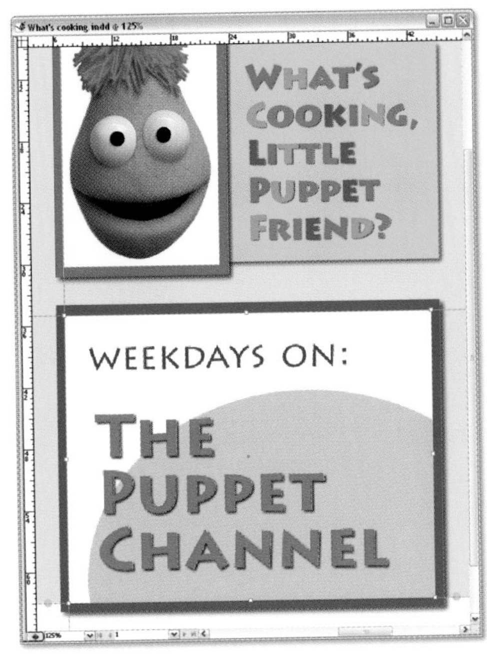

Figure 11-27.

8. *Convert the photo of LPF into an interactive button.* The movie file will play if the poster frame is clicked in the PDF document. But I also want you to create a button that will trigger both the movie and the *Click me.wav* sound file:
   - If the **States** palette isn't still open, choose **Window→Interactive→States**.
   - Select the large photo of LPF's head with the black arrow tool and choose **Object→Interactive→Convert to Button**. A new button appears in the States palette.
   - Change the **Name** to "Big Puppet Head" and press Enter or Return. The result appears in Figure 11-28.

   This time around, we'll forgo adding a rollover or down state to the button. But we do need to apply a few behaviors to it.

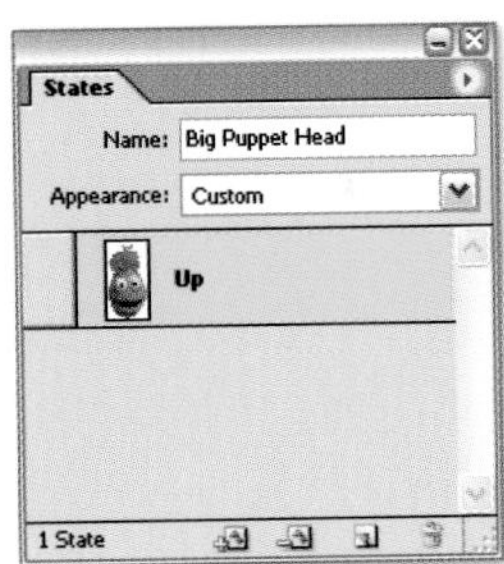

Figure 11-28.

9. *Set options for the button.* Double-click the button in the document window to open the **Button Options** dialog box. Click in the **Description** area and type "Click to play the promo movie." Then switch to the **Behaviors** panel and do the following:
   - First, I want the *Click me.wav* file to play when the cursor rolls over the button. Choose **Mouse Enter** from the **Event** pop-up menu. Then choose **Sound** from the **Behavior** option and **Click me.wav** from the **Sound** option. Check that the last option is set to **Play** and click the **Add** button.

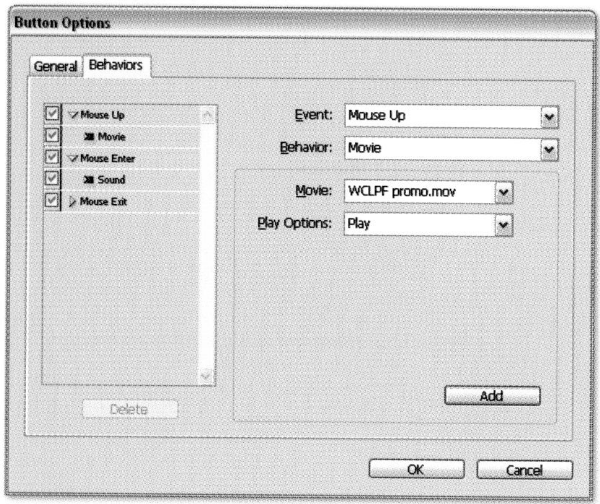

Figure 11-29.

- Next, let's add a behavior that makes the *Click me.wav* file stop playing when the cursor leaves the button area. Choose **Mouse Exit** from the **Event** pop-up menu and **Click me.wav** from the **Sound** pop-up menu. Set the **Play Options** to **Stop**. Then click the **Add** button.
- Our last behavior will make the *WCLPF promo.mov* file play when the reader clicks the photo. Set the **Event** option to **Mouse Up**. Choose **Movie** from the **Behavior** pop-up menu. Make sure the next two options are set to **WCLPF promo.mov** and **Play**, and then click the **Add** button.

Your Button Options settings should match those in Figure 11-29. Assuming that they do, click **OK** to close the dialog box.

10. ***Save your work.*** Congratulations, you have successfully created a multimedia file in InDesign. Granted, we've experienced scant evidence of our labors so far, but that's about to change in the very next exercise. In the meantime, save your work by choosing **File→Save As**, naming the document "What's cooking 1.indd," and clicking **Save**.

Exporting to PDF

My only complaint with InDesign's bevy of interactivity functions is that you have to wait until you export a document as a PDF file to see the functions interact. As a result, you've amassed an entire lesson of delayed gratification, and that's just not healthy. The good news is, now that you've done all that work, it's finally time to sit back and reap the rewards. In this final exercise, you'll export your interactive InDesign documents to the widely acclaimed Portable Document Format. Then you'll click a few buttons and smile. Honestly, I can't imagine a more satisfactory way to end a lesson.

PEARL OF WISDOM

Before you can perform these steps, you'll need to have a working copy of the free Adobe Reader 6 or the commercial Adobe Acrobat 6 (or later) installed on your computer. Adobe Reader is available gratis at *www.acrobat.com*; click the Get Adobe Reader button. Acrobat ships with the Premium edition of the Creative Suite.

1. ***Open both of your interactive documents.*** Open the latest versions of the two documents we've been working on throughout this lesson: *LPF's PB&O cookies 4.indd* and *What's cooking 1.indd*. Your two documents should look like the ones pictured in Figure 11-30. (I switched both of

my documents to the preview mode—by pressing the W key, as you may recall. This hides the guides and the light blue rectangle around the *One cup peanut butter* entry.)

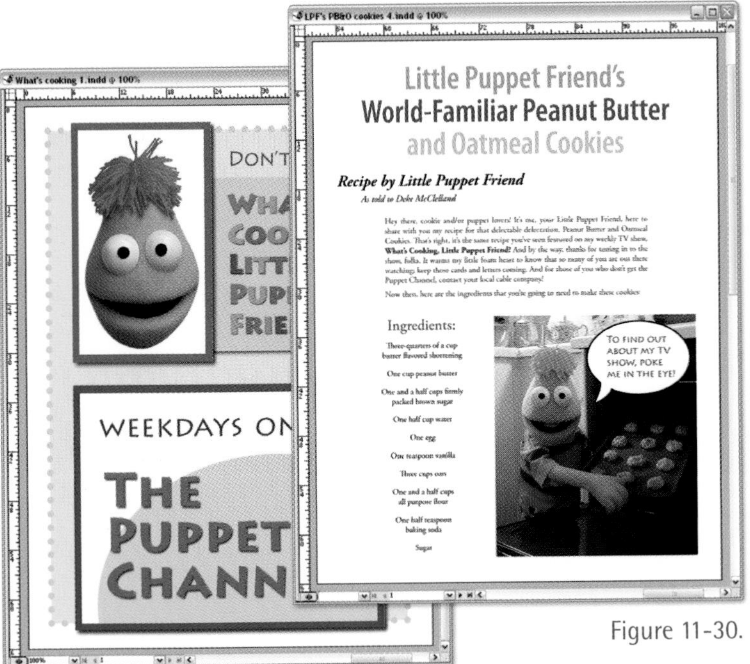

Figure 11-30.

2. ***Bring the Peanut Butter and Oatmeal document to front.*** The cookie recipe (*LPF's PB&O cookies 4.indd*) contains more interactive elements, so we'll start with it.

3. ***Choose the Export command.*** Choose **File→Export** or press Ctrl+E (⌘-E). InDesign displays the **Export** dialog box, which asks you to name the file and select a format. Navigate to the *Lesson 11* folder inside *Lesson Files-IDcs 1on1*. Make sure the **Save as Type** option (**Format** on the Mac) is set to **Adobe PDF**. Change the name of the file to suit your strange and peculiar tastes. I removed the number, that's how weird I am. And then click the **Save** button.

4. ***Load the eBook settings.*** InDesign presents you with the great and powerful **Export PDF** dialog box, which contains six panels of options designed to overwhelm and intimidate. Fortunately, we need to concern ourselves with relatively few of them. For starters, go to the **Preset** pop-up menu and choose **[eBook]**, as in Figure 11-31 on the next page, which selects what Adobe regards as the ideal settings for saving an interactive document. Most importantly, it turns on four of the Include check boxes

at the bottom of the dialog box. The Bookmarks, Hyperlinks, and Interactive Elements options ensure that InDesign saves the results of our labors in the first three exercises. The other check box, eBook Tags, automatically assigns a predefined collection of XML-style tags (like those we learned about in Lesson 9, "Pages, Layers, and XML"), no work necessary. Unfortunately, the free Adobe Reader does not support eBook tags, so most folks can't see them. (If you own Adobe Acrobat, you can view eBook tags by choosing View→Navigation Tabs→Tags.)

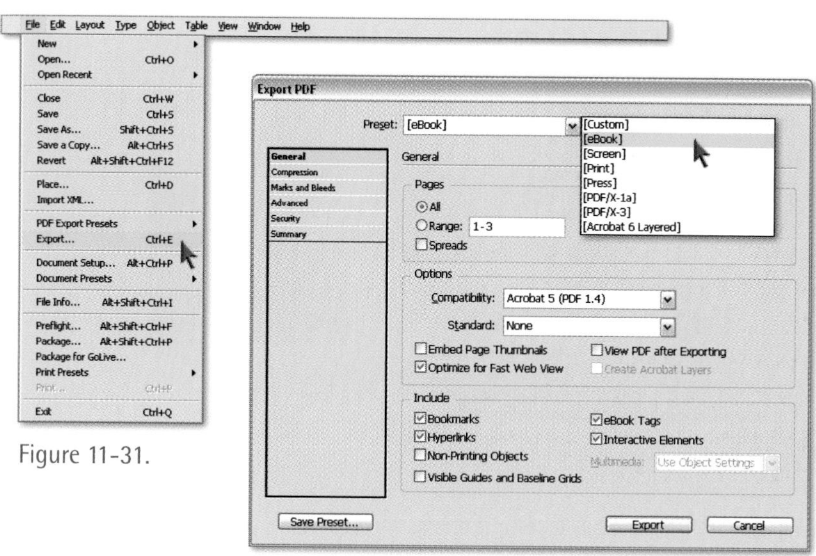

Figure 11-31.

5. ***Change the Compatibility option to Acrobat 6.*** To permit embedded sounds and movies, set the **Compatibility** option to **Acrobat 6 (PDF 1.5)**. This particular document doesn't have a movie, but the next one does. We might as well establish one collection of settings that works for both. This limits compatibility to Adobe Reader 6 or Acrobat 6 (or later), but such is the price of progress.

6. ***Make sure All and Optimize are on.*** We want to export all three pages of this document, so check that the **All** option is turned on. There should also be a checkmark inside the **Optimize for Fast Web View** option. The latter option organizes the exported PDF data so it can be read as soon as the first page is downloaded from a Web site or a server. It also compresses graphics to reduce the final file size (as I explain in Step 8.).

7. *Tell InDesign to open the PDF file when you finish.* I imagine that you'll want to see your PDF file after you finish creating it. You've been waiting all this time, after all. So turn on the **View PDF after Exporting** check box to instruct InDesign to automatically launch Adobe Reader or Acrobat and open the PDF file the moment it gets done exporting the document.

8. *Turn off downsampling for the imported images.* Click **Compression** in the left-hand list or press Ctrl+2 (⌘-2 on the Mac) to advance to the next panel. These options let you reduce the resolution of imported images and specify how InDesign goes about compressing them. Pictured in Figure 11-32, the panel is divided into three sections, which provide you with independent control over color, grayscale, and black-and-white images. Within each section, InDesign offers two or more of the following options:

   - The first pop-up menu lets you *downsample* imported images, which means to reduce the resolution by averaging pixels. Lower image resolutions make for a smaller PDF file, which is faster to download, email, and transmit over a network. If you choose to downsample, the default setting, Bicubic Downsampling to, is the wisest choice. But that's a big if, as I'll explain in a moment.
   - *Compression* is a means of reducing the size of the image data when incorporated into the PDF file. InDesign may choose to eliminate redundant data (so-called *lossless* compression), restructure the image to reduce its complexity (*lossy*), or both. My tests suggest that InDesign is very smart about how it applies compression; therefore, I advise leaving the Compression option set to Automatic so it can work its magic without interference.
   - When saving color and grayscale images, InDesign applies lossy compression according to rules published by the Joint Photographic Experts Group, or *JPEG*. The third pop-up menu, Image Quality, determines how much JPEG compression InDesign applies. More compression results in lower quality images and a smaller PDF file. If file size isn't a concern, you can raise the Image Quality to High or Maximum. Otherwise, leave it set to Medium. Lower-quality settings tend to produce ratty looking images, and no one wants that.

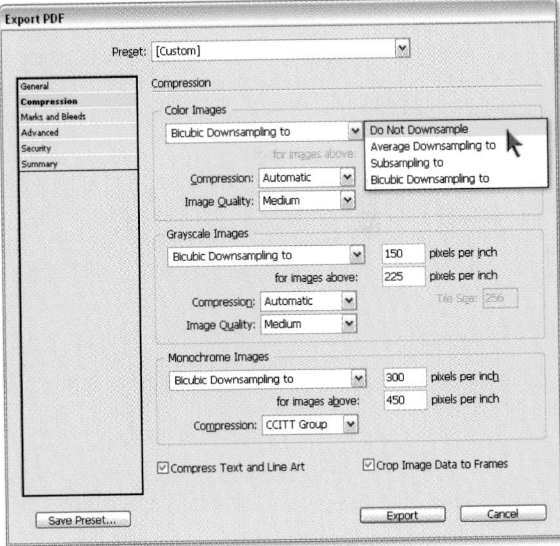

Figure 11-32.

PEARL OF WISDOM

I am an enthusiastic supporter of JPEG compression, which may reduce the size of imported images by factors of 50 to 80 percent with only a slight loss in quality. I am far less enthusiastic about downsampling, which provides comparatively small reductions in file size in return for whopping losses in quality. Downsampling is *never* to be entered into lightly. So when in doubt, turn it off, just as we will now.

The cookie recipe contains a total of four color images—two photos plus LPF's alternative eyes used for the Over and Down button states in the "Making Buttons" exercise. There are no grayscale or black-and-white images, so the second and third sections in the dialog box don't apply. Click the first pop-up menu and choose **Do Not Downsample**. Leave all other settings as you found them.

9. ***Adjust the color space.*** Click **Advanced** in the left-hand list or press Ctrl+4 (⌘-4). This takes you to the Color options, circled in Figure 11-33. An interactive PDF document is meant first and foremost to be viewed on a computer screen, which is an RGB device. So it's only fitting that the Color option is set to RGB. But the colors won't look right without color management, which is unwisely turned off. Here's how to activate it:

    - Turn on the **Include ICC Profiles** check box. (Note that color management must be turned on for this option to be available, according to my instructions in Step 11 on page xvi of the Preface.) This embeds source color profiles, so that Acrobat or some other PDF viewer knows where the document comes from.
    - Both Adobe Reader and Acrobat can read profiles, interpret them, and adjust colors accordingly. But these aren't the only programs that can open PDF files, and those other programs aren't always so clever. To convert the colors in your document so they look halfway decent with or without color management, set the **Destination Profile** option to **sRGB IEC61966-2.1**, as in Figure 11-33. While the previous setting, Adobe RGB (1998), is better suited

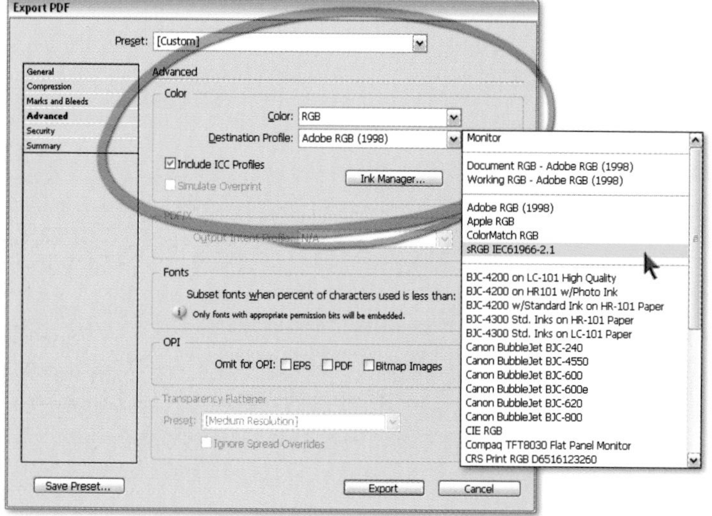

Figure 11-33.

to high-end imaging and print work, the sRGB color space better anticipates the display capabilities of a consumer-grade computer monitor.

10. *Save your settings for later use.* Click the **Save Preset** button in the bottom-left corner of the dialog box. Enter "Interactive Document" and click **OK**. This saves all the settings you assigned in Steps 4 through 9 so that you can retrieve them again without going to all that effort.

11. *Create and test the PDF document.* Now for the moment of ultimate truth. Click the **Export** button. InDesign displays a progress bar as it generates the PDF file. Then it launches Adobe Reader or, if you have it, Adobe Acrobat and opens the spanking-new PDF document, as in Figure 11-34. Here are some things to try:

    - Click the **Bookmarks** tab along the left edge of the window to display the tags you created in the first exercise, "Creating Bookmarks." Click a bookmark name to go to the corresponding entry in the text.
    - Click the hyperlink *One cup peanut butter* to advance to the peanut butter paragraph on page 2. Press the Page Down key a couple of times to go to the bottom of page 3, and then click the *Baking Cookies One-on-One* link. Assuming you're connected to the Internet, this should load the *oneonone.oreilly.com* Web page. (If you get a Specify Weblink Behavior dialog box, select In Web Browser and click OK.)
    - Go back to the beginning of the document and hover your cursor over LPF's eyes. They should get beady. Don't click, however—our destination page isn't done yet.
    - Press Ctrl+spacebar (⌘-spacebar on the Mac) and click a few times inside one of the photos to zoom into it. Thanks to the compression settings you established in Step 8, the high-resolution photographs look great.

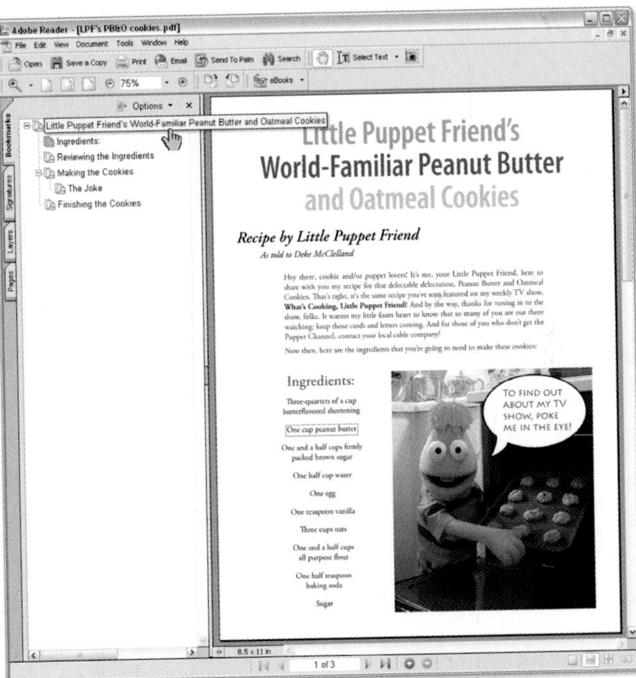

Figure 11-34.

12. *Return to InDesign.* We still have another document to export. So switch back to InDesign and bring the document that contains the movie and sound files to the front.

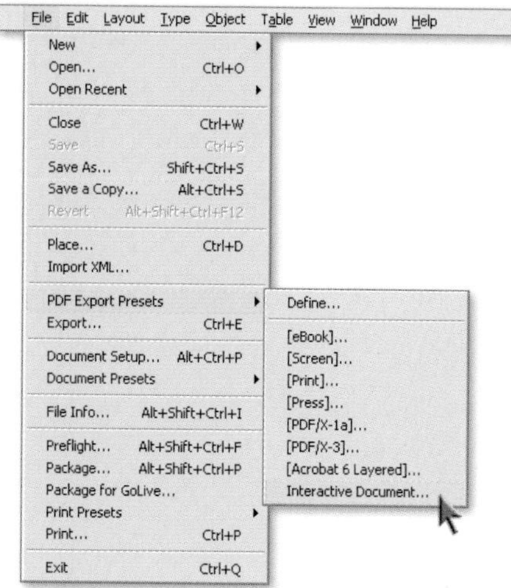

Figure 11-35.

13. ***Choose the Export command.*** Because you saved a preset in Step 10, things are considerably easier this time around:

   - Choose **File→PDF Export Presets→ Interactive Document**, as in Figure 11-35.
   - On the PC, check that **Save as Type** is set to **Adobe PDF**. (On the Mac, InDesign knows you're saving a PDF file.)
   - Name the PDF file "What's cooking.pdf." This ensures that the links function as specified in the previous exercises.
   - Click **Save** to open the **Export PDF** dialog box.
   - This time, turn off **View PDF after Exporting**. Better to load the PDF doc by following the links in the recipe file.
   - Click the **Export** button. If you get a missing or modified links warning, just click OK to move on. InDesign generates the PDF file, but does not switch to Reader or Acrobat.

Figure 11-36.

14. ***Load, listen, and watch.*** Return to the *LPF's PB&O cookies.pdf* file that you have open in Reader or Acrobat. If your computer has speakers, please turn them on. Then click and hold for a moment on LPF's eyes to see them cross. Release the mouse button to load *What's cooking.pdf*. You should hear LPF welcome you to the page. Hover over LPF's image to hear another message. Then click anywhere on his face to start the movie, which I show playing in Figure 11-36. Take pride in a job well done.

As a backup, I've included copies of my PDF files inside the *Final PDFs* folder in the *Lesson 11* folder. If you encounter a problem with getting something to work in your documents, try loading mine and see if it works any better. And if you decide to make the cookies, let me know how they turn out. I'm really curious how they taste.

WHAT DID YOU LEARN?

Match the key concept in the numbered list below with the letter of the phrase that best describes it. Answers appear upside-down at the bottom of the page.

Key Concepts

1. Bookmark
2. Hyperlink
3. Rollover button
4. Create PDF Bookmarks
5. Hyperlink anchor
6. Highlight
7. URL
8. Inherit Zoom
9. The Down state
10. Mouse Up
11. Poster
12. Optimize for Fast Web View

Descriptions

A. Select this check box to tell InDesign to automatically create a bookmark for each entry in the table of contents.

B. Unlike its real world namesake, this is added by the document's creator to point out a section that the creator thinks is important.

C. This option defines the appearance of an embedded sound or movie file when the file is not being played.

D. When selected, this option opens a linked file at the reader's active magnification setting.

E. This Behaviors setting in the Button Options dialog box schedules an event to occur *after* the reader clicks a rollover button.

F. This Appearance option in the New Hyperlink dialog box determines what a hyperlink looks like when it's being clicked.

G. This attribute defines how a rollover button will look during that brief period of time when the reader's mouse button is pressed.

H. Indicated by a ⚓, this destination marker takes you to a very specific location in a document.

I. This animated link changes appearance when the reader moves the cursor over it or clicks on it.

J. When turned on, this option in the Export PDF dialog box organizes a file so it can be read as soon as the first page is downloaded.

K. This can be any text or graphic object, including a single word or character of type; clicking it might take you to a different file, including one posted on the Internet.

L. Typically regarded as the address of a Web page, this can just as easily point to a file on your hard drive.

Answers

1B, 2K, 3I, 4A, 5H, 6F, 7L, 8D, 9G, 10E, 11C, 12J

LESSON 12

Y•85 M•85 C•9 K•42
Y•100 M•100 C•10 K•42
Y•40 M•40 C•4 K•24
Y•55 M•55 C•6 K•24
Y•70 M•70 C•7 K•24
Y•85 M•85 C•9 K•24
Y•100 M•100 C•10 K•24
K•0
C•0 K•0
70 C•0 K•0
M•85 C•0 K•0
5 M•100 C•0 K•0

PRINTING AND OUTPUT

Given its standing as the best page-layout program in a trillion-mile radius, InDesign would be remiss if it didn't supply you with the most sophisticated printing controls in the history of human achievement. Happily, the word "remiss" has no bearing on this topic. InDesign isn't just good at printing, it outprints every other program on the market with equal amounts flair and righteous zealotry. As you will learn in this lesson, InDesign is a program that was born to print.

InDesign supports all variety of printers, from inexpensive inkjet devices to professional-grade imagesetters. It automatically adjusts imported artwork to ensure accurate color, even going so far as to translate RGB photographs to CMYK. It converts translucent objects to a format that the printer can understand, previews color separations on screen, and tests a file to avoid common pitfalls. Finally, InDesign gathers all linked graphics and fonts so that you can hand off the files to a commercial print house, confident that your project is good to go. InDesign is that rare and exceptional program that "has your back" from the beginning of a project to its logical, predictable end.

PostScript versus Inkjet

Printers divide into two camps: those that support the PostScript printing language and those that do not. Virtually all print houses rely on PostScript, thanks to its proven ability to accurately render very high-resolution text and graphics on the page. Most personal printers do not use PostScript because of its high cost and added complexity. InDesign's job is to bring these two worlds into agreement, so that a page printed from a personal printer matches one output from a PostScript device.

ABOUT THIS LESSON

Project Files

Before beginning the exercises, make sure that you've installed the lesson files from the CD, as explained in Step 5 on page xv of the Preface. This should result in a folder called *Lesson Files-IDcs 1on1* on your desktop. We'll be working with the files inside the *Lesson 12* subfolder.

This final lesson covers topics related to inkjet printing, professional PostScript output, and color separations. You'll learn how to:

Video Lesson 12: Previewing Color Separations

If you intend to print hundreds or thousands of copies of a document, then you'll most likely submit your files to a commercial print house for reproduction from an offset or a sheetfed press. To accommodate such a press, the document must be output to multiple color separations, one for each component ink (typically cyan, magenta, yellow, and black).

InDesign CS lets you preview color separations before printing them. To see how this process works, watch the twelfth video lesson on the CD. Insert the CD, click the **Start Training** button, click the Set 4 button, and then select **12, Previewing Color Separations** from the Lessons list. The movie lasts 12 minutes 56 seconds, during which I explain the following operations and shortcuts:

Operation	Windows shortcut	Macintosh shortcut
Print a document	Ctrl+P	⌘-P
Show the Separations Preview palette	Shift+F6	Shift-F6
View a single separation	Click ink in Separations palette	Click ink in Separations palette
View multiple separations	Click 👁 in front of ink	Click 👁 in front of ink
Track exact ink values	Hover cursor over color	Hover cursor over color
Access Graphics→Image Color Settings	Right-click graphic	Right-click (or Control-click) graphic

This is no small task, what with all the differences in the way professional and consumer printers work. Consider the PostScript *imagesetter*, which is a monstrously expensive device that service bureaus and print houses use to output pages to film or some other medium before loading the inks and plates onto the press. An imagesetter prints at resolutions of several million dots per square inch, but it can render just two colors: black and white. Given that every one of the full-color pages in this book was output by an imagesetter, you may find this difficult to believe. That's because the imagesetter fools us into seeing a rich array of colors. Here's how:

- First, the imagesetter prints the document in multiple passes, known as *separations*. When placed on the press, each separation receives a different ink. The ink is applied to the separation and thus imparts a color. Most full-color documents are printed using four separations, one for each of the four *process inks*: cyan, magenta, yellow, and black.
- The inks are translucent and thus blend with each other. But at most this results in eight color variations. (I say at most because black mixed with one ink doesn't look all that different from black mixed with another.)
- So where do all the other color variations come from? The imagesetter simulates shades by assembling printer dots into a grid of *halftone cells*. A single, roughly circular halftone cell may contain 100 printer dots or more. Large, closely packed halftone cells translate to dark colors; small cells with lots of white space around them read as light colors.

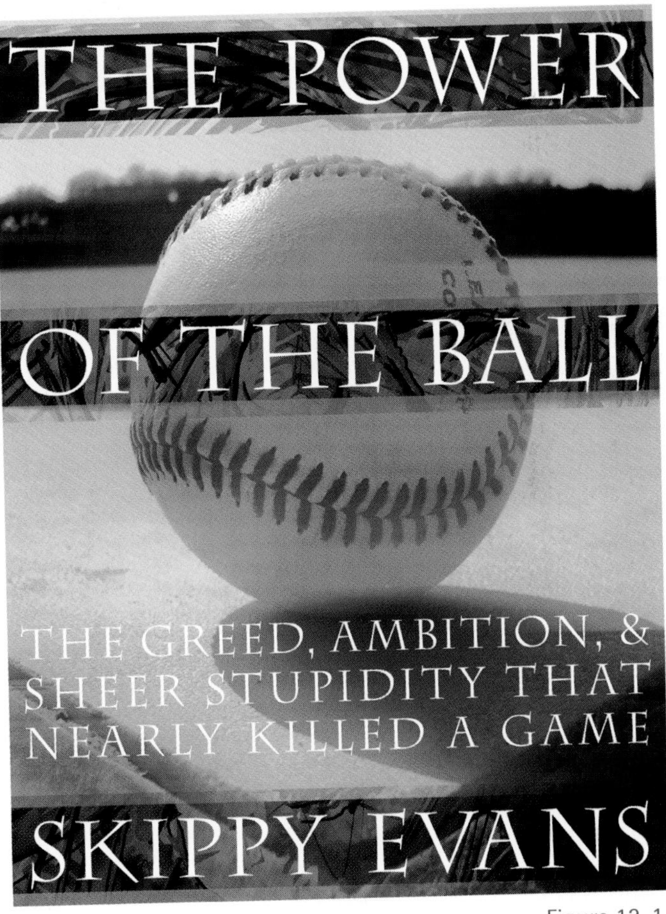

Figure 12-1.

By way of example, take a look at the book cover in Figure 12-1. Although I've confined my artwork to a small range of purples and oranges with occasional bands of muted green, it nevertheless comprises several hundred unique colors. On the next page, Figure 12-2 shows a detail from the cover magnified by a factor of 10. At this size, you can make out the individual halftone cells. The top portion of the figure shows the four layers of halftone cells interacting with each other; the bottom area shows each process color by itself. The right-hand circle zooms in on a sampling of black halftone cells. The cells contain just two colors, black and white, with no variation between them.

A typical inkjet printer uses six or more inks and organizes its dots in a much tighter pattern. Even when separated and magnified by a factor of 50, as in the circle on the right side of Figure 12-3, the dots remain remarkably small and intricately woven. As a result, an inkjet device is able to print a wider color range with smoother variations and better detail. The downside is that inkjet output is not commercially reproducible—except by scanning the page and separating it, which would defeat the purpose. This limits inkjet printers to proofing pages and printing drafts, as explained in the exercise "Printing a Draft of Your Document," which begins on page 435.

Figure 12-2.

PostScript and inkjet prints also differ in how they process data. A PostScript printer is capable of rendering type and vector objects on its own. InDesign conveys the page as a series of mathematical equations; the printer renders the math, even going so far as to adjust curves and character outlines to better suit specific size and resolution ratios. The result is razor sharp text and graphics that print quickly and efficiently, without slowing down the computer or other hardware. (It's worth noting that InDesign limits its support to PostScript Levels 2 and 3, which account for most devices sold since 1990. Comparatively ancient Level 1 printers are out of luck.)

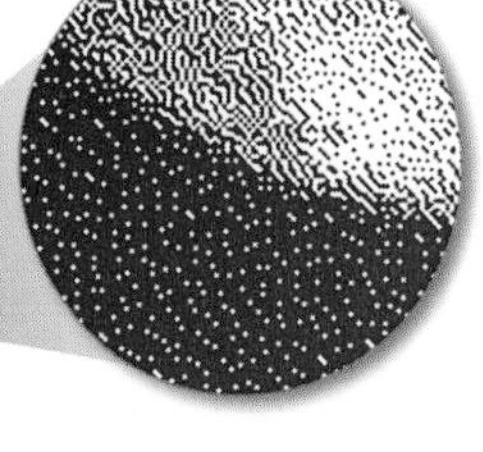

Figure 12-3.

In contrast, printing to a consumer inkjet device requires InDesign to render the entire document to pixels and communicate the colored pixels to the printer. This means everything prints pretty much identically to the way it looks on screen. But it amounts to more work for InDesign and more processing effort on the part of your computer. Hence inkjet documents take longer to print and may slow your computer's performance.

The consequence of all this is that most of InDesign's printing capabilities are designed to support PostScript and generate professional-level color separations. Fortunately, this is precisely the way you want it to be, assuming that you intend to mass-reproduce a document in quantities of 100 copies or more. But InDesign also gives passing attention to non-PostScript devices, permitting you to proof colors, gauge layout and composition, and otherwise monitor the development of a document.

Printing a Draft of Your Document

With the possible exception of interactive PDF files (like those you created in the previous lesson), the world's ever-burgeoning supply of InDesign documents are bound for the printed page. So regardless of what a document looks like on screen, the printer is the final arbitrator, the medium where the pages succeed or fail. Back when I was a thin scrap of a lad, when monitors were black and white and screen renderings were at best rough approximations of a document, this meant I had to print lots of test pages. These *drafts* were often my first reliable means of gauging how a design was coming together—and sadly for a forest or two, I went through a lot of them.

Thankfully, InDesign previews pages a heck of a lot more dependably than the meager applications I grew up with. With its sophisticated color management, high-quality image display, and Separations Preview palette (see Video Lesson 12, "Previewing Color Separations"), InDesign is just plain terrific at accurately translating type and graphics to a color monitor. Even so, it never hurts to print a draft of your document just to be sure. I'm not suggesting that you print one every 10 minutes the way I used to. But one complete printout right at the end is a great way to hunt down typos, confirm the placement of page elements, and assess the appearance of imported graphics. A draft is your opportunity to experience the document from a reader's perspective.

The quality of your draft depends on the quality of the printer itself. In all likelihood, you have an inkjet printer (assuming you have a printer at all). Inkjets are inexpensive, they print a wide range of colors, and they're great at rendering photographic images. On the downside, they're relatively slow, they consume a lot of ink, and you have to use them regularly or the heads clog. If you're feeling flush, you can purchase a more expensive color laser printer. Although these workhorse devices aren't as good at rendering photographs, they are fast, reliable, efficient in their use of toner, and better at printing text and line art (see Figure 12-4 on the next page). And if you want to make a serious investment in your future, look into a PostScript-equipped laser printer. Color PostScript printers cost upwards of $2,000, but they do the best job of matching commercial output, which also relies on PostScript. A PostScript laser printer is also well-suited to small print runs, in the neighborhood of 100 or fewer copies. The upshot is that you can print your document yourself rather than visit a commercial print house.

satura

Inkjet printer

satura

PostScript laser printer

Figure 12-4.

Despite my recommendations, it's my job to help you make the printer you have now work. Because you'll be printing a draft, there's no sense in throwing a lot of expensive paper at this project. For my part, I load the printer with a 20-pound bond in the 80 to 90 brightness range, which is cheap stuff that you can buy in bulk at a warehouse store. If you're trying to impress a boss or client, look for something closer to 26-pound with a brightness rating of 94 or higher. But don't use glossy photo paper or the like—that's just a waste of money and it doesn't provide any better indication of how the job will look when it comes off the press.

PEARL OF WISDOM

Obviously, I have no idea what printer you're using, so your experience may diverge from mine (though I try to give you hints as to when the divergence might occur along the way). And I leave it up to you to make sure your printer is set up properly and in working order. This means that the power is turned on, the printer is connected to your computer, print drivers and other software are installed, the printer is loaded with plenty of ink or toner, and the print head nozzles are clean. For more information on any of these issues, consult the documentation that came with your printer. Finally, it's possible that your default settings are set to something different than what I suggest in the steps. Afford me the usual leap of faith, do as I direct, and all will be fine.

1. ***Open a test document.*** Open the document called *Pages 62-67 reprise.indd*, found in the *Lesson 12* folder inside *Lesson Files-IDcs 1on1*. If InDesign warns you about missing or modified links, click the **Fix Links Automatically** button to find the graphic files and reestablish the links. (Otherwise, the document may not print correctly, so be sure to do it.) Eventually, you'll see the document pictured in Figure 12-5, which is the file you created by the end of the "Setting Up Master Pages" exercise in Lesson 9. Blessed with six pages and lots of color, this document will serve you well in your exploration of printing.

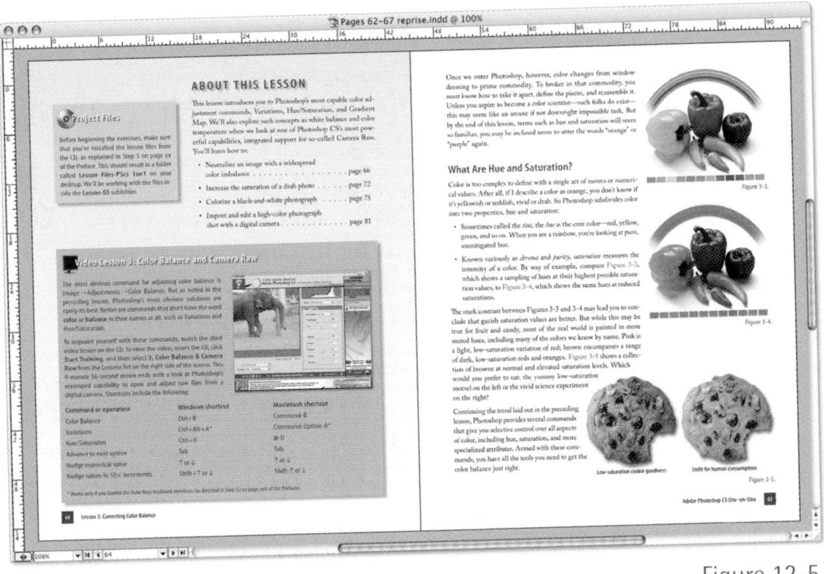
Pages 62-67 reprise.indd @ 100%

ABOUT THIS LESSON

Project Files

Before beginning the exercises, make sure that you've installed the lesson files from the CD, as explained in Step 5 on page xv of the Preface. This should result in a folder called Lesson Files-PScs 1on1 on your desktop. We'll be working with the files inside the Lesson 03 subfolder.

This lesson introduces you to Photoshop's most capable color adjustment commands, Variations, Hue/Saturation, and Gradient Map. We'll also explore such concepts as white balance and color temperature when we look at one of Photoshop CS's most powerful capabilities, integrated support for so-called Camera Raw. You'll learn how to:

- Neutralize an image with a widespread color imbalance . . . . . page 66
- Increase the saturation of a drab photo . . . . . page 72
- Colorize a black-and-white photograph . . . . . page 75
- Import and edit a high-color photograph shot with a digital camera . . . . . page 81

Video Lesson 3: Color Balance and Camera Raw

The most obvious command for adjusting color balance is Image→Adjustments→Color Balance. But as noted in the preceding lesson, Photoshop's most obvious solutions are rarely its best. Better are commands that don't have the word color or balance in their names at all, such as Variations and Hue/Saturation.

To acquaint yourself with these commands, watch the third video lesson on the CD. To view the video, insert the CD, click Start Training, and then select 3, Color Balance & Camera Raw from the Lessons list on the right side of the screen. This 9-minute 36-second movie ends with a look at Photoshop's revamped capability to open and adjust raw files from a digital camera. Shortcuts include the following:

Command or operation	Windows shortcut	Macintosh shortcut
Color Balance	Ctrl+B	Command-B
Variations	Ctrl+Alt+A*	Command-Option-A*
Hue/Saturation	Ctrl+U	⌘-U
Advance to next option	Tab	Tab
Nudge numerical value	↑ or ↓	↑ or ↓
Nudge values in 10× increments	Shift+↑ or ↓	Shift-↑ or ↓

Lesson 3: Correcting Color Balance

Once we enter Photoshop, however, color changes from window dressing to prime commodity. To broker in that commodity, you must know how to take it apart, define the pieces, and reassemble it. Unless you aspire to become a color scientist—such folks do exist—this may seem like an arcane if not downright impossible task. But by the end of this lesson, terms such as hue and saturation will seem so familiar, you may be inclined never to utter the words "orange" or "purple" again.

What Are Hue and Saturation?

Color is too complex to define with a single set of names or numerical values. After all, if I describe a color as orange, you don't know if it's yellowish or reddish, vivid or drab. So Photoshop subdivides color into two properties, hue and saturation:

- Sometimes called the *tint*, the *hue* is the core color—red, yellow, green, and so on. When you see a rainbow, you're looking at pure, unmitigated hue.
- Known variously as *chroma* and *purity*, *saturation* measures the intensity of a color. By way of example, compare Figure 3-3, which shows a sampling of hues at their highest possible saturation values, to Figure 3-4, which shows the same hues at reduced saturations.

The stark contrast between Figures 3-3 and 3-4 may lead you to conclude that garish saturation values are better. But while this may be true for fruit and candy, most of the real world is painted in more muted hues, including many of the colors we know by name. Pink is a light, low-saturation variation of red; brown encompasses a range of dark, low-saturation reds and oranges. Figure 3-5 shows a collection of browns at normal and elevated saturation levels. Which would you prefer to eat: the yummy low-saturation morsel on the left or the vivid science experiment on the right?

Continuing the trend laid out in the preceding lesson, Photoshop provides several commands that give you selective control over all aspects of color, including hue, saturation, and more specialized attributes. Armed with these commands, you have all the tools you need to get the color balance just right.

Figure 3-3.

Figure 3-4.

Low-saturation cookie goodness

Unfit for human consumption

Figure 3-5.

Adobe Photoshop CS One-on-One

Figure 12-5.

2. ***Choose the Print command.*** Choose **File→Print** or press Ctrl+P (⌘-P on the Mac). InDesign displays its highly specialized **Print** dialog box. As you'll see, this dialog box is a mixed bag. On one hand, it provides you with a vast array of options not found in competing programs. But it also hides many of your printer's unique capabilities, which can prove a bit frustrating if you're using an inkjet printer.

3. ***Select your printer model.*** Choose the model of printer that you want to use from the **Printer** pop-up menu. Figure 12-6 on the next page finds me choosing my color PostScript laser printer, a Tektronix Phaser 750N. But I could just as easily choose my consumer inkjet device, the Epson Stylus Photo 1280, or one of the other printers networked to my computer. If you select

a PostScript printer, the PPD setting will be updated to reflect the associated *PostScript printer description* file. Otherwise, the PPD option is blank.

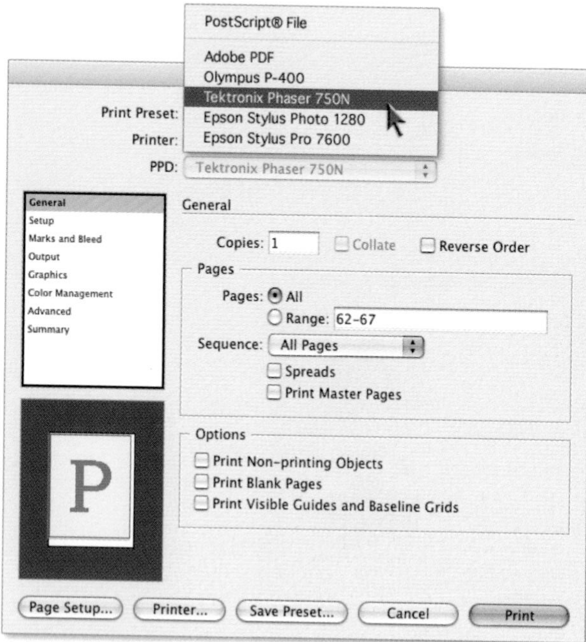

Figure 12-6.

4. *Set the page order.* The Print dialog box is divided into eight panels, only a few of which we'll look at. The first panel, **General**, includes the most basic controls. Here's how I'd like you to set them:

   - Leave **Copies** set to 1. When printing drafts, one copy of each page is enough.
   - Suppose you want to print just those pages that are set against a white background. In our case, this means page 63 as well as pages 65 through 67. Click in the **Range** option box. Then enter "63, 65–67." A comma separates independent pages, a hyphen indicates a range. Spaces are irrelevant.

   When printing to the end of the document, you can omit the final page number, as in "63,65–." If you don't know how a document is numbered, you can enter a + followed by a relative page number, as in "+2,+4–+6" or just plain "+2,+4–" since the sixth page is the last page.

   - To print the last page first and the first page last so the pages are stacked properly when they come out of the printer, select the **Reverse Order** check box.
   - The other check boxes let you output an entire spread on a single page, output master pages independently of their print pages, and print such nonprinting elements as guides. Leave these options off.

5. *Specify the paper size.* In most other programs, you use the Page Setup command to define the size and orientation of the printed page. But in InDesign, you click the **Setup** option along the left side of the Print dialog box. Or press Ctrl+2 (⌘-2 on the Mac). Set the **Paper Size** pop-up option to match the size of the paper you have loaded in your printer (most likely Letter). Then select the first **Orientation** icon, which prints each page upright rather than on its side. Other options let you scale the pages to fit the paper, useful when printing drafts of an oversized document. Leave each of these options set as is.

6. ***Turn on all printer marks.*** Click the **Marks and Bleed** option or press Ctrl+3 (⌘-3) to switch to the third panel, which allows you to print a collection of marks and labels around the perimeter of the page. Select the **All Printer's Marks** check box. This turns on all marks used by professional printers to trim, identify, and gauge pages, which I've labeled for your viewing pleasure in the symbolic Figure 12-7. Frankly, this is overkill for draft prints. But it's easier than picking and choosing just those check boxes that you absolutely need: Page Information, which adds filename and date labels, and Crop Marks, which prints trim lines that you can use to cut the paper down to size. (In Figure 12-7, the dark orange represents the page size; the light orange represents the bleed.)

   Also make sure that **Use Document Bleed Settings** is turned on. The slug is too big to fit on a letter-sized page, so go ahead and turn off **Include Slug Area**.

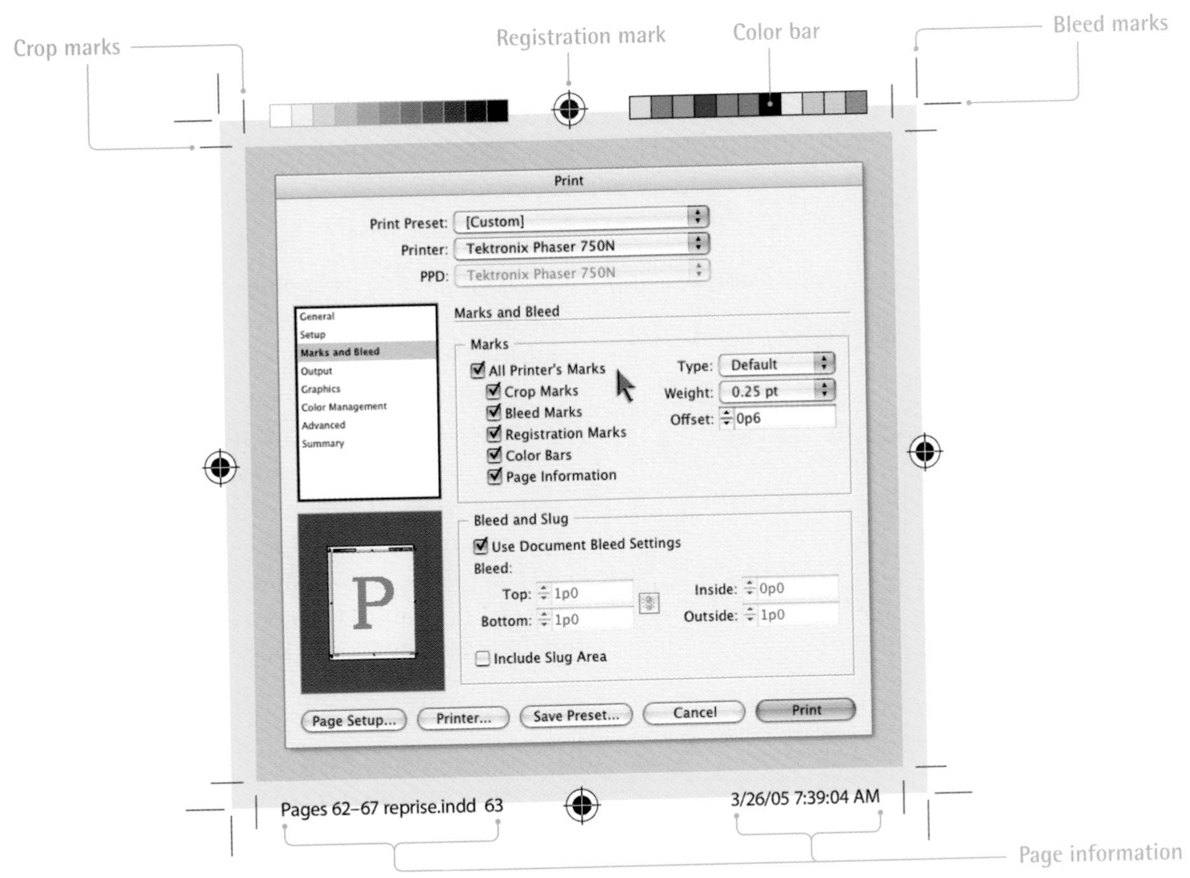

Figure 12-7.

7. ***Select the proper color output settings.*** Click the **Output** option on the left side of the dialog box or press Ctrl+4 (⌘-4) to enter the first of two areas that let you control how InDesign outputs color. The proper settings in this panel vary depending on whether you're printing to a PostScript printer or not:

   - When printing to a typical inkjet or laser printer that does not understand PostScript, set the **Color** option to **Composite RGB**. This leaves the printer driver in charge of translating the document colors from RGB to the printer's native color space. Most inkjet printers offer more inks than the standard CMYK, so limiting yourself to CMYK would produce inaccurate results.
   - When printing to a color PostScript device, set **Color** to **Composite CMYK**. This puts PostScript in charge of the color calculations and thus stands the best chance of matching your final press colors.

   This document contains lots of colored text that I want to print in color, so turn the **Text as Black** check box off. Finally, turn on the lower-right **Simulate Overprint** check box, as I have in Figure 12-8. This blends colors to simulate the effect of any manual traps and overprints you may have established. To learn more, read the next exercise, "Trapping and Overprinting."

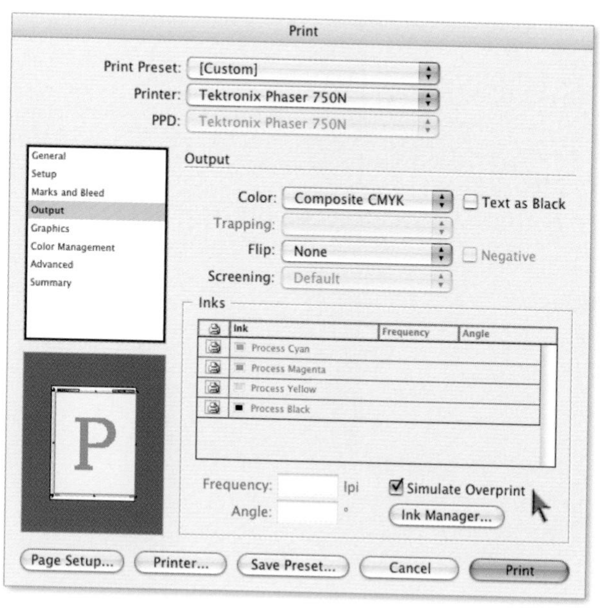

Figure 12-8.

8. ***Turn off the downsampling of graphics.*** As I mentioned in an exercise in the preceding lesson ("Exporting to PDF," Step 8, page 425), I'm strongly opposed to the idea of InDesign or any other layout program automatically reducing the number of pixels within imported images. And yet, InDesign is determined to do just that when printing a document. Ostensibly, it speeds up print times. But it does so only very slightly and at an obscenely high price. Downsampling can harm the definition of high-contrast, high-resolution imagery—and that, my friends, is not acceptable.

   So join me, won't you, as we turn off what I consider to be the most dangerous function inside InDesign:

   - Click the **Graphics** option along the left side of the dialog box. Or press Ctrl+5 (⌘-5).
   - Change the **Send Data** setting from the poorly conceived Optimized Subsampling to **All**, as in Figure 12-9.

The other options in this panel will be dimmed when printing to a non-PostScript printer. If you are lucky enough to be printing to a PostScript device, leave the options set as is.

9. ***If printing to an inkjet printer, switch the print space to sRGB.*** Those of you using a PostScript laser printer, skip to Step 11. The rest of you, click the **Color Management** option or press Ctrl+6 (⌘-6 on the Mac). Then switch the **Profile** setting to **sRGB IEC61966-2.1**, as demonstrated in Figure 12-10. Consumer inkjet printers are factory-calibrated to be compatible with the ubiquitous sRGB color space. Meanwhile, if you followed my instructions in the Preface (Step 11, page xvi), InDesign is set to work in the more flexible Adobe RGB. By switching this Profile setting to sRGB, you instruct InDesign to convert all colors from both CMYK and Adobe RGB to sRGB. InDesign then hands off the sRGB info to the printer driver,

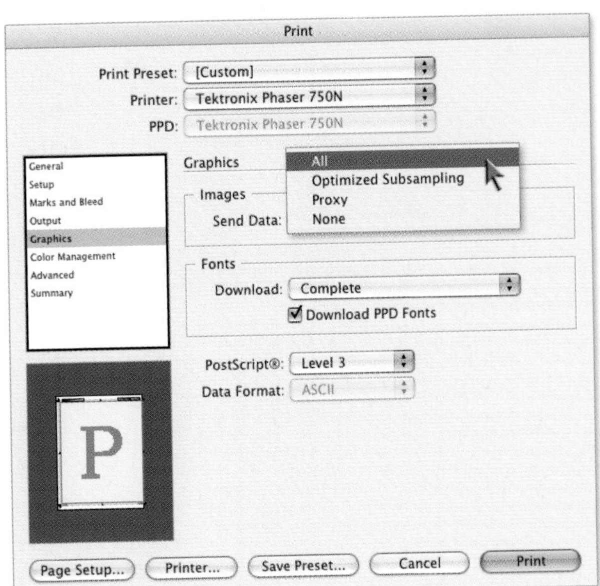

Figure 12-9.

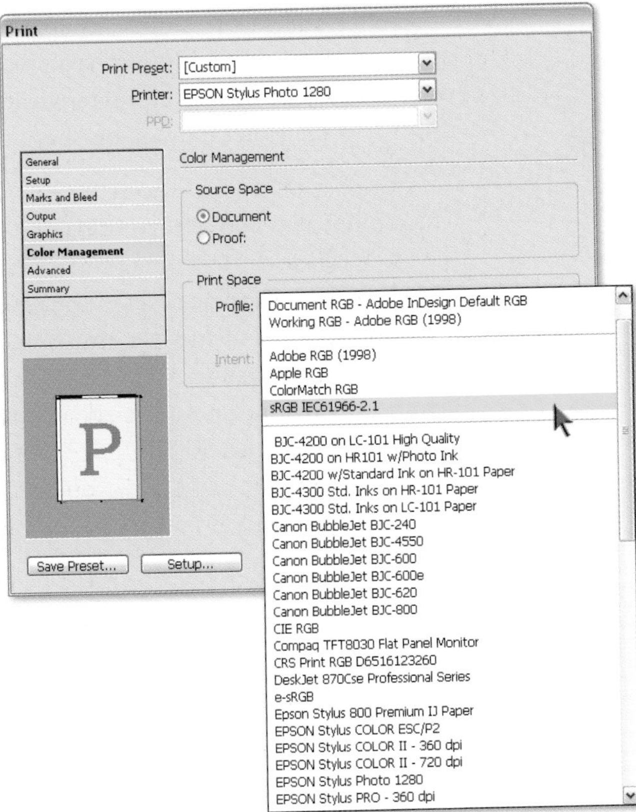

Figure 12-10.

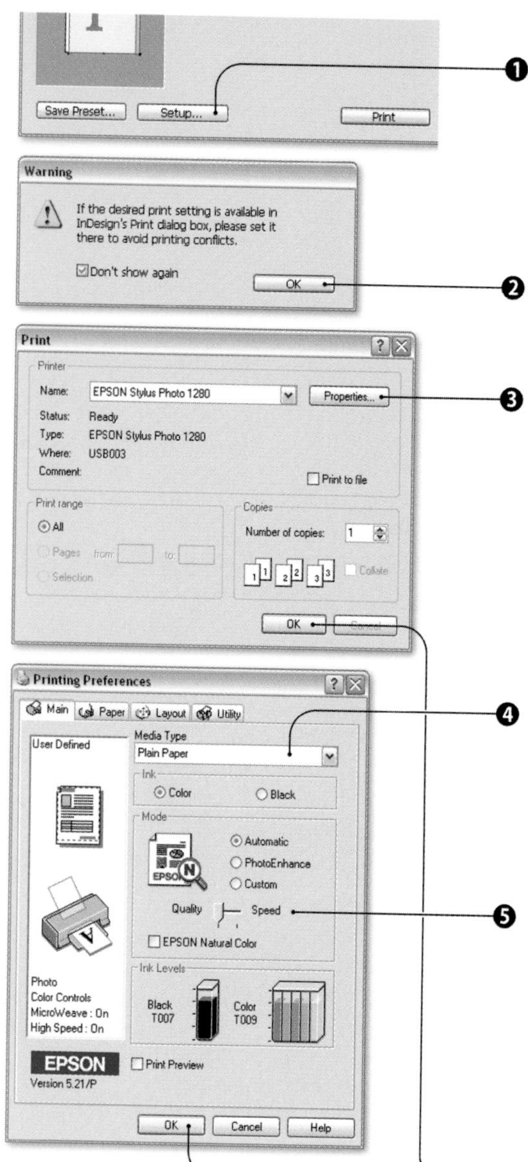

Figure 12-11.

which knows how to convert the colors from there. Note that this is an essential step for inkjet printing—*failing to switch to sRGB is very likely to result in inaccurate colors.*

10. ***Select the paper and quality settings for your inkjet printer.*** Again, those of you who are using a PostScript laser printer should skip to Step 11. You inkjetters, stick with me. You see, inkjet printers permit you to adjust the paper quality and ink standards. That's part of what makes them so versatile. But if you get the combination wrong, it can make a mess of your output. So it's always worth checking to make sure everything's in order. The exact process for doing so varies fairly significantly between the PC and the Mac, as well as from one model of printer to another. Diagrammed for Windows in Figure 12-11 and for the Mac in Figure 12-12, the following is a walk-through based on the behavior of my Epson Stylus Photo 1280:

    - Click the **Setup** button (labeled ❶ in the figures) at the bottom of the Print dialog box. (On the Mac, click the **Printer** button.)
    - InDesign alerts you that it doesn't approve of you adjusting print settings outside the Print dialog box. Turns out, you have no choice. So tell InDesign to take a hike by turning on the **Don't show again** check box and clicking **OK** (❷ in the figures).
    - This dumps you into yet another Print dialog box. On the PC, click either the **Preferences** or **Properties** button (❸ in Figure 12-11), whichever is available. (Windows XP has multiple Print dialog box variations, and you never know which one is going to come up.) On the Mac, choose **Print Settings** or an equivalent option from the third pop-up menu (❸ in Figure 12-12).
    - Look for an option called **Media Type** or the like, and set it to **Plain Paper** (❹) or something equally prosaic. Feel free to raise the quality setting (❺), but steer clear of any Advanced or Custom settings.
    - Click **OK** twice on the PC or click **Print** once on the Mac (❻). This returns you to InDesign's Print dialog box.

11. ***Save your settings as a preset.*** You don't want to have to go through all these steps every time you print a document. To save yourself a lot of repetitious work, click the **Save Preset** button. Name the preset something logical (like "One-on-

One draft") and click **OK**. From now on, you can retrieve all your settings except the page range and the inkjet settings applied in Step 10 by choosing your new preset from the Print Preset pop-up menu at the top of the dialog box.

12. ***Send the print job on its merry way.*** Click the **Print** button to start the document printing. InDesign displays a few progress bars informing you that it's flattening the document and so on. This is nothing to worry about—it all happens on the fly; no change is made to your document. InDesign hands off the document to the operating system, which then spools it to the printer. A few minutes later, the four pages you requested should be waiting for you in your printer's tray, stacked in the proper order.

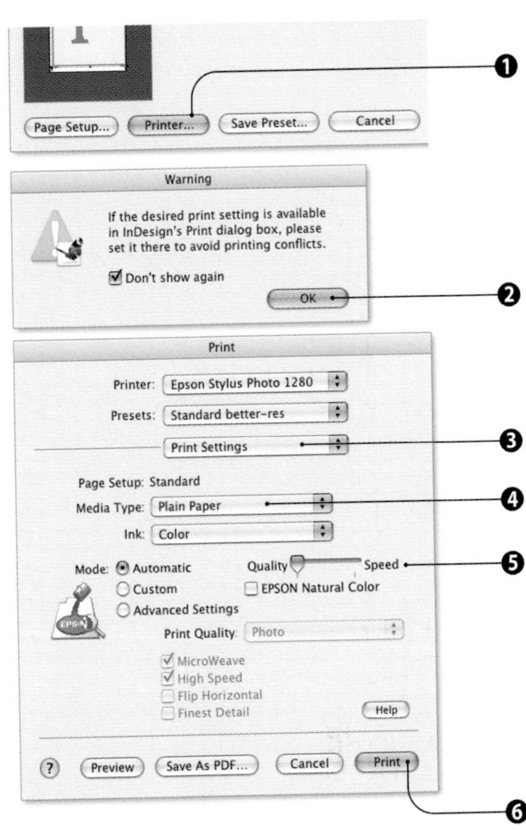

Figure 12-12.

If this were a real-world document, you would read through it to catch any typos, gauge the quality of the graphics, and perhaps even hand it off to others for their approval. If you like the printed colors, you might also consider submitting the pages along with the electronic version of the document to your commercial print house. This way, the press technician has a benchmark that he can use to compare the output. If he's sufficiently conscientious, he may even use your output to tweak a press setting or two.

Trapping and Overprinting

The publishing industry has long been divided into two camps—the designers who create the documents and the technicians who print them. So if InDesign's printing controls strike you as a bit over the top, bear in mind that they weren't intended for you to use in the first place. Adobe has structured InDesign's Print command to conform to the specialized needs of service bureaus, commercial print houses, and other companies that make printing their number-one business. The fact that the command just so happens to work with your inkjet printer is literally an afterthought; InDesign couldn't print reliably to non-PostScript devices until Version 1.5.

When it comes time to commercially reproduce your document, you no longer have to worry about the Print command and its many complexities. Happily, that becomes someone else's responsibility. But you can't expect to ignore the printing process entirely. Your commercial printer will expect you to turn in a document that's ready for output. And that means predicting what can go wrong and accounting for it in advance.

PEARL OF WISDOM

Having spent my formative years working at a PostScript service bureau—where we rendered PageMaker and QuarkXPress files to film in advance of commercial reproduction—I strongly urge you to seek the counsel of a kind, knowledgeable representative from your print house. If no such representative exists, bid that establishment *adieu* and move along to the next one. The people who manage printers for a living know the demands and rigors of their equipment far better than you or I ever will. And if they're wise, they'll be more than happy to warn you about the most common pitfalls and tell you what to do to avoid them.

In this exercise, we'll take a look at one of the most common pitfalls of commercial printing, misregistration. We'll also examine two popular solutions, trapping and overprinting. Be forewarned, these may or may not turn out to be issues you have to contend with. Some print houses trap files automatically; others do not. Either way, you'll be familiar with the process and ready to have a moderately intelligent conversation on the topic.

Tight (good) registration

Loose (bad) registration

Figure 12-13.

Tight registration with trapping

Loose registration with trapping

Figure 12-14.

Because inks are laid down in separate passes (see the sidebar "The Commercial Printing Process" on page 448), each ink must precisely align, or *register*, with the next to accurately reproduce the colors in your text and graphics. But this is not as easy as it may sound. With paper flying through the press at breakneck speeds, some degree of misregistration is bound to occur. And when it does, you end up with gaps between neighboring objects that do not share common inks. Figure 12-13 compares the "tight" registration that I enjoy with this book with the "loose" registration that may occur if press conditions are not closely monitored, as is often the case at bargain print shops. Note that the crown is made up of cyan and black inks, while the background is exclusively magenta and yellow.

Fortunately, you can fill in potential gaps using *trapping*. The easiest way to trap an object is to create a *spread*. First add a stroke that matches the color of the fill. Then set the stroke to *overprint* its background. As pictured in Figure 12-14, overprinting mixes the cyan and black inks with the magenta and yellow inks. The result isn't perfect—the right crown remains out of sync with its background—but it's better than a gap. The other way to trap an object is to stroke the background behind the object. Called a *choke*, this is a harder effect to achieve, as you'll see in the exercise.

PEARL OF WISDOM

Bear in mind, trapping is necessary only when two neighboring objects do not share common inks. Why? Because when as much as a single ink travels from one object to another, it fills in the gap. A great example of an object that never requires trapping is a full-color photograph. Virtually every pixel contains a mixture of CMYK inks, hence no gaps. This is not to say misregistration doesn't hurt a photo—it does. But trapping doesn't help.

In the following steps, we will focus on those objects that do benefit from trapping, vector art and text. In addition to learning how InDesign's trapping controls work, you'll learn how to identify objects that require trapping (only a few kinds of objects do) and which of two trapping solutions (manual or automatic) to use. If later it transpires that your print house provides trapping as part of its standard service, then all the merrier. Instead of scratching your head in bewilderment, you'll know to be grateful. Then again, if you're getting a good deal, and your printer has never heard of trapping (many small printers haven't), you'll recognize which objects might give you trouble and be right raring to fix them.

Figure 12-15.

1. ***Open a document in need of trapping.*** Typically, I try to present you with documents that have at least one foot in the real world. But this time, I present you with one that's purely instructional in nature. The document in question: *Trapping turtles.indd* in the *Lesson 12* folder inside *Lesson Files-IDcs 1on1*. Featured in Figure 12-15, it includes four variations on a turtle illustration set against a multicolored background. As it just so happens, two of these reptiles require trapping and two do not.

2. ***Inspect the colors of the first turtle.*** Select the upper-left turtle with the black arrow tool. Then press F6 to display the **Color** palette. Like all the other turtles, this one offers no stroke. Its chartreuse fill is

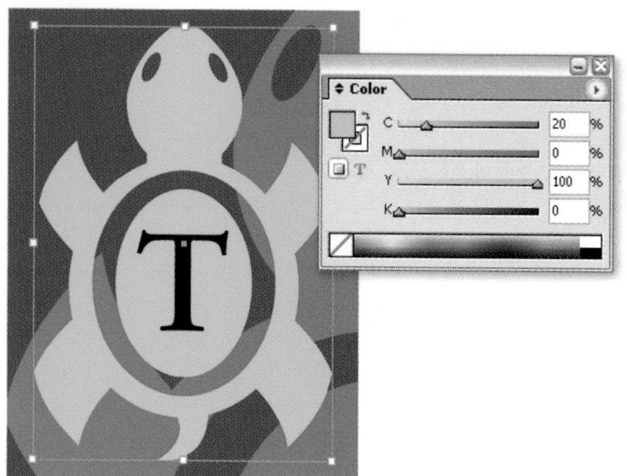

Figure 12-16.

made up of 100 percent cyan and 20 percent yellow, as shown in Figure 12-16. (If you don't see the color values, press the X key to switch focus to the fill.) Although the background exists on a locked layer—making it difficult to confirm its exact colors—we can reasonably assume by its appearance that it contains a generous supply of cyan. I can also tell you that it contains some yellow. So given that the turtle and its background share common inks, I know that there's no need for trapping.

3. ***Inspect the second turtle.*** Now click the upper-right turtle to select it. This guy is 100 percent yellow with no cyan or other ink. Meanwhile, its deep blue background contains equal parts cyan and magenta with a bit of black. The objects share no common color, so we should apply some trapping.

4. ***Assign a yellow stroke.*** The easiest way to trap the yellow turtle is to surround it with a yellow stroke. Click the stroke icon (stroke icon) in the Color palette or press the X key. Then change the **Y** value to 100 to exactly match the fill. (You should be able to click the last color swatch in the bottom-left corner of the Color palette.) By default, the stroke is 1-point thick, which is about right for most press scenarios. But for the time being, I want you to press F10 to display the **Stroke** palette and then increase the **Weight** value to 8 points. This exaggerates the trap so you can better see what's going on.

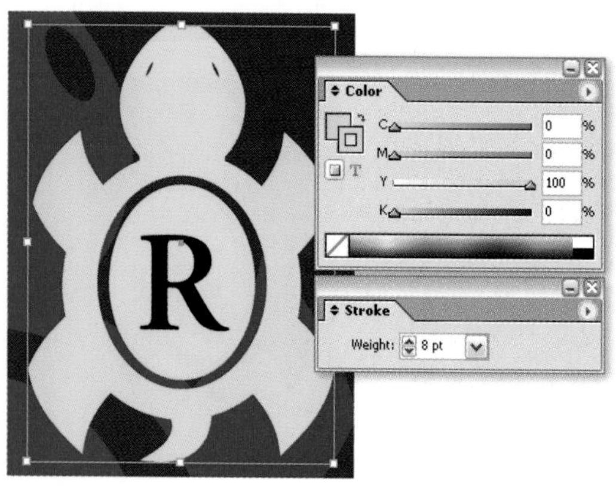

Figure 12-17.

PEARL OF WISDOM

The stroke is centered on the path outline. This means the turtle grows outward half the line weight, or 4 points, as shown in Figure 12-17. If you're clever, it might occur to you that you could also align the stroke to the outside of the path and reduce the Weight value to 4 points. But if you did that, you wouldn't trace the inside of the eyes, which need trapping as much as anything else. A centered stroke set to twice the thickness of the intended trap is your best bet.

5. ***Overprint the stroke.*** So far, we haven't really accomplished anything. The yellow turtle spreads outward 4 points, but the background retreats those same 4 points. Without overprinting, the inks don't overlap and therefore you have no trap.

   To apply overprinting, choose **Window→Attributes** to display the little known **Attributes** palette. Then, with the yellow turtle still selected, turn on the **Overprint Stroke** check box.

6. ***Turn on the overprint preview.*** If you were to print this document to a PostScript printer, the yellow stroke would mix with

the deep blue background. So why is it that on screen, it doesn't look any different? By default, you can't see overprints on screen. Why this is, I can't tell you. Hiding overprints doesn't speed things up and it's highly misleading. Even so, you have to ask to see them. To do just that, go to the **View** menu and choose the first command, **Overprint Preview**. Or press the highly inconvenient shortcut, Ctrl+Shift+Alt+Y (⌘-Shift-Option-Y on the Mac). The yellow turtle collapses to its previous size, and the intersecting inks appear very dark, as in Figure 12-18.

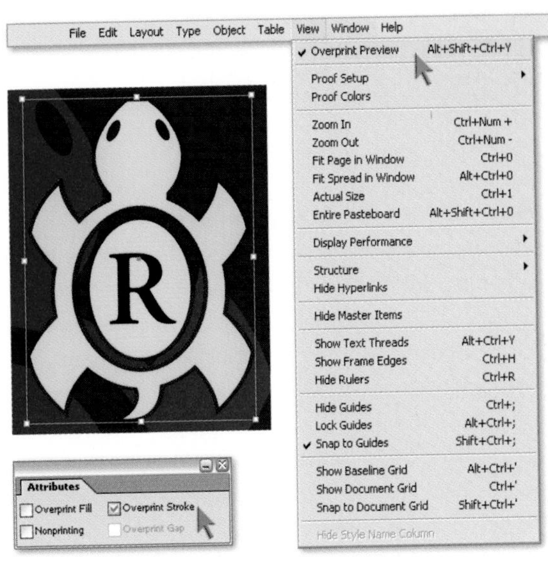

Figure 12-18.

7. ***Reduce the stroke to 1 point.*** Now that you know what the trap looks like, restore the **Weight** value in the Stroke palette to 1 point. This may seem awfully thin—after all, it makes for a narrow ½-point trap. But given that you don't want to see your trap—you just want it to fill in the gaps—it makes sense to keep the value as small as possible. And most professionally minded printers are willing to guarantee their registration within ½ point. I recommend going higher—say, 2 points—only when printing to newsprint, which is more liable to stretch on the press, or when working with a bargain quick-print outfit whose standards may be more lax.

8. ***Select and inspect the first gradient turtle.*** Click the lower-left turtle to select it. As witnessed in Figure 12-19, this graceful terrapin is filled with a gradient. Press the X key to activate the fill icon at the bottom of the toolbox (as in). Then bring up the **Gradient** palette and click either of the color stops. The recipe for the first stop is C:5 M:20; the second includes all four inks. The background not only includes lots of magenta but also is filled with the same gradient as the turtle; the direction is merely reversed. With so many shared colors, no trapping is warranted.

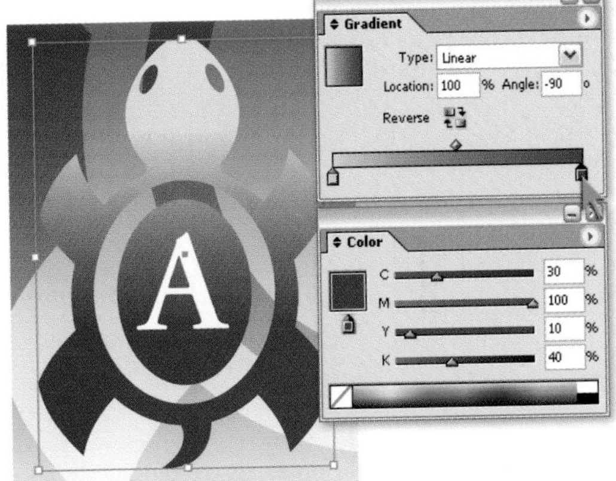

Figure 12-19.

9. ***Take a gander at the last turtle.*** As it just so happens, you rarely need to trap gradients. One exception is when the gradient contains a spot color that will print to a separate plate. Click the lower-right turtle with the black arrow tool. Then click the second color stop in the Gradient palette. Sure enough, this color stop calls for a spot color from the Pantone ink library. The spot color will print to a separate plate, so it should be trapped.

The Commercial Printing Process

Commercial printing is an elaborate, expensive, resource-intensive process. A large printing press costs millions of dollars, is longer than your house, and weighs as much as 50 elephants. And as you might imagine, it's more complicated to operate than an inkjet or a laser printer. Many steps that occur automatically when you print a document in your home or office have to be performed manually by your service bureau or press technician. For example, the technician never outputs a document directly to the printer. Instead, he creates independent pages for each ink, known as *color separations*. The figure at the bottom of this page shows a detail from a full-color document, followed by four separations, one for each of the CMYK inks.

The technician may render the separations to film and then burn the film to flexible, usually aluminum *lithographic plates*; or he may print to the plates directly. The plates are then wrapped around cylinders and installed on the press. For large print runs—a few thousand copies or more—the most popular press technology is *web-offset lithography*, or just plain offset printing. Diagrammed in the simplified illustration at the top of the opposite page, offset printing uses the plate cylinders to transfer ink to continuous rolls of paper. (The term *web* refers to these rolls; it has nothing to do with the World Wide Web.) Water rollers clean the excess ink off the plates. The plate conveys the ink to a rubber *blanket*, which in turn shuttles the ink to the paper. The result is that the plate never touches the paper, hence the term *offset*. Each of the roller groups in the illustration is called a *printing unit*. One printing unit exists for each ink. Standard process-color printing requires four units, one each for cyan, magenta, yellow, and black, as in the illustration. Each spot color adds another unit. Most presses can accommodate at least six printing units, enough for CMYK and two spots.

Each rotation of the plate and blanket lays down what's known as an *impression*, which is typically equal to anywhere from 4 to 12 pages. The big presses—the ones that print newspapers, magazines, and books—can print as many as a dozen impressions per second. No kidding, the paper speeds through the press so rapidly that it manufactures its own breeze and the printed pages look like one big blur. The high-speed snapshots at the bottom of the opposite page show my *Look & Learn Photoshop* (the first project I laid out in InDesign) whizzing

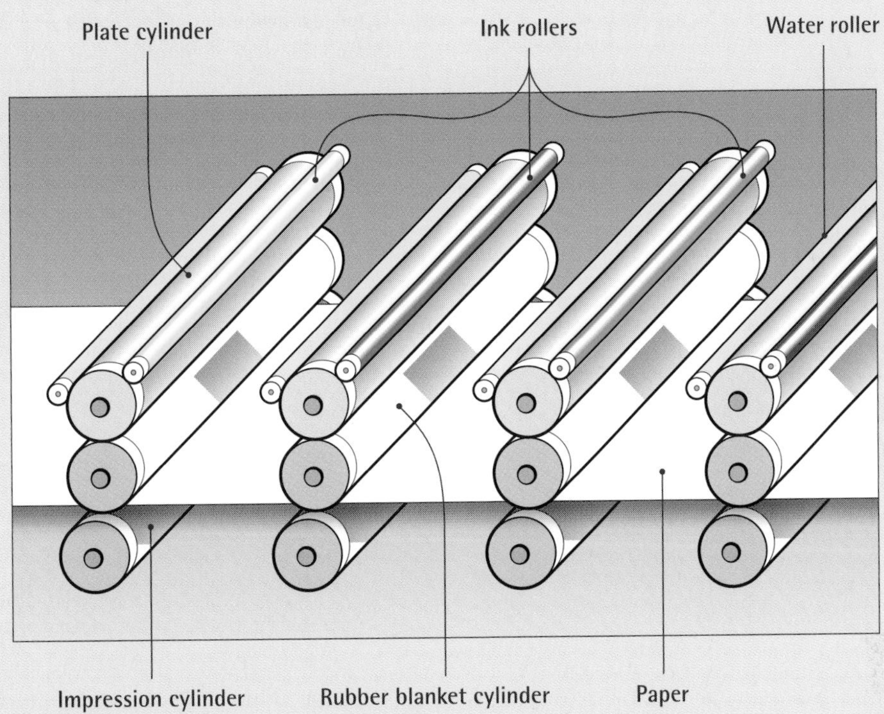

through the press and rolling off as cut, folded pages called *signatures*. Incidentally, this was a two-color job, black and Pantone 285 blue; so it required just two printing units, which resulted in lower press costs.

Smaller print runs are better served by a *sheetfed press*. As with offset printing, a sheetfed press relies on color-separated lithographic plates that convey ink to paper by way of blanket cylinders. But instead of using a web roll, a sheetfed press prints to individual sheets of paper. The process is a little slower, but it's still faster than you might think, with overlapping pages traveling by in a steady stream. A *registration board* ensures that one piece of paper precisely aligns with the next. As a result, a sheetfed press may enjoy tighter registration than its web-offset counterpart and thus require little or no trapping. But as always, this is an issue for you to discuss with your friendly printer representative.

Figure 12-20.

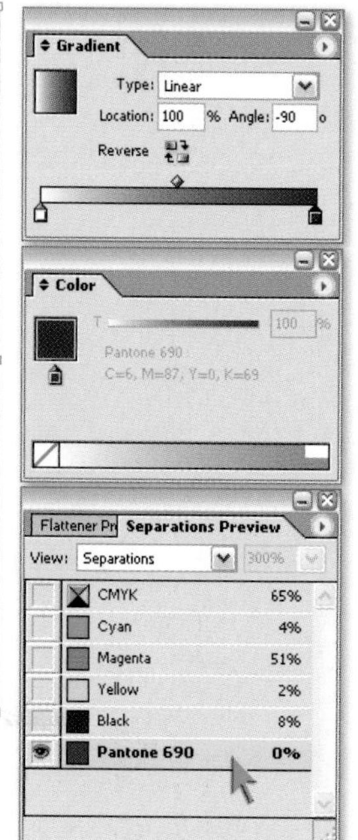

PEARL OF  WISDOM

To see just how isolated this poor turtle is, choose **Window→Output Preview→Separations** or press Shift+F6 to display the **Separations** palette. Then click the last option in the palette, **Pantone 690**. As you may recall from Video Lesson 12, "Previewing Color Separations," the Separations palette lets you view each ink independently or in combination with others. So when you click Pantone 690, you see only those objects that will print on the Pantone 690 plate, which means the bottom-right gradient turtle and nothing else (see Figure 12-20). If you click one of the other inks in the Separations palette, you'll see a white turtle-shaped hole, called a *knockout*. In other words, the gradient turtle exists on the Pantone 690 plate and nowhere else, which means it's just begging for trapping.

10. ***Create a custom trap preset.*** You could trace the turtle with a gradient stroke, but you may find it difficult to exactly align the fill and stroke gradients. The more convenient solution is to create a customized trap preset and apply it to the entire page. This leaves InDesign in charge of making the trapping decisions automatically, which you may prefer in the long run anyway.

    Choose **Window→Trap Presets** to display the **Trap Presets** palette. Then press the Alt key (Option on the Mac) and click the ◳ icon at the bottom of the palette. This displays the **New Trap Preset** dialog box, pictured in Figure 12-21.

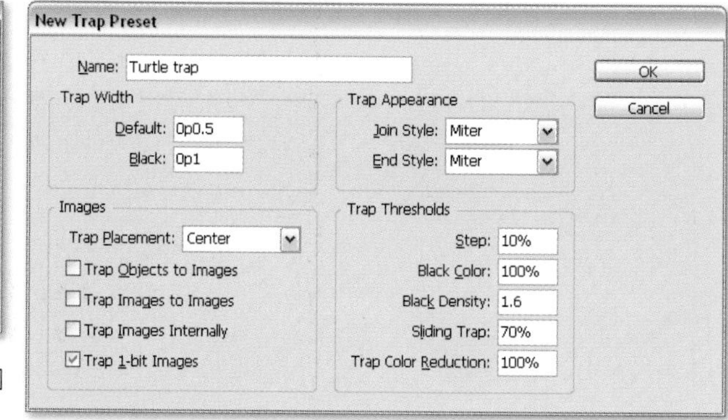

Figure 12-21.

11. ***Enter your preferred trap settings.*** InDesign's trapping controls are nothing if not comprehensive. I could fill another 12 pages with a discussion of this dialog box alone. But I'm not going to for two simple reasons: 1) That discussion would be the most boring thing you would ever read, and 2) it would end with the conclusion, "And that's why most of the settings are fine as is." I recommend you change just five options, so let's save ourselves a lot of tedium and focus on those:

    - Name the new preset "Turtle Trap."
    - Notice that InDesign offers two Trap Width values. The first, **Default**, affects the size of traps that do not involve black ink. InDesign measures the trap in one direction only, so the value should be half as thick as you would use for an overprinting stroke. For example, to match the trap thickness that you established back in Step 7 (see page 447), raise this value to 0p0.5, or ½ point.
    - Very wisely, InDesign does not spread objects on the black plate. First, any such spreading would be overly obvious. Second, most text appears on the black plate, and spreading text can ruin its legibility. Instead, InDesign spreads other inks into black according to the second Trap Width value, **Black**. Because black ink does a better job of covering the others, you can set this value higher. I recommend a value of 0p1 (1 point).
    - As I mentioned in the introduction to this exercise, you don't need to trap images. In fact, doing so takes a lot of time and may even harm your imported photos. So turn off the **Trap Objects to Images** check box, which would otherwise spread vector objects into imported images.
    - Also turn off the exceedingly unwise **Trap Images to Images**, which would attempt to spread overlapping images into each other. The only worse setting is Trap Images Internally, which spreads neighboring pixels inside an image. Fortunately, this one is off by default; leave it that way.

    The other settings are set the way they ought to be set. You now have my permission to click the **OK** button.

12. ***Apply the new trap preset to the page.*** InDesign adds a Turtle Trap item to the **Trap Presets** palette. But just because you made it doesn't mean that it's in force. To apply the preset to the current page, do the following:

   - Click the ⊙ in the upper-right corner of the palette and choose **Assign Trap Preset**, as shown in Figure 12-22.
   - Select **Turtle Trap** from the **Trap Preset** pop-up menu.
   - Click the **Assign** button to apply the preset to all pages in the document (which happen to be just this one).
   - Click the **Done** button. Note that the document won't look any different. I explain why in just a moment.

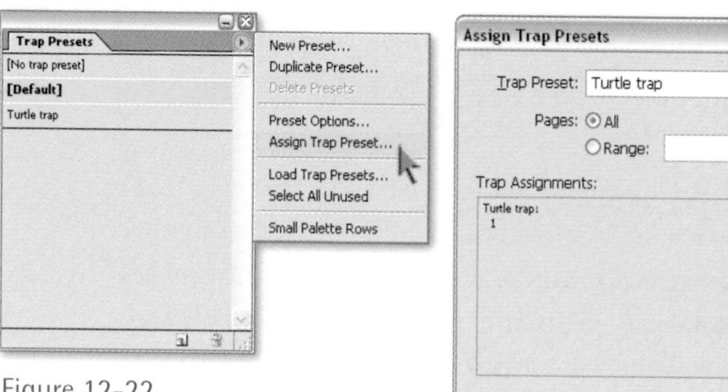

Figure 12-22.

13. ***Set the text to overprint.*** At this point, the document is entirely trapped with one exception. Click the **Yellow** plate in the **Separations Preview** palette and you'll see white knockouts in the shape of the *T* and *R* in the yellow turtles. As I mentioned before, the trapping preset will not spread the letters, but it will choke the yellow turtles into the letters. Turns out, this is not the ideal solution. Given that the letters are 100 percent black, it makes the most sense to overprint them in their entirety against the turtles. This way, you eliminate any chance of misregistration gaps and no trapping is needed.

    To overprint all black objects on the page, press Ctrl+K (or ⌘-K) to display the **General** panel of the **Preferences** dialog box. Then turn on the **Overprint [Black] Swatch at 100%** check box, which I've circled in Figure 12-23. This sets all objects that contain 100 percent black ink without any C, M, or Y to overprint the colors behind them. Click **OK** to accept your changes. The knockouts in the yellow turtles vanish.

Although your head may be swimming, I must ask you to keep in mind two more points: First, there's no way to preview the trapping preset you established in Steps 10 through 12. InDesign's automatic trapping functions come into play only when printing color separations. Second, even though you specifically assigned your Turtle Trap preset in Step 12, InDesign will *not* trap the document until it is specifically told to do so during the printing process. I recommend that you include a little note for your press technician telling him to set the Trapping option in the Output panel of the Print dialog box to Application Built-In. Or better yet, read the final exercise, "Preflight and Packaging," where I'll tell you how to communicate this and much more as you prepare your document for its ultimate destination, the commercial press.

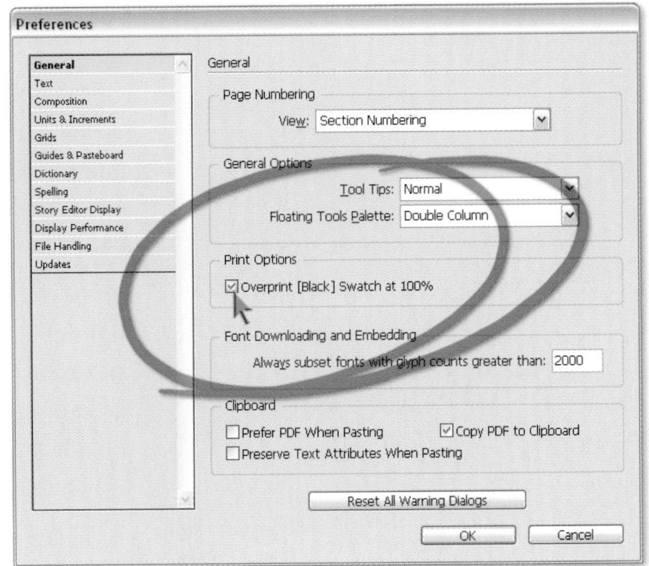

Figure 12-23.

Preflight and Packaging

The glorious day has arrived. You're ready to collect the various pieces of your InDesign document and ship them off to a commercial printer. It's finally someone else's responsibility to worry over your document while you fret about something else for a change. But only if your document is really—and I do mean *really*—rock-solid ready to go. Failing to include so much as a single linked graphic or font file can result in the dreaded phone call from your print rep. It starts with, "Uh, we seem to have a problem," and ends with you making a mad dash across town to avoid getting bumped off the press. Because many printers book out far in advance, missing a press date can throw you a week or more off your deadline.

Fortunately, InDesign provides two tools that help take the fear out of this last-ditch frenzy:

- Before you submit any print job, you can run what's known as a *preflight* inspection. Like the aviation test for which it's named, preflighting is a safety check. But rather than confirming a plane's airworthiness, it examines a document's readiness for professional output.
- Once preflighting is complete, you *package* the document, which hunts down all links and fonts—no matter how far-flung—and collects them inside a single folder. Copy that folder to a CD or server, and your job is ready for takeoff.

InDesign lets you initiate these two distinct operations by choosing either of two commands under the File menu. The Preflight command inspects the document and then offers you the option of packaging it. The Package command starts with a preflight check and then copies the links and fonts to a common location. The upshot is that you have to choose just one command to both preflight and package a document.

Of the two, I prefer File→Package. It interrupts you only if the preflight check finds a problem. Then it automatically moves on to the essential task of packaging. In this final exercise, you'll use the Package command to confirm the press-worthiness of a real-world document, assemble its pieces, and copy the resulting folder to a CD or some other medium.

1. ***Open the reprise document.*** As in the first exercise, open *Pages 62-67 reprise.indd* in the *Lesson 12* folder inside *Lesson Files-IDcs 1on1*. You've output this file to your own printer; now let's get it ready for commercial reproduction. The document happens to link to a total of 17 graphics that are contained in the *Lesson 09* folder. Although InDesign should be able to locate the graphics easily enough, this is poor long-term organization because it means I have to copy the entire *Lesson Files-IDcs 1on1* folder to preserve the links. Better to package the document and collect the files in a central, tidy location, independent of the other lesson files.

2. ***Choose the Package command.*** Choose **File→Package**. If you've made any changes to your document since it was last saved, InDesign will prompt you to update the file on disk. Otherwise, the program flashes a series of progress messages, most of which disappear before you can read them. They tell you that InDesign is rounding up images, looking for fonts, and evaluating the color settings, as in Figure 12-24.

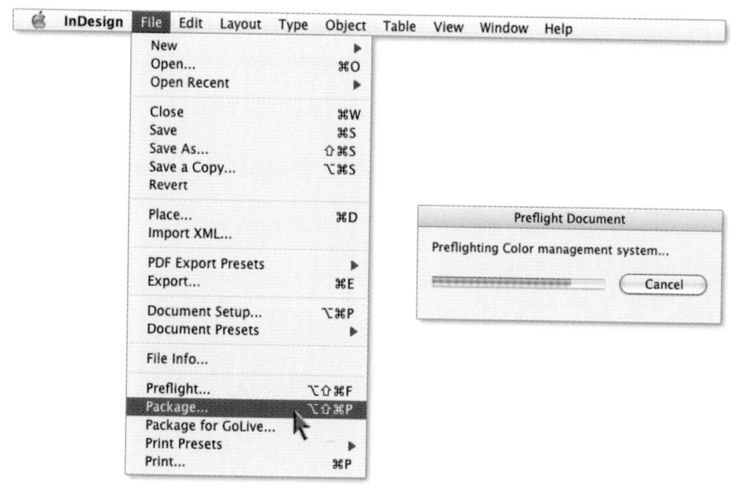

Figure 12-24.

3. ***View the potential preflight problems.*** A moment later, you'll see an alert message warning you that InDesign has encountered "possible problems." Click the **View Info** button to see what those problems might be. InDesign displays the multipaneled **Preflight** dialog box. Pictured in Figure 12-25, the first panel provides a summary of all

preflight issues, including fonts, imported graphics, color settings, and transparency.

4. ***View the Link and Images comments.*** InDesign highlights its "possible problems" with yellow ⚠ icons. In our case, the single ⚠ appears in front of the information about imported graphics. But what exactly is InDesign's concern? To figure that out, we have to dig a little deeper, as follows:

   - Click the **Links and Images** option along the left side of the dialog box or press Ctrl+3 (⌘-3 on the Mac). This brings up the Links and Images panel, which contains detailed information about all imported graphics. The scrolling list below the ⚠ chronicles the 16 Photoshop images linked to the document. (An image is repeated, which is why InDesign lists a total of 17 links.)
   - To refine the list to just the problem graphics, turn on the **Show Problems Only** check box, as in Figure 12-26. This should reduce the list to 11 images. (If not, keep reading; I explain a solution.)
   - Click a graphic in the list to explore it in detail. You'll see the date it was last modified, its original resolution, and the "effective" resolution after factoring in any scaling performed inside InDesign.

The Update and Repair All buttons permit you to refresh outdated links and locate missing files, respectively. If either button is available, click **Repair All** to establish links with the graphic files on disk. For those of you who still saw 17 images in the list, now you have 11.

So what exactly *is* the problem with the outstanding 11? Take a peek at the entries in the second column of Figure 12-26, all of which read *Photoshop RGB*. Here we are, poised to submit a document to a CMYK press, and more than half our linked images are saved in the RGB mode. Conventional wisdom tells us that the only way to maintain accurate color is to convert images to the CMYK mode in Photoshop before importing them into InDesign. (To learn how, see "Preparing a CMYK File for Commercial Reproduction" on page 436 of *Adobe Photoshop CS One-on-One*.) Therefore, InDesign flags the files as problems.

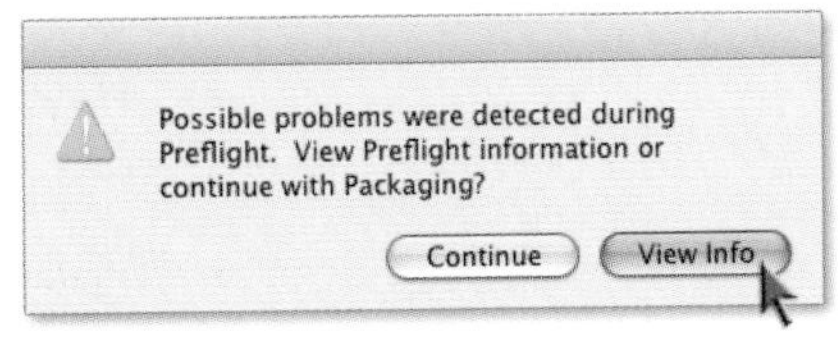

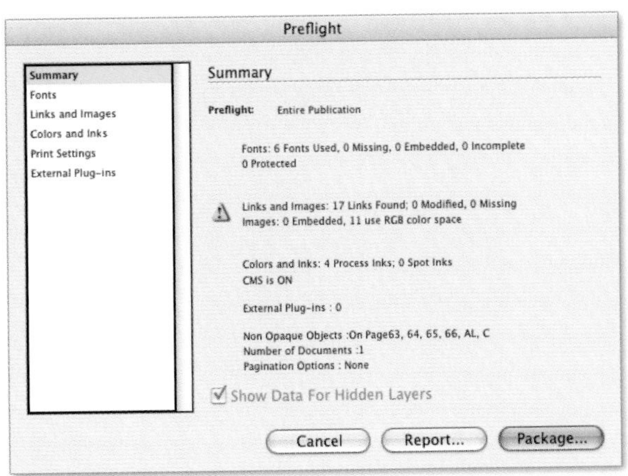

Figure 12-25.

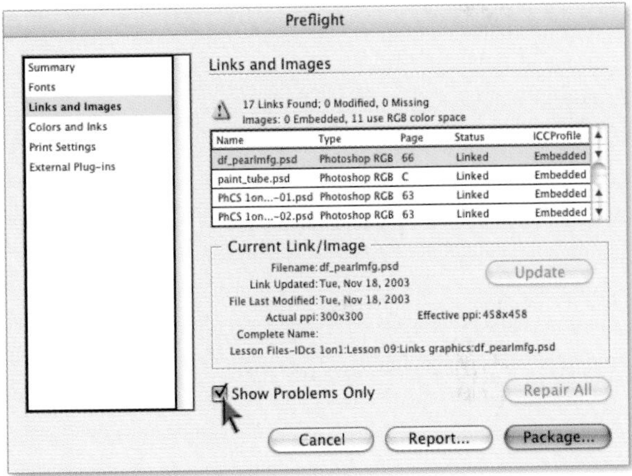

Figure 12-26.

PEARL OF WISDOM

I'm as much a fan of conventional wisdom as the next guy, but in this case, it's only half true. If I were printing an image from PageMaker or QuarkXPress, I'd make darn certain I converted it to CMYK before saving it in Photoshop. But InDesign is more flexible. RGB images work just as well as CMYK, provided that 1) you turned on InDesign's color management function as directed in Step 11 on page xvi of the Preface, and 2) your press technician prints the document directly from InDesign. Because Photoshop and InDesign share a common color engine, a conversion made in one program is identical to a conversion made in another.

Need proof? Look no further than these very pages. Every screen shot and photograph in this book is an RGB image that InDesign converted on the fly during the print process. The advantage of this approach is threefold:

- Photoshop works more quickly when you edit RGB images than CMYK.
- RGB images take up less room on disk than their CMYK counterparts.
- In its capacity as the end-of-the-road output program, InDesign is the better program for making the tricky conversion from RGB to CMYK. Because your technician can fine-tune the CMYK conversion to best suit his particular brand of press, an RGB image is actually *more* likely to provide accurate color than its CMYK equivalent.

5. ***Click the Package button.*** With all that in mind, InDesign's "possible problems" turn out to be no problems at all. If InDesign asks you to save the document, go ahead and do so. Then click the **Package** button at the bottom of the dialog box to say goodbye to preflighting and move on to the more important process of packaging.

6. ***Enter your printing instructions (if any).*** Rather out of the blue, the **Printing Instructions** dialog box invites you to construct a Read Me file for your press technician. Fill in the various options according to your personal tastes and click the **Continue** button to create a plain text file that can be read on any computer.

   - If you have nothing to communicate, do *not* click Cancel. Instead, click the Continue button to close the dialog box and move on. But be aware: this causes InDesign to create an empty file called *Instructions.txt*. Before submitting your project to a commercial printer, I recommend you delete the empty *Instructions.txt* file to avoid confusion.

- Better yet, take a few moments to fill out the print instructions, line for line. Figure 12-27 shows my filled-in dialog box followed by the resulting text file. If you don't like how InDesign organizes your printing instructions, you can modify the text later using a text editor such as NotePad on the PC or TextEdit on the Mac.

7. ***Specify a folder name and location.*** InDesign next asks you what you want to name the folder that contains the packaged files and where you want to put it. Just so we're all on the same page, change the folder name to *My Project* and navigate to the *Lesson 12* folder (see Figure 12-28). Then turn on the first three check boxes (some of which may already be on), which do the following:
    - The first check box copies all font files required to print the document. The *(roman only)* moniker is a bit misleading: Assuming that you're using a Western (non-Asian) font, InDesign includes all type styles that you use and none that you don't.
    - The next check box copies all imported graphics. In our case, it copies the image files from the *Lesson 09* folder.

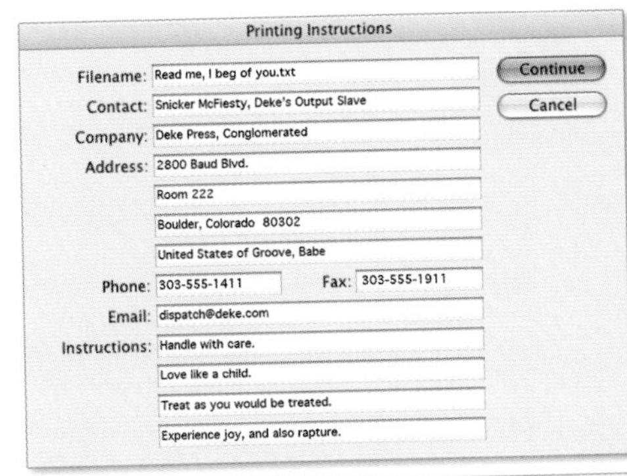

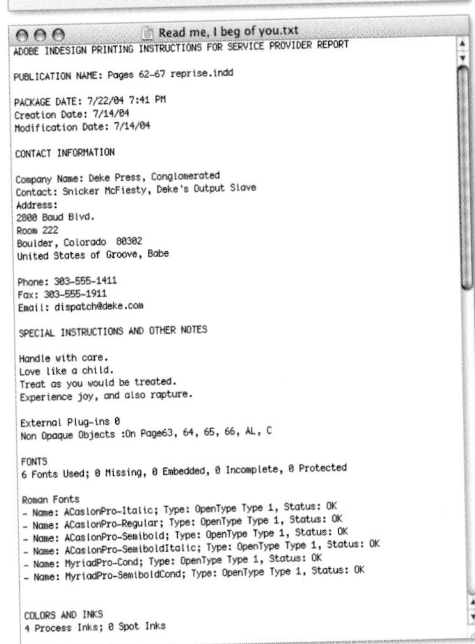
Read me, I beg of you.txt

ADOBE INDESIGN PRINTING INSTRUCTIONS FOR SERVICE PROVIDER REPORT

PUBLICATION NAME: Pages 62-67 reprise.indd

PACKAGE DATE: 7/22/04 7:41 PM
Creation Date: 7/14/04
Modification Date: 7/14/04

CONTACT INFORMATION

Company Name: Deke Press, Conglomerated
Contact: Snicker McFiesty, Deke's Output Slave
Address:
2800 Baud Blvd.
Room 222
Boulder, Colorado 80302
United States of Groove, Babe

Phone: 303-555-1411
Fax: 303-555-1911
Email: dispatch@deke.com

SPECIAL INSTRUCTIONS AND OTHER NOTES

Handle with care.
Love like a child.
Treat as you would be treated.
Experience joy, and also rapture.

External Plug-ins 0
Non Opaque Objects :On Page63, 64, 65, 66, AL, C

FONTS
6 Fonts Used; 0 Missing, 0 Embedded, 0 Incomplete, 0 Protected

Roman Fonts
- Name: ACaslonPro-Italic; Type: OpenType Type 1, Status: OK
- Name: ACaslonPro-Regular; Type: OpenType Type 1, Status: OK
- Name: ACaslonPro-Semibold; Type: OpenType Type 1, Status: OK
- Name: ACaslonPro-SemiboldItalic; Type: OpenType Type 1, Status: OK
- Name: MyriadPro-Cond; Type: OpenType Type 1, Status: OK
- Name: MyriadPro-SemiboldCond; Type: OpenType Type 1, Status: OK

COLORS AND INKS
4 Process Inks; 0 Spot Inks

Figure 12-27.

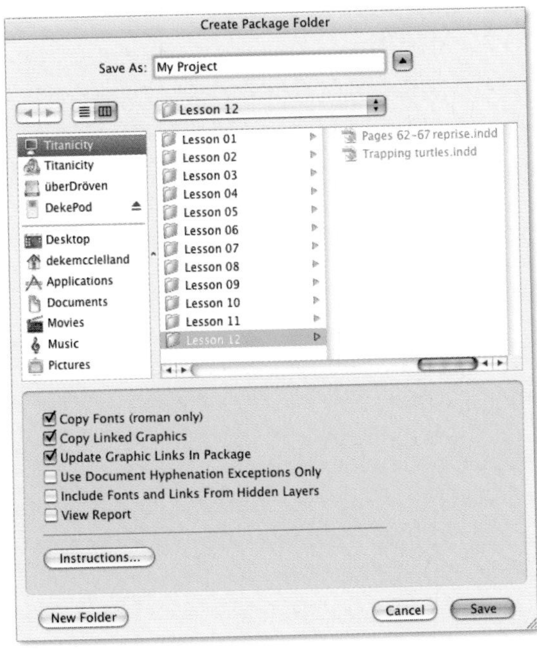

Figure 12-28.

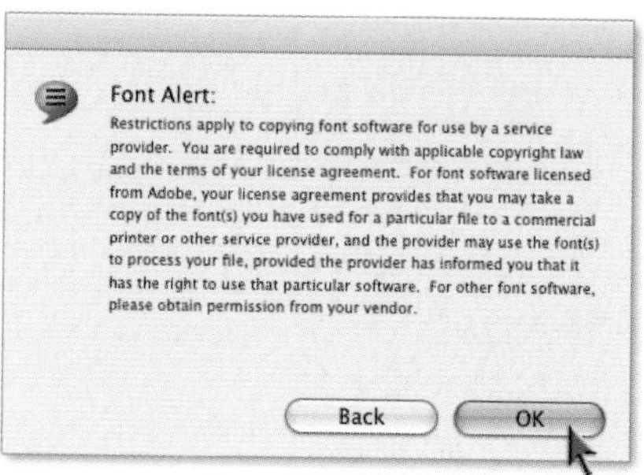

Figure 12-29.

- The third check box links the InDesign document to the graphic files copied by the preceding check box. This option must be on to create a self-contained print job.

When you finish, click **Package** (or **Save** on the Mac) to accept your settings and continue.

8. ***Acknowledge the legal statement.*** Like all modern contrivances, fonts are copyrighted. And as a font vendor, Adobe is keen to make you aware of this fact. So anytime you copy font files, InDesign displays the legal statement pictured in Figure 12-29. If you're curious about what it says, read it. (Summary: It's okay for you to send fonts to your commercial print house as long as they already have the right to use the fonts. Of course, that doesn't quite make sense, but there it is.) Whether you read the statement or not, click the **OK** button to make the infernal thing go away.

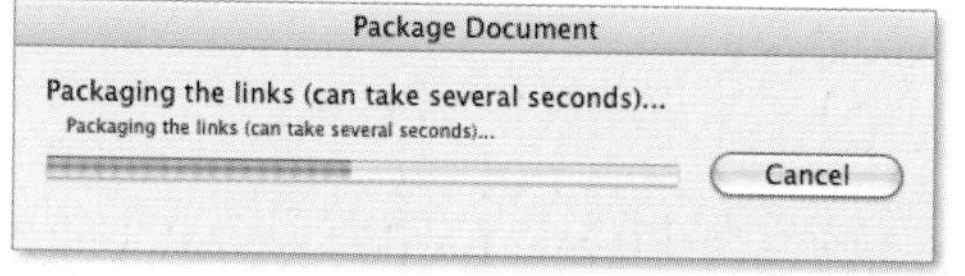

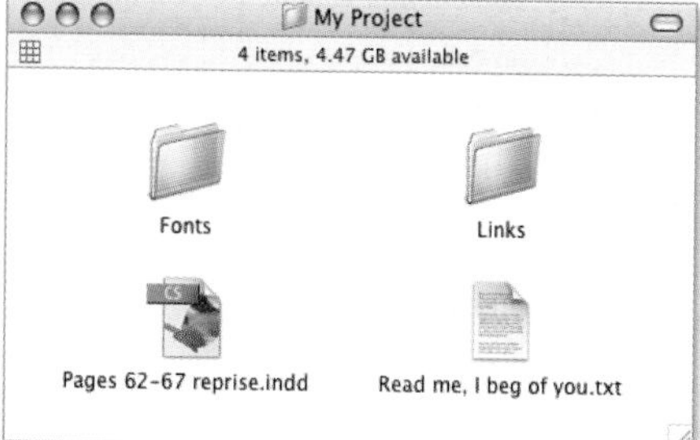

Figure 12-30.

9. ***Examine the packaged folder.*** Once again, InDesign flashes a series of progress messages. When the progress bar disappears, the package is complete. Switch from InDesign to the desktop level of your computer. Open the *Lesson 12* folder inside *Lesson Files-IDcs 1on1*. Then open the *My Project* folder to view the newly packaged items pictured in Figure 12-30:

   - The *Fonts* subfolder contains all fonts used in the document.
   - The *Links* subfolder contains the 16 imported images, both CMYK and RGB.
   - *Pages 62–67 reprise.indd* is a copy of the InDesign document with all links updated to the files inside the *Links* subfolder.
   - The remaining document is the instructions file that you created in Step 6. If you didn't include any instructions, delete this file. Otherwise, leave it where it is.

10. ***Copy the folder to a CD or some other medium.*** The files are now ready to hand off to a commercial print house. If you were seriously ready to do so, you would copy the entire *My Project* folder—which contains about 41MB of files—to a CD-ROM or another disk. Or if you prefer, you could avoid shipping costs by uploading the files to a server or FTP site, or by using some other online solution. To find out what options are available, consult your friendly local print rep.

WHAT DID YOU LEARN?

Match the key concept in the numbered list below with the letter of the phrase that best describes it. Answers appear upside-down at the bottom of the page.

Key Concepts

1. Imagesetter
2. Color separation
3. Halftone cells
4. Composite RGB
5. Misregistration
6. Trapping
7. Spread
8. Overprint Stroke
9. Web-offset lithography
10. Sheetfed press
11. Preflight
12. Package

Descriptions

A. This press technology prints on continuous rolls of paper and is the most popular choice for magazines, books, and other large print runs.

B. This trapping technique adds an overprinting stroke that matches the fill of a foreground object.

C. One of the many passes rendered by an imagesetter when printing a full-color document; each of the passes receives a different ink.

D. Smaller print runs are better served by this press technology, which outputs to individual sheets of paper.

E. The art of filling in the tiny gaps between colors that may occur as a result of misregistration.

F. When printing to an inkjet printer or other non-PostScript device, this option leaves the printer driver in charge of translating colors.

G. This process hunts down all links and fonts contained in a document and collects them inside a single folder.

H. A check box that mixes the outline of an object printed on one plate with an underlying fill or stroke from another plate; to preview the effect, press Ctrl+Shift+Alt+Y (⌘-Shift-Option-Y on the Mac).

I. This pesky output problem occurs when paper slips or plates don't line up perfectly during the commercial reproduction process.

J. Service bureaus and print houses use this monstrously expensive PostScript device to output pages to film or some other medium prior to loading the inks and plates onto the press.

K. This rigorous if occasionally overzealous inspection examines a document's readiness for professional output.

L. An imagesetter simulates shades of color by assembling printer dots into a grid of these.

Answers

1J, 2C, 3L, 4F, 5I, 6E, 7B, 8H, 9A, 10D, 11K, 12G

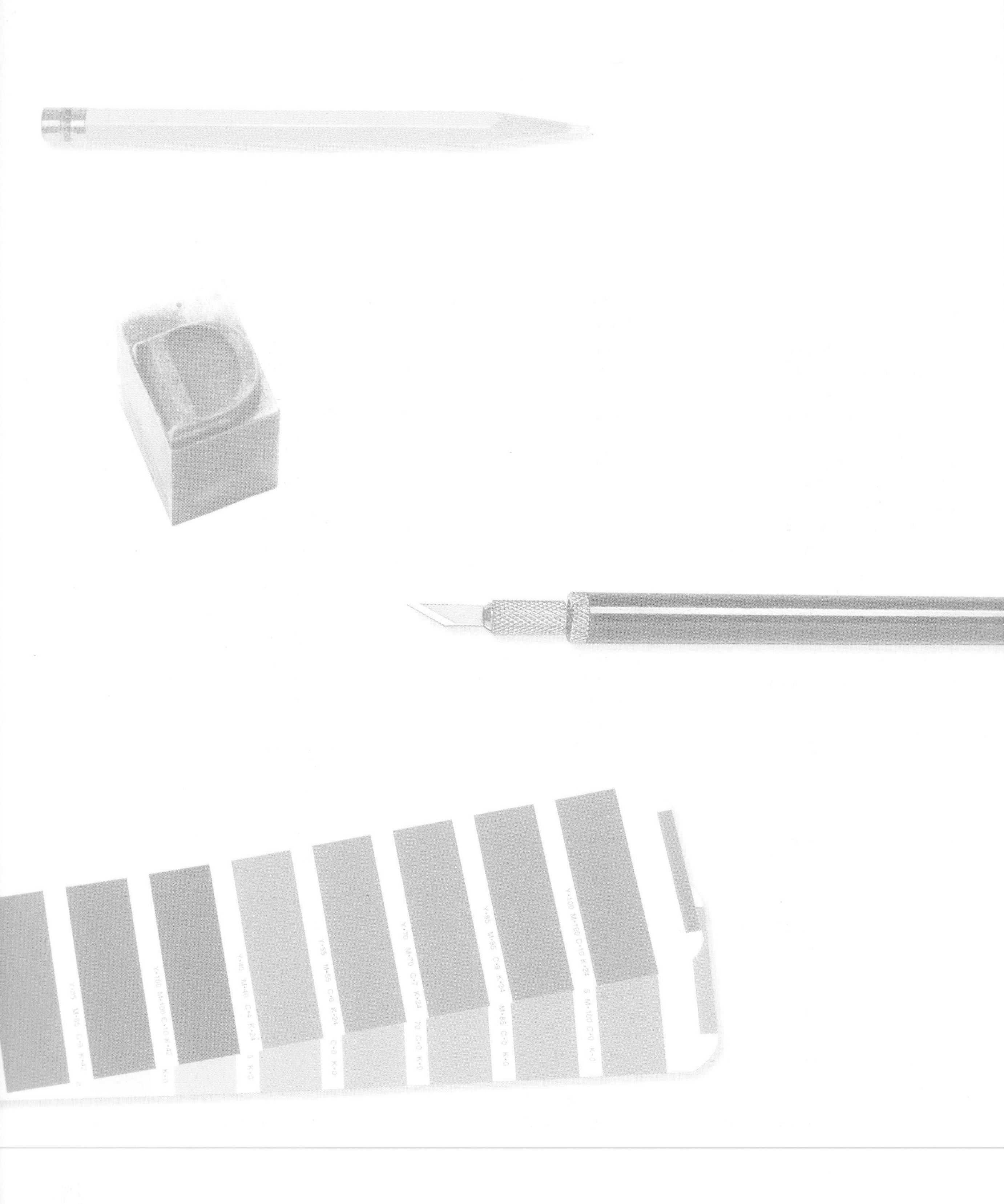

INDEX

E

F

G

H

I

J

K

L

P

Q

R

S

T

U

V

W

X

Z